P9-EMH-629

Ologies and Isms

A Dictionary of Word
Beginnings and Endings

Michael Quinion has had a varied career since gaining his
science degree at Cambridge University rather a long time
ago. He has been a BBC studio manager and producer in
radio, heritage interpreter, audio-visual scriptwriter and
producer, museum curator, tourism consultant, and
computer software writer. He has researched word usage for
the *Oxford English Dictionary* since 1992 and wrote a third of
the entries for the second edition of the *Oxford Dictionary of
New Words*. Since 1997 his World Wide Words website has
intrigued and entertained great numbers of visitors with its
informal but informed analyses of word histories and
language evolution.

Oxford Paperback Reference

The most authoritative and up-to-date reference books for both students and the general reader.

forthcoming

Ologies and Isms

A Dictionary of Word
Beginnings and Endings

MICHAEL QUINION

OXFORD
UNIVERSITY PRESS

OXFORD
UNIVERSITY PRESS

Great Clarendon Street, Oxford OX2 6DP

Oxford University Press is a department of the University of Oxford.
It furthers the University's objective of excellence in research, scholarship,
and education by publishing worldwide in

Oxford New York
Auckland Cape Town Dar es Salaam Hong Kong Karachi Kuala Lumpur
Madrid Melbourne Mexico City Nairobi New Delhi Taipei Toronto
Shanghai

With offices in
Argentina Austria Brazil Chile Czech Republic France Greece
Guatemala Hungary Italy Japan South Korea Poland Portugal
Singapore Switzerland Thailand Turkey Ukraine Vietnam

Oxford is a registered trademark of Oxford University Press
in the UK and in certain other countries

Published in the United States
by Oxford University Press Inc., New York

British Library Cataloguing in Publication Data

Data available

Library of Congress Cataloging in Publication Data

Data available

ISBN 0-19-280640-8
ISBN 978-0-19-280640-6

1

Typeset by SPI Publisher Services, Pondicherry, India
Printed in Great Britain by
Clays Ltd, St Ives Plc

Contents

Introduction

This book is about some of the building blocks of the English language, those beginnings and endings that help form a large proportion of the words we use. Not all word-forming roots are here. If they were, the book would be ten times as big and vastly less digestible. What you will find are those examples that are identifiable as affixes, knowledge of which can then be generalized to help identify unknown words of the same kind, or even perhaps to create new ones.

It was in the summer of 1995, while my former business partner and I were studying the displays in a medical museum in order to advise how to improve them, that he remarked that one of the things needed to enhance visitors' enjoyment would be an explanation of the mysteries of medical terminology: the difference, say, between an -ITIS and an -ALGIA, or between words starting in HAEM- and HEPA-. That conversation stayed with me. Increased exposure to the complexities of technical language, and to the diversification of knowledge that has led to sub-disciplines such as *palaeophytogeography*, *psychoneuroendocroimmunology*, and *ethnotraumapsychopharmacology*, whose names pile element upon element, reinforced a belief that a concise work was needed that interpreted the main word-forming affixes in English.

The entries in this work cover most of those active in the language today, as well as others that have contributed to the language in the past; only the most specialist, obscure or archaic have been left out. However, place-name affixes (-*burgh*, -*ham*, -*thwaite*, -*wick*) have been excluded; you will find information on these in the *Oxford Dictionary of English Place-Names* and elsewhere. Personal name affixes such as *Fitz-*, *Mac-*, and -*son* have also been omitted.

The aim throughout has been to provide many examples, on the principle that it is easier to absorb the subtleties of the way such forms are used when they are seen in action. A second aim has been to show links between words, both grammatically and thematically; where possible (bearing in mind the need not to create an expensive and indigestible doorstop) I have tried to give some background and explain how words have come to mean what they do. So far as possible, technical language has been avoided or explained. But finding a short way to explain the complexities of medical or scientific terminology is not always achievable without using other words that are equally specialist and obscure. A dictionary writer may do so in the comforting knowledge that the reader is already holding the key in his hand. This book doesn't have that advantage; if technical terms send you to the dictionary too often, I apologize, but the alternative would be too wordy to endure. For the same reason, though explanations of the meanings of many technical words are supplied for guidance, they should not be taken as definitive; a large dictionary or specialist work should be consulted in doubtful or subtle cases.

I have deliberately avoided most linguistic or grammatical language. But a few terms are relatively common, and hard to avoid without circumlocution, loquacity, or confusion, so it seemed best to take a deep breath and put them in. A note of their meanings appears on page viii.

It is a truism that all lexicography is plagiarism, since every new work builds on what has gone before. In particular, I acknowledge my debt to the *New Oxford Dictionary of English*, whose presentation of the language on the most modern principles has been invaluable, and to the *Oxford English Dictionary*, whose depth of scholarship is unrivalled in the English language. But many dozens of specialist works have also been trawled, as has the World Wide Web, a resource that might have been invented to help hard-pressed word-searchers.

My thanks go to my editors at Oxford University Press, Elizabeth Knowles and Alysoun Owen, and to Dr Terry Hoad for his help in sorting out many points of detail, in the process greatly improving my Latin and Greek. The person who has been most directly affected is my wife, who has coped in her usual uncomplaining way with a husband at times driven to distraction by the vagaries of English, and who was too often preoccupied with the affix of the moment. I promise to finish the decorating now.

Michael Quinion
Thornbury, South Gloucestershire

Some technical terms in this book

There are four types of affixes:

* A **prefix** is an element placed at the beginning of a word to adjust or qualify its meaning, for example DE-, NON-, and RE-.

* A **suffix** is an element placed at the end of a word to form a derivative, such as -ATION, -FY, -ING, frequently one that converts the stem into another part of speech.

* A **combining form** can be either a prefix or a suffix; the difference is that the combining form adds a layer of extra meaning to the word.

  For example, BIO- adds the idea of life or living things to words, as in *biochemistry*, the study of the chemical processes which occur within living organisms; -CIDE adds the idea of killing or a killing agent, as in *pesticide*. Compare these examples with a prefix such as EX- or a suffix such as -IC, neither of which add meaning, but only modify an existing meaning.

  Combining forms only appear in compounds; by definition, if it can stand alone it is not a combining form. For example, CARBO- only appears in compounds to indicate carbon, but there are many related words that begin with *carbon-*; these are considered to be compound words and *carbon-* is not a combining form. Having said that, in some cases a combining form has at some point in its life taken on the status of a free-standing word (CYBER- is a recent example), but if its primary function is as a combining form, it appears in its place in the text. To be a combining form a word element must be found attached to stems that also have intrinsic meaning; this excludes many stems whose only compounds are grammatical variations, such as *intense* (*intensive*, *intensively*, *intensiveness*).

* An **infix** is placed within a word; these are rare in English, though *cupful* can be made plural as *cupsful* by inserting the plural *s* as an infix; infixes sometimes occur in facetious creations like *absobloodylutely* (which some grammarians would rather describe as tmesis). Infixes frequently appear as linking vowels between prefixes and stems, for example the final letters of NARCO- and CALCI-. They are also found between a stem ending in a consonant and a suffix beginning with one, as with -FEROUS, which frequently appears as -*iferous*, or -LOGY, which is commonly seen as -*ology*. The only examples of such linking vowel infixes in this book are -I- and -O-.

No formal identification is made in the text of the class of affix to which entries belong. The position of the hyphen is sufficient indication whether it is placed at the beginning, in the middle or at the end of a word: NEO-, -I-, -GRAPHY.

Many prefixes that end in a vowel can lose that vowel when attached to a stem that begins in one, as for example *phlebo-* loses its final letter in *phlebitis*. Such cases are marked by enclosing the final letter of the entry headword in parentheses: *phleb(o)-*.

The term **productive** has a special sense throughout the text: it refers to an affix which is active in the language and which is being used by writers today to create new words.

A

a-¹ Before a vowel **an-**. *Not or without.* [Greek *a-*.]

In more or less disguised form, this occurs in a number of words brought over from Greek, such as *abyss* (Greek *bussos*, depth); *anomalous* (Greek *homalos*, even); and *anarchy* (Greek *arkhos*, chief or ruler).

A variety of scientific and medical terms contain it, such as *anaesthetic* (US *anesthetic*) (Greek *aisthēsis*, sensation), something that prevents one feeling pain; *amorphous* (Greek *morphē*, form), without a clearly defined shape; and *anorexia* (Greek *orexis*, appetite), a medical condition in which there is a lack of appetite. Some have been created using native English stems: *apolitical*, not interested or involved in politics; *atypical*, not representative of a type or class.

A few can have slightly different senses to those in other negative prefixes on the same stem: someone who is *immoral* does not conform to moral precepts, but someone *amoral* lacks a moral sense; a person who is *antisocial* acts against the laws and customs of society, but one who is *asocial* is hostile to social interaction.

Despite these examples, the prefix is not often used to make new words.

a-² *Towards, of, in, into, or at; marking some ongoing process or state; movement onwards or away.* [Old English prepositions *of* or *on* (sometimes as unstressed *an*), or the Old English prefix *a-*.]

The Old English prepositions were originally separate words, but became reduced to **a-** and attached to the words they once modified. The process can be seen in *alive*, which in Old English was two words, *on līfe*, literally 'in life'; others of similar type are *aside*, *akin*, and *anew*. Some examples are verbs derived from Old English *a-*, which had an idea about it of an action or an intensification of an action: *arise*, *abide*, and *awake*.

Some adjectives imply a continuing or active state, and have much the same force as a present participle ending in *-ing* (see -ING²): *ablaze*, *abuzz*, *afire*, *afoot*, *aglow*, *astride*. Others combine the prefix with a present participle, usually hyphenated; such words imply an ongoing process or activity: *a-brewing*, *a-roving*, *a-hunting*, *a-wasting*; though they are mostly now archaic, literary, or dialectal, the form has had a small revival in recent decades, as in Bob Dylan's song lyric *The times they are a-changing*.

-a¹ *Forming singular words of various types.* [Derived from a Greek, Latin, or Romance feminine singular ending.]

Many feminine nouns in Greek and Latin had this ending, and a number have been brought over into English unchanged: *area*, *arena*, *camera*, *formula*, *idea*, *lamina*, *peninsula*. Examples from modern Romance languages include *diva*, *marina*, *pasta*, *rumba*, and *siesta*.

Many names for animals or plants derived from or modelled on Latin have this ending: *alga*, *amoeba*, *cicada*, *dahlia*, *fuchsia*, *hyena*, *lobelia*. It is the usual ending for the oxides of metals, as in *alumina*, *magnesia*, and *soda*.

It forms the ending for many female forenames derived from Latin or Latinized forms, such as *Anna*, *Diana*, *Julia*, *Maria*, and *Victoria*. Other female forenames have been created from their male equivalents using **-a**, as in *Alexandra*, *Georgia*, *Joanna*, *Nigella*, and *Roberta*.

A number of geographical terms contain this ending, again taken from Latin precursors, such as *Africa*, *Asia*, *Corsica*, and *Malta*.

However, many English words ending in **-a** come from other sources in which the **-a** does not indicate this suffix: *vodka* is from Russian, *sofa* from Arabic, *pyjama* from Urdu and Persian, *satsuma* from a

Japanese placename, *tea* via Malay from Chinese, and so on.

-a² Also **-ata**. *The plural of certain nouns of Latin or Greek origin.* [From the Latin or Greek neuter plural ending.]

Many nouns from Latin or Greek that end in *-um* or *-on* form their plurals in **-a**, as for example *datum* changes to *data* and *phenomenon* to *phenomena*. Such plurals are now often formed using *-s* instead.

A further group, mostly specialist words, whose singulars already end in **-a**, can form their plurals with **-ata**. Examples are *lemma* (plural *lemmata*), *schema* (*schemata*), *stigma* (*stigmata*), and *trauma* (*traumata*). Here, too, plurals ending in *-s* are now common.

The same plural form occurs in the scientific names of many classes of animals, such as *Mammalia*, *Amphibia*, *Cetacea*, *Crustacea*, *Mollusca*, and *Protozoa* (*see also* -ACEA and -IA).

-a³ *Informal terms in spoken English.* [Taken from rapid or casual pronunciations.]

This ending seeks to represent what happens to various linking words in rapid speech. Most are more common in American English than British.

Examples where it replaces *of* include *kinda* (kind of), *lotsa* (lots of), and *sorta* (sort of). The same happens with *to*, for example in *gonna* (going to), *gotta* (got to), and *wanna* (want to). It can also represent an elided form of *have*, as in *coulda* (could have), *shoulda* (should have), and *woulda* (would have). Others indicate the partial loss of a final unstressed syllable, as with *fella* (from *fellow*).

Characteristically British examples include *cuppa* (cup of, especially a cup of tea, now well established as an informal noun), and *pinta* (pint of, especially of milk, popularized by a slogan used in advertisements by the then National Dairy Council from 1959 on: *drinka pinta milka day*).

ab- Also **abs-**. *Off, away, or from.* [Latin *ab-*, with the same meaning.]

This is not a living prefix; words containing it were imported into the language from Latin, often with a figurative sense.

Some examples are *abdicate* (*dicare*, to declare), to renounce the throne; *aborigine* (*ab origine*, from the beginning), an inhabitant of a place from earliest times; *abort*, to terminate a pregnancy (*oriri*, be born); and *abuse*, to use something improperly (*abuti*, to misuse, from *uti*, to use).

Abs- is used before *c* and *t*, as in *abscess* (*cedere*, to go), *abscond* (*concere*, to hide or stow), and *abstruse* (*trudere*, to push).

abdomin(o)-. *The abdomen.* [Latin *abdomen*, *abdomin-*, abdomen.]

The *abdomen* is the part of the body cavity below the diaphragm, containing the stomach, intestines, kidneys, and other organs. An *abdominoplasty* is an operation to tighten the abdominal muscles and remove excess fat, also called a *tummy tuck*. Several terms refer to the abdomen together with another organ or part of the body: *abdominothoracic*, abdomen and thorax; *abdominoperineal*, abdomen and perineum.

-able Also **-ible** and **-uble**; **-ability**, **-ibility**, and **-ubility**. *Able to be.* [Originally from the Latin adjectival suffix *-bilis*.]

The adjectival suffixes **-able**, **-ible**, and **-uble** have several meanings; the main one, and the usual one in new forms today, indicates an ability to do something (*calculable*, *defensible*, *voluble*), but other senses also exist: suitable for some purpose (*reversible*, *edible*); due to be (*payable*); having a quality expressed by the word stem (*comfortable*, *passable*, *suitable*); subject to (*taxable*); or causing some effect (*terrible*, *horrible*). Several hundred words contain these suffixes, of which a very few other examples are *allowable*, *combustible*, *conceivable*, *enjoyable*, *gullible*, *legible*, *practicable*, *seasonable*, *soluble*, *visible*, and *washable*.

The **-ible** and **-uble** endings are not currently active (and **-uble** is much less common than the others, with only *soluble* and *voluble* being at all common), but **-able** is frequently used to form new words, such as *gluggable*, of a wine that is good to drink; *kebababable*, a meat capable of being kebabed; or in Britain *ISAble*, of an investment that can be made into an ISA, an individual savings account. Part of the popularity of **-able** comes from its similarity to the English word *able*, though the two are not related.

The related suffixes **-ability**, **-ibility**, and **-ubility** form abstract nouns that refer to a quality, such as *capability*, *plausibility*, *solubility*, *suitability*, and *usability*.

A few adjectives have different meanings in their **-able** and **-ible** forms: *contractable* means 'liable to be contracted', as of a habit or a disease, but *contractible* means 'able to be reduced in length'; *forceable* refers to a thing that can be forced open, whereas *forcible* means something executed by means of force; *infusable* is said of something, such as a herb, that can be steeped in water, while *infusible* refers to a thing that cannot be melted or fused.

Some words appear to contain these endings through accidents of spelling: *crucible*, *double*, *parable*, *syllable*, *vegetable*.

abs-: *see* AB-

ac-: *see* AD-

-ac Also **-acal**. *Forming adjectives and nouns.* [Latin *-acus* or French *-aque* from Greek *-akos*.]

All words ending in **-ac** from this source include an *i* from the original Latin or Greek root, so making it in effect *-iac*.

Some are adjectives: *cardiac* (Greek *kardia*, heart), of the heart; *iliac* (Latin *ilia*, entrails), relating to the ilium, a bone in the pelvis, or to the nearby regions of the lower body. Others are nouns: *aphrodisiac*, a food, drink, or drug that stimulates sexual desire; *zodiac*, the belt of the heavens that includes the apparent paths of the sun, moon, and principal planets. Some can be both noun and adjective: *amnesiac*, *hypochondriac*, *insomniac*.

Nouns often have linked adjectives in *-al* (*see* -AL[1]), as in *zodiacal* and *ammoniacal*. In a few cases, adjectives in both forms co-exist, as with *paradisiac* and *paradisiacal*, or *heliac* and *heliacal* (though in both these cases the form in **-acal** is much more common).

Some words in **-ac** have related forms in -IC: *demoniac* and *demonic*, *haemophiliac* and *haemophilic*, *maniac* and *manic*. In each of these cases the form in -IC is an adjective, irrespective of the role of the form in **-ac**. An exception is *amnesiac*, in which *amnesic* can be both adjective and noun.

-acal: *see* -AC

acanth(o)-.   *Spiny or thorny.* [Greek *akantha*, a thorn.]

The *acanthus* is a genus of Mediterranean plants that have prickly leaves; the mineral *acanthite*, a major source of silver, forms slender pointed crystals; *acanthosis* is a thickening of the prickle cells in the skin, as in eczema and psoriasis.

acar(o)- Also **acari-**. *A mite or tick.* [Greek *akari*, mite or tick.]

Mites and ticks belong to the order or subclass, *Acari* (or *Acarina*); a member of the group is an *acarid* and the study of them is *acarology*. A substance that kills mites and ticks is an *acaricide* (Latin *-cida*, from *caedere*, kill).

-acea Also **-acean**. *Groups of animals.* [The neuter plural of the Latin ending *-aceus*, belonging to, or of the nature of.]

Terms in **-acea** are systematic names of animal groups, mostly orders but also classes and a few superfamilies. Examples include *Crustacea*, a class of mostly marine arthropods that includes lobsters, shrimps, crabs, and barnacles; *Cetacea*, the order that includes the whales, dolphins, and porpoises; and *Cumacea* (Greek *kuma*, billow or wave), the order containing the tadpole shrimps.

Names in **-acean** either indicate individual members of these groups or adjectives relating to them. The most common examples are *cetacean* and *crustacean*; another is *larvacean* for a member of the *Larvacea*, a class of minute transparent planktonic animals related to the sea squirts.

See also -AE and -EAN.

-aceae *Families of seed-bearing plants.* [The feminine plural of the Latin ending *-aceus*, belonging to, or of the nature of.]

Examples include *Brassicaceae*, the brassica family, including cabbages, radishes, mustards, and cresses; *Liliaceae*, the lilies, also including tulips, garlics, onions, and leeks; *Orchidaceae*, the orchids; *Taxaceae* (Latin *taxus*, yew), the yews.

See also -ACEOUS, -AE, -ALES, and -ID².

-acean: *see* -ACEA

-aceous *Forming adjectives.* [Latin adjectival ending -*aceus*, of the nature of, plus -OUS.

Some examples are formed from plant family names in -ACEAE: *rosaceous*, of the rose family, the *Rosaceae*; *orchidaceous*, of an orchid, a member of the *Orchidaceae* family; *solanaceous*, of the *Solanaceae*, the nightshade family.

The ending also appears in a variety of words from biology and geology, as in *herbaceous*, relating to plants that are leafy and not woody; *saponaceous* (Latin *sapon*, soap), soapy; *olivaceous*, having a dusky yellowish-green or olive-green colour; *proteinaceous*, of the nature of a protein or consisting of protein; and *sebaceous* (Latin *sebum*, tallow), resembling tallow or fat or secreting a fatty substance.

See also -OUS.

acet(o)-. *Acetic acid or the acetyl group.* [Latin *acetum*, vinegar, whose primary constituent is acetic acid.]

Acetic acid can be made by fermenting ethyl alcohol using *acetobacter* bacteria; an intermediate product is *acetaldehyde*, an important raw material for synthesizing other organic compounds; salts or esters of acetic acid are *acetates*. The radical CH_3CO— from acetic acid is the *acetyl* group and **aceto-** can refer to this group, as in *acetone*, a ketone used as a reagent and solvent; *acetanilide*, a form of the dyestuff aniline; and *acetonitrile*, a colourless and poisonous liquid used as a solvent.

acid(o)- Also **acidi-**. *Acid; sharp or sour.* [Latin *acidus*, from *acere*, to be sour.]

Examples include *acidosis*, an excessively acid condition of the tissues or fluids; *aciduria*, a medical condition in which acid is present in the urine; to *acidify* a substance is to make it *acidic*, while to *acidulate* it is to make it only slightly acid; a substance that is *acidulous* is mildly sharp-tasting or sour (and this adjective can refer in a figurative sense to cutting or bitter remarks); *acidimetry* is the measurement of the strengths of acids; something *acidophilic* (Greek *philia*, fondness) is either easily stained with acid dyes, or grows best in acid conditions.

-acious Also **-acity**. *Inclined to, given to, or having as a capacity.* [Originally and mainly from Latin words in -*ax* or -*ac*-, plus -OUS.]

Words in **-acious** are adjectives. See the LIST opposite for examples. Words ending in **-acity** are corresponding nouns of quality or state (*audacity*, *sagacity*).

acoust(o)- Also **acous-**, **acou-**, and **acoustico-**. *Sound or hearing.* [Greek *akoustikos*, from *akouein*, to hear (**acou-** comes from the latter).]

Acoustics is the branch of physics concerned with the properties of sound; the field of *acoustooptics* studies interactions between very high frequency sound waves and beams of laser light. In medicine, *acousma* (also called *acouasm*) is a non-verbal auditory hallucination, such as a ringing or hissing; *acousticophobia* is fear of noise. *See also* -ACUSIS and AUDIO-.

acr(o)- *A tip, height, or extremity.* [Greek *akron*, a tip or summit.]

An *acrobat* (Greek *bainein*, to walk) is literally someone who walks on tiptoe; an *acropolis* (Greek *polis*, city) was a fortified part of an ancient Greek city, typically on a hill; an *acronym* (Greek *onuma*, name) is a word formed from the initial letters of a phrase.

In medicine, the *acromion* is the outward end of the spine of the shoulder blade. Medical conditions include *acromegaly* (Greek *megas*, great), abnormal growth of the extremities and face caused by excessive production of growth hormone, and *acrophobia*, extreme or irrational fear of heights.

-acious	Inclined to, given to, having as a capacity. *All examples derive from Latin.*	
audacious	willing to take risks	(*audax*, bold)
capacious	having a lot of space inside, roomy	(*capax, capac-*, capable)
efficacious	successful in producing a desired result	(*efficax*, from *efficere*, to accomplish)
loquacious	talkative	(*loquax*, from *loqui*, talk)
mendacious	not telling the truth	(*mendax*, lying, related to *mendum*, a fault)
pertinacious	holding firmly to an opinion or a course of action	(*pertinax*, holding fast)
pugnacious	eager or quick to argue or fight	(*pugnax*, from *pugnare*, to fight)
rapacious	aggressively greedy or grasping	(*rapax*, from *rapere*, to snatch)
sagacious	showing good judgement	(*sagax*, wise)
tenacious	holding fast to something, not easily giving up	(*tenax*, from *tenere*, to hold)
veracious	speaking or representing the truth	(*verax*, from *verus*, true)
vivacious	attractively lively and animated	(*vivax*, lively or vigorous, from *vivere*, to live)
voracious	wanting or devouring great quantities of food	(*vorax*, from *vorare*, to devour)

Some words that look as though they include this prefix actually contain Latin *acer*, pungent or acrid: *acrolein*, a sharp-smelling liquid; *acrimonious*, of an angry or bitter exchange.

acryl(o)- *Acrylic.* [English *acrylic* (from Latin *acer, acri-*, pungent), plus -o-.]

Acrylic acid is a pungent liquid organic acid. It can be polymerized to make synthetic resins; the adjective **acrylic** refers to such polymers; an **acrylate** is a salt or ester of the acid; **acrylonitrile** is its nitrile, a pungent, toxic liquid, used in making artificial fibres and other polymers.

actin(o)- Also **actini-**. *A ray or beam.* [Greek *aktis, aktin-*, ray.]

Some examples refer to rays of light. Radiation that is able to cause chemical reactions, as light does on photographic film, is said to be *actinic*; an **actinometer** is an instrument for measuring the intensity of radiation. *Actinium* is a rare radioactive element (atomic number 89), so named because it glows in the dark; hence **actinide**, a member of the series of radioactive elements, including uranium and plutonium, of which actinium is the first.

Other examples refer to structures that radiate from a centre. Something **actinomorphic**, such as a starfish or the flower of a daisy, has radial symmetry. An **actinomycete** (Greek *mukēs, mukēt-*, fungus) is a bacterium with a filamentous form, which was formerly considered to be a fungus, the *ray-fungus*; this can cause disease in humans and animals; **actinomycin** is a member of a group of antibiotics extracted from soil bacteria of this genus.

-acusis Also **akusis**. *A condition of the hearing.* [Greek *akoustikos*, from *akouein*, to hear.]

The most common example here is **hyperacusis** (Greek *huper*, over, beyond), abnormally acute hearing or painful sensitivity to sounds. Others are **paracusis** (Greek *para*, amiss or irregular), a general term for an abnormality of hearing; **hypoacusis** (Greek *hupo*, under), a reduced sensitivity to sounds; and **diplacusis** (Greek *diplous*, double), a defect of the inner ear so that one sound is heard as two.

-acy: *see* -CY

ad- *Motion or direction to; reduction or change into; addition, increase, or intensification.* [Latin *ad*, to].

Many loanwords from Latin containing this prefix took on a modified or figurative sense in Latin and they retain it in English. For example, *adore* is from Latin *orare*, to speak or pray, via a late Latin form *adorare*, to worship; *addict* originally meant to be assigned by decree to do something (Latin *dicere*, to say), but later shifted sense in English to refer to an attachment to one's own inclinations. Other examples of similar kind are *adolescent*, *adjacent*, *advocate*, and *adequate*.

In Latin the prefix changes according to the initial letter of the word to which it is attached—it can appear as **a-** (before *sc* and *sp*), **ac-** (before *c* and *q*), and as **af-**, **ag-**, **al-**, **an-**, **ap-**, **ar-**, **as-**, and **at-**, in each case before stems beginning with the second letter of the form. A few examples here are *ascribe* (Latin *scribere*, to write), *acquire* (Latin *quaerere*, to seek), *affluent* (Latin *fluere*, to flow), *agglomerate* (Latin *glomus*, a ball), *allocate* (Latin *locare*, location), *annihilate* (Latin *nihil*, nothing), *appetite* (Latin *petere*, to seek), *arrest* (Latin *restare*, remain or stop), *assail* (Latin *salire*, to leap), and *attempt* (Latin *temptare*, to tempt).

-ad¹ *Collective numerals; nymphs.* [Greek *-as*, *-ad-*.]

Examples of collective numerals include *dyad*, something that consists of two elements or parts, and *triad*, of three. A *chiliad* (Greek *khílioi*, a thousand) is either a group of a thousand or a period of a thousand years; a *myriad* is usually a countless or extremely great number (more strictly ten thousand, as it comes from the Greek *murioi* for that number). *Decade*, meaning ten or a period of ten years, retains its final *e* from French. In classical Greece an *Olympiad* was the period of four years between one Olympic Games and the next, though in modern English it often refers to a celebration of the games.

Names of nymphs in Greek classical mythology include *dryad* (Greek *drus*, tree), a nymph inhabiting a tree or a wood, and *naiad* (Greek *naein*, to flow), a water nymph said to inhabit a river, spring, or waterfall.

-ad² *Indicating a direction towards some part of the body.* [Latin *ad*, to or towards.]

A set of adverbs was invented in 1803 by the Scottish anatomist John Barclay (1758–1826) in his book *A New Anatomical Nomenclature*; he created them from adjectives in *-al* (see -AL¹) by replacing that ending with **-ad**, so for example making *ventrad*, towards the abdominal surface of the body, from *ventral*. They are specialist words, mainly confined to zoology. Two further examples are *cephalad* (Greek *kephalē*, head), towards the head, and *caudad* (Latin *cauda*, tail), towards the tail.

-ade *Denoting an action, its result, or something associated with it.* [From Portuguese, Provençal, or Spanish words ending in *-ada*, or Italian words ending in *-ata*, derived from the Latin *-atus*, made of.]

Words in **-ade** have usually come into English through French. The derivation is often less than obvious, as with *barricade*, from Spanish *barrica* for a barrel or cask, as barrels were often used to build barricades. Similarly, *arcade*, a covered passage with arches along one or both sides, is based on Latin *arcus* for a bow, in allusion to the curve of the arches. A *cavalcade*, a kind of procession, ultimately derives from Latin *cavalcare*, to ride. *Lemonade* is from French *limonade*; in imitation English has other names for drinks, such as *cherryade*, *gingerade*, *limeade*, and *orangeade*.

See also -ADO and -CADE.

aden(o)- *A gland.* [Greek *adēn*, a gland.]

The *adenoids* are glandular tissue at the back of the nose, whose surgical removal is *adenoidectomy* (Greek *ektomē*, excision); *adenopathy* (Greek *patheia*, suffering) is a disease or disorder of glandular tissue, usually enlargement of the lymphatic glands; *adenosis* is excessive growth or development of glands; the adjective *adenoid* can refer to the adenoids, but also to glandular tissue in general.

An *adenovirus* is any of a group of DNA viruses first discovered in adenoid tissue, most of which cause respiratory diseases. *Adenine* is one of the four constituent bases of DNA, named because it is found in all glandular tissue; its relative *adenosine*, a compound of it with the sugar ribose, is a nucleoside best known for its derivative *adenosine triphosphate* (ATP), which stores energy in cells.

adip(o)- *Fat or fatty tissues.* [Latin *adeps*, *adip-*, fat.]

The usual adjective is *adipose*, mainly used in medical contexts to describe fatty body tissues; an *adipocyte* is a cell found in connective tissue that stores fat; *adiposity* is fatness, or a tendency to fatness; *adipocere* (Latin *cera*, wax) is a waxy substance sometimes formed by the decomposition of fatty tissue in dead bodies. *See also* LIPO-.

-ado *Forming a variety of words based on Portuguese, Spanish, or Italian originals.* [Spanish and Portuguese *-ado*, or Italian *-ata* or Spanish *-ada*, based on Latin *-atus*, the past participial suffix of verbs ending in *-are*.]

Words in **-ado** form a disparate group whose only link is European languages descended from Latin. Examples include *aficionado*, *amontillado*, *avocado*, *bravado*, *incommunicado*, and *tornado*. *See also* -ADE.

adren(o)-. *The adrenal glands.* [From *adrenal*, formed from AD- plus *renal*, 'of the kidneys', from Latin *renes*, kidney.]

The two *adrenal glands* lie on top of the kidneys. One part of each makes *adrenaline* and *noradrenaline* (in US *epinephrine* and *norepinephrine*), needed to prepare for stress and muscular activity. *Adrenalectomy* (Greek *ektomē*, excision) is surgical excision of all or part of the adrenal glands; the adjective *adrenocortical* refers to the outer portion of the adrenal glands, while *adrenergic* refers to or denotes nerve cells in which adrenaline, noradrenaline, or a similar substance acts as a neurotransmitter.

-ae *Forming plurals.* [From a Latin plural suffix, or representing the Greek plural ending *-ai*.]

The **-ae** suffix is used for the plural of many non-naturalized, specialist, or unfamiliar nouns ending in *-a* (see -A[1]) derived from Latin or Greek: *antennae* is the plural of *antenna*; *larvae* of *larva*; *scapulae* of *scapula*, a shoulder-blade; *pupae* of *pupa*, a chrysalis. It is increasingly common for such words to have plurals in *-as* instead. *See also* -ACEA, -ACEOUS, -IDAE, and -INAE.

-aemia Also **-haemia**. In US **-emia** and **-hemia**. *A substance present in the blood, especially in excess.* [Modern Latin, from Greek *-aimia*, from *haima*, blood.]

A substantial number of such terms exist, mostly from medicine, though a few relate to veterinary ailments. See the LIST on the next page. Forms ending in **-haemia** appear after a stem that ends in *p*, *t*, or *k*, but are rare. Most words ending in **-aemia** can have associated adjectives ending in *-aemic* that describe the condition or a person exhibiting it (*anaemic*, *leukaemic*).

aer(o)- *Air or another gas; the atmosphere; aircraft.* [Greek *aēr*, air.]

Some examples relate to the atmosphere: *aerology* is its study; *aerobiology* is the study of airborne micro-organisms. Others refer to air as a gas, as in *aerate*, to introduce air into something: the form sometimes refers specifically to oxygen: something *aerobic* involves or requires oxygen from the air; *aerobics* is exercise that increases consumption of oxygen. It can refer more broadly to any gas: an *aerosol* is a fine mist dispersed in a gas (it can also be the container that dispenses it).

Aerodynamics is the study of objects moving through the air, such as *aerofoils*, surfaces such as wings shaped to produce lift; *aeronautics* is the science of aerial travel; *aerospace* relates to vehicles that travel both through air and outer space; an *aeroshell* protects a spacecraft during re-entry into the atmosphere.

af-: *see* AD-

afore- *Before or previously.* [Old English *onforan*, from *on-* (see A-[2]) and *foran*, in front, in advance.]

-aemia	A substance present in the blood. _Word origins are from Greek unless otherwise stated._	
anaemia	a deficiency of red blood cells or haemoglobin in the blood	(a-, without)
bacteraemia	the presence of bacteria in the blood	(English _bacterium_)
enterotoxaemia	mostly in veterinary medicine, blood poisoning caused by an enterotoxin	(English _enterotoxin_)
glycaemia,	the presence of glucose in the blood	(_glukus_, sweet)
hyperglycaemia	an excess of glucose in the bloodstream, often associated with diabetes mellitus	(_huper_,over or beyond, plus glycaemia)
hypoglycaemia	deficiency of glucose in the bloodstream	(_hupo_, under, plus glycaemia)
ischaemia	an inadequate blood supply to an organ, especially the heart muscles	(_iskhein_, keep back)
leukaemia	a form of cancer in which increased numbers of leucocytes are produced in the blood	(_leukos_, white)
septicaemia	blood poisoning, especially that caused by bacteria or their toxins	(_sēptikos_, septic)
toxaemia	blood poisoning by toxins from a local bacterial infection	(_toxikon_, poison)
uraemia	a raised level in the blood of urea and other nitrogenous waste compounds	(_ouron_, urine)
viraemia	the presence of viruses in the blood	(English _virus_)

Words beginning with **afore-** are now archaic or formal and in some cases have been replaced by words or phrases employing _before_. Examples are _aforehand_, beforehand, and _aforetime_, in former or past times. _Aforementioned_ and _aforesaid_ refer to a thing or person previously mentioned; _aforethought_, premeditation, now usually appears only in the formal legal term _malice_ aforethought, the intention to kill or harm that distinguishes murder from accidental killing. _Afore_, as a free-standing word meaning 'before', is now only in dialect use.

Afro- _Africa; African and_ …[Latin _Afer_, _Afr-_, African.]

Hyphenated terms often denote a combination of Africa with another country: _Afro-Asiatic_ denotes a family of languages spoken in the Middle East and North Africa; _Afro-American_ (now also in full as _African-American_), refers to black Americans; _Afro-Caribbean_ to a person of African descent living in or coming from the Caribbean. In the US _Afrocentric_ refers to teaching that emphasizes African history and culture. An _Afro_ is a hairstyle reminiscent of the natural hair of some black people.

ag-: _see_ AD-

-age _Forming nouns._ [Old French, based on Latin _-aticum_, neuter form of the adjectival ending _-aticus_.]

Some of the oldest examples came into English from French, such as **language**, **voyage**, or **courage**. Many others have been formed subsequently in English on their models. They are a diverse collection. A few examples of a large group are _coinage_, _cottage_, _damage_, _marriage_, _mileage_, _mortgage_, _peerage_, _plumage_, _postage_, _village_, and _voltage_. Some relatively recent borrowings from French retain their French pronunciation: _entourage_, _montage_.

-agogue In the US often _-agog_. _Leading or promoting._ [Greek _agōgos_, leading.]

A *demagogue* (Greek *demos*, the people) is a political leader who seeks support by appealing to popular desires and prejudices; a *pedagogue* is a teacher, especially a strict or pedantic one (originally from Greek *paidagōgos*, a slave who accompanied a child to school).

The ending appears in medical terms for a substance that induces expulsion or secretion: *cholagogue* (Greek *cholē*, bile), something that promotes the flow of bile; *emmenagogue* (Greek *emmēna*, menses), one that stimulates or increases menstrual flow; *secretagogue*, a substance which promotes secretion.

However, *synagogue* comes from the Greek word for a meeting, from *sun-*, together, plus the related *agein*, bring.

-agra *Pain in some part of the body.* [Greek *agra*, a seizure.]

A few medical terms contain this ending, though it is relatively rare. Examples are *podagra* (Greek *pous*, *pod-*, the foot), gout of the foot, especially of the big toe; *pellagra* (Greek *pelle*, skin, on the pattern of podagra), a vitamin deficiency disease; and *chiragra*, a pain in the hand (Greek *cheir*, hand).

agro- Also **agri-**. *Farming; cultivation.* [Greek *agros* or Latin *ager*, *agr-*, a field.]

The principal term here is *agriculture*. Others are *agrochemical*, a chemical used in agriculture, such as a pesticide or fertilizer; *agroforestry*, agriculture that incorporates the cultivation of trees; *agriscience*, the application of science to agriculture; and *agronomy*, the science of soil management and crop production.

Agribusiness is either agriculture on strictly commercial principles (often by implication having limited regard for nature or landscape conservation) or the industries that deal with agricultural produce and services for farming; *agritourism* (or *agrotourism*) is tourism that involves visitors with the work of farms and rural life, often as a means of economic regeneration. The adjective *agrarian* refers to the cultivation of land or reform of the system of holding land.

-(a)holic Also **-oholic**. *A person exces-* sively fond of something. [The ending of *alcoholic*, a person suffering from alcoholism.]

Many terms in this ending have disparaging or facetious associations and few refer to an addiction in the medical sense. Some common examples are *workaholic*, a person who compulsively works excessively hard and unusually long hours; *chocoholic* (less often *chocaholic*), a person who is excessively fond of chocolate; and *shopaholic*, a compulsive shopper. Words are often created to meet a momentary need: *computerholic*, a person who spends too much time in front of a computer (here the initial *a* of the ending is replaced by the unstressed final *er* of *computer*); *gymaholic*, someone who spends too much time exercising at the gym.

-aire *A person characterized by or linked to the idea in the stem.* [French **-ier** or *-aire*, derived from Latin words in *-arius*.]

Some examples are *millionaire*, a person whose assets are worth one million pounds or dollars or more (and other words formed in imitation of it, such as *billionaire* and *zillionaire*); *commissionaire*, a uniformed door attendant at a hotel or theatre (medieval Latin *commissionarius*, a person in charge); and *concessionaire*, the holder of a concession or grant. *Doctrinaire* is now usually an adjective referring to an attempt to impose a doctrine without regard to practical considerations. *See also* -AR², -ARY, -ER, and -EER.

-akusis: *see* -ACUSIS

al-: *see* AD-

-al¹ Also **-ial**, **-orial**, and **-ual**. *Forming adjectives and some nouns.* [Variously from French *-el* or *-aille*, or Latin *-alis*.]

This suffix can be added to many nouns to create associated adjectives. Several thousand examples exist, often as compound endings with other suffixes. Originally the ending was attached to words from Latin roots (*annual*, *infernal*), but was later extended to those from Greek (*historical*, *comical*), and sometimes native English sources (*tidal*). Other examples are *accidental*, *eternal*, *gradual*, *individual*, *natural*, *paternal*, *universal*, and *visual*.

Adjectives in **-ial** often derive from Latin words in *-ialis*, where the *i* is contributed by the stem: *celestial*, *official*, *partial*, *special*. Adjectives in **-orial** are related to or derived from Latin or English nouns which end in *-or* or *-tor* (*see* -OR¹): *curatorial*, *dictatorial*, *janitorial*, *professorial*, or from Latin words ending in *-oralis*, or English nouns in -ORY: *categorial*, *purgatorial*, *territorial*. Adjectives in **-ual** derive from Latin words ending in *-ualis* (*annual*, *sensual*, *virtual*) or *-uus* (*continual*, *intellectual*, *perpetual*).

Nouns with this ending contain the idea of action or process, usually based on French or Latin verbs, for example *arrival*, the act or action of arriving, and *denial*, the act of denying something. Other common examples are *approval*, *dismissal*, *proposal*, *recital*, *rehearsal*, *survival*, and *trial*.

See also -AR¹, -HEDRON (for *-hedral*), -IC (for *-ical*), -LOGICAL, -METER (for *-metrical*), -OID (for *-oidal*), and -ION.

-al² *An aldehyde.* [The first syllable of *aldehyde* or *alcohol*.]

This is one of the systematic naming rules of the International Union of Pure and Applied Chemistry. The *aldehyde* group is —CHO, formed by the oxidation of alcohols. Some aldehydes were named before the rules were developed, so *ethanal* is better known as *acetaldehyde* and *methanal* as *formaldehyde*; other examples of systematic names are *propanal* and *butanal*; the generic term is *alkanal*. *Chloral*, a colourless, viscous liquid made by chlorinating acetaldehyde, is formally *trichloroethanal*; the name is usually an abbreviation for *chloral hydrate*, once used as a hypnotic and anaesthetic and as knock-out drops. *See also* ALDO-.

alb- *White or bright.* [Latin *albus*, white.]

An *albino* is a person or animal with abnormally white skin and hair, resulting from a lack of pigment, hence *albinism* for the condition; in astronomy, the *albedo* of a celestial body is the extent to which it reflects light, how bright it is;

albumen is egg white, or the protein contained in it.

The same prefix occurs less obviously in *albatross* (from the Spanish *alcatras* for the frigate bird, changed and applied to the albatross under the influence of *albus*, the bird being white); *album* (originally applied in Roman times to a blank, or white, tablet on which public notices were inscribed); and *Albion* as an ancient name for the British Isles, in reference to the white cliffs of Dover.

aldo- *An aldehyde.* [English *aldehyde*.]

The *aldehyde* group is —CHO, formed by the oxidation of alcohols. The *aldoses* are sugars that contain the group, such as ribose; *aldol* (formal name 3-hydroxybutanal) is a viscous liquid obtained when two molecules of acetaldehyde link together in dilute alkali or acid (the name is a blend of *aldehyde* and *alcohol*, since the molecule shows properties of both); *aldosterone* is a hormone containing an aldehyde group which regulates water and salt balance; *aldolase* is an enzyme found in muscle tissue. *See also* -AL².

-ales *Orders of plants.* [The plural of the Latin adjectival suffix *-alis*.]

In the hierarchical classification of plants, orders come immediately below the subclass or superorder (whose names end in -AE), and immediately above the families (whose names end in -ACEAE). Some examples are *Orchidales*, the order containing orchids; *Rosales*, the roses and related plants; *Taxales*, the yews; *Equisetales*, the horsetails; and the *Ranunculales*, the buttercups and related plants.

-algia Also **-algic**. *Pain, usually in a specified part of the body.* [Greek *algos*, pain.]

Most words ending in **-algia** are specialist medical terms, but a few are more generally known, such as *neuralgia*, intense intermittent pain along the course of a nerve. For more examples, *see* the LIST opposite.

One that seems not to fit here is *nostalgia*, a sentimental longing or wistful affection for the past; this first entered the language meaning homesickness (Greek

-algia	Pain.	
	Word origins are from Greek.	
arthralgia	pain in a joint	(*arthron*, a joint)
causalgia	severe burning pain in a limb caused by injury to a peripheral nerve	(*kausos*, heat or fever)
cephalalgia	headache	(*kephalē*, head)
erythromelalgia	a disease associated with burning, redness of the skin, and pain	(*eruthros*, red, plus *melos*, limb)
gastralgia	pain in the stomach	(*gastēr* or *gastr-*, stomach)
mastalgia	pain in the breast caused by congestion during lactation, or other causes	(*mastos*, breast)
myalgia	pain in a muscle or group of muscles	(*mus*, muscle)
neuralgia	intense, typically intermittent pain along the course of a nerve	(*neuron*, a nerve)
ostalgia	a pain associated with some abnormal condition in a bone	(*osteon*, bone)
otalgia	earache	(*ōtalgia*, from *ous* or *ōt-*, ear)
prosopalgia	stabbing pain in the face, also called trigeminal neuralgia	(*prosōpon*, face)
rachialgia	pain in or due to the spine	(*rhakhis*, spine)

nostos, return home), hence having a sense close to 'pain of separation'.

A few terms have linked adjectives in **-algic**, for example **arthralgic**, **myalgic**, **neuralgic**, and **nostalgic**.

algo- *Pain.* [Greek *algos*, pain.]

Algology is the branch of medicine concerned with the study of pain (a word of the same spelling, but from Latin *alga* seaweed, refers to the study of algae); a person who studies this specialism is an *algologist*; *algophobia* is an abnormal fear of pain; and *algolagnia* (Greek *lagneia*, lust) is a desire for sexual gratification through inflicting pain on oneself or others, sadomasochism.

-alia *A collection or group.* [Latin plural ending of adjectives in *-alis*.]

Examples from Latin include *genitalia*, the genitals (Latin *genitalis*, from *gignere*, to beget), *marginalia*, marginal notes (Latin *marginalis*, marginal), and *paraphernalia*, miscellaneous articles, often viewed as superfluous (originally the private property of a married woman, based on Greek *parapherna*, property separate from a dowry). A few words

have been coined in English from Latin roots, such as *orientalia* (Latin *orientalis*, oriental), items characteristic of the Orient.

On their model, especially that of paraphernalia, a few words have been invented in English on stems in which *-alia* indicates a collection, sometimes with implications of triviality; perhaps the best-known is *kitchenalia*, miscellaneous items of kitchenware. Temporary forms appear from time to time, such as *curtainalia* and *tartanalia*, but the ending is not really productive.

See also -IA *and* -LALIA.

all(o)- *Other; different.* [Greek *allos*, other.]

An *allegory* (Greek *-agoria*, speaking, so literally 'speaking otherwise') is a story, poem, or picture in which there is another, hidden meaning; an *allergy* (Greek *ergon*, work, so something working differently) is a damaging immune response by the body to a substance.

Allotropes are the different physical forms in which an element can exist, such as carbon, which can occur as graphite or as diamond; *allopathy* is the treatment of disease with drugs having effects opposed to the symptoms (contrasted with *homeopathy*).

In linguistics, *allographs* are alternative forms of a letter of an alphabet, for example its capital, lower-case, and italic forms; *allophones* are the various ways sounds can be pronounced, which do not contribute to distinctions of meaning.

alumin(o)- *Aluminium.* [Latin *alumen*, *alumin-*, alum, an aluminium compound used in dyeing and tanning.]

Alumino- is comparatively unusual, appearing mainly in *aluminosilicate*, a silicate containing aluminium, as in some clays or feldspars; the adjective *aluminous* describes minerals that contain aluminium; and *alumina*, an ore of aluminium. The *aluminothermic* process (also called the thermite process) reduces metallic oxides to their metals using finely powdered aluminium; a mineral that is *aluminiferous* contains or yields aluminium.

-ama: *see* -ORAMA

ambi- *On both sides; around.* [Latin *ambo*, both, or *ambi-*, on both sides, around.]

In the sense of both, this refers to an equivalence between two opposing ideas or forces, as in *ambidextrous*, of somebody who is able to use the right and left hands equally well, or the psychological term *ambisexual* for a person who is bisexual or androgynous. This has been extended to mean an indefinite small number in words such as *ambiguous* (Latin *agere*, to drive), a matter open to more than one interpretation, or *ambivalent* (Latin *valere*, be worth), having mixed feelings or contradictory ideas about something or someone.

The sense of being or going around appears in *ambient*, relating to the surrounding area or environment, and in *ambit*, the scope, extent, or bounds of something (in both cases from Latin *ambire*, to go around). The idea is more deeply disguised in *ambition*, which comes from the same Latin verb; originally this referred to going around canvassing for votes, or more generally seeking out favour.

amid(o)- *The CONH₂— group in chemical compounds.* [From *amide*, an organic derivative of *ammonia*.]

The group is variously called the *amide group* or *amido group* and occurs, for example, in polymers. *Amidines* are strong bases derived from amides; *amidol* (a trade name for *diamidophenol*) is a photographic developer.

amino- *The amine group, —NH₂.* [From *amine*, an organic derivative of *ammonia*.]

The prefix commonly appears as a freestanding word in *amino acid*, one of a number of organic compounds essential for life; the name comes from the presence of an amine group in each. The *aminoglucosides* are a group of antibiotics that includes streptomycin; *aminophylline* is used to treat asthma; *aminoplastic* resins derive from amine compounds such as urea; *aminocarb* is an insecticide.

amnio- *The amnion.* [Greek *amnion*, caul, a diminutive of *amnos*, lamb.]

The *amnion* is the innermost membrane that encloses the embryo of a mammal, bird, or reptile, for which the adjective is *amniotic*. *Amniocentesis* is the process of sampling that fluid for analysis. Related medical terms include *amniotomy* (Greek *-tomia*, cutting), the artificial rupture of the amnion immediately before birth, and *amnionitis*, an inflammation of the amnion that may be caused by premature rupture of the membrane.

amph(i)- Also **ampho-**. *Variously two, both, on both sides, or around.* [Greek *amphi-* or *amphō*, both.]

This appears in a number of words borrowed from Greek, such as *amphitheatre* (US *amphitheater*), an arena surrounded by spectator seating, and *amphibian* (Greek *amphibios*, living both in water and on land). Modern examples include *amphipathic* (Greek *pathos*, experience), of a molecule which has elements with different properties (such as a detergent, which has molecules with one end soluble in water and one not); a molecule that is **amphoteric** has both acidic and basic properties.

amyl(o)- *Starch.* [Greek *amylon*, starch.]

Amylase is an enzyme that digests starch and glycogen and converts them into simple sugars; *amyloid* is a starch-like protein which is deposited in some soft tissues in certain diseases. Starch occurs in two forms in the body—*amylo-pectin* is the insoluble form, consisting of branched polysaccharide chains, while *amylose* is the soluble form having un-branched chains. *Amyl* refers to the C_5H_{11}— radical of *amyl alcohol* (which was first obtained from fermented grain starch), which appears in a variety of chemical compounds.

an-: *see* A-[1], AD-, and ANA-

-an: *see* -IAN

an(a)- *Variously up, back, or again.* [Greek *ana*, up, back, again, anew.]

Some common words show the variety of senses of the Greek original: an *ana-gram*, a word or phrase formed by re-arranging the letters of another, comes from Greek *ana-* in the sense of 'anew', plus *gramma*, a letter; *anatomy*, the study of bodily structure, is literally 'cutting up' (from *tomia*, a cutting) because dissec-tion is an essential part of that study; an *anachronism*, a thing belonging or appropriate to a period other than that in which it exists, comes from *ana-* in the sense of 'backwards', plus *khronos*, time.

Most words containing this form are technical terms in the arts and sciences. Some examples are *anabolic* (Greek *bal-lein*, to throw), of the metabolic synthesis of molecules in living organisms; *anadro-mous* (Greek *dromos*, running), of a fish, such as the salmon, that migrates up rivers from the sea to spawn; *anode* (Greek *hodos*, way), the positively charged electrode by which the electrons leave an electrical device; *anaphylactic* (Greek *phulaxis*, guarding), of an extreme allergic reaction, for example to a bee sting.

-ana Also **-iana**. *Things associated with a person, place, or field of interest.* [Latin, neu-ter plural ending of adjectives in *-anus*.]

This ending can indicate a collection of interesting or collectible items associated with a person, place, or period: *Ameri-cana*, *Churchilliana*, *Africana*, *Shake-speareana* (sometimes *Shakespeariana*), *Victoriana*; or a collection of notable sayings associated with a person: *John-soniana*, *Swinburneana*. *Ana* sometimes occurs as a free-standing word in the sense of a collection of anecdotes or liter-ary gossip about a person.

-ance Also **-ence**, **-ancy**, and **-ency**. *A state or quality; a process or action.* [French *-ance* or *-ence*, from Latin *-antia* or *-entia*.]

Words in the *a* and *e* spellings have similar meanings. Which spelling is considered correct usually depends on the Latin word from which it derives. But the history of the suffixes is confused and inconsistent; many words have changed spelling in passing through French, and again in English. Modern creations use the spelling of their Latin precursors where one exists; with stems from other sources, the choice of ending is largely arbitrary.

Words with these endings may suggest a quality or state (*confidence*, *ignorance*, *impertinence*, *protuberance*), an amount or degree (*conductance*, *pittance*), or an action or process, or its result (*emergence*, *furtherance*, *performance*, *reference*, *remit-tance*, *vengeance*).

Latin *-antia* and *-entia* are also the source of English words ending in **-ancy** and **-ency**. These endings are more recent than **-ance** and **-ence** and suggest the idea of a quality or state, often an abstract one, without the idea of action or process. Examples are *buoyancy*, *con-stancy*, *efficiency*, *infancy*, *piquancy*, *presi-dency*, *urgency*, and *vacancy*.

Because of the overlap in meaning between words ending in **-ance** and **-ancy** and those in **-ence** and **-ency**, a number of word pairs exist that have closely related senses, though one member is often rarer than the other: *convergence* and *convergency*, *re-pugnance* and *repugnancy*, *irrelevance* and *irrelevancy*, *permanence* and *perman-ency*.

See also -CY and -ESCE (for nouns in *-escence*); *see* -ANT for related adjectives.

anchylo- or **ancylo-**: *see* ANKYLO-

-and *A person or thing to be treated in a specified way.* [Latin verb forms *-andus*, *-anda*, and *-andum*, which function as adjectives.]

Words usually have a passive sense of something or somebody which is to suffer some action. A *multiplicand* (Latin *multiplicandus*, to be multiplied) is a quantity which is to be multiplied by another; an *operand* (Latin *operandum*, on which labour is to be expended) is a quantity on which a mathematical operation is to be carried out; an *ordinand* (Latin *ordinandus*, being put in order) is a person under training to be ordained as a priest or minister.

A small number of modern technical terms have been created using **-and**: *analysand* (from *analyse*), a person undergoing psychoanalysis, *ligand* (Latin *ligandus*, that can be tied), an ion or molecule attached to a metal atom by coordinate bonding, and *proband* (Latin *probandus*, to be proved), a person serving as the starting-point for the genetic study of a family.

andr(o)- *Male or maleness.* [Greek *anēr*, *andr-*, man.]

Medical terms in this prefix include *androgen*, a male sex hormone such as testosterone or *androsterone*, and *andrology*, the study of male health, especially infertility and impotence. Someone *androgynous* (Greek *gunē*, woman) exhibits characteristics both of male and female, usually in the social sense rather than as the result of a medical condition. An *android* in science fiction is either a human-looking robot or a biological construct in human form; it is also an adjective referring to something typically masculine, such as an *android pelvis*, one characteristic of the male.

For its female equivalent, *see* GYNAECO-. *See also* HOMO-[2].

-androus Also **-andry**. *Maleness.* [Modern Latin *-andrus*, from Greek *anēr*, *andr-*, man.]

Forms in **-androus** are adjectives: *polyandrous* (Greek *polloi*, many), referring to a state in which a woman has more than one husband; *protandrous* (Greek *prōtos*, first) in a hermaphrodite flower or animal is a state in which the male reproductive organs come to maturity before the female ones. Corresponding nouns end in **-andry**: *polyandry*, *protandry*, *misandry* (hatred of males; Greek *misos*, hatred). In common with some other words, *husbandry* does not contain this suffix, but is instead formed from *husband* plus *-ry* (*see* -ERY). For the female equivalent, *see* -GYNOUS.

-ane[1] *Saturated straight-chain (aliphatic) hydrocarbons.* [An invented ending, on the model of Greek noun suffixes.]

Early members of the hydrocarbon series are identified using existing common names for related compounds: *methane*, *ethane*, and *butane*; later members are named using number prefixes, based on how many carbon atoms there are in the molecule: *pentane*, *hexane*, *octane*. The general term for a member of the series, of formula C_nH_{2n+2}, is *alkane* (from German *Alkohol*, alcohol). These forms occur widely in chemical names of compounds: *polyurethane*, *isobutane*, *2-methylpentane*. For the related adjectival ending, *see* -YL.

-ane[2] *Forming adjectives.* [Latin adjectival endings *-anus*, *-ana*, *-anum*.]

This is a variant spelling of *-an* (*see* -IAN), which was sometimes introduced to distinguish words from counterparts in *-an*, as in *humane* and *urbane*. Some have no equivalent form in *-an*: *arcane* (Latin *arcanus*, from *arcere*, to shut up), *mundane* (Latin *mundus*, world), *profane* (Latin *profanus*, outside the temple, not sacred, from *fanum*, temple). The word spelled *germane* is a variant of *german*, from Latin *germanus*, genuine, of the same parents. In *balletomane* the ending is *-mane* (*see* -MANIA).

anem(o)- *The wind.* [Greek *anemos*, wind.]

This prefix is most commonly encountered in the *anemometer*, an instrument for measuring the speed of the wind. In botany, an *anemophilous* (Greek *philos*, loving) plant is one that is pollinated by the wind. The name of the *anemone* comes from the Greek word meaning windflower (a name the plant sometimes has in English), so called because it was thought the flowers open only when the wind blows.

-aneous: *see* -OUS

angi(o)- *Blood or seed vessels.* [Greek *angeion*, vessel.]

Angiography is the X-ray examination of blood vessels; *angiocardiography* is a similar examination of the heart and its blood vessels. An *angioma* (plural *angiomata*) is a benign tumour composed of blood vessels or lymph vessels; the production of new blood vessels is called *angiogenesis*; *angiotensin* is an enzyme whose presence in the blood constricts the vessels and raises blood pressure. (The heart condition *angina*, which looks as though it belongs here, derives instead from Greek *ankhonē*, strangling, which describes the pain.) In botany, an *angiosperm* is a plant of a large group that has flowers and produces enclosed seeds.

-angium *A container.* [Greek *angeion*, vessel.]

In botany, a *sporangium* in ferns and lower plants is a receptacle in which asexual spores are formed; a *synangium* (Greek *sun*, with) is a group of united sporangia; a *gametangium* is a specialized organ or cell in which gametes are formed in algae, ferns, and some other plants. In zoology, a *gonangium* (Greek *gone*, generation, seed) is a reproductive polyp of a colonial hydroid.

Anglo- *English or British; English or British and …* [Latin *Anglus*, English.]

The prefix has several meanings depending on context that often reflect a confusion between *England* and *Britain*. Terms often have multiple senses resulting from historical links or sensitivities.

It is frequently used in hyphenated compounds linking England or Britain to another group or nationality: *Anglo-American* can refer to a American citizen of English origin, or relationships between the United States and Britain; *Anglo-Irish* can indicate a link between Britain and Ireland, specifically to the Republic of Ireland (as in the *Anglo-Irish Agreement* of 1995), or to a person of English descent born or resident in Ireland (or one of mixed English and Irish parentage), or to the English language as used in Ireland. *Anglo-Saxon* refers to the Germanic inhabitants of England between the 5th century and the Norman Conquest (and in modern times to individuals of English descent).

Other words containing the prefix include *Anglomania*, excessive admiration for English customs; *Anglophobia*, a hatred or fear of England or Britain; *Anglocentric*, centred on or considered in terms of England or Britain. An *anglophone* is an English-speaking person, or refers to the speaking of English.

anis(o)- *Unequal, asymmetrical, dissimilar.* [Greek *anisos*, unequal.]

Terms are the negatives, using *an-* (*see* A-[1]), of words in ISO-. Examples are *anisotropic* (from Greek *tropē*, turn, turning), having a physical property that is not the same in every direction; *anisometropia* (Greek *metron* measure, plus *ōps*, *ōp-*, eye), inequality of refractive power of the eyes; *anisocytosis* (Greek *kutos*, vessel), abnormal variation in the size of cells, especially of red blood corpuscles; *anisogamy* (Greek *gamos*, marriage), sexual reproduction by the fusion of dissimilar gametes; and *anisophyllous* (Greek *phullon*, leaf), having leaves of different shapes or sizes on either side of a shoot.

ankylo- *Also* **anchylo-** *and* **ancyclo-**. *Bent or crooked; stiff or fixed.* [Greek *ankulos*, crooked.]

Ankylosis (sometimes *anchylosis*) is abnormal stiffening and immobility of a joint due to fusion of the bones; *ankylosing spondylitis* is an inflammatory disease of the spine that often causes it to bend forwards; *ankyloglossia* (Greek *glōssa*, tongue), also called *tongue-tie*, is an impeded motion of the tongue. An *anky-losaur* is a Cretaceous dinosaur (literally, 'crooked lizard'). The spelling **ankylo-** is now the usual one.

-ant Also **-ent**. *Forming adjectives and nouns.* [French *-ant* or *-ent*, taken from Latin present participial forms.]

Such adjectives and nouns often parallel words in *-ance* or *-ence* (*see* -ANCE), and similar confusion accompanies their spelling. Adjectives with these endings include *arrogant*, *convenient*, *different*, *obedient*, *permanent*, *portent*, *reminiscent*, and *resident*. Nouns often denote a person or thing acting in some capacity: *agent*, *applicant*, *contestant*, *deodorant*, *opponent*, *propellant*, *superintendent*, *tenant*. *See also* -ESCE (for *-escent*), -FIC, -FACIENT, -MENT, and -ULENT.

ante- *Before or preceding.* [Latin *ante*, before.]

The sense is either of something placed in front of another or existing earlier in time. The first idea is found in *antechamber*, *anteroom*, and *anterior* (situated towards the front of the body); an *antepenultimate* item is the last but two in a series. The second sense appears in *antenatal* (before birth), *antedate* (to pre-date), *antebellum* (before the war, especially the US Civil War), and *ancestor* (Latin *cedere*, to go, hence to go before or precede). Some that appear to be formed from the equivalent Greek prefix ANTI- actually contain **ante-**: *anticipate*, *antique*. Its opposite is POST-.

antero- *Nearer the front of the body; forward in time.* [English *anterior*.]

The adjective *anterolateral* means in front of and on each side of an object or body; an *anteroposterior* direction is from front to back, typically in reference to the direction of an X-ray beam; something *anterograde* is directed forward in time, especially in *anterograde amnesia*, an inability to remember events that happen after the onset of amnesia, often as a result of a head injury.

anth(o)- *A flower or flowers.* [Greek *anthos*, flower.]

The *anthocyanins* (Greek *kuan(e)os*, dark blue) are pigments that give the red, blue, or purple colour to flowers and fruits; an *anthozoan* is a member of a large class of marine animals that includes the sea anemones and corals, which resemble flowers. An *anthology* is literally a collection of flowers, but figuratively refers to little flowers of composition—poems or epigrams by various authors.

anthrac(o)- Also **anthra-**. *Coal or carbon; a carbuncle.* [Greek *anthrax*, coal.]

A hard type of coal is called *anthracite*, originally the Greek word for a type of gem; the chemical *anthracene*, a valuable raw material for making dyestuffs, was first obtained by distilling coal-tar. The plant diseases collectively called *anthracnose*, caused by a fungus, are so named because dark, sunken spots appear; *anthrax*, a severe infectious disease caused by a bacillus, causes carbuncles among other symptoms.

The shortened prefix **anthra-** denotes compounds obtained originally from coal-tar or related to anthracene: *anthraquinone* is a yellow crystalline compound used to make dyes; another dyestuff precursor is *anthranilic acid*, whose derivative *methyl anthranilate* gives foodstuffs a grape flavour and also appears in perfumes and aromatherapy oils.

anthrop(o)- *Human, or of a human being.* [Greek *anthrōpos*, human being].

Anthropology is the study of human beings; to be *anthropocentric* is to regard humankind as the central or most important element of existence; an *anthropoid* is an animal resembling a human being in form, such as an *anthropoid ape*; *anthropomorphism* (Greek *morphē*, form) is the attribution of human behaviour or characteristics to a god, animal, or object. Something *anthropogenic* results from human activity (usually in reference to pollution or environmental degradation); *anthropometry* is the scientific study of the measurements and proportions of the human body.

-anthropy Also **-anthropist**, **-anth-**

rope, and **-anthropic**. *Human, or human-kind.* [Greek *anthrōpia*, mankind.]

Common examples are *philanthropy* (Greek *philein*, to love), a desire to promote the welfare of others; *misanthropy* (Greek *miso-*, hating), a dislike of humankind; and *lycanthropy* (Greek *lukos*, wolf), the super-natural transformation of a person into a wolf, as recounted in folk tales. Names for the individuals involved are formed in **-anthropist** (*philanthropist*), or some-times **-anthrope** (*misanthrope*); adjec-tives are formed in **-anthropic** (*lycanthropic*).

ant(i)- *Acting against, resisting, or opposing something; the opposite or re-verse of something.* [Greek *anti*, against.]

Many terms in **anti-** are hyphenated if the next element begins with a vowel, though hyphenation is variable. The pre-fix is active, often forming new words that are destined to be temporary. Words may be nouns or adjectives, sometimes both.

One group represents opposition, resistance or aversion: *anti-abortion*, *anti-apartheid*, *antiestablishment*, *anti-government*, *anti-nuclear*, *anti-Semitic*, *antivivisectionist*. Another refers to an agent that acts against something: *anti-aircraft*, *antibiotic*, *antimagnetic*, *anti-freeze*, *anti-static*, *antiseptic*. A third denotes the simple opposite of some-thing: *anticlimax*, *anticlockwise*, *Antarctic* (the opposite side of the world from the Arctic), *antigravity*, *antisocial*.

Subatomic particles have mirror parti-cles with the same mass but opposite values for other properties, such as charge; the prefix is used in the sense of 'opposite' to name them: *antiproton*, *antineutrino*, *antimuon*; the general name is *antiparticle*, and hypothetical matter made up entirely of such particles is *anti-matter*.

Some words in *anti-*, such as *anticipate*, are actually formed using ANTE-.

ap-: *see* AD-

apic(o)- *A point or apex.* [Latin *apex*, *apic-*, a point or tip.]

The usual adjective is *apical*; some-thing *apiculate* has a minute apex or tip;

apicitis is inflammation of the apex of a body structure, such as the root of a tooth.

apo- *Away from; separate from.* [Greek *apo*, off, from, or away.]

The prefix often occurs in words borrowed from Greek, as in *apostasy* (Greek *apostasis*, defection), the abandon-ment or renunciation of a religious or political belief or principle; *apostrophe*, a mark to show where one or more letters have been missed out (Greek *stre-phein*, to turn, so a mark of turning away, an elision); *apostle* (Greek *apostolos*, mes-senger); *apoplexy* (from *plēssein*, to strike, hence 'struck down').

A number of coinages appear in mod-ern scientific English: *apoptosis* (Greek *ptōsis*, falling or a fall, hence a falling away or decay), the death of cells which occurs as a normal part of an organism's development; *apomixis* (Greek *mixis*, min-gling), asexual reproduction in plants; and *apocarpous* (Greek *karpos*, fruit), of a flo-wer or fruit that has its carpels separate.

In astronomy, the prefix referes to the point in its orbit at which a body is fur-thest from its parent, as in *apogee* (**Greek** *gē*, earth), for the moon or a satellite in earth orbit; *aphelion* (Greek *hēlios*, sun; the final *o* of the prefix is lost before *h*), for the sun; *apolune* (Latin *luna*, moon), for the moon. Its opposite is PERI-.

après- *A period following some activity.* [French *après*, after.]

This appears in some informal and hu-morous words that are modelled on the French *après-ski*, the social activities and entertainment following a day's skiing. Examples are *après-board*, relating to snowboarding, *après-surf*, surfing, and *après-shopping*.

aqua- *Also* **aque-** *and* **aqui-**. *Water.* [Latin *aqua*, water.]

The usual adjectives are *aquatic*, relat-ing to an activity that takes place in or on water or to plants or animals that live in water, and *aqueous*, of or containing water, especially as a solvent or medium.

Aquaculture (sometimes *aquiculture*) is fish-farming or other water-based culti-vation; an *aquarium* is a tank of water for keeping aquatic animals or plants or a building containing a number of such tanks; an underwater swimmer may use an *aqualung* in order to breathe; *aquarobics* are aerobic exercises performed in water; an *aquifer* is a rock formation containing extractable water. The stone called *aquamarine* takes its name from Latin *aqua marina*, seawater, because of its light bluish-green colour. *Aqua* itself appears in lists of ingredients to indicate the presence of water.

Words that do not belong here include *aquiline*, having a nose hooked like an eagle's beak (Latin *aquila*, eagle), and *acquaint*, *acquiesce*, and *acquit* (for which *see* AD-).

ar-: *see* AD-

-ar¹ *Forming adjectives.* [Latin adjectival ending *-aris*.]

Latin word stems that ended in *l* employed *-aris* to make their adjectives rather than *-alis*, the source of our -AL suffix. As a result, the majority of adjectives in **-ar** in English have *l* or *ul* before the suffix, such as *angular*, *circular*, *globular*, *jocular*, *polar*, *regular*, *similar*, and *singular* (*see also* -ULE). Other English adjectives derived from Latin words ending in *-aris* include *columnar*, *linear*, *lumbar*, *lunar*, *planar*, and *stellar*. Some English adjectives have been formed using **-ar** that do not have Latin originals in *-aris*, often being based instead on Latin nouns in *-um*: *curricular*, *granular*, *molecular*, *nuclear*, *scapular*. See also -ARY.

-ar² *Forming nouns.* [Latin words ending in *-aris*, *-arius*, *-arium*, or *-are*, or Old French words ending in *-aire* or *-ier*.]

Examples from Latin include *altar*, *bursar*, *cellar*, *exemplar*, *mortar*, *scholar*, and *vicar*. Examples from Old French include *burglar*, *collar*, *pillar*, *poplar*, and *vinegar*. For a few nouns this ending is a variant of *-er* (*see* -ER¹) or *-or* (*see* -OR¹ and -OR²), changed by an accident of spelling history: *liar*, *beggar*. Other nouns have this ending by chance, often through an origin in some other language: *sugar* (from Arabic), *guitar* (Greek), *briar* (Old English), *fulmar* (Old Norse), *jaguar* (Tupi-Guarani).

Others, such as *sonar* and *radar*, are acronyms. *See also* -AIRE and -ARY.

arachn(o)- *A spider or spiders.* [Greek *arakhnē*, spider.]

Somebody frightened of spiders is said to have *arachnophobia*; the study of spiders—and the other *Arachnida*, a class of arthropods that also includes scorpions, mites, and ticks—is *arachnology*; an *arachnid* is a member of this group; the associated adjective is *arachnoid*.

-arama: *see* -ORAMA

arbor(i)- *A tree or trees.* [Latin *arbor*, tree.]

An *arboretum* is a tree garden; *arboriculture* is the culture of trees, especially for ornamental or scientific purposes. An *arbour* (US *arbor*) is a garden alcove shaded by trees or plants trained over a framework. Adjectives include *arborescent*, something tree-like in growth or appearance, such as a crystal, and *arboreal*, living in trees, or of the nature of trees. An *arborization* in anatomy is a fine branching structure at the end of a nerve fibre, like the branches of a tree.

arch- Also **arche-** and **archi-**. *Chief; principal; pre-eminent of its kind.* [Greek *arkhi-* or *arkhe-*, from *arkhos*, chief.]

The main meaning is that of the most important or highest ranking person of a given type, as in *archduke*, *archdeacon*, *archangel*, and *archbishop*. An *architect* is literally the 'chief builder', from Greek *tektōn*, builder.

A secondary sense uses the prefix in a critical or dismissive way to mean somebody who holds extreme views, or is the worst kind of something, or the ringleader of a group. Examples are *arch-enemy*, *arch-fiend*, *arch-criminal*, *arch-reactionary*, *arch-rival*, and *arch-villain*.

An *archegonium* (Greek *gonos*, race) is the female sex organ in mosses, liverworts, ferns, and most conifers. In *archetype* (*tupos*, model), the Greek prefix has a meaning more like 'original' or 'primitive', hence one of its meanings—the original pattern or model for something. The word *architrave* (Latin *trabs*, a beam) came from classical architecture, in which it was a main beam resting across the tops of columns.

Archive comes from a Greek word for public records; it derives from the related *arkhē*, government.

-arch: *see* -ARCHY

archaeo- Also **archae-** (In the US, usually **archeo-** and **arche-**.) *Ancient or prehistoric times.* [Greek *arkhaios*, ancient.]

Archaeology is the scientific study of human history and prehistory through the excavation and study of physical remains. Several terms link another area of study to archaeology: *archaeobotany* is the study of botanical remains in archaeology; *archaeometry* is the application of scientific techniques to the dating of archaeological remains; *archaeostronomy* is the investigation of the astronomical knowledge of prehistoric cultures.

The *archaea* (singular *archaean*) are ancient organisms intermediate between the bacteria and eukaryotes (another name for the group is *archaebacteria*, now thought to be inaccurate). *Archaeomagnetism* is fossil magnetism in a rock laid down when it first cooled, which can be used to date it and its surroundings. *Archaeopteryx* (Greek *pterux*, wing) is the oldest known fossil bird, from the late Jurassic period.

arche- or **archi-**: *see* ARCH-

-archy Also **-arch**. *Government; rule of a particular type; a chief or ruler.* [Greek *arkhēs*, ruler; *arkhein*, to rule.]

Words in **-archy** are abstract nouns for types of government, leadership, or social influence or organization. They correspond to nouns in **-arch** for a person or people who rule or command in that way. For example, a *monarch* (Greek

---

-archy Government or rule.
All word sources are Greek unless otherwise stated.

anarchy	a state of disorder due to absence or non-recognition of authority, or absence of government and absolute freedom of the individual	(*an-*, without)
autarchy	a system of government by one person with absolute power	(*autos* self)
eparchy	a province of the Orthodox Church	(*epi*, above, so 'rule from above')
hierarchy	a system of authority in which members are ranked according to status (the earliest sense was that of a system of orders of angels and heavenly beings)	(*hieros*, sacred)
matriarchy	a system of society or government ruled by a woman or women	(Latin *mater*, mother, on a mistaken analogy with *patriarchy*)
monarchy	a state with a sovereign head of state, especially a king, queen, or emperor	(*monos*, alone or single)
oligarchy	a small group of people having control of a country, organization, or institution; a place or body so ruled	(*oligoi*, few)
patriarchy	government by the father or eldest male	(*patria*, family)
squirearchy	landowners collectively, especially when considered as a class having political or social influence	(English *squire*)
synarchy	joint rule or government by two or more individuals or parties	(*sun-*, together)

monos, alone or single) is a sovereign head of state, in a type of government called *monarchy*.

The ending is somewhat active, with terms being created for occasional use or wordplay, such as *cupidarchy*, a state built on cupidity, or *ergonarchy* (Greek *ergon*, work), one ruled by the work ethic.

For more examples, see the LIST on the previous page. *See also* -CRACY.

-ard Also **-art**. *Forming nouns.* [Old French, from German *-hard* or *-hart*, hard or hardy, often appearing as the last element in personal names, such as *Reginhart*, *Adalhart*, or *Bernhart*.]

Such nouns that relate to people often have a dismissive sense: *bastard*, *coward*, *drunkard*, *laggard*, *sluggard*. These usually derive from adjectives, some of which are now archaic (*coward*, for example, comes from Old French *couard*, a tail, suggesting someone retreating with tail between legs).

Nouns sometimes suggest an object that has been formed as the result of an action: *bollard*, a post for mooring a ship, is from *bole*, the trunk of a tree; *pollard*, a tree trimmed to encourage new growth to feed stock, is from *poll*, to cut the top off something; *standard*, a flag mounted on a pole, is from Old French *estendre*, to extend, whose initial letter was lost in the shift to English. Other examples are *placard*, *mallard*, and *buzzard*.

Rarely, the suffix is spelled **-art**, as in *braggart*.

Some words with this ending come from other sources: *custard* (Old French *crouste*), *hazard* (originally the name of a dice game, the precursor of craps, from Persian *zār* or Turkish *zar*, dice), *leopard* (Greek *leōn*, lion, plus *pardos*, a male panther, the animal at first being thought a hybrid).

See also -WARD.

areo- *The planet Mars.* [Greek *Ares*, the war god equivalent to the Roman god *Mars* after whom the planet is named.]

Most terms containing **areo-** are direct equivalents to ones in GEO- that relate to Earth. Several are late nineteenth-century coinages resulting from increased interest in the planet by astronomers: *areographer*, a person who studies the surface features of Mars; *areology*, the science of the physical structure of the planet. Others are relatively recent inventions resulting from exploration of the planet by space probes or deriving from science fiction: *areosynchronous* refers to a spacecraft in orbit around Mars that stays above the same spot on its surface, and *areobotany* is the study of (hypothetical) Martian vegetation, its *areoflora*.

argent(o)- Also **argenti-**. *Silver.* [Latin *argentum*, silver.]

Argentite is silver sulphide, an important ore of the metal; such silver-bearing minerals are said to be *argentiferous*. In chemistry, *argentic* compounds are those containing divalent silver (for example, *argentic oxide*, AgO); *argentous* compounds contain monovalent silver (for example, *argentous chloride*, AgCl); *Argentina* is the 'Silver Republic' in Spanish, named for the silver jewellery worn by native inhabitants at the time of colonization; in heraldry, *argent* means silvery white, as it can also do in poetic or literary contexts.

-arian *Forming adjectives and corresponding nouns.* [Originally from Latin words ending in *-arius*.]

Examples include *agrarian* (Latin *ager*, a field), relating to cultivated land or cultivation; *antiquarian* (Latin *ante*, before), relating to or dealing in antiques or rare books; *disciplinarian* (Latin *disciplina*, discipline), a person who promotes the orderly observance of rules. Others are *centenarian*, *grammarian*, *librarian*, *proletarian*, and *veterinarian*.

The most common use of this ending is to create adjectives from various English stems that refer to systems of thought or belief, or nouns for people who support or advocate them: *authoritarian*, *contrarian* (opposing or rejecting popular opinion or going against current practice), *doctrinarian*, *egalitarian*, *fruitarian* (a person who lives on fruit only), *humanitarian*, *libertarian*, *sectarian*, *totalitarian*, *Unitarian*, *vegetarian*.

See also -AN.

-arious Connected with; pertaining to. [Originally from Latin adjectives ending in -arius.]

In the same way that many Latin words ending in -us arrived in English through French with the ending changed to -ous, some of those in -arius changed to **-arious** (others took on the endings -ARIAN or -ARY instead).

Words ending in **-arious** are adjectives. Some common examples are *gregarious* (Latin *greg-*, *grex*, a flock or herd), fond of company or sociable; *precarious* (Latin *prex*, *prec-*, prayer), uncertain or insecure; *nefarious* (Latin *nefas*, *nefar-*, wrong), wicked or criminal; *vicarious* (Latin *vicarius*, substitute), of something experienced through the feelings or actions of another person; and *various* (Latin *varius*, changing or diverse).

This suffix has never been active in English; examples that appear to exist have actually been formed by attaching -OUS (or its variant -ious) to a word stem containing -ar-: *burglarious*, *hilarious*, *uproarious*.

-arium A place or container connected with, or employed for, some purpose. [Latin, the neuter ending of adjectives in -arius.]

The first terms in English were for places connected with Roman life, as in *caldarium*, *tepidarium*, and *frigidarium*, respectively the hot, intermediate, and cold rooms of Roman baths.

Several words indicate places containing collections: *aquarium*, a tank for keeping water creatures or a building containing many of them; *herbarium* (Latin *herba*, grass, herb), a collection of dried plants; and *terrarium*, a place in which smaller land animals are kept; the general term for a place in which to keep living things is *vivarium* (Latin *vivere*, to live). More recent examples, such as *dolphinarium* and *oceanarium*, as much suggest a place of public entertainment as one where animals are housed; a *planetarium* is a domed building in which images of the sky are projected for entertainment or education.

Other examples are *honorarium*, a payment given for professional services that are rendered nominally without charge, and *armamentarium* (Latin *armamentarium*, an arsenal) at first the medicines, equipment, and techniques available to a medical practitioner, now more generally a collection of resources available for a given purpose.

-aroo or **-aroonie**: *see* -EROO

arsen(o)- Arsenic. [English *arsenic*, from Greek *arsenikon*, yellow orpiment (arsenic sulphide).]

Arsenic is a semi-metallic element whose compounds are poisonous; the usual adjective is *arsenical*. Compounds in which arsenic has a valency of five are referred to by the adjective *arsenic*; those in which it has a valency of three are said to be *arsenious*. *Arsenopyrite*, also called mispickel, is the main ore of arsenic; *arsenolite* (Greek *lithos*, stone) is a naturally occurring form of arsenic oxide.

Arsenal—a collection of military equipment or a place where armaments are stored and made—is unconnected, originating in an Arabic term for a place of manufacture.

-art: *see* -ARD

arteri(o)- An artery. [English *artery*, from Greek *artēria*, windpipe or artery.]

Terms include *arteriosclerosis* (Greek *sklēroun*, to harden), the hardening of the walls of the arteries, typically in old age; *arteriole*, a small branch of an artery leading into capillaries; *arteriography*, investigation of an artery using radiography; *arteriotomy* (Greek *tomia*, cutting), cutting into or opening an artery; and *arteritis*, inflammation of the walls of an artery. The usual adjective is *arterial*, which also has a figurative sense of an important route in a system of roads, railway lines, or rivers.

arthr(o)- A joint. [Greek *arthron*, joint.]

Arthritis refers to a painful inflammatory condition of the joints, whereas *arthralgia* (Greek *algos*, pain) is pain in a joint not accompanied by swelling; the surgical procedure *arthroplasty* (Greek *plastos*, formed, moulded) is the surgical remodelling of a diseased joint. In zoology, an **arthropod** (Greek *pous*, *pod-*, foot, hence an animal with a jointed foot) is a member of a large group of invertebrate animals that includes insects, spiders, crustaceans, and their relatives.

-ary¹ *Forming nouns.* [Latin *-arius* or *-arium*.]

Some (from Latin words in *-arius*) can refer to a person linked to an activity; examples are **secretary** (Latin *secretarius*, a confidential officer), and **actuary** (Latin *actuarius*, bookkeeper), a person who uses statistics to calculate insurance risks and premiums. **January** derives from *Januarius*, of Janus, the Roman god who presided over doors and beginnings. Other examples are **adversary**, **antiquary**, **beneficiary**, **emissary**, and **notary**.

Some nouns in this ending, from Latin words ending in *-arium*, have no common theme: **aviary** (Latin *avis*, bird); **diary** (Latin *dies*, day); and **salary** (Latin *salarium*, a Roman soldier's allowance to buy salt, from *sal*, salt). Others are **dictionary**, **glossary**, **ovary**, **sanctuary**, and **vocabulary**.

See also -ERY.

-ary² *Forming adjectives.* [French *-aire*; Latin *-aris* and *-arius*.]

Such adjectives broadly have the senses 'of the kind of', 'belonging to', 'connected with', or 'pertaining to'. Many taken from Latin have been brought into English under the influence of French, such as **voluntary**, from Old French *volontaire* and Latin *voluntarius* (itself derived from *voluntas*, will), or **military**, from French *militaire* or Latin *militaris* (from *miles*, *milit-*, a soldier).

Some come from Latin words ending in *-aris*, such as **capillary** (Latin *capillus*, hair), and **exemplary** (Latin *exemplum*, sample or imitation); further examples of like kind are **ancillary**, **epistolary**, **maxillary**, and **salutary**.

Others are from Latin words in *-arius*: **necessary** (Latin *necesse*, needful); **elementary** (Latin *elementum*, principle or rudiment); and **arbitrary** (Latin *arbiter*, judge or supreme ruler). Words of similar source include **contrary**, **honorary**, **mercenary** (which can also be a noun), and **primary**.

The ending is active in English, and a number of adjectives ending in **-ary** have been formed from English nouns. Examples are: **budgetary**, **complimentary**, **discretionary**, **fragmentary**, **inflationary**, **parliamentary**, **revolutionary**, **sedimentary**, **supplementary**, and **visionary**.

as-: *see* AD-

asc(o)- *A bag or sac.* [Greek *askos*, a bag or wineskin.]

In botany, an **ascus** (plural **ascii**) is a sac in which the spores of **ascomycete** fungi develop (Greek *mukētes*, fungi), and the prefix can refer to this sac, as in **ascospore** for one of the spores it holds. In medicine, **ascites** is the accumulation of fluid in the peritoneal cavity, causing abdominal swelling.

Some words beginning in *asc-* do not belong here: *ascetic* comes from another Greek word, *askein*, to exercise; others, such as *ascertain* and *ascend*, contain a variant form of AD-.

-ase *An enzyme.* [The final part of *diastase*, derived from Greek *diastasis*, separation.]

Enzymes are substances produced by living organisms which catalyse biochemical reactions. The first named, in the 1830s, was **diastase**, which appears during the malting of barley and converts starch into sugar (it is now better known as **amylase**, from Latin *amylum*, starch); other examples named on its model were **zymase** (Greek *zumē*, leaven) and **maltase**: together these convert the sugar maltose into alcohol. A very large number of other enzymes has been discovered in the period since, of which a few are given in the LIST opposite.

-asis. Also **-iasis**. *A disease or other medical condition.* [Via Latin from Greek *-asis*.]

The most common examples are words describing diseases caused by an external parasite, frequently tropical or subtropical in origin. Despite its origin, which determines its place in this work, the ending is almost always **-iasis**, incorporating the linking vowel -I-.

-ase An enzyme.
Names are from English nouns unless otherwise stated.

carboxylase	catalyses the addition of a carboxyl group to a specified substrate (the reverse process is carried out by **decarboxylase**)	(*carboxyl*)
cholinesterase	one of a group (especially **acetylcholinesterase**) which hydrolyses esters of choline	(*choline*)
hydrolase	catalyses the hydrolysis of a particular substrate	(*hydrolysis*)
isomerase	converts a compound to an isomer	
lipase	catalyses the breakdown of fats to fatty acids and glycerol or other alcohols	(Greek *lipos*, fat)
polymerase	brings about the formation of a particular polymer, especially DNA or RNA	(*polymer*)
protease	breaks down proteins and peptides	(*protein*)
proteinase, or *endopeptidase*	breaks peptide bonds other than terminal ones in a peptide chain	
reductase	promotes the chemical reduction of a specified substance	(*reduce*)
synthase	catalyses the linking together of two molecules, especially without the direct involvement of ATP	(*synthesis*)
transcriptase	catalyses the formation of RNA from a DNA template during transcription (**reverse transcriptase** does the opposite)	(*transcription*)

Examples are *candidiasis*, infection with candida, a yeast-like parasitic fungus, especially when it causes oral or vaginal thrush; *leishmaniasis*, a tropical and subtropical disease caused by a parasitic protozoan (named after William Leishman, 1856–1926, a British pathologist); *schistosomiasis*, now more commonly called *bilharzia* or *bilharziasis*, a chronic disease caused by infestation with blood flukes; and *elephantiasis*, a condition in which a limb or other part of the body becomes grossly enlarged due to obstruction of the lymphatic vessels, typically by the filarial worms which also cause *filariasis*.

A variety of other medical conditions contain this ending: *lithiasis* (Greek *lithos*, stone), formation of stony concretions, specifically *urolithiasis*, in the bladder or urinary tract, and *cholelithiasis*, gallstones; *psoriasis*, a skin disease marked by red, itchy, scaly patches (Greek *psōra*, itch); *hypochondriasis* is the technical term for hypochondria.

-ast Also **-iast**. *A person connected with a pursuit or activity.* [Greek nouns ending in *-astēs*, often from verbs in *-azein*.]

The most common example here is *enthusiast* (Greek *enthousiastēs*, a person inspired by a god). Others derived directly from Greek words include *gymnast* (Greek *gumnastēs*, trainer of athletes, from *gumnazein*, to exercise naked, the usual practice in classical Greece); *pederast* (Greek *pais*, *paid-*, boy); and *iconoclast* (Greek *eikonoklastēs*, breaker of images, from *eikōn*, image). Modern examples include *cineaste* (borrowed from French and retaining the French spelling) and *ecdysiast* (Greek *ekdusis*, shedding), a humorous term for a striptease performer.

-aster *Inferior; a poor imitation.* [Latin *-aster*, incomplete resemblance.]

Most terms are rare or outdated. The only one much found is *poetaster* (Latin *poeta*, poet), a person who writes inferior poetry. Rarer examples include *criticaster*, a minor or inferior critic; *philosophaster*, a petty philosopher; and *politicaster*, a petty, feeble, or contemptible politician. *Oleaster* (Latin *olea*, olive tree), a small shrub sometimes called the wild olive or Russian olive, was so called because its fruits are like those of the olive. However, the shrub called *cotoneaster* derives its name from ancient *Cydonia* (Canea, in Crete). The ending is not active.

astr(o)- *A star or other celestial body; outer space; star-shaped.* [Greek *astron*, star.]

Common examples include *astronomy* (Greek *nomos*, law) and *astrology* (Greek *logos*, discourse). *Astrophysics* is the study of the nature of stars and other celestial bodies; an *astronaut* (Greek *nautēs*, a sailor) is a person trained to travel in a spacecraft. Some terms imply that a thing has points like the conventional representation of a star: an *astrocyte* is a star-shaped glial cell of the central nervous system; and an *astroid* is a hypocycloid with four cusps, shaped like a square with concave sides.

at-: *see* AD-

-ata: *see* -A[2]

-atable: *see* -ATE[3]

-ate[1] *Forming nouns.* [Old French *-at* or Latin *-atus*, *-ata*, *-atum*.]

One sense, usually derived from Latin originals, is that of an office, rank, or position: *doctorate*, *episcopate*, *baccalaureate* (a university bachelor's degree). Others refer to place: a *consulate* is the place where the function of consul is carried out; a *protectorate* is a state protected or controlled by another. Some signify the office or territory of a ruler: *sultanate*, *caliphate*, *vizierate*.

The suffix can mark a group or collective body: *electorate*, *mandarinate* (often used for a group of powerful civil servants), *rabbinate*, *senate*, *syndicate*, *triumvirate*. Others describe a person who exercises some function: *magistrate*, *advocate*, *candidate*, *curate*, *subordinate*. A *mandate*, an official order or commission to do something, is from Latin *mandatum*, something commanded.

The suffix also indicates salts of acids whose names end in -IC, such as *nitrate* (a

salt of *nitric acid*), *carbonate* (from *carbonic acid*), or *acetate* (from *acetic acid*). Compare -ITE[1]. The related term *hydrate* refers to compounds containing chemically bound water. Several examples indicate the result of some chemical process: *filtrate*, *precipitate*, *condensate*, *distillate*.

-ate[2] *Forming adjectives.* [Latin *-atus*, *-ata*, *-atum*.]

A wide variety of adjectives have been formed from Latin words in these endings; they include *accurate*, *affectionate*, *desperate*, *effeminate*, *legitimate*, *literate*, *ornate*, *roseate*, and *temperate*. Many, such as *elaborate*, *moderate*, *prostrate*, *sedate*, and *separate*, can also be verbs (*see* the next entry) though then said with shifted stress; others, such as *associate* and *duplicate*, commonly also appear as both nouns and verbs. A few, such as *aspirate*, now a noun and verb, came into the language as adjectives, but are so no longer.

-ate[3] *Also* **-atable**. *Forming verbs.* [Latin words ending in *-atus*, *-ata*, *-atum*, or verbs in *-are*.]

Some verbs were formed from adjectives with the same ending (*see* the previous entry), for example *separate* and *associate*. Later, many others were created from Latin verbs: *captivate*, *create*, *demonstrate*, *fascinate*, *hyphenate*, *litigate*, *originate*, *sublimate*, *substantiate*, *vaccinate*.

Others have been formed on words from a variety of sources: *assassinate*, *cerebrate* (to think), *chlorinate*, *curate* (to carry out the functions of a museum or art gallery curator), *eventuate*, *methylate*, *speciate* (to form a new and distinct species in the course of evolution).

The suffix is highly productive in modern English. There is a slight tendency to prefer verbs ending in **-ate** to ones formed on the same stems using other endings, as for instance *administrate* is gaining in popularity compared with *administer*.

Verbs in **-ate** usually form adjectives in **-atable**: *debatable*, *locate*, *rotatable*, but many of more than two syllables lose the *-ate* ending: *demonstrable*, *educable*, *penetrable*, *tolerable*, *venerable*. *See also* -ABLE.

Most of these verbs form nouns in -ATION.

-ateria: *see* -TERIA

ather(o)- *An atheroma.* [Greek *athērōma*, from *athērē*, *atharē*, porridge or groats.]

Atheroma is a medical condition of the walls of the arteries caused by accumulated fatty deposits and scar tissue; it is so called because the fatty deposits are of a porridge-like consistency. The resulting disease is *atherosclerosis*, and the adjective is *atheromatous*; the surgical removal of an atheroma is *atherectomy* (Greek *ektomē*, excision).

-athon After a vowel **-thon**. *An event long in duration, usually for fund-raising purposes.* [The last part of *marathon*, from *Marathōn* in Greece, the scene of a victory over the Persians in 490 BC.]

From the 1930s onwards, the ending of *marathon* was borrowed, originally in the US, to form words relating to some charitable activity. The first examples were *walkathon*, a long-distance walk organized as a fund-raising event, and *radiothon*, a prolonged radio broadcast by a person or group, similarly to raise money.

Many examples have been created since, of which *telethon*, a long television programme to raise money for charity, has gone furthest towards general acceptance. Others are *operathon*, a marathon performance of opera; *preachathon*, an extended sermon; and *swimathon*, a sponsored swimming event.

Some examples are facetious terms indicating an unreasonably extended happening, such as *boreathon*, an interminable occasion; *plugathon*, an extended advertisement for a product or person; and *excuseathon*, an overextended apology for some mishap.

-ati Also **-erati**. *Groups of people.* [Latin plural adjectival ending -ati.]

Early examples are Latin or Italian plurals, such as *literati*, well-educated people interested in literature (the plural of Latin *literatus*, acquainted with letters), or *castrati*, male singers castrated in boyhood (the plural of Italian *castrato*).

In recent years it has become a fashionable ending in popular journalism for groups of people with common interests or characteristics, sometimes with implications of triviality. Early examples were blends of English words with *literati* and it is as yet uncertain whether a genuinely new word-forming element has been created, or whether word coiners are working by analogy. Its vogue may end before its status becomes obvious.

Examples include *digerati*, people with expertise or professional involvement in information technology; *glitterati* (from *glitter*), the fashionable set of people engaged in show business or some other glamorous activity; *soccerati*, those closely interested in or involved with soccer.

Where the root does not already end in *-er*, it is common to insert it: *fasherati*, the set of people concerned with current fashion in clothes; other examples are *poperati* and *neterati*.

-atic *Forming adjectives, and some nouns.* [French *-atique* or Latin *-aticus*, often based on Greek *-atikos*.]

Some of the many adjectives in this ending are *dramatic* (via late Latin from Greek *dramatikos*); *rheumatic* (Old French *reumatique*, or via Latin from Greek *rheumatikos*); *pneumatic* (French *pneumatique* or Latin *pneumaticus*, from Greek *pneumatikos*, from *pneuma*, wind). The ending also appears in adjectives formed from English nouns: *operatic*, *acrobatic*, *lymphatic*.

Some adjectives in **-atic** have become nouns as well, through a shorthand in which—for example—*aquatic plant* has been abbreviated to an *aquatic*, or in geology, an *erratic boulder* became an *erratic*, one thought to have been brought from a distance by glacial action. A few are as often nouns as they are adjectives: *lunatic*, *fanatic*.

For adjectives ending in *-cratic*, *see* -CRACY.

-atile *Possibility, potential, or ability.* [Latin *-atilis*.]

This suffix generates adjectives. Common examples are *versatile*, able to adapt to many different circumstances, and *volatile*, of a substance that is easily evaporated, or a person liable to change rapidly and unpredictably. More specialist terms include *pulsatile*, pulsating or relating to pulsation, and *saxatile*, living or growing among rocks (Latin *saxatilis*, from *saxum*, rock or stone).

-ation *An action, or an instance of an action.* [French *-ation* or Latin *-ation-*.]

The *New Oxford Dictionary of English* records more than 1,400 nouns that contain this suffix. Most are associated with verbs, commonly those in *-ate* (see *-ATE*[3]): *creation*, *deviation*, *moderation*, *navigation*, *perforation*, *pronunciation*, *resuscitation*, *suffocation*, *vibration*. Others are associated with a variety of verbs, all ultimately from Latin: *application* with *apply* (Latin *applicare*); *probation* with *probe* (Latin *probare*, to test or prove); *publication* with *publish* (Latin *publicare*, make public).

Many other words ending in **-ation** appear to derive from English verbs: *alteration*, *consultation*, *embarkation*, *formation*, *plantation*, *taxation*, *temptation*, *vexation*, *visitation*. Though this is accidental, as the English verbs and nouns can all be traced back to Latin sources, this apparent connection was important in developing the idea of **-ation** as a true English suffix, so permitting nouns like *flirtation* to be based on English verbs. However, a number of nouns with this ending do not have an associated verb in English: *duration*, *tribulation*, *ostentation*, *constellation*.

See also -FICATION, -ION, -ITION, -IZE (for *-ization* and *-isation*), and -UTION.

-ative *Characteristic or predisposed.* [From French *-atif*, *-ative* or Latin *-ativus*.]

Examples are often adjectives: *appreciative*, *decorative*, *innovative*, *speculative*, *talkative*, and *vituperative*. Others can equally well be nouns: *formative*, *laxative*, *purgative*, *superlative*. A few longer adjectives formed from nouns ending in *t* can lose the *-at-* element through a process called syncopation; for example *interpretative* can appear as *interpretive* and *preventive* is sometimes preferred to *preventative*. *See also* -IVE.

-ator: *see* -OR[1]

-atory: *see* -ORY[1] *and* -ORY[2]

atto- *In units of measurement, a factor of* 10^{-18}. [Danish or Norwegian *atten*, eighteen, with the ending changed to match that of the other SI (Système International) multiples (see the table of WORDS FOR MULTIPLES on page 127).]

Such quantities are so tiny that they are only needed by scientists investigating extremely short time periods (*attoseconds*), or tiny forces (*attonewtons*). The term *attoparsec* has been used in fun to refer to a distance of slightly more than an inch (3.1 cm).

audi(o)- *Hearing or sound.* [Latin *audire*, to hear.]

Audiometry is measurement of the range and sensitivity of a person's sense of hearing; *audiology* is the branch of science and medicine concerned with the hearing; the adjective is *auditory*. As a free-standing word, *audio* refers to sound, especially sound that has been recorded, transmitted, or reproduced. Several related compounds exist, such as *audio-visual* (often now without the hyphen), using both sight and sound, as in a slide-tape or video presentation; *audiobook*, a recording of the reading of a book; and *audiophile*, a hi-fi enthusiast.

aur(i)- *Gold.* [Latin *aurum*, gold.]

An *auriferous* mineral is one containing gold, while something *aureate* is made of or has the colour of gold. In chemistry, *auric* refers to compounds in which gold has a valency of three and *aurous* those in which it has a valency of one. The *aurora*, the Northern or Southern Lights, derives from *Aurora*, the Roman goddess of the dawn. However, *aura*, a supposed emanation surrounding the body of a living creature, is the Latin word for a breeze. A few words, such as *auricle*, the external part of the ear, derive instead from Latin *auris*, ear.

Austro-[1] *Austria; Austria and…* [From *Austria*.]

Austro-Hungarian usually refers to the former empire of that name; the *Austro-*

Prussian War of 1866 is sometimes called the Seven Weeks' War.

Austr(o)-² Also **austral(o)-**. *Australia; Australia and … ; southern.* [Latin *australis*, southern.]

Australia was originally *Terra Australis*, the southern land. The prefix occurs occasionally in words indicating Australia plus another country, as in *Austro-Malayan* and *Austro-Asiatic*. *Australasia* is the region consisting of Australia, New Zealand, New Guinea, and the neighbouring islands of the Pacific; an *Austronesian* language is one of a family spoken in an area extending from Madagascar in the west to the Pacific islands in the east.

Words in **australo-** refer generally to something in the southern hemisphere. An *australite* in Geology is a glassy fragment, a tektite, often found in Australia. An *australopithecine* (Greek *pithēkos*, ape) is a member of an extinct species of primate found in southern Africa.

aut(o)-¹ *Self; oneself; by itself.* [Greek *autos*, self.]

A person writing the story of their own life produces an *autobiography*; an *autocrat* retains power in himself; an *autodidact* is a self-taught person; something or someone *autonomous* can operate independently; an *autopsy*, a post-mortem examination, literally means 'seeing for oneself' (Greek *autoptēs*, eyewitness, from *optos*, seen).

The form often refers to equipment that operates by itself, *automatically*: an *autopilot* keeps an aircraft on course without the pilot's intervention; a *autofocusing* camera focuses without human assistance; *automation* is the introduction or use of *automatic* equipment in a factory. An *autoclave*, a vessel used to sterilize items, was so called because it was self-fastening (either from Latin *clavis*, key, or *clavus*, nail, nobody seems sure which).

auto-² *An automobile or motor vehicle.* [English *automobile*.]

An *automobile* was named because it seemed to go by itself, not needing an

obvious motive force such as a horse. Some terms refer specifically to the motor car, including *auto* itself: an *autoworker* builds cars in a factory and *autocross* is a competition using motor vehicles. An *autorickshaw* in the Indian subcontinent is a motorized, three-wheeled rickshaw for public hire.

aux(o)- *Growth or increase.* [Greek *auxein*, to increase.]

An *auxin* is a plant hormone which regulates plant growth; an *auxotroph* (Greek *trophos*, feeder) is an organism that needs special nutrients to grow; *auxesis* is growth that results from an increase in cell size rather than of the number of cells; an *auxochrome* is a group of atoms introduced into a dyestuff to intensify its colour. *Auxiliary*, however, comes from Latin *auxilium*, help.

avi- *A bird or birds; flight.* [Latin *avis*, bird.]

Examples are *aviary*, a place to keep birds; *aviculture*, the breeding and rearing of birds; *avifauna*, the birds of a particular region, habitat, or geological period. *Aviation*, the flying or operating of aircraft, comes from the same root via French.

axo- Also **axi-**. *An axis.* [Greek *axōn*, axis.]

This ending appears in a few biological terms: an *axon* is the long thread-like part of a nerve cell along which impulses are conducted from the cell body to other cells; an *axoneme* is the central strand of a cilium or flagellum. In architecture an *axonometric* projection is drawn on a plane inclined to each of the three principal axes of the object, so that it is three-dimensional but without perspective; something *axisymmetric* is symmetrical about an axis. *Axiom*, however, is from a different Greek word, *axios*, worthy.

az(o)- Also **azot(o)-**. *Nitrogen; the chemical radical* $-N\!=\!N-$. [Obsolete English *azote*, nitrogen, from French, generated from Greek *a-*, without, and *zōē*, life (because nitrogen gas does not support life).]

Some terms beginning in **azo-** refer generally to the presence of nitrogen, or to compounds containing nitrogen: an *azide* is a compound containing the unstable N_3 radical, such as *sodium* azide, NaN_3.

More specifically, the suffix refers to the presence of the group $-N{=}N-$ (the *azo* group) in chemical compounds, for example in *azobenzene*, an orange-red, crystalline powder with the formula $C_6H_5N{=}NC_6H_5$.

Compounds containing **azoto-** include *azotobacter*, an aerobic nitrogen-fixing bacterium. In medicine, *azotemia* is the retention of excessive amounts of nitrogenous compounds in the blood.

See also NITRO-.

-azole: *see* -OLE[1]

bacill- *A bacillus.* [Latin *bacillus*, diminutive of *baculum*, rod or stick.]

A *bacillus* (plural *bacilli*) is a rod-shaped bacterium, often causing disease. Taking its meaning directly from its Latin source, something *bacilliform* is rod-shaped. However, compounds in medicine usually refer to the presence of disease-causing bacilli, as in *bacillaemia* (US *bacillemia*) (in the blood), or *bacilluria* (in the urine), in both cases as a result of infection; the adjective *bacillary* refers particularly to an infection caused by bacilli. *See also* BACTERIO-.

-bacter *A genus of bacteria.* [The first part of English *bacterium*.]

Most such genus names are the province of specialists, spelled by convention with a capital letter: *Azotobacter* (obsolete *azote*, nitrogen), a free-living genus of soil bacteria able to fix nitrogen; *Enterobacter* (Greek *enteron*, intestine), a genus whose members are commonly found in faeces and sewage. A few have become more widely known and are commonly spelled without an initial capital letter: *acetobacter*, bacteria that oxidize organic compounds to acetic acid, as in vinegar formation; *campylobacter* (Greek *kampulos*, bent), a type of bacterium which sometimes causes abortion in animals and food poisoning in humans.

bacteri(o)- Also **bacter-**. *Bacteria.* [English *bacterium*, from Greek *baktērion*, diminutive of *baktēria*, staff or cane (because the first bacteria to be discovered were rod-shaped).]

Bacteria are members of a large group of single-celled micro-organisms, including some which can cause disease. *Bacteriology* is the study of them; a *bactericide* is a substance which kills them; a *bacteriophage* (Greek *phagein*, eat) is a virus which attacks bacteria; a *bacteriostat* (Greek *statos*, standing) is a substance that prevents the multiplying

of bacteria without destroying them; *bacteraemia* (US *bacteremia*) is the presence of bacteria in the blood, while *bacteriuria* is their presence in the urine. *See also* BACILL-.

baro- Also **bary-**. *Pressure.* [Greek *baros*, weight; Greek *barus*, heavy.]

A *barometer* measures atmospheric pressure; a *baroreceptor* is one of a set of nerve endings that monitor changes in blood pressure; *barotrauma* is damage to the ear caused by changes in air pressure, as experienced during air travel or deep-sea diving; a *barostat* (Greek *statos*, standing), is a device that maintains constant atmospheric pressure in a closed vessel. The **bary-** equivalent is less common; examples are *barycentric*, relating to a centre of gravity, and *barysphere*, the dense interior of the earth, under the lithosphere.

basi- *A base or basis.* [Latin *basis*, base or pedestal, from Greek.]

In plants, growth or development that is *basipetal* (Latin *petus*, seeking) is towards the base or point of attachment; something *basifixed* is attached at or near the base. In medicine *basioccipital* refers to the base of the occiput, the back of the head; the adjective *basilar* refers to something situated at the base of a part of the body, especially of the skull, or of the organ of Corti in the ear. A *basilect* is a less prestigious dialect or variety of a particular language.

Basilisk and *basilica*, on the other hand, derive from Greek *basileus*, king.

basidio- *A basidium.* [Greek *basidion*, a diminutive of *basis*, base or pedestal.]

A *basidium* is a microscopic club-shaped spore-bearing structure produced by fungi called *basidiomycetes* (Greek *mukēs*, *mukēt-*, fungus or mushroom), such as the smuts, rusts, mushrooms, and puffballs; **basidio-** refers to the presence of a basidium, as in *basidiospore*, a spore formed in one, or *basidiocarp*, the fruiting body of basidiomycetes that produces them.

bathy- Also **batho-**. *Depth.* [Greek *bathus*, deep.]

A *bathysphere* is a manned spherical chamber for deep-sea observation; a *bathymeter* measures the depth of water in seas or lakes; *bathypelagic* (Greek *pelagios*, of the sea) refers to organisms inhabiting the deep sea. Words beginning in **batho-** derive from the related Greek *bathos*, depth: *bathochromic* (Greek *khrōma*, colour), relating to or denoting a shift of the absorption spectrum of a compound towards longer wavelengths (figuratively, deeper ones); *batholith* (Greek *lithos*, stone), a very large igneous intrusion extending to an unknown depth in the earth's crust.

be- *Forming verbs and adjectives.* [Old English, weak form of *bī*, by.]

This prefix has been productive in the past, but is rarely used to make new words today. It appears in some adverbs and prepositions that indicate position, as in *behind*, *below*, *beneath*, *between*, and *beyond*.

Its main function has been to create transitive verbs, ones able to take a direct object, from nouns or adjectives: *befoul*, *befriend*, *beguile*, *belittle*, *besiege*, *bewitch*. In some cases, it changes an existing verb from being intransitive to transitive: *becloud*, *bemoan*, *bestride*. It can also intensify the action of an existing verb, suggesting that something is happening thoroughly or excessively: *bedazzle*, *belabour*, *besmear*, *bewail*.

In combination with -ED[2] it forms participial adjectives from nouns, often implying that an object or person is furnished with something: *bejewelled*, *beribboned*, *bespectacled*, *bewhiskered*.

bene- *Good; well.* [Latin *bene*, well.]

Bene- is present in a number of English words, but is not an active word-forming element. Examples include *benefaction* (Latin *facere*, do), a donation or gift; *benediction* (Latin *dicere*, say), the utterance or bestowing of a blessing; and

benevolent (Latin *velle*, to wish), well-meaning and kindly.

benz(o)- *Benzene.* [The first part of English *benzoic* plus -o-, from gum *benzoin*, based on Arabic *lubānjāwī*, incense of Java.]

This indicates compounds that contain a six-membered ring of carbon atoms, a derivative of benzene. Examples include *benzaldehyde*, a colourless liquid aldehyde smelling of bitter almonds, used to make dyes and perfumes; *benzodiazepine*, a member of a group of tranquillizers, such as Librium or Valium; *benzopyrene*, the major carcinogen present in cigarette smoke; and *benzoquinone*, a yellow crystalline compound.

bi- Also **bin-** and **bis-**. *Two; having two; doubly.* [Latin, *bi-*, doubly, having two; *bini*, two together; *bis*, twice.]

To *bisect* a thing (Latin *secare*, to cut) is to divide it into two parts; a person who is *bisexual* is sexually attracted to both men and women; a *bipedal* animal uses only two legs for walking; a *biplane* has two pairs of wings, one above the other; a system or circuit that is *bistable* has two stable states; a *binomial* (Greek *nomos*, part or portion) is an algebraic expression of the sum or difference of two terms. In names of chemical compounds, **bi-** indicates the presence of two atoms or groups of a given kind: *bicarbonate*, *bisulphite*.

A *biennial* event takes place every other year; a plant is so described if it takes two years to grow from seed to fruition and die; something *biannual* occurs twice a year. Other time terms in **bi-** are ambiguous (*biyearly*, either every two years or twice a year; *bimonthly*, twice a month or every two months; *biweekly*, every two weeks or twice a week).

Examples using **bin-** include *binocular* (Latin *oculus*, eye), adapted for or using both eyes; *binaural*, involving both ears; *binary*, expressed in a system of numerical notation that has 2 rather than 10 as a base.

Bis- is used in the names of chemical compounds containing two secondary groups identically substituted or coordinated, as in *bisphenol A*, an organic compound formed from acetone by adding two molecules of phenol. A *biscuit* is literally a twice-cooked thing (via French from Latin *coquere*, to cook), because biscuits were first baked and then dried out in a slow oven so that they would keep.

biblio- *A book or books.* [Greek *biblion*, book.]

A *bibliography* (Greek -*graphia*, writing) is a list of the books referred to in a scholarly work; a *bibliophile* (Greek *philos*, loving) is a person who collects or has a great love of books, while *bibliomania* is a passionate enthusiasm for collecting and possessing books; *bibliometrics* is the statistical analysis of books, articles, or other publications; *bibliomancy* (Greek *manteia*, divination) is the practice of foretelling the future by interpreting a randomly chosen passage from a book, especially the Bible.

bili- *Bile.* [Latin *bilis*, bile.]

The adjective *biliary* refers to bile or the bile duct; to be *bilious* is to be affected by nausea or vomiting. Breakdown products of haemoglobin excreted in bile include the orange-yellow *bilirubin* (Latin *ruber*, red) and the green *biliverdin* (Latin *viridis*, green); *biliurea* is the presence of bile in the urine, and *bilirubinaemia* (US *bilirubinemia*) is an excess of bilirubin in the blood.

-bility: *see* -ABLE

bin-: *see* BI-

bio- *Life; living things.* [Greek *bios*, (course of) human life.]

Though the Greek precursor of this form referred only to human life, the sense has been extended to mean life in general, especially in the key term *biology*, the study of living organisms. The form is extremely active in the language, and only a few of the more common examples of compounds are given in the LIST on the next page. The great importance and potential of biological topics has resulted in many terms for cross-disciplinary subjects of study—a few examples appear in the list.

-biosis Also **-biont** and **-biotic**. *A mode of life.* [Greek *biōsis*, mode of life.]

Terms in **-biosis** include *symbiosis* (Greek *sun*, with), interaction between two organisms living in close physical association, typically to the advantage of both (outside science, it can have the sense of a mutually beneficial relationship between different people or groups); *cryptobiosis* (Greek *kruptos*, hidden), a physiological state in which metabolic activity is reduced to an undetectable level without disappearing altogether; *necrobiosis* (Greek *nekros*, corpse), gradual degeneration and death of cells in the body tissues.

The form **-biont** indicates an individual organism living in this way: *symbiont* (from *symbiosis*); *mycobiont* (Greek *mukēs*, fungus, mushroom) and *phycobiont* (Greek *phukos*, seaweed, hence alga), respectively the fungal and algal components of a lichen. *See also* -ONT.

Words ending in **-biotic** are adjectives and nouns (deriving from Greek *biōtikos*, fit for life), either relating to a mode of living described by a word ending in **-biosis** (*cryptobiotic*, *symbiotic*), or to a way of acting on living things: *antibiotic*, a medicine that inhibits the growth of or destroys micro-organisms; *xenobiotic* (Greek *xenos*, stranger, foreigner), of a substance, typically a synthetic chemical, that is foreign to the body or to an ecological system.

bis-: *see* BI-

-blast Also **-blastic**. *An immature or embryonic cell.* [Greek *blastos*, germ or sprout.]

Examples include *erythroblast* (Greek *eruthros*, red), an immature erythrocyte, a red blood cell; *neuroblast*, an embryonic cell from which nerve fibres originate; and *fibroblast*, a cell in connective tissue which produces collagen and other fibres. Sometimes the ending refers to an abnormality, as in *lymphoblast*, an abnormal cell resembling a large lymphocyte, produced in large numbers in a form of leukaemia. It can also denote a germ layer of an embryo: *epiblast* (Greek *epi*, upon), the outermost layer of an

> **bio-** Life; living things.
> *Terms mainly derive from English stems.*
>
> **General terms**
>
> | | |
> |---|---|
> | *bioavailability* | the proportion of a drug or other substance which is able to have an active effect in the body |
> | *biodegradable* | capable of being decomposed by bacteria or other living organisms and thereby avoiding pollution |
> | *biodiversity* | the variety of plant and animal life in the world or in a particular habitat |
> | *biofeedback* | the use of electronic monitoring of a normally automatic bodily function in order to train someone to acquire voluntary control of that function |
> | *biogas* | gaseous fuel, especially methane, produced by the fermentation of organic matter |
> | *biohazard* | a risk to human health or the environment arising from biological work |
> | *biome* | a large naturally occurring community of flora and fauna occupying a major habitat, such as forest or tundra |
> | *biomedical* | of or relating to both biology and medicine |
> | *bioremediation* | the use of micro-organisms to consume and break down environmental pollutants |
> | *biosphere* | the regions of the surface and atmosphere of the earth or another planet occupied by living organisms |
>
> **Subjects of study**
>
> | | |
> |---|---|
> | *biochemistry* | of the chemical and physico-chemical processes which occur within living organisms |
> | *biocomputing* | of the design and construction of computers using biochemical components |
> | *biogeography* | of the geographical distribution of plants and animals |
> | *biomathematics* | of the application of mathematics to biology |
> | *biomechanics* | of the mechanical laws relating to the movement or structure of living organisms |
> | *biophysics* | of the application of physics to biology |
> | *biotechnology* | the exploitation of biological processes for industrial and other purposes. |

embryo before it differentiates into ectoderm and mesoderm; ***trophoblast*** (Greek *trophē*, nourishment), a layer of tissue on the outside of a mammalian embryo, supplying it with nourishment and later forming the major part of the placenta. A mature cell is indicated by -CYTE.

Words such as *counterblast* or *sandblast* are compounds of the English word *blast*.

Forms in **-blastic** are adjectives (*see* -IC) that may be derived from nouns in **-blast**: *erythroblastic*, *lymphoblastic*, *trophoblastic*. They may also denote a thing that has undergone a particular kind of development: ***poikiloblastic*** (Greek *poikilos*, variegated, varied), of the texture of

a metamorphic rock in which small crystals of a mineral occur within crystals of its metamorphic product; ***diploblastic*** (Greek *diplous*, double), having a body derived from only two embryonic cell layers (ectoderm and endoderm, but no mesoderm), as in sponges and coelenterates.

blasto- *Germination.* [Greek *blastos*, germ or sprout.]

Examples include ***blastocyst***, a mammalian blastula (an embryo at the early stage of development when it is a hollow ball of cells) in which some differentiation of cells has occurred; ***blastoderm*** (Greek *derma*, skin), a blastula having the form of a disc of cells on top of the yolk; and *blastomere* (Greek *meros*, part), a cell formed by cleavage of a fertilized ovum.

-ble: *see* -ABLE

blephar(o)- *The eyelid.* [Greek *blepharon*, eyelid.]

Examples are *blepharitis*, inflammation of the eyelid; *blepharoplasty*, surgical repair or reconstruction of one; *blepharospasm*, involuntary tight closure of the eyelids; *blepharophimosis* (Greek *phimosis*, muzzling), a small aperture between them.

bor(o)- *Boron.* [English *boron*, from *borax*, a white mineral which contains boron.]

The element *boron* was named in imitation of carbon, which it resembles in some respects. Examples of compounds include *borosilicate* glass, a low-melting glass made from a mixture of silica and *boric* oxide; *borohydride*, a compound containing the radical —BH$_4$; *borate*, a salt in which the anion contains both boron and oxygen, as in borax; and *borane*, one of a set of unstable binary compounds of boron and hydrogen.

-bot *Automatic or autonomous device or software program.* [The ending of English *robot*.]

Robot, an automatic or programmable machine, originally one resembling a human being, derives from Czech *robota*, forced labour.

One sense, directly derived from the concept of a robot, is that of an autonomous device, usually mobile, with a degree of awareness derived from computer technology; many examples are found in scientific or science fiction contexts, but few have become widely known. Examples include *nanobot* (Greek *nanos*, dwarf), a hypothetical robot of molecular dimensions; *cryobot* (Greek *kruos*, frost), a NASA-invented device for penetrating deep ice layers to examine what lies beneath; *killerbot*, an autonomous military killing machine; *biobot*, a robot which mimics biological behaviour.

The more common sense is of a semi-autonomous software program, usually linked to networking and especially to the Internet and the World Wide Web. Well-known examples include *cancelbot*, a program that searches for and deletes specified mailings from Internet newsgroups; *knowbot*, a program which has reasoning and decision-making capabilities; and *spambot*, a program which scans Web pages in order to harvest e-mail addresses to which unsolicited commercial advertising (spam) can be sent.

Bot also exists as a word in its own right, in reference to a device of either kind.

botry(o)- *A bunch of grapes.* [Greek *botrus*, bunch of grapes.]

The mould *botrytis* is deliberately cultivated (as noble rot) on the grapes used for certain wines; *botryomycosis* is a disease of horses, which produces granular masses; the adjective *botryoidal* describes minerals that look rather like a cluster of grapes.

brachi(o)- *An arm.* [Latin *brachium* or Greek *brakhiōn*, arm.]

An ape that is *brachiate* moves by using the arms to swing from branch to branch; a *brachiosaurus* (Greek *sauros*, lizard) was a herbivorous dinosaur with especially long forelegs; a *brachiopod* (Greek *pous*, *pod-*, foot) is a member of a phylum of marine invertebrates, the lamp shells; *brachioplasty* (Greek *plastos*, formed, moulded) is a surgical procedure to tighten the skin of the upper arm; the adjective *brachiocephalic* refers to the arm and head considered together, especially in the *brachiocephalic artery* (also called the *innominate artery*) which feeds blood from the heart to the head, neck, and arms.

brachy- *Shortness.* [Greek *brakhus*, short.]

Someone who is *brachycephalic* has a relatively broad, short skull; *brachydactyly* is abnormal shortness of the fingers and toes; *brachytherapy* is a type of radiotherapy in which radioactive materials are implanted into or close to a tumour to give intense radiation for short periods.

brady- *Slowness.* [Greek *bradus*, slow.]

Terms mostly occur in medicine in reference to an abnormal state: *bradycardia*

(Greek *kardia*, heart) is abnormally slow heart action; *bradykinesia* (Greek *kinēsis*, motion) is a condition in which body movements are abnormally slow; *bradyphasia* (Greek *phanai*, speak) is abnormal slowness of speech, often linked with mental illness; *bradykinin* (Greek *kinēsis*, motion) is a compound released in the blood in some circumstances which causes contraction of smooth muscle and dilation of blood vessels.

branchio- *Gills.* [Greek *brankhia*, gills.]

The *branchia* are the gills of fish and some invertebrate animals; the adjective relating to them is *branchial*. A *branchiopod* (Greek *pous*, *pod-*, foot) is a member of a class of crustaceans (the *Branchiopoda*) that includes water fleas and fairy shrimps, which have gills on the feet; the adjective *branchiostegal* (Greek *stegē*, covering) relates to the covering of gills.

Brit- *British.* [The first element of *British*.]

Though the abbreviated form *Brit* for a British person has been known since the beginning of the 20th century, it was only from the late 1980s that it began to be used in a variety of compound terms relating to aspects of British cultural life, such as *Britart*, *Britculture*, *Britfashion*, *Britpop*, and *Britrock*. Terms are often hyphenated, sometimes with the second element capitalized.

brom(o)- *Bromine.* [The first part of English *bromine* plus -o-.]

The form is widely employed in chemistry to mark a bromine derivative of a compound, as in *bromoacetone*, *bromobenzene*, and *bromoform*, the bromine analogue of chloroform. *Bromides* are compounds of bromine with another element or group, while *bromates* are salts of *bromic acid*, $HBrO_3$. To *brominate* a chemical compound is to combine bromine with it.

In medicine, *bromocriptine*, a bromine–containing synthetic analogue of the ergot alkaloids, is used in the treatment of Parkinsonism and other conditions; *bromsulphthalein* (also called *sulphobro-* *mophthalein*) is a blue dye used in tests of liver function; *brompheniramine* is an antihistamine.

The element's name derives from Greek *brōmos*, a stink, because it has a heavy, irritating smell. The same root occurs in *bromhidrosis*, the secretion of foul-smelling sweat, body odour.

bronch(o)- *The bronchi.* [Greek *bronkho-*, from *bronkhos*, windpipe.]

The *bronchi* (singular *bronchus*) are the major air passages of the lungs which split off from the windpipe. *Bronchitis* is inflammation of the mucous membrane in the *bronchial* tubes; it typically causes coughing and *bronchospasm*, a spasm of bronchial smooth muscle, producing narrowing of the bronchi. A *bronchodilator* is a drug that causes widening of the bronchi, such as those taken to alleviate asthma; *bronchiectasis* is abnormal widening of the bronchi or their branches, causing a risk of infection; a *bronchiole* is one of the minute branches into which a bronchus divides.

bryo- *Moss.* [Greek *bruon*, moss.]

Bryology is the study of mosses and liverworts, small flowerless green plants called *bryophytes* that belong to the botanical division *Bryophyta*; *Bryozoa* (Greek *zōia*, animals) is a phylum of aquatic invertebrates that comprises the moss animals, sedentary colonial aquatic animals found chiefly in the sea. However, the name of *bryony*, the climbing Eurasian hedgerow plant, derives ultimately from the related Greek *bruōnia*, a wild vine.

bucco- *The cheek.* [Latin *bucca*, cheek.]

The adjective *buccal* relates to the cheek; *buccolingual* (Latin *lingua*, tongue) to the cheek and tongue; *buccopharyngeal* to the cheek and pharynx or the mouth and pharynx; *buccinator*, a flat thin muscle in the wall of the cheek, derives from the related Latin *buccinare*, to blow a trumpet. However, *buccaneer*, a pirate, comes from French *boucan*, a frame on which to cook or cure meat.

but- Also **butyro-**. *Four-carbon chains of atoms.* [The first element of English *butyric*, from Latin *butyrum*, butter.]

The first chemical compound named from this Latin source was **butyric acid**, C_3H_7COOH, a colourless organic acid, so named because it was found in rancid butter. Names for other four-carbon compounds have since been created, such as the hydrocarbons **butane**, **butadiene**, and **butylene**, and the organic alcohol **butanol**. The adjective is **butyl**, in reference to the radical —C_4H_9, as in butyl *rubber* and in butyl *acetate*, an important solvent in lacquers.

The longer form **butyro-** is now relatively uncommon, but appears, for example, in **butyrophenone**, one of a small group of tranquillizers used to relive symptoms of serious psychiatric disorders. A **butyrometer** is an instrument for estimating the percentage of butter-fat in milk.

by- *Subordinate; incidental; secondary.* [English *by*.]

In Britain, a **by-election** is the election of an MP or local councillor to fill a vacancy arising during a term of office. A **byroad** or **byway** is a minor road or track; a **by-catch** is the unwanted fish and other marine creatures trapped in nets during fishing for a different species; a **byname** is a sobriquet or nickname, especially one given to distinguish a person from others with the same given name; a **by-product** is an incidental or secondary product; **byplay** is secondary or subsidiary action or involvement in a play or film.

In **bypass**, a road that passes by a congested area to provide an alternative route, or **bystander**, a person who is present at an event or incident but does not take part, the sense is that of 'aside'. A **by-law** (also **bye-law**), a rule made by a company or society to control the actions of its members (in Britain, a regulation made by a local authority) may instead derive from Old Norse *býjar*, genitive singular of *býr*, town.

C

cac(o)- *Unpleasant, bad, or incorrect.* [Greek *kakos*, bad or evil.]

The most common word here is *cacophony* (Greek *phōnē*, sound) a discordant mixture of sounds. In medicine, *cachexia* (Greek *hexis*, habit) is the dramatic weight loss that can occur in cancer patients. Other examples are *cacodemon* (Greek, *daïmon*, spirit), a malevolent spirit or person; and *cacography* (invented on the pattern of *orthography*), bad handwriting or spelling.

-cade *A procession or show.* [The last syllable of *cavalcade*.]

Cavalcade, a formal procession of people on horseback or in (originally horse-drawn) vehicles, derives from Latin *caballus*, horse. The ending is actually -ADE, but was wrongly analysed. A few words have been formed on its model, mostly in the US, such as *aquacade* (Latin *aqua*, water), a spectacle involving swimming and diving, and *motorcade*, a procession of motor vehicles. Temporary formations also appear: *camelcade*, *tractorcade*.

calc(i)- Also **calcareo-**. *Lime or calcium.* [Latin *calx*, *calc-*, lime.]

Calcium is the chemical element present in chalk, limestone, gypsum, and *calcite*. The adjectives *calciferous* and *calcareous* refer to minerals that contain calcium or lime. A *calcicole* (Latin *colere*, inhabit) is a plant that needs a soil containing lime. *Calciferol* (from calciferous plus -OL) is the formal name for Vitamin D, essential for metabolizing calcium in the body; conversely, *calcitonin* is a hormone that reduces calcium levels in the blood. The Latin word for a small stone, *calculus*, is used in medicine for a stone in the kidney or gall bladder; small stones were used as markers on Roman counting tables and the English mathematical terms *calculate* and *calculus* derive from this.

calli- Also **cali-**. *Beautiful.* [Greek *kallos*, beauty.]

Calligraphy (Greek *graphein*, write) is decorative handwriting or handwritten lettering; *callisthenics* (US *calisthenics*) (Greek *sthenos*, strength) are gymnastic exercises to achieve bodily fitness and grace of movement; a person or statue that is *callipygian* or *callipygean* (Greek *pūgē*, buttocks) has well-shaped buttocks; the *callistemon* (Greek *stēmōn*, thread or stamen), the bottlebrush plant, is so named because of its attractive long red or yellow stamens.

carb(o)- *Carbon.* [English *carbon*, from Latin *carbo*, coal or charcoal.]

Carbohydrates are a large group of compounds that include sugars and starches, which contain carbon together with hydrogen and oxygen in the same proportions as in water (hence *hydrate*, from Greek *hudōr*, water). A *carbide* is a compound of carbon with a metal, such as *calcium carbide*, once used to generate acetylene gas in vehicle lamps; *carbazole* is a colourless substance obtained from coal-tar, used in dye production; *carbamazepine* is a synthetic benzodiazepine, used as an anticonvulsant and analgesic drug.

carboxy- *The carboxyl group.* [CARBO- plus OXY-.]

The *carboxyl* group is the organic acid radical —COOH; a *carboxylic acid* is an organic acid containing one or more carboxyl groups, which form esters called *carboxylates*. In medicine a *carboxylase* is an enzyme which causes a carboxyl group to be added to a compound; *carboxyhaemoglobin* is a compound formed in the blood by binding carbon monoxide to haemoglobin, which prevents it from transporting oxygen; *carboxymethylcellulose* is a polymer derived from cellulose, used as a stabilizer for various foods and an appetite suppressant.

carcino- *Cancer.* [Greek *karkinos*, crab or ulcerous sore.]

The Greek word is said to have been applied to cancerous tumours because the swollen veins around them resemble the limbs of a crab. A *carcinogen* (Greek *genēs*, born) is a substance capable of causing cancer in living tissue; a *carcinoma* is a cancer arising in the epithelial tissue of the skin or of the lining of the internal organs; *carcinogenesis* is the initiation of cancer formation.

-cardial: *see* -CARDIUM

cardi(o)- *The heart.* [Greek *kardia*, heart.]

The medical study of the heart is *cardiology*, practised by a *cardiologist*; an *electrocardiogram* (Greek *graphein*, write), or ECG, is a record or display of a person's heartbeat, created by an *electrocardiograph*. Several adjectives relate to the heart as part of the wider body system; these include *cardiovascular* (Latin *vasculum*, a little vessel) for the heart and its blood vessels, *cardiopulmonary* (Latin *pulmo*, *pulmon-*, lung) for the heart and lungs, and *cardiothoracic* (Greek *thōrax*, chest) for the heart and chest. Outside medicine the most common compound is *cardioid* for a heart-shaped curve in mathematics.

-cardium Also **-cardial**. *Tissue related to the heart.* [Greek *kardia*, heart.]

The oldest such term, the model for the others, is *pericardium* (Greek *peri*, around), the membrane enclosing the heart. Other examples are *epicardium* (Greek *epi*, upon, near to) a membrane that forms the innermost layer of the pericardium, attached to the muscles of the wall of the heart; *endocardium* (Greek *endon*, within), the thin, smooth membrane which lines the inside of the chambers of the heart and forms the surface of the valves; and *myocardium* (Greek *mus*, *mu-*, muscle), the muscular tissue of the heart. Associated adjectives are formed in **-cardial** (*endocardial*, *myocardial*).

-carp *A fruit or fruiting body.* [Greek *karpos*, fruit.]

The *pericarp* (Greek *peri-*, around) is the part of the fruit formed from the wall of the ripened ovary; in some fungi and related plants the *sporocarp* (Greek *spora*, spore) is the fruiting body in which spores form; a *schizocarp* (Greek *skhizein*, to split) is a dry fruit that splits into single-seeded parts when ripe.

caryo-: *see* KARYO-

cat(a)- Also **cath-** and **kata-**. *Movement downwards; figuratively, wrong or inferior.* [Greek *kata-*, down.]

Many English words beginning in **cata-** entered the language from Greek with the prefix already attached: *cataract* (Greek *kataraktēs*, down-rushing); *cataclysm* (Greek *kataklusmos*, deluge—the word was originally applied to the Biblical flood); *catarrh* (Greek *katarrhein*, flow down); *catapult* (Greek *katapeltēs*, hurling down); and *catastrophe* (Greek *katastrophē*, a sudden overturning or down-turning).

Among modern formations are *catabolism* (Greek *ballein*, to throw), the process of breaking down food to release energy, and *catalyst* (Greek *luein*, loosen), a substance that speeds up a chemical reaction without itself being consumed.

The variant form **cath-** is used before *h*, as in *catheter* (Greek *hienai*, to let go); *cathode* (Greek *hodos*, way), the electrode through which electrons enter a device.

Cata- is not an active word-forming element; recent examples tend to be spelt **kata-** and some technical terms in **cata-** have alternative forms in *k*. Examples include *katabatic*, a local wind flowing down a hillside at night, and *kataplexy* (also spelt *cataplexy*), a state imitating death adopted by some animals when alarmed.

-cele Also **-coel** and **-coele**. *A tumour, swelling, or hernia.* [Greek *kēlē*, a tumour or hernia.]

Examples are *bronchocele* (Greek *bronkhos*, windpipe), a swelling of the thyroid gland, as in goitre; *enterocele*, a hernia of the pouch of Douglas, between the rectum and uterus; *gastrocele*, a hernia of the stomach; *hydrocele*, a tumour containing fluid, especially in the scrotum; *meningocele*, a protrusion of the meninges (the outer membranes of the brain) through the skull; and *varicocele*, a mass of varicose veins in the spermatic cord.

Words in **-cele** are sometimes spelled *-coel* or *-coele*, though this ending strictly derives from a different Greek root (*see* -COEL); the confusion between spellings is accentuated by their relative closeness of meaning and the existence of a few words in both spellings with different senses, such as *enterocele* and *enterocoel*. *See also* COELO-.

celo-: *see* COELO-

-cene *A division of geological time.* [Greek *kainos*, new.]

The ending generates adjectives for divisions of the Cenozoic period (a name that derives from the same Greek root, plus Greek *zōion*, animal), dating from 65 million years ago to the present day. The most recent is the *Holocene* (Greek *holos*, whole, complete), 10,000 years ago to the present day; in increasing distance back in time are the *Pleistocene* (Greek *pleistos*, most), *Pliocene* (Greek *pleiēn*, more), *Miocene* (Greek *meiēn*, less), *Oligocene* (Greek *oligos*, small, few), *Eocene* (Greek *ēōs*, dawn), and *Palaeocene* (US *Paleocene*) (Greek *palaios*, ancient).

-centesis *A puncture or perforation of a body cavity.* [Greek *kentēsis*, pricking.]

This forms medical terms that relate to making a puncture in order to remove liquid or gas for diagnostic or therapeutic purposes. Examples are *amniocentesis* (Greek *amnion*, caul), a process in which amniotic fluid is sampled using a hollow needle inserted into the uterus, to screen for abnormalities in the developing fetus; *paracentesis* (Greek *para*, beside), the perforation of a body cavity, especially with a hollow needle to remove liquid or gas; and *pericardiocentesis*, removal of excess fluid from within the pericardium, the sac surrounding the heart.

centi- *One hundredth; a multiple of a hundred.* [Latin *centum*, a hundred.]

In current usage, **centi-** always denotes a fractional unit, as in *centimetre* for one hundredth of a metre, or *centilitre*

(**centiliter** in US) for a hundredth of a litre. It is one of the standard SI (Système International) multiples (see the table of WORDS FOR MULTIPLES on page 127). There are a few older words in which the form represents a hundred, as in *centipede* (Latin *pes, ped-*, foot) for an insect with (supposedly) a hundred legs, or the *centigrade* scale of temperature (now officially called the *Celsius* scale), in which the range between the freezing and boiling point of water is divided into one hundred parts.

centr(i)- Also **centro-** *A centre.* [Latin *centrum*, centre.]

A *centripetal* force (Latin *petere*, seek) is one that moves or tends to move towards a centre, the opposite of *centrifugal* (Latin *fugere*, flee), acting away from a centre. A *centrifuge* is a rotary device that separates fluids of different densities by applying centrifugal force. In mathematics, a *centroid* is the centre of mass of an object. In biology, the *centrosome* (Greek *sōma*, body) is a small body near the nucleus of a cell, and a *centromere* (Greek *meros*, part) is the point on a chromosome by which it is attached to a spindle fibre during cell division.

-centric *Having a specified centre.* [English *centre*, from Latin *centrum* or Greek *kentron*.]

Well-established examples include *concentric* (Latin *con-*, together), denoting things that share the same centre; *heliocentric* (Greek *hēlios*, sun), having or representing the sun as the centre, as in the accepted astronomical model of the solar system; and *eccentric* (literally, not placed centrally, from Greek *ek*, out of).

The ending also has a figurative sense of having a certain point of view or being mentally focused on some topic. Examples are *egocentric* (Latin *ego*, I), thinking only of oneself; *Afrocentric*, regarding African or black culture as pre-eminent; *Eurocentric*, centred or focused on European culture. This sense has become fashionable, especially in the computer industry, with many formations appearing that may not survive (**network-centric**, **UNIX-centric**, **webcentric**).

Among the better established are **PC-centric** (concerning or promoting the personal computer or PC to the exclusion of other types of computer) and **customer-centric** (focused on the needs of the customer).

centro-: *see* CENTRI-

-cephalic Also **-cephalous**, **-cephalus**, and **-cephaly**. *The head.* [Greek *kephalē*, head.]

Adjectives in **-cephalic** and **-cephalous** are usually equivalent in meaning, though the former is more common. Examples are *hydrocephalic* (literally, having water on the head) in reference to a child suffering from an enlarged head because of fluid retention; *brachycephalic* (Greek *brakhus*, short), having a relatively broad, short skull; *microcephalic* (Greek *mikros*, small), abnormal smallness of the head, a congenital condition associated with incomplete brain development; *bicephalous* (Latin *bi*, having two), having two heads.

Nouns ending in **-cephalus** or **-cephaly** refer to the condition: *hydrocephalus*; *microcephaly*; *macrocephalus*; *plagiocephaly* (Greek *plagios*, slanting), oblique deformity of the head. With the exception of *hydrocephalus*, forms in **-cephalus** are generally less common than those in **-cephaly**.

cephal(o)- *The head.* [Greek *kephalē*, head.]

Cephalic is the adjective relating to the head, *cephalometry* is the study and measurement of the head and face, and *cephalin* is a phospholipid found in the brain. An *electroencephalogram* (Greek *graphein*, write) is a record of brain activity produced by an *electroencephalograph*.

-cephalous, **-cephalus**, or **-cephaly**: *see* -CEPHALIC

cerato-: *see* KERATO-

cerebr(o)- *The brain.* [Latin *cerebrum*, brain.]

The adjective relating to the brain is *cerebral*, both physically and with reference to its powers of reasoning; the *cerebrum* is the pair of lobes at the front of the brain responsible for complex sensory tasks; the *cerebellum* (literally the little cerebrum), controls balance and movement; to *cerebrate* is to think. *Cerebrospinal* refers to the brain and spinal cord viewed together; *cerebrovascular* (Latin *vasculum*, a little vessel) similarly refers to the brain and its blood vessels.

cervic(o)- *The cervix; the neck.* [Latin *cervic-*, *cervix*, the neck.]

Though the Latin root sense is that of the neck, this form refers more commonly to the *cervix*, the neck of the womb. However, the adjective *cervical* can refer to both, as in *cervical smear*, a specimen of cellular material taken from the neck of the womb to test for cancer, or *cervical vertebrae*, the top seven vertebrae of the spinal column. On rare occasions the form refers to another kind of neck, as in *cervicolabial*, of the side of the neck of a tooth nearer the cheek. Examples relating to the cervix include *cervicitis*, inflammation of the neck of the womb, and *cervicotomy* (Greek *-tomia*, cutting), an incision into the cervix. Examples relating to the neck include *cervicodynia* (Greek *odune*, pain), pain in the neck; *cervicofacial*, relating to the neck and face, and *cervicogenic*, of a condition originating in the cervical vertebrae.

cet(o)- *A whale.* [Latin *cetus*, from Greek *ketos*, whale or sea-monster.]

A *cetacean* is a member of an order of marine mammals that comprises the whales, dolphins, and porpoises; *cetology* is the branch of zoology dealing with whales and dolphins. *Cetane* is a hydrocarbon present in petroleum spirit, so named because related compounds were first derived from spermaceti, which is often used as a standard against which to measure the ignition properties of diesel fuel.

-chaete (US **-chete**). *A bristle or seta.* [Greek *khaitē*, long hair, mane.]

Examples include *polychaete* (Greek *polu-*, many), a member of a class of marine annelid worms which comprises the bristle worms; *oligochaete* (Greek *oligoi*, few), a member of a class of annelid worms which includes the earthworms, which have simple bristles projecting from each segment; *spirochaete*, a flexible spirally twisted bacterium, especially one that causes syphilis.

chaet(o)- *Hair.* [Greek *khaitē*, long hair.]

A *chaeta* (plural *chaetae*) is a stiff bristle made of chitin, especially in an annelid worm; a *chaetognath* is a member of a small phylum of marine invertebrates with bristles around the mouth; the order *Chaetophorales* consists of freshwater algae that have slender thread-like flagella. *See also* SETI-.

chalc(o)- *Copper.* [Greek *khalkos*, copper or brass.]

Two important ores of copper are *chalcopyrite* and *chalcocite*; the *Chalcolithic* was a transitional period at the end of the Neolithic when copper tools were beginning to be used; *chalcography* is the craft of engraving on copper. *See also* CUPRO-.

cheil(o)- In the US **chil(o)-**. *A lip.* [Greek *kheilos*, lip.]

The form appears in some medical terms: *cheilosis* refers to swollen and cracked lips, caused by a vitamin deficiency; *cheilitis* is inflammation of the lips; and *cheiloplasty* is plastic surgery on the lips. The *Chilopoda* (Greek *pous*, *pod-*, foot) is a class of arthropods which comprises the centipedes, so called because the foremost pair of legs are jaw-like appendages.

cheiro-: *see* CHIRO-

chel(i)- *A claw.* [Greek *khēlē*, claw.]

A *chela* (plural *chelae*) is a pincer-like claw, especially of a crab or other crustacean; a *chelicera* (plural *chelicerae*) (Greek *keras*, horn) is either of a pair of appendages in front of the mouth in arachnids and some other arthropods, usually modified as pincer-like claws; the *Chelicerata* are a large group of arthropods (arachnids, sea spiders, and horseshoe crabs), all of which possess a pair of chelicerae. In chemistry, a *chelate* is a compound in which a central metal atom is bound to an organic molecule in two or more places, so named because the metal is figuratively gripped like a claw; a *chelating agent* uses a chelate to treat heavy metal poisoning.

chem(o)- Also **chemi-** *Chemistry; chemical compounds; chemical reactions.* [English *chemical*.]

The more common form is **chemo-**, as for example in *chemotherapy*, the chemical treatment of disease; *chemoreceptor*, a cell responsive to a chemical stimulus; *chemosynthesis*, the creation of chemical substances from inorganic material by bacteria; and *chemoprophylaxis*, the use of drugs to prevent disease. Two examples using **chemi-** are *chemiluminescence*, light created chemically without heat, as fireflies do, and *chemisorption*, absorption of a substance held in place by chemical bonds.

-chete: *see* -CHAETE

chili- *A thousand.* [Greek *khilioi*, thousand.]

This is the less common equivalent of KILO-, from the same Greek root. A *chiliad* is a group of a thousand things; a *chiliast* is more commonly called a *millenarian*, a person who believes that Christ will return to reign on earth for a thousand years; *chiliarch* is an historical term, especially in ancient Greece, for a commander of a thousand men; a *chiliagon* is a plane figure with a thousand faces.

chilo-: *see* CHEILO-

chiro- Also **cheiro-**. *A hand.* [Greek *kheir*, hand.]

Two common examples are *chiropody* (Greek *pous*, foot), treatment of the feet, and *chiropractor* (Greek *praktikos*, practical), a therapist who manipulates the joints using the hands. **Cheiro-** is an alternative spelling mainly restricted to natural history, as in *Cheirotherium* (Greek *thērion*, animal), an extinct animal whose footprints resemble a human hand.

chlor(o)- *The colour green.* [Greek *khlōros*, green.]

The pigment in plants that absorbs sunlight, *chlorophyll* (Greek *phullon*, leaf), is so called because it is green; it is held in the leaves in *chloroplasts*, which contain the plant's photosynthetic machinery. The gaseous element *chlorine* was named in 1810 by the chemist Sir Humphry Davy (1778–1829) because it is greenish-yellow; **chloro-** can refer to chemical compounds containing chlorine, such as *chlorides*, the salts of hydrochloric acid; the anaesthetic *chloroform*; and the anti-malaria drug *chloroquine*.

choan(o)- *A funnel.* [Greek *khoanē*, funnel.]

A *choanocyte* (Greek *kutos*, vessel) is a cup- or funnel-shaped cell which lines the internal chambers of sponges; the part of the sponge that contains them is the *choanosome*. A *choana* (plural *choanae*) is a funnel-like opening, especially used of the two openings between the back of the nose and the pharynx. The adjective is *choanal*.

chol(e)- Also **cholecyst-**. *Bile or gall.* [Greek *cholē*, bile.]

Cholera was so named because it was originally thought to be a disease of bile; *cholesterol*, an important sterol in the body, was first found in the gall bladder; *hypercholesterolaemia* (Greek *haima*, blood) is an abnormal increase in the levels of cholesterol in the blood; *choline*, a base present in the bile, regulates the deposition of fat in the liver (its derivative *acetylcholine* is an important transmitter of impulses between nerves).

The compound form **cholecyst-** (Greek *kutos*, a bladder) refers to the gall bladder, as in *cholecystitis* for inflammation of it, *cholecystography* for an X-ray examination of it, and *cholecystectomy* (Greek *ektomē*, excision) for its removal.

chondr(o)- Also **chrondri-**. *A cartilage; a grain.* [Greek *khondros*, a grain or cartilage.]

An example referring to cartilage is *achondroplasia* (Greek *a-*, without; *plasis*, moulding), abnormal formation of cartilage leading to a type of dwarfism. *Hypochondria*, literally 'below the cartilage (of the breast bone)', came from the old belief that melancholy originated in the liver and associated organs (the medical term for abnormal anxiety about one's health is now *hypochondriasis*). The sense of a grain is found in *chondrule*, a spherical grain or nodule of silica embedded in a type of meteorite called a *chondrite* and in the class name for certain fossil seaweeds, *Chondrus*.

chori(o)- *The chorion or choroid.* [Greek *khorion*, the membrane enclosing the foetus.]

The *chorion* is the outer membrane surrounding an embryo, which in mammals develops into the placenta. Hence *choriocarcinoma*, a malignant tumour of the uterus originating in the chorion of a foetus. The related adjective is *chorionic* (as in *human chorionic gonadotrophin* (HCG), a hormone secreted during pregnancy, and *chorionic villus sampling* (CVS), a test made to detect congenital abnormalities in the foetus).

The *choroid* is the pigmented layer of the eyeball in front of the retina, so named because it also contains many blood vessels. Some words beginning in **chorio-** refer to this: *chorioretinopathy*, an eye disease that affects both the choroid and the retina; *choriocele*, a hernia or protrusion of the choroid layer.

Christo- *Christ.* [Latin *Christus* or Greek *Khristos*, Christ.]

Examples are *Christology*, that part of theology which relates to Christ; *Christocentric*, centring on Christ; *Christogram*, a symbol of Christ such as the chi-rho figure (a monogram formed from the first two Greek letters of *Khristos*); and *Christophany*, an appearance of Christ, as after the Resurrection.

-chroic Also **-chroism**. *Having colour of a given type.* [Greek *khrēs*, colour.]

A crystal that is *pleochroic* (Greek *pleon*, more) shows different colours when viewed in polarized light at various angles, depending on the underlying structure of the crystal; specifically, a *dichroic* (Greek *di-*, twice) crystal has two such directions, a *trichroic* one has three. Synthetic dichroic material in flat sheets is used in some kinds of sunglasses. Forms ending in **-chroism** are nouns for the property concerned: *dichroism*.

chromato-: *see* CHROMO-

-chrome *Colour.* [Greek *khroma*, colour.]

A *cytochrome* (Greek *kutos*, vessel) is one of several coloured compounds that play an important role in cell respiration; a *phytochrome* (Greek *phuton*, a plant) is a blue-green pigment found in plants. Something *monochrome* (Greek *monos*, alone) is of a single colour, as opposed to *polychrome* (Greek *polus*, much), of many colours.

chrom(o)- *Colour; chromium.* [Greek *khroma*, *khromat-*, colour.]

A *chromophore* (Greek *pherein*, to bear) is a chemical group responsible for the colours of dyestuffs; the *chromosphere* is a reddish layer in the atmosphere of a star; *chromatin* is a readily stained material in the cell nucleus that contains wrapped-up DNA, RNA, and proteins; the DNA part of it, the *chromosome*, was called that because it, too, is easily stained.

The element *chromium* was named (via French *chrome*) because of the brilliant colours of its compounds. *Chromic* compounds contain trivalent chromium and are usually green or violet, while divalent *chromous* ones are usually blue; *chromates* contain the group —CrO_4 and are usually yellow; *chromite* is a brownish-black ore of chromium.

-chronic Also **-chronous**, **-chrony**, and **-chronism**. *Time.* [Greek *khronos*, time.]

The endings **-chronic** and **-chronous** both generate adjectives, but when both forms exist they usually have distinct senses. For example, *synchronous* (Greek *sun*, with) refers to events existing or happening at the same time, while *synchronic* refers to the study of a language as it exists at one point in time, the opposite of a *diachronic* approach, which focuses on the way a language has developed through its history. Another example is *isochronous*, referring to events that take equal amounts of time. Related nouns are

formed using **-chrony** (*synchrony*; *diachrony*), or **-chronism** (*synchronism*; *anachronism*, from Greek *ana-*, backwards, a thing belonging or appropriate to a period other than that in which it exists).

chron(o)- *Time.* [Greek *khronos*, time.]

Events may be *chronological* or be listed in date order in a *chronology*; a related term from the same root is *chronicle*, a record of events in the order in which they occurred. The adjective *chronic* is commonly used in medicine for a condition that lasts a long time or constantly recurs (in contrast to *acute*, of short duration but typically severe). A *chronometer* is a clock designed to keep accurate time in spite of motion or variations in temperature, humidity, and air pressure, as for example at sea.

-chrony: *see* -CHRONIC

chrys(o)- Also **crys(o)-**. *Gold; gold-coloured.* [Greek *khrusos*, gold.]

The *chrysanthemum* was given that name because its flowers were gold in colour; the Greeks named the pupa of an insect a *crysalis* because some that they knew had a metallic gold sheen; *chrysotherapy* is the treatment of certain diseases, especially rheumatoid arthritis, with gold compounds; *crysolite*, *crysotile*, and *chrysoberyl* are minerals that are sometimes yellowish in colour.

-cide Also **-cidal**. *A person or substance that kills; an act of killing.* [Latin *-cidium* and *-cidere*, from *caedere*, to strike down or slay.]

One set of words refers to the killing of one human being by another, or self-killing in the case of *suicide* (*sui*, of oneself); terms here either describe the act of killing or the person who kills (so *infanticide* is either the killing of an infant or someone who kills an infant). Another group concerns the destruction of organisms considered undesirable, a general word for which is *pesticide* and common group terms *insecticide*, *fungicide*, and *herbicide*; terms here denote the agent that kills. Adjectives are formed using **-cidal** (*fratricidal*, *homicidal*). See the LIST opposite.

-cide Names for persons or organisms killed by some agent.
All word origins are from Latin unless otherwise stated.

algicide	algae	(*alga*, seaweed)
bactericide	bacteria	(Greek *baktēria*, staff or cane)
biocide	living organisms	(Greek *bios*, life)
deicide	gods	(*deus*)
fratricide	a brother	(*frater*)
fungicide	fungi	(English *fungus*)
germicide	a disease germ	(English *germ*)
genocide	an ethnic or national group	(Greek *genos*, race, stock, kind)
herbicide	weeds and grasses	(*herba*, herb)
homicide	murder	(*homo*, man, in practice gender-neutral)
infanticide	a baby or infant	(*infant*)
insecticide	insects	(English *insect*)
matricide	one's mother	(*mater*)
microbicide	microbes	(Greek *mikros*, small, plus *bios*, life)
parricide	a parent	(*parricidium*, murder of a parent)
pesticide	a pest	(*pestis*, plague)
regicide	a king or other ruler	(*rex*)
rodenticide	rodents, especially rats or mice	(*rodere*, to gnaw)
spermicide	sperm	(Greek *sperma*, seed)
suicide	self-killing	(*sui-*, of oneself)

cine- Also **ciné-**. *The cinema; film.* [English *cinematographic*, through French from Greek *kinēma*, movement.]

A *cineaste* or a *cinephile* is a devotee of the cinema. A *cineplex* is a term in the US for a cinema with several separate screens. Several terms refer to the technology of moving pictures: *cine-projector*, *cine-camera*, *cine-film*. In medicine *cineradiography* records a moving X-ray image. *Cine* can also stand alone as an adjective. Some terms are on occasion written with an accent, such as *cinéaste*, reflecting the immediate French origin of the form, but this is now much less common than it once was. *See also* KINESIO-.

-cion: *see* -ION

circum- *Around or about.* [Latin *circum*, around.]

Many words in this form have been adopted, usually in a figurative sense, from Latin words already containing it: to *circumvent* (Latin *venire*, to come) is to avoid or find a way around some obstacle; to be *circumspect* (Latin *specere*, to look) is to be wary or careful; *circumscribe* (Latin *scribere*, write) can still literally mean to draw a line round something, but usually means to restrict within limits.

To *circumnavigate* the world is to travel all the way round it; a *circumcircle* is a circle that touches all the vertices of a geometrical figure. Several adjectives denote moving around a celestial body, such as *circumsolar* (the Sun) and *circumlunar* (the Moon); *circumpolar* refers to moving around the pole, especially a *circumpolar star*, one that never sets.

cirr(o)- *A tuft, curl, or tendril.* [Latin *cirrus*, a tuft or curl.]

Cirrus is the meteorological term for those very high, wispy clouds also called mare's tails; *cirrocumulus* (Latin *cumulus*, a heap) is a broken layer of high cloud, and *cirrostratus* (Latin *stratus*, strewn) a thin, high layer of hazy cloud. Cirrus is also a term in zoology or botany for a tendril, so the form can refer to this, as in *cirrose*, bearing tendrils. However, *cirrhosis*, a disease of the liver, comes instead from the Greek *kirrhos*, tawny, from its colour when affected.

cis- *On this side of; on the side nearer the speaker.* [Latin *cis*, on this side of.]

The adjective *cisalpine* refers to the southern side of the Alps (from the perspective of Rome, since the Romans invented the term); *cisatlantic* refers to the speaker's side of the Atlantic; something *cismontane* is on this side of a mountain; *cislunar* means this side of the Moon, between the Earth and the Moon.

The form also indicates isomers of chemical compounds in which substituents at opposite ends of a carbon-carbon double bond are on the same side of the bond, as in *cisplatin*, an anti-tumour drug, or in formal chemical names such as *cis*–2–butene. Its opposite is TRANS-.

clad(o)- *A branch or branching.* [Greek *klados*, a branch or shoot.]

A set of terms in biology refers to a method of classifying organisms according to physical or genetic characteristics they share with common ancestors; the theory is *cladistics*, adherence to the theory is *cladism*, and a *cladogram* is a diagram of the relationships concerned. A *cladode* (also known as a *cladophyll* or *phylloclade*) is a flattened leaf-like stem that can photosynthesize; a *cladoceran* is a crustacean, a water-flea, so called because it has a bivalve shell from which the head and antennae branch.

-clase *Minerals showing characteristic cleavage.* [Greek *klasis*, breaking.]

Orthoclase (Greek *orthos*, straight) is a common rock-forming feldspar mineral that has two characteristic cleavages at right angles; *plagioclase* (Greek *plagios*, slanting) is a white form of feldspar, also common in rocks, having two cleavages at an oblique angle; *periclase* (Greek *peri*, utterly) is a colourless mineral occurring chiefly in marble and limestone, so named because it cleaves perfectly; *eu-*

clase (Greek *eu*, well) is a brittle mineral sometimes valued as a gemstone.

-cle: *see* -CULE

-clinic Also **-cline** and **-clinal**. *Oblique, reclining, at an angle.* [Greek *klinein*, to slope.]

An *isoclinic* line on a map connects points where the dip of the earth's magnetic field is the same (Greek *isos*, equal); a *monoclinic* crystal (Greek *monos*, alone) has three unequal axes, one of which is inclined to the others at an angle, so it has only one plane of symmetry. The ending **-cline** forms nouns: *anticline*, a ridge or fold of stratified rock in which the strata slope downwards from the crest; *monocline*, a bend in rock strata that are otherwise uniformly dipping or horizontal. Such nouns have associated adjectives in **-clinal**: *anticlinal*.

clino- Rarely **klino-**. *Inclined; monoclinic.* [Greek *klinein*, to slope.]

The first sense appears in *clinometer*, a device for measuring the angle of a slope; *clinostat* (also *klinostat*), a device to rotate a growing plant during an experiment to cancel out the effects of gravity; and *clinodactyly*, a congenital inward bending of a finger.

The form is used to indicate that a mineral forms *monoclinic* crystals (see the previous entry). Some examples: *clinopyroxene*, a general term for the monoclinic minerals of the pyroxene group; *clinozoisite*, hydrous calcium aluminum silicate, a variety of epidote; *clinochlore*, a hexagonal variety of chlorite.

co-: *see* COM-

cocci- Also **cocco-**. *A small spherical body.* [Greek *kokkos*, grain or berry.]

Most words in **cocci-** derive from one or other of the systematic names for roughly spherical microscopic living things. One is *coccidia*, a broad term for several types of parasitic protozoa. *Coccidioides* is a genus of fungus, which has given its name to *coccidioidomycosis*, a serious infection of the lungs and other tissues, also known as *San Joaquin Valley fever*. A *coccolithophore* is a single-celled marine organism with a calcareous shell, whose tiny platelets are called *coccoliths*.

-coccus Also **-coccal** *A spherical bacterium.* [Greek *kokkos*, grain or berry.]

Many of these bacteria cause disease in humans and animals. Examples include *enterococcus* (Greek *enteron*, intestine), a type which occurs naturally in the intestine but causes disease if introduced elsewhere in the body; *staphylococcus* (Greek *staphulē*, a bunch of grapes, from the way the bacteria clump together), a cause of many diseases; *streptococcus* (Greek *streptos*, twisted, from the shape of the bacteria), which causes infections such as scarlet fever. All have plurals in *-i* (*staphylococci*, *streptococci*) and adjectives in **-coccal** (*gonococcal*, *meningococcal*).

-coel Also **-coele** and **-cele**. *A body cavity.* [Greek *koîlos*, hollow or cavity.]

Words with these endings are technical terms in zoology that are related to *coelom* (Greek *koîloma*, cavity) (US sometimes *celom*), the principal body cavity in most animals.

Examples include *blastocoel* (Greek *blastos*, sprout), the central cavity of a blastula, an animal embryo at the early stage of development when it is a hollow ball of cells; *gastrocoel*, another name for the archenteron, the rudimentary alimentary cavity of an embryo; *enterocoel* (Greek *enteron*, intestine), a body cavity in some invertebrates, which has developed from the wall of the archenteron; *pseudocoel* (Greek *pseudes*, false), a body cavity which is not part of the true coelom. Less commonly, such terms appear with a final *e*: *blastocoele*, *enterocoele*, though the spelling without it is now standard. The spelling **-cele** also occurs, though this is easily confused with words from a different Greek root (*see* -CELE), a confusion that is accentuated by relative closeness of meaning.

coel(o)- Also **coelio-**. In the US, **cel(o)-** or **celio-**. *A cavity.* [Greek *koîlia*, belly; *koîlos*, hollow; *koîlōma*, cavity.]

The usual medical sense is of the abdomen: *coelioscopy* is a technique of viewing abdominal organs through an incision in the abdominal wall; the usual adjective relating to the abdomen is *coeliac*. The *coelom* (US sometimes *celom*) is the principal body cavity in most animals, located between the intestinal canal and the body wall. Animal examples include the *coelacanth* (Greek *akantha*, spine, so 'having hollow spines'), an ancient species of fish, and *coelenterate* (Greek *enteron*, intestine), a member of a group that includes jellyfish and sea-anemones. However, the astronomical instrument called a *coelostat*, comes—irregularly—from a different root, Latin *caelum*, sky.

col-: *see* COM-

col(o)- *The colon.* [Greek *kolon*, the large intestine.]

Colitis is inflammation of the colon; *colotomy* (Greek *-tomia*, cutting) is an incision into it; *colectomy* (Greek *ektomē*, excision) is the removal of all or part of it; and *colostomy* (Greek *stoma*, mouth) is a surgical procedure whereby the colon is cut and diverted to the abdominal wall. *Colorectal* refers to the colon and rectum as one unit.

-colous Also **-coline** and **-cole**. *Living in or preferring a given environment.* [Latin *colere*, inhabit.]

A plant or animal that is *saxicolous* (Latin *saxum*, rock) lives or grows among rocks; a *terricolous* plant or animal grows or lives on the ground or soil (Latin *terra*, earth); a *calcicolous* plant is one that grows best in calcareous soil. The ending **-coline** is a rarer variant of **-colous**, as in *saxicoline*. Words ending in **-cole** indicate a plant or animal of the given type: *calcicole*, *terricole*.

colpo- *The vagina.* [Greek *kolpos*, womb.]

A *colposcope* is a surgical instrument used to examine the vagina and the cervix of the womb. A *colpotomy* (Greek *-tomia*, cutting) is any surgical incision into the wall of the vagina; *colporrhaphy* (Greek *rhaphē*, a seam) is an operation to remove lax and redundant vaginal tissue in cases of prolapse of the vaginal wall. *See also* VAGINO-.

com- Also **co-**, **col-**, **con-** and **cor-**. *Joint; mutual.* [Latin *cum*, with.]

Which form is used depends on the initial letter of the stem: **com-** is usual before *b*, *m*, and *p*, some vowels, and sometimes *f* (*combine*, *commerce*, *compact*, *comestible*, *comfort*); **co-** before vowels, *h*, and *gn* (*coerce*, *cohabit*, *cognate*); **col-** before *l* (*collect*); **cor-** before *r* (*correct*); and **con-** before other consonants (*concede*, *connect*, *contain*). Many words of these types were created in Latin and brought over into English; in many of them the form has the effect of intensifying the root word. The form **co-** often makes a hyphenated pair with another English word, indicating some activity taken in common or jointly: *co-author*, *co-driver*, *co-education*, *co-pilot*, *co-producer*, *co-purchaser*.

contra- *Against, contrary.* [Latin *contra*, against.]

Most words beginning with **contra-** were created in Latin or Italian and have a figurative or abstract sense: *contradict* (Latin *dicere*, to speak); *contravene* (Latin *venire*, come); *contraband* (Italian, from *bando*, proclamation or ban), goods imported illegally. Compounds created in English include *contraflow*, *contraception*, and *contraindication*. Some are commonly hyphenated: *contra-rotating*. See *also* COUNTER-.

copro- *Dung or faeces.* [Greek *copros*, dung.]

A *coprolite* is fossilized dung; *coprophagous* (Greek *phagein*, eat) means feeding on dung, as some beetles do; *coprosma* is a genus of New Zealand evergreen shrubs (from Greek *osme*, smell, because their leaves emit a putrid odour when bruised); *coprophilia* is an abnormal interest in faeces and defecation; *coprolalia* (Greek *lalia*, speech or chatter) is the involuntary and repetitive use of obscene language.

cor-: *see* COM-

-core *A musical genre.* [English *core*.]

The ending derives from *hard core*, the most active, committed, or unyielding members of a group or movement, which derives from its sense in British English of rubble and other stony material used for the foundations of buildings. The term, (usually as *hard-core* or *hardcore*) also refers to pornography of an explicit kind (contrasted with *softcore*, which is suggestive or erotic but not explicit).

The musical form called *hardcore* is a uncompromising, experimental, and harsh form of techno. Other terms for musical genres were invented in the 1980s and 1990s on its model: *queercore*, a punkish and aggressive musical style favoured by some young homosexuals; *loungecore*, a dismissive term for an easy-listening style with no strong character; *grindcore*, a type of fast heavy metal music incorporating harsh noise; and *thrashcore*, a noisy, thrashing punk style.

cosmo- *The world; the universe.* [Greek *kosmos*, order, world.]

The original sense of *kosmos* was order, but was applied to the world following the teaching of Pythagoras that its creation was orderly; so a *cosmopolitan* (Greek *politēs*, citizen) is a person familiar with many cultures and at ease with them. More recently the form has been applied to the whole universe: *cosmology* is the science of the origin and development of the universe; *cosmogenesis* refers to its origin; a *cosmogony* is a theory or myth about the birth of the universe. *Cosmonaut* derives from Russian *kosmonaut*, the Soviet equivalent of an *astronaut*; this has generated other words mainly used about the Soviet space programme, such as *cosmodrome* for a launching site for spacecraft.

cost(o)- *A rib or ribs.* [Latin *costa*, a rib.]

Several adjectives describe the ribs plus another part of the body: *costocervical*, of ribs and neck; *costoclavicular*, of the ribs and the clavicle or shoulder-blade; *costosternal*, of the ribs and the sternum or breastbone. The usual adjective relating to the ribs is *costal*. The adjective *costive* means constipated and is not a member of this set.

counter- *Opposition, retaliation, or rivalry.*

[Anglo-Norman French *countre-*, from Latin *contra*, against.]

Examples include *counterbalance*, *counterculture*, *counterfactual*, *counterfoil*, *counterpart*, *counterpoint*, and *counterweight*. A small number originated in French from Latin roots, such as *counterfeit* (Latin *facere*, to make) and *counterpoise* (Latin *pensum*, weight). Some are usually hyphenated: *counter-attack*, *Counter-Reformation*, *counter-espionage*, *counter-intuitive*. See also CONTRA-.

-cracy Also **-crat**, **-cratic**, and **-cratical**. *Government, rule, or influence.* [Greek *-kratia*, power or rule.]

Many terms ending in **-cracy** have been coined, though only a small number are at all well known; most can mean either a system of influence or rule or a society so ruled, as with *democracy*, rule through elected representatives; a few can also refer to the rulers as a group, as with *aristocracy* (Greek *aristos*, best), rule by members of the highest social class. See the LIST below.

The form is active, used to create words for influential groups with characteristics in common: *punditocracy*, media commentators; *adhocracy*, a loose group of influential advisers; *meritocracy*, government or the holding of power by people selected on the basis of their ability.

All can have associated adjectives in **-cratic** (*bureaucratic*, *meritocratic*), and nouns ending in **-crat** for a member of the relevant class or group (*aristocrat*, *autocrat*). A few can also have adjectives ending in **-cratical** (*aristocratical*, *democratical*), but these are much rarer than the corresponding forms ending in **-cratic**.

See also -ARCHY and -CY.

crani(o)- *The cranium.* [Greek *kranion*, skull.]

In medicine, *cranioscopy* is the observation and examination of the skull; *craniectomy* (Greek *ektomē*, excision) is surgical removal of a portion of it; *craniotomy* (Greek *-tomia*, cutting) is any surgical incision into it, say to reduce pressure; and *cranioplasty* is plastic surgery carried out on it. The usual adjective is *cranial*.

cross- *Movement or position across something; transverse; interaction; cross-shaped; marked with a cross.* [English *cross*.]

Cross has many meanings; the prefix reflects that, to the extent it is not always possible to tease out clearly defined and distinct senses for it. Examples where it has the idea of movement across something include *crossfire*, *cross-channel*, *cross-border*, *crossover*, *cross-fade*, *cross-country*. Other words suggest two things

---

-cracy   Government, rule, or influence.

aristocracy	rule by the highest social class	(Greek *aristos*, best)
autocracy	rule by one person with absolute power	(Greek *autos*, self)
bureaucracy	government in which officials take most of the decisions	(French *bureau*, office)
democracy	rule by all citizens	(Greek *dēmos*, the people)
gerontocracy	rule by old people	(Greek *gerōn*, old man)
mediocracy	rule by mediocre people or a system in which mediocrity is rewarded	(Latin *mediocris*, middling)
meritocracy	rule by those selected on the basis of ability	(English *merit*)
mobocracy	rule by the mob	(English *mob*)
plutocracy	rule by the rich	(Greek *ploutos*, wealth)
technocracy	control of society by technical experts	(English *technology*)
teledemocracy	democracy mediated or operated by telecommunications or television	(Greek *tēle-*, far off)
thalassocracy	rule over the seas	(Greek *thal*, sea)
theocracy	rule by priests	(Greek *theos*, God)

lying across each other at an angle: *cross-legged*, *cross-eyed*, *cross-grained*, *cross-ply*, *crossbill*. Some denote an interaction between two things: *cross-pollinate*, *cross-breed*, *cross-fertilize*, *cross-examine*, *cross-index*, *cross-check*, *cross-refer*, *cross-subsidize*. The idea of something transverse appears in *crossbar* and *crosspiece*. An implication that the form of a cross is present is found in *crossbones* (as in *skull and crossbones*), *cross-bun*, *crossbow*, *crossroads*, and *crossword*.

cryo- *Involving or producing cold.* [Greek *kruos*, frost.]

The usual adjective relating to very low temperatures is *cryogenic*, as in *cryogenic freezing*, in which tissues or foodstuffs are plunged into liquid nitrogen to preserve them; a *cryostat* maintains materials at a predefined low temperature; *cryogenics* is the study of materials at very low temperatures; *cryosurgery* uses intense cold to free and kill unwanted tissue; the *cryosphere* is that part of the planet that experiences persistent low temperatures, say at the poles or at high altitudes.

crypt(o)- *Concealed or secret.* [Greek *kruptos*, hidden.]

One set of words relates to the production of messages intended only to be understood by the intended recipient, or to methods for illicitly reading them. Text containing such a private message is a *cryptogram* and the process of creating it is *encryption*; the art of preparing or reading codes or ciphers is *cryptography*; the techniques of cracking codes or ciphers to discover messages are collectively called *cryptanalysis*.

The form also appears in the biological sciences. A *cryptogam* (Greek *gamos*, marriage) is a plant that reproduces by spores, so named because the means of reproduction were not obvious at the time; some organisms survive dry conditions through *cryptobiosis*, in which their metabolic activity becomes undetectably low; *cryptozoology* is the search for species of animal whose existence is disputed.

A third group has the idea of some membership, allegiance, or belief kept secret, as in *crypto-communist*, *crypto-fascist*, or *crypto-semite*.

cryso-: *see* CHRYSO-

crystall(o)- *A crystal or crystals.* [Latin *crystallum*, crystal, from Greek *krustallos*, ice, crystal.]

Crystallography is the branch of science concerned with the structure and properties of crystals; metamorphic rocks can have a *crystalloblastic* structure (Greek *blastos*, germ, sprout) caused by crystals grown in the solid medium; the protein *crystallin* is present in the lens of the eye.

cten(o)- *A comb.* [Greek *kteis*, *kten-*, comb.]

A *ctenidium* is a comb-like structure, especially a respiratory organ or gill in a mollusc; a *ctenoid* fish scale has many tiny projections on the edge like the teeth of a comb; *Ctenophora* is a small phylum of aquatic invertebrates that comprises the comb jellies. The initial letter is silent.

-cule Also **-cle**, **-icle**, and **-culus**. *Forming nouns.* [French *-cule*, derived from Latin *-culus*, *-cula* or *-culum*.]

The original sense of the Latin endings was as a diminutive, though this has largely been lost in English. Words ending in **-cule** include *graticule* (Latin *cratis*, a hurdle), a series of fine lines used as a measuring scale; *molecule* (Latin *moles*, mass), a group of atoms bonded together. Words ending in **-cle** (of which **-icle** is a variant in which the *i* is contributed by the Latin stem) include *article*, *particle*, *carbuncle*, *cubicle*, *manacle*, and *testicle*.

Some words exist in more than one form, with those in **-(i)cle** being more general than those in **-cule** or **-culus** (the latter perpetuating the masculine form of the Latin ending), which are commoner in scholarly contexts. An example is *fascicle* (from Latin *fascis*, a bundle) for an instalment of a printed book, which sometimes appears as *fascicule*; in anatomy and biology the word is more commonly *fasciculus* for a bundle of structures, such as nerve fibres or conducting vessels.

Words that primarily exist with the **-ulus** ending include *homunculus* (Latin *homo*, man), a very small human figure; the genus of the bindweed, *convolvulus* (literally a little thing bound together); and *apiculus*, a minute point or tip.

-culture Also **-cultural**. *Cultivation or husbandry.* [Latin *cultura*, growing, cultivation.]

The first words in this form to appear were *agriculture* (Latin *ager*, field) and *horticulture* (Latin *hortus*, garden). On their model many other terms for the cultivation or growing of specific plants or animals have since been created. See the LIST below for some examples. Related adjectives are formed ending in **-cultural** (*agricultural*, *horticultural*).

Terms in which *-culture* refers to a group or section within society that has certain characteristics in common (*counterculture*, *technoculture*) are usually regarded as compounds of the noun *culture*.

-culus: *see* -CULE

cupr(o)- *Copper.* [Latin *cuprum*, copper.]

Two adjectives relating to copper compounds are *cuprous*, containing monovalent copper (as in *cuprous sulphate*), and *cupric*, containing divalent copper (as in *cupric chloride*). An example of an ore yielding copper is *cuprite*, a dark

red mineral; *cuprammonium* is a solution of cupric hydroxide in ammonia, a solvent for cellulose; *cupro-nickel* is an alloy of copper with nickel. *See also* CHALCO-.

-cy Also **-acy**. *An abstract state, condition, or quality; a rank or status.* [Originally from French *-cie* or *-tie*, Latin *-cia* or *-tia*, or Greek *-k(e)ia* or *-t(e)ia*.]

Words with these suffixes are a subset of those ending in -Y³; they derive from word stems that end in *t*, *c*, or *k*. Those ending in **-acy** derive from stems that have an *a* before the final consonant. Many words ending in **-cy** contain the compound suffixes *-ancy*, *-ency* (for both, *see* -ANCE), -CRACY, and -MANCY.

Nouns formed from stems ending in *-t* usually convert the *t* into a *c*, as with *diplomacy*, *idiocy*, or *secrecy*; a few do not, as with *bankruptcy*, *baronetcy*, or *viscountcy*.

Most nouns denote an abstract state associated with the adjective or noun from which they were formed, often originally in Latin or Greek. Examples are *accuracy*, the condition of being *accurate*, or *celibacy*, the state of being *celibate*; other examples are *conspiracy*, *delicacy*, *effeminacy*, *fallacy*, *lunacy*, *piracy*, and *privacy*.

A smaller proportion indicate a rank or status. These usually add the **-cy** suffix to

---

-culture Cultivation or husbandry.
All word sources are from Latin, unless otherwise stated.

agriculture	farming	(*ager*, field)
apiculture	bee-keeping	(*apis*, bee)
aquaculture	aquatic animals or plants	(*aqua*, water)
arboriculture	ornamental trees	(*arbor*, tree)
aviculture	birds	(*avis*, bird)
floriculture	flowers	(*flos*, flower)
horticulture	gardening	(*hortus*, garden)
mariculture	sea fish or other marine life	(*mare*, sea)
monoculture	cultivation of only one sort of crop	(Greek *mono*, alone)
permaculture	sustainable agriculture	(a blend of *permanent* and *agriculture*)
sericulture	silk and silkworms	(*sericum*, silk)
silviculture	trees	(*silva*, wood)
vermiculture	earthworms	(*vermis*, worm)
viticulture	grapevines	(*vitis*, vine)

an English noun, often modifying its stem, as in *candidacy*, from *candidate*, or *magistracy*, from *magistrate*; other examples are *captaincy*, *chaplaincy*, and *prelacy* (Anglo-Norman French *prelacie*).

cyan(o)- *The colour blue, especially dark blue; cyanide or a derivative.* [Greek *kuan(e)os*, dark blue.]

The poisonous gas *cyanogen* (C_2N_2), though itself colourless, was named in 1815 by the French chemist Joseph Gay-Lussac (1778–1850) because he found it was chemically related to the dark-blue dyestuff Prussian Blue. The group —CN is now called the *cyano* group. Inorganic or mineral compounds containing it are *cyanides* (organic salts are *nitriles*). *Cyanoacrylates*, cyanide derivatives of acrylates, are quick-setting adhesives.

The colour *cyan* is a light greenish-blue, one of the three principal secondary colours (the others being magenta and yellow), complementary to red. *Cyanosis* is a blueness of the skin owing to poor circulation or inadequate oxygenation of the blood. A *cyanobacterium* is the modern name for what used to be called a *blue-green alga*; it is a bacterium capable of photosynthesis.

cyber- *Computer-mediated electronic communications.* [From the first element of *cybernetics*, the science of communications and automatic control systems, itself derived from Greek *kubernētēs*, steersman.]

Cyber- is one of the newest and in the 1990s also one of the most fertile combining forms in the language. The science-fiction writer William Gibson coined *cyberspace* in the early 1980s to describe a shared but intangible virtual reality space within computers. At about the same time *cyberpunk* came into being to describe the genre characterized by William Gibson's work, set in lawless future societies dominated by computer technology.

When public interest in the Internet blossomed in the early 1990s, journalists and commentators borrowed **cyber-** to refer to the online world, shifting its sense so it referred to electronic communications in general. This form became fashionable in the mid-1990s, with many hundreds of coinages recorded; only a few are likely to have a lasting place in the language. *Cyber*, as an adjective for electronic communication, is now also a word in its own right. For examples, See the LIST opposite. *See also E-.*

cyclo- *A circle, circular movement, or regular repetition.* [Either Greek *kuklos*, circle, or English *cycle* or *cyclic*.]

Words that include the idea of a circle include *cyclorama*, originally a large cylindrical picture designed to be viewed from inside, today usually a curved backdrop in a theatre, and *cyclostome*, an eel-like animal with a circular sucking mouth, such as a lamprey.

Other examples suggest circular movement: a *cycloid* is a curve marked out by a point on a circle rolling along a straight line, such as a point on a moving vehicle wheel; a *cyclotron* is a circular device for accelerating atomic and subatomic particles. A few compounds refer to a cyclic recurring condition, as in *cyclothymia*, a mental state in which the sufferer swings repeatedly between depression and elation.

In chemistry, the form marks a compound that contains a closed chain or ring of carbon atoms, as in *cyclohexane*, a colourless liquid used as a paint solvent. In medicine, *cyclosporin* (Greek *spora*, spore), a cyclic peptide derived from a fungus, is used to prevent rejection of grafts.

cyno- *A dog.* [Greek *kuōn*, dog.]

Examples include *cynodont*, a fossil carnivore with dog-like teeth, and *cynophilia*, a love of dogs (with its opposite, *cynophobia*). A *cynosure*, now anything which is the centre of attention or admiration, derives from Greek *kunosoura*, literally 'dog's tail', the Greek name for the constellation that contains the pole star, long used for navigation.

cyst(o)- *The urinary bladder.* [Greek *kustis*, bladder.]

Cystitis is inflammation of the urinary bladder, a *cystoscope* is a device for in-

cyber-   Computer-mediated electronic communications.
             All terms are based on English stems.

cyberart	art using computers or computer visualization methods
cybercash	electronic money stored in a smart card
cybercitizen	either a member of the online Internet community, or someone who uses the Net to exercise democratic rights in their community, say through electronic discussion forums or electronic voting
cybercommerce	an older term for *electronic commerce* (see E-)
cybercrime	in theory any criminal activity carried out using electronic communications, but principally electronic theft of money or identity or industrial espionage
cyberdemocracy	another name for *electronic democracy*, exercised by a cybercitizen
cyberian	a high-tech hippy who embraces technology
cyberlawyer	either someone versed in the law applying to electronic communications, or one who studies its implications for the law
cyberpunk	a sub-genre of science fiction, relating to lawless future societies dominated by computer technology
cybershopping	buying things via the Net, electronic shopping
cyberspace	(adjective *cyberspatial*) the notional environment in which communication over computer networks occurs
cybersquatting	registering an Internet domain name with the sole purpose of selling it on at a profit
cybersurfer	someone who surfs the Internet
cyberterrorism	the use of electronic techniques to cause damage to the computer systems or communications of an opposition group
cyberwar	using electronic methods to knock out the command systems of an enemy

specting it, *cystography* is a method for examining it by introducing a liquid opaque to X-rays, a *cystocoele* (Greek *kēlē*, tumour) is a hernia in it, and a *cystectomy* (Greek *ektomē*, excision) is its surgical removal. *Cyst* comes through Latin from the same Greek source, but in medicine has a wider meaning of any sac or cavity in the body; though the adjective *cystic* can refer to the urinary bladder, it can also be used in reference to the gall bladder or to cysts in general.

-cyte Also **-cytosis**. *A cell.* [Greek *kutos*, vessel]

This ending usually indicates a mature cell, as opposed to an immature or embryonic cell, whose name ends in -BLAST. For examples, see the LIST overleaf. Nouns ending in **-cytosis** refer to an action or condition relating to a cell: *phagocytosis* (Greek *phagein*, to eat), the ingestion of bacteria or other material by phagocytes and amoeboid protozoans; *endocytosis* (Greek *endon*, within), the taking in of matter by a living cell by turning its cell membrane inside out to form a vacuole.

cyto- *A cell.* [Greek *kutos*, vessel.]

Examples are *cytology*, the branch of biology that deals with living cells, *cytoplasm*, material inside a cell but outside the nucleus, and *cytoskeleton*, a network of protein in the cytoplasm of many cells that gives them shape; *cytoarchitecture* is the arrangement of cells in a tissue; a *cytokine* is a type of chemical messenger that acts on other cells; something *cytotoxic* is poisonous to cells.

-cyte   A cell.

adipocyte	a cell that stores fat	(Latin *adeps*, fat)
astrocyte	a star-shaped cell of the nervous system	(Greek *astron*, star)
erythrocyte	a red blood cell	(Greek *eruthros*, red)
granulocyte	a circulating white blood cell having prominent granules	(Latin *granulum*, a little grain)
hepatocyte	a liver cell	(Greek *hēpar*, liver)
keratinocyte	a cell in the skin that produces keratin	(Greek *keras*, horn)
leucocyte	a white blood cell	(Greek *leukos*, white)
lymphocyte	a small white blood cell found in the lymph	(Latin *lympha*, water)
melanocyte	a cell in the skin producing dark pigment, as in hair colour or tanning	(Greek *melas*, black)
oocyte	a cell in an ovary which may divide to become an ovum	(Greek *ōion*, egg)
phagocyte	a cell that absorbs bacteria and other small particles	(Greek *phagein*, to eat)
spermatocyte	a cell formed during the creation of spermatozoa	(Greek *sperma*, seed)
thrombocyte	a blood cell fragment involved in clotting, a platelet	(Greek *thrombos*, blood clot)

D- or d-: *see* DEXTRO-

dacryo- *Tears.* [Greek *dakruon*, tear.]

Dacryoadenitis (Greek *adēn*, gland) is inflammation of the gland that produces tears; *dacryocystitis* (Greek *kustis*, bladder) is inflammation of one of the sacs between the eye and the nose in which tears collect; *dacryocystorhinostomy* (Greek *rhis*, *rhin-*, nose; *stoma*, mouth) is an operation to restore passage from this sac into the nose through the drainage duct.

-dactyl or -dactyla: *see* -DACTYLY

dactyl(o)- *Fingers or toes.* [Greek *daktulos*, finger.]

A person with *dactylomegaly* (Greek *megas*, *megal-*, great) has one or more abnormally large fingers or toes; *dactylitis* is inflammation of a finger or toe; *dactylology* is the representation of speech by finger movements, sign language; *dactylography* is the study of fingerprints for identifying individuals. A *dactyl* is a unit of poetical metre consisting of three syllables, so called from the three bones of a finger that are taken to represent the three syllables; the associated adjective is *dactylic*.

-dactyly Also **-dactyla**, **-dactyl** and **-dactylous**. *Having fingers or toes of a given type.* [Greek *daktulos*, finger, plus -Y³.]

An animal or person exhibiting *syndactyly* (Greek *sun*, with) has some or all of the fingers or toes united, either naturally, as in web-footed animals, or as a malformation; *brachydactyly* (Greek *brakhus*, short) is the state of having abnormally short fingers or toes; in zoology *polydactyly* (Greek *polloi*, many) is the state of having more than five fingers on a hand or toes on a foot.

Words ending in **-dactyla** are names of orders of hoofed mammals: *Artiodactyla* (Greek *artios*, even) comprises those with an even number of toes, such as pigs, camels, deer, and cattle; *Perissodactyla* (Greek *perissos*, uneven) comprises those with an odd number, such as zebras, horses, and tapirs. Other systematic names with this ending are obsolete.

The ending **-dactyl** either marks adjectives relating to the state indicated by **-dactyly** or **-dactyla**, or nouns indicating an individual of that nature: *polydactyl*, *syndactyl*, *artiodactyl*, *perissodactyl*. One example always a noun is *pterodactyl* (Greek *pteron*, wing), a fossil flying reptile of the Jurassic and Cretaceous periods. The **-dactylous** ending (*see* -OUS) generates adjectives with a similar sense to **-dactyl**, but which are less common: *polydactylous*, *zygodactylous*.

de- *Forming verbs and their derivatives.* [Latin *de*, off or from; less commonly via French *dé-*, Old French *des-*, from the Latin negative prefix *dis-*, in which it implies removal or reversal (*see* DIS-).]

Examples of the first origin include *decay* (Latin *de-*, fall down or off, plus *cadere*, fall); *defend* (Latin *de-*, off, plus *-fendere*, to strike); and *desist* (Latin *de-*, down from, plus *sistere*, to stop). Examples of the second origin are *defame* (Latin *dis-*, expressing removal, plus *fama*, report); *debate* (Latin *dis-*, expressing reversal, plus *battere*, to fight); and *deploy* (Latin *plicare*, to fold).

The prefix has several meanings. In older words, adopted from French or directly from Latin roots, it can contain the idea of 'down' or 'away', often figuratively, as in *descend*, *depress*, *degrade*, and *depose*. Sometimes it implies something done completely or thoroughly, as with *denude*, *devour*, or *derelict*. It often has negative implications, as with *deceive*, *delude*, *deride*, and *detest*.

When **de-** is used to form verbs on English stems, it has a sense of undoing the action of the stem verb—by removal, reversal, or separation—a sense closely related to UN-: *debrief*, *decertify*, *decriminalize*, *defrost*, *dehumidify*, *de-ice*, *delouse*, *desegregate*, *deselect*. The prefix is often hyphenated before a vowel or in new creations. It is very active and examples from recent decades are *de-archive*, *delayer* (to reduce the number of levels in an organizational hierarchy of employees), *deinstall* (removal of a piece of computer software from a system), *demutualize* (change the status of a mutual organization such as a building society to a different kind).

dec(a)- Also **dek(a)-**. *Ten.* [Greek *deka*, ten.]

A *decade* is a period of ten years; a *decathlon* (Greek *athlon*, contest) is an athletic contest of ten events; a *decagon* is a plane figure with ten straight sides and angles. *Decane* is a colourless liquid hydrocarbon of the alkane series, whose molecule contains ten carbon atoms; a *decapod* (Greek *pous*, *pod-*, foot) is a crustacean with five pairs of walking legs, such as shrimps and crabs. The form appears in units of measurement (*decalitre*, *decametre*) and is one of the standard SI (Système International) multiples (see the table of WORDS FOR MULTIPLES on page 127); the standard specifies that it should be spelled **deca-**. The spelling with *k* is used in the US. *See also* the next entry.

decem- *Ten.* [Latin *decem*, ten.]

This is the less common Latin alternative to the Greek DECA-. The only common example is *December*, originally the tenth month of the Roman year. *Decennium*, a decade (with its adjective *decennial*) derives from the related Latin *decennis*, of ten years, from *annus*, year.

deci- *One tenth.* [Latin *decimus*, tenth.]

The *decimal* system of counting is based on the number ten; to *decimate* originally meant to kill one in every ten of a group, but in current usage it refers to any large proportion; a *decile* is each of ten equal groups into which a population can be divided according to the distribu-

tion of values of a variable. For *decillion* see the table of NUMBER WORDS on page 162. A *decibel* (one tenth of a *bel*, a unit too large for practical convenience) is used to measure the intensity of a sound or an electrical signal by comparing it with a given level on a logarithmic scale; other examples in units of measurement include *decilitre* and *decimetre* (US *deciliter* and *decimeter*). It is one of the standard SI (Système International) multiples (see the table of WORDS FOR MULTIPLES on page 127).

-decker *Having a specified number of decks or layers.* [English *deck* plus -ER[1].]

Examples are *four-decker*, a ship with four decks; *three-decker*, of a Victorian novel in three volumes; *triple-decker*, a sandwich containing three slices of bread with fillings between; *double-decker*, something, especially a bus, that has two floors or levels.

dehydro- *Loss of hydrogen.* [DE- plus HYDRO-[2].]

In chemical naming this indicates the loss of one or more hydrogen atoms, a process called *dehydrogenation*; examples include *dehydrocholesterol*, a derivative of cholesterol present in the skin that is converted to vitamin D by sunlight, and *dehydroacetic acid*, a cyclic compound derived from acetic acid that is sometimes used as a fungicide. A *dehydrogenase* is an enzyme that catalyses the removal of hydrogen atoms from a particular molecule, examples being *glucose dehydrogenase*, *choline dehydrogenase*, and *alcohol dehydrogenase*. To *dehydrate*, to lose water from the body, comes directly from Greek *hudros*, *hudr-*, water.

-delic Also **-delia**. *Of attitudes or activities relating to a given type of experience.* [Greek *dēlos*, clear, manifest, plus -IA.]

The first example, from the 1950s but especially linked to the sixties hippie era, was *psychedelic* (Greek *psukhē*, breath, life, soul), relating to or denoting drugs (especially LSD) that produce hallucinations and apparent expansion of consciousness. On its model, a few others have been created, though none has achieved great popularity and the meaning of the ending is variable and often imprecise: *funkadelic*, relating to the collective experience of making and playing funk music; *cyberdelic*, of a Northern Californian subculture that attempts to reconcile the information revolution with 1960s counterculture. Other, more transient, examples are *dancedelic* and *sampladelic* (centred on sampled musical sounds), and *shagadelic* (British vulgar slang *shag*, have sexual intercourse with), popularized by the Mike Myers film *Austin Powers: The Spy Who Shagged Me*. Related nouns are formed using **-delia** (*psychodelia*, *cyberdelia*, *funkadelia*).

demi- *Half; partially.* [Latin *dimidius*, half.]

Words in **demi-** have come into English through French and many examples retain a strong French flavour. It is found especially in subject areas that contain much vocabulary derived from French, such as heraldry, fortifications, armour, and costume. It is not a living prefix, its role having almost entirely been taken over by SEMI-.

In many terms, the prefix means either a half, or something of lesser or reduced size: *demilune* (French, literally 'half-moon'), a crescent or half-circle, or a thing of this shape; *demitasse* (French, literally 'half-cup'), a small coffee cup; *demisemiquaver*, in British music notation, a note having the time value of half a semiquaver, a thirty-second note; *demi-pension* (French, literally 'half board'), hotel accommodation with bed, breakfast, and one main meal per day.

In others, **demi-** suggests something of a lesser degree: *demigod*, a being with partial or lesser divine status; *demimonde* (French, literally 'half-world'), in 19th-century France, the class of women considered to be of doubtful social standing and morality.

However, *demiurge*, a being responsible for the creation of the universe, derives from Greek *dēmios*, public; *demijohn*, for the container, is probably from French *dame-jeanne* 'Lady Jane'.

demo- *The people.* [Greek *dēmos*, the people.]

The only two common words here, not counting their compounds and relatives, are *democracy*, a system of government by essentially the whole population, and *demography*, the study of statistics that illustrate the changing structure of human populations.

demon(o)- *Demons.* [Greek *daimon*, demon.]

Examples include *demonology*, the study of demons or demonic belief; *demonize* or *demonise*, to portray someone as wicked and threatening; *demonolatry* (Greek *-latria*, worship), the worship of demons; *demonism*, belief in the power of demons; and *demonomania*, a form of mental disturbance in which a person believes he or she is possessed by a demon or spirit. *Demonstrate* is not a member of this set, as it comes instead from Latin *demonstrare* (*de-*, entirely, plus *monstrare*, to show).

dendro- Also **dendri-**. *A tree or trees.* [Greek *dendron*, tree.]

Dendrochronology is a method of dating objects by using the patterns of annual growth rings in timber and tree trunks; *dendrology* is the scientific study of trees; something *dendriform* is tree-shaped. Some examples use the branching shape of a tree as an analogy, as in *dendrogram*, a diagram with branches like a family tree to show relationships, and *dendrite*, a short branched extension of a nerve cell.

-dendron *A shrub or tree.* [Greek *dendron*, tree.]

This appears in a few common names of trees and shrubs, such as *rhododendron* (Greek *rhodon*, rose), a shrub or small tree with large clusters of bell-shaped flowers; *philodendron* (Greek *philos*, loving), a tropical American climbing plant; *liriodendron* (Greek *leirion*, lily), a tree of a small genus which includes the tulip tree; *fremontodendron*, a Californian shrub, also called the flannel bush.

dent(i)- Also **dento-**. *A tooth; tooth-like.* [Latin *dens*, *dent-*, tooth.]

A *dentist* looks after one's teeth; a *denture* is a plate containing artificial teeth;

dentition is the arrangement or condition of the teeth in the mouth; a *dentifrice* (Latin *fricare*, to rub) is a paste or powder for cleaning the teeth; *dentine* is the hard dense bony tissue forming the bulk of a tooth, beneath the enamel. The adjective *dentofacial* refers to teeth and jaws together and by extension to the shape of the face, *dentogingival* to the teeth and gums.

Something *dentate* has a tooth-like or serrated edge, while something *denticulate* (Latin *denticulus*, small tooth) is finely dentate, for example the edge of a leaf, or has *dentils*, small rectangular blocks resembling teeth, used as a decoration under the moulding of a cornice in classical architecture. *See also* ODONTO-.

deoxy- *Loss of oxygen.* [DE- plus OXY-².]

This appears in names of substances to indicate that the molecule has lost one or more oxygen atoms compared with a precursor compound, a process sometimes called *deoxygenation*. Examples include *deoxyribonucleic acid* (DNA), a self-replicating material, the carrier of genetic information in the chromosomes; part of its structure is *deoxyribose*, a sugar derived from ribose by replacement of a hydroxyl group by hydrogen; *deoxycholic acid* is one of the bile acids; *deoxycorticosterone* is a corticosteroid hormone involved in regulating the salt and water balance in the body.

-derm Also **-dermatous**. *Skin; covering.* [Greek *derma*, skin, hide.]

Several terms refer to an embryo, such as *blastoderm* (Greek *blastos*, germ or sprout), a blastula (an embryo at an early stage of development) that has the form of a disc of cells on top of the yolk; and the set *ectoderm* (Greek *ektos*, outside), *mesoderm* (Greek *mesos*, middle), and *endoderm* (Greek *endon*, within), respectively the outermost, middle, and inner layers of cells of an embryo in early development. In botany, the *periderm* (Greek *peri*, about, around) is the corky outer layer of a plant stem formed in secondary thickening or as a response to injury or infection. A *pachyderm* (Greek *pakhus*, thick) is a very large mammal

with thick skin, especially an elephant, rhinoceros, or hippopotamus.

Other examples are the names of existing or fossil species of animal, such as *echinoderm* (Greek *ekhinos*, hedgehog, sea urchin), a member of a group of marine invertebrates which includes starfishes, sea urchins, and sea cucumbers; *placoderm* (Greek *plax*, *plak-*, flat plate), a fossil fish of the Devonian period.

Linked adjectives are formed in **-dermatous**, though these are relatively rare: *echinodermatous*, *pachydermatous*.

-derma *A disorder of the skin.* [Greek *derma*, skin, hide.]

Examples include *leucoderma* (Greek *leukos*, white), another name for vitiligo, in which whitish patches form on the skin; *pyoderma* (Greek *puon*, pus), a skin infection with formation of pus; *scleroderma* (Greek *sklēros*, hard), a chronic hardening and contraction of the skin and connective tissue; *xeroderma* (Greek *xēros*, dry), any disease in which the skin becomes very dry.

dermat(o)- Sometimes **derm(o)-**. *The skin.* [Greek *derma*, *dermat-*, skin or hide.]

Dermatology is the branch of medicine concerned with the diagnosis and treatment of skin disorders, such as *dermatitis*, a condition of the skin in which it becomes red, swollen, and sore; *dermabrasion* is the removal of superficial layers of skin with a rapidly revolving abrasive tool, as a technique in cosmetic surgery; *dermatoglyphics* is the study of skin markings or patterns on fingers, hands, and feet, and its application, especially in criminology.

The form **dermo-** was once common but has been now largely replaced by **dermato-**; surviving examples include *dermoid*, relating to the skin, usually found in dermoid *cyst*, an abnormal growth containing skin cells, hair follicles, and sebaceous glands; and *dermographism* (Greek *-graphia*, writing), a local reaction caused by pressure on the skin, such that it can be 'written' on, producing welts.

desm(o)- *A bond or chain.* [Greek *desmos*, a chain or fetter; *desme*, bundle.]

A *desmosome* is a structure by which two adjacent cells are attached, formed from protein plaques in the cell membranes linked by filaments; *desmoid* denotes a type of fibrous tumour of muscle and connective tissue, typically in the abdomen; a *desmid* is a single-celled freshwater alga which appears to be composed of two rigid cells with a shared nucleus.

deuter(o)- Sometimes **deuto-**. *Second; secondary.* [Greek *deuteros*, second.]

Examples where the form means 'second' include *deuteragonist* (Greek *agōnistēs*, actor), the person second in importance to the protagonist in a drama; *Deuteronomy* (Greek *nomos* law), the fifth book of the Old Testament, so named because it contains a repetition of the decalogue and the laws given in Exodus; and *deuterium*, a stable second isotope of hydrogen.

The idea of something secondary appears in *deuterocanonical*, of sacred books or literary works that form a secondary canon; and *deuterostome* (Greek *stoma*, mouth), an organism, such as a starfish, whose mouth develops from a secondary embryonic opening.

Deuto- is now uncommon, appearing for example in *deutoplasm*, sometimes used for the yolk of an egg.

dextr(o)- Also **D-** and **d-**. *On or to the right.* [Latin *dexter*, *dextr-*, right.]

Dextral refers to the right side or the right hand (the opposite of *sinistral*, see SINISTRO-); the adjective *dexterous* (or *dextrous*) strictly also means 'on the right', but usually means that a person is skilful (left-handed people were once thought clumsy); someone *ambidextrous* (Latin *ambi-*, on both sides) is able to use the right and left hands equally well; *dextrocardia* is a congenital condition in which the position of the heart is a mirror image of normal, with the apex of the ventricles pointing to the right.

Many chemical compounds rotate polarized light to the right (clockwise facing the oncoming radiation) and are then said to be *dextrorotatory*. In chemical names, the dextrorotatory form is sometimes indicated by **d-**, for example *d-ribose* or *d-gluconic acid*. The optical activity of a compound reflects the arrangement of the atoms in its molecules; the prefix **D-** has been used to refer to one whose shape is consistent with that of *D-glyceraldehyde*; however, **d-** forms are not necessarily also **D-** forms and both prefixes have largely been replaced by other naming conventions. A few chemical names include a reference to optical activity of this kind, such as *dextrose*, the dextrorotatory form of glucose. The opposite to **dextro-** in this sense is LAEVO-.

di- *Twice, two, double.* [Greek *dis*, *di-*, two or twice.]

Some older examples derive from Greek words already containing the prefix, such as *diphthong*, a sound formed by the combination of two vowels in a single syllable (Greek *diphthongos*, from *phthongos*, voice or sound), or *dilemma*, a situation in which a difficult choice has to be made between two or more equally undesirable courses of action (Greek *dilēmma*, from *lēmma*, premise).

On these models, a number of English forms have been created, mostly technical terms. Examples include *dipole*, a pair of equal and oppositely charged or magnetized poles separated by a distance; *Diptera* (Greek *pteron*, wing), a large order of insects that comprises the two-winged or true flies; *dimer* (formed on the pattern of *polymer*) a molecule or molecular complex consisting of two identical molecules linked together; *dioecious* (Greek *-oîkos*, house), describes a plant or invertebrate animal that has the male and female reproductive organs in separate individuals.

In chemistry, **di-** is used to indicate the presence of two atoms or groups of a specified kind, as in *dioxide*, *dichromate*, *disulphide* and many others. It is also used to make compound affixes indicating that a radical appears twice in a molecule, as in *dichloro-*, *-diene*, *dihydro-*, *dimethyl-*, *-dione*, and *diphenyl-*. All of these except the last have separate entries under the radical name without the preceding **di-**.

For *dichotomy*, see DICHO-. Some words beginning in *di-* contain instead the Latin prefix meaning 'apart', derived from DIS-: *digest*, *dilapidated*, *divert*. Other examples are in the next entry.

See also BI-.

di(a)- *Through, across.* [Greek *dia*, through.]

Most words beginning in **dia-** are based directly on Greek terms that already contain it. Some examples are *diagnosis* (Greek *diagignōskein*, distinguish or discern, from *gignōskein*, recognize or know), the identification of the nature of an illness by examining symptoms; *diagonal* (Greek *gōnia*, angle), joining two opposite corners; *diagram* (Greek *diagraphein*, mark out by lines, from *graphein*, write); and *dialogue* (Greek *dialegesthai*, converse with, from *legein*, speak). *Diabolic* is a less obvious example, as it derives ultimately from Greek *diabolos*, slanderer, from *ballein*, to throw (the name of a toy, *diabolo*, is a close relative via Latin and Italian).

A smaller proportion of words can be said unequivocally to have been generated using **dia-** as an English word-forming element. Among them are *dielectric*, having the property of transmitting electric force without conduction; *diathermy* (Greek *thermon*, heat), a therapeutic technique involving heating part of the body by high-frequency electric currents; *diamagnetic*, of a substance or body that tends to become magnetized in the opposite direction to the applied magnetic field; and *epidiascope* (Greek *epi*, upon, plus *skopein*, look at), an optical projector capable of giving images of both opaque and transparent objects.

Diamond was originally *adamans* in Latin (the source also of our *adamant*) but was altered in late Latin under the influence of Greek words beginning with **dia-**.

diazo-: *see* DI- and AZO-

dichloro-: *see* DI- and CHLORO-

dich(o)- *In two parts; paired.* [Greek *díkho-*, apart, in two.]

The most common example of this rather rare form is *dichotomy* (Greek *-tomia*, cutting), a contrast between two things that are opposed or entirely differ-

ent; others are *dichogamy* (Greek *gamos*, marriage), referring to the ripening of the stamens and pistils of a flower at different times, so that the flower cannot fertilize itself; and *dichotic* (Greek *ous*, *ōt-*, ear), involving or relating to the simultaneous stimulation of the right and left ear by different sounds.

dictyo- *A net.* [Greek *díktuon*, net.]

The *Dictyoptera* (Greek *pteron*, wing, from their veined appearance) are an order of insects that comprises the cockroaches and mantises; a *dictyostele* in some ferns and dicotyledons is a stele, the central core of the stem, which is so interrupted by leaf-gaps as to resemble a network of strands; a *dictyosome* (Greek *sōma*, body) is the set of flattened membranes in a Golgi body (a complex of vesicles and folded membranes within the cytoplasm), that resembles a stack of plates.

dif-: *see* DIS-

digit(i)- *A finger.* [Latin *digitus*, finger or toe.]

A mammal that is *digitigrade* (Latin *-gradus*, walking) walks on its toes, as a cat does, not touching the ground with its heels; something *digitate* is shaped like a spread hand; *digital*, literally relating to the fingers, now more commonly refers to signals or information represented by discrete values (the related Latin word *digit* has come to mean a numeral, because people counted on their fingers). It is found less obviously in *digitalis*, a drug from the dried leaves of foxgloves that stimulates the heart muscle; this derives from the modern Latin genus name of the foxglove, given it because the flower resembles a finger stall or thimble.

dihydro-: *see* DI- and HYDRO-

dihydroxy-: *see* DI- and HYDROXY-

dino- *Terrible, frightful.* [Greek *deinos*, terrible.]

Easily the most common example is *dinosaur* (Greek *sauros*, lizard), a fossil reptile of the Mesozoic era; another fossil type is *dinotherium* (Greek *thēr*, beast), a mammal like an elephant from the later Tertiary Period. A few words use **dino-** in the sense of dinosaur, such as *dinoturbation*, the effect on the formation of sedimentary rocks of dinosaurs churning up the ground, and *dinomania*, an excessive interest in dinosaurs. However, *dinoflagellate*, a single-celled organism with two flagella, derives from Greek *dinos*, whirling.

-dione: *see* DI- and -ONE

-dioic: *see* DI- and -OIC

diplo- *Double.* [Greek *diplous*, double.]

A *diplococcus* (Greek *kokkos*, berry) is a roughly spherical bacterium that occurs in pairs, such as pneumococcus; *diplopia* (Greek *ōps*, *ōp-*, eye) is the technical term for double vision; a cell that is *diploid* contains two complete sets of chromosomes, one from each parent; a *diplontic* alga or other lower plant has a life cycle in which the main form is diploid. *Diploma* derives from the Greek word for a folded paper, hence an official document; *diplomat* comes from the same source (somebody who carries state papers).

dis- Also **dif-**. *Expressing a variety of negative senses.* [Latin *dis-*, sometimes via Old French *des-*.]

The prefix had various linked senses in Latin, such as reversal, moving apart, removal or separation; sometimes it could express simple negation. For example, in *dissuade* it indicates reversal, as the stem verb *suadere* means to advise or persuade; in *dissipate*, from *supare*, to throw, it has the sense of 'apart', so literally 'to scatter'; in *discharge*, from Latin *discarricare*, to unload, it signals the opposite of *carricare*, to load.

As a prefix in English, it can have any of these senses. It indicates reversal in *disaffirm*, *disconnect*, *disappear*, *disembark*, *disestablish*, *disown*, *dispossess*, *disqualify*; removal in *disbud*, *disburden*, *disembowel*; negation in *disability*, *dishonour*, *dislike*, *dissimilar*.

The prefix is active, for instance in recent decades forming *disambiguate*, to remove the ambiguity from some situation; *disintermediation*, eliminating

intermediaries from a chain of suppliers or traders; *disinformation*, false information which is intended to mislead.

In a few examples in Latin, **dis-** could intensify the action of the stem. In English, a few examples exist, but they are unusual: *disannul*, to make null and void; *dissever*, to divide or sever something.

Before stems beginning with *f*, the prefix became **dif-** in Latin, examples of which in English include *differ*, *difficulty*, *diffident*, *diffract*, and *diffuse*.

Though *dismal* looks like a member of this set, it actually derives from medieval Latin *dies mali*, evil days.

disco- *A disc; disc-shaped.* [Greek *diskos*, a disc.]

Words in this form are closely related to English *disc* (US *disk*) and *discus*, both of which entered the language through Latin. One group refers to gramophone records, such as *discotheque* (French *discothèque*, originally a record library, from which *disco* derives by abbreviation), *discography*, a descriptive catalogue of musical recordings, and *discophile*, a collector of records. The form appears in some names of organisms, such as *discomycete* (Greek *mukēs*, fungus), a member of a class of fungi that have a cup-shaped or disc-shaped fruiting body. Something *discoid* or *discoidal* is shaped like a disc.

dithio-: *see* DI- and THIO-

docu- *A documentary programme.* [The first element of English *documentary*.]

In recent decades several words have been formed for types of television entertainment containing documentary elements. Early examples were blends of *documentary* with other words (especially *docutainment*, entertainment that includes documentary materials), but recent creations suggest that **docu-** is evolving into a combining form. Examples include *docudrama*, a dramatized television programme based on real events; *docusoap*, a television soap based on factual elements. These seem well-established; less so are *docucomedy* and *docu-fiction*.

dodec(a)- *Twelve.* [Greek *dodeka*, twelve.]

A *dodecahedron* (Greek *hedra*, seat, base) is a three-dimensional shape having twelve plane faces, while a *dodecagon* is a plane figure with twelve straight sides and angles. The *Dodecanese* is a group of twelve islands in the SE Aegean. The term *dodecaphonic* refers to a system of musical composition, also called the twelve-note or twelve-tone system.

In chemistry, *dodecane* is the straight chain (aliphatic) hydrocarbon $C_{12}H_{26}$; *dodecyl* (*see* -YL) relates to the radical —$C_{12}H_{25}$, as in dodecyl aldehyde, also called lauric aldehyde or *dodecanal* (*see* -AL[2]), used in perfumery; *dodecanoic acid* (*see* -OIC), or lauric acid, occurs in many vegetable fats and is used to make soaps and cosmetics.

dolicho- *Long.* [Greek *dolíkhos*, long.]

A skull that is *dolichocephalic* is relatively long compared to its width; a *dolichocolon* is an excessively long colon; *dolichol* is a long-chain unsaturated compound whose phosphate is important in converting proteins into sugars in the body. *Dolichos* is a genus of leguminous plants, so named because members have long seed pods; *Dolichotis* (Greek *ous*, *ōt-*, ear) is a genus of South American rodents with long ears (*Dolichotis patagonum* is the Patagonian hare).

-dom *Forming abstract or collective nouns.* [A Germanic root related to the Old English *dom*, originally a decree or judgement.]

Older examples imply a state or condition (as in *freedom*, the state of being free, or *wisdom*, the condition of being wise) or denote a rank or an area controlled by a person of that rank (so *earldom* is either the rank of an earl, or the domain controlled by one; other examples are *fiefdom* and *kingdom*). The suffix is active, but modern creations most often describe a class of people, or of attitudes linked to them, such as *officialdom*. Some of these—such as *stardom* or *fogeydom*—have achieved a permanent or semi-permanent status. But many transient compounds are created in popular writing, most of them destined to be used just once: *groupiedom*, *touchie-feeliedom*, *wifedom*. One relatively new example that might achieve permanence is *computerdom*, for the whole group of people associated with computers and computing.

-dont, **-dontia**, **-dontics**, or **-dontology**: *see* -ODONT

dors(i)- Also **dorso-**. *The back.* [Latin *dorsum*, back.]

The historical distinction between these forms, in which **dorsi-** refers to the back, while **dorso-** alludes to the back plus another part of the body, is not now observed.

The adjective *dorsal* relates to the upper side or back of an animal, plant, or organ; something *dorsolateral* involves the dorsal and lateral surfaces; *dorsiflex* is a verb meaning to bend something, typically the hand or foot, dorsally or towards its upper surface. The *dorsum* is the dorsal part of an organism or structure. *Dorsiventral* (Latin *venter*, *ventr-*, belly) is used mainly in botany for a leaf or other part of a plant that has dissimilar dorsal and ventral surfaces, while *dorsoventral* mainly appears in anatomy and biology to denote an axis joining the dorsal and ventral surfaces (these senses are sometimes interchanged).

-dox *An opinion or view.* [Greek *doxa*, opinion.]

This has never been an active word-forming element, but appears in a few words of Greek origin: *paradox*, from Greek *paradoxon*, a contrary opinion, from *para-*, distinct from; *orthodox*, from Greek *orthos*, straight or right; *heterodox*, from Greek *heteros*, other.

-drome Also **-dromic** and **-dromous**. *Running or racing; proceeding in a given way.* [Greek *dromos*, course; running.]

Examples of the first sense include *hippodrome* (Greek *hippos*, horse), originally a course for chariot or horse races in ancient Greece or Rome, but in English a grandiose name for a circus, later applied to theatres or concert halls; *velodrome* (French *vélo*, bicycle), a cycle-racing track; *aerodrome*, a British term for a small airport or airfield; *cosmodrome* (Greek *kosmos*, world), a launching site for spacecraft in the countries of the former USSR.

The idea of proceeding in a given way appears in the medical terms *syndrome* (Greek *sun-*, together), a group of symptoms which occur together or a condition with such a set of symptoms, and *prodrome* (Greek *pro*, before), an early symptom indicating the onset of a disease or illness. It also occurs in *palindrome* (Greek *palin*, again), a word, phrase, or sequence that reads the same backwards as forwards, and *loxodrome* (Greek *loxos*, slanting), an imaginary line on the earth's surface cutting all meridians at the same angle.

Adjectives corresponding to these nouns are formed in **-dromic** (*see* -IC): *loxodromic*, *palindromic*. A few adjectives exist ending in **-dromous** (*see* -OUS), but these do not have associated nouns ending in **-drome**: *anadromous* (Greek *ana-*, up), of a fish, such as the salmon, that migrates up rivers from the sea to spawn, the opposite of which is *catadromous* (Greek *kata*, down), of ones that migrate downstream, as the eel does.

drom(o)- *Movement; speed.* [Greek *dromas, dromad-*, runner.]

This appears in *dromedary*, an Arabian camel, especially one of a light and swift breed trained for riding or racing; an agent that is *dromotropic* influences the speed of conduction of electrical impulses, say to the heart; someone with *dromomania* has a pathological impulse to roam or run.

du(o)- *Two; having two.* [Latin *duo*, two.]

A *duet*, a performance by two people, and *dual*, consisting of two parts, both derive from this Latin source, the former via Italian *duetto*. A *duologue* (Greek *logos*, word) is a play or part of a play with speaking roles for only two actors; a *duopoly* (Greek *pōlein*, sell) is a situation in which two suppliers dominate the market for a commodity or service.

Some related words are based on Latin *duplex, duplic-*, from *duo* plus *plicare*, to fold; examples include *duplicate*, and *duplicity*, deceitfulness or double-dealing, as well as *duplex* itself, something having two parts.

duodeci- *Twelve; twelfth.* [Latin *duodecim*, twelve; *duodecimo*, twelfth.]

This form appears relatively rarely, the Greek DODECA- being more common. Examples include *duodecimal*, of a system of counting or numerical notation that has twelve as a base; *duodecimo*, a size of book in which each leaf is one twelfth of the size of the printing sheet; *duodecennial*, relating to a period of twelve years; *duodecad* (rarely *duodecade*), either a group of twelve or a period of twelve years.

duoden(o)- *Duodenum.* [Latin *duodeni*, in twelves.]

The *duodenum*, the first part of the small intestine immediately beyond the stomach, was so named because it was as long as about twelve finger widths. *Duodenitis* is inflammation of the duodenum; *duodenostomy* (Greek *stoma*, mouth), is the surgical creation of an opening to the duodenum through the abdominal wall; *duodenectomy* (Greek *ektomē*, excision) is surgical removal of the duodenum.

dynam(o)- Also **dyna-**. *Power.* [Greek *dunamis*, power.]

The Greek root is present in *dynamic* and its relatives, relating to a process or system that undergoes constant change, activity, or progress; a *dynamo* (originally a *dynamo-electric machine*), converts mechanical energy into electrical energy; a *dynamometer* measures the power output of an engine. The name of the explosive *dynamite* contains the same root, as does *dyne*, a unit of force in the obsolete CGS system, equivalent to 10^{-5} of a newton.

-dynia: *see* -ODYNIA

dys- *Bad; difficult.* [Greek *dus-*, hard, bad.]

This form appears most commonly in medical terms, such as *dyspepsia* (Greek *duspeptos*, difficult to digest), indigestion; *dysphagia* (Greek *phagein*, eat), difficulty or discomfort in swallowing, as a symptom of disease; *dyslexia* (Greek *lexis*, speech, through a confusion with Latin *legere*, to read), a general term for dis-orders that involve difficulty in learning to read or interpret words, letters, and other symbols.

A **dysphemism** (Greek *phēmē*, speaking) is a derogatory or unpleasant term used instead of a pleasant or neutral one, the opposite of *euphemism*; a **dystopia** (Greek *topos*, place) is an imagined place or state in which everything is unpleasant or bad, the opposite of *utopia*; **dysfunctional** refers to something not operating nor-mally or properly, or someone unable to deal adequately with normal social rela-tions; the chemical element **dysprosium** (*see* -IUM) was so named from the related Greek *dusprositos*, hard to get at.

Its opposite is EU-.

E

e-¹ *Electronic communications.* [The first letter of *electronic*.]

The oldest form is *e-mail*, short for *electronic mail*, first recorded in 1982. From the early 1990s, others began to appear that signify types of information or transaction in digital electronic format, frequently transmitted over computer networks such as the Internet. It is a close relative of CYBER-; however, each has its own constituency of compounds which do not much overlap.

Examples include *e-cash* and *e-money* (electronic analogues of money used for purchases online), *e-banking* (using the Internet to carry out banking transactions), *e-auction*, *e-business*, *e-commerce*, *e-shopping* (various Internet-mediated commercial activities). An *e-book* is one in electronic form which can be purchased and downloaded from the Net, an *e-zine* is a magazine distributed by e-mail, and an *e-journal* is an academic journal published in electronic form; *e-text* is a general term for a text made available in digital electronic form. Some are rhyming inventions: *e-tailing* (*electronic retailing*); *e-lance*, an *electronic freelance*, who works from home, relying on e-mail, fax, and telephone to stay in touch with clients.

Of these, only *e-mail* is at all commonly written without a hyphen, and the only one to have become a verb.

e-²: *see* EX-¹

-ean *Forming adjectives and some nouns.* [Latin *-aeus*, *-eus* or Greek *-aios*, *-eios*, plus *-an*.]

The ending most often appears in adjectives derived from proper names and place-names. The ending is no longer productive, new forms being created ending in -IAN instead.

Many derive from names associated with the classical periods via their Greek or Latin adjectival forms. For example,

Euclidean, of the system of geometry based on the work of the Greek mathematician Euclid, comes from the Greek adjectival form *Euklideios*. Others are *Herculean*, from *Hercules*, via Latin *herculeus*, and *Pythagorean*, from *Pythagoras*. Some, derived from proper names of classical times but now usually written with lower case initial, are *cyclopean* (from the one-eyed giant *Cyclops*), *protean* (from the Greek sea god *Proteus* who could change shape at will), and *terpsichorean* (from the Greek muse of lyric poetry and dance, *Terpsichore*).

Some adjectives have been formed from place names that derive from Latin or Greek: *European* (Latin *europaeus*, based on Greek *Eurōpē*, Europe) and *Mediterranean* (Latin *mediterraneus*, from *medius*, middle, plus *terra*, land).

A few adjectives in **-ean** do not come from proper names: *subterranean*, existing, occurring, or done under the earth's surface, comes from Greek *subterraneus*, below the earth; *hyperborean*, of an inhabitant of the extreme north, is from late Latin *hyperboreanus*, from Greek *huperboreos*, 'beyond the north wind'.

A few adjectives relating to places have been created in English: *Andean, Antipodean, Caribbean* (also a noun), *Hebridean, Ecuadorean, Tyrolean*. Some other adjectives derived from personal or place names actually contain *-an* added to a word ending in *e* or *ea*: *Boolean, Carlylean, Eritrean, Kampuchean, Shakespearean, Zimbabwean*.

See also -ACEA (for *-acean*).

ec-: *see* EX-²

echin(o)- *Spiny.* [Greek *ekhinos*, hedgehog, sea urchin.]

The *echinoderms* (Greek *derma*, skin) belong to a group which includes starfishes, sea urchins, and sea cucumbers. An *echinococcus* (Greek *kokkos*, seed, grain) is a parasitic tapeworm found in the intestines of dogs, whose intermediate stage (consisting of hooked cysts) infects sheep, pigs, and sometimes humans, and causes the disease *echinococcosis*. An *echinacea* is a plant of the daisy family, whose flowers have a raised cone-like centre which appears to consist of soft spines.

eco- *Ecology; the natural environment.* [Greek *oikos*, house.]

Ecology deals with the relations of organisms to one another and to their physical surroundings. Several terms in science use the prefix in this strict sense: *ecosystem*, a biological community of interacting organisms and their physical environment; *ecosphere*, the biosphere of the earth or other planet, especially when the interaction between the living and non-living components is emphasized; *ecotype*, a distinct form or race of a plant or animal species occupying a particular habitat.

The prefix is more common in a broader sense that refers to the natural environment, especially something that aids its preservation; in this sense it is intimately linked to green issues and the environmentalist movement. A product that is *eco-friendly* does not harm the environment; *ecotourism* is tourism directed towards exotic, often threatened, natural environments, especially to support conservation efforts and observe wildlife; *ecoterrorism* is violence carried out to further environmentalist ends; *ecofeminism* is a philosophical and political theory and movement which parallels and combines environmental concerns with feminist ones.

ecto- *Outer; external; on the outside.* [Greek *ektos*, outside.]

Most terms are in scientific use: the *ectoderm* (Greek *derma*, *dermat-*, skin, hide) is the outermost layer of cells or tissue of an embryo in early development; an *ectoparasite* is a parasite, such as a flea, that lives on the outside of its host; *ectoplasm* (Greek *plasma*, formation) is the more viscous, clear outer layer of the cytoplasm in amoeboid cells (it can also be a substance that appears during a

spiritualistic trance); an *ectomorph* (Greek *morphē*, form) is a person with a lean and delicate build of body. The adjective *ectopic*, used in medicine to denote something in an abnormal place or position (as in *ectopic pregnancy*) comes from Greek *ektopos*, out of place. Its opposite is ENDO-. *See also* EXO-.

-ectomy *Surgical removal of all or part of a specified organ.* [Greek *ektomē*, excision, from *ek*, out, plus *temnein*, to cut.]

A large number of medical terms contain this suffix; for a selection see the LIST opposite. The suffix is active in the language, well enough known outside its medical context that it is sometimes used facetiously, as in *parentectomy*, cutting off contact with one's parents, or *humorectomy*, of a supposed operation that has removed somebody's sense of humour. *See also* -STOMY *and* -TOMY.

-ed¹ *Having; possessing; affected by; characteristic of.* [Old English *-ede*.]

These adjectives are formed from nouns; a few examples of a large group are: *cultured*, *diseased*, *flowered*, *grained*, *hooded*, *jagged*, *jaundiced*, *knotted*, *leisured*, *matted*, *ragged*, *ridged*, *scented*, *talented*, *toothed*. In principle, most nouns can add **-ed** in this way to create new adjectives: *architected*, *liposuctioned*, *polymered*, *touristed*.

This construction is common with hyphenated phrases consisting either of an adjective and a noun or a pair of nouns: *able-bodied*, *absent-minded*, *barrel-chested*, *deep-rooted*, *high-spirited*, *oil-fired*, *rose-tinted*, *semi-skimmed*, *well-timed*.

For adjectives ending in **-ed** formed from verbs, see the next entry.

-ed² *Also* **-t**. *Forming the past tense and past participles of regular (weak) verbs.* [Old English *-ed*, *-ad*, *-od*.]

Examples from a large group include *addressed*, *behaved*, *cheated*, *defeated*, *ironed*, *judged*, *lived*, *sorted*, and *toasted*. Some verbs instead use **-t**, either after certain consonants (*crept*, *sent*) or when there is an internal change of vowel (*felt*, *slept*).

Many past participles ending in **-ed** can also be used as adjectives: *excited*,

| **-ectomy** | Surgical removal of all or part of an organ. |
| | *Terms are mainly derived from English nouns; otherwise, origins are from Greek unless otherwise stated.* |

appendectomy	the appendix	
cholecystectomy	the gall bladder	(Latin *cholecystis*, gall bladder)
cystectomy	urinary bladder or a cyst	(*kustis*, bladder)
endarterectomy	the inner lining of an artery plus any obstructions	(*endon*, within, plus *artery*)
hysterectomy	the womb	(*hustera*, womb)
keratectomy	a section or layer of the cornea	(*keras, kerat-*, horn)
laminectomy	the back of one or more vertebrae	(Latin *lamina*, layer)
lumpectomy	a cancerous lump from the breast	
mastectomy	a breast	(*mastos*, breast)
orchidectomy	one or both testicles	(*orkhis*, testicle)
prostatectomy	the prostate gland	
splenectomy	the spleen	
thyroidectomy	removal of the thyroid gland	
tonsillectomy	the tonsils	
vasectomy	cutting the vas deferens	(Latin *vas*, vessel)

certified, collapsed, devoted, measured, moisturized, organized, pierced, scrambled, soiled, typed, wounded. The sense is not always exactly that of the verb: *accomplished*, highly trained or skilled in a particular activity, comes from *accomplish*, to achieve or complete something successfully.

A number of verbs have forms in both **-ed** and **-t** (*dwelled, dwelt; kneeled, knelt; leaped, leapt; spelled, spelt*). As a broad rule, the **-t** forms are more common in British English and the **-ed** ones in American English, though the **-ed** forms are increasingly found also in British English. When the past participles are used as adjectives, the forms in *-t* are preferred (*burnt toast, spilt milk, spoilt child*).

-ee *Forming nouns from verbs.* [Anglo-Norman French *-é* or *-ee*, from Latin *-atus* (past participial ending).]

Words in **-ee** mark the passive recipient of an action, or a person affected in some way by the action of the verbs from which they have been formed: *abductee, amputee, detainee, employee, inductee, internee, interviewee, licensee, nominee, patentee, trainee.* In many cases, the active agent is marked by *-er* (see **-ER**[1])

or **-OR**, as in *interviewer* or *abductor*; such pairs are common in legal usage, in which the **-OR** form is common: *lessor/lessee, vendor/vendee.* A **committee** was originally a person to whom some duty has been committed; it can still have the legal sense of a person entrusted with the charge of someone else's property.

Some examples seem active rather than passive, and have been criticized for that reason: an *absentee* has actively absented him- or herself; an *escapee* has escaped, say from prison; a *returnee* has returned, perhaps from active military service overseas. However, several of these, especially *escapee* and *returnee*, have a useful nuance of an action completed rather than in process.

The suffix is active in the language, often being used to create words for a single use: *apologee, embalmee, introducee, phonee, suggestee, vaccinee.*

Other nouns ending in *-ee* come from a variety of languages. Some are from Hindi words ending in *-i*: *dungaree, puttee, puggaree.* Words such as *debauchee, fricassee, grandee, jubilee, marquee, squeegee,* and *trochee* derive from French, Spanish, and other languages. The origins of *bungee, filigree, jamboree,* and *settee* are uncertain.

For some examples of affectionate or diminutive terms ending in **-ee**, see -Y[2].

-een *Forming diminutive nouns.* [Irish diminutive suffix *-ín*.]

Most words ending in **-een** are characteristically Irish, though many are now more widely known: a *colleen* (Irish *cailín*, diminutive of *caile*, countrywoman) is a girl or young woman; *poteen* (Irish *(fuisce) poitín*, little pot (of whiskey), diminutive of *pota*, pot) is alcohol made illicitly, typically from potatoes; a *shebeen* (Anglo-Irish *síbín*, from *séibe*, mugful) is an unlicensed establishment or private house selling alcoholic liquor; *smithereens* (Irish *smidirín*, a small fragment), small pieces.

A few words come instead from the French ending *-in* or *-ine*: *canteen*, *tureen*; some names for materials were formed in English in imitation of *bombazeen*, an older spelling of *bombazine*, for example *velveteen* and *sateen*. The modern equivalent of this ending is *-ine* (see -INE[2]).

See also -TEEN.

-eer *Forming nouns and verbs.* [French *-ier*, from Latin *-arius*.]

Most words ending in **-eer** are nouns denoting a person concerned with or engaged in an activity: *auctioneer*, *mountaineer*, *mutineer*, *puppeteer*. Others can be verbs denoting concern for or involvement with an activity, sometimes with negative associations: *commandeer*, *domineer*, *electioneer*. Some examples can be both nouns and verbs: *engineer* (Old French *engigneor*), *profiteer*, *volunteer*. *Gazetteer*, a geographical index or dictionary, was originally a French word for a journalist who worked on a *gazette*, a news-sheet.

The suffix is mildly active in the language, usually forming nouns. Some relatively recent examples are *imagineer* (a creative person, in particular one who devises the attractions in Walt Disney theme parks); *rocketeer* (a person who works with space rockets; a rocket enthusiast); *supermarketeer* (organizations that operate supermarkets, or their directors); *tabloideer* (someone who writes for or manages a tabloid newspaper).

Terms such as *overseer*, *sightseer*, and *seer* come from *see* plus -ER[1]; *veneer* is German but from a French root; *career* in both noun and verb senses derives from French *carrière*.

See also -IER.

ef-: *see* EX-[1]

eicos-: *see* ICOS-

eigen- *Proper; characteristic.* [German adjective *eigen*, own.]

Terms are confined to mathematics and physics and often mimic German formations. Examples include *eigenfrequency*, one of the natural resonant frequencies of a system; *eigenfunction*, each of a set of independent functions which are the solutions to a given differential equation; and *eigenvalue*, each of a set of values of a parameter for which a differential equation has a non-zero solution (an eigenfunction) under given conditions.

-ein: *see* -INE[3]

eka- *Unknown elements.* [Sanskrit *eka*, one.]

Dmitri Mendeleev (1834–1907), the Russian chemist who developed the periodic table, used this prefix to name elements that his scheme predicted but which were then unknown. He added it to the name of the preceding element in the same group: *eka-selenium* (now called *technetium*), *eka-aluminium* (now *gallium*). As all naturally occurring chemical elements have now been identified and named, the form is mostly of historical interest. It appears occasionally in names for previously unidentified transuranic elements (for example, *eka-lead* for element 114); however, a formal naming scheme for these exists, rendering the prefix unnecessary.

-el: *see* -LE[1]

elast(o)- *Elastic.* [English *elastic* (from Greek *elastikos*, propulsive), plus -O-.]

Examples include *elastin*, an elastic, fibrous glycoprotein found in connective tissue; *elastomer*, a natural or synthetic polymer having elastic properties, such as rubber; *elastofibroma*, a type of benign, elastic tissue that can develop in older people; *elastography*, an ultrasonic imaging technique for measuring the elasticity of soft tissues; and *elastosis*, the degeneration of fibres in connective tissues and skin.

electr(o)- *Relating to, caused by, or connected with electricity.* [Latin *electrum*, amber, from Greek *ēlektron*.]

The Latin word was borrowed by William Gilbert in 1600 because amber produces static electricity when rubbed. The usual adjectives are *electric* and *electrical*. Examples of the form are *electromagnetic*, relating to the interrelation of electric and magnetic phenomena; *electrode* (Greek *hodos*, way), a conductor through which electricity enters or leaves some region; and *electrolysis* (Greek *lusis*, loosening), chemical decomposition produced by passing an electric current through a liquid or solution.

The *electron* was given that name because it acts as the primary carrier of electricity, hence *electronics*, originally the study of the movement of electrons in a vacuum or materials, but now the design and application of complex electrical circuits; the adjective is *electronic*.

In medicine, the prefix appears in the name of several instruments that measure and record electrical activity in the body: *electrocardiography* (Greek *kardia*, heart), in the heart; *electroencephalography* (Greek *kephalē*, head), in the brain; *electromyography* (Greek *mus*, *mu-*, muscle) in muscle tissue. *Electroconvulsive* therapy is a method of treating mental illness by the application of electric shocks to the brain.

-ella *Genera of bacteria and algae.* [Latin diminutive ending *-ella*.]

This forms the genus and informal names of a variety of bacteria and algae. Examples include *Chlorella* (Greek *khlōros*, green), a single-celled green alga; *Legionella* (first identified following an outbreak at a meeting of the American *Legion*), the bacterium which causes legionnaires' disease; *Salmonella* (Daniel E. Salmon, 1850–1914, an American veterinary surgeon), a bacterium that causes food poisoning; *Shigella* (Kiyoshi *Shiga*, 1870–1957, Japanese bacteriologist), a bacterium, some kinds of which cause dysentery.

Many other words ending in **-ella** occur in English. Some are Latin diminutives: *rubella*, the medical term for German measles (Latin *rubellus*, reddish); *lamella*, a thin layer (Latin *lamina*, thin plate). Others are plurals of Latin words ending in -ELLUM: *flagella*, *cerebella*. Another group are Italian diminutives adopted into English: *umbrella* (Latin *umbra*, shade; at first it kept off the sun rather than rain); *mortadella*, a type of sausage (Latin *murtatum*, seasoned with myrtle berries); *villanella*, an Italian rustic-style part-song (*villano*, peasant).

-elle *Forming nouns.* [Latin diminutive suffix *-ella*.]

Some examples derive directly from Latin, but most have come via French words ending in *-elle*. Examples include the game *bagatelle* (French, from Italian *bagatella*, perhaps from *baga*, baggage, or from a diminutive of Latin *baca*, berry); *nacelle* (French, from late Latin *navicella*, diminutive of Latin *navis*, ship), a streamlined housing or tank on the outside of a vehicle; *organelle* (modern Latin *organella*, diminutive of *organum*, instrument, tool), any of a number of specialized structures within a living cell; *gazelle* (French, probably via Spanish from Arabic *ghazāl*), a type of antelope.

-ellum *Forming nouns.* [Latin diminutive suffix *-ellum*.]

This occurs mainly in technical terms for parts of animals or plants: the *cerebellum* (Latin, diminutive of *cerebrum*, brain) is a part of the brain at the back of the skull in vertebrates; a *flagellum* (Latin, diminutive of *flagrum*, scourge) is a microscopic whip-like appendage which enables many single-celled animals to swim; a *cribellum* (Latin, diminutive of *cribrum*, sieve) is an additional spinning organ in some spiders; a *labellum* (Latin, diminutive of *labrum*, lip) is one of a pair of lobes at the tip of the proboscis in some insects, or a central petal at the base of an orchid flower. These all have plurals ending in *-a* (see *-a*[2]): *labella*, *flagella*.

However, *antebellum*, occurring or existing before a particular war, especially the US Civil War, and the equivalent *post-bellum*, both derive from Latin *bellum*, war, which is not a diminutive; *vellum*, fine parchment made originally from the skin of a calf, comes from Old French *velin*.

em-: *see* EN-[1] and EN-[2]

embryo- *An embryo.* [Late Latin *embryo*, fetus.]

Embryology is the branch of biology and medicine concerned with the study of embryos and their development; *embryogenesis* is the formation and development of an embryo; *embryoscopy* is the examination of an embryo in early pregnancy by using an endoscope; an *embryopathy* is an anomaly in the development of an embryo. The usual adjective is *embryonic*, which also has a figurative sense of something that is in a rudimentary stage with potential for further development.

-eme Also **-emic**. *Linguistic units that are in systemic contrast with one other.* [The ending of *phoneme*.]

A *phoneme* (Greek *phōnēma*, sound, speech) is one of the perceptually distinct units of sound in a language that distinguish one word from another. On its model, a number of other terms have been formed, of which examples include *morpheme* (Greek *morphē*, form), a meaningful unit that cannot be further divided; *lexeme* (Greek *lexis*, word), a basic unit of language consisting of one word or several words, the elements of which do not separately convey the meaning of the whole; *grapheme* (Greek *graphē*, writing), a minimal unit in a writing system, consisting of one or more symbols serving to represent a phoneme. Adjectives are formed ending in **-emic**: *morphemic*, *phonemic*. Some other words end in *-eme* through accidents of spelling: *blaspheme*, *extreme*, *raceme*, *supreme*, *trireme*.

-emia: *see* -AEMIA

-emic: *see* -EME or -AEMIA

en-[1] Also **em-**. *Forming verbs.* [French, from Latin *in-*.]

The prefix can be added to nouns, adjectives, and verbs. **Em-** is a variant used before the consonants *b*, *m*, and *p*.

One set suggests putting something into or on another (*embed*, *enshrine*, *enthrone*); others have a sense of confining or restricting (*ensnare*, *entwine*), or of surrounding something or placing it within something (*embrace*, *enclose*, *encapsulate*, *encircle*, *enfold*, *engulf*, *envelop*). A large group has a broad sense of 'put into some state or condition': *embarrass*, *embitter*, *encode*, *endanger*, *enlarge*, *enrage*, *enrich*, *enslave*, *entreat*. Rarely, it can suggest going into or on to something, as in *enplane*. Some are figurative terms derived from French or Latin roots, in which the origin of the meaning is no longer easily recognizable: *emphasize*, *endeavour*, *ensure*, *endure*.

Some words beginning in **en-** and **em-** actually contain a variant of EX-: *emancipate* is from Latin *mancipium*, slave; *enunciate* from Latin *nuntius*, a messenger; *ennervate* from Latin *nervus*, a sinew.

See also IN-[2], particularly for words that can be spelled both **en-** and *in-*.

en-[2] Also **em-**. *Within; inside.* [Greek *en-*.]

Words in this prefix were mostly created in Greek. **Em-** is a variant used before *b*, *m*, *p*, and *ph*.

Examples created in classical Greek include: *energy* (Greek *energeia*, from *ergon*, work); *enthusiasm* (Greek *enthousiasmos*, from *enthous*, possessed by a god, based on *theos*, god); *empathy* (Greek *empatheia*, from *pathos*, feeling); *enema* (Greek *enienai*, send or put in, from *hienai*, send); *endemic* (Greek *endēmios*, native, based on *dēmos*, people).

Examples formed on Greek roots include the thermodynamic quantity *entropy* (Greek *tropē*, transformation); and *engram* (Greek *gramma*, letter of the alphabet), a hypothetical permanent change in the brain accounting for the existence of memory; a memory trace.

-en¹ *Forming verbs from nouns and adjectives.* [Old English *-nian*, of Germanic origin.]

Such verbs have the sense of creating, developing, or intensifying the state signalled in the noun or adjective from which they derive. Examples from adjectives include *brighten*, *cheapen*, *fasten*, *loosen*, *moisten*, *redden*, *sweeten*, and *widen*. Examples from nouns include: *frighten*, *heighten*, *lengthen*, *strengthen*, and *threaten*. The ending is not active in the language.

-en² *Also* **-n**. *Forming adjectives from nouns.* [Old English, of Germanic origin.]

Adjectives refer to an object made of or consisting of the material described by the noun, as in *earthen* or *woollen*. In most cases, the literal sense is now given by the noun, with the adjective having a poetical or metaphorical meaning, as in the difference between *a gold watch* (literal) and *a golden harvest* (metaphorical). Adjectives often used metaphorically include *ashen*, *flaxen*, *leaden*, *oaken*, *silken*, and *wooden*. A few have lost the *e* of the ending following a final *r* in the stem: *silvern*.

-en³ *Also* **-n**. *Forming past participles of strong verbs.* [Old English, of Germanic origin.]

Strong verbs indicate their past tenses by a change of vowel within the stem (as *sing* has past tense *sang* and past participle *sung*). Some of them mark their past participles by adding **-en**. Examples include *broken*, *chosen*, *frozen*, *spoken*, *stolen*, *sunken*, *taken*, and *woven*. American English retains *gotten* as the past participle of *get*. A number have lost the *e* from the ending following a final *r* in the stem: *born*, *shorn*, *sworn*. These forms can be used as adjectives, as can some whose participial use is now rare or archaic, such as *proven* and *drunken*; however, the second of these has the restricted sense of having drunk too much alcohol.

-en⁴ *Forming noun plurals.* [Middle English reduction of the earlier suffix *-an*.]

The few examples (*brethren*, *children*, *oxen*) are survivals of a plural inflexion that was once common, until *-s* (*see* -S¹) displaced it in Middle English.

-en⁵ *Forming diminutives of nouns.* [Old English, of Germanic origin.]

A few examples exist (*chicken*, *kitten*, *maiden*), but the suffix is not active. (Chicken comes from an Old English word that originally meant a young or small bird of the species; *chick* is an abbreviation of it.)

enantio- *Opposite, opposing.* [Greek *enantios*, opposite.]

Two crystals or molecules are *enantiomorphic* (Greek *morphē*, form) if they are mirror images of each other and so cannot be superimposed; *enantiomers* (Greek *meros*, part) are pairs of molecules of this type. Two other examples are *enantiodromia* (Greek *dromos*, running), the tendency of things to change into their opposites, especially as a supposed governing principle of natural cycles and of psychological development; and *enantiosis* (Greek, a contradiction), a figure of speech in which what is meant is the opposite of what is said.

-ence: *see* -ANCE

encephalo- *The brain.* [Greek *enkephalos*, inside the head.]

Encephalitis is inflammation of the brain, caused by infection or an allergic reaction, an *encephalopathy* is a disease that affects the way the brain functions (as in *bovine spongiform encephalopathy*, BSE or *mad cow disease*), and *encephalomyelitis* (Greek *muelos*, marrow) is inflammation of the brain and spinal cord, typically due to acute viral infection. *Encephalography* is a technique for recording the structure or electrical activity of the brain, whose results may be recorded on an *encephalogram*. In anatomy and zoology, the *encephalon* is the formal name for the brain; the usual adjective is *encephalic*.

-enchyma *Also* **-enchyme** *and* **-enchymal**. *Cellular tissue.* [Greek *enkhuma*, infusion, from *khūmos*, juice.]

The most common example is *parenchyma* (Greek *para-*, beside), in anatomy the functional tissue of an organ as distinguished from the connective and supporting tissue. Others include *sclerenchyma* (Greek *skléros*, hard), strengthening tissue in plants formed from cells with thickened walls; and *collenchyma* (Greek *kolla*, glue), plant tissue strengthened by thickened cell walls.

Less commonly, such terms appear spelled **-enchyme**: *collenchyme*, *parenchyme*. *Mesenchyme* (Greek *mesos*, middle) is more common in this spelling than in *mesenchyma*; it refers to loosely organized embryonic tissue which develops into connective and skeletal tissues, including blood and lymph. All form adjectives ending in **-enchymal** (*mesenchymal*, *parenchymal*, *sclerenchymal*).

-ency: *see* -CY and -ANCE

-end Also **-endum**. *Forming nouns.* [Latin *-endus*, *-enda*, *-endum*, endings of gerunds.]

This ending has never been active in the language, and the only examples are those that have been drawn directly from Latin gerunds, verb forms that function as adjectives with the sense of something that should or must be done.

Apart from *dividend* and *reverend*, examples are specialist or archaic; in mathematics, the *subtrahend* is a quantity or number to be subtracted from another, the *minuend*; a *prebend* (Latin *praebere*, to grant), now only historical, was the portion of the revenues of a cathedral or collegiate church granted to a canon or member of the chapter as salary or expenses.

The neuter gerund ending **-endum** is preserved in a number of Latin words brought over into English: *addendum* (literally 'that which is to be added') is an item appended to the end of a book or other publication; *corrigendum* (Latin, from *corrigere*, bring into order) is something to be corrected, typically an error in a printed book; *referendum* (Latin *referre*, carry back) is a general vote by the electorate on a political question. For their plurals, *see* -A[2].

end(o)- *Internal; within.* [Greek *endon*, within.]

An *endoscope* is an instrument which can be introduced into the body to give a view of its internal parts; an *endoskeleton* is an internal skeleton, such as that of vertebrates; the *endocardium* (Greek *kardia*, heart) is the thin, smooth membrane which lines the inside of the chambers of the heart; the *endometrium* (Greek *mētra*, womb) is the mucous membrane lining the womb; *endarterectomy* (Greek *ektomē*, excision) is surgical removal of part of the inner lining of an artery.

The adjective *endogenous* refers to something having an internal cause or origin; *endothermic* to a reaction or process in chemistry accompanied by or requiring the absorption of heat; *endocrine* (Greek *krinein*, sift) refers to glands which secrete hormones or other products directly into the blood; *endemic*, restricted to a certain country or area, was formed in Greek (*endēmios*, native, based on *dēmos*, people).

Endo- is closely related to ENTO-; its opposite is ECTO- or EXO-.

-endum: *see* -END

-ene[1] Also **-diene**, **-triene**, and **-ylene**. *Hydrocarbons.* [Greek *-ēnos*.]

A variety of common names for hydrocarbons containing a double or triple carbon-carbon bond contain this ending: *anthracene*, *benzene*, *naphthalene*, *styrene*, *toluene*, *xylene*. It is frequently added to the adjectival form of the stem (*see* -YL): *acetylene*, *ethylene*, *propylene*, *allylene*, *butylene*. The artificial fibre called *terylene* was named by inverting parts of its chemical name (*polyeth)ylene ter(eph-thalate)*.

In systematic chemical naming, the **-ene** suffix is restricted to open-chain (aliphatic) hydrocarbons that contain a double bond: *heptene*, *cyclopentene*. Some chemical compounds have both a systematic and a common name: *ethene* is the systematic name for ethylene, *propene* for propylene, and so on. The general term for a member of the series, with chemical formula C_nH_{2n}, is *alkene* (German *Alkohol*, alcohol). The ending **-ylene** is used in systematic naming only to describe the groups —CH_2— (*methylene*),

—C_2H_4— (ethylene), and —C_6H_4— (*phenylene*).

Molecules that contain two double carbon-carbon bonds are named using **-diene**: *butadiene*, *cyclopentadiene*; those that contain three use **-triene**: *hexatriene*, *cycloheptatriene*. Such compounds are known generically as *dienes* and *trienes* respectively.

-ene² *An inhabitant.* [Greek *-ēnos*.]

Examples include: *Cairene*, an inhabitant of Cairo; *Hellene*, of Greece (Greek *Hellēn*, a Greek); *Nazarene*, of Nazareth, referring specially to Christ or, figuratively, to Christians (Greek *Nazarēnos*, from *Nazaret*, Nazareth); *Damascene*, of Damascus. Most examples can also be adjectives referring to the place or an inhabitant. A *Gadarene* is literally an inhabitant of Gadara, but is usually an adjective referring to a headlong or potentially disastrous rush to do something, from the Gospel story of the *Gadarene swine* (New Testament Greek *Gadarēnos*).

Other words ending in *-ene* come from a variety of sources: *gangrene* from Greek *gangraina* and *epicene* from Greek *epikoinos* (based on *koinos*, common); *contravene*, *intervene*, and *supervene* all derive from Latin *venire*, come; *obscene* comes from Latin *obscaenus*, ill-omened or abominable.

-enne Also **-ienne**. *Nouns denoting females.* [French feminine ending *-enne*.]

Such words are formed as the female equivalents of nouns in -IAN, or sometimes *-an*. A small group exists: *comedienne* (a female comedian), *tragedienne* (an actress who specializes in tragic roles, the feminine form of *tragedian*), *equestrienne* (a woman horse-rider), *doyenne* (a woman who is the most respected or prominent in a particular field, the female equivalent of *doyen*). However, the feminine forms of other words in *-ian* do not exist—there is no equivalent to *pedestrian* or *thespian*, for example. As a result of changing views about gender equality, the masculine forms of these words now often do service for both men and women, though only *comedienne*

is common in any case. *See also* -ESS, -ETTE, -STRESS, and -TRIX.

ennea- *Nine.* [Greek *ennea*, nine.]

An *enneagram* is a nine-sided figure used in one system of analysis to represent the spectrum of possible personality types; an *enneagon* (Greek *-gōnos*, angled) is a nine-sided plane figure; an *enneahedron* (Greek *hedra*, seat, base) is a solid figure having nine faces; *ennead* is a group or set of nine. *See also* NONA- and the table of NUMBER PREFIXES on page 161.

-ennium *A period of years.* [Latin *annum*, year.]

Terms are based on Latin number prefixes (see the table of NUMBER PREFIXES on page 161): *biennium*, a period of two years; *triennium*, of three; *quadrennium*, four; *quinquennium*, five; *decennium*, ten; and *millennium*, a thousand years.

eno-: *see* OENO-

ent-: *see* ENTO-

-ent: *see* -ANT

enter(o)- *The intestine.* [Greek *enteron*, intestine.]

Enteritis is inflammation of the intestine; an *enteropathy* (Greek *patheia*, suffering, feeling) is a disease of it; an *enterovirus* is one of a group that occur in the gastrointestinal tract; an *enterotoxin* is a toxin affecting the intestines, such as those causing food poisoning or cholera; *enterobiasis* is an infection of the intestines, especially of children, caused by a threadworm; the adjective relating to the intestines is *enteric* (*enteric fever* is an old name for typhoid fever).

ent(o)- *Within; inside.* [Greek *entos*, within.]

A visual image that is *entoptic* occurs or originates inside the eye; an *entamoeba* is an amoeba that typically lives harmlessly in the gut; the *Entoprocta* is a small phylum of sedentary aquatic invertebrates (Greek *prōktos*, anus, the anus being within a ring of tentacles). Other examples are relatively rare or are variant forms of those in ENDO-.

entom(o)- *An insect or insects.* [Greek *entomon*, neuter (denoting an insect) of *entomos*, cut up, segmented.]

The science or study of insects is *entomology*; the *entomofauna* of an area is its insect life; an *entomophilous* (Greek *phílos*, loving) plant or flower is one pollinated by insects; *entomophagy* (Greek *phagein*, eat) is the practice of eating insects, especially by people.

eo- *Early, primeval.* [Greek *ēōs*, dawn.]

The *Eocene* geological period is the second epoch of the Tertiary period, between the Palaeocene and Oligocene epochs; the *eohippus* (Greek *hippos*, horse) is an older name for the *hyracotherium*, the earliest fossil ancestor of the horse; *Eoanthropus* (Greek *anthrōpos*, human being, so 'dawn man') is the genus to which the now-discredited Piltdown man was assigned; an *eolith* (Greek *lithos*, stone) is a roughly chipped flint found in Tertiary strata, originally thought to be an early artefact but probably of natural origin. The red fluorescent dye *eosin* uses the Greek literally, since its colour was thought to resemble a reddish sunrise; derived from this is *eosinophil*, a white blood cell containing granules that are readily stained by eosin, plus several other terms. *Eolian*, however, is the standard US spelling of British English *aeolian*, relating to or arising from the action of the wind, from Greek *Aiolos*, the god of the winds.

-eous: *see* -OUS

ep(i)- *Upon; above; in addition.* [Greek *epi*, upon, near to, in addition.]

A number of English words have been introduced from Greek, often via Latin and French, with the prefix already attached: *epidemic* (Greek *epidēmia*, prevalence of disease, from *dēmos*, the people) plus *epidemiology* and related terms; *epilepsy* (Greek *epilambanein*, seize or attack, from *lambanein*, take hold of); *epidermis* (Greek *derma*, skin), the outer layer of cells covering an organism; an *epitaph* is literally something on a tomb (Greek *taphos*, tomb); an *epigram* (Greek *epigramma*, from *gramma*, a thing written) is a pithy saying or remark expressing an idea in a clever and amusing way.

Examples coined in English using the prefix include *epidural* (Latin *dura*, hard), relating to an anaesthetic introduced into the space around the dura mater of the spinal cord; *epiphenomenon*, a secondary effect or by-product; and *epiphyte* (Greek *phuton*, plant), a plant that grows on another plant.

equi- *Equal; equally.* [Latin *aequi-*, from *aequus*, equal.]

Two things that are *equiangular* have equal angles; though it has other meanings, the key sense of *equity* is equality, fairness, and impartiality; an *equipoise* is a balance of forces or interests.

Other examples come from Latin words with the prefix already attached: *equilateral* (Latin *aequilaterus*, equal-sided, from *latus*, *later-*, side), having all its sides the same length; *equilibrium* (Latin *aequilibrium*, from *libra*, balance), a state in which opposing forces or influences are balanced; *equinox* (*aequinoctium*, from *nox*, *noct-*, night), a date on which day and night are of equal length.

However, *equine* and its relatives come from Latin *equus*, horse, as does *equisetum*, a plant of a genus that comprises the horsetails; *equip* is probably from Old Norse *skipa*, to man a ship.

-er¹ *Forming nouns.* [Variously from Old English *-ere*, of Germanic origin; French *-ier*, from Latin *-arius*, *-arium*; Latin *-aris*; Old French *-eure* from Latin *-atura*; Old French *-eor* from Latin *-atorium*; Anglo-Norman French *-eour* or Old French *-eor*; Anglo-Norman French infinitive ending.]

This is a common and productive suffix, with several senses.

One large set comprises words for people who are concerned with a specified object, concept, or action, often as a trade or occupation, but frequently in some broader sense: *abuser, banker, carpenter, designer, explorer, farmer, inspector, observer, philosopher, swimmer, writer.* Many hyphenated forms exist: *asset-stripper, house-hunter, record-breaker, theatre-goer, window-shopper.*

A second group refers to a person who lives in a specified place: *Londoner*, *Icelander*, *New Yorker*, *New Zealander*. More broadly, it includes people who live in a certain type of place or who have an attribute related to place: *city-dweller*, *foreigner*, *northerner*, *villager*; *insider* and *outsider* are usually figurative rather than directly related to position.

Some informal, complimentary terms refer mainly to women: *looker*, *stunner*, *goer*, *smasher* (the sense overlaps with that discussed in -ER³). Some, often of obscure formation, are abusive coarse slang: *bleeder*, *bugger*, *fucker*, *nigger*, *tosser*.

Some examples, chiefly in law, denote verbal action or a document effecting such action: *disclaimer*, *waiver*. These come from Anglo-Norman French infinitive endings, as do *supper* and *dinner*.

The ending also denotes objects that perform a specified action or activity, or have a given attribute: *blotter*, *cutter*, *gasholder*, *lawnmower*, *liquidizer*, *roller*, *sweater*. Again, many examples are hyphenated: *back-hander*, *air-freshener*, *lemon-squeezer*, *quarter-pounder*.

Some nouns ending in **-er** are accidental spellings, mostly from early English or Scandinavian sources: *boulder*, *ladder*, *sewer* (in the drainage sense), *summer*, *tinder*, *tuber*, *winter*; some US spellings are equivalent to British English *-re*: *specter*, *theater*.

See also -AR, -EER, -FER, -GRAPHY (for *-grapher*), -IER, -IZE (for *-izer* or *-iser*), -LATRY (for *-later*), -LOGY (for *-loger*), -MONGER, -NOMY (for *-nomer*), -OR¹, and -STER.

-er² *Forming the comparative of some adjectives and adverbs.* [Old English suffix *-ra* (adjectival), *-or* (adverbial), of Germanic origin.]

The adjectives that make their comparatives with **-er** are generally those of one syllable: *brighter*, *greater*, *harder*, *older*, *richer*, *tighter*. Most of those with two syllables that end in *-le*, *-er* or *-ow* also add **-er**, as do those in *-y* or *-ly* (when the *y* changes to an *i*): *simpler*, *cleverer*, *narrower*, *angrier*, *livelier*. Most adjectives of two syllables or more form their comparatives with *more* instead.

A few adverbs are identical in form to the adjectives from which they derive, and follow the same rules for forming comparatives: *he runs faster*, *I'll see you later*. A few others, without corresponding adjectives, do the same: *sooner*, *farther/further*.

For the superlative form, *see* -EST¹.

-er³ Also **-ers**. *Colloquial or humorous nouns and adjectives.* [Probably an extended use of -ER¹.]

Examples are *footer* (football), *rugger* (rugby), *brekker* (breakfast), and *soccer* (the last from an abbreviated and clipped form of *Association Football*). The style is to abbreviate—and often to distort—the root word, and then add **-er**. This was originally Rugby School slang, later adopted at Oxford University about 1875, then extended into general use. Most examples have since disappeared; only *soccer* has become standard English. A few are spelled **-ers** (*Twickers* for the rugby ground at Twickenham), though most with this ending are adjectives: *bonkers* and *crackers* (mad), *preggers* (pregnant), *starkers* (stark naked).

-er⁴ *Forming verbs.* [Old English *-erian*, *-rian*, of Germanic origin.]

Such verbs have an idea about them of repeated action: *batter*, *clamber*, *flicker*, *flitter*, *flutter*, *glitter*, *shimmer*, *shiver*, *shudder*. Some are imitative of a noise: *blatter*, *chatter*, *clatter*, *mutter*, *splutter*, *twitter*.

-erati: *see* -ATI

-erel: *see* -REL

-ergic *Involving, releasing, or mimicking a specified substance as a neurotransmitter.* [Greek *ergon*, work, plus -IC.]

Some examples: *adrenergic*, relating to or denoting nerve cells in which adrenalin or a similar substance acts as a neurotransmitter, as contrasted with *cholinergic* cells, in which acetylcholine acts as a neurotransmitter; *dopaminergic*, releasing or involving dopamine as a neurotransmitter; *purinergic*, involving a purine derivative; *peptidergic*, designating a neurone which releases one or more particular neuropeptides when stimulated.

The same root is present in *synergic* (from *synergy*, the creation of something greater than the sum of its parts). However, in *lysergic* (as in *lysergic acid diethylamide* or LSD) the root is *ergot*, a fungal disease of cereals; in *allergic* the ending is an accident of spelling.

ergo- *Work; energy.* [Greek *ergon*, work.]

Ergonomics is the study of people's efficiency in their working environment, a practitioner being an *ergonomist*; an *ergometer* is an apparatus which measures work or energy expended during a period of physical exercise; an *erg* is a unit of work or energy in the older centimetre-gram-second system. However, *ergosterol*, a compound present in many fungi, derives instead from *ergot*, a fungal disease of cereals.

-erie: *see* -ERY

-eroo Also **-aroo**, **-aroonie**, and **-eroonie**. *An informal and often humorous intensifier of nouns.* [A fanciful formation of uncertain origin.]

This ending is most common in North America, Australia, and New Zealand. It appeared in the US in the 1930s, but its origin is not known. It may be that it was influenced by the older *buckaroo*, a cowboy, which derives from Spanish *vaquero*; its acceptance in Australia and New Zealand may have been helped by the model of *kangaroo*, *wallaroo*, and other words. It sometimes implies something sizeable, overwhelming, remarkable, or unexpected.

Examples include *boozeroo* (sometimes *boozaroo*), New Zealand slang for a drinking spree; *jackaroo* or *jackeroo* (from the proper name *Jack*), a learner or tyro at any occupation, especially a young man working on a sheep or cattle station in Australia to gain experience (the rarer female equivalent is a *jillaroo*); *flopperoo*, a complete failure or flop, especially with theatre, cinema, or TV audiences or critics; and *smackeroo*, in the US variously a

hard smack, a kiss, or a sum of money. The extended forms **-aroonie** and **-eroonie** (adding the diminutive suffix **-ie**, *see* -Y²) have been current in the US since the 1960s, for example in *smackeroonie*.

erot(o)- *Sexual desire or excitement.* [Greek *erōs*, *erōt-*, sexual love.]

Examples include *eroticism*, the quality or character or being *erotic*, arousing sexual desire or excitement; *erotica*, literature or art intended to arouse sexual desire; *erotology*, the study of sexual love and behaviour; *erotomania*, excessive sexual desire. The adjective *erogenous*, which refers to a part of the body sensitive to sexual stimulation (as in *erogenous zone*), comes from the same Greek root.

-ers: *see* -ER³

-ery Also **-ry** and **-erie**. *Forming nouns.* [French *-erie*, based on Latin *-arius* and *-ator*.]

It is often unclear whether words contain this suffix by borrowing from French, or whether they have been created in English from nouns ending in *-er* by adding *-y* (*see* -ER¹ and -Y³). The **-ry** form is a shortened version of **-ery**.

The suffix has several meanings that can be broadly classified, though not all words fit neatly into one of the groups. One very broad set denotes a class or kind of objects: *confectionery*, *crockery*, *cutlery*, *finery*, *greenery*, *machinery*, *scenery*. Another marks places where some occupation, trade, or activity is carried on: *bakery*, *brewery*, *cemetery*, *distillery*, *fishery*, *grocery*, *nunnery*, *nursery*. A third indicates an occupation, state, condition, or behaviour: *archery*, *bravery*, *butchery*, *devilry*, *mastery*, *rivalry*, *slavery*, *treachery*; sometimes a depreciatory reference is meant: *knavery*, *tomfoolery*. A fourth denotes a place set aside for an activity or a place to keep things, animals or the like: *fernery*, *piggery*, *orangery*, *rookery*, *shrubbery*, *swannery*, *vinery*.

The form **-erie** sometimes signals a direct import from French: *boulangerie*, *charcuterie*, *menagerie*, *patisserie*, *rotisserie*; it can also mark an informal, affectionate or dismissive version of a form in

-ery, as with *eaterie* for *eatery*; some of this latter sort have been created directly with **-erie**: *niterie* for a night club, *nosherie* for a restaurant, *drinkerie* for a bar or public house.

Not all examples come from French *-erie*. Words such as *skulduggery* and *sitooterie* are of Scots origin; *country* is from Old French *cuntree*, based on Latin *contra*, against, opposite; *lottery* is probably from Dutch *loterij*; *gantry* probably from Middle English dialect *gawn*.

See also -ARY.

erythro- Redness. [Greek *eruthros*, red.]

An **erythrocyte** is a red blood cell; **erythropoiesis** (Greek *poiēsis*, making) is the production of red blood cells; **erythropoietin** is a hormone that increases this rate; the adjective **erythroid** refers to erythrocytes; an **erythroblast** is an immature erythrocyte; **erythromelalgia** (Greek *melos*, limb, plus *algos*, pain) is painful distension of the blood vessels of the skin, usually in the extremities; **erythrophobia** is a morbid fear of blushing or of the colour red.

-es: see -S¹

-esce Also **-escent**, **-escence**, and **-escency**. Forming verbs, often denoting the initiation of an action. [Verbs ending in **-esce** are from or suggested by Latin verbs ending in *-escere*; adjectives in **-escent** are from French or Latin *-escent-* (the present participial stem of verbs ending in *-escere*); nouns in **-escence** derive from the related French *-escence* or Latin *-escentia*.]

Examples of the verb include *coalesce*, *convalesce*, *effervesce*, *fluoresce*, and *phosphoresce*. In some cases the sense has shifted away from that of its Latin precursor: *acquiesce* means to accept something reluctantly but without protest, but its Latin original implies an active change of state, 'to put at rest' (*ad-*, to or at, plus *quiescere*, to rest).

The ending **-escent** forms adjectives related to the verbs: *deliquescent*, *effervescent*, *incandescent*, *phosphorescent*. In some cases adjectives derive instead from verbs ending in -FY; *frutescent* (*fruc-*

tify); *putrescent* (*putrefy*); *tumescent* (*tumefy*). A few adjectives, such as *adolescent*, can also be nouns. The ending **-escence** forms nouns that correspond to the adjectives or verbs or both: *adolescence*, *convalescence*, *excrescence*, *fluorescence*, *luminescence*, *obsolescence*, *putrescence*, *senescence*.

A few nouns in **-escency** exist: *effervescency*, *quiescency*, but they are much less common than the equivalents in **-ence**.

-ese Forming adjectives and nouns. [Old French *-eis*, based on Latin *-ensis*.]

Adjectives denote an inhabitant or language of a city or country: *Cantonese*, *Japanese*, *Maltese*, *Nepalese*, *Taiwanese*, *Vietnamese*, *Viennese*. *Pekinese*, from an older transliteration of the name of the city now usually called *Beijing*, often refers to a breed of dog brought to Europe from that city; *Siamese* is from an older name of the country now called *Thailand*, and now usually refers to a breed of cat or to twin babies conjoined at birth.

Nouns are often derogatory, referring in particular to written language from a given source that is considered to be in a poor style: *journalese*, *officialese* (and *bureaucratese*), *legalese*, *novelese* (a style of writing supposedly characteristic of inferior novels). New examples continue to be formed: *computerese* (the supposedly incomprehensible technical jargon of computing), *jargonese*. A rare example that is not derogatory is *mother-ese* (child-directed speech).

-esis Nouns of action or process. [Greek *-ēsis*.]

Most examples are direct imports into English of Greek words: *diaeresis* (Greek, separation), a mark placed over a vowel to indicate that it is sounded separately; *exegesis* (Greek, interpretation, guidance), critical explanation or interpretation of a text, especially of scripture; *genesis* (Greek, generation, creation, nativity, horoscope), the origin or mode of formation of something; *kinesis* (Greek, movement), movement or motion, *nemesis* (Greek, retribution), retribution; *thesis* (Greek, a placing, a proposition). Some—such as *diuresis* and *synthesis*—have corresponding adjectives ending in -ETIC. *See also* -OSIS.

esophago-: *see* OESOPHAGO-

-esque *In the style of; resembling.* [From French, via Italian -*esco* from medieval Latin -*iscus*.]

This suffix is commonly attached to personal names to form adjectives that indicate a creative work in that person's style: *Caravaggesque* (from the Italian painter Caravaggio), *Chaplinesque*, *Disneyesque* (usually today the organization rather than the late Walt Disney himself), *Felliniesque*, *Kafkaesque*, *Pinteresque*, *Tolkienesque*. It can also be attached to names of periods of architecture (*Romanesque*) and generates words referring to the beliefs or personal characteristics of an individual, usually in politics: *Clintonesque*, *Majoresque*, *Thatcheresque*. Such terms are frequently created at need and are often ephemeral.

Other examples are formed from nouns: *carnivalesque*, *grotesque* (originally, resembling something in a grotto, from Italian *grottesca*), *picturesque*, *statuesque*. Some examples are now themselves nouns: *arabesque* (literally, something in an Arab style), *burlesque* (a parody or comically exaggerated imitation of something, from Italian *burlesco*, from *burla*, mockery; this can also be a verb).

-ess *Forming nouns denoting the female gender.* [From French -*esse*, via late Latin from Greek -*issa*.]

Many examples exist: *actress*, *countess*, *duchess*, *enchantress*, *hostess*, *lioness*, *ogress*, *peeress*, *poetess*, *princess*, *waitress*. In some cases, it can mean 'wife of': *ambassadress*, *mayoress*. Such forms are now often seen as sexist or patronizing; many have been replaced to a greater or lesser extent by the stem term, taken to be neutral in gender (*poets*, for example, may be either male or female). Some examples are now mainly of historical or poetic relevance, such as *abbess*, *goddess*, *priestess*, and *shepherdess*.

See also -ENNE, -ETTE, -STRESS, and -TRIX.

-est¹ *Forming the superlatives of some ad-* *jectives and adverbs.* [Old English -*ost-*, -*ust-*, -*ast-*.]

Examples of adjectival superlatives include *clearest*, *greatest*, *oldest*, *shortest*, *strongest*, *widest*, *youngest*; of adverbial superlatives *fastest*, *latest*, *soonest*. Many longer adjectives and adverbs instead form their superlatives using *most*. For the comparative form, *see* -ER².

-est² *Also* **-st**. *Forming the second person singular of verbs.* [Old English -*est*, -*ast*, -*st*.]

This ending, like -*eth* for the third person singular (*see* -ETH²) is archaic. Examples include *canst*, *comest*, *goest*, *knowest*, *sayest*.

-et *Forming nouns, originally diminutives.* [Old French -*et*, -*ete*.]

An example is *target*, etymologically speaking a small *targe* or shield. Others of similar kind are *banquet* (French *banc*, bench), *crotchet* (French *croc*, hook), *hatchet* (French *hache*, axe), *pocket* (French *poke*, pouch), and *turret* (French *tour*, tower). More recent formations such as *facet* have come from French words ending in -ETTE, an ending many retain (*cigarette*, sometimes spelled *cigaret* in US English). A few words have been created in English on native roots: *cabinet* derives from *cabin* and *midget* from *midge*. The suffix is no longer productive of new words, though *nymphet*, an attractive and sexually mature young woman, was created by Vladimir Nabokov in his novel *Lolita* in 1955. *See also* -LET.

-eteria: *see* -TERIA

eth- *A two-carbon chain of atoms.* [English *ether* (Greek *aithēr*, upper air, because the ether was believed to occupy all space beyond the sphere of the moon).]

This form is used to represent the *ethyl* radical, a chain of two carbon atoms (*ether* is the common name for *diethyl ether*, which contains two such chains separated by an oxygen atom); this appears in a few names of organic compounds, such as *ethene*, *ethyne*, *ethambutol* (a synthetic compound used to treat tuberculosis), and *ethacrynic acid*, a powerful diuretic drug. *See also* ETHOXY-.

-eth¹: *see* -TH¹

-eth² *Forming the third person singular of the present tense of verbs.* [Old English -*eth*, -*ath*, -*th*.]

This ending is archaic, familiar only from older writings, such as the King James Bible: 'For I am a man under authority, having soldiers under me: and I say to this man, Go, and he *goeth*; and to another, Come, and he *cometh*; and to my servant, Do this, and he *doeth* it'. For the equivalent second person form, *see* -EST².

ethno- *A nation, people, or culture.* [Greek *ethnos*, nation.]

Ethnology is the study of the characteristics of different peoples and the differences and relationships between them; *ethnicity* is the fact or state of belonging to a social group that has a common national or cultural tradition; *ethnocentric* refers to evaluating other peoples and cultures according to one's own assumptions or preconceptions; the adjective *ethnic* relates to a population group with a common national or cultural tradition.

The form is commonly found in names for cross-disciplinary studies or sciences: *ethnoarchaeology*, the study of present-day societies in order to draw conclusions about past ones; *ethnolinguistics*, the part of linguistics that deals with the relations between linguistic and cultural behaviour; *ethnobotany*, the scientific study of the traditional knowledge and customs of a people concerning plants; *ethnomusicology*, the study of the music of different cultures.

ethox(y)- *The ethoxyl radical.* [ETH- plus OXY-².]

The *ethoxyl* radical is $CH_3CH_2O—$, derived from ethyl alcohol. Ether, more formally *diethyl ether*, has the systematic chemical name *ethoxyethane*; an *ethoxide* is a salt or simple compound containing this radical, for example *sodium ethoxide*; a compound into which the radical has been introduced is said to have been *ethoxylated*. The form also appears as an element in the systematic names of compounds: *3-ethoxy-2-fluorohexane*. *See also* METHOXY-.

-etic *Forming adjectives and some nouns.* [Greek -*etikos* or -*ētikos*.]

For example, *cosmetic* comes from Greek *kosmētikos*, from *kosmos*, order or adornment; *ascetic* from Greek *askētikos*, from *askētēs*, a monk. Others similarly formed include *aesthetic*, *apologetic*, *athletic*, *diuretic*, *energetic*, *pathetic*, *prophetic*, *synthetic*, and *theoretic*. Such adjectives often have corresponding nouns in -ESIS. *See also* -ATIC, -ITIC, -OTIC, and -IC.

-etidine: *see* -IDINE

-ette *Forming nouns.* [Old French -*ette*, feminine of -*ET*.]

Early examples of the use of **-ette** to indicate the feminine gender date from the sixteenth and seventeenth centuries in words imported from French: *brunette* (French, feminine of *brunet*, a diminutive of *brun*, brown); *coquette* (French, feminine of *coquet*, wanton, a diminutive of *coq*, cock). However, it was only in the early 20th century that similar words began to be created in English, beginning with *suffragette* (from *suffrage*, the right to vote in political elections); others are *usherette* and *drum majorette*. The move towards gender-neutral terms in recent decades means that new words ending in **-ette** with this sense are often deliberately dismissive or flippant: *bimbette* (from *bimbo*), *ladette* (a female *lad*, in the British colloquial sense of a man who is boisterously macho in his behaviour or actions), *punkette*, *yobette*.

A common use is to suggest a diminutive: *kitchenette*, a small kitchen or part of a room equipped as a kitchen; *statuette*, a small statue or figurine; *diskette*, a small removable computer data storage disk; *novelette*, a frequently derogatory term for a short novel; *courgette* (French *courge*, gourd), in British English the immature fruit of a vegetable marrow, a zucchini. However, many words that once had this sense have lost it: *cigarette*; *omelette* (literally, a little knife blade, from its flatness; French *amelette*, from *lemele*, knife blade). Others never had it: *launderette*; *etiquette* (French *étiquette*, a list of ceremonial observances of a court).

The suffix can also denote an imitation or substitute; many are now only historical, such as *beaverette*, *cashmerette*, or *poplinette*; examples still in use include *flannelette*, a napped cotton fabric resembling flannel; *leatherette*, an imitation leather, and *winceyette* (Scots *wincey*, an alteration of *woolsey* in *linsey-woolsey*, a cheap fabric of wool and cotton), a lightweight napped flannelette.

Silhouette is an eponym, named after Étienne de *Silhouette* (1709–67), a French author and politician, though nobody knows why.

See also -ET and -LET.

eu- *Well; easily.* [Greek *eu*, well, from *eus*, good.]

Examples derived directly from Greek words include *euphony*, the quality of being pleasing to the ear (Greek *euphōnia*, based on *phōnē*, sound)—the valved brass musical instrument called the *euphonium* derives from the same root; *eulogy*, a speech or piece of writing that praises someone or something highly (Greek *eulogia*, praise); *euphoria*, a feeling or state of intense excitement and happiness (Greek *euphoros*, borne well, healthy, from *pherein*, to bear).

Examples created in English on Greek roots include *euthanasia*, the painless killing of a patient suffering from an incurable and painful disease (Greek *thanatos*, death, so literally 'easy death'); *eutrophication*, excessive richness of nutrients in a body of water (Greek *trephein*, nourish); *eubacterium*, the 'true' bacteria and cyanobacteria, as distinct from archaea.

The opposite is DYS-. *See also* EURY-.

Eur(o)- *European; Europe or European plus another country; Europe; the European Union.* [English *Europe* plus -O-.]

Examples in which it refers to Europe plus another part of the world, or Europeans plus another nationality, include *Euro-American*; *Eurafrican* refers to Europe and Africa, or to a person of mixed European and African parentage or descent.

The form may refer to Europe in general: *Eurobond*, an international bond issued in Europe or elsewhere outside the country in whose currency its value is stated; *Eurovision*, a network of European television production administered by the European Broadcasting Union; *Euratom*, the European Atomic Energy Community; *Eurotunnel*, the Channel tunnel; *Eurocommunism*, the theory of communism advocated by communist parties in western European countries; something or someone that is *Eurocentric* focuses on European culture or history to the exclusion of a wider view of the world.

The most common usage is now in reference to the European Union: a *Euromarket* is a financial market which deals with *Eurocurrencies*, the currencies of members of the European Union; the *Euro* is the single European currency; a *Euro-MP* is a member of the European Parliament; a *Europhile* is a supporter of the EU, its opposite being a *Europhobe*. In political journalism, transitory formations referring to the EU appear widely: *Euro-enthusiasm*, *Euro-farming*, *Euro-influenced*, *Euro-lunacy*, *Euromyth*.

eury- *A wide variety or range of something.* [Greek *eurus*, wide.]

Several terms in ecology refer to organisms that can tolerate a wide range of conditions, for example *euryhaline* (Greek *halinos*, of salt), tolerating a wide range of salinity; *eurytopic* (Greek *topos*, place), tolerating a variety of habitats or ecological conditions; *eurythermal* (Greek *thermē*, heat), tolerating a wide range of temperatures. These are usually contrasted with terms in STENO-.

Other than these, **eury-** most frequently appears in the names of organisms, such as *euryapsid* (*apsis*, *apsid-*, arch), an extinct marine reptile of the Mesozoic period; *eurypterid* (Greek *pteron*, wing), a giant fossil marine arthropod; *Eurycephalus*, a genus of beetles.

ex-¹ Also **ef-** and **e-**. *Out; upward; thoroughly; removal or release; former.* [Latin *ex*, out of.]

This prefix is common, appearing in a variety of verbs, adjectives, nouns, and the occasional adverb. However, virtually all instances have been derived from Latin sources, mostly verbs, that already contain the prefix. Apart from its hyphenated form meaning 'former' (see below), it has only rarely been used in English to create new words.

In verbs, the most common sense is a literal or figurative one based on the meaning of its Latin source, as in *exclude* (Latin *excludere*, from *claudere*, to shut) or *export* (Latin *exportare*, from *portare*, carry); it may suggest a figurative movement upwards, as in *exalt* (Latin *exaltare*, from *altus*, high); sometimes it expresses the idea of thoroughness, as in *excruciate* (Latin *excruciat-*, tormented, based on *crux*, *cruc-*, a cross), or making something worse, as in *exacerbate* (Latin *exacerbat-*, made harsh, from *acerbus*, harsh, bitter); it may suggest removal or release, as in *excommunicate* (ecclesiastical Latin *excommunicat-*, excluded from communication with the faithful, from *communis*, common to all); it may suggest the inducement of a state, as in *exasperate* (Latin *exasperat-*, irritated to anger, from the verb *exasperare*, derived from *asper*, rough).

Other verbs containing various of these senses are: *excel*, *excuse*, *extend*, *export*, *express*, and *extort*. Some examples of adjectival forms are *exorbitant*, *exquisite*, *extant*, *extinct*, and *extravagant*. Nouns include *example*, *exertion*, *exhilaration*, *expert*, *expletive*, *explosion*, and *exploration*.

In hyphenated words attached to names of offices or functions, it means 'former': *ex-wife*, *ex-mayor*, *ex-president*, *ex-serviceman*, *ex-parrot*.

The spelling **ex-** appears in Latin before vowels; before *f* it becomes **ef-**: *effervesce*, *effigy*, *effort*, *effusive*; before consonants it becomes **e-**: *ebullient*, *edict*, *elect*, *emaciated*, *enormity*, *erupt*, *escape*.

ex-² Also **ec-**. *Out*. [Greek *ex*, out of.]

This prefix is closely related to its Latin equivalent (see the previous entry) but is much rarer. Examples are *exarch* (Greek *exarkhos*, from *arkhos*, ruler), a bishop of the Orthodox Church, *exodus* (Greek *exodos*, from *hodos*, way), and *exorcize* (ecclesiastical Latin *exorcizare*, from Greek *exorkizein*, from *horkos*, oath).

Before consonants it was replaced in Greek by *ek-*, which has become **ec-** in English, for example in **eccentric** (Greek *kentron*, centre), *eclipse* (Greek *ekleipein*, fail to appear, be eclipsed, from *leipein*, to leave), *ecstasy* (Greek *ekstasis*, standing outside oneself, based on *histanai*, to place), and *eczema* (Greek *ekzein*, boil over, break out, from *zein*, boil).

A few specialist modern formations exist, such as *exergonic* (Greek *ergon*, work), a biochemical reaction that proceeds with release of energy, and *exstrophy* (Greek *strophē*, turning), a birth defect resulting in the turning inside-out of a hollow organ, but the prefix is hardly productive.

Words such as *exotic* contain EXO- instead.

exa- *In units of measurement, a factor of 10^{18}.* [Based on the Greek prefix *hexa-*, six, by deleting the first letter.]

This is one of the standard SI (Système International) decimal prefixes (see the table of WORDS FOR MULTIPLES on page 127). This form is rarely met with in general scientific usage; an example is *exajoule*. It is occasionally used in discussions predicting very fast computers in the future, as in *exaflop* (*see* -FLOP), or large amounts of data: *exabyte*.

exbi-: see the table of WORDS FOR MULTIPLES on page 127

exo- *External; from outside.* [Greek *exō*, outside.]

The great majority of words here are in modern technical and scientific usage; exceptions are *exotic*, which derives via Latin from Greek *exōtikos*, foreign, and *exogamy* (Greek *gamos*, marriage), the custom of marrying outside a community, clan, or tribe. Some examples of technical terms are *exoskeleton*, a rigid external covering for the body in some invertebrate animals; *exothermic*, of a chemical reaction or process that is accompanied by the release of heat; *exogenous*, developing from external factors; *exobiology*, the branch of science that deals with the possibility and likely nature of life on other planets or in space.

Its opposite is ENDO-; *see also* ECTO-. Words such as *exorbitant* or *exonerate* instead contain Latin *ex-* (*see* EX-¹); some, such as *exodus* or *exorcize*, come from Greek (*see* EX-²).

extra- *Outside; beyond.* [Latin *extra*, outside.]

Extraordinary comes from the Latin phrase *extra ordinem*, outside the normal course of events; an *extramural* course of study derives from Latin *extra muros*, outside the walls; *extravagant* from Latin *vagari*, wander; *extraneous* from *extraneus*, external; something *extramarital* occurs outside marriage, especially a sexual relationship.

Technical terms derived from the same source include *extrapolate* (**extra**-plus the second part of *interpolate*), to infer or estimate by extending or projecting known information; *extraterrestrial*, of or from outside the earth or its atmosphere (or a hypothetical or fictional being from outer space, especially an intelligent one); *extravehicular*, relating to work performed outside a spacecraft; *extravasation* (Latin *vas*, vessel), the escape of fluids from the vessels that naturally contain them.

A number of words contain Latin *ex-* instead, for example *extract* and *extradition*; *see* EX-¹. The opposite is INTRA-.

extro- *Outwards.* [An alteration of Latin *extra*, outside.]

This is an invented prefix designed to generate words that are the opposites of those beginning in INTRO-. The only common word containing it is *extrovert* (Latin *vertere*, to turn) for an outgoing, socially confident person, though the original form *extravert* is found in psychology. Other examples, such as *extrospection*, the consideration and observation of things external to the self, are rare.

-ey: *see* -Y¹

F

-facient *Producing a specified action or state.* [Latin *facient-*, doing or making.]

Terms in **-facient** are usually adjectives that relate to or describe an induced change. Some were formed in Latin, such as *stupefacient*, inducing stupor, and *rubefacient* (Latin *rubellus*, reddish), causing the skin to go red, say during medical treatment. Others have been created in English, including *abortifacient*, productive of abortion. Such terms can often also be nouns that identify the agent causing the change. A few words ending in **-facient** have related verbs in -FY (*liquify*, *stupify*); these and others have nouns ending in -FACTION that describe the action in the abstract (*putrefaction*, *tumefaction*).

faci(o)- *The face.* [Latin *facies*, face, appearance.]

A few specialist medical terms contain this form, most commonly *facioscapulohumeral*, referring to the face, shoulder blade (the *scapula*) and upper arm (whose bone is the *humerus*), as in *facioscapulohumeral muscular dystrophy* (FSHD), the term for a type of muscular dystrophy that mainly affects this area; the adjective *faciolingual* refers to the face and tongue considered together; *facioplegia* is paralysis of the face. The Latin original *facies* is in English a medical term for a facial expression typical of a disease or condition; it is also a geological term for the appearance or character of a rock formation, and a general word for the appearance or composition of something.

-faction *Nouns of action or associated state.* [Latin *facere*, to do or make.]

English has adopted most words with this ending from Latin originals that already contain the root, such as *benefaction*, the making of a gift or donation (literally, 'doing good to', from Latin *bene*, well); *satisfaction* (Latin *satisfacere*,

satisfy), fulfilment of one's wishes or expectations; *stupefaction* (Latin *stupefacere*, be amazed), the action or state of being stunned or insensible. Many have related verbs ending in -FY and adjectives in -FACIENT.

falc- *Sickle-shaped.* [Latin *falx*, *falc-*, sickle.]

Something *falciform* or *falcate* is hooked or curved like a sickle; a *falx* (plural *falces*) is a sickle-shaped fold in the membrane enveloping the brain and spinal cord; *falciparum* is the most severe form of malaria, caused by infection with *Plasmodium falciparum*.

fasci(o)- *A bundle.* [Latin *fascis*, bundle; *fascia*, band.]

The name of the authoritarian governmental system *fascism* derives from the *fasces* (plural of *fascis*), a bundle of rods with a projecting axe blade, carried by a lictor in ancient Rome as a symbol of a magistrate's power. In anatomy, *fascia* has a specific sense of a thin sheath of fibrous tissue enclosing a muscle or other organ; linked words are *fasciculation*, a brief spontaneous contraction affecting a small number of muscle fibres, and *fasciitis*, inflammation of the fascia of a muscle or organ. A *fascicle* (or *fascicule*) can be a separately published instalment of a printed work or, in anatomy and biology, a bundle of structures, such as nerve or muscle fibres or conducting vessels in plants, for which an alternative term is *fasciculus*. *Fascioliasis*, infestation of a human or an animal with the liver fluke, *Fasciola hepatica*, derives from the related Latin *fasciola*, a small bandage.

-fashion *In some specified manner.* [English *fashion*.]

A small number of hyphenated compounds include this ending, such as *Bristol-fashion*, in good order (after the British seaport of Bristol, now almost always as part of the set phrase *all shipshape and* Bristol-fashion); *parrot-fashion*, reciting something mechanically, without thought or understanding, as a parrot says words it has learned; and *spoon-fashion*, of a couple lying snugly together head to foot, as a pair of spoons might be fitted together.

febr(i)- *Fever.* Latin *febris*, fever.

The adjective is *febrile*, usually meaning feverish or relating to fever, but with a subsidiary sense of showing nervous excitement; a *febrifuge* (Latin *fugare*, drive away) is a medication that dispels or reduces fever; a *febricule* is a brief fever; *febriphobia* is fear of contracting a fever.

femor(o)- *The thigh or thigh bone.* [Latin *femur*, *femor-*, thigh.]

The adjective *femoral* refers to the thigh bone or *femur*. The *femoropopliteal* artery runs down the thigh and behind the knee; the adjective *femorotibial* relates both to the thigh and the leg below the knee (the *tibia* being one of the two bones of the lower leg). The last two terms are also seen hyphenated.

femto- *In units of measurement, a factor of 10^{-15}.* [Danish or Norwegian *femten*, fifteen.]

This is one of the standard SI (Système International) decimal prefixes (see the table of WORDS FOR MULTIPLES on page 127), which occurs in compounds such as *femtogram*. Since chemical reactions take place in periods of time measured in *femtoseconds* (one femtosecond is to a second as a second is to 32 million years), a speciality called *femtochemistry* has grown up using techniques such as ultrafast laser pulses to observe their progress directly.

-fer *Bearing or carrying.* [Latin *ferre*, to carry or bear.]

Nouns include *conifer* (Latin *conus*, cone, so 'cone-bearing'); *crucifer* (Latin *crux*, *cruc-*, a cross), a type of plant having four petals arranged in the shape of a cross; *umbellifer* (Latin *umbella*, parasol, from the shape of the flowers), a plant of the parsley family. A rare example

created in English is *aquifer* (Latin *aqua*, water, so 'water-bearing'), a body of permeable rock that can contain or transmit groundwater.

Verbs ending in **-fer** are usually figurative: *transfer* (from *trans*, across, so literally to carry across); *defer* and *differ* (both from Latin *dis-*, apart); and *confer* (Latin *con-*, together). The form is not active in the language.

Some words derive from accidents of spelling: *duffer*, an incompetent or stupid person, is from Scots *dowfart*, a stupid person; *gaffer*, a person in charge of others, is probably a contraction of *godfather* or *grandfather*. Others are from stems ending in *f* that contain the suffix -ER (as in *golfer* from *golf*).

-fera *Also* **-ifera**. *Animal orders or phyla.* [Modern Latin, the neuter plural of *ferre*, to bear.]

Though the ending from the Latin source is **-fera**, examples all contain the linking vowel -I-: *Foraminifera* (Latin *foramen*, an opening or passage), an order of single-celled planktonic animals; *Rotifera* (Latin *rota*, wheel), a phylum of minute aquatic animals with a characteristic wheel-like ciliated organ used in swimming and feeding; and *Loricifera* (Latin *lorica*, breastplate), a minor phylum of minute marine invertebrates, resembling rotifers and living in gravel.

ferri-: *see* FERRO-

-ferous *Also* **-iferous**. *Having, bearing or containing something.* [Latin *ferre*, to carry or bear, plus -OUS.]

Many words have been formed in this ending, especially in the life and earth sciences; for some examples see the LIST opposite. Strictly the ending is **-ferous** from its Latin origin, but in every case there is an *i* before the ending (see -I-) so that the usual form is **-iferous**. *See also* -FERA.

ferr(o)- *Also* **ferri-**. *Iron.* [Latin *ferrum*, iron.]

The more general of the prefixes is **ferro-**: *ferroconcrete*, concrete reinforced with steel; *ferrocene*, a crystalline compound containing iron between

-ferous   Having, bearing or containing.
All word origins are from Latin unless otherwise stated.

auriferous	of rocks or minerals that contain gold	(*aurum*, gold)
carboniferous	containing or bearing carbon, especially in reference to the geological period in which coal measures were laid down	(English *carbon*)
coniferous	of a type of tree that bears cones	(*conus*, cone)
cruciferous	denoting plants of the cabbage family, the Cruciferae	(*crux*, cross; flowers have four petals arranged crosswise)
floriferous	of a plant producing many flowers	(*flos, flor-*, a flower)
fossiliferous	describing rocks that contain fossils	(English *fossil*)
luminiferous	producing or transmitting light	(*lumen*, light)
metalliferous	bearing or producing metal	(*metallum*, metal)
odoriferous	having or giving off a smell, especially an unpleasant one	(*odor*, smell or scent)
pestiferous	harbouring infection and disease, or figuratively, being a pest or nuisance	(*pestifer*, bringing pestilence)
seminiferous	producing or conveying semen	(*semen*, seed)
splendiferous	splendid	(English *splendour*)
umbelliferous	bearing flowers arranged in clusters or umbels	(*umbella*, sunshade, from *umbra*, shadow)
vociferous	vehement or clamorous	(*vox, voc-*, voice)

two flat layers of atoms; the adjective *ferruginous* describes a substance containing iron oxides or rust. The usual adjective is *ferrous* (but see below).

A few metals can be strongly and permanently magnetized; because this was first observed in iron, it is called *ferromagnetism*, though it is also shown by nickel and cobalt and their alloys.

In chemistry, **ferro-** refers specifically to iron compounds in which the iron is divalent, as in *ferrocyanide*, for which the adjective is *ferrous*; **ferri-** is used for chemical compounds that contain iron in its trivalent state, as in *potassium ferricyanide*, and here the adjective is *ferric*.

-fest *A festival, gathering, or activity.* [From German *Fest*, festival.]

This ending was first used by German immigrants to the United States, on the model of words such as *Octoberfest* for the Munich beer festival, and is still most common there.

Early examples were *gabfest*, a gathering at which there is a lot of conversation (from *gab*, speech, as in *gift of the gab*); *songfest*, an informal or spontaneous gathering at which people sing; and *slugfest*, a tough and challenging contest, especially in boxing or baseball.

More recent creations include *gloomfest*, any unhappy gathering; *campfest*, a celebration by gays; and *rockfest*, a rock festival. The sense of activity is often broadly interpreted: *gorefest*, a type of excessively bloodthirsty film; *flamefest*, a bout of insults ('flames') exchanged between individuals online.

feto- Also **feti-** and **foeto-**. *The fetus.* [Latin *fetus*, pregnancy, childbirth, offspring.]

A *fetoprotein* is an antigen that occurs naturally in fetuses, but in adults only as a result of certain diseases; *feticide* (Latin *-cida*, from *caedere*, kill) is destruction or abortion of a fetus; something *fetotoxic* is poisonous to a fetus; *fetoscopy* is the direct observation of the uterus and fetus using a fibre-optic instrument; *fetology* is the branch of medicine concerned with the study and treatment of the fetus. Spellings beginning in

foeto- (*foetus*, *foeticide*) are now found only in non-technical contexts in Britain.

fibrino- *Fibrin.* [English *fibrin* (from *fibre*), plus -O-.]

When blood clots, *fibrin*, a stringy protein, is deposited as an insoluble mesh that holds the clot together; it is generated as needed from *fibrinogen*, a soluble protein in the blood, through the action of the enzyme thrombin. The adjectives *fibrinoid* and *fibrinous* refer to the nature or properties of fibrin. The natural process of breaking down fibrin by enzymes is called *fibrinolysis* (Greek *lusis*, loosening); the agent that breaks it down is another enzyme, *fibrinolysin*.

fibr(o)- *Fibres.* [Latin *fibra*, fibre.]

The names of many medical conditions contain this form. Examples are *fibrosis*, the thickening and scarring of connective tissue, usually because of injury; *fibrositis*, an inflammation of fibrous connective tissue, typically causing back pain; *fibrillation*, the uncoordinated contraction of muscle fibres in the heart, giving rise to an irregular and inefficient heartbeat; a *fibroid* is a fibrous growth in the uterus; a *fibroma* is a benign tumour of connective tissue. In geology, *fibrolite* is a variety of sillimanite, a felted fibrous mass of small crystals.

-fic Also **-ific** and **-(i)ficent**. *Forming adjectives of action.* [Latin *-ficus*, ultimately from *facere*, to do or make].

The **-fic** ending marks adjectives that relate to an activity, often a continuing one, as in *beatific*, feeling or expressing blissful happiness; *honorific*, of something given as a mark of respect; *horrific*, causing horror; *prolific*, producing much of something; and *soporific*, tending to induce drowsiness or sleep.

Some have moved some way away from literalness—*terrific* now often refers to something wonderful or excellent, but it once meant 'inducing terror', from Latin *terrere*, to frighten; *calorific* (Latin *calor*, heat) literally means 'producing heat', but now usually refers to the amount of energy contained in food or fuel.

The ending **-ficent** (*see* -ANT) forms a few adjectives from nouns ending in *-ence* (*see* -ANCE) that relate to an action or activity, such as *beneficent*, doing good or conferring benefits; *magnificent*, making a splendid appearance or show; and *munificent*, acting generously.

Virtually all these words contain the linking vowel -I- before the suffix, so that the currently active forms are taken to be **-ific** and **-ificent**. *See also* -FY and -IC.

-fication Also **-ification**. *Forming nouns of action.* [Latin *-fication-*, from verbs ending in *-ficare*.]

These nouns derive from verbs ending in -FY. There are several hundred examples in English, almost all of which contain the linking vowel -I- before the ending. They indicate an action or the result of an action. A few examples are *amplification*, the action of amplifying sound, or the results of doing so; *classification*, the act of classifying, or the results of classifying; *commodification*, the action of turning something into a commodity; *gratification*, the state of being gratified or the act causing it; *magnification*, the action of magnifying something, or the result of doing so; and *simplification*, the action of simplifying, or its result.

See also -ATION, -ION, and -IZE (for *-isation* and *-ization*).

-fid *Divided in a specified way or into a specified number of parts.* [Latin *fidus*, cleft or split.]

Something *trifid* (Latin *tri-*, three), less commonly *trefid*, is partly or wholly split into three divisions or lobes (not to be confused with a *triffid*, a predatory plant moving on three legs, invented by John Wyndham in *The Day of the Triffids*); similarly something *bifid* (Latin *bi-*, two) is divided by a deep cleft or notch into two parts; a leaf that is *pinnatifid* (Latin *pinnatus*, feathered) has leaflets arranged on either side of the stem, but not divided all the way down to the central axis.

Finno- Also **Fenno-**. *Finland, the Finns or the Finnic languages.* [From *Finn* or *Finnic*.]

This form occurs in only a few terms and is mainly used in the linguistic terms *Finno-Ugric* and *Finno-Ugrian*, which relate to the group of Uralic languages of which Finnish and Hungarian are important members. The **Fenno-** form appears in *Fennoscandia*, a land mass in NW Europe comprising Finland, Scandinavia, and the adjacent area of NE Russia, for which the related adjectives are *Fennoscandian* and *Fennoscandinavian*.

flav(o)- *Yellow or yellow-tinted.* [Latin *flavus*, yellow.]

Something *flavescent* is yellowish or turning yellow; *flavin* is a yellow dye made from the bark of a North American oak tree; a *flavoprotein* is a protein containing flavin that takes part in cell respiration and metabolism; *flavone* is a colourless crystalline compound which is the basis of a number of white or yellow plant pigments; *flavonoids* are compounds related to flavone that, despite their name, include most of those that give flowers their red and blue colours; it has been suggested their presence in food helps to maintain health.

-flop Also **-flops**. *Measures of computing speed.* [A partial acronym of *floating-point operations (per second)*.]

A *floating-point operation* in computing is a calculation carried out on numbers whose format allows the binary equivalent of the decimal point to move about, or 'float'. The speed of a computer can be measured by counting the rate at which it can do such calculations. The original form of this suffix was **-flops**, as in *megaflops*, *gigaflops*, or *teraflops* (see the list of WORDS FOR MULTIPLES on page 127) but the final *s* (for *second*) was frequently taken to indicate a plural and is now often dropped.

flor(i)- *A flower or flowers.* [Latin *flos, flor-*, a flower.]

Floristics is the branch of geography that studies the vegetation of an area; *florescence* is the process of flowering; a *floret* is one of the small flowers making up a composite flower head; *floriculture*, on the model of *horticulture*, is the cultivation of flowers; a *floribunda* (Latin *floribundus*, freely flowering) is a type of rose which bears dense clusters of flowers; *floriferous* means producing many flowers.

-florous *Having flowers of a certain type.* [Latin *flos, flor-*, a flower, plus -OUS.]

This ending appears in a few uncommon adjectives. Examples are *cauliflorous* (Latin *caulis*, stem), having flowers on the stem, as a cauliflower plant does; *multiflorous*, having many flowers (with its opposite *uniflorous*, having only one flower); and *ramiflorous* (Latin *ramus*, branch) flowering on the branches.

fluor(o)- Also **fluo-**. *Fluorine; fluorescence.* [Latin *fluor*, a flux, from *fluere*, to flow.]

The mineral *fluorspar* was so called because it was used as a flux in metal working; the element *fluorine* was first isolated from it. Organic chemical compounds that contain fluorine and chlorine are *chlorofluorocarbons*, now known to be largely responsible for the depletion of the ozone layer in the upper atmosphere; fluorine compounds are added to toothpastes and drinking water to help harden teeth, by a process called *fluoridation*, but excess of it can lead to *fluorosis*, marked by a mottling of the teeth.

Some names for inorganic fluorine compounds mark the presence of fluorine with **fluo-**, as in *fluoborate* or *fluosilicate*.

Some substances exhibit *fluorescence*, in which they emit light when they are irradiated with radiation such as ultraviolet; the phenomenon was so named because it was first demonstrated in fluorspar. Several words beginning in **fluoro-** refer to it: *fluorography* is photography in which the image is formed through fluorescence; a *fluoroscope* has a screen that *fluoresces* when hit by X-rays, so the image can be viewed directly; *fluorimetry* is a method of analysis using fluorescence.

fluvi(o)- *River.* [Latin *fluvius*, river.]

The general adjective relating to rivers is *fluvial*; something associated with or formed by rivers is *fluviatile*. In geology, *fluvioglacial* refers to meltwater streams that flow from glaciers, and to the erosion or deposition they cause; similarly, *fluvio-lacustrine* (Latin *lacus*, lake) refers to sediments caused by both rivers and lakes.

foeto-: *see* FETO-

-fold *A number of parts or facets; multiplied by such a number; relating to folding or to a folded object.* [Old English *-fald*, *-feald*, related to *fold*.]

This suffix forms adjectives and adverbs from the cardinal or counting numbers, so *twofold*, *eightfold*, *hundredfold*, *thousandfold* and many others. Related words are *bifold*, double or twofold; and *manifold*, many and various, or a thing with many different parts or forms (*manyfold* is a more recent equivalent with the sense of something increased many times).

The suffix also has the sense of folding: a *gatefold* is an oversized page in a book, folded inside but designed to be opened out to be looked at; in the US a *billfold* is a wallet designed to hold folded dollar bills. Other examples are *linenfold*, an ornamental motif resembling folded linen that is carved on panelling; and *fanfold*, continuous stationary folded concertina-fashion.

Blindfold does not belong here, as it is a modified form, on the model of words ending in **-fold**, of the Old English *blindfeld*, to cover the eyes or make blind; *scaffold* is another with a different origin — the unrelated Anglo-Norman French *(e)schaffaut*.

for- *Forming verbs and adjectives.* [Old English *for-*, *faer-*.]

This is no longer a living prefix, and many words formed with it are either obsolete (*forwalk*, *forirk*), archaic (*fordo*), or formal, poetic, or literary (*forbear*, *forfend*, *forswear*).

It was used to give increased force to a word (*forlorn*, pitifully sad and abandoned, from Old English *lēosan*, lose), indicate a prohibition (*forbid*), or variously suggest neglect, abstention or renunciation (*forget*, *forgo*, *forsake*, *forgive*).

Some words beginning with *for-*, such as *foreign*, *forest*, and *forfeit*, derive from other Latin roots. Others appear to contain it through accidents of spelling: *forage* (Old French *fuerre*, straw) and *forceps* (the Latin word for tongs or pincers).

fore- *Before, beforehand, going before, in front of, leading.* [Old English *fore*.]

Verbs, adjectives, and nouns containing this form have a general sense of being in front of something else, either in time or place. It can indicate a front part of the body: *forehead*, *forearm*, *forebrain*, *foreleg*, *forelock*. Several refer to parts of a sailing ship near the bows, such as *foremast*, *foresail*, *forecastle* (abbreviated to *fo'c'sle*), and *forestay*. Examples relating to time include *forecast*, *foretell*, *foresee*, *forebear*, *forefather*, and *forestall*. A *foreword* is an introduction to a book; a *forecourt* is an open area in front of a building; a *foreman* or *forewoman* is a person in charge of others or one who presides over a jury; someone or something that is *foremost* is the most prominent in rank, importance, or position.

-form *Also* **-iform**. *Having a specified form or number of forms.* [Latin *forma*, a mould or form.]

This ending is active in English and frequently forms adjectives in botany and zoology that describe the shape of a plant or animal or some part of it. Though the spelling is strictly **-form** because of the Latin original, adjectives created using it usually have a *i* before the ending (*see* -I-). A selection of varying application is given in the LIST on the opposite page.

Verbs ending in **-form**, including *form* itself, are from Latin *formare*, to form (based on *forma*); hence *conform*, *deform*, *inform*, *reform*, and *transform*. An exception is *terraform*, to make a planet more like Earth, from Latin *terra*, earth, plus the English verb *form*. However, *perform* is from Old French *par*, through or to completion, plus *fournir*, to furnish or provide.

-form   Having a specified form or number of forms.
All word sources are from Latin unless otherwise stated.

Relating to animal or plant shapes:

coliform	belonging to a set of rod-shaped bacteria typified by *Escherichia coli*, common in the gastrointestinal tract	(*coli*, of the colon)
cribriform	having an anatomical structure pierced by holes, such as the spinnerets of some kinds of spiders	(*cribrum*, sieve)
filiform	thread-like	(*filum*, thread)
spongiform	having a porous structure resembling that of a sponge	(English *sponge*)
vermiform	resembling a worm	(*vermis*, a worm)

Indicating a number of forms or parts:

multiform	existing in many forms	(*multus*, much or many)
uniform	all of one kind or form	(*unus*, one)
variform	of a group of things that vary from one another in form	(*varius*, diverse)

Other examples:

cirriform	of the form of clouds composed of ice crystals, such as cirrus	(*cirrus*, a curl)
cruciform	having the shape of a cross	(*crux*, cross)
cuneiform	wedge-shaped characters in some ancient Middle-East writing systems; wedge-shaped	(*cuneus*, wedge)
stratiform	arranged in layers	(*stratum*, something strewn or laid down)

Nouns ending in **-form** are from a variety of sources and similarly are not examples of the combining form: *chloroform* is from CHLORO- plus the first part of *formic acid*; *platform* comes from the French *plateforme*, a ground plan (literally a flat shape); *landform* and *microform* both derive from the English noun *form*.

-formes   Also **-iformes**. *Orders of animals.* [Latin, plural of *forma*, form.]

Terms here are systematic names, mainly for orders of birds, but also fish. All contain the linking vowel -i- before the ending. Examples are *Perciformes* (Latin *perca*, perch), a large order of nearly half of all bony fishes, including perch; *Anguilliformes* (Latin *anguilla*, eel), an order comprising the eels; *Passeriformes* (Latin *passer*, sparrow), a large order of birds with feet adapted for perching, including all songbirds; *Ciconiiformes* (Latin *ciconia*, stork), the order that includes the herons, storks, and egrets; and *Psittaciformes* (Latin *psittacus*, parrot), the order of the parrots, parakeets, and budgerigars.

Franco-   *France or French.* [Medieval Latin *Francus*, a Frank.]

This prefix sometimes appears hyphenated with an adjective for another country to suggest a combined or linked character, as in *Franco-German* or *Franco-Russian*, or in phrases such as *Franco-Prussian War*. Other instances include *Francophile*, a lover of France and things French; and *francophone*, French-speaking, as of some African countries or French-speaking Canada.

franken-   *Genetically modified.* [The first element of the name of Baron Victor *Frankenstein*, from Mary Shelley's novel

Frankenstein, or the Modern Prometheus of 1818.]

Activists sometimes describe genetically modified foods as *Frankenstein foods*, evoking Frankenstein's creation of a living being, in popular understanding a terrifying monster who turns on his creator and destroys him. The first element of his name appears in various invented words—*frankenfood*, *frankencrop*, *frankenfruit*, *frankenplant*—with the technology known generically as *frankenscience* (all are often written with initial capital letter). They are all deeply pejorative.

-free *Free of or from something indicated by the first element.* [English *free*.]

This suffix is active in the language, frequently forming adjectives: *duty-free*, *gluten-free*, *cruelty-free*, *fat-free*, *lead-free*, *nuclear-free*, *sugar-free*, and *GM-free* (not containing ingredients derived from *genetically modified* crops). More oblique examples are *post-free*, carried by post or mail free of charge to the customer, and *hands-free*, not needing to be held to operate, as of a mobile phone. Most such forms are hyphenated; those that are not mainly derive from first elements that end in a vowel: *carefree*, *smokefree*, *wirefree* (using infra-red or radio communication instead of wires).

fronto- Also **fronti-** *The forehead or front part of something.* [Latin *frons*, *front-*, front or forehead.]

The most common word here is *frontispiece* (Latin *specere*, to look, so unrelated to *piece*), an illustration facing the title-page of a book. Some examples are terms in anatomy or surgery: *frontocortical*, of the front of the cerebral cortex; *frontoparietal*, of the frontal bone or lobe. In meteorology, *frontogenesis* is the formation or development of a weather front, whose opposite is *frontolysis* (from Greek *luein*, loosen).

fruct(i)- Also **fructo-**. *Fruit; fructose.* [Latin *fructus*, fruit.]

An insect or animal that is *fructivorous* eats fruit; to *fructify* is to make something

fruitful or to bear fruit. *Fructose* is fruit sugar, so called because it is found in fruit juices as well as in honey; several terms relate to its presence in the body: *fructokinase* is an enzyme involved in its metabolism; *fructosemia* is the presence of fructose in the blood; and *fructosuria* is similarly its presence in the urine.

-fuge Also **-fugal**. *An agent that dispels, drives away, or eliminates something.* [Latin *-fugus*, from *fugare*, to drive away or to put to flight.]

Some terms here are medical: *febrifuge*, a drug or treatment that reduces or prevents fever; *vermifuge*, one that removes parasitic worms. A *calcifuge* (Latin *calx*, *calc-*, lime) is a plant that is not suited to soil containing lime, and so is figuratively driven away by it. Derived adjectives are formed with **-fugal** (*febrifugal*, *vermifugal*).

A *centrifuge* is a rotating device that separates substances; this derives from the related Latin verb *fugere*, to flee. Two other similarly formed common words are *refuge* and *subterfuge*.

-ful *Full of; having given qualities.* [English *full*.]

Adjectives formed in this ending can mean 'full of': *beautiful*, *colourful*, *graceful*, *painful*, *powerful*, *youthful*. In other cases it means 'having the qualities of': *careful*, *helpful*, *lawful*, *restful*, *spiteful*, *thoughtful*, *truthful*, *useful*. Some, taken from English verbs, have the senses 'apt to, able to, accustomed to': *boastful*, *forgetful*, *mournful*, *wakeful*, *watchful*. Over time some have become figurative: *grateful* (formerly 'agreeable, acceptable', from Latin *gratus*, pleasing), now means 'feeling or showing an appreciation of kindness'; *hateful* (once 'full of hate', now 'generating hate'), *joyful* (originally 'full of joy', rather than the more modern 'causing or evoking joy').

The ending generates nouns indicating an amount needed to fill a given container or holder: *armful*, *basketful*, *cupful*, *handful*, *hatful*, *spadeful*. A few examples of this type are figurative: *earful*, literally an ear-filling amount, but usually a severe reprimand; *eyeful*, a good look, but often describing somebody striking or attractive; and *skinful*, enough alcoholic drink to make one drunk.

fung(i)- *Fungus.* [English *fungus*.]

A *fungicide* (Latin *-cida*, from *caedere*, kill) is a chemical compound that destroys a fungus; something *fungiform* is in the shape of a fungus or mushroom; a *fungistatic* substance is one that inhibits the growth of fungi; *fungaemia* (US *fungemia*) is the presence of a fungus in the bloodstream; an animal that is *fungivorous* (Latin *vorare*, devour) feeds on fungi.

-fy Also **-ify**. *Make or produce; transform into; become.* [Latin *-ficare* and *-facere*, from *facere*, to make or do.]

Many verbs with this ending exist, formed either from nouns or adjectives. Some examples are *amplify*, *certify*, *dignify*, *exemplify*, *horrify*, *identify*, *liquefy*, *magnify*, *pacify*, *ratify*, *satisfy*, *stupefy*, *testify*, and *verify*.

The ending is in active use, forming verbs both from nouns and adjectives. Because many existing examples contain the linking vowel -I-, its form is usually taken to be **-ify** rather than **-fy**.

Verbs are sometimes created with humorous intent, as in *trendify*, to make trendy or fashionable, and *yuppify*, to make an area attractive to *yuppies*; others of similar kind are *cutify*, *uglify*, and *youthify*.

Many verbs ending in **-fy** have associated adjectives in -FIC and nouns in -FICATION. *See also* -ESCE.

G

galact(o)- *Milk; galactose.* [Greek *gala*, *galakt-*, milk.]

The sugar *galactose* derives from milk. The form sometimes marks its presence in a chemical compound, for example *galactoside*, a glycoside, and *galactan*, which occurs in seaweeds and some other plants. In medicine, a *galactagogue* (Greek *agōgos*, eliciting) is a food or drug that induces the flow of a mother's milk. The adjective *galactic* can refer to milk, but more commonly alludes to galaxies, originally the band of stars across the heavens called the Milky Way.

Gallo- *France or French; French and....* [Latin *Gallus*, a person from Gaul.]

This prefix usually appears hyphenated with an adjective for another country to suggest an association or link, as in *Gallo-German* or *Gallo-American*. Rarely it appears unhyphenated, as in *Gallomania*, an unreasoning attachment to French customs or ways. It is now more common to use FRANCO- instead.

galvan(o)- *Electric current.* [From the name of the Italian anatomist Luigi *Galvani* (1737–98).]

Galvani discovered that electric currents cause muscles to twitch, and so to *galvanize* somebody is to provoke them into sudden action as though shocked by electricity; the verb can also mean to cover iron with zinc (so producing *galvanized* iron), because the zinc was at first deposited from solution using an electrical current. *Galvanism* can refer either to electricity produced by chemical action or to the therapeutic use of electric currents. A device to measure small electric currents is a *galvanometer*. The usual adjective is *galvanic*.

gam(o)- Also **gamet(o)-**. *Marriage or union, fertilization or reproduction.* [Greek *gamos*, marriage.]

A *gamete* is a mature germ cell, male or female, able to undergo sexual reproduction, *gamogenesis*; petals of a flower that are *gamopetalous* are joined together.

The prefix **gameto-** refers specifically to gametes, as in *gametocyte* (Greek *kutos*, vessel), a cell that divides to make a gamete; *gametangium* (Greek *angeion*, a vessel), the cell or organ in which gametes are formed; *gametophyte*, the gamete-producing phase of the life cycle of plants with alternating generations.

-gamy Also **-gamous** and **-gamic**. *Marriage, fertilization, or reproduction.* [Greek *gamos*, marriage.]

Some common words ending in **-gamy** refer to human marriage customs, such as *monogamy* or *bigamy*. Others are terms from zoology or biology that relate to reproduction. For more examples, see the LIST opposite. The endings **-gamous** and **-gamic** form related adjectives (*monogamous*, *cryptogamic*).

ganglio- *Ganglion.* [English *ganglion*, from Greek.]

A *ganglion* is a structure containing a number of nerve cell bodies, often forming a swelling on a nerve fibre; the related adjective is *ganglionic*, less often *ganglionar*. A *ganglioside* is one of a group of complex lipids particularly abundant in nerve cell membranes; a *gangliocytoma* is a tumour involving ganglionic cells.

gastr(o)- *The stomach; feeding.* [Greek *gastēr*, stomach.]

In medicine, *gastritis* is inflammation of the stomach lining and a *gastroscope* is a device for examining its interior. *Gastronomy* is the art of choosing, cooking, and eating good food. A *gastropod* (Greek *pous*, *pod-*, foot) is a mollusc that feeds through its foot—the mouth aperture is in the muscular foot so it can feed from the rocks it creeps over. However, the

-gamy   Marriage, fertilization, or reproduction.
              Word origins are from Greek unless otherwise stated.

Relating to human marriage customs:

bigamy	illegal marriage to more than one person at a time	(Latin *bi-*, twice)
endogamy	marriage only within one clan or tribe	(*endon*, within)
exogamy	the custom of marrying only outside one's clan or tribe	(*exō*, outside)
monogamy	marriage to only one person at a time	(*monos*, alone)
polygamy	marriage to more than one person at a time	(*polloi*, many)

Relating to reproduction in plants or animals:

autogamy	self-pollination	(*autos*, self)
cryptogamy	having no flowers but reproducing by spores	(*kruptos*, hidden)
homogamy	simultaneous maturation of the stamens and pistils of a flower, the opposite of *dichogamy*; inbreeding	(*homos*, same)
karyogamy	the fusion of the nuclei of cells	(*karuon*, kernel)
plasmogamy	fusion of the cytoplasm of two or more cells	(*plasma*, a thing moulded)
syngamy	the fusion of two cells in reproduction	(*sun*, with)
xenogamy	fertilization of a flower by pollen from another, non-identical, plant	(*xenos*, stranger or foreigner)

gastrocnemius (Greek *knēmē*, leg), is the chief muscle of the calf of the leg which causes the calf to bulge (figuratively like the belly).

A set of words refer to the stomach together with another part of the digestive system: *gastroduodenal*, stomach and duodenum; *gastroenteric*, stomach and intestines. A more common adjective for the latter is now *gastrointestinal*, but a specialist in those parts of the body is always a *gastroenterologist* and a bacterial or viral infection of the stomach and intestines is *gastroenteritis*.

-gate *A scandal, especially a political one.* [The second part of *Watergate*, the Washington office building containing the national headquarters of the Democratic Party, which was burgled in 1972.]

The impact of *Watergate* was so great that the word became a model for many others that describe a scandal associated with politics. Most examples are short-lived, but a few that refer to particularly significant events have survived, such as *Irangate* and *Contragate* (in reference to covert sales of arms by the USA to Iran and use of the proceeds to aid the Contras in Nicaragua).

-gen Also **-gene**, **-geny**, **-genics**, **-genicity**, and **-genic**. *Generation or creation.* [Via French *-gène* from Greek *genos*, a kind.]

The ending **-gen** can denote substances from which others are generated: *glycogen* (Greek *glukus*, sweet), a polysaccharide in body tissues that yields glucose on hydrolysis; *collagen* (Greek *kolla*, glue), the main structural protein found in animal connective tissue, which yields gelatin when boiled. It can also indicate substances which cause or induce some effect: *carcinogen*, a substance capable of causing cancer in living tissue; *pathogen* (Greek *pathos*, suffering or disease), a micro-organism that can cause disease. The first examples were names for gaseous chemical elements borrowed from French, of which two are *hydrogen* (Greek *hudōr*, water, so literally 'water-maker'), and *nitrogen* (Greek *nitron*, nitre or saltpetre), a gaseous element, so named because it combines to form nitrates.

Examples formed using **-gene** include *indigene* (Latin *indigina*, a native, from *gignere*, to beget), a person native to a place, and *phosgene*, a poisonous gas (Greek *phōs*, light; it was first produced by the action of sunlight on a mixture of carbon monoxide and chlorine). *Gene*, a sequence of nucleotides forming part of a chromosome, ultimately comes from the same Greek root. Some words ending in **-gene** are regarded as compounds of this word rather than examples of the ending, such as *oncogene* (Greek *onkos*, mass), a gene which can transform a cell into a tumour cell.

Nouns ending in **-geny** refer to the origin or development of something, or the mode by which it is produced: *cosmogeny* (Greek *kosmos*, order, world), the origin or evolution of the universe; *orogeny* (Greek *oros*, mountain), the process of forming a mountain range. They can sometimes refer also to the study of the processes involved, though for most there are related terms ending in *-ology* (*see* -LOGY), or a few in **-genics**, such as *cryogenics* (Greek *kruos*, frost), the branch of physics concerned with very low temperatures.

The adjectival ending **-genic** has a distinct sense of being well suited to something. The first example was *photogenic* in the 1920s—literally 'producing or emitting light', but used figuratively to mean a person who photographed well. By imitation it has since given rise to *telegenic*, *mediagenic*, and others.

geo- *The Earth.* [Greek *gē*, earth.]

Words that refer to the Earth include *geopolitics*, politics with implications for the whole world, and *geosynchronous*, of an orbit for a satellite that keeps it apparently stationary over one point. Several sciences relate to the Earth, as in *geography*, *geology*, and *geomorphology* (the study of the physical features of the surface of the Earth and how they relate to its geology); these and others are the *geosciences*. *Geometry* literally means 'earth measuring'. The idea of soil occurs in *geophagy*, the practice of eating it, and less obviously so in *geomancy*, which can refer to divination using signs derived from earth, such as by scattering soil.

Germano- *German or Germany.* [Latin *Germanus*.]

Examples are *Germanophile*, a lover of Germany or German ways (with its opposite *Germanophobe*), and *Germanophone*, German-speaking.

geront(o)- Also **ger-**. *Old age or old people.* [Greek *gerōn*, old man; *gēras*, old age.]

The medical study of ageing and old age is *gerontology*; *gerontocracy* is rule by old people or a country or group so ruled; the adjective *gerontic* relates to old age, elderly people, or senescence, while *geriatric* (Greek *iatros*, doctor) refers to the medical care of old people, with *geriatrics* for the branch of medicine concerned; *gerodontics* (Greek *odont-*, tooth), is the special study of the dental problems of ageing or elderly people.

-gerous Also **-igerous**. *Bearing some specified thing.* [From Latin *-ger*, bearing.]

Examples include *dentigerous* (Latin *dens*, *dent-*, tooth), having teeth; *ovigerous* (Latin *ovum*, egg), bearing or carrying eggs; and *setigerous* (Latin *seta*, bristle), having bristles. A word from outside science is *armigerous*, entitled to bear heraldic arms (Latin *arma*, arms). However, *dangerous* comes from a different source.

-geusia *The sense of taste.* [Greek *geusis*, taste.]

Examples include *dysgeusia* (Greek *dus-*, bad or difficult), an impairment of the sense of taste; *ageusia* (Greek *a-*, not or without), inability to taste things; and *hypogeusia* (Greek *hupo*, under), a diminished acuteness in that sense.

gibi-: see the table of WORDS FOR MULTIPLES on page 127

giga- *In units of measurement, a factor of one thousand million or 10^9. In computing, often a factor of 2^{30} (1,073,741,824).* [Greek *gigas*, giant.]

This is one of the standard SI (Système International) decimal prefixes (see the table of WORDS FOR MULTIPLES on page 127), which appears in such compounds as **gigahertz** and **gigawatt**. Computer science has borrowed the unit—as it has with others—to refer to powers of 2 rather than 10, so that a **gigabyte**, for example, is usually taken to be 2^{30} bytes. This is true also of other computer terms such as **gigabit** or **gigaflops** (strictly 2^{30} floating-point operations per second).

gigant(o)- *Great size or extent.* [Greek *gigas*, *gigant-*, giant.]

Gigantism is excessive growth due to hormonal imbalance; something **gigantesque** is befitting or suggestive of a giant; **Gigantopithecus** (Greek *pithēkos*, ape) is a very large fossil Asian ape of the Upper Miocene to Lower Pleistocene epochs; in Greek mythology, **gigantomachy** (Greek *makhia*, fighting) was the struggle between the gods and the giants.

gingiv(o)- *The gums.* [From Latin *gingiva*, gum.]

Gingivitis is inflammation of the gums; the adjective **gingival** refers to the gums; a **gingivectomy** (Greek *ektomē*, excision) is the surgical removal of gum tissue, and **gingivostomatitis** (Latin *stoma*, mouth) is a virus infection of the gums and mucous membranes of the mouth.

glacio- *Glaciers.* [Latin *glacies*, ice.]

Glaciology is the study of the internal dynamics and effects of glaciers; **glaciofluvial** (Latin *fluvius*, river), less commonly *fluvioglacial*, refers to the action of streams that originate in glacial ice; **glacioeustatic** denotes changes in sea level (*eustasy*) caused by changes in the size of ice sheets (this also appears hyphenated).

glio- *The glia.* [Greek *glia*, glue.]

The *glia*, also called the neuroglia, is the connective tissue of the nervous system, consisting of several different types of cell associated with neurons. A *glioma* is a malignant tumour of the glial tissue and a **glioblastoma** is a highly invasive glioma in the brain; *gliosis* is a proliferation of certain **glial** cells that may appear as a sign of healing after damage to the central nervous system; **gliomatosis**

is a diffuse extra growth of neuroglia in the brain or spinal chord.

-globin *A globin compound.* [Latin *globus*, spherical object, globe.]

Globins are the protein parts of various molecules concerned with oxygen transport in the blood; examples are **haemoglobin** (US **hemoglobin**) (Greek *haima*, *haimat-*, blood), a red protein bound with iron, responsible for transporting oxygen in the blood; **myoglobin** (Greek *mus*, *mu-*, muscle), a simpler relative which carries and stores oxygen in muscle cells; **haptoglobin** (Greek *haptein*, fasten), a protein in plasma that binds with free haemoglobin so it can be removed by the liver; **methaemoglobin** (US **methemoglobin**), an oxidized form of haemoglobin which cannot transport oxygen around the body.

-glossia *Speech or language.* [Greek *glōssa*, tongue.]

Examples include **ankyloglossia** (Greek *ankulos*, crooked), the state of being tongue-tied, **diglossia**, the presence of two parallel forms of a language in one society for different functions, and **heteroglossia**, the presence of two or more voices or expressed viewpoints in one artistic work.

gloss(o)- Also **glott(o)-**. *The tongue; speech or language.* [Greek *glōssa* or *glōtta*, tongue.]

Some examples are medical terms, such as **glossitis**, inflammation of the tongue, and **glossodynia** (Greek *odunē*, pain), pain in it. The adjective **glossopharyngeal** refers to a nerve that controls both the tongue and pharynx. The *glottis* is the part of the larynx that contains the vocal cords.

A second group refers to a function of the tongue, the power of speech or language, for example **glossolalia**, the ability apparently to speak in unknown languages; **glottochronology**, the use of statistical techniques to date when languages diverged from their common sources; a **glossary** is an alphabetical list with brief explanations of terms used in a special field.

-glot *Language.* [Greek *glōtta*, tongue.]

Two common adjectives contain this form: *monoglot* (Greek *monos*, alone), knowing or using only one language, as opposed to *polyglot* (Greek *polloi*, many) for several (both words can also be nouns to identify individuals with these characteristics).

glotto-: *see* GLOSSO-

gluco-: *see* GLYCO-

glut- *Gluten.* [From Latin *gluten*, glue.]

Gluten is a sticky nitrogenous protein material present in wheat flour. Words beginning in **glut-** refer to related chemical compounds, such as the amino acids *glutamine* and *glutamic acid*; salts of the latter are *glutamates*, as in the taste-enhancing food additive *monosodium glutamate*; *glutaminase* is an enzyme that breaks down glutamine to glutamic acid.

gluteo- Before a vowel **glut-**. *The buttocks.* [Greek *gloutos*, buttock.]

Gluteus (plural *glutei*) is the name given to any of the three large muscles in each buttock which move the thigh, for which the related adjective is *gluteal*; *gluteofemoral* refers to the buttock and thigh considered together.

glyc(o)- Also **gluc(o)-**. *Sugar.* [Greek *glukus*, sweet.]

The first substance named using **glyco-** was *glycerine* (now more usually *glycerol*, especially in scientific contexts), because it tasted sweet. **Gluco-** was first used in the name of the important sugar *glucose*.

In modern chemistry **glyco-** is more common than **gluco-**, and refers to the sugars, which in combination make up the carbohydrates and starches. So a *glycoside* is a compound produced from any of the simple sugars, a *glycogen* is a substance deposited in bodily tissues as a store of carbohydrates and a *glycoprotein* is a protein with carbohydrate groups attached.

Some compounds in **gluco-** relate to any sugar, such as *glucocorticoid*, one of a group involved in the metabolism of carbohydrates. However, most current words including it refer specifically to glucose: a *glucoside* is a glycoside that derives from glucose alone, a *glucan* is a complex sugar containing only glucose units, and *glucagon* is a hormone in the pancreas that promotes the breakdown of glycogen to glucose.

gnath(o)- *The jaw.* [Greek *gnathos*, jaw.]

The *gnathion* is the lowest point of the midline of the lower jaw; *gnathology* is the dental study of the process of chewing; the adjectives *gnathal* and (less commonly) *gnathic* refer to the jaw. In biology, *Gnathostoma* (Greek *stoma*, mouth) is a genus of parasitic nematodes.

-gnomy *Knowledge.* [Greek *gnōmē*, an opinion or maxim.]

The only common word in this form is *physiognomy*, a person's facial features, especially as a guide to character or origin. Rarer examples include *chirognomy* (Greek *kheir*, hand), the art of estimating character by inspecting the hand, and *craniognomy*, the study of the form and character of the skull.

-gnosis Also **-gnostic**. *Knowledge; recognition.* [Greek *gnōsis*, knowledge.]

Diagnosis (Greek *dia*, apart) is the identification of an illness by examining its symptoms, while a *prognosis* (Greek *pro-*, before) is a forecast of the likely outcome of a disease. *Gnosis* itself refers especially to spiritual knowledge. Other examples are *stereognosis*, the ability to perceive the form of solid objects by touch, and *telegnosis*, the psychic perception of events happening at a distance. Adjectives are formed using **-gnostic**: *diagnostic*, *gnostic* (hence *agnostic*, from Greek *a-*, not or without, relating to a belief that nothing is known or can be known of the nature of God). All these can also be nouns.

-gogue: *see* -AGOGUE

gon-: *see* GONO-

-gon *A plane figure with a specified number of straight sides.* [Greek *-gōnos*, angled.]

Terms mainly use Greek numerals to indicate the number of sides (see the table of NUMBER PREFIXES on page 161):

pentagon, *hexagon*, *dodecagon*; *polygon*, many sided. A few employ Latin equivalents: *octagon*, *nonagon*. For the equivalent solid figures, *see* -HEDRON.

gonado-: *see* GONO-

gonio- *Angle.* [Greek *gōnia*, angle.]

A *goniometer* is an instrument that measures angles, especially those between the faces of crystals; *goniometry* is the study of such angular relationships. In medicine, a *gonioscope* is an optical instrument used for viewing otherwise hidden structures within the eye; *goniotomy* (Greek *-tomia*, cutting) is an eye operation for congenital glaucoma in which an incision is made at the junction of the cornea and sclera within the eye.

gon(o)- Also **gonado-**. *Sexual; reproductive.* [Greek *gonos*, semen, seed, generation.]

A *gonad* (*see* -AD[1]) is an organ such as a testis or ovary that produces mature germ cells; in invertebrates, a *gonopore* is an opening through which eggs or sperm are released; *gonorrhoea* (US *gonorrhea*) (Greek *rhoia*, flux) is a contagious infection of the genital tract caused by a bacterium called a *gonococcus*. The form **gonado-** derives from gonad by adding the linking vowel -o-; an example is *gonadotrophin* (Greek *trophē*, nourishment), a hormone secreted by the pituitary which stimulates the action of the gonads.

-gonium *Organs of reproduction.* [Greek *gonos*, race.]

Examples are *archegonium* (Greek *arkhegonos*, founder of a race), the female reproductive organ in ferns and mosses; *oogonium* (Greek *ōion*, egg), either the female sex cells of certain algae and fungi, or the immature female reproductive cells in animals; and *spermatogonium*, a cell produced in the early stages of formation of spermatozoa. An unrelated word is that for the shrubby plant called the *pelargonium*, whose name comes from the Greek *pelargos*, a stork, plus the final part of *geranium*.

-gony *Production, genesis or origination.* [Greek *-gonia*, begetting.]

Cosmogony (Greek *kosmos*, world) is a theory about the creation of the universe, or the branch of science concerned; *sporogony* is the asexual process of spore formation in parasitic sporozoans; *schizogony* (Greek *skhizein*, to split) refers to asexual reproduction by multiple fission; *theogony* (Greek *theos*, god) is the genealogy of a group or system of gods. Whilst *agony* also comes from Greek, it has a different source: *agōn*, contest.

-grade *A division; a method of locomotion.* [Latin *gradus*, a step.]

The sense of a division appears in *centigrade*, having a hundred divisions, particularly as applied to the thermometer scale. The sense of locomotion occurs in *retrograde*, directed or moving backwards, and figuratively in *anterograde* (Latin *ante*, before), directed forwards in time.

The ending often appears in adjectives that indicate methods of animal locomotion: *digitigrade*, walking on the toes or digits; *orthograde*, walking upright (the opposite is *pronograde*, going on all fours; Latin *pronus*, prone); *plantigrade*, walking upon the soles of the feet; and *tardigrade*, moving slowly (Latin *tardus*, slow), a term sometimes applied to the sloths.

Graeco-. In the US, **Greco-**. *Greece; Greek and …* [Latin *Graecus*.]

Examples of a bilateral relationship are *Graeco-Turkish* and *Graeco-Roman*, the latter relating to classical Greece and Rome taken together. *Graecomania* is a passion for all things Greek.

-gram Also **-gramme**. *Something written or recorded in a particular way.* [Greek *gramma*, something written, from *graphein*, to write.]

A few examples came into English through French and retained the French spelling *-gramme*. Modern usage prefers **-gram** and this is now standard in scientific terminology and US English. The only common word in British English that retains the longer form is *programme*, and not even then in computing.

In many cases, a word ending in -*graph* (*see* -GRAPHY) refers to an instrument that produces a written record described by **-gram**—a *cardiogram* is produced by a *cardiograph*, and a **seismogram** by a *seismograph*. A **telegram** is a message sent by *telegraph*. In other cases, they are different names for the same thing, as *pictogram* or *pictograph*, a pictorial symbol for a word or phrase. More rarely, the members of a pair have different senses: a *hologram* is a three-dimensional image formed using laser light but a *holograph* is something handwritten by its author; a *monogram* is a motif formed by intertwined letters, while a *monograph* is a detailed written study on a single specialized topic.

For examples in various senses, see the LIST below.

A number of words have been invented on the model of telegram for greetings messages delivered by a person, often in costume, that are intended to surprise or embarrass the recipient; examples are **kissogram**, **gorillagram**, and **strippergram**.

-gram Something written or recorded in a particular way.

Terms for word skills, or manipulating text, language, or symbols:

anagram	a word formed from another by rearranging its letters	(Greek *ana*, up)
cryptogram	a text written in a code or cipher	(Greek *kruptos*, hidden)
epigram	a brief and pointed witty saying	(Greek *epi*, upon, near to)
lipogram	a composition from which the writer deliberately omits a letter of the alphabet	(Greek *leipein*, to leave out)
monogram	a motif formed by intertwined letters	(Greek *monos*, single)
pictogram	a pictorial symbol for a word or phrase, as in early forms of writing	(Latin *pict-*, painted)

Types of visual representation:

diagram	a simplified graphical representation	(Latin *diagramma*, from Greek *diagraphein*, to mark out by lines)
histogram	a diagram formed from rectangles used in statistics	(Greek *histos*, mask or web)
hologram	a three-dimensional image formed using laser light	(Greek *holos*, whole)
parallelogram	a four-sided plane figure with opposite sides parallel	(Greek *parallēlos*, alongside another)
pentagram	a five-pointed star, often a mystical or magical symbol	(Greek *pente*, five)
stereogram	an image that gives a three-dimension representation of an object, or a stereo radiogram.	(Greek *stereos*, solid)

Words for the written results of tests or investigations:

audiogram	a written record of a test of a person's hearing	(Latin *audire*, hear)
cardiogram	a record of muscle activity within the heart produced by a *cardiograph*	(Greek *cardia*, heart)
mammogram	an image of the breast formed using X-rays	(Latin *mamma*, breast)
seismogram	a record of earthquakes produced by a seismograph	(Greek *seismos*, earthquake)
spectrogram	a record of a spectrum	(Latin *specere*, to look)

Words ending in **-gram** for weights or masses, such as *kilogram*, are compounds of the unit of mass, *gram*, with a prefix indicating a multiple (see the table of WORDS FOR MULTIPLES on page 127). These derive from the Latin *gramma*, weight.

grand- Also **great-**. *The second degree of parentage or descent.* [From Latin *grandis*, great]

English borrowed this prefix from French, in which it refers only to parentage, as in English *grandfather* and *grandmother* for the parents of one's parent (in general *grandparent*). In French the corresponding term for degrees of descent is *petit*, little, but English adopted **grand-** for both situations, as in *grandson* or *granddaughter* for the child of one's child, or more generally *grandchild*.

Further degrees of separation by generations are indicated by prefixing **great-**: *great-grandfather*, *great-granddaughter*. Both can sometimes be used for relationships at one remove: *great-aunt* (also *grand-aunt*), the aunt of one's father or mother; *great-nephew* (also *grand-nephew*), the son of one's nephew or niece.

grano- *Granite.* [English *granite*.]

This appears in a few terms in mineralogy, such as *granodiorite*, a coarse-grained rock lying between granite and diorite in composition; *granophyre* (Greek *porphureos*, purple), a granitic rock consisting of intergrown feldspar and quartz crystals; *granolithic*, of concrete containing fine granite chippings, used to render floors.

granulo- *A granule.* [Latin *granulum*, granule.]

A *granulocyte* (Greek *kutos*, vessel) is a white blood cell with secretory granules in its cytoplasm; *granulocytosis* is an abnormal increase in their number in the blood; a *granuloma* is a mass of granulation tissue, typically produced in response to infection, inflammation, or the presence of a foreign substance. The adjective *granulometric* relates to the size, distribution, or measurement of grain sizes in sand, rock, or other deposits.

graph(o)- *Writing; the production of images.* [Greek *graphein*, to write, *graphē*, writing.]

Some examples refer specifically to writing: *graphology* is the study of handwriting, for example to infer a person's character; in linguistics, a *grapheme* is the smallest meaningful contrastive unit in a writing system; *graphemics* is the branch of knowledge that deals with systems of written symbols in relation to spoken language; *graphite* is a form of carbon so called because it is used to write or draw with as the main constituent of pencil 'leads'.

In other terms, the sense has been extended to refer to the production of images: *graph*, a diagram showing the relationship between variable quantities; *graphics*, the products of the graphic arts, especially commercial design or illustration; *graphicacy*, on the model of *literacy* or *numeracy*, is the ability to understand maps, graphs, and the like, or to present information by means of diagrams. The adjective *graphical* refers to graphs or visual images; the adjective *graphic* refers to visual art, but also has a figurative sense of giving a vivid picture with explicit detail.

-graphy Also **-graph**, **-graphic**, **-graphical**, and **-grapher**. *Writing; the production of images; descriptive sciences or studies.* [Greek *graphein*, to write.]

The set of words ending in **-graphy** is extremely varied. Terms relate to writing, to the transmission of messages or information over a distance, the production of images of various kinds, a descriptive science or study, or a list. For examples, see the LIST overleaf.

It is common for these terms to have linked words ending in **-graph**, often for the result of the process (as *photography* produces a *photograph*), but sometimes for an instrument involved in a process (*seismograph*, *telegraph*); the names of records produced in such cases often end in -GRAM.

Adjectives may be formed from words ending in **-graphy** or **-graph**, either ending in **-graphic** (*choreographic*,

-graphy   Writing; the production of images; descriptive sciences.
            All word origins are from Greek unless otherwise stated.

Relating directly to writing or the transmission of messages:

biography	an account of a person's life	(*bios*, life)
cryptography	the art of preparing or reading codes or ciphers	(*kruptos*, hidden)
lexicography	the practice of compiling dictionaries	(*lexis*, word)
orthography	spelling, especially correct spelling	(*orthos*, straight)
stenography	writing and transcribing shorthand	(*stenos*, narrow)
telegraphy	the science of transmitting information over a distance	(*tēle-*, far off)

The production of images, graphs, or diagrams:

cartography	the science of drawing maps	(*khartēs*, papyrus leaf)
cinematography	the art of making motion pictures	(*kinēma*, movement)
photography	the taking of photographs	(*phōs*, light)
pornography	writing and images designed to stimulate sexual excitement	(*pornographos*, writing about prostitutes)
radiography	the production of images by X-rays, gamma rays, etc.	(Latin *radius*, a ray)
tomography	a technique for producing a cross-section of the human body by X-rays or ultrasound	(*tomos*, slice or section)
xerography	a dry copying process	(*xēros*, dry)

A descriptive science or study:

choreography	the art of designing steps in ballet or another staged dance, or its associated written notation	(*khoros*, chorus)
cosmography	the science of the universe	(*kosmos*, order, world)
demography	the study of statistics charting changing human populations	(*dēmos*, the people)
ethnography	the study of different peoples	(*ethnos* nation)
geography	the science of the physical features of the earth and their relation to human populations	(*gē*, earth)
oceanography	the science of the sea	(from *ocean*)
petrography	the study of rocks	(*petros*, stone)

A descriptive list of titles, authors, or performers on a specific topic:

bibliography	books	(*biblion*, book)
discography	musical recordings	(English *disc*, a gramophone record)
filmography	films	(English *film*)
webliography	a listing of pages on the World Wide Web	

topographic) or **-graphical** (*geographical, stratigraphical*). In many cases both forms exist. The name of a person engaged in the activity or discipline ends in **-grapher** (*lexicographer, stenographer*). *See also* GRAPHO-, -AL[1], and -Y[3].

gravi- *Weight; gravity.* [Latin *gravitas*, weight.]

Gravimetry is the measurement of weight; *gravitation* is the mutual force of attraction between masses (adjective *gravitational*); the *graviton* is a hypothetical quantum of gravitational energy, regarded as a particle.

great-: *see* GRAND-

Greco-: *see* GRAECO-

gymn(o)- *Bare or naked.* [Greek *gumnos*, naked.]

In classical Greece, a *gumnasion* was a place where young men exercised naked, from which English has derived *gymnasium* and its relatives *gymnast, gymnastic,* and *gymnastics*. The *gymnosophists* (literally, 'naked wise men', from Greek *sophistēs*, a teacher of philosophy) were members of an ancient Hindu sect, known for ascetic behaviour that included wearing few clothes. The prefix appears in a number of biological and botanical terms, including *gymnosperm* for a class of plants—including conifers, cycads, and the ginkgo—whose seeds are not protected by an ovary or fruit.

gynaeco- (In the US **gyneco-**). Also **gynandro-** and **gyn(o)-**. *Female; relating to women.* [Greek *gunaïk-*, from *gunē*, woman or female.]

The branch of medicine that deals with diseases and functions specific to women, especially of the reproductive system, is *gynaecology*. *Gynaecomastia* (Greek *mastos*, breast) is abnormal enlargement of the breasts in men.

The related **gyno-** relates generally to women, as in *gynocentric*, centred on or taking a female or feminist view; *gynarchy* or *gynaecocracy*, rule by women or a woman; and *gynophobia*, extreme or irrational fear of women. In botany, a *gy-*

noecium is the female part of a flower, containing the carpels.

A few words combine the Greek *gunē* with *andros*, man, to make **gynandro-**, to suggest a plant or animal that combines male and female characteristics, as in *gynandromorph*, an abnormal individual, usually an insect, that does so.

-gynous Also **-gyny**. *Of women; female organs.* [Greek *gunē*, woman or female.]

The adjective *misogynous* (Greek *misos*, hatred) refers to hatred of women by men; *polygynous* (Greek *polloi*, many) means having more than one wife; and *androgynous* (Greek *anēr, andr-*, man) means partly male and partly female or of indeterminate sex.

Examples from botany include *epigynous* (Greek *epi*, near to), of a plant or flower that has the ovary enclosed, with the stamens and other floral parts above, as opposed to *hypogynous* (Greek *hupo*, under) in which the situation is reversed, and *perigynous* (Greek *peri*, about, around), where they are at the same level. In social insects such as ants, *monogynous* (Greek *monos*, alone) refers to the state of having only one functioning queen in a colony at a time.

Some terms ending in **-gynous** have related nouns ending in **-gyny** (*see* -Y[3]), as in *androgyny, misogyny,* and *polygyny*.

gyro- *Rotation.* [Greek *guros*, a circle or ring.]

A *gyroscope* is a spinning device used as a navigational device in ships and aircraft (a *gyrocompass*) and as a way to keep an object stable (a *gyrostabilizer*). A rotating charged particle generates a magnetic field, a principle called *gyromagnetism*. A *gyrocopter* (formed on the model of *helicopter*) has an unpowered rotating wing. Someone practising the form of divination called *gyromancy* walked in a circle until they fell down from dizziness, the place in the circle at which they fell giving the required indication.

haem(o)- Also **haema-** and **haemat(o)-**. *Blood.* [Greek *haima, haimat-*, blood.]

Many medical terms contain these forms; in the US, they all begin *hem-*. A few examples of **haemo-**: *haemorrhage* (Greek *rhēgnunai*, burst), a profuse escape of blood from a ruptured blood vessel; *haemoglobin*, a red protein responsible for transporting oxygen in the blood, of which the iron-containing part is the *haem* (US *heme*); *haemophilia* (Greek *philia*, fondness or undue inclination), a medical condition in which the blood does not clot properly.

The longer form **haemato-** is found in *haematocrit* (Greek *kritēs*, judge), the ratio of the volume of red blood cells to the total volume of blood, or an instrument for measuring this; *haematemesis* (Greek *emesis*, vomiting) is vomiting of blood; *haematuria* is the presence of blood in urine.

The ore of iron called *haematite* was so named—from Greek *haimatitēs (lithos)*, blood-like (stone)—because it is a reddish-black mineral.

See also SANGUI-.

-haemia: *see* -AEMIA

hagi(o)- *Saints or holiness.* [Greek *hagios*, holy.]

Hagiography is writing about the lives of saints, or a biography that idealizes its subject; *hagiology* is literature dealing with the lives and legends of saints, while *hagiolatry* (Greek *-latria*, worship) is their worship. A *hagioscope* is a squint, an opening in the wall of a church permitting a view of the altar.

hal(o)- *Halogens; salinity or salt.* [Greek *hals, halo-*, salt or the sea.]

The *halogens* are a group of chemically similar elements that includes fluorine and chlorine, so named because they form salts (called *halides*) with metals; *halogenation* is the substitution of hydrogen atoms in methane by halogen atoms, leading to a *haloform* compound such as chloroform.

The sense of salinity appears in *halophile* (Greek *philos*, loving), an organism, especially a micro-organism, that grows in or can tolerate saline conditions, and *halophyte* (Greek *phuton*, a plant), a plant adapted to growing in saline conditions, for example in a salt marsh.

False friends include *halitosis*, bad breath, from Latin *halitus*, breath; although the *halibut* is a sea fish, its name is actually Middle English for 'holy flatfish', because it was often eaten on holy days; and *halo* comes from Greek *halōs*, in reference to the disc of the sun or moon.

haplo- *Single or simple.* [Greek *haploos*, single.]

In genetics, a *haploid* cell is one that has only a single set of unpaired chromosomes, for example a sperm or egg cell in humans. Organisms which are *haplodiploid* have females which develop from fertilized (diploid) eggs and males from unfertilized (haploid) ones. *See also* DIPLO-.

In writing, *haplography* is the inadvertent omission of a repeated letter or letters (for example, writing *philogy* instead of *philology*, or *Missipi* for *Mississippi*); in speech, *haplology* is a similar omission of a sound or syllable (for example, saying *probly* when *probably* is meant).

hapt(o)- *Binding or fastening; touching.* [Greek *haptein*, fasten.]

A *haptoglobin* is a protein present in blood serum which binds to and removes free haemoglobin from the bloodstream; a *hapten* is a small molecule that can combine with a protein in the body to form an antigen which provokes the production of antibodies. The adjective *haptic* refers to the sense of touch, and *haptics* is the study of that sense and its applications.

-head *The head, in various senses, often figurative.* [English *head*.]

One set of words indicates the front or top part of something: *masthead*, *spearhead*, *warhead*, *pithead*. Another comprises terms for people, frequently derogatory, of which a few are *airhead*, *blockhead*, *chucklehead*, *skinhead*, *egghead*, *fathead*, *slaphead* (a bald person), and *deadhead* (a boring or unenterprising person; in the US also a passenger carried free, or a member of an audience with a free ticket, or a follower of the band *The Grateful Dead*). A third group contains words indicating a person is addicted to some drug: *crackhead*, *pothead*, *hophead* (a drug addict or, in Australia and New Zealand, a heavy drinker). Some indicate a condition or quality (*Godhead*, *maidenhead*), for which the more common suffix is now -HOOD.

hect(o)- Also **hekto-**. *One hundred.* [French; an irregular contraction of the Greek *hekaton*, hundred.]

This is one of the standard SI (Système International) decimal prefixes (see the table of WORDS FOR MULTIPLES on page 127) and appears in such terms as *hectolitre* and *hectometre*. One *hectare* is one hundred ares (an area ten metres square, inconveniently small for land measurement); the associated noun is *hectarage*, equivalent to *acreage*. The spelling **hekto-** is now rare.

-hedron Also **-hedra** and **-hedral**. *A geometrical solid with a specified number of plane faces.* [Greek *hedra*, seat, base.]

A *tetrahedron* is a solid having four plane triangular faces, a triangular pyramid; similarly, other solids with increasing numbers of plane faces have names that are usually based on Greek number prefixes (see the list of NUMBER WORDS on page 162): *octahedron* (eight), *decahedron* (ten), *dodecahedron* (twelve), *icosahedron* (twenty). In general, a *polyhedron* is any solid figure with many plane faces. A few terms relate to the shape of the faces rather than their number: *rhombohedron*,

one with six equal rhombuses as faces; *trapezohedron*, one whose faces are trapeziums or trapezoids. Plurals are traditionally formed ending in **-hedra** (*polyhedra*, *tetrahedra*), but now often in *-s* instead. Related adjectives end in **-hedral** (*octahedral*, *dodecahedral*). For flat geometric figures, *see* -GON.

hekto-: *see* HECTO-

heli- *Helicopter.* [English *helicopter*.]

This was created through an incorrect analysis of *helicopter* as a compound of *heli* and *copter*, though it actually contains HELICO-. A *helipad* is a landing and take-off area for helicopters, often private; a *heliport* is the equivalent of an airport for helicopters. *Heli-skiing* is a sport in which skiers are taken to the top of a mountain by helicopter and ski down from there.

helic(o)- *Spiral; screw.* [Greek *helix*, *helik-*, spiral.]

A *helix* is a spiral formed by a wire wound in a single layer around a cylinder or cone, with constant pitch. Something *helical* is spiral in shape, but something *helicoid* is more specifically in the form of a helix. A *helicopter* (Greek *pteron*, a wing) is an aircraft with a rotating wing that behaves like a screw propeller. The plant called the *helichrysum* (Greek *khrusos*, gold) has yellow spiral flowers.

helio- *The Sun.* [Greek *hēlios*, sun.]

The Sun is at the centre of the solar system, which is therefore *heliocentric*; the *heliosphere* is the volume of space, enclosing the solar system, in which the solar wind has a significant influence. A *heliograph* is either a type of telescope for photographing the Sun, or a signalling device that reflects sunlight off a mirror. *Heliotherapy* is the therapeutic use of sunlight. *Heliotrope* (Greek *trepein*, to turn) is a plant of the borage family whose flowers turn towards the Sun; it has purple flowers, so the word can also refer to that colour. A beautiful variety of clear yellow beryl is called *heliodor* (literally 'a gift from the Sun', from Greek *dōron*, gift).

hema- or **hemato-**: *see* HAEMO-

hemi- *Half; a part.* [Greek *hēmi-*, half.]

A *hemisphere* is half a sphere; a *hemicycle* is a semicircular shape or structure (adopted for the seating in the European Parliament); *hemiplegia* (Greek *plēgē*, stroke) is paralysis of one side of the body. In poetry, a *hemistich* (Greek *stikhos*, line of verse) is half a line of verse and in British musical usage a *hemidemisemiquaver* is a note with the time value of half a demisemiquaver, a 64th note.

Rather than strictly one half, it can sometimes mean 'part of' or 'a lesser constituent', as in *hemicellulose*, substances which occur in the cell walls of plants and are polysaccharides of simpler structure than cellulose, and *hemiparasite*, a plant which obtains or may obtain part of its food by parasitism but which also photosynthesizes (an example is mistletoe).

See also DEMI- and SEMI-.

-hemia: *see* -AEMIA

hemo-: *see* HAEMO-

hendeca- *Eleven.* [Greek *hendeka*, eleven.]

This form is rare, the only words at all met with being *hendecasyllable*, a line of verse containing eleven syllables; *hendecagon*, a plane figure with eleven straight sides and angles; and *hendecahedron*, a solid figure with eleven faces. Its Latin equivalent UNDECA- is often preferred.

hepat(o)- Occasionally **hepar-**. *The liver.* [Greek *hēpar*, *hēpat-*, liver.]

Hepatitis is inflammation of the liver; a *hepatoma* is a cancer of its cells; *hepatectomy* (Greek *ektomē*, excision) is its removal; *hepatocytes* are the principal cell type in it; *hepatology* is its study; an *hepatotoxic* agent is damaging to liver cells; the usual adjective referring to the liver is *hepatic*. The anticoagulant drug *heparin* is so called because it was first isolated from the liver. Some terms refer to the liver plus another part of the body: *hepatojugular*, *hepatoduodenal*.

hepta- *Seven.* [Greek *hepta*, seven.]

A *heptagon* is a plane figure with seven sides; a *heptahedron* is a solid one with seven faces. A *heptarchy* (Greek *arkhia*, rule) is a state or region consisting of seven smaller, autonomous regions, or government by seven rulers; a *heptathlon* (Greek *athlon*, contest) is an athletics contest in which competitors take part in a set of seven events. *Heptachlor* is a chlorinated hydrocarbon used as an insecticide whose molecule contains seven chlorine atoms; the *heptoses* are a group of sugars whose molecules each contain seven carbon atoms. *See also* SEPTI-.

hernio- *Hernia.* [English *hernia*.]

Herniography is the radiological examination of a hernia; a *herniorrhaphy* (Greek *rhaptein*, to stitch or sew) or *hernioplasty* (Greek *plastos*, formed, moulded) is an operation to repair a hernia; a *herniotomy* (Greek -*tomia*, cutting) is a surgical procedure to reduce a hernia by cutting.

hetero- *Different or other.* [Greek *heteros*, other.]

This prefix is common and active and is often contrasted with HOMO-, the same. An example is *heterosexual*, of a person who is sexually attracted to the opposite sex, as opposed to *homosexual*. A *heterodox* (Greek *doxa*, opinion) opinion is one that does not conform to accepted or orthodox standards; something *heterogeneous* (Greek *genos*, race or kind) is diverse in character or content, or composed of parts of different kinds; *heterogametic* refers to the sex that produces different types of sex chromosomes (in humans the male, in birds, the female); *heterozygous* describes an individual having two different alleles of a particular gene or genes, and so giving rise to varying offspring.

hex(a)- *Six.* [Greek *hex*, six.]

A *hexagon* is a six-sided plane figure, while a *hexahedron* is a solid figure with six plane faces. A *hexameter* (Greek *metron*, measure) is a line of verse that consists of six metrical feet. In architecture a *hexastyle* is a six-columned portico (Greek *stulos*, column); in music, a *hexachord* is a scale of six notes. A *hexad* is a group or set of six. In computing, the *hexadecimal* number system is one based on sixteen. In chemistry, *hexane* is a hydrocarbon containing six carbon atoms; a *hexose* is a member of a group of simple sugars whose molecules contain six carbon atoms, such as glucose and fructose. *See also* SEXI-.

Hibern(o)- *Irish; Irish and*…[Latin *Hibernus*, Irish.]

The adjective *Hibernian* refers to or concerns Ireland, and can also be a noun indicating a native of Ireland (the word is now most common in set names, such as *Royal Hibernian Academy*); some hyphenated terms refer to varieties of a language as spoken or written in Ireland: *Hiberno-English*, *Hiberno-Saxon*, *Hiberno-Latin*.

hidro- *Sweat.* [Greek *hidrōs*, sweat.]

Hidrosis is the medical term for sweating, but it more commonly occurs in compounds relating to abnormal medical conditions: *hyperhidrosis* (Greek *huper*, over, beyond), excessive sweating, and *anhidrosis* (Greek *an-*, not or without), inadequate sweating; a *hidrocystoma* is a benign cyst containing fluid.

hier(o)- *Sacred or holy.* [Greek *hieros*, sacred.]

Most common terms are figurative: *hierarchical* refers to people or things arranged in order of rank in a *hierarchy* (Greek *arkhein*, to rule; the earliest sense was of a system of orders of angels and heavenly beings); a *hieroglyph* (Greek *gluphē*, carving) is a stylized picture representing a word, syllable, or sound, of which early examples occurred in ancient Egyptian sacred writings; similarly, the adjective *hieratic*, priestly, can often refer to the ancient Egyptian writing of abridged *hieroglyphics*. A *hierophant* (Greek *phainein*, reveal) is a person, especially a priest, who interprets sacred mysteries or esoteric principles; *hierocracy* (Greek *kratia*, rule) is rule by priests.

hind- *At the back; posterior.* [Middle English *hind*, at the back.]

Some examples relating to parts of a body are *hindquarters*, *hindwing*, and *hindbrain* (the lower part of the brain-

stem). Something or someone *hindmost* is the furthest back; *hindsight* is understanding a situation only after it has happened. A *hindrance*, something causing resistance or delay, comes from the related verb *hinder*.

hipp(o)- *Horse.* [Greek *hippos*, horse.]

Most terms are figurative: *hippodrome* now occurs in the names of theatres, but in ancient Greece or Rome it was a course for chariot or horse races (Greek *dromos*, race or course); etymologically speaking, the large semi-aquatic African mammal called a *hippopotamus* is a river horse (Greek *potamos*, river); the *hippocampus* (Greek *kampos*, sea monster) is one of the elongated ridges in each lateral ventricle of the brain, so called because it was thought to look like a fish called the seahorse. Literal terms are rare: *hippuric acid* is a compound present in the urine of herbivores and other mammals, especially horses, from which it was first obtained. The *Hippocratic* oath taken by doctors comes instead from the name of the classical Greek physician Hippocrates.

Hispan(o)- *Spanish; Spanish and*…[Latin *Hispanus*, Spanish.]

A *Hispanophile* is a lover of Spain or the Spanish people or language; a *Hispanist* (less often *Hispanicist*) is an expert in or student of the language, literature, and civilization of Spain and the Spanish-speaking countries of South America; an *Hispanic* is a Spanish-speaking person, especially one of Latin American descent, living in the US. Terms such as *Hispano-American* and *Hispano-German* refer to links between countries or peoples.

hist(o)- *Organic tissue.* [Greek *histos, histion*, web or tissue.]

Histology is the study of the microscopic structure of tissues, while *histochemistry* is the study of their chemical constituents; *histocompatibility* refers to compatibility between the tissues of individuals, so that one can accept a graft from the other without inducing an immune reaction; *histamine* is a compound present in most body tissues which is released in response to injury and in allergic and inflammatory reactions. *Histogram*, a diagram consisting of rectangles whose area is proportional to the frequency of a variable, comes from the same Greek root in its sense of a web.

-holic: *see* -AHOLIC

hol(o)- *Whole or complete.* [Greek *holos*, whole.]

Though *holocaust* (Greek *kaustos*, burnt) literally means something entirely consumed by fire, it is usually applied to destruction or slaughter on a mass scale, particularly the mass murder of Jews and others under the German Nazi regime; *holistic* refers to the view that the whole is greater than the sum of its parts, especially in medicine, where it refers to treatment of the whole person and their circumstances; a *hologram* is a three-dimensional image formed by the interference of light, so named because it captures the whole scene, including information about depth and position. A *holograph* is a manuscript entirely hand-written by its author.

homeo- Also **homoio-** and **homoeo-**. *Similar.* [Greek *homoios*, like or similar.]

In *homeopathy* (Greek *patheia*, suffering or feeling) disease is treated by minute doses of substances that in a healthy person would produce symptoms of the disease, so treating like with like. *Homeostasis* is the tendency for plant and animal populations to remain in stable equilibrium; two geometrical figures are *homeomorphic* if they are topologically equivalent, as a circle can be converted to a square.

Most words once written using **homoeo-** (*homoeopath*, *homoeobox*) or **homoio-** (*homoiothermic*) are now usually spelled with **homeo-** instead. Exceptions are those that are mainly historical in application, such as *homoiousian*, a person who held that God the Father and God the Son are of like but not identical substance.

homo-¹ *The same.* [Greek *homos*, same.]

Things that are *homogeneous* are of the same kind or alike; to *homogenize* something is to make all its parts uniform or similar (as in bringing the fat droplets in milk to a common small size so it emulsifies); things that are *homocentric* have the same centre (but see the next entry); those that are *homologous* (Greek *logos*, ratio or proportion) are of the same essential nature.

Someone *homosexual* is sexually attracted to a person of his or her own sex (as opposed to *heterosexual*, *see* HETERO-). The link between **homo-** and *homosexuality* is sufficiently strong that in a few terms the prefix relates specifically to it: *homoerotic*, concerning or arousing sexual desire centred on a person of the same sex; and *homophobia*, an irrational aversion to homosexuality and homosexuals.

This and the sense explained in the next entry are sometimes confused.

hom(o)-² *Man; human being.* [Latin *homo*, man.]

The adjective *homocentric* refers to a view that humankind is the central or most important element of existence; a *hominid* is a primate of a family which includes humans and their fossil ancestors; *homage* originally referred to the ceremony by which a vassal declared himself to be his lord's 'man'; a *homunculus* is a very small human or humanoid creature; *human* comes from the same root. See also the previous entry as well as ANDRO- and -ANDROUS.

-hood *A group of people; a condition or quality.* [Old English *-hād*, originally an independent noun meaning 'person, condition, quality'.]

Examples in which the sense is of a group include *brotherhood*, *sisterhood*, and *priesthood*. In *neighbourhood*, it now has a weaker sense of an area of a town rather than the group of one's neighbours. The more common usage is of a condition or quality, as in *childhood*, *adulthood*, *motherhood*, *falsehood*, *likelihood*, and *livelihood*. *See also* -HEAD.

hyal(o)- *Glassy or transparent.* [Greek *hualos*, glass.]

Hyalin is a clear substance produced especially by the degeneration of epithelial or connective tissues; something *hyaline* has a glassy, translucent appearance, as does *hyaloid*, which often refers particularly to the vitreous humour of the eye. The mineral *hyalite* is a translucent, colourless variety of opal.

hydr(o)-¹. *Water.* [Greek *hudōr*, *hudro-*, water.]

A *hydrant* supplies water for fire-fighting; a *hydroelectric* system generates electricity using flowing water; a *hydrofoil* is a boat fitted with shaped vanes or foils which lift the hull clear of the water at speed; *hydrophobia* is fear of water, especially as a symptom of rabies in humans; *hydroponics* (Greek *ponos*, labour) is the process of growing plants using liquid nutrients without soil. *Hydrocephalus* is a condition in which fluid accumulates in the brain. A *hydrate* is a compound in which water molecules are chemically bound to another compound or an element; *hydrolysis* is the chemical breakdown of a compound by reaction with water. In some terms, the sense has been broadened to 'liquid' or 'fluid', as in *hydraulic*, relating to operation of a machine by a fluid under pressure, or *hydrodynamics*, the branch of science concerned with forces acting on or exerted by fluids of any type.

hydr(o)-² *Hydrogen.* [Greek *hudōr*, *hudro-*, water.]

Hydrogen is the 'water maker' because it produces water when burned in air or oxygen; *hydrochloric acid* is a strongly acidic solution of the gas hydrogen chloride in water; the *hydroxonium* ion is H_3O^+, the hydrated hydrogen ion. A *hydrocarbon* is a compound of hydrogen and carbon; a *hydride* is a binary compound of hydrogen with a metal; *hydrazine* (**hydro-** plus AZO- and -INE) is a fuming liquid often used as a rocket fuel; *hydrogenation* is the chemical addition of hydrogen to a substance. *See also* DEHYDRO-.

hydroxy- Also **hydroxo-**. *Hydroxyl; hydroxide.* [English *hydroxyl*.]

The *hydroxyl* group is the radical —OH; a *hydroxide* is a compound of a metal with it; generally a *hydroxylic* compound contains the hydroxyl radical; to *hydroxylate* a compound is to introduce the hydroxyl group into it. The mineral *hydroxyapatite*, a complex form of calcium phosphate, is the main inorganic constituent of tooth enamel and bone. Several drug names indicate the presence of a hydroxyl group: *hydroxocobalamin* is a cobalt-containing drug administered in cases of vitamin B_{12} deficiency; *hydroxyprogesterone* is a synthetic female sex hormone.

hygr(o)- *Moisture or humidity.* [Greek *hugros*, wet.]

A *hygrometer* is an instrument that measures humidity; a *hygrostat* is an apparatus that maintains constant humidity; a *hygroscopic* substance is one that tends to absorb moisture from the air.

hylo- *Woodlands or wood; matter.* [Greek *hulē*, wood, material, or matter.]

Some instances refer to wood or woodlands, as in *Hylobates* (Greek *bainein*, to go), the genus of the tree-living gibbons. The broader sense of 'matter' appears in *hylomorphism* (Greek *morphē*, form) the doctrine that matter is the first cause of the universe and that physical objects result from the combination of matter with form, and *hylozoism* (Greek *zōē*, life), the doctrine that all matter has life.

hymen(o)- *A membrane; the hymen.* [Greek *humēn*, membrane.]

The *hymen* is a membrane which partially closes the opening of the vagina in virginal women; *hymenectomy* (Greek *ektomē*, excision) is its surgical excision. In some fungi, the *hymenium* is a surface consisting mainly of spore-bearing structures; any fungal structure which bears one is a *hymenophore*. The *Hymenoptera* (Greek *pteron*, wing) is a large order of insects that includes the bees, wasps, and sawflies, so called because its members have transparent or membranous wings.

hyper- *Excessive; above normal.* [Greek *huper*, over or beyond.]

A person who is *hypercritical* is excessively and unreasonably critical, while someone or something *hypersensitive* is abnormally or exceedingly sensitive. *Hyperbole* (Greek *ballein*, to throw) is exaggerated statements or claims not meant to be taken literally. In medicine, *hypertension* is abnormally high blood pressure; *hyperthermia* is the condition of having a body temperature greatly above normal; a patient who *hyperventilates* breathes at an abnormally rapid rate.

The basis of the World Wide Web is *hypertext*, a tagging system that goes beyond text to allow cross-referencing between related material. A *hypercube* is a geometrical figure similar to a cube but in four or more dimensions; *hyperspace* is space of more than three dimensions, or in science fiction a notional space–time continuum in which it is possible to travel faster than light.

Hyper can also be a word in its own right—a shortening of *hyperactive*—for someone who is unusually energetic.

Hyper- can easily be confused with its opposite HYPO-, because they are pronounced similarly in compounds. *See also* SUPER-.

hypn(o)- *Sleep; hypnosis.* [Greek *hupnos*, sleep.]

The adjective *hypnagogic* (or *hypnogogic*) refers to the semiconscious state immediately before falling asleep (Greek *agōgos*, leading to); its opposite is *hypnopompic* (Greek *pompē*, sending away); in medicine, a *hypnotic* is one of a class of drugs that induces sleep; *hypnopaedia* is learning by listening to recordings during sleep.

Hypnosis is a trance-like state that resembles sleep, induced by the monotonous repetition of words or gestures. Some terms beginning in **hypno-** refer to the state: *hypnogenesis* is its induction, and *hypnotherapy* is its use as a therapeutic technique; hypnotic can also be an adjective relating to this state, or to something compelling or soporific.

hypo- *Under; below normal; slightly.* [Greek *hupo*, under.]

A *hypodermic* syringe (Greek *derma*, skin) is one that injects a drug below the skin; *hypotension* is abnormally low blood pressure; *hypoglycaemia* is deficiency of glucose in the bloodstream; *hypothermia* is the condition of having a low body temperature, usually dangerously so.

Several words were imported from Greek, and the sense in these is usually figurative: *hypothesis*, a provisional explanation, comes from Greek *hupothesis*, foundation; *hypocrite*, someone claiming to have better standards or beliefs than is the case, is from Greek *hupokrinesthai*, to play a part or pretend, from *krinein*, to judge; *hypochondriac*, somebody abnormally anxious about their health, derives from Greek *hupokhondria*, the soft body area below the ribs in which melancholy was once thought to be based.

In chemistry, the prefix refers to a compound containing an element with an unusually low valency, as in the bleaching agent *hypochlorite*, or the photographer's *hypo* from sodium *hyposulphite* (now more usually *sodium thiosulfate*).

The prefix is sometimes confused with HYPER-.

hypso- *Height; elevation.* [Greek *hupsos*, height.]

Hypsography is the measurement and mapping of heights above sea level; a *hypsometer* is an instrument for measuring the altitude of points on the earth's surface by testing the boiling point of water; a *hypsodont* (Greek *odous*, *odont-*, tooth) is a tooth having a high crown and a short root.

hyster(o)- *Uterus.* [Greek *hustera*, womb.]

A *hysterectomy* (Greek *ektomē*, excision) is removal of the uterus; a *hysteroscope* (or *uteroscope*) is an instrument for inspecting the interior of the uterus; *hysterography* is the use of X-rays and related techniques to assess the condition of the uterus. The medical condition called *hysteria* involving exaggerated or uncontrollable emotion or excitement was once thought to be exclusively a female condition, due to a malfunction of the womb. *Hysteresis*, a retardation or lagging of the production of an effect after its cause, comes instead from Greek *husteros*, later.

-i¹ *Forming plurals.* [Latin or Italian plural endings.]

Some Latin nouns ending in *-us* that form their plurals in *i* usually retain that plural form in English: *bacilli*, *fungi*, *gladioli*, *narcissi*, *stimuli*. Many, however, have adopted English plurals completely (*viruses*), or can use either (*foci* or *focuses*; *radii* or *radiuses*).

Other examples are plurals of Italian nouns, either those ending in *-e* (*cognoscenti*, *dilettanti*), or in *-o* (*bambini*, *divertimenti*). Some Italian plurals for things that are not individually counted have become mass nouns, grammatically singular (*confetti*, *macaroni*, *spaghetti*); at one time *graffiti* seemed to be going the same way, but the singular *graffito* is now often encountered. Some examples are acknowledged to be plurals but their singulars are uncommon (*biscotti*).

Other English nouns ending in *-i* derive from other languages: Japanese (*origami*, *sushi*), Arabic (*alkali*), Urdu (*biriani*), Hindi (*basmati*).

-i² *Adjectives and nouns relating to countries.* [Semitic and Indo-Iranian adjectival endings.]

The countries are in the Near or Middle East or South Asia, and the forms can either be adjectives relating to the country, or nouns for a native or national of the country: *Azeri*, *Azerbaijani*, *Bangladeshi*, *Bengali*, *Hindi*, *Israeli*, *Kuwaiti*, *Nepali*, *Pakistani*.

-i- *A connecting vowel.* [From Latin.]

In Latin this is a regular part of word formation. As a result, it occurs in many words borrowed into English either directly from Latin or through French, for example *omnivorous*, *uniform*, and *pacific*. On the model of these and others, it has come to be used in words created in English. These can be formed from words which are ultimately of Latin origin, such as *calciferous* (containing or produc-

cing calcium salts, from Latin *calx*, *calc-*, lime), ultimately from Greek, such as *amoebiform* (like an amoeba, from Greek *amoïbē*, change, alternation), or even from those not of classical origin, such as *tickicide* (a substance that kills ticks, *see* -CIDE). It occurs particularly before an ending of Latin origin such as -ANA, -FEROUS, -FIC, -FORM, -FY, -GEROUS, or *-vorous* (*see* -VORE). See also -O-.

-ia *Forming nouns.* [Latin or Greek noun endings.]

Some nouns with this ending have been adopted unchanged from classical Latin or Greek: *fascia*, *mania*, *militia*, *onomatopoeia* (the formation of a word from a sound associated with what is named). Some terms created in recent centuries but based on Latin or Greek also contain it: *encyclopedia*, *utopia*.

A second set comprises names of medical states and disorders which are derived from Latin or Greek roots: *anorexia*, *catatonia*, *chlamydia*, *diphtheria*, *dyslexia*, *hysteria*, *paraplegia*, *pneumonia*.

The ending occurs in many names for living things, which are often derived from proper names. Most are of plants: *dahlia*, *gardenia*, *lobelia*, *magnolia*, *poinsettia*, *wisteria*. A few are of other organisms: *latimeria* (a genus of coelacanth), *leishmania* (a genus of a single-celled parasitic protozoan). See also -A².

A number of country and other place names end in **-ia**: *Bohemia*, *Cambodia*, *India*, *Nigeria*, *Russia*, *Sardinia*, *Virginia*. It also marks the names of some oxides of metallic elements whose names end in -IUM: *lithia*, *magnesia*, *thoria*, *zirconia*.

See also -AEMIA, -ALIA, -ALGIA, -DELIC (for *-delia*), -MANIA, -OPIA, -PHILE (for *-philia*), -PHOBIA, -TERIA, and -URIA.

-iac: *see* -AC

-ial: *see* -AL

-ian Also **-an**. *Forming adjectives and nouns.* [Latin adjectival endings *-anus*, *-ana*, *-anum*, 'of or belonging to something'.]

The original form was **-an**, as in *urban* (Latin *urbanus*, from *urbs*, city) and *Roman* (Latin *Romanus*, from *Roma*, Rome). However, many Latin words had an *i* before the ending (as in *meridian*, from Latin *meridianum*, noon; *see* -I-) and other examples ending in **-ian** come from French words ending in *-ien* (as in *civilian*, from Old French *civilien*) that are derived from Latin. As a result, the usual form is now **-ian**, though it is truncated to **-an** if the stem ends in a vowel.

One set is of adjectives that refer to places: *Australian*, *Chicagoan*, *Indian*, *Kenyan*, *Malayan*, *Nebraskan*, *Parisian*, *Puerto Rican*, *Scandinavian*, *Tibetan*, and so on. Some modify the stem: *Glaswegian*, *Norwegian*, *Peruvian*. Most can also be nouns that identify a person from that place.

Some adjectives derive from individuals' names and refer to a style or characteristic associated with that person. Many examples exist; new ones are created freely according to need. Some examples are *Chestertonian*, *Clintonian*, *Hogarthian*, *Johnsonian*, *Nabokovian*, and *Orwellian*. Some relate to periods of history named after monarchs: *Edwardian*, *Elizabethan*, *Victorian*.

Some personal names appear in adjectives and nouns that refer to systems of thought or belief, the founders of such systems, or their proponents: *Copernican*, *Darwinian*, *Freudian*, *Hegelian*, *Lutheran*. Others with related meanings are formed on a variety of stems: *Episcopalian*, *Presbyterian*, *Puritan*, *Republican*, *utopian*.

The endings also occur in nouns that denote someone who engages in, uses, or works with whatever is referenced by the stem: *comedian*, *equestrian*, *historian*, *pedestrian*, *sacristan*, *thespian*.

See also -ANE, -ARIAN, -EAN, -ENNE, -ICIAN, -MAN, and -WOMAN.

-iana: *see* -ANA

-iasis: *see* -ASIS

-iast: *see* -AST

-iatric Also **-iatrical**, **-iatrics**, **-iatrician**, **-iatrist**, and **-iatry**. *Medical practice or treatment.* [Greek *iatros*, doctor.]

Forms ending in **-iatric** are adjectives: *geriatric* (Greek *gēras*, old age), of the health care of old people; *paediatric* (US *pediatric*) (Greek *pais*, *paid-*, child, boy), of the care of children and their diseases; *psychiatric* (Greek *psukhē*, soul or mind), of mental illness or its treatment; **-iatrical** is a rarer equivalent (*psychiatrical*). Nouns for the medical specialisms are formed with **-iatrics** (*geriatrics*) or **-iatry** (*psychiatry*). Names for the specialists end in **-iatrist** (*psychiatrist*) or **-iatrician** (*geriatrician*). *See also* -IC, -ICS, -IAN, -IST, and -Y.

iatro- *A physician or medical treatment.* [Greek *iatros*, physician.]

The only common term here is *iatrogenic*, relating to illness caused by medical examination or treatment. *Iatrochemistry* is a school of thought of the 16th and 17th centuries which sought to understand medicine and physiology in terms of chemistry; *iatrology* is a rare term for the science of medicine.

-iatry: *see* -IATRIC

Ibero- *Iberian; Iberian and …* [Greek *Iberia*.]

This can refer to *Iberian* in any of its senses: of ancient Iberia in the Caucasus (*Ibero-Caucasian*, a group of languages spoken in the region); of the countries of Spain and Portugal (as in *Ibero-French*); of the extinct Romance language spoken in the Iberian peninsula (sometimes called *Ibero-Romance*); or of the similarly extinct Celtic language of the area.

-ibility, **-ible**, or **-ibly**: *see* -ABLE

-ic Also **-ick**, **-ique**, **-ical**, and **-icity**. *Forming adjectives and some nouns.* [French *-ique*, Latin *-icus*, or Greek *-ikos*.]

A very large number of adjectives ending in **-ic** exist, of which a few examples are *aquatic*, *bucolic*, *chronic*, *drastic*, *electric*, *heroic*, and *terrific*.

In chemistry, the **-ic** ending forms adjectives indicating an element in a higher valency compared with a form ending in -OUS: *cupric*, *ferric*, *nitric*, *sulphuric*.

Some examples, though principally adjectives, can also be nouns (*cosmetic*, *lunatic*, *lyric*); some are now primarily nouns (*arithmetic*, *mechanic*, *mimic*, *picnic*, *sceptic*), though a number can also act as adjectives. Some noun examples mark a particular instance of a noun that ends in -ICS (*aesthetic*, *ethic*, *mnemonic*, *statistic*, *tactic*).

Nouns ending in -**ic** often have linked adjectives ending in -**ical** (*lyrical*, *tactical*). Many other examples of adjectives with this ending exist, such as *chemical*, *farcical*, *practical*, and *vertical*. In many cases both forms exist (*classic* and *classical*; *historic* and *historical*); sometimes these have slightly different senses, but often they are interchangeable (*comic* or *comical*; *geographic* or *geographical*; *symmetric* or *symmetrical*) and the choice is often personal, or set by a house style, or to suit the rhythm of the sentence.

The ending -**icity** forms abstract nouns indicating a quality or condition (*authenticity*, *electricity*, *toxicity*).

The spelling -**ick** (*Gothick*, *musick*) is now archaic or deliberately used as an archaism. A few words retain the French spelling -**ique** (*mystique*, *physique*, *unique*).

See also -ICIAN, -ICS, -ITIC, -ITY, -LY, and -OIC.

-**ice** *Forming nouns.* [Old French -*ice*, from Latin -*itia*, -*itius*, -*itium*.]

Examples include *avarice*, *cowardice*, *jaundice*, *justice*, *malice*, *notice*, *novice*, *precipice*, and *service*. Some words have come from other sources and have taken on the same ending by a process of assimilation: *accomplice*, *apprentice*, *crevice*, *lattice*, *poultice*, and *practice*. *See also* -ISE[2].

ichthyo- *Fish; fishlike.* [Greek *ikhthus*, fish.]

Ichthyology is the branch of zoology that deals with fishes; *ichthyosis* is a congenital skin condition which causes the epidermis to become dry and horny like fish scales; an *ichthyosaur* is a fossil marine reptile of the Mesozoic era; some-

one who is *ichthyophagous* (Greek *phagein*, eat) eats a lot of fish.

-**ician** *Also* -**icist**. *Nouns denoting occupations.* [Mainly from English words ending in -IC or -ICS.]

Some examples ending in -**ician** are *clinician*, *electrician*, *magician*, *mathematician*, *optician*, and *technician*. Examples ending in -**icist** include *ceramicist*, *geneticist*, and *lyricist*. The two forms are equivalent in meaning and there is no clear rule about which is used on which stem; *physician* and *physicist* both derive from Latin *physica*, natural things, but by different routes and have very different senses. A few words ending in -**ician** have been formed on other English stems, mainly in American English: *beautician*, *mortician*. *See also* -IAN and -IST.

-**ick**: *see* -IC

-**icle**: *see* -CULE

icono- *An image or likeness.* [Greek *eikēn*, likeness.]

Iconology is the study of visual imagery and its symbolism and interpretation, while *iconography* (Greek -*graphia*, writing) is the use or study of images or symbols in the visual arts. An *iconoclast* (Greek *klan*, to break), originally someone who destroyed religious images, is now usually a figurative term for a person who attacks cherished beliefs or institutions; an *iconostasis* (Greek *stasis*, standing, stopping) is a screen bearing icons, separating the sanctuary of many Eastern churches from the nave.

icos- *Also* **eicos-** *Twenty.* [Greek *eikosi*, twenty.]

An *icosahedron* is a solid figure with twenty plane faces, especially equilateral triangular ones; an *icosidodecahedron* (Greek *dodeka*, twelve) is a solid with 32 faces, 20 of them equilateral triangles and 12 regular pentagons. *Eicosapentaenoic acid*, so named because it contains 20 carbon atoms, is a fatty acid found especially in fish oils, a metabolic precursor of prostaglandins; the *eicosanoids* are a group of hormones and other biologically active substances similarly containing 20 carbon atoms, including leucotrienes, prostaglandins, and thromboxanes.

-ics *A subject of study or branch of knowledge.* [French *-iques*, Latin *-ica*, or Greek *-ĭka*, all plural forms.]

A large number of such terms exist, of which a few are *classics*, *ethics*, *genetics*, *mathematics*, *obstetrics*, *politics*, and *statistics*. These are considered to be singular when referring to a subject (*behavioural economics is a young science*), but can be plural if they are used more generally, or preceded by words such as *the*, *his*, *such*, or *their* (*the classics are hardly read these days*). An instance of the subject can sometimes be formed by losing the final letter, so a *statistic* is a statistical item; *see* -IC.

-id¹ *Forming adjectives.* [French *-ide* from Latin *-idus*.]

Examples include *acrid* (Latin *acer*, *acri-*, sharp or pungent), *morbid* (Latin *morbidus*, from *morbus*, disease), *putrid* (Latin *putridus*, from *putrere*, to rot), *stupid* (Latin *stupidus*, from *stupere*, be amazed or stunned), and *torrid* (Latin *torridus*, from *torrere*, parch or scorch). *See also* -OID and -PLOID.

-id² *Forming nouns.* [Either French *-ide*, via Latin *-idis*, or Latin *-ides*, in both cases derived from Greek.]

This ending forms the names of some plants whose family name ends in -ACEAE (*orchid*, family Orchidaceae); of some animals whose taxonomic name ends in -IDAE (*felid*, a mammal of the cat family, Felidae; *noctuid*, a moth of the family Noctuidae); or of plants or animals in classes whose name ends in -IDA (*arachnid*, a member of the class Arachnida).

It is also used to form the names of structural constituents in biology (*chromatid*, each of the two thread-like strands into which a chromosome divides during cell division; *plasmid*, a genetic structure in a cell that can replicate independently of the chromosomes).

In astronomy it can denote a meteor in a shower radiating from a specified constellation (*Geminids*, from Gemini; *Leonids*, from Leo); a *cepheid* is a variable

star like the first one observed, Delta Cephei.

The ending can also indicate a member of a dynasty or family (*Abbasid*, a member of a dynasty of caliphs who ruled in Baghdad from 750 to 1258; *Sassanid*, a member of a dynasty that ruled Persia from the early 3rd century AD until the Arab Muslim conquest of 651).

See also -OID.

-ida Also **-idan**. *Taxonomic groups.* [Latin, the neuter plural of *-ides*, offspring of, from Greek.]

Examples occur in both botany (*Bryopsida*, the class of the true mosses; *Candida*, a genus of yeast that can cause thrush) and zoology (*Arachnida*, the class containing the spiders, mites, and related species; *Pentastomida*, a class of worms that are parasites of the respiratory tract of vertebrates). Adjectives are formed using **-idan** (*arachnidan*).

-idae *Taxonomic groups.* [Latin, from Greek *-idai*, plural of *-idēs*, offspring of.]

In animal classifications, the ending indicates a family (a group of genera): the *Laridae* family contains the gulls and terns; *Amoebidae* the amoebas; *Felidae* the cats, including the lions and tigers. In plants, such names usually refer to a higher classification variously called a superorder or subclass. For example, the *Liliidae* contains the lilies and orchids and the *Rosidae* the roses and many other plants. *See also* -AE and -INAE.

ideo- *Idea.* [Greek *idea*, form.]

An *ideology* is a system of ideas and ideals; an *ideogram* is a character that represents the idea of a thing without indicating the sounds used to say it (examples are numerals and Chinese characters); in medicine the adjective *ideomotor* relates to involuntary movements caused by an idea. This form is easily confused with IDIO-.

-ides Also **-oides**. *Plant and animal genera.* [Greek plural ending *-eidēs*, related to *eidos*, form.]

Terms often contain the linking vowel -o-, present in many Greek source words.

Examples are *Anthropoides*, the genus of the demoiselle cranes; *Lampides*, the genus containing the long-tailed blue butterfly; *Bacteroides*, a genus of bacteria, normally living in the body, which can cause severe infection.

-idine Also **-etidine**, **-iridine**, and **-olidine**. *Organic ring compounds containing nitrogen.* [From -IDE plus -INE³.]

Such names often imply a compound derived from another; for example *toluidine* is toluene plus a nitrogen-containing amino group; *xylidine*, a dye intermediate, is similarly xylene with an amino group added.

These examples are derivatives of monocyclic hydrocarbons; the ending also appears in names for compounds with two rings, such as *benzidine*, another dyestuff intermediate, formed from biphenyl. It also occurs in some names of alkaloids (*quinidine*, an isomer of quinine), certain nucleosides (*cytidine*, a nucleoside obtained from RNA by hydrolysis), and some heterocyclic compounds (*piperidine*, a peppery-smelling liquid used as a solvent).

In systematic chemical naming, the derived forms **-iridine**, **-etidine**, and **-olidine** refer to saturated heterocyclic rings containing nitrogen with respectively three, four, and five atoms in the ring (examples are *aziridine*, *phenetidine*, and *pyrrolidine*).

idio- *Personal; own.* [Greek *idios*, own, distinct.]

Something *idiosyncratic* (Greek *sun*, with, plus *krasis*, mixture) is peculiar to an individual; an *idiom* (Greek *idiōma*, private property, peculiar phraseology) is a group of words established by usage as having a meaning not deducible from those of the individual words; an *idiolect* is the speech pattern peculiar to a particular person; in medicine *idiopathic* denotes any disease or condition which arises spontaneously or for which the cause is unknown. *Idiot* derives from the same root, via Greek *idiōtēs*, a private person, layman, or ignorant person. This form is easily confused with IDEO-.

-idium *A structure in a plant or animal.* [Greek diminutive suffix *-idion*.]

Examples are *antheridium* (Greek *anthos*, flower), the male sex organ of algae, mosses, ferns, fungi, and other non-flowering plants; *basidium* (Greek *basis*, stepping), a microscopic club-shaped spore-bearing structure produced by certain fungi; *nephridium* (Greek *nephros*, kidney), an excretory organ in many invertebrates; *pyxidium* (Greek *puxis*, box), a seed capsule that splits open so that the top comes off like the lid of a box. *See also* -IUM.

-ie: *see* -Y²

-ienne: *see* -ENNE

-ier Also **-yer**. *A person engaged in an occupation or activity.* [Either from Middle English, or via French *-ier* from Latin *-arius*.]

In examples from Middle English, the ending is a variant of -ER¹: *glazier* (Old English *glæs*, glass); *brazier* (Old English *bræs*, brass), a worker in brass. In words like *carrier* and *occupier* the ending is -ER¹ with the *i* converted from the final *y* of the stem. A few are spelled **-yer**, usually following a stem ending in *w*: *lawyer*, *sawyer*.

From the 16th century onwards, many French words ending in **-ier** have been brought into English: *brigadier*, *cavalier*, *costumier*, *croupier*, *financier*, *fusilier*, *hotelier*. *See also* -EER.

-ifera: *see* -FERA

-iferous: *see* -FEROUS

-ific or **-ificent**: *see* -FIC

-ification: *see* -FICATION

-iform: *see* -FORM

-iformes: *see* -FORMES

-ify: *see* -FY

-igerous: *see* -GEROUS

il-: *see* IN-¹ and IN-²

-ile Also **-il** and **-ility** *Forming adjectives and some nouns.* [Via French from Latin *-ilis*.]

Most words ending in **-ile** from this source are adjectives: *agile*, *docile*, *ductile*, *fertile*, *fragile*, *juvenile*, *mobile*, *versatile*, *volatile*. Several in statistics derive from Latin ordinal numerals, as in *decile*, each of ten equal groups into which a population can be divided; others are *quartile*, *quintile*, and *percentile*. A few nouns ending in **-ile** come from Latin words ending in *-ilis*: *reptile* (Latin *reptilis*, from *repere*, crawl), *textile* (Latin *textilis*, from *texere*, to weave). Others (like *exile*, *facsimile*, and *imbecile*) come from different Latin sources.

A few nouns ending in **-il** also derive from Latin *-ilis* (*fossil*, Latin *fossilis*, dug up; *utensil*, Latin *utensilis*, usable). However, most nouns with this ending derive from a variety of other sources, some from Old English (*nostril*), others from various French and Latin sources (*fibril*, *lentil*). The only common adjective ending in **-il** derived from a Latin word in *-ilis* is *civil*.

Abstract nouns are formed from adjectives ending in either **-ile** or **-il** by adding -ITY: *agility*, *civility*, *mobility*, *volatility*. *See also* -PHILE.

ile(o)- *The ileum.* [Medieval Latin *ileum*, a variant of *ilium*, a flank or side, perhaps by confusion with *ileus*, colic.]

The *ileum* is the lowest of the three portions of the small intestine. *Ileitis* is inflammation of the ileum; *ileocolitis* is inflammation of the ileum and the colon; *ileostomy* (Greek *stoma*, mouth) is a surgical operation in which a damaged part is removed and the cut end diverted to an artificial opening in the abdominal wall. Several adjectives refer to the ileum plus another part of the body: *ileocaecal* (US *ileocecal*), ileum plus caecum; *ileoanal*, ileum plus anus; *ileorectal*, ileum plus rectum.

ili(o)- *The ilium.* [Latin *ilium*, flank or side.]

The *ilium* is the large broad bone forming the upper part of each half of the pelvis, the haunch or hip bone. The *iliacus* is a triangular muscle which passes from the pelvis through the groin on either side; the *iliopsoas* is a complex muscle comprising this and the psoas muscle. The usual adjective referring to the ilium is *iliac*; other adjectives refer to it plus another part of the body, often in reference to bands of tissue: *iliotibial* and *iliofemoral*, ilium plus the tibia and femur respectively, the two bones in the lower leg; *ilioinguinal*, the hip plus the groin (the inguinal area).

-ility: *see* -ILE

-ily: *see* -LY

im-: *see* IN-^{1} and IN-^{2}

-im *A plural ending of words from Hebrew.*

Examples include the angelic beings *cherubim* (Hebrew *krūb*) and *seraphim* (Hebrew *srāpīm*), as well as *kibbutzim* (Hebrew *qibbūs*, gathering), communal settlements in Israel, and *goyim* (Hebrew *gōy*, people, nation), an offensive name for a non-Jew.

Some other examples (such as *literatim*, of the copying of a text letter by letter; *passim*, of allusions or references be found at various places throughout the text of a published work; and *seriatim*, taking one subject after another in regular order) derive instead from a Latin adverbial ending.

-imeter: *see* -METER

imid(o)- Also **imin(o)-**. *Various amine derivatives.* [An arbitrary alteration of *amide*.]

Imido- is the combining form relating to *imide*, an organic compound containing the group —CONHCO—. Similarly **imino-** indicates the presence of an *imine* group —C=NH or —C=NR, where R is an alkyl or other group. However, the two are sometimes confused, especially with *iminoester*, a compound containing the group —C(NH)OR, which should strictly be an *imidoester*. **Imido-** is also applied unsystematically to heterocyclic nitrogen compounds such as *imidazole*, an anti-fungal drug, which has a five-membered ring with two nitrogen atoms in it, or *imidocarb*, used to treat tick-borne diseases in domestic animals.

immuno- *Immune or immunity.* [English *immune* plus -O-.]

Immunology is the branch of medicine and biology concerned with immunity; a drug that is *immunosuppressive* partially or completely suppresses the immune response of an individual; a substance that is *immunogenic* is able to produce an immune response; *immunodefic-iency*, as in the *human immunodeficiency virus* (HIV), is failure of the immune system to protect the body adequately from infection; an *immunoglobulin* is one of a class of proteins present in the serum and cells of the immune system, which function as antibodies.

in-¹ Also **il-**, **im-**, and **ir-**. *Not; without.* [Latin *in-*.]

This prefix is added to adjectives to give a negative sense (*infertile*, *inarticu-late*, *inexpensive*, *invariable*) and to nouns to indicate a lack of something (*inatten-tion*, *incapacity*, *insensitivity*). Many examples exist, but **in-** is not a living form, new words instead being created using **un-**, to which it is closely related in sense. There is no clear rule deciding which should be used: *see* **un-** for more information. *See also* the next entry.

The prefix is spelled **il-** before stems beginning in *l* (*illegitimate*, *illiberal*), **im-** before *b*, *m*, and *p* (*imbalance*, *immoral*, *impossible*), and **ir-** before *r* (*irrational*, *irregular*).

in-² Also **il-**, **im-**, and **ir-**. *In, into.* [English *in* or Latin *in-*.]

Words beginning in **in-** that derive from Latin are to various degrees figura-tive; sometimes the prefix gives add-itional force or emphasis. Examples include *incantation*, *incarcerate*, *indoc-trinate*, *induce*, *infect*, *influx*, and *inundate*. In other cases the prefix derives from English *in*, as with *income*, *inlet*, *insight*, and *intake*; with these the literal sense of *in* is more often retained.

A distinction between this and the pre-vious sense is not always obvious: *im-mense* looks as though it has *in-* as an intensifier, but actually it derives from Latin *in-* in the sense of 'not', plus *mensus*, measured. Similarly, *inflammable* looks as though it might mean 'not capable of burning', but it really means

'easily set on fire' (this is such a poten-tially disastrous confusion that *flammable* has replaced it in safety instructions).

The Latin form became *en-* in French (*see* **en-¹**), and many English words either now contain that spelling, or have done so in the past: *enable* used to be spelled *inable*; *entail* was once *intail*. Some words can exist in both forms: *inquire* is the usual spelling in the US, while in Britain *enquire* is more common. Sometimes dif-ferences in usage exist: *insure* usually means 'protect oneself by insurance', while *ensure* means 'make sure'. In other cases, one or the other form predomin-ates, as *enclose* does over *inclose*.

The prefix is spelled **il-** before stems beginning in *l* (*illuminate*, *illustrate*), **im-** before *b*, *m*, and *p* (*imbibe*, *immerse*, *imper-sonate*), and **ir-** before *r* (*irradiate*, *irri-gate*).

-in¹: *see* **-ine³**

-in² *A gathering of people having a common purpose, typically as a form of pro-test.* [English *in*.]

The first examples, *sit-ins*, were strikes in the US in the 1930s, in which buildings were occupied as a form of protest; the sense was extended to Black protests in the early 1960s against racial segrega-tion. The ending became very common in the mid-1960s (*sleep-in*, *love-in*, *pray-in*, *bed-in*, *teach-in*) but is now mainly his-torical. The form is modelled on words like *lie-in*, *stand-in*, *drive-in*, *plug-in*, and *shoo-in*, all of which predate the 1930s.

-ina *Forming nouns.* [Italian, Spanish, or Latin feminine suffixes.]

Some examples are feminine terms and titles (*ballerina*, *Latina*, *signorina*, *tsarina*), female personal names (*Chris-tina*, *Georgina*, *Wilhelmina*), or occasion-ally place-names derived from such personal names (*Carolina*). Others are musical instruments (*concertina*, *oca-rina*), or compositions (*sonatina*).

The ending also appears in the taxo-nomic names of some plant and animal groups; here it derives from the neuter plural of Latin adjectives ending in *-inus* (often with *animalia*, animals, understood). Examples are *Casuarina*, a genus of trees native to Australia and SE Asia; *Globigerina*, a genus of planktonic marine protozoans with calcareous shells; *Spirulina*, a genus of filamentous cyanobacteria.

Others come from a variety of unconnected sources: for example, *pashmina*, a fine-quality material made from goat's wool, is from Persian *pam*, wool.

See also -INE² *and* -INO.

-inae *Animal subfamilies.* [Latin, the feminine plural of words ending in -*inus*.]

In systematic naming, an animal subfamily is a collection of genera within one family (whose name ends in -IDAE). Examples include *Bovinae*, which includes wild and domestic cattle and bison, a subfamily of the *Bovidae*; *Falconinae*, the true falcons, such as the peregrines; and *Felinae*, which includes the domestic cats and many wild cats, such as the ocelot, lynx, and puma.

indi-: *see* INDO-²

Indo-¹ *India; India and…* [Latin *Indus*, from Greek *Indos*, Indian.]

The link may be geographical (*Indo-China*; *Indo-Pacific*, relating to the Indian Ocean and the adjacent parts of the Pacific; *Indo-jazz*, a jazz style modified by the musical styles and instruments of the Indian sub-continent), ethnological (*Indo-Malaysian* or *Indo-Malayan*, an ethnological region comprising Sri Lanka, the Malay peninsula, and the Malaysian islands), or linguistic (*Indo-European*, of the family of languages spoken over the greater part of Europe and Asia as far as northern India).

ind(o)-² *Also* **indi-**. *A chemical substance related to indigo or an indole.* [English *indigo*, via Portuguese from Greek *indikos*, of India.]

Indigo is a tropical plant from which a blue dye is obtained; its main constituent is a crystalline compound either called *indigotin* or *indigo blue*, which also occurs in woad; *indirubin*, *indigo red*, is an isomer. Sometimes **indo-** refers to the colour, as in *indicolite*, an indigo-blue gem variety of tourmaline, or the element *indium*, called that because there are two characteristic indigo lines in its spectrum.

Indole is a crystalline organic compound with an unpleasant odour, present in coal-tar and in faeces, first obtained artificially from indigo blue; *indene* (*indole* plus -ENE¹) is a colourless liquid hydrocarbon, obtained from coal-tar and used in making synthetic resins; the *indoxyl* radical —ONC_8H_6 is derived from indole and is present in indigotin; *indoleacetic acid* is an acetic acid derivative of indole, especially found in plants.

-ine¹ *Forming adjectives.* [French -*in*, -*ine*, or from Latin -*inus*, sometimes derived from Greek -*inos*.]

This suffix appears in adjectives derived from Latin: *asinine*, *clandestine*, *divine*, *feminine*, *genuine*, *marine*, *masculine*, *supine*. It also appears in some adjectives from proper names or placenames: *Levantine*, *Saturnine*.

It also forms adjectives related to or formed from the taxonomic names of families, subfamilies, or genera: *bovine* (genus *Bos*, cattle), *feline* (family *Felidae*, the cats), *colubrine*, snake-like (family *Colubridae*).

Other examples are adjectives formed from the names of minerals, plants, and the like: *coralline*, *crystalline*, *hyacinthine*.

-ine² *Forming feminine nouns.* [French, via Latin -*ina* from Greek -*inē*, or from German -*in*.]

The only common example is *heroine*; *chatelaine* (French, feminine of *châtelain*, the governor of a castle) is a woman in charge of a large house, *margravine* is a historical term for the wife of a margrave, the hereditary title of some princes of the Holy Roman Empire; *chorine*, a chorus girl, was formed from *chorus*. It is possible that the humorous name for the former British prime minister Margaret Thatcher, *leaderene*, was influenced by this ending, even though the spelling derives from female names ending in -*ene*. *See also* -EEN, -INA, *and* -INO.

-ine³ *Also* **-in**. *Forming nouns.* [French, from the Latin feminine form -*ina*.]

One group is of abstract nouns: *discipline*, *doctrine*, *famine*, *medicine*, *rapine*, *routine*. Other examples from the same source are *concubine* and *urine*. A few are diminutives: *figurine*.

Many are names of products, often derived from something they are supposed to resemble or imitate (*nectarine*, a type of peach whose flavour was thought to be like nectar) or from which they derive (*caffeine*, a compound found especially in tea and coffee, from French *café*; *dentine*, the bony tissue forming the bulk of a tooth, from Latin *dens*, *dent-*, tooth). The ending has been used with no clear system to name substances (*gasoline*, *margarine*, *quinine*, *turpentine*), and also appears in the trade names of products (*plasticine*, *vaseline*).

In systematic chemical naming, **-ine** is used for alkaloids and basic substances (*aconitine*, *nicotine*, *strychnine*). It is regarded as distinct from **-in**, which appears in the names of neutral substances, such as glycerides, glucosides, and colouring matters (*albumin*, *casein*, *chitin*, *pepsin*). This distinction is not always strictly observed. In some cases, the non-scientific spelling in **-ine** exists alongside the systematic name in **-in** (*gelatine* and *gelatin*; *glycerine* and *glycerin*); however, US usage often prefers the forms ending in **-in**. *Vitamin*, originally *vitamine*, is so spelled everywhere.

The ending **-ine** was used to name the halogens (*fluorine*, *chlorine*, *bromine*, *iodine*, *astatine*) and this spelling has been preserved; **-ine** is also used systematically to form the names of certain six-membered monocyclic compounds having a nitrogen atom in the ring, as in *azine*, the source of a group of dyestuffs. See also -IDINE.

-iness: *see* -NESS

infra- *Below, underneath, beneath.* [Latin *infra*, with the same meaning.]

Examples include *infrared*, that part of the spectrum lying below visible light in frequency; *infrastructure*, the physical and organizational substructure or foundations (such as roads, buildings, and power supplies) needed for the operation of a society; *infrasound*, sound which is too low in frequency to be audible by human ears. *Infrarenal*, lying below the kidney, and *infraorbital*, situated below the orbit of the eye, are two examples of a group of medical terms. *Infra* on its own is used in documents to refer to something further on in the text; *infra dig*, an abbreviation of Latin *infra dignitatem*, beneath (one's) dignity, is an informal term for something demeaning.

-ing¹ *Forming nouns derived from verbs.* [Old English *-ung*, *-ing*, of Germanic origin.]

Such nouns express the action of a verb (*fighting*, *muttering*, *shaving*, *thinking*, *working*), often relating to some occupation or skill (*banking*, *fencing*, *glassblowing*, *modelling*, *silversmithing*, *welding*); sometimes they indicate a single instance of the action (a *ruling*, a *scolding*, a *wedding*). They may also denote a material used for a process, or associated with it (*bedding*, *cladding*, *clothing*, *flooring*, *piping*, *wadding*); a few of these are formed from other nouns without a corresponding verb (*sacking*, *scaffolding*). For nouns such as *sibling* or *weakling*, *see* -LING.

-ing² *Forming the present participle of verbs, and adjectives from nouns.* [Middle English: variation of earlier *-ende*, later *-inde*, subsequently completely identified with -ING¹.]

The present participle is the form of the verb used to make a continuous tense, as in *he is climbing*, *they are walking*, *stop what you are doing*. Any verb can form its present participle by adding **-ing** in this way. Such participles are often used as adjectives: *he is a charming man*, *she is his golfing partner*. Some adjectives of this type are formed from nouns instead: *cunning*, *hulking*, *swashbuckling*.

-ing³ *Forming nouns.* [Old English, of Germanic origin.]

This is a very old form, long since ceasing to make new words. It has the sense of a thing belonging to or having the quality of something. It appears in the name of coins and fractional parts: *farthing* (Old English *fēorthing*, from *fēortha*, fourth), *riding* (Old Norse *thrithi*, third, with the initial sound lost in English through being absorbed into the ending of *west*, *north*, and *east*), one of three former administrative divisions of Yorkshire. Other examples may be *gelding*, *herring*, *whiting*, and *wilding* (a wild plant, especially an apple tree descended from cultivated varieties), though the early history of several of these is unclear.

ino- *Fibrous tissue or muscle.* [Greek *is*, *in-*, fibre, muscle.]

The adjective *inotropic* refers to something that modifies the force or speed of contraction of muscles, especially the heart; *inositol* is a simple carbohydrate which occurs in animal and plant tissue, especially muscle; *inosine* is a nucleoside found in animal tissue which is used in kidney transplantation to provide a temporary source of sugar; an *inosilicate* is a silicate mineral in which the silicate groups are connected in parallel chains like fibres.

-ino *Forming diminutives.* [Italian diminutive form.]

Some terms have been taken over from Italian or are familiar from that language: *bambino*, baby (a diminutive of *bambo*, silly); *cappuccino*, coffee made with milk that has been frothed up with pressurized steam (literally 'a Capuchin', because its colour resembles that of a Capuchin's habit); *casino*, a public room or building where gambling games are played (a diminutive of *casa*, house). The ending appeared in scientific use following the naming of the *neutrino* (Italian, diminutive of *neutro*, neutral), a small uncharged nuclear particle, by the Italian physicist Enrico Fermi (1901–54). Others coined in imitation include *photino*, the hypothetical supersymmetric counterpart of the photon, and *virino*, a hypothetical infectious particle postulated as the cause of scrapie, BSE, and CJD. *See also* -INA and -INE².

inter- *Between or among; mutually or reciprocally.* [Old French *entre-* or Latin *inter*, between, among.]

Many examples derive from Latin words already containing the prefix: *interest* (Latin *interesse*, differ, be important, from *esse*, be); *intercept* (Latin *intercept-*, caught between, from *capere*, take); *internecine* (Latin *internecinus*, from *necare*, to kill).

Based on this model, the prefix has become a common and active one in English, forming adjectives (*intercontinental*, *interfaith*, *intermolecular*, *interwar*), nouns (*intercom*, *interface*, *Internet*), and verbs (*interoperate*, *intermarry*).

In the sense of 'between or among', examples are *intercity*, *interglacial*, and *international*; in that of 'mutual or reciprocal', examples are *interdependent*, *intermingle*, and *interrelation*. However, these senses are often not clearly distinguishable in any given case.

intra- *On the inside; within.* [Latin *intra*, inside.]

This form is widely used in scientific fields, especially biology and medicine: *intracellular*, located within a cell or cells; *intramolecular*, existing or taking place within a molecule; *intramuscular*, situated or taking place within, or administered into, a muscle; *intrauterine*, within the uterus; *intravenous*, existing or taking place within, or administered into, a vein or veins. Other examples are *intramural*, situated or done within the walls of a building, or one institution; *intrapreneur*, a manager within a company who promotes innovative product development and marketing (from *entrepreneur*). The opposite is EXTRA-.

However, *intransigent* contains Latin *in-*, not, plus *transigere*, come to an understanding; *intractable* similarly derives from Latin *tractabilis*, from *tractare*, to handle.

intro- *Into; inwards.* [Latin *intro*, to the inside.]

Examples brought in from Latin with the prefix attached include *introduce* (Latin *introducere*, from *ducere*, to lead), *introspection* (Latin *introspicere*, to look into), and *introvert* (originally a verb meaning to turn one's thoughts inwards in spiritual contemplation, from Latin *vertere*, to turn; its use as a term in psychology dates from the early 20th century). A very few words have been created in English, such as *introjection*, in psychoanalysis the unconscious adoption of the ideas or attitudes of others (invented on the pattern of *projection*). *See also* EXTRO-.

iod(o)- *Iodine.* [French *iode*, iodine, from Greek *iōdēs*, violet-coloured.]

The element *iodine* was so named from the colour of its vapour. In medicine, *iodism* is iodine poisoning; *iodopsin* is a photosensitive violet pigment that occurs in the cones of the retina; an *iodophor* (Greek *pherein*, to bear) is one of a group of disinfectants containing iodine in combination with a detergent. A compound that has been *iodinated* has had iodine introduced into it; *iodides* are compounds of iodine with another element or group. The form is used in names of organic compounds containing the radical —I, for example *iodobenzene* or *iodoform*, a yellow crystalline compound with antiseptic properties.

-ion Also **-cion**, **-sion**, **-tion**, and **-xion**. *Forming nouns denoting verbal action.* [Via French from Latin *-ion-* or words ending in *-io*.]

Examples have been formed from Latin verbs, adjectives, and past participles. The main sense is that of an action related to a verb, as *communion* is the action of communing; *rebellion* is similarly related to the verb to *rebel*, *fusion* to *fuse*, and *infliction* to *inflict*. Nouns can often refer as much to a condition resulting from an action as to the action itself, as *pollution* can be the action of polluting, or the presence of some harmful substance as a result of the action. In some cases, the noun refers more particularly to the result rather than the action, as in *explosion*.

Many examples are preceded by a letter derived from the stem of the Latin participle: mainly *s* (*immersion*, *persuasion*) or *t* (*evolution*, *solution*), less often by *c* (*suspicion*) or *x* (*fluxion*).

A small group derived from Latin nouns have variously been spelled either **-xion** or **-ction**. With a few, the first spelling is standard (*complexion*, *transfixion*). With others both forms exist (*connection/connexion*; *inflection/inflexion*); in these cases the spelling ending in **-ction** predominates, partly because of the way the associated verb is spelled (*connect*, *inflect*) but also because there are so many nouns ending in **-tion** that this spelling has influenced them.

None of these endings are active in the language; new examples are formed using -ATION or -ITION. *See also* -IZE (for *-isation* and *-ization*). *Compare* -MENT and -NESS.

-ior Also **-or**. *Forming adjectives of comparison.* [From Latin comparatives.]

Examples are *anterior*, *exterior*, *inferior*, *junior*, *posterior*, *prior*, and *ulterior*. Some do not have the intermediate *i*, such as *major* (Latin, comparative of *magnus*, great). Some can also be nouns indicating a person or thing having that quality. However, *warrior* derives instead from a variant of Old French *guerreior*, from *guerre*, war; others (*behavior*, *savior*) are US spellings of words ending in *-our* (*see* -OR[2]).

-ious: *see* -OUS

-ique: *see* -IC

ir-: *see* IN-[1] and IN-[2]

-iridine: *see* -IDINE

irid(o)- *The rainbow; the iris.* [Via Latin from Greek *iris*, rainbow, iris.]

The Greek word could refer to the rainbow (*Iris* was the female messenger of the gods who appeared as the rainbow), to a type of lily, and to the coloured part of the eye surrounding the pupil. All these senses appear in various English compounds. Something *iridescent* shows luminous colours that seem to change when seen from different angles; the metallic element *iridium* was so named because it forms compounds of various colours; *iridaceous* refers to plants of the iris family (*Iridaceae*).

However, the larger number are medical terms referring to the iris of the eye, as in *iridocyclitis* (Greek *kuklos*, circle), inflammation of the iris and ciliary body of the eye; *iridectomy* (Greek *ektomē*, excision), a surgical procedure to remove part of the iris; *iridodialysis* (Greek *dialusis*, from *dialuein*, split, separate), a tear caused to the connection between the iris and the ciliary body as a result of an injury.

-isation: *see* -IZE

ischio- *The ischium.* [Latin, from Greek *iskhion*, hip joint.]

The *ischium* is the curved bone forming the base of each half of the pelvis. Anatomical terms refer to the ischium plus another part of the body: *ischiorectal*, *ischiopubic*, *ischiofemoral*, *ischioanal*.

-ise¹: *see* -IZE

-ise² *Forming nouns.* [Old French *-ise*, from Latin *-itia*, *-itius*, *-itium*.]

Most words from these Latin endings were spelled with *-ice* in French and this spelling became the usual one in English (*see* -ICE). However, a small number of words adopted **-ise** instead: *exercise*, *expertise*, *franchise*, *merchandise*.

-ish¹ *Forming adjectives.* [Old English *-isc*, of Germanic origin; related to Old Norse *-iskr*, German and Dutch *-isch*, also to Greek *-iskos* (a suffix forming diminutive nouns).]

This suffix forms adjectives from nouns and from other adjectives.

One set from nouns is of adjectives for a member of a nation (*British*, *Cornish*, *Irish*, *Netherlandish*, *Polish*, *Swedish*, *Turkish*), occasionally of a religious or other group, as with *Jewish*. Rarely, the ending has been reduced to *-sh*, as in *Welsh*.

A second set from nouns is of adjectives that indicate its qualities or characteristics (*boyish*, *folkish*, *gypsyish*). Many are formed from proper names, often for a single use: *Ayckbournish*, *Hockneyish*, *Thurberish*. Though these examples are neutral in tone, the great majority are derogatory: *babyish*, *Bunterish*, *bookish*, *boorish*, *childish*, *Eeyorish*, *foolish*, *freakish*, *Micawberish*, *priggish*, *selfish*, *sluttish*.

Examples formed from other adjectives suggest some quality that is roughly or somewhat like that of the adjective (*coldish*, *dullish*, *loudish*, *moreish*, *oldish*, *sweetish*, *tallish*, *weakish*). In particular, the ending can suggest an approximate age (*fiftyish*) or time of day (*sevenish*, *latish*).

-ish² *Forming verbs.* [French *-iss* (from stems of verbs ending in *-ir*), from Latin *-isc-* (a suffix forming verbs that express the beginning of an action).]

Examples deriving directly from such French verbs include *abolish*, *banish*, *burnish*, *establish*, *flourish*, *furnish*, *impoverish*, *nourish*, and *punish*. Some, from French verbs with other endings, have adopted the ending by analogy, such as *astonish*, *distinguish*, *publish*, and *varnish*.

-ism *Forming nouns.* [French *-isme*, via Latin from Greek *-ismos*, *-isma*.]

This is one of the most prolific word-creating elements in the language. Beyond the 2,000 or more that are recorded in large dictionaries, many others are formed as need arises, often for a single use.

The sense nearest to its Greek roots is that of some action or its result: *baptism*, *criticism*, *exorcism*, *ostracism*, *plagiarism*, *volcanism*. Derived from that is the sense of some state or quality: *barbarism*, *egotism*, *heroism*, *hypnotism*, *isomerism*, *magnetism*, *organism*.

As a further stage in its development it has come to denote a system, principle, practice, doctrine, or ideological movement. This is now its main sense, to the extent that *ism* was created in the late 17th century for a distinctive practice, system, or philosophy, typically a political ideology or an artistic movement, often with derogatory undertones. For a few common examples, see the LIST opposite.

Examples of some recent, often temporary, formations (out of a very large group) include *hacktivism* (the movement comprising people who hack into and damage computer systems as a political act, modelled on *activism*), *knee-jerkism*, *New Labourism*, *presenteeism* (the princi-

-ism	Forming nouns
	In most cases, terms are based on English stems.

absenteeism	the practice of regularly staying away from work or school without good reason
activism	the policy or action of using vigorous campaigning to bring about political or social change
Buddhism	a widespread Asian religion or philosophy
Catholicism	the faith and practice of the Roman Catholic Church
creationism	belief in the literal truth of the Biblical story of the creation of the world and living things
environmentalism	concern for the environment and active advocacy of its protection
evangelism	the spreading of the Christian gospel by public preaching or personal witness
expressionism	an artistic movement which emphasized subjective emotional experience
feminism	the advocacy of women's rights on the basis of the equality of the sexes
Hinduism	a major religious and cultural tradition of the Indian subcontinent
idealism	the practice of forming or pursuing ideals, especially unrealistically
imperialism	a policy of extending a country's power and influence through colonization, use of military force, or economic means
Judaism	the monotheistic religion of the Jews
liberalism	a political or social philosophy that favours political, civil, and personal liberty
Marxism	the political and economic theories of Karl Marx and Friedrich Engels, especially as the basis for communism
nationalism	patriotic feeling, principles, or efforts, often in an extreme form marked by a feeling of superiority over other countries
Protestantism	the faith and practice of the Protestant Churches
racism	the belief that race accounts for differences in human character or ability and that a particular race is superior to others; discrimination or prejudice based on race
Romanticism	a late 18th-century artistic movement, emphasizing inspiration, subjectivity, and the primacy of the individual
shamanism	the animistic religion of some peoples of northern Asia and North America in which mediation between the visible and spirit worlds is effected by shamans
Taoism	a Chinese philosophy based on the writings of Lao-tzu, advocating humility and religious piety
volunteerism	the use or involvement of volunteer labour, especially in community services in the USA
Zionism	originally a movement for the re-establishment of a Jewish nation in what is now Israel; today its development and protection

ple of staying at work for excessive hours out of anxiety for one's job, the opposite of *absenteeism*), *rejectionism* (a political viewpoint in which the whole of a policy is rejected without possibility of compromise), *shopaholism* (the state of being addicted to shopping), *youthism* (an emphasis in fashion and the media on young people to the exclusion of other age groups).

Two other specific senses are worth noting. Some stand for a peculiarity in language (*colloquialism*, *syllogism*), especially that of a particular group (*Americanism*, *Cockneyism*, *Irishism*) or some point of style characteristic of a writer

(*Hitchcockism*, of the film director Alfred Hitchcock; *Pratchettism*, of the writer Terry Pratchett). Some denote a pathological condition: *alcoholism*, *cretinism*, *embolism*.

For related nouns and adjectives, *see* -IST.

iso- *Equal; isomeric.* [Greek *isos*, equal.]

In meteorology, an **isobar** (Greek *barus*, heavy) is a line on a map connecting points having the same barometric pressure; a triangle that is **isosceles** (Greek *skelos*, leg) has two sides of equal length; something **isomorphic** (Greek *morphē*, form) is similar in form and relations to another; an object or substance that is **isotropic** (Greek *tropos*, a turn) has a physical property which has the same value when measured in different directions; **isotopes** are forms of the same element that contain different numbers of neutrons in their nuclei (Greek *topos*, place, because the forms occupy the same place in the periodic table of elements).

Its opposite is ANISO-.

In chemistry, **iso-** indicates that a compound is **isomeric** with another, indicating that it has the same number and kind of atoms but that they are arranged differently in the molecule: **isooctane**, a liquid hydrocarbon used as a standard in the system of octane numbers; **isocyanide**, an organic compound containing the group —NC, isomeric with cyanides; **isoleucine**, an amino acid. *See also* CIS- and TRANS-.

Isolate and its relatives come instead from Italian *isolato*, which is derived from Latin *insula*, island.

-ison *Forming nouns.* [Old French *-a(i)son* or *-e(i)son*, from Latin *-atio(n)-*, *-etio(n)-*, or *-itio(n)-*.]

A small number of such nouns exists, of which the most common are *comparison*, *jettison* (usually now a verb), and *venison*. *See also* -ATION, which is now the active suffix from the same source.

-ist *Also* -istic *and* **-istical** *Forming personal nouns and some related adjectives.* [Old French *-iste*, Latin *-ista*, from Greek *-istēs*.]

One large group consists of words linked to nouns ending in -ISM, so suggesting a person who adheres to a system of beliefs or principles, or practices some art, skill, or activity (*communist*, *hedonist*, *Marxist*, *realist*, *socialist*, *spiritualist*, *tourist*, *ventriloquist*), or subscribes to some prejudice or practises discrimination (*ageist*, *racist*, *sexist*, *sizeist*). A second group is of agent nouns associated with verbs ending in -IZE, many of which also have related nouns ending in -ISM: *antagonist*, *Baptist*, *evangelist*, *exorcist*, *plagiarist*.

On their model a large number of terms have been generated from a variety of nouns, or sometimes from adjectives or verbs, to indicate a member of some profession or business activity, or a person engaged in some pursuit or activity: *artist*, *cyclist*, *dentist*, *dramatist*, *florist*, *humorist*, *idealist*, *linguist*, *motorist*, *novelist*, *organist*, *scientist*, *trombonist*. Some refer to students of the language or culture of a region: *Americanist*, *Hebraist*, *Hellenist*, *Latinist*, *Orientalist*.

The suffix is often used to form new words, often for a single occasion: *everythingist*, *garbageologist* (a person who investigates household rubbish as a marker of social status or aspirations), *oppositionalist* (a member of a political party who rigorously opposes some aspect of policy), *rebuttalist* (one who rebuts another), *road-ragist* (a person who exhibits road rage).

It is common to form related adjectives using the compound suffix **-istic** (-ist plus -IC): *atheistic*, *evangelistic*, *idealistic*, *realistic*. A few nouns also have adjective forms ending in **-istical**: *egoistical*, *pietistical*, though these are less common.

See also -LOGIST.

-ista *A supporter of a person or organization.* [Spanish *-ista*, derived from Latin.]

The Spanish suffix is that language's equivalent of English -IST. It became known in the latter part of the 20th century through several Spanish terms for political groupings, especially *Sandinista*, a member of a left-wing Nicaraguan political organization, named after a similar group founded by Augusto César Sandino (1893–1934); *Fidelista*, an adherent of Fidel Castro in Cuba; and *Peronista*, a supporter of Juan Perón in Argentina.

A small number of English colloquial terms have been created using it, always with derogatory implications: *Blairista*, a supporter of the British prime minister, Tony Blair; *Guardianista*, a reader of the Guardian newspaper or one whose opinions correspond to its liberal outlook; *Portillista*, a follower of or someone sympathetic to the views of the British Conservative politician Michael Portillo.

-it: *see* -ITE[2]

Italo- *Italian; Italian and .…* [English *Italy* plus -O-.]

An *Italophile* is a person who admires Italian culture and traditions; someone *Italophone* speaks Italian; *Italo-Grecian* refers to Greek settlers or Greek civilization in Italy in the classical period; *Italo-Byzantine* refers to Byzantine art as developed in Italy.

-ite[1] *Forming nouns.* [French *-ite*, via Latin *-ita* from Greek *-ītes*.]

Some examples are the names of an inhabitant of a place or country: *Canaanite*, *Israelite*, *Muscovite*, *Seattleite*. Others refer to a follower of a movement or doctrine, especially one marked by -ISM: *Hitlerite*, *Jacobite*, *Labourite*, *Luddite*, *Thatcherite*, *Pre-Raphaelite*, *Shiite*, *Trotskyite*.

In Greek, words were often adjectives describing a mineral, with *lithos*, stone, understood, and the ending has become common as a mark of minerals (*andesite*, *bauxite*, *chondrite*, *dolomite*, *graphite*, *lignite*) and fossils (*ammonite*, *stromatolite*, *trilobite*) (*See also* -LITE). By extension, it has been used to form names for manufactured substances, especially explosives and hard materials (*Bakelite*, *cordite*, *dynamite*, *ferrite*, *gelignite*, *vulcanite*).

Some examples are names for constituent elements of an organism or body: *cellulite*, persistent subcutaneous fat; *catabolite*, a product of catabolism; *dendrite*, a short branched extension of a nerve cell; *somite*, each of a number of body segments containing the same internal structures.

In chemistry, names ending in **-ite** are salts of acids whose names end in -OUS: *chlorite*, *chromite*, *nitrite*, *phosphite*, *sulphite*. *Compare* -ATE[1].

-ite[2] *Also -it. Forming adjectives, nouns, and verbs.* [Latin *-itus*, past participle of verbs ending in *-ere* and *-ire*.]

Such words have nothing in common except their source. Adjectives include *composite*, *contrite*, *definite*, *erudite*, *exquisite*, *favourite*, *finite*, *opposite*, *polite*, and *requisite*. Some of these can also be nouns, and a few others are wholly or mainly so: *appetite*, *requisite*. Others are verbs: *expedite*, *ignite*, *unite*. Some have lost the final *e*: *circuit*, *elicit*, *implicit*, *solicit*.

By no means all words ending in **-ite** have this Latin origin. Most short words, such as *smite* and *write*, are of Germanic origin; *hypocrite* and *parasite* come from Greek; others, such as *respite* and *satellite*, come from different Latin sources.

-itic *Forming adjectives and nouns.* [French *-itique*, via Latin *-iticus* from Greek *-itikos*.]

One group of adjectives derives from nouns ending in *-ite* (*see* -ITE[1]), of which a few examples are *anthracitic*, *bauxitic*, *dendritic*, *graphitic*, *parasitic*, *Semitic*, and *stalagmitic*. Another set comes from nouns ending in -ITIS: *arthritic*, *bronchitic*, *laryngitic*, *meningitic*. A few come from other sources, such as *syphilitic*, *Sanskritic*, or *Cushitic* (of a group of East African languages whose name derives from *Cush*, grandson of Noah). A few of these adjectives can also be nouns. *See also* -IC.

-ition *Forming nouns.* [French, or from Latin *-itio(n)-*.]

This suffix may be considered to be a combination of -ITE[2] and -ION and is equivalent to -ATION. Some examples are *audition*, *condition*, *definition*, *disposition*, *edition*, *inhibition*, *nutrition*, *prohibition*, *sedition*, *tradition*, and *volition*. Some form associated adjectives ending in -ITIOUS.

-itious *Forming adjectives.* [Either from

nouns ending in -ITION, or from Latin *-itius*, alteration of Latin *-icius*.]

Examples from nouns ending in -ITION arise by losing the last two letters and adding the suffix -OUS; they include *ambitious*, *nutritious*, *repetitious*, and *seditious*. Examples from the Latin ending *-itius* include *adventitious* (happening or carried on according to chance), *fictitious*, and *supposititious* (based on assumption rather than fact).

-itis *Inflammatory disease.* [Greek feminine form of adjectives ending in *-itēs*.]

In Greek, such adjectives were often used alone, with a following noun understood, especially *nosos*, disease. For example, though *nephritis* in classical Greek strictly meant 'of the kidneys', it actually referred to a disease of that organ. Application specifically to inflammations occurred in English from the 18th century onwards. A large number of such terms now exists, of which a few are given in the LIST below.

The ending is often used facetiously in temporary formations that refer to some state of mind or tendency viewed as a disease: *celebritis*, excessive admiration for celebrities; *electionitis*; *lotteryitis*; *millenniumitis*.

-itive *Forming adjectives.* [French *-itif*, *-itive* or Latin *-itivus* (from past participial stems ending in *-it*).]

Examples include *cognitive*, *definitive*, *fugitive*, *genitive*, *inquisitive*, *positive*, *punitive*, and *transitive*. Some of these can also be nouns.

-itol *Polyhydric alcohols.* [A combination of -ITE[1] and -OL.]

This is used for the sugar alcohols, derived from a variety of four-, five- and six-carbon carbohydrates by reduction. Many of these were originally named with -ITE, but this has been systematically changed to **-itol** to indicate the presence of the extra hydroxyl group —OH. Examples include *mannitol* (formerly *mannite*), found in many plants and used as a diuretic; *sorbitol*, found in some fruits and first isolated from the berries of the mountain ash, *Sorbus aucuparia*, used by diabetics as an alternative to cane sugar; and *xylitol*, derived from *xylose*, present in some

-itis	Inflammatory disease.	
appendicitis	inflammation of the appendix	(English *appendix*)
arthritis	disease causing inflammation of the joints	(Greek *arthron*, joint)
bronchitis	inflammation of the mucous membrane in the bronchial tubes	(Greek *bronkhos*, windpipe)
colitis	inflammation of the lining of the colon	(English *colon*, from Greek *kolon*)
conjunctivitis	inflammation of the conjunctiva, the mucous membrane that covers the front of the eye	(Latin *conjungere*, join together)
cystitis	inflammation of the urinary bladder	(Greek *kustis*, bladder)
dermatitis	an inflammatory condition of the skin	(Greek *derma*, *dermat-*, skin)
encephalitis	inflammation of the brain	(Greek *enkephalos*, brain)
gastritis	inflammation of the lining of the stomach	(Greek *gastēr*, *gastr-*, stomach)
hepatitis	inflammation of the liver	(Greek *hēpar*, *hēpat-*, liver)
mastitis	inflammation of the mammary gland in the breast or udder	(Greek *mastos*, breast)
meningitis	inflammation of the meninges, the membranes that line the skull	(Greek *mēninx*, *mēning-*, membrane)
poliomyelitis	an infectious viral disease that can cause paralysis	(Greek *polios*, grey, plus *muelos*, marrow)

plant tissues and used as an artificial sweetener in foods. The ending also appears in the names of some cyclic hexanes, such as *inositol*, which occurs in animal and plant tissue and is a vitamin of the B group.

-ity Also **-itous**. *A quality or condition.* [French *-ité*, from Latin *-itas*, *-itatis*.]

Examples from a large set include *dignity* (Latin *dignitas*), *humility* (Latin *humilitas*), and *opportunity* (Latin *opportunitas*). Others are *chastity*, *hostility*, *lucidity*, *prosperity*, *timidity*, and *vulgarity*.

In some cases adjectives can be created from nouns ending in **-ity** by losing the final *y* and adding -OUS, corresponding to French words ending in *-iteux* that come from Latin ones ending in *-itosus*: *calamitous*, *fortuitous*, *precipitous*, *ubiquitous*.

See also -ABLE (for *-ability*, *-ibility*, and *-ubility*), -ACIOUS (for *-acity*), -IC (for *-icity*), -OSITY, and -TY[1].

-ium *Forming nouns.* [Via Latin from Greek *-ion*.]

This ending appears in a wide range of words, often in technical and scientific use, some of which are unchanged from their Latin forms: *alluvium*, *colloquium*, *delirium*, *geranium*, *odium*, *proscenium*.

It has also been used to form the names of most of the chemical elements discovered or isolated since the beginning of the 19th century, when Sir Humphry Davy (1778–1829) used it for *sodium*, *potassium*, *magnesium*, and *aluminium* (US *aluminum*, based on the older Latinate form *-um*); some others are *cadmium*, *iridium*, *lithium*, *osmium*, *palladium*, *rhodium*, *titanium*, and *uranium*. The ending has also been used for various cationic forms (able to take the role of metals in reactions), such as *ammonium*.

A further set marks names for parts of the body, commonly derived via modern Latin from Greek precursors: *cranium* (Greek *kranion*, skull); *epithelium* (Greek *epi*, above, plus *thēlē*, teat), the thin tissue forming the outer layer of a body's surface; *ilium* (Latin, singular of *ilia*, flanks), the large broad bone forming the upper part of each half of the pelvis; *pericardium* (Greek *peri*, around, plus *kardia*,

heart), the membrane enclosing the heart.

Others are names for botanical and biological structures: *archegonium* (Greek *arkhegonos*, founder of a race), the female sex organ in mosses, liverworts, ferns, and most conifers; *ommatidium* (Greek *omma*, *ommat-*, eye), each of the optical units that make up the compound eye of an insect; *uropygium* (Greek *orros*, sacral bone, plus *pugē*, rump), the rump of a bird, supporting the tail feathers. *See also* -ORIUM.

-ive Also **-ivity** and **-iveness**. *Showing a quality or tendency.* [French *-if*, *-ive*, from Latin *-ivus*.]

Most examples of words with this ending are adjectives: *active*, *attractive*, *consecutive*, *corrosive*, *destructive*, *extensive*, *passive*, *subversive*, and *vindictive*. Some can act both as adjectives and nouns: *captive*, *corrective*, *explosive*, *native*, *sedative*, *subjunctive*. A few are nouns only: *adjective*, *incentive*, *locomotive*, *missive*. Related abstract nouns are created using either **-iveness** (*decisiveness*, *furtiveness*, *restiveness*) or **-ivity** (*activity*, *captivity*, *festivity*).

See also -ATIVE and -ITIVE.

-ivore: *see* -VORE

-ize Also **-ise**, **-ization** and **-isation**, **-izer** and **-iser**. *Forming verbs.* [French *-iser*, via late Latin *-izare* from Greek verbs ending in *-izein*.]

Verbs with this ending are a large and diverse set. Very broadly, one group is of verbs that take a direct object, which describe acting on something or treating it in a given way, so causing it to change its state (*baptize*, *computerize*, *dramatize*, *fossilize*, *oxidize*, *pasteurize*, *privatize*, *sterilize*, *terrorize*). A second set, of verbs that do not take a direct object, refers to following some line of behaviour, action, practice, or policy (*agonize*, *apologize*, *extemporize*, *moralize*, *realize*, *theorize*).

In French, the spelling is uniformly *-iser* and this has influenced English spelling. In the US the *z* form is standard, but in Britain spellings with *z* are largely restricted to formal and academic usage; elsewhere in the English-speaking world, **-ise** is usual. Whatever policy is adopted, some verbs must be spelled using in **-ise**, including *advertise*, *advise*, *arise*, *chastise*, *despise*, *disguise*, *exercise*, *revise*, and *surprise*.

The ending is commonly used to make new verbs from adjectives or (especially) nouns and has done for centuries. In the 20th century some people objected to new forms such as *finalize*, *prioritize*, or *hospitalize*. However, such formations are now widely accepted, and new ones appear as needed (*incentivize*, *medicalize*, *strategize*, *technologize*), though not always with hopes of long-term survival (*angularize*, *flexibilize*, *graf-*

fitize, *radarize*). Many apparently new forms, such as *ceremonialize* and *novelize*, actually have a long history.

These verbs frequently have related abstract nouns ending in **-ization** (*criminalization*, *fertilization*, *liberalization*, *optimization*, *rationalization*) though in the case of some modern examples, the noun came first and the verb was derived from it. *See also* -ATION, -ITION, and -ION.

Action nouns are formed ending in **-izer**: *atomizer*, *fertilizer*, *memorizer*, *sympathizer*, *womanizer*. *See also* -ER[1].

Related endings are -ISM and -IST.

jejun(o)- *The jejunum.* [Latin, neuter of *jejunus*, fasting.]

The *jejunum* is the part of the small intestine between the duodenum and ileum; the link with the Latin word is that it is usually found to be empty after death. A *jejunostomy* (Greek *stoma*, mouth) is a surgical operation in which the jejunum is brought through the abdominal wall and opened; the adjective *jejunoileal* refers to the jejunum and the ileum, usually with reference to a bypass operation in which they are connected.

Judaeo- (US **Judeo-**) *Jewish; Jewish and…* [Latin Judaeus, Jewish]

The most common term here is *Judaeo-Christian*, of the shared traditions of the Jewish and Christian religions; another is *Judaeo-Spanish*, the language of some Sephardic Jews based on medieval Spanish, which is more commonly known as Ladino or Judezmo.

juxta- *Near to.* [Latin *juxta*, next.]

The only common non-specialist word containing this form is *juxtapose* and its derivatives, to place close together for contrasting effect (French *juxtaposer*, from *poser*, to place). Other examples are mostly specialist terms in medicine, such as *juxta-articular*, situated near a joint; *juxtaglomerular*, denoting a group of structures that secrete hormones into the small artery that leads into a cluster of nerve endings (a *glomerulus*) in the kidney; *juxta-spinal*, situated by the side of the spine.

K

karyo- Also **caryo-**. *The nucleus of a cell.* [Greek *karuon*, kernel.]

The *karyotype* is the number and visual appearance of the chromosomes in the cell nuclei of an organism or species; *karyogamy* is the fusion of cell nuclei during fertilization; *karyokinesis* (Greek *kinēsis*, movement), is division of a cell nucleus during mitosis, normal cell reproduction. Rarely, the spelling **caryo-** is found, as in *caryopsis* (Greek *opsis*, appearance), a dry one-seeded fruit, typical of grasses and cereals, a grain.

kata-: *see* CATA-

kibi-: *see* the table opposite

kerat(o)- Also **keratino-** and **cerato-**. *Horny tissue; the cornea.* [Greek *keras*, *kerat-*, horn.]

Keratin is a fibrous protein that forms the main structural constituent of hair, feathers, hoofs, horns, and the like. Several terms in **kerato-** refer to keratin, such as *keratosis*, a horny growth, especially on the skin. The rarer form **keratino-** derives from *keratin* by adding the linking vowel -o-; an example is *keratinocyte*, an epidermal cell which produces keratin. Occasionally the spelling is **cerato-**: *ceratopsian* (Greek *ops*, face), a herbivorous Cretaceous dinosaur such as triceratops, with a beaked and horned head.

Several medical terms refer to the cornea, the transparent layer forming the front of the eye (whose name derives from *cornu*, the Latin equivalent of Greek *keras*). Examples are *keratectomy* (Greek *ektomē*, excision), surgical removal of a section or layer of the cornea, usually performed using a laser; and *keratoplasty* (Greek *plastos*, formed, moulded), surgery carried out on the cornea, especially corneal transplantation.

ket(o)- Also **keton-**. *Ketone.* [English *ketone*.]

Ketones are organic chemical compounds that contain a carbonyl group —CO— bonded to two alkyl groups and whose names have the systematic ending -ONE. The production of ketones during the metabolism of fats is termed *ketogenesis*; *ketosis* is the presence of raised levels of ketones in the body. The form sometimes appears as **keton-** before a vowel, as in *phenylketonuria*, an inherited inability to metabolize phenylalanine.

In chemistry, a *keto acid* is a compound whose molecule contains both a carboxyl group (—COOH) and a ketone group, such as α–*ketoglutaric acid*, which occurs in the metabolism of proteins; *ketamine* is a synthetic compound used as an anaesthetic and analgesic drug and also (illicitly) as a hallucinogen.

kilo- *In units of measurement, a factor of a thousand.* [Greek *khílioi*, thousand.]

This is one of the standard SI (Système International) decimal prefixes (see the table of WORDS FOR MULTIPLES opposite). Examples are *kilogram* (sometimes also *kilogramme*), the SI unit of mass; *kilometre*, a distance of a thousand metres; *kilowatt*, one thousand watts of electrical power. In computing, the form is commonly (and confusingly) used to refer to 2^{10} or 1,024 instead, as in *kilobit*, 1,024 binary bits of data or memory, or *kilobyte*, 1,024 bytes. *See also* CHILI-.

-kin Also **-kins**. *Forming diminutive nouns.* [Middle Dutch -*kijn*, -*ken*, Middle Low German -*kīn*.]

A *manikin*, a person who is very small, derives from Dutch *manneken*, diminutive of *man* (the store dummy called a *mannequin* is the French spelling of the same word); a *bodkin*, a thick, blunt needle with a large eye, is historically most probably a small *bod*, an Irish word for a dagger; *gherkin* is a diminutive of a Dutch word for a cucumber; *larrikin*, an Australian term for a boisterous, often

WORDS FOR MULTIPLES

The standard system of prefixes for multiples is that laid down in SI units
(Système International D'Unités), an international agreement dating from
1960, which defines standard units for quantities and the names for the
decimal prefixes to use with them.

The standard SI multiples:

DECA-	10	(Greek *deka*, ten)
HECTO-	100	(Greek *hekaton*, hundred)
KILO-	10^3	(Greek *khílioi*, thousand)
MEGA-	10^6	(Greek *megas*, great)
GIGA-	10^9	(Greek *gigas*, giant)
TERA-	10^{12}	(Greek *teras*, monster)
PETA-	10^{15}	(Greek *penta-* five, this being the fifth prefix in the series, by analogy with tera-)
EXA-	10^{18}	(Based on the Greek prefix *hexa-*, six, by deleting the first letter)
zetta-	10^{21}	(Adapted from the Italian *setta*, seven)
yotta-	10^{24}	(Adapted from the Italian *otto*, eight)

The standard SI submultiples:

DECI-	one-tenth or 10^{-1}	(Latin *decimus*, a tenth)
CENTI-	one-hundredth or 10^{-2}	(Latin *centum*, a hundred)
MILLI-	10^{-3}	(Latin *mille*, thousand)
MICRO-	10^{-6}	(Greek *mikros*, small)
NANO-	10^{-9}	(Greek *nanos*, dwarf)
PICO-	10^{-12}	(Spanish *pico*, literally a little bit)
FEMTO-	10^{-15}	(Danish or Norwegian *femten*, fifteen)
ATTO-	10^{-18}	(Danish or Norwegian *atten*, eighteen)
zepto-	10^{-21}	(Adapted from SEPTI-, seven, on the pattern of other multiples)
yocto-	10^{-24}	(Similarly adapted from OCTO-, eight)

The prefixes *hecto-*, *deca-*, *deci-*, and *centi-* are generally avoided in scientific work.

Binary multiples for computer purposes

The use of decimal prefixes to describe the closely-similar—but not identical
—binary multiples used in computing (such as **megabyte** or **terabit**) has caused
confusion—for various reasons, a *megabyte* can be 1,048,576, 1,024,000, or
1,000,000. In 1998 the International Electrotechnical Commission (IEC) agreed an
international standard for a new group of prefixes that removes the ambiguity;
names use the first two letters of the SI decimal prefix, followed by the letters *bi*,
for binary. These are only very slowly coming into use.

kibi-	2^{10}
mebi-	2^{20}
gibi-	2^{30}
tebi-	2^{40}
pebi-	2^{50}
exbi-	2^{60}

badly behaved young man, is possibly a diminutive of the given name *Larry*; *napkin* is a diminutive of Old French *nappe*, tablecloth. Words ending in **-kins** express endearment, as in *babykins*, *bunnykins*, *mouseykins*.

kinesio- Also **kinesi-**, **kinema-**, and **kineto-**. *Movement.* [Greek *kinēsis*, movement; *kinētos*, movable; *kinēma*, *kinēmat-*, motion; all from *kinein*, to move.]

The spelling of English words derived from the Greek roots has been very variable. *Kinesiology* is the study of the mechanics of body movements; *kinaesthesia* (Greek *aisthēsis*, sensation) (US *kinesthesia*) is awareness of the position and movement of the parts of the body by means of sensory organs in the muscles and joints; *kinematics* is the branch of mechanics concerned with the motion of objects without reference to the forces which cause the motion; the adjective *kinetic* concerns motion; a *kinetoscope* is an early motion-picture device in which the images are viewed through a peephole. *See also* CINE-.

-kinesis Also **-kinesia**, **-kinetic**, and **-kinetics**. *Movement.* [Greek *kinēsis*, motion; *kinētos*, movable; both from *kinein*, to move.]

Terms ending in **-kinesis** are nouns indicating movement, as in *hyperkinesis* (Greek *huper*, over, beyond), a muscle spasm, or a disorder of children marked in part by hyperactivity; *psychokinesis*, the supposed ability to move objects by mental effort alone; *telekinesis* (Greek *tēle-*, far off), a similar ability to move objects at a distance; *kinesis* itself means movement or motion.

Nouns ending in **-kinesia** are closely related: *dyskinesia*, abnormality or impairment of voluntary movement; *akinesia*, loss or impairment of the power of voluntary movement. Sometimes they are alternate forms of terms ending in **-kinesis**: *hyperkinesia*.

Adjectives are formed ending in **-kinetic** (*see* -IC), linked to either of these noun forms: *dyskinetic*, *hyperkinetic*, *psychokinetic*, *telekinetic*.

Kinetics is the branch of chemistry or biochemistry concerned with measuring and studying the rates of reactions; recently formed examples of compound terms include *pharmacokinetics* (Greek *pharmakon*, drug, medicine), studying reaction rates of drugs in the body, and *toxicokinetics* (Greek *toxicon*, poison), similarly studying toxic substances.

kineto-: *see* KINESIO-

-kinin *A hormone.* [Greek *kinēsis*, motion, plus -*in* (*see* -INE[3]).]

The first example, and the model for others, was *bradykinin* (Greek *bradus*, slow), a peptide hormone that causes blood vessels to dilate and smooth muscle to contract (as it were, to set them in motion); *tachykinin* (Greek *takhus*, swift), any of a class of substances having a rapid stimulant effect on smooth muscle. *Kinin* (formed from *bradykinin*) is the general term for this group of substances, formed in body tissue in response to injury; in botany that term indicates a plant hormone (also called a *cytokinin*) that promotes cell division and growth and inhibits ageing.

klepto- *Thieving.* [Greek *kleptēs*, thief.]

Kleptomania is a recurrent urge to steal, typically without regard for need or profit; a *kleptoparasite* is an animal which habitually steals food from animals of other species; a *kleptocracy* (Greek -*kratia*, power, rule) is literally government by thieves, one in which those in power exploit national resources to personal profit.

klino-: *see* CLINO-

kypho- *Humped.* [Greek *kuphos*, bent, hunchbacked.]

In medicine, *kyphosis* is an excessive outward curvature of the spine, causing hunching of the back; *kyphoscoliosis* (Greek *skolios*, bent) is a condition in which the spinal column is bent both backward and sideways, a combination of *kyphosis* and *scoliosis*.

L

L- or **l-**: *see* LAEVO-

labi(o)- *The lips.* [Latin *labium*, lip.]

The adjective referring to the lips is **labial**. In phonetics several terms indicate a sound involving the lips, as in *labiodental*, with the lips and teeth, for example *f* and *v*, or *labiovelar*, with the lips and soft palate, for example *w*. A *labium* is a lip-like structure, say part of the mouth of an insect or the lower lip of the flower of a plant.

lact(o)- Also **lacti-**. *Milk; lactic acid or lactose.* [Latin *lac*, *lact*-, milk.]

Lactation refers to the secretion of milk by the mammary glands; something *lactiferous* forms or conveys milk or milky fluids; a hormone or other substance that is *lactogenic* induces the secretion of milk; a person who is a *lacto-ovo-vegetarian* (Latin *ovum*, egg) eats vegetables, eggs, and dairy products but does not eat meat.

A sugar characteristically present in milk is *lactose* or *milk sugar*. Fermentation of it by a *lactobacillus* produces *lactic acid*. *Lactoprotein* is the general name for the protein component of milk, constituents of which include *lactoferrin*, *lactoglobulin*, and *lactalbumin*.

laevo- In the US, **levo-**. Also **l-** and **L-**. *On or to the left.* [Latin *laevus*, left.]

Many chemical compounds rotate polarized light to the left (that is, anticlockwise facing the oncoming radiation) and are then said to be **laevorotatory**. A number of compounds include **laevo-** or **levo-** in their names to indicate they are laevorotatory, for example *laevulose* (another name for the sugar fructose), the antibiotic *levofloxacin*, and *levodopa*, used in the treatment of Parkinson's disease. In chemical names, the laevorotatory form is sometimes indicated by **l-**. The optical activity of a compound reflects the arrangement of the atoms in its molecules; the prefix **L-** has been used to refer to one whose shape is consistent with that of *L-glyceraldehyde*; for example, levodopa is usually abbreviated to *L-dopa*. However, **l-** forms are not necessarily also **L-** forms and both prefixes have largely been replaced by other naming conventions. The opposite to **laevo-** is DEXTRO-.

-lagnia *Morbid sexual arousal.* [Greek *lagneia*, lust.]

These are principally technical terms in psychiatry. Examples include **urolagnia** (Greek *ouron*, urine), a tendency to derive sexual pleasure from the sight or thought of urination; *algolagnia* (Greek *algos*, pain), desire for sexual gratification through inflicting pain on oneself or others; *coprolagnia* (Greek *kopros*, dung), sexual arousal by the thought or sight of faeces.

-lalia *A speech condition or disorder.* [Greek *lalia*, speech.]

Instances are mostly from psychiatry and medicine and include *coprolalia* (Greek *kopros*, dung), the involuntary use of obscene language, as a symptom of mental illness or organic brain disease; *echolalia* (Greek *ēkhō*, echo), uncontrollable repetition of another person's spoken words as a symptom of psychiatric disorder; *glossolalia* (Greek *glōssa*, language, tongue), apparently speaking in an unknown language, especially in religious worship, speaking in tongues; *palilalia* (Greek *palin*, again), a speech disorder characterized by involuntary repetition of words, phrases, or sentences.

lamelli- *A thin scale, plate, or layer.* [Latin *lamella*, diminutive of *lamina*, a thin plate.]

This form is in limited use, mainly in zoology. An animal that is *lamellibranch* (Greek *brankhia*, gills), has plate-like gills, as do the bivalves, which include the oysters, mussels, and scallops; *lamellicorn*

(Latin *cornu*, horn), is an older term for a member of a large group of beetles that includes the cockchafer, now usually called *scarabaeoids*; a *lamellipodium* is a flattened extension of a cell, by which it moves over or adheres to a surface.

lamin(o)- *A thin layer.* [Latin *lamina*, a thin plate]

The word *lamina* (plural *laminae*) refers to thin plates of various kinds, such as scales, layers, or flakes; something *laminar* consists of thin layers; to *laminate* a surface is to overlay it with a layer of plastic or some other protective material; *laminitis* is inflammation of sensitive layers of tissue inside the hoof in horses and other animals; a *laminectomy* (Greek *ektomē*, excision) is a surgical operation to remove the back of one or more vertebrae. In phonetics, *laminal* refers to a consonant formed with the blade of the tongue touching the alveolar ridge.

lapar(o)- *The abdominal wall.* [Greek *lapara*, flank.]

A *laparoscope* is a fibre optic instrument which is inserted through the abdominal wall to view the organs in the abdomen, a procedure called *laparoscopy*; a *laparotomy* (Greek *-tomia*, cutting) is a surgical incision into the abdominal cavity, for diagnosis or in preparation for major surgery.

laryng(o)- *The larynx.* [Greek *larunx*, larynx.]

The *larynx* is the hollow organ that conveys air to the lungs and contains the vocal cords; *laryngitis* is inflammation of the larynx; *laryngology* is the branch of medicine that deals with the larynx and its diseases; a *laryngoscope* is an instrument for examining it, or for inserting a tube through it; a *laryngectomy* (Greek *ektomē*, excision) is surgical removal of all or part of it; the usual adjective is *laryngeal*, which in phonetics also refers to a speech sound made in the larynx with the vocal cords partly closed.

latero- Also **lateri-**. *Lateral; to one side.* [Latin *latus*, *later-*, side.]

The **latero-** form appears in a number of specialist medical terms, often hy-

phenated. Some refer to lateral displacement: *lateroflexion*, bending or curvature of a body part to one side; *lateroversion* (Latin *vertere*, to turn), displacement of an organ (especially the uterus) to one side. Others refer to the side of a specified structure: *laterocervical* (Latin *cervix*, *cervic-*, neck), the side of the neck; *laterodorsal* (Latin *dorsum*, back), the side of the back of an organ, especially in a part of the brain called the *laterodorsal tegmental nucleus*; *lateroventral* (Latin *venter*, *ventr-*, belly), similarly the side of the front of an organ. The **lateri-** form is rare, the only example at all met with being *laterigrade*, walking sideways, as some species of spiders do.

-latry Also **-later**. *Worship of a specified thing.* [Greek *-latria*, worship; *-latrēs*, worshipper.]

Most words formed using these endings have negative implications. Examples include *idolatry* (Greek *eidōlon*, from *eidos*, form, shape), worship of idols; *Mariolatry*, idolatrous worship of the Virgin Mary; *hagiolatry* (Greek *hagios*, holy), the worship of saints, or undue veneration of a famous person; *demonolatry*, the worship of demons; *bardolatry* is a humorous term for excessive admiration of the Bard, Shakespeare. Names for worshippers end in **-later**: *bardolater*, *idolater*.

-le¹ Also **-el**. *Forming nouns.* [Either from Old English, or from Middle English *-el*, *-elle* (partly from Old English and partly from Old French words based on Latin forms).]

One group, from Old English, contains the names of agents or instruments: *handle*, *saddle*, *shuttle*, *sickle*, *thimble*, *whistle*; less commonly it is used for animals and plants, or parts of them: *apple*, *beetle*, *bramble*, *bristle*, *cockle*.

A second set either have or originally had a diminutive sense: *castle* (a diminutive of Latin *castrum*, a fort), *cobble* (from *cob*, a rounded lump), *girdle* (probably from *gird*), *nozzle* (from *nose*), *puddle* (from Old English *pudd*, a ditch or furrow).

In some cases, the older form **-el** has been retained where the rules of English spelling and pronunciation do not permit the change to **-le** after certain letters: *satchel*, *angel*, *kennel*, *kestrel*, *bushel*, *brothel*, *shovel*. *See also* -REL.

The suffix is not used to make new words.

-le² *Apt to; liable to.* [Middle English: from earlier *-el*, of Germanic origin.]

The few examples are adjectives, formed from older verbs, for example *brittle*, *fickle*, and *nimble*. The suffix is not used to make new words.

-le³ *Forming verbs.* [Old English *-lian*, of Germanic origin.]

Many examples express a repeated action or movement: *babble*, *crackle*, *hobble*, *mingle*, *paddle*, *prattle*, *sparkle*, *tangle*, *tinkle*, *wriggle*. Some are based on echoic roots: *cackle*, *gabble*, *giggle*, *mumble*. The suffix is not used to make new words.

-lecithal *Having an egg yolk of a given kind.* [Greek *lekithos*, yolk of an egg.]

This suffix is found most commonly in developmental biology. Examples are: *alecithal*, relating to an egg with little or no food-yolk; *centrolecithal*, having the yolk near the centre of the egg; *isolecithal* (Greek *isos*, equal), having the yoke distributed throughout the egg; and *telolecithal* (Greek *telos*, near), having the yolk near one end of the egg.

lecith(o)- *Egg yolk.* [Greek *lekithos*, yolk of an egg.]

Lecithin is another name for phosphatidylcholine, a substance widely distributed in animal tissues and egg yolk; *lecithinase* is another name for phospholipase, an enzyme which hydrolyses phosphatidylcholine; in zoology, *lecithotrophic* refers to the larvae of certain marine invertebrates that feed on the yolk of the egg from which they have emerged.

-lect *A variety within a language.* [The second element of *dialect*.]

The base term, *dialect* (Greek *dialektos*, discourse, way of speaking), is the form of a language which is peculiar to a specific region or social group. Other words

have been derived from it, including *acrolect* (Greek *akron*, summit), the most prestigious dialect or variety of a particular language; *idiolect* (Greek *idios*, own, distinct), the speech habits peculiar to a particular person; and *sociolect* (Latin *socius*, companion), the dialect of a particular social class.

leio- *Smooth.* [Greek *leios*, smooth.]

In pathology, a *leiomyoma* is a benign tumour made up of smooth muscle fibre; someone *leiotrichous* (Greek *trikho-*, from *thrix*, hair) has smooth or straight hair; from the same Greek source, the *leiothrix* is an Asian bird of the babbler family.

-lent *Full of; characterized by.* [Latin *-lentus*, *-lens*, *-ful*.]

Examples are *pestilent* (Latin *pestilentus*, from *pestis*, plague), *redolent* (Latin *redolens*, from *olere*, to smell), *somnolent* (Latin *somnolentus*, from *somnus*, sleep), and *violent* (Latin *violentus*, violent). Most of the others are compounds of Latin words ending in *-volent*, 'wishing' (*benevolent*, *malevolent*), or *-valent* (*see* -VALENT), 'being worth' (*equivalent*, *prevalent*). *See also* -ULENT.

lepid(o)- *Scales.* [Gk *lepis*, *lepid-*, a scale.]

The *Lepidoptera* (Greek *pteron*, wing) are the butterflies and moths, so called because they have scale-covered wings; hence a *lepidopterist* is a person who studies or collects butterflies and moths; *lepidolite* is a mineral of the mica group, occurring in layers; a plant that is *lepidote* is covered with scale-like hairs. The word *leper* (Greek *lepra*, scaly) for a person suffering from leprosy came about because of the characteristic skin lesions.

-lepsis Also **-leptic**. *A figure of speech.* [Greek *lēpsis*, a seizing, from *lambanein*, take hold of.]

Words ending in **-lepsis** derive from medieval terms in rhetoric. A *syllepsis* (Greek *sullēpsis*, taking together) is a figure of speech in which a word is applied to two others in different senses (for example, *he caught the train and a bad cold*); *prolepsis* (Greek *prolēpsis*, from *prolambanein*, anticipate, from *pro*, before, plus *lambanein*, take) can refer to anticipating and answering possible objections in rhetorical speech, or to a literary device in which something is presumed to have existed before it actually happened, as in *he was a dead man when he entered*; **metalepsis** (Greek *metalepsis*, from *metalambanein* to substitute, from *meta*, with, across, or after) is a form of metonymy of an indirect kind in which the substitution is of a word that is already being used figuratively. Adjectives are formed using **-leptic**: *syleptic*, *proleptic*.

-lepsy Also **-leptic**. *A seizure.* [Greek *lēpsis*, a seizing, from *lambanein*, take hold of.]

Common examples relate to medical conditions: **epilepsy** (Greek *epilēpsia*, from *epilambanein*, seize, attack), involving sudden recurrent episodes of sensory disturbance, loss of consciousness, or convulsions; **catalepsy** (Greek *katalēpsis*, from *kata*, down), a condition of trance or seizure with loss of sensation and consciousness in which the body becomes rigid; **narcolepsy** (Greek *narkē*, numbness, on the pattern of *epilepsy*), a condition in which those affected show an uncontrollable tendency to fall asleep. More rarely, it can refer to other sorts of seizures: **nympholepsy** (Greek *numphē*, nymph, bride), a poetic or literary term for a passion aroused in men by beautiful young girls. Adjectives are formed ending in **-leptic**: *epileptic*, *nympholeptic*.

lept(o)- *Small; narrow.* [Greek *leptos*, fine, thin, delicate.]

This form appears in a variety of terms in the sciences: **leptin** is a protein which regulates fat storage in the body (so named because an excess makes an animal thin); a **lepton** is a small subatomic particle, such as an electron or muon, which does not take part in the strong interaction; **leptospirosis** (Greek *speira*, coil, from the shape of the bacterium) is an infectious bacterial disease that can be transmitted to humans; the **leptomeninges** are the inner two layers that cover the brain and spinal cord, between which the cerebrospinal fluid circulates; in statistics, a frequency distribution that is **lep-**

tokurtic (Greek *kurtos*, bulging) is concentrated about the mean.

-less Also **-lessness**. *Without; unaffected by; failure or inability.* [Old English *-lēas*, from *lēas*, devoid of.]

Words ending in **-less** are nearly all adjectives. The great majority come from nouns and have the sense of lacking or being without that thing or quality: *bottomless*, *childless*, *defenceless*, *lawless*, *pointless*, *spineless*, *strapless*, *toothless*. The comparatively few that originate in verbs indicate something that is unaffected by the action or the verb, or some failure or inability to carry out that action: *dauntless*, *quenchless*, *relentless*, *resistless*, *tireless*.

The suffix is freely used to create new adjectives at need, to the extent that only a proportion of them can be recorded in dictionaries. Many are invented to fill a momentary need: *girlfriendless*, *handbrakeless*, *monarchless*, *passwordless*, *sidewalkless*.

Corresponding nouns are formed by adding -NESS: *childlessness*, *fearlessness*, *tastelessness*.

-let *A thing of a smaller or lesser kind.* [Originally from French *-ette*, added to nouns ending in *-el*.]

Some words were formed in medieval times from French diminutive nouns, but that sense has largely been lost in English. Examples include **bracelet** (French *bras*, arm), **gauntlet** (French *gant*, glove), **hamlet** (French *hamel*, little village), **tablet** (Old French *tablete*, from a diminutive of Latin *tabula*, table), and **toilet** (French *toile*, cloth).

The ending became popular in the 18th century; in the 19th century it became—and remains—a common word-forming element in the language. Most suggest something small of its kind, though this idea has softened in some with the passage of time. Examples include **booklet**, **cloudlet**, **droplet**, **hooklet**, **leaflet**, **moonlet**, **notelet**, **piglet**, **ringlet**, **rootlet**, **starlet**, **statelet**, **streamlet**, and **wavelet**.

A **doublet** was originally a man's short close-fitting padded jacket; later it came to mean either of a pair of similar things, which gave rise by imitation to *triplet* and *quadruplet*.

On the model of *bracelet*, some other words for articles of adornment have been created: *anklet*, *armlet*, *necklet*, *wristlet*.

See also -ET *and* -ETTE.

leuc(o)- Also **leuk(o)-**. *White; whiteness.* [Greek *leukos*, white.]

Leukaemia (US *leukemia*) (Greek *haima*, blood) is a disease in which increased numbers are produced of immature or abnormal white blood cells called *leucocytes* (also spelled *leukocyte*); *leucine* is an amino acid, a white crystalline compound, essential in the human diet; *leucoderma* (also called *vitiligo*) is a condition in which the pigment is lost from areas of the skin, causing whitish patches; a *leucoma* is a white opacity in the cornea of the eye; a *leucistic* animal has whitish fur, plumage, or skin due to a lack of pigment.

levo-: *see* LAEVO-

ligno- Also **ligni-**. *Wood.* [Latin *lignum*, wood.]

The adjective *ligneous* refers to something consisting of or resembling wood; *lignite* is a soft brownish coal that still shows traces of plant structure; *lignin* is a complex organic polymer deposited in the cell walls of many plants, making them rigid and woody; *lignocellulose* is a complex of lignin and cellulose present in the cell walls of woody plants; the local anaesthetic *lignocaine* was named to indicate its chemical similarity to xylene, derived from wood. *See also* XYLO-.

limn(o)- *Fresh water.* [from Greek *limnē*, lake.]

This form is most commonly found in *limnology*, the study of the features of bodies of fresh water, and in its compounds. Other examples are *limnic*, of a sediment laid down in fresh water such as a lake or swamp; *Limnaea*, the genus of freshwater pond snails; and *limnoplankton*, plankton that prefer freshwater.

-ling *Forming nouns, often with diminutive or depreciatory implications.* [Old English or Old Norse.]

Nouns have been formed from other nouns, or from adjectives, adverbs, or verbs. In older formations, the sense is of a person or thing connected with the stem: *foundling*, *hireling*, *nestling*, *suckling*. In many cases the stem is rare or archaic and the link is now unclear: *sibling* originally meant a relative, from the Old English *sib*, related by descent; *sterling*, British money, derives from Middle English *steorra*, star, because some early Norman pennies bore a small star.

The ending has long had implications of smallness, especially when speaking of the young of animals or plants: *duckling*, *gosling*, *fledgling*, *hatchling*, *oakling*, *spiderling*, *yearling*. Occasionally terms are meant affectionately, as in *darling* (Old English *dēore*, beloved). More commonly, the associations are negative: *underling*, *weakling*, *princeling*, *lordling*, *godling*.

The suffix is now only used to make new words in this depreciatory sense, and not often even then: *tycoonling*, *weedling* (a person who is weedy, or weak of stature).

lip(o)- *Fat.* [Greek *lipos*, fat.]

In cosmetic surgery, *liposuction* removes excess fat from under the skin by suction; *lipids* are a class of organic compounds that include many natural oils, waxes, and steroids; *lipase* is an enzyme that catalyses the breakdown of fats; a *lipoma* is a benign tumour of fatty tissue; *lipogenesis* is the normal formation of fat in the body; *lipolysis* (Greek *lusis*, loosening) is the breakdown of fats and other lipids to release fatty acids. *See also* STEATO-.

A *lipogram*, a composition from which the writer systematically omits one or more letters of the alphabet is instead based on Greek *leipein*, to leave (out).

-lite *A mineral or fossil.* [Greek *lithos*, stone.]

This ending appears in a number of mineral names as an alternative to *-ite* (*see* -ITE[1]) when following a vowel. A few examples are: *cryolite* (Greek *kruos*, frost; the main deposits are found in Greenland), a mineral added to bauxite as a flux in aluminium smelting; *oolite* (Greek *ōion*, egg), limestone consisting of a mass of rounded grains made up of concentric layers; *rhyolite* (Greek *rhuax*, lava stream), a general name for fine-grained volcanic rocks typically occurring in lava flows; *zeolite* (Greek *zein*, to boil, because examples swell when heated), any of a large group of minerals consisting of hydrated aluminosilicates.

The ending is less commonly used to create the names of fossils: *coprolite* (Greek *kopros*, dung), fossilized dung; *stromatolite* (modern Latin *stroma*, *stromat-*, layer, covering), a calcareous mound built up of layers of lime-secreting cyanobacteria and trapped sediment; *graptolite* (Greek *graptos*, marked with letters, because impressions resemble markings with a slate pencil), a fossil marine invertebrate animal of the Palaeozoic era.

lith-: *see* LITHO-

-lith *A stone or stony structure.* [Greek *lithos*, stone.]

Examples in which this ending refers to types of rock include *regolith* (Greek *rhēgos*, rug, blanket), the layer of unconsolidated solid material covering the bedrock of a planet; *batholith* (Greek *bathos*, depth), a very large igneous intrusion extending to an unknown depth in the earth's crust; *laccolith* (Greek *lakkos*, reservoir), a mass of igneous rock that has been intruded between rock strata, causing uplift in the shape of a dome.

Words in which the sense is of something constructed of stone include *megalith* (Greek *megas*, great), a large stone that forms a prehistoric monument or part of one; and *monolith* (Greek *monos*, single), a large single upright block of stone, especially a pillar or monument.

Other examples occur in the life sciences, including *otolith* (Greek *ous*, *ōt-*, ear), a small calcareous body in the inner ear, involved in sensing gravity and movement; *phytolith* (Greek *phuton*, a plant), either a minute mineral particle formed inside a plant, or a fossilized particle of plant tissue; *gastrolith*, a small stone swallowed by an animal to aid digestion in the gizzard, or in medicine a hard concretion in the stomach.

For related adjectives, see the next entry.

-lithic *Stone.* [Greek *lithos*, stone.]

This ending mainly appears in adjectives formed from nouns ending in -LITH: *megalithic*, *otolithic*. However, *trilithic* derives from *trilithon* (sometimes *trilith*), a structure consisting of two upright stones and a third across the top as a lintel, as in Stonehenge. *Lithic* exists as a standalone adjective, in reference to stone or the nature of stone.

The ending also occurs in adjectives and nouns relating to periods of the Stone Age; examples include *Palaeolithic* (US *Paleolithic*) (Greek *palaios*, ancient), the early phase, when primitive stone implements were used; *Mesolithic* (Greek *mesos*, middle), its middle part; *Neolithic* (Greek *neos*, new), the later part, when ground or polished stone weapons and implements prevailed.

lith(o)- *Stone.* [Greek *lithos*, stone.]

The *lithosphere* is the rigid outer part of the earth, consisting of the crust and upper mantle; a *lithophyte* (Greek *phuton*, a plant) is a plant that grows on bare rock or stone.

The printing process called *lithography* is so called because the flat printing surface was originally a specially prepared stone; *lithophane* (Greek *-phanēs*, appearing) is a kind of ornamentation of porcelain visible when held to the light.

The form also applies to various stony materials which develop in the body, such as kidney stones or gallstones: *lithiasis* is their process of formation; *lithotomy* (Greek *-tomia*, cutting) is their surgical removal; *lithotripsy* (Greek *tripsis*, rubbing) is the surgical technique of breaking a stone into pieces using ultrasound shock waves.

-log: *see* -LOGUE

-loger: *see* -LOGIST

-logical Also **-logic**. *Relating to a branch*

of knowledge or experience. [Formed from nouns ending in -LOGY by replacing the last letter with *-ical* or *-ic.*]

Many examples exist, of which a few are: *astrological*, *biological*, *ecological*, *ideological*, *mineralogical*, *numerological*, *seismological*, *sociological*, *theological*, and *zoological*.

Though **-logical** is the standard way of forming such adjectives, a few are also formed using **-logic**, such as *hydrologic*, *morphologic*, and *physiologic*. Adjectives sometimes exist in both spellings: *geological* and *geologic*; *pharmacological* and *pharmacologic*. In such cases, there is no clear distinction of sense, but the one ending in **-logical** is substantially more common.

-logist Also **-loger**. *A person skilled in, or involved in, a branch of study.* [Formed from nouns ending in -LOGY by replacing the last letter with -IST.]

Many examples exist, of which a few are *archaeologist*, *biologist*, *entomologist*, *futurologist*, *geologist*, *meteorologist*, *ornithologist*, *pathologist*, *psychologist*, *technologist*, and *zoologist*. The form is actively used to make new words as required.

At one time, the form **-loger** with the same sense was common (*see* -ER¹), but most examples have been replaced by others ending in **-logist**. A rare surviving example is *astrologer*.

logo- *Words or speech.* [Greek *logos*, word or speech.]

A *logotype* is a single piece of type that prints a word or group of separate letters, or an emblem or *logo* (its abbreviated form); *logopaedics* (US *logopedics*) is speech therapy and the study of defects and disabilities of speech; somebody who is *logocentric* regards words and language as a fundamental expression of an external reality; a *logogram* is a sign or character representing a word or phrase, such as those used in shorthand and some ancient writing systems.

-logue In the US usually **-log**. *A type of communication or debate.* [French *-logue*, from Greek *-logos*, *-logon*, word or speech.]

Examples include *monologue* (Greek *monos*, alone), a long speech by one actor, or one by someone monopolizing a conversation; *dialogue* (Greek *dia*, through), a conversation between two or more people or groups, often to resolve some problem; *travelogue*, a film, book, or illustrated lecture describing travels; *epilogue* (Greek *epi*, in addition), a concluding part to a book or play; *Decalogue* is another name for the Ten Commandments in Christian theology.

In *catalogue* (Greek *katalogos*, from *katalegein*, pick out or enrol), it has the rare sense of a compilation; a few modern formations are based on it, including *magalogue*, a blend of *magazine* and *catalogue*, a promotional catalogue or brochure designed to resemble a high-quality magazine.

Rarely, the ending is equivalent to -LOGIST: *ideologue*.

-logy Also **-ology**. *A subject of study or interest; speech or language.* [French *-logie* or medieval Latin *-logia*, from Greek *logos*, word or speech.]

Many examples relating to a field of study exist, of which a selection is given in the LIST overleaf. Almost all precede the ending with -O-; two common exceptions are *genealogy* and *mineralogy*, but under the influence of the majority these are also often seen spelled with *o*.

The ending is active in forming new words. It is often used to create temporary or humorous forms, as with *gizmology*, the subject of gizmos or gadgets; *sleazology*, the investigation or study of sordid and corrupt behaviour; *mindology*, a facetious alternative to psychology. *Ology* has existed since the early 19th century as an informal term for any subject of study or branch of knowledge.

A second, less common, sense is related to that of -LOGUE, indicating some characteristic of speech or language, or a type of discourse. Examples include *terminology* (medieval Latin *terminus*, a term); *tautology* (Greek *tauto-*, same), the saying of the same thing twice over in different words; *symbology*, the study or use of symbols; and *apology* (Greek *apolo-*

-logy A subject of study or interest.
Origins are from Greek unless otherwise stated.

anthropology	the study of humankind	(*anthrōpos*, human being)
archaeology (US also *archeology*)	the study of human history and prehistory through the excavation of sites and the analysis of physical remains	(*arkhaios*, ancient)
astrology	the study of the movements and relative positions of celestial bodies interpreted as having an influence on human affairs	(*astron*, star)
biology	the study of living organisms	(*bios*, life)
biotechnology	the exploitation of biological processes for industrial and other purposes	(*bios*, life, plus *technē*, art, craft)
chronology	the study of historical records to establish the dates of past events	(*khronos*, time)
ecology	the branch of biology that deals with the relations of organisms to one another and to their physical surroundings	(*oîkos*, house)
geology	the science which deals with the physical structure and substance of the earth, their history, and the processes which act on them	(*gē*, earth)
gynaecology (US *gynecology*)	the branch of physiology and medicine which deals with the functions and diseases specific to women and girls, especially those affecting the reproductive system	(*gunē, gunaik-*, woman, female)
meteorology	the branch of science concerned with the processes and phenomena of the atmosphere, especially as a means of forecasting the weather	(*meteōron*, of the atmosphere)
microbiology	the branch of science that deals with micro-organisms	(*mikros*, small, plus *bios*, life)
neurology	the branch of medicine or biology that deals with the anatomy, functions, and organic disorders of nerves and the nervous system	(*neuron*, nerve, sinew, tendon)
pathology	the science of the causes and effects of diseases	(*pathos*, suffering, disease)
pharmacology	the branch of medicine concerned with the uses, effects, and modes of action of drugs	(*pharmakon*, drug)
physiology	the branch of biology that deals with the normal functions of living organisms and their parts	(*phusis*, nature)
psychology	the scientific study of the human mind and its functions, especially those affecting behaviour in a given context	(*psukhē*, breath, soul, mind)
sociology	the study of the development, structure, and functioning of human society	(Latin *socius*, companion)
technology	the application of scientific knowledge for practical purposes, especially in industry	(*technē*, art, craft)
theology	the study of the nature of God and religious belief	(*theos*, god)
topology	the study of geometrical properties and spatial relations unaffected by the continuous hange of shape or size of figures	(*topos*, place)
zoology	the scientific study of animals	(*zōion*, animal)

gia, a speech in one's own defence, from *apo*, away). *Anthology* comes from the related Greek suffix *-logia*, a collection, plus *anthos*, flower, because it originally meant a collection of flowers of verse, choice epigrams and the like. *See also* -LOGIST and -LOGICAL.

lopho- *Crested.* [Greek *lophos*, crest.]

Terms in **lopho-** are mostly specialist ones in zoology: a *lophophore* (Greek *-phoros, -phoron*, bearing, bearer) is a horseshoe-shaped structure bearing ciliated tentacles around the mouth in certain small marine invertebrates; a bacterium that is *lophotrichous* has several flagella in a crest or bundle at one end of the cell; an animal that is *lophodont* (Greek *odous, odont-*, tooth) has transverse ridges on the grinding surfaces of its teeth.

lumbo- *The lower back or loin.* [Latin *lumbus*, loin.]

The adjective that refers to the lower back is *lumbar; lumbosacral* refers to the lumbar and sacral regions, *lumbocostal* (Latin *costa*, rib) to the lumbar region and the ribs, *lumbodorsal* to the lumbar region and the back (these sometimes appear hyphenated); *lumbago* is pain in the muscles and joints of the lower back.

lute(o)- *Yellow; the corpus luteum.* [Latin *luteus*, yellow, or *luteum*, yolk of egg.]

The first sense is comparatively rare. It can apply to various shades of orange or yellow—something *luteous* can be a deep orange-yellow or a greenish yellow colour; *lutescent* refers to something yellowish in colour.

The *corpus luteum* (Latin, literally 'yellow body') is a hormone-secreting structure that develops in an ovary after an egg has been discharged; the process of formation is *luteinization*; ovulation is stimulated by *luteinizing hormone*; *lutein* is a deep yellow pigment found in the corpus luteum, among other places; the adjective *luteal* relates to the corpus luteum.

-ly Also **-ily**. *Forming adjectives and adverbs.* [Old English adjectival ending *-lic* or adverbial ending *-līce*, of Germanic origin.]

One set of adjectives indicates a quality of some kind. They usually derive from nouns, though some are based on other adjectives: *beastly*, *cleanly*, *cowardly*, *deadly*, *evenly*, *gladly*, *heavenly*, *neighbourly*, *rascally*, *scholarly*, *weakly*. Many can also be adverbs, though some, such as *miserly* and *unruly*, are restricted to adjectival use. A second set indicate something recurring at an interval: *hourly*, *daily*, *weekly*, *monthly*, *quarterly*, *yearly*; these can all act as adverbs.

The **-ly** ending most characteristically marks adverbs, and is the usual way of forming them from adjectives. A very large number exist, of which a few examples are *apparently*, *commonly*, *electrically*, *essentially*, *foolishly*, *freely*, *greatly*, *immediately*, *occasionally*, *surprisingly*, *thankfully*, and *wrongly*.

Adverbs formed from adjectives that end in *y* preceded by a consonant replace the *y* by an *i* to make the ending **-ily**: *busily*, *drowsily*, *floppily*, *hastily*, *lazily*, *primarily*, *wittily*.

lymph(o)- Also **lymphaden(o)-** and **lymphangi(o)-**. *Lymph.* [Latin *lympha, limpa*, water.]

Lymph is a fluid containing white blood cells, which drains through the *lymphatic* system into the bloodstream; lymph nodes are small swellings in the lymphatic system where lymph is filtered and *lymphocytes* are formed, small white blood cells with a single round nucleus; a *lymphoma* (plural *lymphomas* or *lymphomata*) is a cancer of the lymph nodes, of which an example is Hodgkin's disease; *lymphoblasts* are abnormal cells resembling large lymphocytes, produced in a form of leukaemia.

The compound form **lymphadeno-** (Greek *adēn*, gland) refers specifically to the lymph nodes; examples include *lymphadenopathy*, a disease affecting them, and *lymphadenitis*, inflammation of them. Another compound form **lymphangio-** (Greek *angeion*, vessel) refers to a lymphatic vessel, as in *lymphangioma*, a localized collection of distended lymphatic vessels that may result in a cyst, and *lymphangitis*, inflammation of lymph vessels.

lyo- *Dispersion; dissolution.* [Greek *luein*, loosen or dissolve.]

-lysis   Disintegration or decomposition.
Origins are from Greek unless otherwise stated.

analysis	detailed examination of the elements or structure of something, typically as a basis for discussion or interpretation	(*analusis*, from *ana-*, up)
catalysis	the acceleration of a chemical reaction by a substance that does not itself undergo any permanent chemical change	(*katalusis*, from *kata-*, down)
cryptanalysis	the art or process of deciphering coded messages without being told the key	(*kruptos*, hidden)
dialysis	the separation of particles in a liquid on the basis of differences in their ability to pass through a membrane, especially the clinical purification of blood by this technique	(*dialusis*, from *dia*, apart)
electrolysis	chemical decomposition produced by passing an electric current through a liquid or solution containing ions	(English *electric*, plus -O-)
glycolysis	the breakdown of glucose by enzymes, releasing energy and pyruvic acid	(*glukus*, sweet)
hydrolysis	the chemical breakdown of a compound due to reaction with water	(*hudōr*, water)
paralysis	the loss of the ability to move	(*paralusis*, from *para*, beside)
photolysis	the decomposition or separation of molecules by the action of light	(*phōs*, *phōt-*, light)
psychoanalysis	a system of psychological theory and therapy	(*psukhē*, breath, soul, mind)
pyrolysis	decomposition brought about by high temperatures	(*pur*, fire)
thermolysis	the breakdown of molecules by heat	(*thermos*, hot)
thrombolysis	the dissolution of a blood clot, especially as induced artificially by infusion of an enzyme into the blood	(*thrombos*, blood clot)

A *lyophilic* colloid is one readily dispersed by a solvent and not easily precipitated, its opposite being *lyophobic*; to *lyophilize* a substance is to freeze-dry it; a *lyotropic* material is one whose phase is determined by its concentration.

lys- or **lysi-**: *see* LYSO-

-lysis Also **-lyse**, **-lyze**, **-lyte**, **-lytic**, and **-lyst**. *Disintegration or decomposition.* [Greek *lusis*, loosening.]

The ending **-lysis** forms nouns. They can either describe the agent by which the process takes place, as with *hydrolysis*, reaction with water, or *photolysis*, with light; alternatively they can suggest the thing acted upon, as in *glycolysis*, the breakdown of glucose by enzymes, or *proteolysis*, of proteins. Some can specify the nature of the process, as with *autolysis*, self-destruction of cells by their own enzymes. *Analysis* and its compounds stand at one remove, since the modern sense is figurative, based on Greek *analusis*, an unloosening, from *ana-*, up. *Lysis* can be a noun in its own right for the disintegration of a cell by rupture of its cell wall or membrane. See the LIST above for more examples.

Related verbs are formed using **-lyse**: *analyse*, *catalyse*, *hydrolyse*, *paralyse*, *psychoanalyse*; *breathalyse* is a rare example where no corresponding noun-ending in **-lysis** exists. These forms are all spelled

-lyze in North America. The ending **-lyte** forms nouns identifying substances that can be decomposed by a specified process, as in *electrolyte*. Related adjectives are created using **-lytic**: *catalytic*, *hydrolytic*, *psychoanalytic*. A few nouns indicating the agent involved in the process are formed using **-lyst**: *catalyst*, *psychoanalyst*.

lys(o)- *Disintegration of cells.* [Greek *lusis*, loosening.]

A *lysosome* is an organelle in cells containing enzymes that digest substances in the cell; a *lysozyme* is an enzyme which catalyses the destruction of the cell walls of certain bacteria, and occurs notably in tears and egg white; *lysis* is the disintegration of a cell by rupture of the cell wall or membrane; *lysin* is an antibody, bacterium, or other substance able to cause this.

m-: *see* META-

-machy *Fighting.* [Greek *-makhia*, -fighting.]

Some rather rare terms contain this ending, such as *sciamachy* (Greek *skia*, shadow), an archaic term for sham fighting for exercise or practice; *tauromachy* (Greek *tauros*, bull), bullfighting or a bullfight; *gigantomachy* (Greek *gigas*, *gigant-*, giant), the struggle in Greek mythology between the gods and the giants; *logomachy* (Greek *logos*, word), an argument about words; and *theomachy* (Greek *theos*, god), a war or struggle against God or among or against the gods.

macro- *Long; large.* [Greek *makros*, long, large.]

This combining form is widely distributed, especially in scientific and technical contexts. The *macrocosm* (Greek *kosmos*, world) is the universe or the whole cosmos; a *macromolecule* contains a very large number of atoms, such as a protein, nucleic acid, or synthetic polymer; *macrophotography* produces photographs of small items larger than life size; *macroevolution* is major evolutionary change. *Macro* can appear as a free-standing word, as in macro *lens*, one used in macrophotography, or as an abbreviation of the computer term *macro instruction*, a single instruction that expands into a set to perform a given task. Also related is *macron*, a written or printed mark (ˉ) used to indicate a long vowel or a stressed vowel in verse. **Macro-** is often contrasted with MICRO-.

magneto- *Magnetism or a magnet.* [English *magnet* plus -o-.]

A *magneto-optical* device employs both optical and magnetic technologies, as some computer storage media do; the adjective *magneto-electric* refers to the electric currents generated in a material by its motion in a magnetic field; *magnetoresistance* is the dependence of the electrical resistance of a body on an external magnetic field; the *magnetosphere* surrounding the earth is the region in which its magnetic field predominates over others.

magn(i)- *Large; great.* [Latin *magnus*, great.]

Though several English words contain this form, it is not in active use. Examples are *magnify*, to make larger; *magnate*, a wealthy and influential person; *magnanimous* (Latin *animus*, soul), very generous or forgiving; *magniloquent* (Latin *-loquus*, -speaking), using high-flown or bombastic language. The Latin original is perhaps best known from *Magna Carta*, the *Great Charter*, signed by King John of England in 1215.

mal- Also **male-**. *Improperly; badly; wrongly.* [French *mal*, from Latin *male*, badly.]

Some words acquired via French include *malady* (Latin *habitus*, having as a condition); *maladroit* (French *à droit*, properly); *maltreat* (French *maltraiter*); and *malcontent* (French *content*, pleased).

Many terms have been formed on English stems, of which a few examples are *malnourished*, affected by a bad or insufficient diet; *maladjusted*, failing or unable to cope with the demands of a normal social environment; *malfunction*, a failure to function normally or satisfactorily; *malpractice*, improper, illegal, or negligent professional activity or treatment; *malodorous*, smelling very unpleasant.

Some early examples were spelled **male-**, though this is long defunct as an active ending: *malediction* (Latin *dicere*, to speak); *malefactor* (Latin *facere*, do); *malevolent* (Latin *volent-*, wishing).

-malacia *Abnormal softening of a tissue.* [Greek *malakos*, soft.]

Examples include *osteomalacia* (Greek *osteon*, bone), softening of the bones, typically through a deficiency of vitamin D or calcium; *chondromalacia* (Greek *khondros*, cartilage), degeneration of cartilage at a joint, in particular the knee; and *tracheomalacia*, erosion of the trachea. *Malacia* also exists, with the general sense of softening of some organ or tissue.

malaco- *Soft.* [Greek *malakos*, soft.]

This form occurs in only a few words; easily the most common is *malacology*, the branch of zoology that deals with the soft-bodied molluscs. Others are *malacostracan* (Greek *ostrakon*, shell), relating to a large class of crustaceans, the *Malacostraca*, which includes crabs, shrimps, and lobsters; and *malacoplakia* Greek *plax*, *plak-*, flat plate), inflammation of an organ (especially the urinary bladder) accompanied by formation of soft flat lesions.

Malayo- *Malay; Malay and…* [English *Malaya* plus -o-.]

The only term here that is at all common is *Malayo-Polynesian*, another term for the Austronesian languages, a group spoken in an area extending from Madagascar in the west to the Pacific islands in the east.

male-: *see* MAL-

mamm(o)- *A breast or breasts.* [Latin *mamma*, breast.]

In medicine, *mammography* uses X-rays to diagnose and locate tumours of the breasts, producing images called *mammograms*; *mammoplasty* is plastic surgery on the breasts; the *mammilla* (also spelled *mamilla*), from a diminutive of *mamma*, is the nipple of a woman's breast; something *mammillary* (also spelled *mamillary*) is rounded like a breast or nipple; the usual adjective is *mammary*, which can also be another word for breast. *Mammal*, for warm-blooded animals that suckle their young, comes from the same source. *See also* MASTO-.

-man *A male person of a specified type.* [English *man*]

This form has long been used to name a man from a given place (*Frenchman*, *Corn-*

ishman), belonging to a certain group (*clansman*), having some specified job or role (*businessman*, **lifeboatman**, **nightwatchman**, *salesman*), or possessing some specified quality (*layman*, *madman*). With changes to the status of women in society, many are being replaced by equivalent forms in -PERSON (*chairperson*, *layperson*), or with other gender-neutral terms such as *firefighter*. (*See also* -WOMAN and -MANSHIP.)

The ending also appears in terms for types of sailing ship, now historical, such as *merchantman* or *Indiaman*, which comes from the word *man* used for a ship.

-mancy Also **-mantic** and **-mancer**. *Divination.* [Greek *manteia*, divination.]

Though many words exist in this ending, most are rare; among common ones are *geomancy* and *necromancy*. For these, and other commonly encountered ones, see the LIST on the next page. Some have corresponding adjectives ending in **-mantic** (*geomantic*, *necromantic*) and a few have related forms in **-manter** for a person who practices divination in that way (*cartomancer*, *necromancer*).

Some words seem to include this ending through an accident of spelling: *adamancy*, *dormancy*, and others contain -CY but not **-mancy**.

-mane: *see* -MANIA

mangan(o)- *Manganese.* [English *manganese*, plus -o-.]

Compounds of manganese with a valency of two are described as *manganous*, while those with a valency of three are *manganic*; salts of the anion $MnO_4{}^{2-}$ are *manganates*; a mineral that is *manganiferous* contains manganese, such as *manganite*, an ore of manganese consisting of manganese oxide.

-mania Also **-maniac** and **-mane**. *Mental abnormality or obsession; extreme enthusiasm or admiration.* [Greek *mania*, madness.]

The ending is common in psychiatry to name various kinds of mental problems (*megalomania*, *nymphomania*) as is *mania* itself as a general term. For more details and examples, see the LIST on page 143.

-mancy	Divination.	
	Word origins are from Greek.	
aeromancy	prediction by observing weather conditions	(*aēr*, air)
arithmancy	divination using numbers, especially by counting the number values of letters in names	(*arithmos*, number)
bibliomancy	telling the future by interpreting a randomly chosen passage from a book, especially the Bible	(*biblion*, book)
cartomancy	fortune telling by interpreting a random selection of playing cards	(French *carte*, card)
chiromancy	the prediction of individuals' future from the lines on the palms of their hands; palmistry	(*kheir*, hand)
geomancy	divination from the configuration of a handful of earth or random dots	(*gē*, earth)
hydromancy	foretelling the future using a reflective object or surface, such as that of water in a bowl; scrying	(*hudōr*, water)
necromancy	communicating with the dead, especially in order to predict the future; more generally, witchcraft or sorcery	(*nekros*, corpse)
oneiromancy	the interpretation of dreams in order to foretell the future	(*oneiros*, dream)
pyromancy	divination by fire	(*pur*, fire)

It is also used more loosely for an enthusiasm so great that those showing it seem almost unbalanced; examples here include *Beatlemania*, *balletomania*, and *Anglomania* (excessive admiration of English customs). In this sense, the ending is frequently used in journalism to create words for short-term purposes, as in *Euromania*, enthusiasm for European integration regarded as excessive, or *lotterymania*, an extreme desire to take part in lotteries.

Someone exhibiting such characteristics, in either sense, can be described by a word ending in **-maniac** (*dipsomaniac*, *megalomaniac*, *nymphomaniac*), or, more rarely, by one ending in **-mane**, of which the only common example is *balletomane*.

Examples that seem to contain the ending through accidents of spelling include *leishmania*, a single-celled parasitic protozoan (from the proper name *Leishman*), and some names of countries: *Romania*, *Tasmania*.

-manship Also **-womanship**. *Skill in a subject or activity.* [English -MAN plus -SHIP.]

Traditionally, terms ending in **-manship** indicate a skill and are formed from words ending in -MAN, as *craftsmanship* derives from *craftsman*. Other examples are *chairmanship*, *horsemanship*, *seamanship*, *showmanship*, and *swordsmanship*.

Following Stephen Potter's invention from 1947 onwards of various humorous terms (*gamesmanship*, *lifemanship*, *oneupmanship*), the ending has taken on a sense in its own right, since in these cases related terms ending in -MAN usually do not exist (*lifeman*, *one-upman*). Its sense is that of a skill deployed in order to disconcert a rival or opponent, as in *committeemanship*. Another example is *brinkmanship*, invented by Adlai Stevenson in 1956.

With the changes in the role of women in society in the second half of the 20th century, some of the traditional terms have been amended to provide female equivalents, in effect creating the ending

-mania	Mental abnormality or obsession.	
	Word origins are from Greek unless otherwise stated.	
Beatlemania	frenzied enthusiasm for the 1960s pop group the *Beatles*	
bibliomania	passionate enthusiasm for collecting and possessing books	(*biblion*, book)
egomania	obsessive egotism or self-centredness	(Latin *ego*, I)
erotomania	excessive sexual desire	(*erōs, erōt-*, sexual love)
hypomania	a mild form of mania, marked by elation and hyperactivity	(*hupo*, under)
kleptomania	a recurrent urge to steal	(*kleptēs*, thief)
megalomania	obsession with the exercise of power, especially in the domination of others	(*megas, megal-*, great)
metromania	a mania for writing poetry	(*metron*, metre)
monomania	exaggerated or obsessive enthusiasm for or preoccupation with one thing	(*monos*, alone)
nymphomania	uncontrollable or excessive sexual desire in a woman	(Latin *nympha*, nymph)
pyromania	an obsessive desire to set fire to things	(*pur*, fire)
trichotillomania	a compulsive desire to pull out one's hair	(*thrix, trikho-*, hair, plus *tillesthai*, to pull out)
tulipomania	a craze for tulips, especially that in Holland in the 17th century	

-womanship (*craftswomanship, sportswomanship*). Sometimes, forms ending in **-personship** are seen, such as *chairpersonship*. Words in either of these last two endings are comparatively rare.

mast(o)- *Breast.* [Greek *mastos*, breast.]

A *mastectomy* (Greek *ektomē*, excision) is a surgical operation to remove a breast; *mastology* is the medical study of the human breast; *mastitis* is inflammation of the mammary gland in the breast or udder; a *mastodon* (Greek *odous, odont-*, tooth) is an extinct elephant-like mammal whose molar teeth had nipple-shaped tubercles on their crowns. The *mastoid process*, a conical prominence behind the ear to which the neck muscles are attached, derives its name from Greek *mastoeidēs*, breast-shaped. *See also* MAMMO-.

matr(i)- Also **matro-**. *A mother.* [Latin *mater, matr-*, mother.]

Kinship that is *matrilineal* is based on the mother or the female line; a *matriarch* is a woman who is the head of a family or tribe, or an older woman powerful within a group; *matricide* (Latin *caedere*, to strike down or slay) is either the killing of one's mother, or a person who kills their mother; *matrimony* and *matron* derive from the same Latin root.

maxi- *Very large or long.* [English *maximum*, from Latin *maximus*, the superlative of *magnus*, great.]

This form was created on the model of MINI- at the beginning of the 1960s. Some early terms related to clothing (*maxi-coat, maxi-skirt, maxi-dress*). Others are *maxi-single*, a record with two tracks on each side instead of just one; *maxi-CD*, an audio CD of extended duration or number of tracks; *maxi-yacht*, in Australian usage, a yacht of about twenty metres length or more. Many terms are written without the hyphen (*maxiskirt*); *maxi single* is often seen written thus as two words; *maxi* alone is an abbreviated form of *maximum*, or sometimes of maxi-skirt.

maxillo- *The jaw.* [Latin *maxilla*, jaw.]

The only common term is *maxillofacial*, of or relating to the jaws and face. Others are *maxillomandibular*, relating to both the upper and lower jaws, and *maxillopalatine* (Latin *palatum*, palate), of the jaw and the palate. All frequently occur hyphenated.

mechano- *Mechanical.* [Greek *mēkhanē*, machine.]

A *mechanoreceptor* is a sense organ or cell that responds to mechanical stimuli such as touch or sound; something *mechanosensitive* is sensitive to mechanical stimuli, such as the proteins in some cell membranes that open a conductance pore in response to mechanical stress; *mechanochemistry* is concerned with the direct conversion of chemical energy into mechanical energy; *mechanotherapy* is the use of mechanical equipment in physiotherapy. Though these and other terms can be hyphenated, such forms are less common.

mebi-: see the table of WORDS FOR MULTIPLES on page 127

medico- *Medicine plus another field.* [Latin *medicus*, physician.]

The term *medicolegal* (also *medico-legal*) refers to the legal aspects of the practice of medicine; *medico-social* (less often *medicosocial*) relates to the social issues surrounding medicine; *medico-economic* refers to the economic implications and costs of medical provision; *medico-chirurgical* (Latin *chirurgia*, surgery) indicates matters relating both to medicine and to surgery.

medio- *Middle.* [Latin *medius*, middle.]

A *mediolateral* position is along the middle of the side of the body; a *mediodorsal* one is similarly along the centre line of the back. These and other examples often appear hyphenated.

meg(a)- Also **megalo-**. *Large or great; a factor of one million; a factor of 2^{20}.* [Greek *megas*, *megal-*, great.]

The sense of largeness appears in *megaphone* (Greek *phōnē*, sound, voice), a device that amplifies and directs the voice; *megalithic* (Greek *lithos*, stone), of prehistoric monuments made of or containing *megaliths*, large stones; *megatherium* (Greek *thērion*, animal), an extinct giant ground sloth; *megastore*, a very large retail store.

This sense is also the usual one for **megalo-**. Examples include *megalomania* (literally a passion for big things), an obsession with the exercise of power, especially in the domination of others; *megalopolis* (Greek *polis*, city), a very large, heavily populated city or urban complex; *megaloblast*, a large, abnormally developed red blood cell typical of certain forms of anaemia.

Mega- is also used as one of the standard SI (Système International) multiples (see the table of WORDS FOR MULTIPLES on page 127), indicating a factor of one million, as in the units *megahertz*, *megawatt*, *megohm*, and *megaton*; other examples include *megabuck*, a million dollars (or more loosely any very large dollar sum), and *megadeath*, a unit used to count the casualties of nuclear war, equal to the deaths of one million people. Since the 1980s, *mega* has become an adjective in its own right for something very large or excellent, or as a general-purpose intensifier.

In computing, **mega-** usually represents the binary multiple 2^{20} or 1,048,576, as in *megabit* and *megabyte*, though these and related terms are also used more loosely in the sense of one million.

-megaly Also **-megalia** and **-megalic**. *Abnormal enlargement of part of the body.* [Greek *megas*, *megal-*, great.]

Examples include *acromegaly* (Greek *akron*, tip, extremity), abnormal growth of the hands, feet, and face; *cardiomegaly* (Greek *kardia*, heart), abnormal enlargement of the heart; and *hepatomegaly* (Greek *hēpar*, *hēpat-*, liver), of the liver. The spelling **-megalia** is a rarer alternative: *hepatomegalia*, *cardiomegalia*. Related adjectives in either case are formed in **-megalic**: *acromegalic*, *cytomegalic*, characterized by enlarged cells, especially with reference to a disease caused by a cytomegalovirus.

meio- Also **mio-**. *Less or fewer.* [Greek *meiōn*, less or smaller.]

Meiosis is cell division that results in two daughter cells each with half the chromosome number of the parent cell; *meiofauna* are minute animals living in soil and aquatic sediments; *meiobenthos* (Greek *benthos*, depth of the sea) are small organisms living at the bottom of the sea.

Mio- is an alternative spelling, as in *Miocene* (Greek *kainos*, new, so literally 'the lesser new [period]'), relating to the fourth epoch of the Tertiary period, between the Oligocene and Pliocene epochs; or *miogeoclinal* (less often *miogeosynclinal*), of a geosyncline that is situated between a larger, volcanic one and a stable area of the crust.

The medical term *miosis* for an excessive constriction of the pupil of the eye comes instead from Greek *muein*, to shut the eyes.

-meister *A person regarded as skilled or prominent in a specified activity.* [German *Meister*, master.]

The original is found in German words such as *Bürgermeister*, a mayor, and *Kapellmeister* (German *Kapelle*, court orchestra), the leader or conductor of an orchestra or choir. Modern terms ending in **-meister** are American in origin, derived from German under the influence of Yiddish. A well-established example is *schlockmeister* (Yiddish *shlog*, wretch, untidy person), someone who sells cheap or trashy goods; a less common one is *webmeister*, a person who runs a World Wide Website, a webmaster. The form is also used to make transient terms, sometimes mildly derogatory: *gagmeister*, *pornmeister*, *talkmeister* (a radio talk-show host).

melan(o)- *Black.* [Greek *melas*, *melan-*, black.]

Most examples occur in medical contexts, such as *melanin*, a dark brown to black pigment that is responsible for tanning; a *melanocyte* (Greek *kutos*, vessel) is a mature melanin-forming cell, typically in the skin; a *melanoma* is a tumour of such cells; *melatonin* is a hormone which inhibits melanin formation and is thought to be concerned with regulating the reproductive cycle. *Melancholy* derives from Greek *kholē*, bile, since an excess of *black bile*, one of the four humours of ancient medicine, was thought to cause depression.

-melia *An abnormal condition of a limb.* [Greek *melos*, limb]

The ending appears in a few terms, including *phocomelia* (Greek *phōkē*, seal), a rare congenital deformity in which the limbs are underdeveloped or absent, and *amelia* (Greek *a-*, without), absence of arms or legs. *Ectromelia* (Greek *ektrōsis*, miscarriage) and *meromelia* (Greek *meros*, part) are general terms for such congenital defects of the limbs.

mening(o)- *The meninges.* [Greek *mēninx*, *mēning-*, membrane.]

The *meninges* are the membranes that line the skull and enclose the brain and spinal cord; *meningitis* is an often severe disease involving inflammation of them, perhaps caused by the bacterium *meningococcus* (Greek *kokkos*, berry); a *meningocele* (Greek *kēlē*, tumour) is a protrusion of the meninges through a gap in the spine due to a congenital defect.

meno- *Menstruation.* [Greek *mēn*, month.]

The *menopause* is the ceasing of menstruation; *menorrhoea* (Greek *rhoia*, flow, flux) is the flow of blood at menstruation; *menorrhagia* (Greek *-rrhag-*, stem of Greek *rhēgnunai*, to burst), is abnormally heavy bleeding at menstruation. Terms such as *menstruation* and *menstrual* derive from the Latin equivalent *mensis*, via *menstrua*.

-ment *Forming nouns.* [Latin *-mentum* or French *-ment*.]

The Latin and French endings were originally added to verbs. Two words based on Latin verbs are *ornament* (Latin *ornare*, adorn) and *testament* (Latin *testamentum*, a will, from *testari*, to testify). Two based on French verbs are *appeasement* (Old French *apaisier*, from *pais*, peace), and *encouragement* (French *encourager*, based on *corage*, courage).

English has usually followed suit by adding the ending to verbs. Many nouns ending in **-ment** indicate either the result of an action or the process involved: *acknowledgment*, *curtailment*, *excitement*, *harassment*, *treatment*, *wonderment*.

Comparatively few words have been formed since the 17th century (two that have are *recruitment* and *secondment*), though it is occasionally used to make short-lived forms like *chortlement*. It is rare to find terms based on other parts of speech, though *merriment* has been created from *merry* and *oddment* from *odd*.

-mer Also **-mere**, **-meric**, and **-merous**. *Part or segment.* [Greek *meros*, part.]

Terms ending in **-mer** often denote substances whose molecules are built up from a number of identical simpler molecules, a *polymer* (Greek *polloi*, many), each of the component parts of which is a *monomer* (Greek *monos*, alone). The number of units can be given by a prefix: *dimer*, a molecule formed from two identical smaller molecules; *trimer*, three; and so on. An *oligomer* (Greek *oligoi*, few) has relatively few such units. Some refer to molecules that are closely related: *isomers* (Greek *isos*, equal) are compounds with the same formula but different arrangements of atoms and different properties; *enantiomers* (Greek *enantios*, opposite), are pairs of molecules that are mirror images of each other.

Related adjectives are formed ending in **-meric**: *dimeric*, *isomeric*, *polymeric*. Adjectives ending in **-merous** refer to an organism made up of a given number of parts: *heptamerous* (Greek *hepta*, seven), having parts arranged in groups of seven; *polymerous*, having or consisting of many parts; *isomerous*, having or composed of parts that are similar in number or position.

Terms ending in **-mere** refer to elements of biological structures, as in *telomere* (Greek *telos*, end), a compound structure at the end of a chromosome; and *blastomere* (Greek *blastos*, germ, sprout), a cell formed by cleavage of a fertilized ovum. Related adjectives here are formed ending in **-meric**: *centromeric*, *telomeric*.

mercapto- *The chemical radical —SH.* [English *mercaptan*, an abbreviation of modern Latin *mercurium captans*, capturing mercury.]

The *mercaptans* (also called *thiols*; *see* THIO-) are a group of organic compounds containing this radical, analogous to the organic alcohols (such as *methyl mercaptan* or *methanethiol*, CH_3SH); frequently they have powerful smells. The drug *mercaptopurine* is used to prevent the growth of cancer cells, especially in leukaemia; *mercaptobenzthiazole* is a fungicide.

mero- *Partly or partial.* [Greek *meros*, part.]

Terms are widely distributed but specialist. A *merozoite* (Greek *zōion*, animal, hence 'partial animal') is a cell produced by asexual fission, as an intermediate stage in reproduction in some protozoa; *meroplankton* are aquatic organisms that spend only part of their life cycle as free-swimming plankton; in mathematics, a *meromorphic* complex function is differentiable except for some singularities, so only partially analytic; a *meronym* is a term which denotes part of something but which is used to refer to the whole of it, for example *faces* when used to mean people.

-merous: *see* -MER

mesio- *A midline.* [Formed irregularly from Greek *mesos*, middle.]

The adjective *mesial* refers to a direction or position towards the middle line of a body. Compounds of **mesio-** appear mainly in dentistry: *mesiobuccal* (Latin *bucca*, cheek), between the mesial and buccal surfaces of a tooth, or *mesiodens* (Latin *dens*, *dent-*, tooth), an extra tooth that develops in the midline of the palate, between the central incisors.

meso- *Middle; intermediate.* [Greek *mesos*, middle.]

Mesopotamia (Greek *potamos*, river) is an ancient region of SW Asia in present-day Iraq, lying between the Rivers Tigris and Euphrates; *Meso-America* is the central region of America, from central

Mexico to Nicaragua. The *mesoderm* is the middle layer of an embryo in early development. The *Mesolithic* (Greek *lithos*, stone) is the middle stone age, between the Palaeolithic and Neolithic, while the *Mesozoic* (Greek *zōion*, animal) is the era between the Palaeozoic and Cenozoic eras, comprising the Triassic, Jurassic, and Cretaceous periods. A *mesomorph* (Greek *morphē*, form) is a person whose build is compact and muscular, intermediate between an ectomorph and an endomorph. A *meson* is a subatomic particle which is intermediate in mass between an electron and a proton.

met(a)- Also **m-**. *Change of position or condition; behind, after, or beyond; of a higher or second-order kind; chemical substitution.* [Greek *meta*, with, across, or after.]

The principal sense in classical Greek was change or transformation; this occurs in a variety of English words, such as *metamorphosis* (Greek *morphē*, form), a change of the form or nature of a thing or person into a completely different one; *metabolism* (Greek *metabolē*, change), the chemical processes that occur within a living organism in order to maintain life; and *metathesis* (Greek, from *metatithenai*, transpose, change the position of), the transposition of sounds or letters in a word.

Other senses have developed in English. One is that of position behind, after, or beyond another, as in *metacarpus*, the group of five bones of the hand between the wrist (*carpus*) and the fingers, or *metatarsus* (Greek *tarsos*, flat of the foot), the group of bones between the ankle and the toes.

The term *metaphysics*, the branch of philosophy that deals with the first principles of things, was interpreted to mean a subject that is beyond or transcends physics. Other terms have since been formed with this sense of a higher level or something once removed: *metalanguage*, a form of language used to describe or analyze another language; *metapsychology*, speculation concerning mental processes and the mind–body relationship, beyond what can be studied experimentally.

In chemistry, **meta-**, usually abbreviated to **m-**, refers to substitution at two carbon atoms in a benzene ring that have one other carbon atom between them: *meta-xylene*; *metadichlorobenzene*; *metanilic acid*, a dyestuff intermediate. *See also* ORTHO- and PARA-. A few names refer to polymers: *metaldehyde*, a solid made by polymerizing acetaldehyde, used in slug pellets and as a fuel for portable stoves; *metaphosphoric acid*, a glassy deliquescent polymeric solid obtained by heating orthophosphoric acid.

metall(o)- *A metal.* [Greek *metallon*, metal.]

Metallurgy (Greek *-ourgia*, working) is the branch of science and technology concerned with metals; something *metallized* has been coated with a thin layer of metal; a *metalliferous* (Latin *-fer*, producing) mineral or ore contains or produces metal; a *metallophone* (Greek *phōnē*, sound) is a musical instrument in which the sound is produced by striking metal bars of varying sizes. A *metalloprotein* is a protein that contains metal atoms in its molecule and a *metalloenzyme* is similarly an enzyme containing metal atoms.

-meter Also **-metre**. *Measuring instrument; unit of measurement.* [Greek *metron*, measure; *-metrēs*, measurer.]

There are several hundred terms ending in **-meter** for various kinds of measuring instrument, a few of the more common of which are in the LIST overleaf. The general term *meter* refers to any device that measures and records the quantity, degree, or rate of something.

Terms ending in **-metre** refer to units of measurement based on the *metre*: *centimetre*, *kilometre*. Forms such as *kilometer* and *centimeter* are the equivalent US spellings.

The words *diameter* (Greek *dia*, across), *geometer*, a person skilled in geometry (Greek *gē*, earth, because the first were land surveyors), and *perimeter* (Greek

-meter   An instrument for measuring something.

altimeter	altitude	(Latin *altus*, high)
barometer	atmospheric pressure	(Greek *baros*, weight)
calorimeter	heat involved in a chemical reaction	(Latin *calor*, heat)
dosimeter	absorbed doses of ionizing radiation	(English *dose*)
interferometer	wavelength, using the interaction of two or more waves of the same frequency	(English *interfere*)
potentiometer	electromotive force using potential difference	(English *potential*)
radiometer	the intensity or force of radiation	(Latin *radius*, a ray)
spectrometer	spectra of electromagnetic radiation	(Latin *spectra*, image, apparition)
speedometer	the speed of a vehicle	(English *speed*)
sphygmomanometer	blood pressure	(Greek *sphugmos*, pulse, plus *manos*, thin)
tachometer	the working speed of an engine	(Greek *takhos*, speed)
thermometer	temperature	(Greek *thermē*, heat)
voltmeter	electric potential in volts.	(English *volt*)

peri-, around) come from the same Greek root. The ending also appears in a set of words for lines of verse containing a specified number of metrical feet, as in *hexameter* (Greek *hex*, six), *tetrameter* (Greek *tetra-*, four), or *octameter* (Greek *oktō*, eight).

meth(o)- *The methyl radical,* —CH₃. [English *methylene*, derived from Greek *methu*, wine, plus *hulē*, wood, because methyl alcohol was first prepared by the destructive distillation of wood.]

Meth- occurs in a variety of common names for chemical substances, many of them drugs, such as *methamphetamine*, a methyl derivative of amphetamine, a synthetic drug used illegally as a stimulant; *methadone*, used in the treatment of morphine and heroin addiction; and *methicillin*, a semi-synthetic form of penicillin. Examples of drug names on invented stems that include the longer form **metho-** are *methoserpidine*, used to lower blood pressure; and *methotrexate*, a treatment for leukaemia. *Methene* (*see* -ENE¹) is the systematic name for the methylene radical —CH₂.; *methacrylic acid* is used in the manufacture of synthetic resins.

methoxy- *The methoxyl radical,* CH₃O— [METHO- plus OXY-.]

Examples include **methoxychlor**, the common name for a relative of DDT used as a veterinary insecticide, and **methoxyethanol**, a jet fuel de-icer and a solvent for cellulose acetate. It occurs most frequently in systematic chemical names, such as **3,6-dichloro-2-methoxybenzoic acid**, sold under various trade names as a herbicide, or **4-methoxyaniline**, an intermediate in making azo dyes and pigments. *See also* ETHOXY-.

-metre: *see* -METER

-metric   Also **-metrical**,   **-metry**, **-metrics**, **-metrist**, and **-metrician**. *Measurement.* [Greek *metron*, measure; *-metrēs*, measurer.]

Nouns ending in **-metry** denote procedures and systems that correspond to the names of instruments ending in -METER: *calorimetry*, *dosimetry*, *interferometry*, *thermometry*. Other words with this ending connected with measurement are *geometry*, *symmetry* (Greek *sun-*, with), and *trigonometry* (Greek *trigō-nos*, three-cornered).

Nouns ending in **-metrics** (usually considered to be singular) are of topics of study concerned with measurement, as with *econometrics*, concerned with mathematical methods used to describe economic systems; and *psychometrics*, the science of measuring mental capacities and processes. Practitioners of these disciplines (and some whose names end in **-metry**) have names ending in **-metrist** (*psychometrist*) or **-metrician** (*econometrician*).

Nouns ending in **-meter**, **-metry**, and **-metrics** have corresponding adjectives ending in **-metric** (*barometric*, *geometric*, *psychometric*) or less commonly in **-metrical** (*diametrical*, *symmetrical*), sometimes both.

metr(o)-¹ *The uterus.* [Greek *mētra*, womb.]

Metritis is inflammation of the womb; *metrorrhagia* (Greek *-rrhag-*, stem of *rhēgnunai*, to burst) is abnormal bleeding from the womb; *metroplasty* (Greek *plastos*, formed, moulded) is reconstructive surgery on the uterus.

metr(o)-² *Measurement.* [Greek *metron*, measure.]

Metrology is the scientific study of measurement; a *metronome* (Greek *nomos*, law), marks regular intervals of time, especially for musicians; a *metre* (US *meter*) is the fundamental unit of length in the metric system.

metro-³ *A capital city or other large urban area.* [The first part of *metropolis*, from Greek *mētēr*, *mētr-*, mother, plus *polis*, city.]

Someone or something *metrocentric* is biased towards the affairs or interests of a capital city; and a *metroplex* (*see* -PLEX) is a very large metropolitan area, especially one which is an aggregation of two or more cities. The form has become a word in its own right, *metro* (originally as French *métro*), to describe an underground or light railway system in a large urban area.

-metropia Also **-metropic**. *A condition of the eye.* [Greek *metron*, measure, plus *ōps*, eye.]

This ending appears in a few medical terms relating to the ability of the eye to form images: *hypermetropia* (Greek *huper*, over, above) is long-sightedness; *anisometropia* (Greek *anisos*, unequal) refers to an inequality in the refractive power of the

two eyes; *ametropia* (Greek *a-*, not, without) is faulty refraction of light rays by the eye, as in astigmatism or myopia; *emmetropia* (*see* EN-²) is the normal refractive condition of the eye, in which the rays of light are accurately focused on the retina. Associated adjectives end in **-metropic** (*emmetropic*, *hypermetropic*).

micro- *Small; a factor of one millionth.* [Greek *mikros*, small.]

This form is common and highly productive. Often it has a straightforward sense of something small or low in quantity: *microprocessor*, an integrated circuit that contains all the functions of a central processing unit of a computer; *microcosm* (Greek *kosmos*, world), something that encapsulates in miniature the characteristic qualities of something larger; *micronutrient*, a chemical substance required in trace amounts for normal growth.

The meaning is often affected by association with *microscope* and its derivatives, relating particularly to things too small to be seen by the unaided eye: *microfilm*, film containing very small images of documents; *microcyte*, an unusually small red blood cell, associated with certain anaemias; *micro-organism*, a very small organism, especially a bacterium, virus, or fungus; *microfossil*, a fossil or fossil fragment that can only be seen with a microscope.

The sense is sometimes of some tool or technique that is designed to deal with things or quantities of small size, as with microscope itself, and also such terms as *microsurgery*, intricate surgery performed using miniaturized instruments and a microscope, and *microtome* (Greek *tomos*, slice, section), an instrument for cutting extremely thin sections of material for examination under a microscope.

Some terms refer to a localized area, to a limitation in scope, or to a focus on a restricted subject area (often the opposite of MACRO-): *microeconomics*, the part of economics concerned with single factors and the effects of individual decisions; *microbrewery*, a brewery which produces limited quantities of beer, typically for consumption on its own premises; *micro-manage*, to manage or control every part, however small, of some enterprise or activity.

A *microphone* (Greek *phōnē*, sound, voice) does not necessarily deal with small sounds; it was named by analogy with *microscope*, the implication being that it enlarges sound, a function that strictly belongs to other parts of the audio system.

Micro- is also used as one of the standard SI (Système International) decimal prefixes (see the table of WORDS FOR MULTIPLES on page 127), indicating a factor of one millionth, as in the units *microgram*, *micrometre*, and *microsecond*.

mid- *Middle; medium; half.* [Old English *midd*, of Germanic origin.]

Examples include *midwinter*; *midfield*; *midweek*; *midstream*; *midway*; *midlife*, the central period of a person's life, say between 45 and 60 years old; *midriff* (Old English *hrif*, belly), the region between the chest and the waist; and *mid-Atlantic*, in the middle of the Atlantic ocean. In *mid-air* the sense is less precise. In *midwife* the first element comes from the obsolete Middle English preposition *mid*, with.

midi- *Medium-sized; of medium length.* [English *mid* or *middle*.]

This form was created in the second half of the 20th century to provide an intermediate between MINI- and MAXI-, mainly in connection with fashion, and occurs only in a few terms, such as *midilength*, an item of clothing of medium leg length, such as a *midi-skirt*. A *midi-system* is a stacked music reproduction system of medium size; a *midi-computer* is a computer system smaller than a mainframe but larger than a microcomputer. The form also exists in another sense, usually capitalized, in which it is short for *Musical Instrument Digital Interface*, a widely used standard for interconnecting electronic musical instruments and computers.

milli- *One thousandth; a thousand.* [Latin *mille*, thousand.]

This is one of the standard SI (Système International) decimal prefixes (see the table of WORDS FOR MULTIPLES on page 127). Examples are *milligram*, *millimetre* (US *millimeter*), and *milliwatt*. In a very few terms, the sense of the Latin stem is preserved, the only common one being *millipede*, an invertebrate with (figuratively) a thousand legs. The Latin stem also appears in *million* (Latin *mille* plus the augmentative suffix *-one*), and in *milliard*, an old British term for one thousand million. However, *milliner*, a person who makes or sells women's hats, derives from the name of the Italian city of Milan.

mini- *Very small of its kind.* [English *miniature*, reinforced by *minimum*.]

Mini- was in demand throughout the 20th century but especially so since the 1960s as a result of names given to fashionable items of the time, especially *minicars* and then *miniskirts*. Since then, many terms have appeared, as it is often added to nouns to indicate something fashionably or notably small. A few examples are *minibar* (a selection of alcoholic drinks in a hotel room), *mini-break* (a short holiday of a few days), *minibus*, *minicam* (a miniaturized camera), *minimart*, *miniseries*, and *minivan*.

It is also now commonly a word in its own right, as in *mini rugby* and the British *mini roundabout*, and as an abbreviation for *miniskirt*, *minicar* (particularly as a tradename, *Mini*), and *minicomputer*, a computer of medium power, more than a microcomputer but less than a mainframe.

mio-: *see* MEIO-

mis- *Various senses with negative implications.* [Old English, of Germanic origin; Old French *mes-* (based on Latin *minus*).]

Words from the two sources eventually became the same in both meaning and form, though those from Old French *mes-* are less common. Both forms imply something is awry, wrong, bad, or unsuitable.

Examples from Old English and Old French include *misadventure*, *misbehave*, *mischance*, *mischief*, *misdeed*, *misfortune*, *mishap* (from the archaic *hap*, chance or good fortune), *mislead*, *mismanage*, *misprint*, and *misrepresent*.

The form is currently active and some modern examples are *mislabelling*, incorrect labelling of goods; *mis-selling*, selling something to a customer for whom it is an inappropriate purchase; and *misaligned*, imperfectly or badly aligned.

Miscellaneous is from Latin *miscere*, to mix. For *misanthropy*, see the next entry.

mis(o)- *Hatred for or a hater of something.* [Greek *misos*, hatred.]

A man who is *misogynistic* (Greek *gunē*, woman) hates women; *misandry* (Greek *aner*, *andr-*, man) is hatred of men; *misanthropy* (Greek *anthropos*, man), is a dislike of humankind in general; *misology* (Greek *logos*, reason) is a hatred of reason, reasoning, or knowledge.

-mo *Book sizes.* [The final syllable of the masculine ablative singular of Latin ordinal numbers.]

Book sizes are determined by the number of leaves into which a sheet of paper has been folded. Older examples are formed on Latin ordinal numbers, such as *duodecimo* (Latin *in duodecimo*, in a twelfth, from *duodecimus*, twelfth), a size of book in which each leaf is one twelfth of the size of the printing sheet. More recently, equivalent terms have been formed using English cardinal numbers: *twelvemo*, *sixteenmo*, *thirty-two-mo*.

-monas Also **-monad**. *Simple microorganisms.* [Greek *monas*, *monad-*, unit, from *monos*, alone.]

The ending appears in genus names, especially of bacteria, protozoa, and algae. Examples are *Pseudomonas* (Greek *pseudēs*, false), a genus of bacteria which occurs in soil and detritus, including a number that are pathogens of plants or animals; *Chlamydomonas* (Greek *khlamus*, *khlamud-*, cloak), a genus of common single-celled green algae which typically have two flagella for swimming, living in water and moist soil; *Trichomonas* (Greek *thrix*, *trikho-*, hair), a parasitic protozoan that infests the urogenital or digestive system. Terms for individual organisms may be formed using **-monad** (*pseudomonad*, *trichomonad*), though these are relatively uncommon.

-monger *A dealer or trader.* [Old English *mangere*, based on Latin *mango*, dealer.]

A variety of terms exist for persons who sell goods, such as *cheesemonger*, *costermonger* (originally an apple seller, from *costard*, a large cooking apple), *fishmonger*, and *ironmonger* (in British usage, a seller of hardware such as tools and household implements, originally of iron). The term has broadened to refer to a person who promotes or disseminates something, often in a negative sense: *newsmonger*, *scaremonger*, *scandalmonger*, *warmonger*. The form is somewhat active, with words like *fearmonger*, *powermonger*, and *smutmonger* appearing in recent years, mainly in journalism.

mon(o)- *One; alone; single.* [Greek *monos*, alone.]

Examples include *monocle* (Latin *oculus*, eye), a single eyeglass; *monologue*, a long speech by a single actor; *monophonic*, of sound reproduction that uses only one channel, as compared with *stereophonic*; *monopoly* (Greek *pōlein*, sell), the exclusive possession or control of the supply or trade in a commodity or service; *monorail*, a railway in which the track consists of a single rail; *monotone*, a sound, especially of someone's voice, that varies in pitch only slightly (the quality of sameness this implies has led to a common sense of *monotonous* and *monotony* for a lack of variety or a tedious routine).

In chemistry, **mono-** refers specifically to a substance that contains only a single instance of an atom or group, as in *monoxide*, an oxide containing one atom of oxygen in its molecule; *monoamine*, a compound having a single amine group in its molecule; *monomer*, a molecule that can be bonded to other identical molecules to form a polymer.

-mony *Forming nouns.* [Latin *-monia*, *-monium*.]

Nouns ending in **-mony** are formed from Latin verbal stems, and indicate an action, state, or quality: *ceremony*, *harmony*, *matrimony*, *parsimony*, *sanctimony*, *testimony*. The ending is not active in the language.

morph-: *see* MORPHO-

-morph Also **-morphic**, **-morphous**, **-morphism**, **-morphy**, and **-morphosis**. *A specified form or character.* [Greek *morphē*, form.]

Terms ending in **-morph** are nouns describing a person or object with the shape, structure, or character concerned, as for example a *pseudomorph* (Greek *pseudēs*, false) is a crystal consisting of one mineral but having the form of another. For more examples see the LIST below.

Such words have adjectives ending in **-morphic** or **-morphous**, frequently both: *allomorphic*, *enantiomorphic*, *isomorphous*, *pseudomorphous*. A few adjectives with these endings do not have corresponding nouns ending in **-morph**, of which one is *zygomorphic* (Greek *zugon*, yoke), of a flower that has only one plane of symmetry, as in a pea or snapdragon.

Terms ending in **-morphism** and **-morphy** are abstract nouns for the state or condition concerned: *anthropomorphism* (Greek *anthrōpos*, human being), the attribution of human characteristics or behaviour to a god, animal, or object; *gynandromorphy* (Greek *gunandros*, of doubtful sex), a condition, especially in insects, in which an individual

---

-morph	A specified form or character. *All word origins are from Greek.*	
allomorph	in linguistics, any of two or more actual representations of a morpheme, such as the different pronunciations of the plural ending *-s*	(*allos*, other)
biomorph	a decorative form or object based on or resembling a living organism	(*bios*, here meaning organic life)
ectomorph	a person with a lean and delicate build of body, in which physical structures from the *ectodermal* layer of the embryo predominate	(*ektos*, outside)
enantiomorph	each of two crystalline or other geometrical forms which are mirror images of each other	(*enantios*, opposite)
endomorph	a person with a soft round build of body and a high proportion of fat tissue, in which physical structures from the *endodermal* layer of the embryo predominate	(*endon*, within)
isomorph	two objects having the same form; also, a line in a linguistic atlas connecting places exhibiting closely similar morphological forms	(*isos*, equal)
mesomorph	a person whose build is compact and muscular, in which physical structures from the *mesodermal* layer of the embryo predominate	(*mesos*, middle)
metamorph	something that has been transformed in some way; in science fiction an organism that can change appearance at will	(*meta*, here meaning change)
palynomorph	something of the shape of a pollen grain	(*palunein*, sprinkle)
polymorph	an organism or inorganic object or material which takes various forms	(*polu-*, many)
pseudomorph	a crystal consisting of one mineral but having the form of another	(*pseudēs*, false)

can have some male and some female characteristics.

A few nouns exist ending in **-morphosis** referring to a change of state: *anamorphosis* (Greek *ana*, back), a distorted projection or drawing which appears normal when viewed from a particular point or with a suitable mirror or lens; *metamorphosis*, a change of the form or nature of a thing or person into a completely different one.

-morpha *Animal groupings.* [Greek *morphē*, form.]

Some systematic biological names contain this ending, such as the *Lagomorpha* (Greek *lagōs*, hare), an order of mammals that comprises the hares and rabbits; *Nematomorpha* (Greek *nēma*, *nēmat-*, thread) a small phylum of the horsehair worms; *Myomorpha* (Greek *mus*, *mu-*, mouse), a major division of the rodents that includes the rats, mice, voles, hamsters, and their relatives.

-morphic: *see* -MORPH

morph(o)- *Form or character.* [Greek *morphē*, form.]

A few examples exist in technical contexts, such as *morphology*, the study of the forms of things, such as living organisms or words, in particular inflected forms; *morphogenesis*, the origin and development of the forms of organisms, or the formation of landforms or other structures; *morphallaxis* (Greek *allaxis*, exchange), regeneration by the transformation of existing body tissues.

Morph also exists as a standalone noun (each of several variant forms of an animal or plant, or of a word) and as a verb (to change smoothly from one image to another by small steps using computer animation techniques).

In linguistics, **morpho-** refers to *morphemes*, meaningful units of a language that cannot be further divided, as in *morphophoneme*, one of the variant phonemes which belong to the same morpheme, and *morphosyntactic*, involving both morphology and syntax.

-morphosis, **-morphous**, and **-morphy**: *see* -MORPH

-most *Superlative adjectives and adverbs.* [Old English *-mest*.]

Such superlatives are formed from prepositions, adjectives, and comparatives that indicate some relative position, either literal or figurative: *easternmost*, *foremost*, *hindmost*, *innermost*, *topmost*, *utmost* (Old English *ūt*, out).

muco- *Mucus.* [English **mucus** plus -o-.]

The adjective *mucocutaneous* (Latin *cutis*, skin) refers to the mucous membranes and the skin together; the *mucopolysaccharides* are a group of compounds which are components of connective tissue; an agent that is *mucolytic* (Greek *-lutikos*, able to loosen) dissolves or breaks down mucus; something *mucopurulent* (Latin *pus*, *pur-*, pus) contains both mucus and pus.

multi- *More than one; many.* [Latin *multus*, much, many.]

A few words derive directly from Latin—examples are *multitude*, *multiply*, *multifarious* (of many and various types), and *multiplex* (consisting of many elements in a complex relationship). Many others have been created on English stems, especially in the past century, and the form is very active. A few examples: *multicultural*, of several cultural or ethnic groups within a society; *multidisciplinary*, combining or involving several academic disciplines or professional specializations; *multifaith*, involving or characterized by a variety of religions; *multilingual*, involving several languages; *multimillionaire*, a person with assets worth several million pounds or dollars; *multiracial*, made up of or relating to people of many races.

musculo- *Muscle.* [Latin *musculus*, muscle.]

Terms containing this form are adjectives for muscles plus another part of the body, of which the most common example is *musculoskeletal*, denoting the musculature and skeleton together. Others are *musculotendinous*, muscles and tendons; *musculocutaneous* (Latin *cutis*, skin), muscles and skin. These are often hyphenated, though *musculoskeletal* is usually written as one word.

my-: *see* MYO-

myc-: *see* MYCO-

-myces Also **-mycete**, *-mycetes*, **-mycotina**, and **-mycota**. *Bacteria or fungi.* [Greek *mukēs*, *mukēt-*, fungus or mushroom.]

In systematic biological terminology, words ending in **-mycota** are names of divisions, those in **-mycotina** a subdivision, **-mycetes** a class or subclass, and **-myces** a genus.

Example are *Ascomycota* (Greek *askos*, sac), the sac fungi, which include the morels and truffles; *Basidiomycotina*, fungi whose spores develop in *basidia*, which include the majority of familiar mushrooms and toadstools; and *Hymenomycetes* (Greek *humēn*, membrane), which includes the common poisonous and edible mushrooms.

Despite the Greek ending, genus names ending in **-myces** sometimes refer to bacteria, because they were originally thought to be fungi. Examples are *Saccharomyces* (Greek *sakkharon*, sugar), the genus of fungi that includes baker's and brewer's yeasts, and *Streptomyces* (Greek *streptos*, twisted), a genus of bacteria, several of which are important sources of antibiotics.

Terms ending in **-mycete** are non-systematic names for groups of organisms that belong to divisions and classes of the fungi and sometimes of bacteria. Examples are *basidiomycete*, *ascomycete*, and *streptomycete*.

myceto-: *see* MYCO-

-mycin *An antibiotic compound derived from fungi.* [Greek *mukēs*, *mukēt-*, fungus or mushroom.]

Examples include *erythromycin* (Greek *eruthros*, red), an antibiotic similar in its effects to penicillin; *vancomycin*, used against resistant strains of streptococcus and staphylococcus; and *streptomycin*, the first drug to be successful against tuberculosis.

myc(o)- Also **mycet(o)-**. *Fungi or fungal.*

[Greek *mukēs*, *mukēt-*, fungus or mushroom.]

Mycology is the scientific study of fungi; a fungus that is *mycorrhizal* (Greek *rhiza*, root) grows in association with the roots of a plant; *mycosis* is a disease caused by infection with a fungus, such as ringworm or thrush; *mycoprotein* is protein derived from fungi, especially that produced for human consumption; a *mycotoxin* is any toxic substance produced by a fungus.

The longer form **mycet(o)-** is much less often encountered, the most common term here probably being *mycetoma*, a chronic inflammation of the tissues caused by infection with a fungus or with certain bacteria. Another example is *mycetozoa*, a group of fungal organisms.

-mycota or **-mycotina**: *see* -MYCES

myel(o)- *Bone marrow; the spinal cord.* [Greek *muelos*, marrow.]

Terms that refer to bone marrow include *myeloma*, a malignant tumour of it; *myelofibrosis*, the replacement of bone marrow by fibrous tissue in some diseases; *myelocyte*, a cell of the bone marrow that develops into a granulocyte, a type of white blood cell; and *myelin*, a whitish insulating sheath around many nerve fibres, so named because it resembles marrow.

Myelo- came to refer to the spinal cord because of the concentration of grey matter and nerve fibres associated with it. Examples include *myelitis*, inflammation of the spinal cord; *myelopathy* (Greek *patheia*, suffering), a disease of it; and *myelography*, X-ray examination of the spinal canal inside the cord by injecting a radio-opaque substance into it.

The adjective *myeloid* can refer either to bone marrow or to the spinal cord.

my(o)- *Muscle.* [Greek *mus*, *mu-*, mouse or muscle.]

Myoglobin is a red protein which carries and stores oxygen in muscle cells; a *myopathy* (Greek *patheia*, suffering) is a disease of muscle tissue; the *myocar-*

dium is the muscular tissue of the heart; *myalgia* (Greek *algos*, pain) is pain in a muscle or group of muscles; *myasthenia* (Greek *asthenēs*, weak) is a condition causing abnormal weakness of certain muscles.

myring(o)- *The eardrum.* [Latin *myringa*, eardrum.]

A few medical terms contain this form: *myringotomy* (Greek *-tomia*, cutting), an incision into the eardrum to relieve pressure or drain fluid; *myringoplasty* (Greek *plastos*, formed, moulded), surgical repair of a perforated eardrum by grafting; *myringitis*, inflammation of the eardrum.

myrmeco- *An ant or ants.* [Greek *murmex*, *murmek-*, ant.]

Myrmecology is the branch of entomology that studies ants; *Myrmecophagidae* (Greek *phagein*, eat) is the family name for the anteaters; a *myrmecophile* (Greek *philos*, loving) is an invertebrate or plant which has a symbiotic relationship with ants.

mytho- *Myth.* [Greek *muthos*, myth, or English *myth* plus -o-.]

A *mythographer* is a writer or collector of myths; *mythopoeia* is the making of a myth or myths; *mythomania* is an abnormal or pathological tendency to exaggerate or tell lies.

myx(o)- *Mucus.* [Greek *muxa*, slime, mucus.]

The rabbit disease called *myxomatosis* is so named because it causes swelling of the mucous membranes and inflammation and discharge around the eyes. In medicine, a *myxoedema* (US *myxedema*) is a swelling of the skin and underlying tissues giving a waxy consistency; a *myxoma* is a benign tumour of connective tissue containing mucous or gelatinous material; a *myxovirus* is one of a group of RNA viruses including the influenza virus. A *myxomycete* is a type of slime mould.

n- *Normal; number; negative.* [The initial letter of these words.]

In chemical formulae, often with a capital letter, this prefix indicates an unbranched chain of carbon atoms: *n-hexane*, *N-acetylcysteine*. In mathematics, it is a symbol for an unspecified or variable number; *n-gon*, a polygon with an unspecified number of sides; *n-tuple*, an entity or set consisting of an unspecified number of parts or elements. It can also be an abbreviation of *negative*: *n-type*, denoting a region in a semiconductor in which electrical conduction is due chiefly to the movement of electrons, as opposed to *p-type*.

-n: *see* -EN[2] and -EN[3]

nano- *In units of measurement, a factor of 10^{-9}.* [Via Latin from Greek *nanos*, dwarf.]

This form occurs in scientific units, for example in *nanosecond*, one thousand millionth of a second, or *nanometre*, the equivalent sub-multiple of a metre. It is one of the standard set of SI (Système International) prefixes (see the table of WORDS FOR MULTIPLES on page 127).

As nanometre measurements are comparable with the size of atoms and molecules, since the 1980s **nano-** has taken on an idea of molecular dimensions; *nanotechnology*, for example, refers to the manipulation of individual atoms and molecules; this term is often abbreviated to *nanotech* or *nano*. Other examples include *nanocomputer*, a computer with molecular-sized switching elements; *nanomachine*, a general term for a very small mechanical device, perhaps including gears and springs; and *nanoscale*, any measurement or activity on scales close to a nanometre.

An unusual case is that of *nanosatellite*, an aerospace jargon term for an artificial satellite weighing less than 10kg; this may prefigure a wider use of **nano-** in a similar way to MICRO- to mean something small of its kind.

-nap *Abduct in order to extract a ransom.* [The second element of *kidnap*, a variant of *nab*, to seize or steal.]

The ending has been used in recent decades to create a number of short-lived facetious terms: *artnap*, *gnomenap* (stealing garden gnomes), *petnap*.

naphth(o)- *Napthalene.* [Latin *naphtha*, from Greek, of Iranian origin.]

Naphtha is a flammable oil containing various light hydrocarbons, obtained by distillation of coal, shale, or petroleum. Compounds related to it, both chemically and linguistically, include *naphthalene* (used in mothballs and as a raw material for chemical manufacture); the *naphthenes* (cyclic aliphatic hydrocarbons such as cyclohexane, isolated from naphtha); the *naphthoquinones* (a set of six isomeric compounds, one of which is a precursor to a vitamin K analogue); and *naphthol*, used as an antiseptic and to make dyes.

narco- *Stupor, drowsiness, or insensibility; the illicit production and use of drugs.* [Greek *narkē*, numbness.]

The first sense appears in *narcolepsy* (created on the pattern of *epilepsy*), a condition in which a person has an extreme tendency to fall asleep; the state of *narcosis* is of stupor or unconsciousness, usually induced by drugs; hence a *narcotic* is, in medical usage, a drug which induces this state. In the early part of the 20th century this last word developed a broader sense of an illegal drug that affects mood or behaviour. This has given rise to a number of terms, such as *narcoterrorism*, terrorism associated with the trade in illicit drugs, *narco-trafficker*, a person who deals in such drugs, *narcodemocracy* or *narco-state*, a country whose leaders are in collusion with drugs producers or dealers.

nas(o)- Also **nasi-** *The nose.* [Latin *nasus*, nose.]

The adjective *nasal* relates to the nose; the *nasion* is the point on the bridge of the nose at the centre of the suture between the nasal and frontal bones. Several terms in medicine indicate the nose plus another part of the body: a *nasogastric* tube reaches or supplies the stomach via the nose; the *nasopharynx* is the upper part of the pharynx, connecting with the nasal cavity above the soft palate; *nasolabial* refers to the nose and lip; *nasolacrimal* (Latin *lacrima*, tear) refers to the nasal cavity and the associated tear ducts.

-nasty Also **-nastic**. *Nastic movement.* [Greek *nastos*, squeezed together, plus -Y[3].]

In botany, a *nastic* movement is one made by a plant in response to an external stimulus that does not dictate the direction of the movement (one that does is a *tropism*); an example is the opening of flowers in response to increasing temperature. A few nouns indicate types of nastic behaviour: *epinasty* (Greek *epi*, upon, near to), the bending downward of a part of a plant caused by increased growth on its upper surface; *nyctinasty* (Greek *nux*, *nukt-*, night), periodic movement of flowers or leaves caused by nightly alterations in light intensity or temperature; *seismonasty* (Greek *seismos*, earthquake), a movement made in response to a mechanical shock. Related adjectives are formed using **-nastic**: *hyponastic*, *nyctinastic*,

natro- Also **natri-**. *Sodium.* [French *natron*, via Spanish and Arabic from Greek *nitron*, saltpetre.]

Natron is a mineral salt found in dried lake beds, consisting of hydrated sodium carbonate; *natrolite* (Greek *lithos*, stone) is a hydrated silicate of sodium and potassium; *natrojarosite* (a variety of *jarosite*, named after a place in Spain) is a basic sulphate of sodium and iron; *natrium* is an archaic chemists' name for sodium (supplying its chemical symbol, Na); *natriuresis* (Greek *ourēsis*, urination) is the excretion of sodium in the urine.

necro- *Death; a corpse.* [Greek *nekros*, corpse.]

A *necropolis* (Greek *polis*, city) is a cemetery, especially a large one belonging to an ancient city; *necromancy* (Greek *manteia*, divination) is the supposed practice of communicating with the dead, especially in order to predict the future; *necrosis* is the death of cells in an organ or tissue due to disease, injury, or failure of the blood supply; the adjective *necrotizing* refers to something accompanied by necrosis, as in *necrotizing fasciitis*, an acute disease in which inflammation of the *fasciae* (the sheaths enclosing muscles or other organs) results in destruction of overlying tissues; *necrology* in medicine is the study of the phenomenon of death; *necrophilia* (Greek *philia*, fondness) is sexual intercourse with or attraction towards corpses.

nega- *Negative.* [An abbreviation of *negative*.]

This appears occasionally and informally to indicate a reduced or negative requirement for energy, as in *negademand*, and in names for units of energy saved as a result of conservation measures: *negawatt* (created by analogy with *megawatt*).

nemat(o)- *Thread-like in shape.* [Greek *nēma*, *nēmat-*, thread.]

Nematodes are species of worms that include the roundworms, threadworms, and eelworms, which belong to the zoological phylum *Nematoda*; a *nematocide* (also *nematicide*) is a substance used to kill nematode worms; *nematology* is the scientific study of them. A *nematocyst* is a specialized cell in the tentacles of a jellyfish or other coelenterate that projects the stinging threads. The adjective *nematic* refers to a state of a liquid crystal in which the molecules are oriented in parallel thread-like lines but not arranged in well-defined planes.

neo- *New.* [Greek *neos*, new.]

The *Neolithic* period, literally 'New Stone (Age)' (Greek *lithos*, stone), is the later part of the Stone Age, when ground or polished stone weapons and implements prevailed; a *neologism* (Greek *logos*, word) is a newly coined word or expression; a *neophyte* is a person who is new to a subject, skill, or belief (in Greek, literally 'newly planted', from *phuton*, plant); *neoteny* (Greek *teinein*, extend, using **neo-** in the sense of youth) is the retention of juvenile features in the adult animal; in medicine a *neonate* (Latin *nat-*, born) is a newborn child.

An important secondary sense is that of a new or revised form of some movement in the arts, sciences, or politics: *neoclassicism* is the revival of a classical style or treatment; *neo-Darwinism* is the modern version of Darwin's theory of evolution by natural selection, incorporating the findings of genetics; *neo-liberal* refers to a modified form of liberalism tending to favour free-market capitalism. Other examples are: *neo-fascist*, *neo-Gothic*, *neo-Nazi*, and *neo-paganism*.

nepho- Also **nephelo-**. *Cloud.* [Greek *nephos*, cloud.]

Nephology is the study of clouds, a *nephoscope* is a device that measures the altitude of clouds and the direction and speed of their movement, and *nephanalysis* is the analysis of the resulting data, often in graphical form. A *nephelometer* is a device for measuring the cloudiness of liquids. The associated adjective is *nepheloid*, as for example in *nepheloid layer*, a layer just above the bottom of a body of water that is cloudy owing to suspended mineral matter and nutrients.

nephr(o)- *A kidney or the kidneys.* [Greek *nephros*, kidney.]

Nephritis is inflammation of the kidneys; something *nephrotoxic* is damaging or destructive to them; *nephrectomy* (Greek *ektomē*, excision) is surgical removal of one or both of them; *nephrology* is the branch of medicine that deals with their physiology and diseases; the adjective relating to the kidneys is *nephritic*. *Nephrite* is a form of jade, so named because it was once thought to cure kidney disease.

-ness Also **-iness**. *A state or condition.* [Old English *-nes(s)*, of Germanic origin.]

This suffix forms nouns, mainly from adjectives. Several thousand examples exist, of which a very few are **alertness**, **baldness**, **greenness**, **idleness**, **lightness**, **neatness**, **quietness**, **richness**, **swarthiness**, **tameness**, and **weakness**. Some are formed from compound adjectives: *cold-bloodedness*, *feeble-mindedness*, *wrong-headedness*. A few come from pronouns (*I-ness*, the reference of all things to one's own consciousness) or adverbs (*nowness*, the quality of taking place in the present time). The ending is frequently added to words already containing other suffixes, as with *blamelessness*, *curvaceousness*, or *thankfulness*.

The suffix is active in the language, though words coined with it are often of transitory existence: *alongsidedness*, *bedworthiness*, *chickenheartedness*, *gung-ho-ishness*, *megastarriness*, *short-sleevedness*.

Words such as *governess* contain -ESS attached to a stem ending in *n*.

neur(o)- *Nerves or the nervous system.* [Greek *neuron*, nerve, sinew, tendon.]

This form appears widely in medicine and related fields. *Neuralgia* (Greek *algos*, pain) is a pain along the course of a nerve, often in the head or face; *neurasthenia* is an ill-defined medical condition characterized by lassitude, headache, and irritability; the adjective *neuromuscular* refers to nerves and muscles. *Neurology* is the study of the anatomy, functions, and organic disorders of nerves and the nervous system. A *neuron* is a specialized cell transmitting nerve impulses; a *neuroleptic* drug tends to reduce nervous tension by depressing nerve functions. A *neurosis* in medical usage is a relatively mild mental illness that is not caused by organic disease, while in non-technical use it refers to excessive and irrational anxiety or obsession (adjective *neurotic*). The form appears in several compound terms for medical sub-specialities, such as *neurophysiology* and *neuropharmacology*. The usual adjective is *neural*.

neutr(o)- *Neutral.* [English *neutral*.]

Examples include **neutrophil** (Greek *philos*, loving), a type of white blood cell that is **neutrophilic**, which can be readily stained only by neutral dyes; **neutropenia** (Greek *penia*, poverty), a lack of neutrophils in the blood. A **neutron** is a subatomic particle of about the same mass as a proton but without an electric charge; a **neutrino** (*see* -INO) is another neutral particle with a mass close to zero.

nigr(o)- Also **nigri-** *Black.* [Latin *niger*, *nigr-*, black.]

Words with this prefix are comparatively rare. The **nigrosines** are a class of dyes used to make printing inks and to dye shoe polish, wood, and textiles; something **nigrescent** is blackish; **nigritude** is blackness.

-nik *A person associated with a specified thing or quality.* [A Yiddish and Russian suffix.]

The ending had been known in English before the mid 1950s, notably in the Yiddish **nudnik** for a person who pesters or bores, **kibbutznik** for a member of a kibbutz, and in proper names such as **Chetnik**, a member of a guerrilla force in the Balkans. However, it was **Sputnik** (literally 'fellow-traveller' in Russian), a satellite launched in October 1957, that introduced the ending to a wider English audience. Examples include **beatnik**, a member of the Beat generation; **refusenik**, a Jew in the former Soviet Union who was refused permission to emigrate to Israel; **neatnik**, a person neat in his habits, the opposite of a beatnik; and **peacenik**, a member of a pacifist movement. The form has since lost much of its novel force; the rare new examples tend to follow *neatnik* and *peacenik* in being facetious or mildly derogatory: **nogoodnik**, **allrightnik**.

nitr(o)- Also **nitri-**. Also **nitros(o)-**. *Containing nitrogen, nitric acid, or nitrates.* [Latin *nitrum*, from Greek *nitron*, saltpetre.]

Nitrogen (Greek *genes*, -born) was so named because it is a component of *nitre*, an old name for saltpetre. The adjectives **nitrous** and **nitric** can generally refer to nitrogen, but in chemistry the former has a specific meaning of mono-valent nitrogen (as in *nitrous oxide*, N_2O), while the latter refers to nitrogen in higher combining states (as in *nitric oxide*, NO, or *nitric acid*, HNO_3). Salts of nitrous acid are **nitrites**, those of nitric acid are **nitrates**. *Nitriles* are cyanides derived from alkanes, straight-chain hydrocarbons; **nitrides** are compounds of metals with nitrogen. *Nitroso* compounds contain the **nitrosyl** radical —NO, for example **nitrosamines**, compounds containing the group =NNO attached to two organic groups.

The ending **nitro-** occurs in the names of many organic compounds, usually indicating the presence of one or more *nitro* groups, $-NO_2$, the introduction of which into a compound is **nitration**: **nitrobenzene** is a yellow oily liquid made by nitrating benzene; **nitrocellulose** is a highly flammable material made by treating cellulose with concentrated nitric acid, used to make explosives and celluloid. *See also* AZO-.

noci- *Pain.* [Latin *nocere*, to hurt or harm.]

Two examples are known from medicine: **nociceptive**, referring to nerve cells concerned with pain, and **nociceptor**, a sensory receptor for painful stimuli. The adjectives *innocuous* and *innocent* come from the same root.

noct(i)- *Night.* [Latin *nox*, *noct-*, night.]

Noctilucent (Latin *lucent-*, shining) refers to something glowing by night, especially noctilucent *clouds*, occasionally seen at night in summer in high latitudes; something **nocturnal** is done, occurring, or active at night; a **nocturne** is either a picture of a night scene or a musical composition of a dreamy nature; a **noctambulist** (Latin *ambulare*, walk) is now usually a facetious term for a sleepwalker; the **noctule** (via Italian *nottola*, bat) is the largest British species of bat.

-nomic or **-nomical**: *see* -NOMY

nomo- *Law.* [Greek *nomos*, law.]

The adjective **nomothetic** relates to the study or discovery of general scientific laws; something **nomological** denotes law-like principles, especially laws of nature, of which the study is **nomology**.

A *nomogram* is a diagram representing the relations between three or more variable quantities by means of a number of scales. A *nomarchy* (Greek *arkhē*, government) is an administrative division of modern Greece, formerly a province. Words such as *nomenclature* and *nominate* come instead from Latin *nomen*, name.

-nomy Also **-nomic**, **-nomical**, and **-nomous**. *A specified area of knowledge or the laws governing it.* [Greek *-nomia*, related to *nomos*, law.]

Examples include *astronomy*, the branch of science which deals with celestial objects and the physical universe; *gastronomy* (Greek *gastēr*, *gastr-*, stomach), the practice or art of choosing, cooking, and eating good food; *agronomy* (Greek *agros*, field), the science of soil management and crop production; *taxonomy* (Greek *taxis*, arrangement), the classification of organisms; *taphonomy* (Greek *taphos*, grave), the branch of palaeontology that deals with the processes of fossilization.

Some terms derive from the related Greek *nemein*, to manage or to give what is due: *economy* from Greek *oikos*, house; *autonomy*, the right of self-government, from Greek *autos*, self. *Physiognomy*, a person's facial features or expression, especially when regarded as indicative of character or ethnic origin, derives from *gnōmōn*, a judge, interpreter.

Related adjectives are formed ending in **-nomic** (*gastronomic*, *taxonomic*), **-ical** (*astronomical*), less often ending in **-nomous** (*heteronomous*, subject to a law or standard external to itself, from Greek *heteros*, other).

See also -LOGY.

non- *Not.* [Latin *non*, not.]

This prefix is more widely used to form negatives than any other. It is freely added to nouns, adjectives, and adverbs, and also to verbs used to form adjectives. In general the sense is neutral, without the implications often present with compounds beginning in *a-*, *in-*, or *un-*; for example *inhuman*, **non-human**, and *unhuman* all refer to something lacking human qualities, but the first is usually pejorative, implying cruelty or barbarism, while the latter two are neutral; *amoral* and *immoral* usually imply a value judgement, while **non-moral** does not.

However, negatives beginning in **non-** can contain the idea of pretence, inadequacy, or unimportance, as in *non-event*, *non-story*, *non-hero*, *non-issue*. Some adjectives formed from verbs have a sense of not causing something (*non-crease*, *non-skid*, *non-stick*), or not requiring something (*non-iron*).

A very few further examples with various senses are: *non-believer*, *nonconformism*, *nonentity*, *non-fattening*, *non-linear*, *non-negotiable*, *non-partisan*, *non-returnable*, *nonsense*, *non-smoking*, *non-stop*, *non-uniformly*, *non-violent*.

See also A-[1], DIS-, IN-[1], and UN-.

nona- *Nine; having nine.* [Latin *nonus*, ninth.]

A *nonagon* is a plane figure with nine straight sides and nine angles; a *nonet* is a group of nine people or things, especially musicians; *nonane* is a hydrocarbon of the alkane series with nine carbon atoms; in the Roman Catholic Church a *novena* is a form of worship consisting of special prayers or services on nine successive days. A few words are based on the related Latin word *nonaginta*, ninety, such as *nonagenarian*, a person who is between 90 and 99 years old. *See also* ENNEA- and the table of NUMBER PREFIXES opposite.

noo- *The mind.* [Greek *noos*, mind.]

The *noosphere* is the name given by the Christian mystic Pierre Teilhard de Chardin (1881–1955) to a postulated stage of evolutionary development dominated by consciousness, the mind, and interpersonal relationships; its coming into being is *noogenesis*. The adjective *nootropic* refers to a drug used to enhance memory or other cognitive functions; *noology* is a semi-archaic word for the study of the mind.

nor- *An organic compound that is the parent of another.* [The first element of *normal*.]

This denotes the normal or parent form of the organic compound named in the stem, one which lacks one or more methyl groups. Examples are *noradrenaline* (in the US *norepinephrine*), a hormone that functions as a neurotransmitter; *nortriptyline*, a tricyclic antidepressant drug; and *norgestrel*, a synthetic progestin.

normo- *Normal; close to the average.* [English *normal.*]

This form is mainly found in medicine. Examples of adjectives are *normotensive*, having or denoting a normal blood pressure; *normocytic*, having red blood cells of normal size; and *normochromic* (Greek *khrōma*, colour, plus -ic), having red blood cells of normal colour because they contain the usual amount of haemoglobin. *Normoglycaemia* (US *normoglycemia*) is a normal concentration of sugar in the blood.

noso- *Disease.* [Greek *nosos*, disease.]

A *nosocomial* disease (Greek *nosokomos*, person who tends the sick) is one that originates in a hospital; *nosography* is the systematic description of diseases; *nosology* is the branch of medical science dealing with the classification of diseases; *nosophobia* is a morbid fear of disease. In homeopathy, a *nosode* is a preparation of substances secreted in the course of a disease, used in the treatment of that disease.

nuci- *A nut.* [Latin *nux, nuc-*, nut.]

A rare form. A tree or bush that is *nuciferous* (Latin *-fer*, producing) bears nuts, while an animal that is *nucivorous* (Latin *vorare*, to devour) eats them. Something *nuciform* is nut-shaped.

nucleo- *Nucleus; nuclear; nucleic acid.* [Latin *nucleus*, inner part, kernel.]

In a cell, the *nucleolus* is a small dense spherical structure in the nucleus which disappears during cell division; the *nucleoplasm* is the substance of the cell nucleus; a *nucleoprotein* is a compound occurring in cells, a nucleic acid bonded to a protein. In biochemistry, *nucleotides* form the basic structural unit of nucleic acids such as DNA, and consist of phosphate groups attached to *nucleosides*, which consist of purine or pyrimidine bases linked to sugars. *Nucleonics* is the branch of science and technology concerned with atomic nuclei and *nu-*

NUMBER PREFIXES

The following are the more common number prefixes derived from Latin and Greek:

Number	Latin	Greek
Half	SEMI-, DEMI-	HEMI-
One	UNI-	MONO-
Two	BI-	DI-
Three	TRI-	TRI-
Four	QUADRI-	TETRA-
Five	QUINQUE-, QUINTI-	PENTA-
Six	SEXI-	HEXA-
Seven	SEPTI-	HEPTA-
Eight	OCTO-	OCTO-
Nine	NONA-	ENNEA-
Ten	DECEM-	DECA-
Eleven	UNDECA-	HENDECA-
Twelve	DUODECI-	DODECA-
Twenty	VIGINTI-	ICOS-
Hundred	CENTI-	HECTO-
Thousand	MILLI-	CHILI-

See also see the table of WORDS FOR MULTIPLES on page 127.

NUMBER WORDS

By a curious historical confusion, two different systems for naming large numbers exist, one in the US and the other in Britain and other parts of the English-speaking world. This could be troublesome, but these days such large numbers are much more often given in unambiguous scientific notation, and the US usage is in any case coming to dominate, as it has almost completely with **billion**.

The original scheme, invented in France in the 16th century, started with **million** and multiplied 1 by that number the required number of times. The name of the unit was then based on the number of multiplications, using Latin numerals. So a **sextillion** was 1 multiplied by a million six times, making a number expressed by 1 followed by 36 zeroes (10^{36} in scientific notation). In the 18th century French mathematicians changed to multiples of a thousand instead, but took over the existing number names; the Latin numbers then marked one less than the number of multiplications, so that **trillion** was 1 multiplied by 1000 four times. The US system was based on the thousands scheme, but the British stayed with the older millions one.

The following table gives some names and values in the two systems:

Number word	Millions scheme	Thousands scheme
million	10^6	10^6
billion (Latin *bi-*, twice)	10^9	10^{12}
trillion (Latin *tres*, three)	10^{12}	10^{18}
quadrillion (Latin *quattour*, four)	10^{15}	10^{24}
quintillion (Latin *quinque*, five)	10^{18}	10^{30}
sextillion (Latin *sex*, six)	10^{21}	10^{36}
septillion (Latin *septem*, seven)	10^{24}	10^{42}
octillion (Latin *octo*, eight)	10^{27}	10^{48}
nonillion (Latin *nonus*, ninth)	10^{30}	10^{54}
decillion (Latin *decem*, ten)	10^{33}	10^{60}

---

cleons (protons and neutrons), especially the exploitation of nuclear power; *nucleosynthesis* is the cosmic formation of atoms more complex than the hydrogen atom.

nudi- *Naked.* [Latin *nudus*, nude.]

A *nudibranch* (Greek *brankhia*, gills) is a member of an order of shell-less marine molluscs which comprises the sea slugs, the *Nudibranchia*; an animal that is *nudicaudate* (Latin *caudia*, tail) has a hairless tail, for example a rat.

nulli- *Nothing.* [Latin *nullus*, no, none.]

To *nullify* is to make legally null and void or make of no use or value; a *nullipara* (Latin *parere*, bear children) (plural *nulliparae*) is a woman (or female animal) that has never given birth; a *nulligravida* (Latin *gravidus*, laden, pregnant) is one that has never been pregnant; *nullifidian* is a rare word for a person having no faith or religious belief. The *Nullarbor Plain*, a vast arid area in SW Australia, derives its name from the Latin *nullus arbor*, no tree.

nyct(o)- Also **nycti-** *Night.* [Greek *nux, nukt-*, night.]

Nyctalopia (Greek *alaos*, blind, *ōps*, eye) is the inability to see in dim light or at night; *nyctophobia* is an extreme or irrational fear of the night or of darkness; *nyctinastic* (Greek *nastos*, pressed) refers to the periodic movement of flowers or leaves caused by nightly changes in light intensity or temperature.

-nym: *see* -ONYM

o-1: *see* OB-

o-2: *see* ORTHO-

-o- *A linking vowel.* [From Greek.]

This appears as the final vowel of many prefixes, such as CHLORO-, INDO-, PNEUMO-, SCHIZO-, and TECHNO-. It comes ultimately from its use as a linking vowel in classical Greek combinations, which were borrowed into Latin and thereafter arrived in English via French. It is often used in English as a connecting vowel irrespective of the source of the word elements it links. However, it is often left off if the following element begins with a vowel (as, for example, with PHLEBO-, a vein, where the **-o-** is lost in forming *phlebitis*, inflammation of the walls of a vein). In English the vowel also often acts as a link between a stem and an ending, as in *cottonocracy* or *speedometer*. In this book it is the Greek source stem that is decisive in placing an ending in its alphabetical sequence, so that entries (to take two common examples) are listed as -CRACY rather than *-ocracy* and -LOGY rather than *-ology*; however, -ONYM appears in that form because it derives from Greek *onoma*, name. Entries are cross-referenced where confusion might arise.

-o *Marking informally shortened or slang nouns.* [Perhaps from the interjection *oh!*, or the use of *-o* in ballads to terminate lines; its use has been reinforced by shortened forms ending in the linking vowel *-o-*.]

Though a wide variety of nouns in English end in **-o**, this suffix occurs only in words that have been formed from other native words in one of two specific ways. One method is to informally abbreviate a longer term, of which a few examples out of many are *ammo*, *condo*, *hippo*, *limo*, and *photo*. Others are based on an adjective or noun, to which the suffix is added to create a colloquial or slangy term, which is often—but by no means always—derogatory: *beano* (from *beanfeast*), *boyo*, *cheapo*, *kiddo*, *pervo* (from *pervert*), *pinko*, *righto*, *sicko*, *weirdo*, *wino*.

oario-: *see* OVARIO-

ob- Also **o-**, **oc-**, **of-**, **op-**, and **os-**. *Towards, to, on, over, or against.* [Latin *ob*, towards, against, in the way of.]

Most words with this prefix are based on Latin words which already contain it, often in a figurative sense. Examples include *obtrude* (Latin *trudere*, to push), to become noticeable in an unwelcome or intrusive way; *obverse* (Latin *vertere*, to turn), the side of a coin or medal bearing the head or principal design; *obsolete* (Latin *solere*, be accustomed); *obese* (Latin *esus*, the past participle of *edere*, to eat); *obey* (Latin *audire*, hear); *obstacle* (Latin *stare*, stand).

The prefix also appears in assimilated forms in which it is reduced to **o-** followed by a duplication of the first letter of the stem. It becomes **oc-** before stems beginning in *c* (*occasion*, *occlude*), **of-** before *f* (*offend*), and **op-** before *p* (*oppress*, *opponent*). Without the duplicated consonant, it sometimes becomes **os-** (*ostensible*) and sometimes just **o-** (*omit*).

The prefix appears in a few specialist technical terms. These may be linked to *obverse*, in which it seems to mean 'inversely'; the idea is of something that is in a direction or manner that is contrary to the usual. Examples are *obduction*, a term in geology for the movement of the edge of a crustal plate over the margin of an adjacent plate, the opposite of *subduction*; *obcordate*, used especially of a heart-shaped leaf that has its attachment at the apex; and *obovate*, of something that is *ovate*, like the outline of an egg, but with the narrower end at the base.

occipito- *The occipital bone.* [Medieval Latin *occipitalis*, from *ob-*, against, plus *caput*, *capit-*, head.]

The *occipital bone* is the saucer-shaped bone at the back and base of the cranium. Words beginning in **occipito-** are adjectives that mainly refer to this bone plus another part of the skeleton, as in *occipitotemporal*, of or relating to the occipital and temporal bones, which lie in the temples; others are *occipitoparietal*, occipital and parietal bones, which form the central side and upper back part of each side of the skull; *occipitofrontal*, occipital and frontal bones; and *occipitoatlantal*, occipital bone and the atlas vertebra, the topmost vertebra of the backbone. All these terms frequently appear hyphenated.

-ock *Forming nouns.* [Old English *-uc*, *-oc*.]

This suffix is now only historical. In some cases it had a diminutive sense, but that has largely been lost—the only one retaining it is *hillock*, a small hill. Other examples are *buttock*, originally a small *butt*, in the sense of backside, and *bullock*, literally *little bull*, a castrated male animal raised for beef. Several terms for animals may originally have been diminutives, though the evidence is unclear: *dunnock*, the hedge sparrow, perhaps 'the little dun-coloured (bird)', and *haddock* and *pollock*, two species of fish. Two British dismissive slang terms may include it, though their origins are uncertain: *slummock*, a dirty, untidy, or slovenly person; *wazzock*, a stupid or annoying person. *Pillock*, however, probably derives from *pillicock*, an old name for the penis. Other words with this ending come from a variety of sources, seemingly unconnected either with the suffix or each other: *bannock*, a round, flat loaf; *futtock*, each of the middle timbers of a ship's frame; *hassock*, a cushion for kneeling on in church; *hammock* comes through Spanish from Taino *hamaka* with the ending altered in imitation of **-ock**.

-ocracy: *see* **-CRACY**

octo- Also **octa-**. *Eight; having eight.* [Latin *octo* or Greek *oktō*, eight.]

Words beginning in **octo-** are usually of Latin origin, ones in **octa-** from Greek. An *octopus* has eight arms; the month of *October* was originally the eighth month of the Roman year; an *octuple* consists of eight parts or things; an *octocentenary* is the eight-hundredth anniversary of a significant event; an *octave* is a series of eight notes occupying the interval between (and including) two notes, one being half the frequency of the other; an *octagon* is a plane figure with eight straight sides and eight angles; an *octahedron* is a three-dimensional shape having eight plane faces. *Octogenarian*, a person in their eighties, derives from Latin *octoginta*, eighty.

oculo- *The eye or the sense of vision.* [Latin *oculus*, eye.]

A common term is *oculomotor*, of or relating to the motion of the eye; others include *oculogyric*, causing or concerned with movements of the eye; *oculoplethysmography* (Greek *plēthus*, fullness, plus *graphos*, writing), measurement of the pressure inside the eyeball, as an indicator of the presence of glaucoma; and *oculonasal*, of the eye and nose.

-ode[1] *Like; of the nature of.* [Greek adjectival ending *-ōdēs*.]

This appears in several technical terms formed from Greek words ending in *-ōdēs*, such as *geode* (Greek *geōdēs*, earthy, from *gē*, earth), a small cavity in rock lined with crystals or other mineral matter; *phyllode* (Greek *phullōdēs*, leaf-like, from *phullon*, leaf), a winged leaf stalk which functions as a leaf; *trematode* (Greek *trēmatōdēs*, perforated, from *trēma*, hole), a member of a class of flatworms; *cladode* (Greek *kladōdēs*, with many shoots, from *klados*, shoot), a flattened leaf-like stem. Others created in imitation in English are *nosode* (Greek *nosos*, disease), a preparation of substances secreted in the course of a disease, used in homeopathy to treat that disease, and *staminode*, a sterile or abortive stamen, frequently resembling a stamen without its anther.

-ode[2] *A conductor of electricity.* [Greek *hodos*, way.]

The ending was invented by William Whewell in 1834 when advising Michael Faraday on names for the conductors by which electricity enters or leaves a medium (originally a solution). He proposed *cathode* (Greek *kata-*, down) for the negatively charged pole by which electrons enter the medium, and *anode* (Greek *ana*, up) for the other. Faraday invented *electrode* from *electric* as a general term for either conductor. A set created later on their model describes thermionic valves with a given number of electrodes: *diode*, *triode*, *tetrode*, *pentode*; the first two now more usually refer to types of semiconductor device.

-odont Also **-odon** and **-odontia**. *Teeth; toothed*. [Greek *odous*, *odont-*, tooth.]

The ending **-odont** appears in adjectives that refer to the type of teeth possessed by animals. Examples are *labyrinthodont*, having the enamel deeply folded to form a labyrinthine structure; *bunodont* (Greek *bounos*, mound), having molar teeth with crowns in the form of rounded or conical cusps; *diphyodont* (Greek *dis*, twice, plus *phuein*, come into being), having two sets of teeth during its development, as humans do.

Since teeth survive better than any other part of the skeleton, many fossil animals have names that describe them in terms of their teeth. Examples ending in **-odont** are *cynodont* (Greek *kuōn*, *kun-*, dog), a fossil carnivorous reptile of the late Permian and Triassic periods, with dog-like teeth; *glyptodont* (Greek *gluptos*, carved), a fossil South American mammal of the Cenozic era with fluted teeth; *thecodont* (Greek *thēkē*, case), a fossil reptile of the Triassic period, ancestral to the dinosaurs, whose teeth are fixed in sockets in the jaw.

Words ending in **-odon** have the same sense: *mastodon*, a large extinct elephant-like mammal of the Miocene to Pleistocene epochs (Greek *mastos*, breast, because it has nipple-shaped tubercles on the crowns of its molar teeth); *iguanodon*, a large herbivorous dinosaur of the early to mid-Cretaceous period,

named thus because its teeth resemble those of the iguana.

A variety of systematic names for animals end in **-odontia**, such as *Aplodontia* (Greek *aplos*, simple), the genus containing the mountain beaver; *Diprotodontia* (Greek *dis*, twice, plus *prōtos*, first), the largest order of marsupials that have two large incisor teeth in the lower jaw. See the next entry for another sense of **-odontia**.

-odontics Also **-odontology** and **-odontia**. *Specialisms in dentistry*. [Greek *odous*, *odont-*, tooth.]

Examples include *paedodontics* (US *pedodontics*) (Greek *pais*, *paid-*, child) which deals with children's teeth; *prosthodontics*, concerning prosthetic replacements for teeth; *orthodontics* (Greek *orthos*, straight, right), the treatment of irregularities in the teeth and jaws. Some dental specialisms contain **-odontology** instead: *gerodontology* (Greek *gerōn*, *geront-*, old man), the dental treatment of elderly people. Some specialisms, especially in the US, can be described by equivalent terms ending in **-odontia**, though these are less common: *endodontia* (Greek *endon*, within) deals with diseases of the dental pulp; *periodontia* (Greek *peri*, about, around) is concerned with diseases that affect the structures surrounding and supporting the teeth. For another sense of **-odontia**, see the preceding entry.

odont(o)- *A tooth or teeth*. [Greek *odous*, *odont-*, tooth.]

Odontology is the scientific study of the structure and diseases of teeth; an *odontogenic* tumour is one composed of dental tissue; *odontalgia* (Greek *algos*, pain) is the technical term for toothache; an *odontoblast* (Greek *blastos*, germ, sprout) is a cell in the pulp of a tooth that produces dentine; the *odontoid*, or *odontoid process*, is a tooth-like projection from the second cervical vertebra on which the first can pivot.

-odynia *Pain*. [Greek *odunē*, pain.]

Pleurodynia (Greek *pleura*, side, *pleuron*, rib) is severe pain in the muscles between the ribs or in the diaphragm; *mastodynia* (Greek *mastos*, breast) is pain in the breast; *coccygodynia* is pain in the coccyx, the triangular bone at the base of the spinal column.

oen(o)- In the US, often **eno-** *Wine.* [Greek *oinos*, wine.]

The study of wines is *oenology*; an *oenophile* is a connoisseur of wines; *oenanthic acid* (a seven-carbon organic acid also called *heptanoic acid*) contributes part of the characteristic smell of wine and is used in perfumery; *oenocyanin* is an extract from red grapes, containing tannins and a blue colouring matter, which is sometimes added to wine to give extra body; an *oenocyte* is a large wine-coloured cell in insects, usually occurring in groups associated with the epidermis or the fat body.

oesophag(o)- Also **esophag(o)-** *The oesophagus.* [Greek *oisophagos*, gullet.]

The *oesophagus* is the gullet, the tube that connects the throat to the stomach. An *oesophagoscope* is an instrument for the inspection or treatment of it; *oesophagitis* is inflammation of it, heartburn; *oesophagectomy* (Greek *ektomē*, excision) is its surgical removal; *oesophagostomy* (Greek *stoma*, mouth) is an operation in which it is opened into the neck, usually as a temporary measure to allow feeding. In the US, it is common to use the spelling **esophago-** instead.

of-: *see* OB-

-ogen: *see* -GEN

-ography: *see* -GRAPHY

-oholic: *see* -AHOLIC

-oic Also **-dioic**. *A carboxyl group or its derivative.* [From -o- plus -IC.]

Though the ending is strictly only a variant of -IC, it has been formalized by chemists to be the standard ending for organic acids in which the carboxyl group, —COOH, replaces the methyl group, —CH3. Some examples from a large group: *valproic acid* (a name indirectly derived from the plant called *valerian*), a synthetic crystalline compound

used in the treatment of epilepsy; *caproic acid* (Latin *caper, capr-*, goat, because of its smell), a liquid fatty acid present in milk fat and coconut and palm oils; *benzoic acid* (from *gum benzoin*), a white crystalline substance used as a food preservative.

Many such names are formal chemical alternative names for compounds with common names, as *ethanoic acid* is the formal name of *acetic acid*. When two carboxyl groups are attached to one molecule, the ending becomes **-dioic** (Greek *dis*, twice), as in *ethanedioic acid*, the systematic name for *oxalic acid*, or *hexanedioic acid*, common name *adipic acid*, a crystalline fatty acid used especially in the manufacture of nylon. In complex systematic names, the form can appear as the final element in a hyphenated sequence, as in *11-oxo-5α-cholan-24-oic acid*.

Words whose meanings lie outside chemistry contain the ending as an accident of spelling in which -IC follows a stem ending in *o*: *echoic, heroic, paranoic*.

See also -YL and -ZOIC[1].

-oid Also **-oidea** and **-oidal**. *Like; resembling.* [Greek *-oidēs*; related to *eidos*, form.]

Words with this ending are adjectives and nouns that indicate a form or resemblance, sometimes an imperfect or incomplete one. A few members from a large group: *android* (Greek *anēr, andr-*, man), an artificial biological lifeform with a human appearance; *cardioid* (Greek *kardia*, heart), in the shape of a heart, especially a heart-shaped curve; *dendroid* (Greek *dendron*, tree), tree-shaped or branching; *factoid*, either something that is reported and repeated so often that it becomes accepted as fact, or a brief or trivial item of news or information; *meteoroid*, a small body moving in the solar system that would become a meteor if it entered the earth's atmosphere.

The ending can also indicate an animal that is a member of a systematic taxonomic grouping that ends in **-oidea**, usually a superfamily, a category that ranks above the family and below the order: a *salmonoid* is a fish of the superfamily

Salmonoidea that includes the salmon; a *hominoid* (Latin *homo, homin-,* human being) is a primate of the superfamily *Hominoidea* that includes humans, their fossil ancestors, and the great apes; *scarabaeoid* is a beetle of a large group, the *Scarabaeoidea,* that includes the scarab and stag beetles.

Adjectives are formed with **-oidal** (*see* -AL¹): *cuboidal,* of the nature of a *cuboid,* a roughly cube-shaped figure; *adenoidal,* relating to the *adenoids* (Greek *adēn,* gland), a structure between the back of the nose and the throat.

See also -PLOID.

-oides: *see* -IDES

-ol *An alcohol or phenol.* [The final element of *alcohol.*]

An *alcohol* is an organic compound containing a hydroxyl group, —OH; a *phenol* is a compound containing that group linked directly to a benzene ring, with phenol itself being the simplest example. Some others are *glycerol* (Greek *glukeros,* sweet), an alcohol containing three hydroxyl groups, a viscous liquid formed as a by-product in soap manufacture; *cholesterol* (Greek *kholē,* bile, plus *stereos,* stiff), a substance found in most body tissues, of which high concentrations in the blood are thought to promote atherosclerosis; *mannitol,* a compound found in many plants which is used in various foods and medical products. Some of the more frequently encountered aliphatic (straight carbon chain) alcohols have systematic names ending in **-ol** in addition to their common ones: *ethanol* is better known as *ethyl alcohol* or just *alcohol*; *propanol* is also known as *propyl alcohol*.

See also -OLE¹.

-ola *Diminutives; trade names; humorous or dismissive formations.* [Latin words ending in *-ola* or *-ula*.]

A few words with this ending come directly from Latin, usually with a diminutive sense: *areola* (Latin, diminutive of *area,* area), a small circular area, in particular the ring of pigmented skin surrounding a nipple; *cupola* (Latin *cupula,* small cask or burying vault, diminutive of *cupa,* cask), a rounded dome forming or adorning a roof or ceiling; *pergola* (Latin *pergula,* projecting roof, from *pergere,* come or go forward), an archway in a garden or park.

This diminutive sense may have been the inspiration for various US trade names (*Pianola,* a mechanical piano; *Victrola,* a type of phonograph; *Moviola,* a type of film-editing machine; *Granola,* a kind of breakfast cereal), mostly now generic or obsolete.

From the 1920s in the US the ending began to be added to a variety of nouns and adjectives to make humorous slang terms. Many of these were only temporary, but two of several that have survived are *boffola* (from slang *boff,* a hearty laugh), a joke or a line in a script meant to get a laugh, and *crapola* (from *crap,* excrement), total rubbish. One that has become standard English is *payola,* the practice of bribing someone to use their influence or position to promote a particular product, from which have evolved *drugola,* payola in the form of drugs, and *plugola,* payment to get favourable mention or display (a *plug*) for a product in a film or on radio or television. The ending is mainly limited to the US.

-ole¹ Also **-azole** and **-ol**. *Organic chemical compounds.* [Latin *oleum,* oil.]

This is a systematic ending in chemistry for unsaturated heterocyclic compounds containing a five-membered ring. Examples are *indole* (from *indigo,* from which it was first synthesized), a compound with an unpleasant odour, present in coal-tar and in faeces, and *pyrrole* (Greek *purrhos,* reddish, because a red colour is produced when its vapour comes into contact with concentrated hydrochloric acid), a sweet-smelling liquid present in bone oil and coal-tar.

When the ring contains nitrogen, the ending strictly becomes **-azole** (*see* AZO-). Examples include *thiazole* (Greek *theion,* sulphur), a foul-smelling liquid whose molecule contains a ring of one nitrogen, one sulphur, and three carbon atoms; and *carbazole* (from *carbon*), a compound obtained from coal-tar and used in making dyes, which contains three rings, one with nitrogen in it. The ending **-azole** is sometimes found in the invented generic names of drugs, such as the antibiotics **metronidazole** and **sulphamethoxazole**.

The ending **-ole** also appears in the names of esters, such as **safrole**, **anisole**, and **phenetole**, some of which are used in perfumery.

Some names (though not those of the drugs) can appear spelled **-ol** instead, as with **eucalyptol**, an oil obtained from eucalyptus leaves, also spelled **eucalyptole** (and which has the alternative name **cineole**).

-ole² *Forming nouns.* [Latin *-olus*, *-ola*, *-olum*.]

Some examples are formed from words that were originally Latin diminutives; others have been created in French or as modern Latin coinages: *areole* (via French from Latin *areola*, diminutive of *area*), a small circular area, especially one bearing spines or hairs on a cactus; *centriole* (modern Latin *centriolum*, diminutive of *centrum*, centre), each of a pair of minute cylindrical organelles near the nucleus in animal cells; *vacuole* (French, diminutive of Latin *vacuus*, empty), a space or vesicle within the cytoplasm of a cell; *fumarole* (Latin *fumariolum*, a vent, a diminutive based on Latin *fumus*, smoke), an opening in or near a volcano, through which hot sulphurous gases emerge; *casserole* (French, diminutive of *casse*, spoon-like container), a kind of slowly-cooked stew or the dish it is cooked in.

See also -ULA and -ULE.

-olatry or **-olater**: *see* -LATRY

ole(o)- *Relating to or containing oil.* [Latin *oleum*, oil.]

An *oleograph* is a print textured to resemble an oil painting; something *oleaginous* is oily or greasy, figuratively obsequious or smarmy; a seed that is *oleiferous* (Latin *-fer*, bearing) produces oil; *oleic acid* is an unsaturated fatty acid present in many fats and soaps. The Latin word *oleum* is used for a form of concentrated sulphuric acid, because it is an oily liquid.

-olidine: *see* -IDINE

olig(o)- *A small number; having few.* [Greek *oligos*, small, *oligoi*, few.]

An *oligarchy* is a small group of people having control of a country, organization, or institution. An *oligopoly* was formed on the pattern of *monopoly* and is a state in which a market is shared by a small number of producers or sellers (the opposite situation, in which there are few buyers, is called *oligopsony*, from Greek *opsōnein*, buy provisions). Several terms in biochemistry refer to molecules which contain a relatively small number of component units, such as *oligopeptide*, a peptide whose molecules contain a relatively small number of amino acid units.

-ological: *see* -LOGICAL

-ologist: *see* -LOGIST

-ology: *see* -LOGY

-oma *A tumour or other abnormal growth.* [Modern Latin, from Greek *-ōma*, a noun ending denoting the result of an action.]

Some examples derive directly from Greek, such as *carcinoma*, cancer, now specifically a cancer arising in the epithelial tissue of the skin or of the lining of the internal organs (Greek *karkinōma*, from *karkinos*, crab, because the swollen veins around the tumour resembled the limbs of a crab); *sarcoma* (Greek *sarkōma*, from *sarx*, *sark-*, flesh), a malignant tumour of connective or other non-epithelial tissue. On the model of these, many others have been formed in English, such as *lymphoma*, cancer of the lymph nodes, typically a malignant tumour associated with skin cancer; *fibroma* (Latin *fibra*, fibre, filament), a benign fibrous tumour of connective tissue; *mesothelioma* (Greek *mesos*, middle, plus *thēlē*, teat), a cancer of mesothelial tissue; *xanthoma* (Greek *xanthos*, yellow), an irregular yellow patch or nodule on the skin, caused by deposition of lipids. See the next entry. *See also* ONCO-.

-ome *Having a specified nature.* [Greek *-ōma*, a noun-ending denoting the result of an action.]

This is an Anglicized form of -OMA and usually indicates some part of a plant having a given nature. Unlike that ending it indicates a normal part of the organism. A *rhizome* (Greek *rhiza*, root) is a continuously growing horizontal underground stem which puts out lateral shoots at intervals; a *trichome* (Greek *trikhoun*, cover with hair) is a small hair or other outgrowth from the epidermis of a plant; a *phyllome* (Greek *phullon*, leaf) is a part of a plant that is regarded as a modified leaf. In ecology, a *biome* (Greek *bios*, life) is a large naturally occurring community of flora and fauna occupying a major habitat.

However, *genome*, the complete set of genetic material present in a cell or organism, derives from a blend of *gene* and *chromosome* (Greek *sōma*, body). A couple of terms have been formed on its model: *proteome*, the complete set of proteins produced from the instructions coded in a cell's genetic material, and *metabolome* (from *metabolism*), the complete set of metabolic processes within a cell. These seem to have been created partly by blending and partly by analogy with the older sense of the ending.

ombro- *Rain; moisture.* [Greek *ombros*, rain shower.]

An *ombrotrophic* environment, such as a bog or its vegetation, is dependent on atmospheric moisture; an *ombrophile* is a plant able to survive in wet conditions; an *ombrometer* is a formal word for a rain-gauge.

omni- *Of all things; in all places.* [Latin *omnis*, all.]

Examples include *omniscient* (Latin *scire*, to know), knowing everything; *omnipotent* (Latin *potens*, *potent-*, power), having unlimited power; *omnicompetent*, able to deal with all matters or solve all problems; and *omnipresent*, present everywhere at the same time (said especially of God). An *omnivore* (Latin *vorare*, devour) eats a variety of food of both plant and animal origin; an *omnibus* (literally 'for all', the dative plural of *omnis*) comprises several items or editions, or is a rather old-fashioned term for *bus*, its abbreviation; an *omnidirectional* antenna receives or transmits radio signals in all directions.

omphal(o)- *The navel; the umbilical cord.* [Greek *omphalos*, navel.]

Omphalitis is inflammation of the naval, especially in newborn infants; an *omphalocele* is a hernia in which abdominal organs protrude into a baby's umbilical cord; the adjective *omphalomesenteric* (sometimes hyphenated) refers to the navel and the mesentery, a fold of the peritoneum which attaches the stomach and other organs to the wall of the abdomen. The Greek word *omphalos* is also a poetic or literary term for the centre or hub of something.

-on¹ *Subatomic particles or quanta; molecular units.* [Originally from *electron*, probably from the ending of *ion* and influenced by Greek *on*, being.]

An *electron* is a stable subatomic particle with a negative charge. On its model, **-on** has become the dominant ending with which to label elementary particles and groups of such particles (for another, *see* -TRON); examples include *proton* (Greek, neuter of *prōtos*, first), a particle with a positive electric charge equal to that of an electron; *meson* (Greek *mesos*, middle), a particle intermediate in mass between an electron and a proton; *baryon* (Greek *barus*, heavy), a particle with a mass equal to or greater than that of a proton.

Names for quanta include *photon* (Greek *phōs*, *phōt-*, light), a particle representing a quantum of light or other electromagnetic radiation; *graviton*, a hypothetical quantum of gravitational energy, regarded as a particle; *phonon* (Greek *phōnē*, sound), a quantum of energy or a quasi-particle associated with a compressional wave such as sound or a vibration of a crystal lattice.

The ending has been adopted in molecular biology for entities regarded as units, such as *codon* (from *code*), a sequence of three nucleotides which together form a unit of genetic code in a DNA or RNA molecule; *intron* (Latin *intra*, inside), a segment of a DNA or RNA molecule which does not code for proteins and interrupts the sequence of genes; and *operon* (French *opérer*, to effect, work), a unit made up of linked genes which is thought to regulate other genes responsible for protein synthesis.

-on² *Inert gases.* [The Greek neuter ending *-on*.]

Argon was the first of the inert gases to be discovered; its name was taken from Greek, the neuter of *argos*, idle, from *a-* without, plus *ergon*, work. Others were named in imitation: *neon* (Greek, literally 'something new', neuter of the adjective *neos*), *krypton* (Greek *krupton*, neuter of *kruptos*, hidden); *xenon* (Greek, neuter of *xenos*, strange); *radon* (from *radium*).

onco- *A tumour.* [Greek *onkos*, mass.]

Oncology is the study and treatment of tumours; something *oncogenic* causes development of a tumour; an *oncogene* is a gene which in certain circumstances can transform a cell into a tumour cell; *oncolysis* (Greek *lusis*, loosening) is the destruction of a tumour, usually in response to treatment; the adjective relating to tumours is *oncotic*, but it can also refer to an increase in volume or pressure. *See also* -OMA.

-one *Various chemical compounds, especially ketones.* [Greek patronymic *-ōnē*.]

A *ketone* is an organic compound containing a carbonyl group —CO— bonded to two alkyl groups. The simplest such compound is *acetone* (formal name *propanone*); another is *butanone*, methyl ethyl ketone; in systematic naming, the ending often appears hyphenated: *3,5-dimethylheptan-4-one*.

A variety of more complex organic compounds contain the same ending, as for example *benzoquinone*, a yellow crystalline compound related to benzene; *dithizone* (more fully *diphenylthiocarbazone*), a synthetic compound used as a reagent for the analysis and separation of lead and other metals; *glutathione*,

a compound involved as a coenzyme in oxidation-reduction reactions in cells.
See also -ONIC and -STERONE.

oneir(o)- *Dreams or dreaming.* [Greek *oneiros*, dream.]

Oneiromancy is the interpretation of dreams in order to foretell the future; *oneirology* is the study of dreams; *oneirism* is a formal term for day-dreaming; the adjective *oneiric* refers to dreams or dreaming.

-onic *Organic acids.* [From -ONE plus -IC.]

Some examples are *sulphonic acid* (US *sulfonic*), a member of a group of organic acids containing the group —SO_2OH; *phosphonic acid*, a crystalline dibasic acid of formula $HPO(OH)_2$; *propionic acid* (Greek *pro*, before, plus *piōn*, fat, it being the first member of the fatty acid series to form fats), a liquid organic acid produced in some forms of fermentation and used for inhibiting the growth of mould in bread; *arachidonic acid*, a polyunsaturated fatty acid present in animal fats, important in metabolism.

-ont *An individual or cell of a specified type.* [Greek *ont-*, being, the present participle of *eimi*, be.]

A *schizont* (Greek *skhizein*, to split) is a cell that divides by *schizogony*, asexual reproduction by multiple fission, to form daughter cells; a *haplont* (Greek *haploos*, single) has a life cycle in which the main form is haploid, with a diploid zygote being formed only briefly, as opposed to a *diplont* (Greek *diplous*, double), in which the main form, except for the gametes, is diploid.

onto- *Existence or being.* [Greek *ōn, ont-*, being.]

Ontogenesis (Greek *genesis*, birth) is the development of an individual organism or anatomical or behavioural feature from the earliest stage to maturity; *ontogeny* is the branch of biology that deals with ontogenesis, while *ontology* is the branch of metaphysics dealing with the nature of being.

-onychia *A condition of the nails.* [Greek *onux, onukh-*, nail or claw, plus -IA.]

Paronychia (Greek *para*, beside) is an inflamed swelling of the fold of skin at the margin of a nail; *koilonychia* (Greek *koilos*, hollow) is a condition in which the fingernails become thin, brittle, and concave instead of convex, also called *spoonnail*; *pachyonychia* (Greek *pakhus*, thick) is a rare genetic disorder in which, among other symptoms, the nails become thickened; *onychia* is inflammation of the bed of a nail.

onycho- *The nails.* [Greek *onux*, *onukh-*, nail or claw.]

Onychomycosis (Greek *mukēs*, fungus) is a fungal infection of the nails; *onycholysis* (Greek *lusis*, loosening) is the separation or loosening of a nail from its bed; *onychogryphosis* (Gk *grupōsis*, hooking of the nails) is the thickening and curving sideways of a nail, usually of the big toe; *onychophagia* (Greek *phagein*, to eat) is the formal term for biting one's nails.

-onym Also **-onymy**, **-onymic**, and **-onymous**. *A name.* [Greek *onuma*, name.]

The ending principally appears in words that describe kinds of words. See the LIST below for some examples. Abstract nouns for the state or concept are formed in **-onymy**: *homonymy*, *metonymy*, *toponymy*. Adjectives are formed in **-onymic** or **-onymous**, sometimes both, though the former is rather more common (*eponymous*, *metonymic*, *synonymous*, *toponymic*).

oo- Also **oö-**. *An egg or ovum.* [Greek *ōion*, egg.]

Terms are mainly specialist ones in biology, such as *oocyte* (Greek *kutos*, vessel), a cell in an ovary which may undergo meiotic division to form an ovum; *oogamous* (Greek *gonos*, generation), relating to or denoting reproduction by the union of mobile male and

---

-onym A name for a type of word.
All word origins are from Greek.

acronym	a word formed from the initial letters of other words	(*akron*, end, tip)
anonym	an anonymous person or publication, or a pseudonym	(*an-*, without)
antonym	a word opposite in meaning to another	(*anti-*, against)
cryptonym	a code name	(*kruptos*, hidden)
eponym	a person after whom a discovery, invention, place, or the like is named	(*epi*, upon)
heteronym	each of two or more words which are spelled identically but have different sounds and meanings	(*heteros*, other)
homonym	each of two or more words having the same spelling or pronunciation but different meanings and origins	(*homos*, same)
hyponym	a word of more specific meaning, a subcategory of a more general class	(*hupo*, under)
metonym	a word, name, or expression used as a substitute for something else with which it is closely associated	(*metōnumia*, change of name)
pseudonym	a fictitious name, especially one used by an author	(*pseudēs*, false)
synonym	a word or phrase that means the same as another word or phrase in the same language	(*sun-*, with)
toponym	a place name, especially one derived from a topographical feature	(*topos*, place)

immobile female gametes; *ootheca* (Greek *thēkē*, receptacle), the egg case of cockroaches, mantises, and related insects. However, it also occurs in geology in reference to egg-shaped masses, as in *oolite* (Greek *lithos*, stone), a limestone consisting of a mass of rounded grains (*ooliths*) made up of concentric layers. The form may occasionally be seen written with a dieresis (**oö-**) to indicate that the two vowels are pronounced separately: *oögamous*, *oölite*. *See also* OVI-.

-oon *Forming nouns and derived verbs.* [Originally from French words having the final stressed syllable *-on*; sometimes via the equivalent Italian *-one*.]

Examples from French include *bassoon* (French *basson*); *dragoon* (French *dragon*, a type of musket, thought of as breathing fire like a dragon, now a member of any of several British cavalry regiments; *pontoon* (French *ponton*), a flat-bottomed boat used to support a temporary bridge or floating landing stage. Examples from Italian include *lagoon* (Italian, and Spanish, *laguna*) and *cartoon* (Italian *cartone*). Some can be either nouns or verbs: *cocoon*, *lampoon*. The only common word formed in English using this ending is *spitoon*.

A few words come from other languages and are unconnected: *tycoon* (Japanese *taikun*, great lord), *monsoon* (Portuguese *monçāo*, from Arabic *mawsim*, season), *raccoon* (Virginia Algonquian *aroughcun*).

See also -ZOON.

oophor(o)- *The ovary.* [Latin *oophoron*, ovary.]

The only two relatively common medical terms in this form are *oophorectomy* (Greek *ektomē*, excision), surgical removal of one or both ovaries, and *oophoritis*, inflammation of an ovary. *See also* OVARIO-.

op-: *see* OB-

-opedia: *see* -PEDIA

ophi(o)- *A snake.* [Greek *ophis*, snake.]

The *Ophidia* is a group of reptiles which comprises the snakes; *ophiology* is the study of snakes. The obsolete mu-sical instrument called the *ophicleide* (Greek *kleis*, *kleid-*, key) was given that name because of its twisted shape. In geology, *ophiolite* is an igneous rock consisting largely of serpentine, the latter called that because of its mottled appearance, like a snake's skin.

ophthalm(o)- *The eyes.* [Greek *ophthalmos*, eye.]

Ophthalmology is the branch of medicine concerned with the study and treatment of disorders and diseases of the eye, a specialist in which is an *ophthalmologist*; an *ophthalmoscope* is an instrument for inspecting the retina and other parts of the eye; *ophthalmitis* is inflammation of the eye; *ophthalmoplegia* (Greek *plēgē*, stroke) is paralysis of the muscles within or surrounding the eye.

-opia *A visual disorder.* [Greek *ōps*, *ōp-*, eye, face.]

Examples include *myopia* (Greek *muein*, to shut), short-sightedness, whose opposite is *hypermetropia* (Greek *huper*, over, above, plus *metron*, measure) or *hyperopia*, long-sightedness; *presbyopia* (Greek *presbus*, old man) is long-sightedness caused by loss of elasticity of the lens of the eye, occurring typically in middle and old age; *diplopia* is the technical term for double vision. Several examples refer specifically to impairment of colour vision, as in *protanopia* Greek *prōtos*, first), insensitivity to red light; *deuteranopia* (Greek *deuteros*, second), insensitivity to green; *tritanopia* (Greek *tritos*, third), insensitivity to blue; these are named on the basis that red, green, and blue are respectively the first, second, and third primary colours.

See also -OPSIA, -TOPIA.

opistho- *Behind; to the rear.* [Greek *opisthen*, behind.]

In medicine, *opisthotonos* (Greek *tonos*, tension) or *opisthotonus* is spasm of the muscles causing backward arching of the head, neck, and spine; in zoology, an *opisthosoma* (Greek *sōma*, body) is the abdomen of a spider or other arachnid; an *opisthobranch* (Greek *brankhia*, gills) is a member of a group of molluscs, the

Opisthobranchia, which includes the sea slugs and sea hares, so called because their gills are placed well back on the body.

-opsia *A defect of vision.* [Greek *-opsia*, seeing, from *ōps*, *ōp-*, eye, face.]

Achromatopsia (Greek *a-*, without, plus *khrōma*, *khrōmat-*, colour) is total colour blindness, while *chromatopsia* is abnormally coloured vision, a rare condition of varied cause; *hemianopsia* (or *hemianopia*) is blindness over half the field of vision; *micropsia* (Greek *mikros*, small) is a condition in which objects appear smaller than normal; *metamorphopsia* (Greek *metamorphoun*, transform, change shape) is a defect in which objects appear distorted. *See also* -OPIA.

-opsis *Observation or perception; likeness.* [Greek *opsis*, sight, appearance.]

A figurative example formed in Greek is *synopsis* (from *sun-*, together), a brief summary or general survey of something. Examples formed in English are varied but not especially common: *stereopsis* (Greek *stereos*, solid), the perception of depth produced by the reception in the brain of visual stimuli from both eyes in combination; *thanatopsis* (Greek *thanatos*, death), a view or contemplation of death. The ending appears in several names for plants to indicate a resemblance: *coreopsis* (Greek *koris*, a bug, because of the bug-like shape of the seed), a plant of the daisy family; *meconopsis* (Greek *mēkōn*, poppy), a Eurasian poppy-like plant which is sometimes grown as an ornamental; *ampelopsis* (Greek *ampelos*, vine), a bushy climbing plant of the vine family.

-opsy *Medical examination.* [Greek *optos*, seen.]

The earliest example was *autopsy* (Greek, *autoptēs*, eyewitness, from *autos*, self), a post-mortem examination. On its model have been derived *necropsy* (Greek *nekros*, corpse), another term for an autopsy, and *biopsy*, an examination of tissue removed from a living body to discover the presence, cause, or extent of a disease.

opto- Also **opti-**. *Vision; light.* [Greek *optos*, seen.]

Optometry is the occupation of measuring eyesight, prescribing corrective lenses, and detecting eye disease. The form appears in a few terms relating to the use of light in electronics, especially *optoelectronics* (or *optronics*), the branch of technology concerned with the interconversion of electronics and light; and *optocoupler*, a device containing light-emitting and light-sensitive components, used to couple isolated circuits.

Words beginning in **opti-** come from Latin *opticus* or *optica*, which derive from the same Greek source. Examples are *optic* and *optical*, of or relating to the eye or vision; *optics*, the scientific study of sight and the behaviour of light; and *optician*, a person qualified to prescribe and dispense glasses and contact lenses, and to detect eye diseases.

-or¹ Also **-our**. *Someone or something that performs a given action.* [From Latin, sometimes via Anglo-Norman French *-eour* or Old French *-eor*.]

A wide variety of such nouns exist in English. A few examples in which it refers to a person are *actor*, *author*, *commentator*, *creator*, *doctor*, *editor*, *inventor*, *navigator*, *oppressor*, *sculptor*, *translator*, and *visitor*. Some of those in which it refers to a device or machine are *accumulator*, *capacitor*, *carburettor*, *motor*, *percolator*, *refrigerator*, *reflector*, *rotor*, and *tractor*.

The ending is for most purposes identical in sense and usage with *-er* (see -ER¹). There is a tendency for words ending in **-or** to be preferred for an agent that is an intangible entity (*descriptor*; *sensor*, *vector*) and in legal terms (*lessor*, *mortgagor*, *vendor*), for which matching terms ending in -EE usually exist for the other party to the transaction. However, differences are slight and there is no rule to determine which ending is correct in any given case. Both the forms *adviser* and *advisor* are widely used, though the former is much more common in British English.

A very few such words are spelled **-our** in British English, particularly *saviour*, though this spelling is also sometimes used in American English when it refers to Jesus Christ.

-or² Also **-our**. *Forming nouns denoting an abstract state or condition.* [From Latin, sometimes via Old French *-or*, *-ur*.]

Examples are *error*, *horror*, *pallor*, *stupor*, *terror*, and *tremor*. Many of these were once spelled **-our** and this spelling persists in some examples in British English (*behaviour*, *colour*, *fervour*, *honour*, *valour*, *vigour*), which—in part as a result of spelling reforms advocated by Noah Webster—are now spelled **-or** in the US: *behavior*, *color*, *fervor*, etc.

Some words in British English that are spelled **-our** lose the *u* when forming derivatives (*clamorous*, *coloration*, *glamorize*), but others keep it (*behaviourist*, *honourable*).

-or³: *see* -IOR

-orama Also **-(r)ama**. *A display or spectacle.* [The final element of *panorama* or *cyclorama*.]

Panorama was invented about 1789 by the Irish painter Robert Barker to describe a very large cylindrical landscape painting which one could stand inside. He derived it from Greek *pan*, all, plus *horama*, view. It became famous, and a fashion developed of creating imitative terms for similar displays (*cyclorama*, *cosmorama*, *georama*, *diorama*). *Cyclorama* has survived to mean an illuminated stage backcloth, *diorama* is now usually a model representing a scene with three-dimensional figures. *Futurama* was an exhibit at the New York World's Fair in 1939. The introduction of the film projection system *Cinerama* in the 1950s sparked off a second series of imitations, this time of shorter-lived terms to indicate some spectacle. Their heyday was the 1960s and 1970s, but the ending has survived. Examples are *sensorama*, *Scout-O-Rama* (used in the US for large annual Scout events), and *odourama* and *smellorama* (adding scents to films, museum exhibits, and other media).

orchid(o)- Also **orch(i)-**. *Testicle; orchid.* [Greek *orkhis*, testicle.]

An *orchiectomy* or *orchidectomy* (Greek *ektomē*, excision) is surgical removal of a testicle; *orchitis* is inflammation of one or both of the testicles; *orchidopexy* (Greek *-pexia*, *pexis*, fixing together) is an operation to fix an undescended testicle in position.

The form has been applied to orchids because their tubers were thought to resemble testicles; hence *orchidaceous*, relating to plants of the orchid family; *orchidist*, a grower or fancier of orchids; *orchidology*, their study.

organo- *Bodily organs; organic chemical compounds.* [Either Greek *organon*, organ, or English *organic*.]

Examples relating to organs include *organoleptic* (Greek *lēptikos*, disposed to take), involving the use of the sense organs; *organogenesis*, the production and development of the organs of an animal or plant; and *organotherapy*, the treatment of disease with extracts from animal organs, especially glands.

In chemistry, the prefix is used to make names for groups of organic compounds which contain a particular element or group, frequently a metal or other inorganic radical: *organochlorine*, any of a large group of pesticides and other synthetic organic compounds containing chlorine; *organophosphorus*, denoting synthetic organic compounds containing phosphorus, especially pesticides and nerve gases; an *organometallic* compound contains a metal atom bonded to an organic group or groups.

-orial: *see* -AL¹

-orium *A place for a particular function.* [Latin neuter ending of words ending in *-orius*.]

Examples from a small group include *crematorium* (Latin, from *cremare*, burn), a place where a dead person's body is cremated; *auditorium* (Latin, neuter of *auditorius*, relating to hearing), the part of a theatre or concert hall in which the audience sits; *sanatorium* (Latin *sanare*, heal), an establishment for the medical treatment of people who are convalescing or have a chronic illness. Though *mora-*

torium, a temporary prohibition of an activity, was created on the same model (Latin neuter *moratorius*, delaying) it does not share the sense of the others; *emporium*, a large retail store, derives through Latin from Greek *emporion*, market. *See also* -ORY and -IUM.

ornith(o)- *A bird or birds.* [Greek *ornis*, *ornith-*, bird.]

The scientific study of birds is *ornithology*; an *ornithopod* (Greek *pous*, *pod-*, foot, hence 'bird-footed') is a mainly bipedal herbivorous dinosaur; the adjective *ornithischian* (Greek *iskhion*, hip joint) denotes herbivorous dinosaurs of an order distinguished by having a pelvic structure resembling that of birds. An *ornithopter* (Greek *pteron*, wing) was a machine designed to achieve flight by means of flapping wings. The amino acid *ornithine* was given that name because it is related to a substance first found in bird excrement.

oro-¹ *Mountains.* [Greek *oros*, mountain.]

Terms include *orogeny* (adjective *orogenic*), a process in which a section of the earth's crust is folded and deformed by lateral compression to form a mountain range; the adjective *orographic* refers to mountains, especially as regards their position and form; and an *orocline* (Greek *klinein*, to slope) is an orogenic system in which rocks have been flexed into a horseshoe shape.

oro-² *The mouth.* [Latin *os*, *or-*, mouth.]

In medicine, the adjective *oropharyngeal* refers to the part of the pharynx that lies between the soft palate and the hyoid bone; *orofacial* refers to the mouth and face; *oronasal* to the mouth and nose. Related general terms are *oral*, of the mouth or of things spoken rather than written; *orotund*, of a voice or phrasing that is full and imposing (Latin *ore rotundo*, with rounded mouth); and *orifice* (Latin *facere*, make), an opening, particularly one in the body.

ortho- Also **o-**. *Straight; correct; upright.* [Greek *orthos*, straight, right.]

Orthodox literally means having the correct opinion (Greek *doxa*, opinion); *orthoepy* (Greek *epos*, *epe-*, word) is the correct or accepted pronunciation of words, or the study of it; *orthodontics* (Greek *odous*, *odont-*, tooth) is the treatment of irregularities in the teeth and jaws; something *orthogonal* (Greek *gōnia*, angle) involves right angles.

In chemistry, the form indicates substitution at two adjacent carbon atoms in a benzene ring (*orthodichlorobenzene*, *ortho-aminoanisole*), as opposed to the other two possible positions, META- and PARA-. It is often abbreviated to **o-**: *o*-tolidine, *o*-hydroxybenzaldehyde.

The form can also denote a compound in the highest state of hydration, containing the maximum number of hydroxyl groups: an example is an *ortho acid* such as *orthosilicic acid*. Such acids are often unstable and lose water to form compounds designated by META-, as *orthophosphoric acid* becomes *metaphosphoric acid* on heating.

-ory¹ *A place having a particular function or character.* [Latin *-oria*, *-orium*, sometimes via Anglo-Norman French *-orie*, Old French *-oire*.]

Some examples relating to the function of a place are *dormitory* (Latin *dormitorium*, from *dormire*, to sleep); *lavatory* (Latin *lavatorium*, place for washing, from *lavare*, to wash); *observatory* (Latin *observatorium*, from *observare*, to watch). Some relating to the character of a place are *promontory* (Latin *promontorium*, from the verb *prominere*, be prominent) and *territory* (Latin *territorium*, from *terra*, land). *History*, however, derives from Greek *historia*, finding out, narrative, history. *See also* -ORIUM.

Associated adjectives are sometimes formed in **-orial** (*lavatorial*, *territorial*); *see* -AL¹.

-ory² Also **-atory**, **-sory**, **-tory**. *Relating to or involving an action.* [Latin *-orius*, Latin *-orius*, sometimes via Anglo-Norman French *-ori(e)*.]

Examples are primarily adjectives. They often contain *at*, *s*, or *t* before the ending, derived from the stem of Latin precursor words. Some examples are *compulsory*, *defamatory*, *mandatory*, *obligatory*, *preparatory*, and *sensory*. They can sometimes also be nouns: *accessory*, *purgatory*. One that is now always a noun is *directory*.

os-: *see* OB-

-oscope: *see* -SCOPE

-ose¹ Also *-oseness. Having a specified quality.* [Latin ending *-osus*.]

Some examples are *bellicose* (Latin *bellicosus*, from *bellum*, war), demonstrating aggression and willingness to fight; *morose* (Latin *morosus*, peevish, from *mos*, *mor-*, manner), sullen and ill-tempered; *verbose* (Latin *verbosus*, from *verbum*, word), using more words than are needed.

Others have been formed in English on various stems, such as *comatose* (Greek *kōma*, *kōmat-*, deep sleep), in a state of deep unconsciousness for a long period. Many are specialist: *nodulose*, having nodules; *strigose* (Latin *striga*, swath, furrow), covered with short stiff hairs that lie closely against the body; *squamulose* (Latin *squamula*, diminutive of *squama*, scale), having small scales.

Corresponding nouns are formed ending in **-oseness** (*moroseness*, *verboseness*), or in -OSITY. *See also* -OUS.

-ose² *Sugars and other carbohydrates.* [From the ending of *glucose*, the first example, which was named in French from Greek *gleukos*, sweet wine.]

Examples of sugars are *fructose* (Latin *fructus*, fruit), found especially in honey and fruit; *dextrose* (Latin *dexter*, *dextr-*, on the right), the dextrorotatory form of glucose, the predominant naturally occurring form; *maltose*, produced by the breakdown of starch, for example by enzymes found in malt and saliva. More complex carbohydrates, formed of sugar units, include *cellulose*, which is the main constituent of plant cell walls and of vegetable fibres such as cotton.

-osis Also **-sis**. *Abstract nouns of action, state, or process.* [Greek *-ōsis* or *-sis*, verbal noun endings.]

In classical Greek, the ending formed abstract nouns from verbs, of which a number have been brought over into

English, such as *metamorphosis* (Greek *metamorphōsis*, from *metamorphoun*, transform, change shape), a change into a completely different form or nature; *narcosis* (Greek *narkōsis*, from *narkoun*, make numb), a state of stupor or unconsciousness produced by drugs; and *gnosis* (Greek *gnōsis*, knowledge, related to *gignōskein*, know), knowledge of spiritual mysteries.

English words ending in **-osis** are commonly names for diseases, diseased conditions, or pathological states: *neurosis*; *tuberculosis*; *thrombosis*; *nephrosis* (Greek *nephros*, kidney), kidney disease; *silicosis*, a disease of the lung caused by inhaling dust containing silica.

Adjectives commonly end in -OTIC. *See also* -ASIS, -CYTE (for *-cytosis*), -ESIS, and -LYSIS.

-osity *Forming nouns.* [French *-osité* or Latin *-ositas*.]

Nouns in **-osity** are formed from adjectives. One set comes from those ending in *-ose* (*see* -OSE¹), such as *adiposity* (from *adipose*, body tissue used for the storage of fat), *bellicosity* (from *bellicose*, warlike), or *verbosity* (from *verbose*). A second set derives from adjectives ending in -OUS, such as *curiosity* (from *curious*), *generosity* (from *generous*), *monstrosity* (from *monstrous*), and *pomposity* (from *pompous*). *See also* -ITY.

osmo- *Osmosis.* [Greek *ōsmos*, a push.]

Osmosis is the diffusion of a solvent through a semipermeable membrane into a more concentrated solution, so tending to equalize concentrations on both sides of the membrane. Words relating to this sense include *osmolality*, the number of *osmotically* effective dissolved particles per unit quantity of a solution; *osmometer*, an instrument for demonstrating or measuring osmotic pressure; *osmoregulation*, the maintenance of constant osmotic pressure in the fluids of an organism by the control of water and salt concentrations.

Rarely, words beginning in **osmo-** derive instead from Greek *osmē*, odour, as in *osmic*, the adjective relating to odours or the sense of smell, or *osmium*, a chemical element, which was named from the pungent smell of its tetroxide. See also the next entry.

-osmia *An abnormal condition of the sense of smell.* [Greek *osmē*, odour.]

The most common term in a specialist medical set is *anosmia*, the loss of the sense of smell, either total or partial; others are *hyposmia* (Greek *hupo*, under), a condition in which the sense of smell is abnormally weak; *dysosmia* (Greek *dus-*, bad or difficult), an impairment of the sense of smell; and *parosmia* (Greek *para*, beside), any disorder of the sense of smell.

oste(o)- *The bones.* [Greek *osteon*, bone.]

Some relatively common instances from an extensive set of medical terms are *osteopathy* (Greek *patheia*, suffering, feeling), treatment of medical disorders through the manipulation and massage of the skeleton and musculature; *osteoarthritis*, degeneration of joint cartilage and the underlying bone, most common from middle age onward; *osteoporosis* (Greek *poros*, passage, pore), a condition in which the bones become brittle and fragile from loss of tissue; *osteomyelitis*, inflammation of bone or bone marrow, usually due to infection; *osteology*, the study of the structure and function of the skeleton and bony structures.

-ostomy: *see* -STOMY

-otic *Forming adjectives and nouns.* [French *-otique*, via Latin from the Greek adjectival ending *-ōtikos*.]

Such words usually correspond to nouns ending in -OSIS, such as *hypnotic*, *narcotic*, *neurotic*, *osmotic*, and *symbiotic*. Some do not have nouns which end in that form: *erotic*, *exotic*. *Chaotic* was formed from *chaos* on the model of *hypnotic*. A few are accidental formations in which -IC has been added to a stem ending in -ot, such as *idiotic* or *patriotic*.

oto- *The ears.* [Greek *ous*, *ōt-*, ear.]

Oto- is found in a variety of medical terms, including *otology*, the study of the anatomy and diseases of the ear; *otoscope*, an instrument designed for visual exam-

ination of the eardrum and the passage of the outer ear; *otolaryngology*, the study of diseases of the ear and throat (*larynx*); *otolith* (Greek *lithos*, stone), each of three small bodies in the inner ear that are involved in sensing gravity and movement; and *otoplasty* (Greek *plastos*, formed, moulded), a surgical operation to restore or enhance the appearance of an ear or the ears.

-otomy: *see* -TOMY

-our *Forming nouns.* [Derived from various sources.]

For the most part, words ending in **-our** are variants of those ending in **-or** (*see* -OR¹ and -OR²). However, there are some that derive from a variety of other sources, such as *endeavour* (late Middle English, in the sense 'exert oneself'; from the phrase *put oneself in devoir*, do one's utmost), *harbour* (Old English *herebeorg*, shelter, refuge), *neighbour* (Old English, from *nēah*, near, plus *gebūr*, inhabitant, peasant, farmer), and *parlour* (Anglo-Norman French *parlur*, place for speaking, from Latin *parlare*, speak). All these are usually written *-or* in American English.

-ous *Also* **-eous**, **-ious**, *and* **-ulous**. *Forming adjectives.* [Latin *-osus*.]

The **-ous** ending is extremely common and is a standard way of forming adjectives, either from words of French or Latin origin (in the latter case usually from nouns ending in *-us*), or from native English nouns. Examples include *cancerous*, *dangerous*, *generous*, *libellous*, *mountainous*, *ominous*, *poisonous*, *thunderous*, and *wondrous*.

The form **-ious** is a variant from Latin *-iosus*, often via French *-ieux* (*cautious*, *curious*, *delirious*, *mysterious*, *precious*, *spacious*, *vivacious*); examples ending in **-eous** are from Latin words ending in *-eus* (*aqueous*, *calcareous*, *extraneous*, *instantaneous*, *simultaneous*, *vitreous*). Those ending in **-ulous** are usually from Latin words ending in *-ulosus* or *-ulus* (*fabulous*, *miraculous*, *populous*, *ridiculous*).

The **-ous** ending frequently appears in compound suffixes, separate entries for which are at -ACEOUS, -ANDROUS,

-FEROUS, -GEROUS, -GYNOUS, and -PAROUS. *See also* -CEPHALIC (for -*cephalous*), -MER (for -*merous*), -PHAGY (for -*phagous*), -PHILE (for -*philous*), -PHORE (for -*phorous*), and -VORE (for -*vorous*).

In chemistry, **-ous** specifically denotes an element having a lower combining power: *cuprous*, *ferrous*, *nitrous*, *sulphurous*. In such cases, the higher valency is marked by -IC.

See also -OSE[1].

out- *Surpassing; external; away from.* [English *out.*]

This prefix forms a great number of compounds—nouns, adjectives, verbs, and adverbs—with a variety of senses. The most common one is that of surpassing or exceeding some norm—being more successful, enduring longer, and so on—frequently appearing in transitive verbs: *outbid*, *outfight*, *outgrow*, *outlast*, *outperform*, *outshine*, *outstay*. It forms nouns, adjectives, and adverbs describing a position or situation external to or separated from some place: *outside*, *outdoors*, *outfield*, *outbuilding*, *outpost*, *outpatient*, *outcast*. It can suggest movement away from some location or position: *outwards*, *outbound*; this can often be figurative in sense: *outcry*, *outgoing*, *outgrowth*, *outpouring*, *output*.

ovari(o)- *An ovary.* [Modern Latin *ovarium*, from Latin *ovum*, egg.]

An *ovariectomy* (Greek *ektomē*, excision) is surgical removal of one or both ovaries, a procedure also known as *ovariotomy* (Greek -*tomia*, cutting) or *oophorectomy*; *ovaritis* is inflammation of an ovary. An *ovariole* is one of the egg tubes in insects of which the ovary is composed. *See also* OOPHORO- and OVI-.

over- *Excessively; extra; outer; above.* [English *over.*]

The form has several of the senses of the preposition *over* and appears in a very large number of compounds that can be nouns, adjectives, verbs, or adverbs. **Over-** can be freely prefixed to other words for a momentary need. Its meanings are rather variable and diffuse, and difficult to categorize.

Having said that, there are some groupings that are commonly encountered. The one most often found refers to something beyond what is usual or desirable, even excessively so (*overambitious*, *overcareful*, *overexert*, *overindulgence*, *overfull*, *overprecise*, *overprepared*, *overweight*), which leads into a rarer sense of 'utterly' or 'completely' (*overawed*, *overjoyed*). In others, the form has a spatial sense of something above or higher up, which broadens into a figurative sense of something that is superior (*overhang*, *overbridge*, *overarching*, *overlook*, *overtone*, *overlord*, *overrule*). A fourth set of words in which the meaning is of something upper, outer, or extra (*overcoat*, *overshoes*, *overtime*). Another sense is of motion forward and down, and hence of inversion (*overturning*, *overbalance*, *overthrow*, *overboard*). The form can also suggest covering a surface (*overpaint*, *overgrow*).

ovi- *Also* **ovo-**. *Eggs, ova.* [Latin *ovum*, egg.]

Terms here are mainly found in zoology rather than medicine. Examples include *oviduct*, the tube through which an ovum or egg passes from an ovary (in humans more commonly called a *Fallopian tube*); *oviparous*, producing young by means of eggs which are hatched after they have been laid by the parent, as in birds (as opposed to *ovoviviparous*, in which young are produced by means of eggs hatched within the body of the parent, as in some snakes); *ovipositor*, a tubular organ through which a female insect or fish deposits eggs; *ovotestis*, an organ producing both ova and spermatozoa, especially in some gastropod molluscs. Something *oviform* is egg-shaped.

Ovine, relating to sheep, comes instead from Latin *ovis*, a sheep.

oxa- *or* **oxo-**: *see* OXY-[2]

oxy-[1] *Sharp, acid.* [Greek *oxus*, sharp.]

An *oxymoron* (Greek *oxumōros*, pointedly foolish, from *mōros*, foolish) is a figure of speech in which apparently contradictory terms appear in conjunction, such as *faith unfaithful*; *oxytocin* (Greek *tokos*, childbirth) is a hormone released by the pituitary gland during labour. The Greek root is also the origin of *oxygen*, originally thought to be essential for the formation of all acids (see the next entry for terms beginning in **oxy-** involving oxygen), and *oxalic acid*, named via Latin from Greek *oxalis*, wood sorrel, because of its sharp-tasting leaves that contain the acid.

ox(y)-² Also **oxa-** and **oxo-** *Oxygen*. [The first element of *oxygen* (see the previous entry).]

In *oxyacetylene* and *oxyhydrogen* the form denotes welding or cutting techniques using a very hot flame produced by mixing acetylene or hydrogen with oxygen; *oxyhaemoglobin* is a bright red substance formed by the combination of haemoglobin with oxygen, present in oxygenated blood; an *oxyacid* is an inorganic acid whose molecules contain oxygen, such as sulphuric or nitric acid; an *oxide* is a binary compound of oxygen with another element or group; *oxidation* originally referred to a chemical combination with oxygen, but is now usually understood as a reaction by which electrons are lost from an atom.

The forms **oxo-** and **oxa-** have specific meanings in the systematic rules for naming chemical compounds; the former refers to the presence of a carbonyl group, $=CO$, anywhere in an organic molecule: *oxodecanoic acid*, *3-oxohexanal*; the latter to an oxygen atom appearing in a heterocyclic molecule, assumed to replace a $—CH_2—$ group: *6-oxa-3-thiadecanenitrile*.

See also DEOXY-, ETHOXY-, and METHOXY-.

-oyl: *see* -YL

-ozoa: *see* -ZOON

p-: *see* PARA-

pachy- *Thick.* [Greek *pakhus*, thick.]

A *pachyderm* (Greek *derma*, skin) is a very large mammal with thick skin, such as an elephant, rhinoceros, or hippopotamus, while *pachyderma* is a condition in which the skin becomes thickened; a *pachymeter* is a device for measuring the thickness of thin structures, especially the cornea of the eye; a *pachycephalosaur* (Greek *kephalē*, head, plus *sauros*, lizard) is a bipedal herbivorous dinosaur of the late Cretaceous period, with a thick domed skull.

-paedia: *see* -PEDIA

paed(o)- Also **ped(o)-**, especially in the US. *Child; relating to children.* [Greek *pais*, *paid-*, child, boy.]

The part of medicine called *paediatrics* deals with children and their diseases, while *paedodontics* (Greek *odous, odont-*, tooth) is the branch of dentistry that deals with children's teeth. A *pedagogue* is an old term for a teacher, especially a strict or pedantic one, but in ancient Greece meant a slave (*paidagōgos*) who accompanied a child to school (Greek *agōgos*, guide). A *paedophile* is a person sexually attracted to children, while *pederasty* (less commonly *paederasty*) (Greek *erastēs*, lover) is sexual activity involving a man and a boy. In zoology, *paedogenesis*, also called *neoteny*, refers to an animal that becomes sexually mature while it is still in its larval or juvenile form.

-pagus *Conjoined twins.* [Greek *pagos*, something firmly fixed.]

This ending is used in a few medical terms for ways in which twins can be born joined together: *thoracopagus*, joined at the thorax, *craniopagus*, at the head, *pygopagus* (Greek *pugē*, rump) at the buttocks or lower back, and *xiphopagus* (Greek *xiphos*, sword), at the xiphoid process, the cartilaginous section at the lower end of the breastbone.

palae(o)- In the US **pale(o)-**. *Ancient.* [Greek *palaios*, ancient.]

The names of several divisions of geological time contain this form, such as the *Palaeozoic* (Greek *zōē*, life), the era between the Precambrian aeon and the Mesozoic era, and the *Palaeolithic* (Greek *lithos*, stone), the early phase of the Stone Age, lasting about 2.5 million years.

It is also widely used to generate names of scientific disciplines that deal with such periods, as in *palaeontology* (Greek *onta*, beings), that concerned with fossil animals and plants, *palaeoanthropology*, the branch of anthropology concerned with fossil hominids, *palaeoclimatology*, the study of climates prevalent at a particular time in the geological past, and *palaeomagnetism*, the branch of geophysics concerned with the magnetism in rocks that was induced by the earth's magnetic field at the time of their formation; other examples are *palaeobiology*, *palaeobotany*, *palaeoecology*, and *palaeogeography*.

Other examples: the *Palaearctic* is a region comprising parts of Europe and Asia, the northern region of the 'Old World'; *Palaeo-Indian* denotes the earliest human inhabitants of the Americas, to *c.* 5000 BC.

palato- *Palate.* [Latin *palatum*, palate.]

This is used in medicine to form adjectives that refer to the palate plus another part of the body, as in *palato-pharyngeal*, the palate and pharynx, and *palato-glossal*, palate and tongue. (These and other examples are often written unhyphenated.) Other medical terms using it include *palatoplasty*, plastic surgery on the palate, and *palatoschisis* (Greek *skhisma*, cleft), the formal name for a cleft palate.

Some other terms are used in phonetics, such as *palato-alveolar* (also seen unhyphenated and as the reversed *alveo-palatal*), of a consonant sounded with a constriction from the alveolar ridge to the palate, and *palatography*, a technique for recording the position of the tongue during articulation from its contact with the hard palate.

pali(n)- Rarely **palim-**. *Again.* [Greek *palin*, again.]

Some examples: *palindrome* (Greek *dramein*, to run) is a word or sequence of words that reads the same backwards as forwards; a *palimpsest* (Greek *palimpsēstos*, from *psēstos*, rubbed smooth) is a parchment which has been written on twice, the later text superimposed on earlier writing that has been rubbed out; a *palinode* (Greek *ōidē*, song) is a poem in which the poet retracts a view or sentiment expressed in a former poem; in medicine, *palilalia* (Greek *lalia*, speech, chatter) is a speech disorder characterized by involuntary repetition of words, phrases, or sentences.

pan- Also **pant(o)-**. *All-inclusive.* [Greek *pan*, *pant-*, respectively the neuter and oblique forms of *pas*, all.]

A *panacea* (Greek *akos*, remedy) is a solution or remedy for all difficulties or diseases; a *pandemic* (Greek *dēmos*, people) is an outbreak of a disease over a whole country or the world; *pandemonium* (Greek *daimōn*, demon), is wild and noisy disorder or confusion, originally from the place of all demons in Milton's *Paradise Lost*; a *pantheon* (Greek *theion*, holy) is the set of all the gods of a people or religion; *pansexual* refers to somebody uninhibited in sexual choice with regard to gender or activity.

Pan- is widely used in terms, often hyphenated, that relate to all the peoples or countries of an area, as in *pan-American*, of all the countries of North and South America; *pan-African*, of all people of African birth or descent, all the peoples of Africa, or all African countries; *Panhellenic*, of all people of Greek origin or ancestry; *pan-Arabism*, the principle or advocacy of political alliance or union of all the Arab states.

Panto- has the same sense, and occurs in words such as *pantograph* (Greek *-graphos*, writing) which was originally a system of hinged and jointed rods for copying a plan or drawing on a different scale, now often a similar-shaped structure for conveying electric power to a vehicle from overhead wires; the British *pantomime* (Greek *mimos*, a mime) was historically an entertainment executed entirely in mime; *pantothenic acid* is a vitamin of the B complex, named from Greek *pantothen* (from every side), as it occurs so widely.

pancreat(o)- Also **pancreatico-**. *The pancreas.* [Greek *pankreas*, *pankreat-*, from *pan*, all, plus *kreas*, flesh.]

Pancreatitis is inflammation of the pancreas; a *pancreatectomy* (Greek *ektomē*, excision) is its surgical removal; *pancreatin* is a mixture of enzymes obtained from animal pancreases, given as a medicine to aid digestion; *pancreatography* is examination of the pancreas by X-rays, ultrasound, or other means. The adjective relating to the pancreas is *pancreatic*; the less common alternative form **pancreatico-** has been formed from it by adding the linking vowel -o-: *pancreaticoduodenal* refers to the pancreas and duodenum considered together.

panto-: *see* PAN-

papillo- *A papilla.* [Latin *papilla*, a nipple, diminutive of *papula*, a small protuberance.]

A *papilla* is a small rounded protuberance on a part or organ of the body. A *papilloma* is a small wart-like growth on the skin or on a mucous membrane; *papillomatosis* is a condition in which many papillomas grow in one place; *papilloedema* (US *papilledema*) (Greek *oidein*, to swell) is a swelling in the first part of the optic nerve, the optic papilla, while *papilitis* is inflammation of it; *papillotomy* (Greek *-tomia*, cutting) is a surgical incision in the papilla of the duodenum.

papulo- *A papule.* [Latin *papula*, a small protuberance.]

A *papule* is a small, raised, solid pimple or swelling, often forming part of a rash on the skin, typically inflamed but not producing pus. A rash that is *papulosquamous* (Latin *squama*, scale) is both papular and scaly; one that is *papulovesicular* (Latin *vesica*, bladder) has both papules and vesicles, small blisters full of clear fluid; a skin eruption that is *papulopustular* has both papules and pustules. Less commonly, these compounds appear hyphenated.

par(a)-¹ Also **p-**. *Beside; adjacent to.* [Greek *para*, beside.]

A number of words from Greek contain this form: *parallel* (Greek *parallēlos*, from *para*, alongside, plus *allēlos*, one another); *paragraph* (Greek *paragraphos*, a short horizontal stroke written below the beginning of a line in which a break of sense occurs, from *graphein*, write). The Greek form often had a sense of something amiss, faulty, irregular, or subsidiary, which appears in *parasite* (Greek *parasitos*, eating at another's table, from *sitos* food); *parish* (literally a subsidiary place, from Greek *oíkos*, dwelling); and *parody* (Greek *parōidia*, a burlesque poem, from *ōidē*, an ode).

The sense of something irregular, or outside what is considered normal, appears in several English words: *parapsychology*, the study of mental phenomena outside orthodox scientific psychology, such as hypnosis or telepathy; *paranormal*, of topics such as telekinesis or clairvoyance that are beyond the scope of normal scientific understanding; *parainfluenza*, a disease caused by any of a group of viruses which resemble influenza; *paramagnetic*, of something very weakly attracted by the poles of a magnet, but not retaining any permanent magnetism; *paranoia* (Greek *noos*, mind, hence 'irregular mind'), a mental condition characterized by delusions of persecution; *parasuicide*, apparent attempted suicide without the actual intention of killing oneself.

The form is also used for occupational roles considered to be ancillary or subordinate; *paramedic*, a person who is trained to do medical work, but is not a fully qualified doctor; *paralegal*, a person

trained in subsidiary legal matters but not fully qualified as a lawyer; a more general term is *paraprofessional*. Such terms are in general more common in North America than in Britain. Sometimes the sense is of something irregular: *paramilitary*, of an unofficial force organized on military lines.

Para- can refer to something beside or adjacent, as in *parathyroid*, a gland next to the thyroid; *parhelion* (Greek *hēlios*, sun), a bright spot in the sky appearing on either side of the sun; *paracrine* (Greek *krinein*, to separate), of a hormone which has effect only in the vicinity of the gland secreting it.

In chemistry, the form indicates that a benzene ring has been substituted at diametrically opposite carbon atoms, as in *paradichlorobenzene*, a moth repellent, and *para-aminobenzoic acid*, a crystalline acid which has been used to treat rickettsial infections. It is frequently abbreviated to **p-** (*p-xylene*; *p-nitrotoluene*). Substitution in other positions is indicated by ORTHO- and META-. In chemical compounds such as *paraformaldehyde*, *paraldehyde*, and *paranthracene*, whose molecules do not contain benzene rings, **para-** is used unsystematically in the sense of 'altered' to refer to a polymer of the compound.

Some words do not belong here: *pariah* comes from Tamil; *parade* from Latin *parare*, prepare; *paradise* from a Persian word meaning an enclosed space; *paramour* from Old French *par amour*, by love.

para-² *Protection; parachuting.* [Via French from Italian *parare*, defend or shield, derived from Latin *parare*, to prepare.]

The main examples of the first sense are *parachute* (French *para-*, protection against, plus *chute*, fall) and *parasol* (via French from Italian *parasole*, from *para-*, protecting against, plus *sole*, sun).

Several terms contain **para-** as a combining form derived from parachute: *paratroops*, troops equipped to be dropped by parachute from aircraft (hence the abbreviated form *paras*); *para-*

drop, a descent or delivery by parachute; *paragliding*, a sport in which the rider hangs from a specially designed canopy like a parachute (called a *parafoil*) that enables him or her to glide down from a height; *parawing*, a type of parachute or kite having a flattened shape like a wing, to give greater manoeuvrability.

parieto- *Body cavity; hollow structure.* [English *parietal*, from Latin *paries*, *pariet-*, wall.]

The adjective *parietal* is used in medicine to refer to the wall of a body cavity or hollow structure. A few compound adjectives refer to such a structure plus another part of the body: *parieto-occipital*, of the parietal bone (which forms the central side and upper back part of each side of the skull) together with the occipital bone (the one that forms the back and base of the skull); *parieto-visceral*, pertaining to the abdominal wall and abdominal organs. Such forms also occur unhyphenated.

-parous Also **-parity** and **-para**. *Bearing; producing.* [Latin *-parus*, bearing, plus *-ous*.]

Most adjectives ending in **-parous** describe ways in which an organism reproduces: *viviparous* (Latin *vivus*, alive), bringing forth live young; *fissiparous*, reproducing by fission; *oviparous* (Latin *ovum*, egg), producing young by means of eggs which are hatched after they have been laid by the parent, as in birds; *ovoviviparous*, producing young by means of eggs which are hatched within the body of the parent.

Others describe a state relating to reproduction: *nulliparous*, of a woman or female animal that has never given birth; *primiparous*, one who is giving birth for the first time; *multiparous*, having borne more than one child, or habitually producing more than one young at a birth; *iteroparous* (Latin *iterum*, again), giving birth more than once during a lifetime.

Nouns for the concepts—less common than the adjectives—are formed in **-parity** (*nulliparity*, *oviparity*). The feminine form, **-para**, of the Latin root

appears in a few nouns used in medicine to describe a woman with a given characteristic: *nullipara*, *primipara*.

partheno- *Without fertilization.* [Greek *parthenos*, virgin.]

Parthenogenesis (Greek *genesis*, creation) is reproduction from an ovum without fertilization, a normal process in some invertebrates and lower plants; *parthenocarpy* (Greek *karpos*, fruit) is the similar development of a fruit; a *parthenospore* is a spore produced without previous sexual fusion.

-path, -pathic, or **-pathist** *see* -PATHY

path(o)- *Disease.* [Greek *pathos*, suffering, disease.]

A *pathogen* (Greek *gen-*, root of *gignomai*, be born, become) is a bacterium, virus, or other micro-organism that can cause disease; *pathology* is the science of the causes and effects of diseases; the adjective *pathological* refers to a physical or mental disease, but sometimes has the sense of somebody compulsive or obsessive; *pathogenesis* is the manner of development of a disease; *pathognomonic* (Greek *gnōmōn*, judge) refers to a sign or symptom that indicates a particular disease or condition. *Pathos*, a quality that evokes pity or sadness, and *pathetic*, arousing pity, come from the same source.

-pathy Also **-path**, **-pathic**, and **-pathist**. *Disease or disorder; treatment of disease.* [Greek *patheia*, suffering, feeling.]

Several common terms ending in **-pathy** have been imported entire from Greek and relate to feelings: *antipathy*, *apathy*, *empathy*, *sympathy*. Apart from these, the ending frequently indicates a disease or disorder (*cardiopathy*, *psychopathy*) or a method of treating a disorder (*homeopathy*, *osteopathy*). For more details and examples, see the LIST overleaf.

Terms that refer to systems of treatment can have agent nouns ending in **-path** for a practitioner (*naturopath*, *osteopath*); less commonly, terms ending in **-pathy** for disorders have nouns ending in **-path** for a sufferer from the condition (*psychopath*, *sociopath*, though

-pathy	Disease or disorder; treatment of disease. *All word sources are from Greek unless otherwise stated.*	
adenopathy	enlargement or disease of any gland	(*adēn*, gland)
allopathy	the treatment of disease by conventional means, that is, with drugs having effects opposite to the symptoms	(*allos*, other)
arthropathy	disease of the joints	(*arthron*, joint)
cardiopathy	a disease or disorder of the heart	(*kardia*, heart)
enteropathy	a disease of the intestine, especially the small intestine	(*enteron*, intestine)
homeopathy	a system of complementary medicine in which disease is treated by minute doses of substances that in a healthy person would produce symptoms of the disease	(*homoios*, like)
hydropathy	the treatment of illness through the use of water	(*hudōr*, water)
myelopathy	disease of the spinal cord	(*muelos*, marrow)
myopathy	a disease of muscle tissue	(*mus*, *mu-*, muscle)
osteopathy	a complementary medicine that treats medical disorders through the manipulation and massage of the skeleton and musculature	(*osteon*, bone)
psychopathy	mental illness or disorder	(*psukhē*, breath, soul, mind)
retinopathy	disease of the retina which results in impairment or loss of vision	(Latin *rete*, net)
sociopathy	a personality disorder involving extreme antisocial attitudes and behaviour	(English *social*)
telepathy	the supposed communication of thoughts or ideas by means other than the known senses	(*tēle-*, far off)

the former in common usage refers to a sufferer from a chronic mental disorder with abnormal or violent social behaviour). Rarely, terms for therapists are formed with **-pathist** (*homeopathist, hydropathist*).

Adjectives end in **-pathic**: *apathetic, hydropathic, myopathic, sympathetic*.

patr(i)- *Father.* [Latin *pater, patr-*, father; Greek *patēr, patr-*, father.]

Examples are *patrimony* (from Latin), property inherited from one's father or male ancestor; *patronymic* (Greek *onuma*, name), a name derived from the name of a father or male ancestor; *patricide* (Latin *caedere*, kill), the killing of one's father, or a person who kills his or her father; *patrilineal*, based on relationship to the father or descent through the male line.

Related words include *paternal*; *patrician* (Latin *patricius*, having a noble father), an aristocrat or nobleman or characteristic of those classes; *patriot* (Greek *patris*, fatherland); *patron* (Latin *patronus*, protector of clients, a defender); and *patriarch* (Greek *patria*, family), the male head of a family or tribe.

pebi-: see the table of WORDS FOR MULTIPLES on page 127

ped-: *see* PAEDO- and PEDI-

-ped Also **-pede** and **-pedia**. *Having feet of a given type or number.* [Latin *pes, ped-*, foot.]

Common examples are *biped* (Latin *bi-*, having two), an animal that uses only two legs for walking; *quadruped* (Latin *quadru-*, four), an animal with four feet, especially an ungulate mammal. *Centi-*

pede (Latin *centum*, hundred) and *milli-pede* (Latin *mille*, thousand) refer to invertebrates with long segmented bodies and many legs, though not literally either a hundred or a thousand.

A few systematic names in zoology end in the Latin neuter plural **-pedia**: *Pinni-pedia* (Latin *pinna*, wing, fin), an order of carnivorous aquatic mammals with flipper-like limbs which comprises the seals, sea lions, and walrus; *Cirripedia* (Latin *cirrus*, a curl, because of the form of the legs), a class of crustaceans that comprises the barnacles. (For another sense of **-pedia**, *see* -PEDIA.) The usual name for a member of these groups is respectively *pinniped* and either *cirripede* or *cirriped*.

A *velocipede* (Latin *velox*, *veloc-*, swift) was an early form of bicycle.

See also -POD.

pedi- *Foot.* [Latin *pes*, *ped-*, foot.]

A *pedicure* (Latin *curare*, attend to) is a cosmetic treatment of the feet and toenails; a *pedicab* is a small pedal-operated vehicle; a *pedipalp* is one of the second pair of appendages or palps in scorpions, spiders, and other arachnids; a *pedicel* (Latin *pedicellus*, small foot) is a small stalk bearing an individual flower in an inflorescence.

-pedia Also **-paedia** *Compendium of information.* [Greek *paideia*, education.]

The term from which others derive is *encyclopedia*, which comes via Latin from the pseudo-Greek word *enkuklopaideia*, more correctly *enkuklios paideia*, all-round education. The spelling ending in **-pae-dia** is archaic and appears only in the titles of long-established works such as the *Encyclopaedia Britannica*. *Cyclopedia* is an abbreviated form. A few terms have been created on its model, such as the irregularly-formed *Weblopedia*, an encyclopedia accessible through the World Wide Web, and *rockopedia*, one containing information on rock music.

pedo-¹ *Soil or soil types.* [Greek *pedon*, ground.]

Pedology is another name for soil science; the adjective *pedogenic* refers to processes occurring in soil or leading to the formation of soil, while *pedogenesis* is the process of soil formation; a *pedocal* soil (Latin *calx*, lime) is one rich in carbonates or lime.

pedo-²: *see* PAEDO-

pelvi- *The pelvis.* [English *pelvis*.]

Pelvimetry is measurement of the size of the pelvis, undertaken chiefly to help determine whether a woman can give birth normally, while *pelviscopy* is surgical examination of the pelvis, similarly as part of reproductive medicine. Less commonly, **pelvi-** occurs in adjectives for the pelvis plus another part of the body, such as *pelvirectal*, of the pelvis and rectum, or *pelvifemoral* (Latin *femur*, *femor-*, thigh), of the structures of the hip joint.

pen(e)- *Almost; nearly.* [Latin *paene*, almost.]

A *peninsula* (Latin *insula*, island) is a piece of land almost surrounded by water; something *penultimate* (Latin *ultimus*, last) is last but one in a series of things; a *penumbra* (Latin *umbra*, shadow) is the partially shaded outer region of a shadow cast by an opaque object; a *peneplain* is a more or less level land surface produced by erosion over a long period; a process in geology that is *penecontemporaneous* occurs immediately after deposition of a particular stratum, almost contemporary with it.

-penia *Deficiency in a component of the blood.* [Greek *penia*, poverty.]

Examples include *thrombocytopenia*, a deficiency of thrombocytes or platelets; *leucopenia* (also *leukopenia*) (Greek *leukos*, white), similarly of white cells; *lymphopenia*, of lymphocytes; *pancytopenia* (Greek *pan*, all, plus *kutos*, vessel), a deficiency of all three cellular components of the blood: red cells, white cells, and platelets.

pent(a)- *Five; having five.* [Greek *pente*, five.]

A *pentagon* is a plane figure with five straight sides and five angles; the athletic event called the *pentathlon* comprises five different events for each competitor; a *pentameter* is a line of verse containing five metrical feet; a *penta-gram* is a five-pointed star, often used as a mystic and magical symbol; the *Penta-teuch* (Greek *teukhos*, implement, book) is the collective name for the first five books of the Old Testament.

In chemistry, a *pentavalent* atom or group has a combining power of five; a *pentoxide* is an oxide containing five atoms of oxygen in its molecule or empirical formula; a *pentose* is any of the class of simple sugars whose molecules contain five carbon atoms, such as ribose and xylose.

See also QUINQUE- and QUINTI-.

per- *Through; all over; completely.* [Latin *per*, through, by means of.]

Words containing this combining form have frequently come directly from Latin or through French with the initial **per-** already attached; it is not an active word-forming element.

Examples in which it means 'through' or 'all over' include *perforate* (Latin *perforare*, from *forare*, to pierce); *perambulate* (Latin *perambulare*, from *ambulare*, to walk); *pervade* (Latin *pervadere*, from *vadere*, to go); and *peroration* (Latin *perorat-*, spoken at length, from *orare*, speak). It can suggest an action taken to completion, as in the verb *perfect* (Latin *perficere*, from *facere*, to do). It can sometimes imply destruction, as in *perdition* (Latin *perdere*, to destroy, from the base of *dare*, to put) or *perish* (Latin *perire*, pass away, from *ire* to go). *Peremptory*, insisting on immediate attention or obedience, originally meant decisive (Latin *peremptorius*, deadly, decisive, from *perempt-*, destroyed, cut off, from *emere*, to take).

In chemistry **per-** implies that an element is present in the maximum proportion possible, or that the principal atom is in a higher state of oxidation than usual, as in *peroxide*, *perchlorate*, *permanganate*, or *perborate*; in this sense **per-** forms compound prefixes such as *perchloro-*, *perfluoro-*, and *peroxy-*. In modern systematic naming, specific prefixes are preferred (manganese *dioxide* to manganese *peroxide*; *tetrachloroethylene* to *perchloroethylene*, and so on), though many names

beginning in **per-** are preserved in popular use.

perchloro- or **perfluoro-**: *see* PER-

peri- *Round; about.* [Greek *peri*, about, around.]

Many examples were formed in Greek and have reached English through Latin and French, such as *peripatetic*, travelling from place to place (Greek *peripatētikos*, walking up and down), or *periphery* (Greek *periphereia*, circumference, from *pherein*, to bear).

The form is common in modern scientific and medical terms. A *pericarp* (Greek *karpos*, fruit) is the part of a fruit formed from the wall of the ripened ovary; a *periglacial* area is one adjacent to a glacier or ice sheet or otherwise subject to repeated freezing and thawing; the *pericardium* (Greek *kardia*, heart) is the membrane enclosing the heart; *peri-odontics* (Greek *odous*, *odont-*, tooth) is the branch of dentistry concerned with the structures surrounding and supporting the teeth; a *periurban* area is countryside immediately adjacent to a built-up area.

In astronomy, **peri-** refers to the point in the orbit of a celestial object or spacecraft at which it is nearest to its parent body, so *perihelion* (Greek *hēlios*, sun), the point in an orbit closest to the sun; *peri-lune* (Latin *luna*, moon), the point at which a spacecraft in lunar orbit is closest to the moon; *perigee* (Greek *gē*, earth), similarly the point in its orbit around the earth at which a satellite or spacecraft is closest to it. Its opposite is APO-.

pero- *Deformity.* [Greek *peros*, damaged.]

This occurs in a few medical terms, such as *perochirus* (Greek *kheir*, hand), a foetus or individual with deformed hands, and *peromelia* (Greek *melos*, limb), a congenital deformity of a limb. The general term is *peronia*, a congenital deformity or anomaly of development.

peroxy-: *see* PER-

-person *Gender-neutral alternative to 'man' in compounds.* [English *person*.]

Terms such as *craftsperson*, *chairperson*, *salesperson*, or *spokesperson* are sometimes used to avoid the implied sexism of terms ending in -MAN (*chairman*, *spokesman*). These have not achieved general acceptance, as they are often seen as clumsy or unnecessary. Other terms are frequently sought instead, such as *firefighter* for *fireman*, or *fresher* in place of *freshman*. For a note on the compound form *-personship*, *see* -MANSHIP.

peta- *In units of measurement, a factor of 10^{15}.* [Adapted from PENTA-, five, on the pattern of other SI (Système International) multiples (see the table of WORDS FOR MULTIPLES on page 127).]

The prefix appears most often in measures of computer data, such as *petabyte*; outside this field it is rare, though *petagram* (a multiple of a thousand million metric tonnes) sometimes appears in discussions of the global carbon cycle.

-petal *Seeking; moving towards.* [Latin *petus*, seeking, from *petere*, seek.]

The most common term in this ending is *centripetal*, moving or tending to move towards a centre, the opposite of *centrifugal*. In botany, growth or development that is *basipetal* is downwards towards the base or point of attachment, its opposite being *acropetal* (Greek *akron*, tip); *corticopetal* refers to something originating outside the cerebral cortex and running into it.

petro- Also **petri-.** *Rocks; petroleum.* [Greek *petros*, stone, *petra*, rock.]

To *petrify* something is literally to turn it into stone, though it is more frequently used figuratively to refer to somebody so frightened that they are unable to move or think; a *petroglyph* (Greek *glyphē*, carving) is a rock carving, especially a prehistoric one; *petrography* is the systematic description of the composition and properties of rocks based on observation; *petrology* is the study of rocks, including their origins, structure, and composition

Petroleum derives from Latin *oleum*, oil, so literally 'oil from the rocks'. A number of terms beginning in **petro-** refer to petroleum, for example *petrochemicals*,

substances obtained by the refining and processing of petroleum or natural gas, and *petrodollar*, a notional unit of currency earned by a country from the export of petroleum.

-pexy *Surgical operation for fixing an organ in position.* [Greek *-pexia*, *pexis*, fixing or putting together.]

Examples include *mastopexy* (Greek *mastos*, breast), an operation to lift and fix the breast; *orchidopexy* (also *orchiopexy*) (Greek *orkhis*, testicle), an operation to move an undescended testicle into the scrotum and fix it there; *gastropexy*, surgical attachment of the stomach to the intestinal wall.

phaco- Also **phako-.** *Lens of the eye; lens shaped.* [Greek *phakos*, a lentil (from the shape of the seeds).]

The most common term here is *phacoemulsification*, the use of ultrasound to break up a cataract so it can be removed through a small incision. Others are *phacoanaphylactic*, of an allergic reaction to protein released from the crystalline lens of the eye; *phacomatosis*, a hereditary condition which produces benign tumour-like nodules in the eye and other parts of the body; and *phacolite*, a colourless zeolite which is often lens-shaped. The spelling **phako-** appears mainly in the US.

phaeo- Also **pheo-.** *Dusky.* [Greek *phaios*, dusky.]

A *phaeochromocytoma* is a small vascular tumour of the adrenal gland, so called because cells in it are a dusky colour; *phaeohyphomycosis* is a fungal infection caused by darkly pigmented moulds; the class of lower plants called the *Phaeophyceae* (Greek *phukos*, seaweed) comprises the brown algae. Forms beginning in **pheo-** are standard US spellings.

phag(o)- *Feeding, eating.* [Greek *phago-*, eating.]

A *phagocyte* is a type of cell capable of absorbing bacteria and the like, a process called *phagocytosis* (Greek *kutos*, vessel); a *phagosome* is a vacuole in the cytoplasm of a cell, containing a *phagocytosed* particle enclosed within a part of the cell membrane; *phagotrophy* in botany is a type of nutrition in which cells ingest solid food particles.

-phagy Also **-phagia**, **-phagic**, **-phagous**, **-phage**, and **-phagia**. *Feeding or subsisting on a specified food.* [Greek *phagein*, to eat.]

The noun-ending **-phagy** indicates the eating of a specified food, as with *coprophagy* (Greek *kopros*, dung), the eating of faeces or dung; *anthropophagy* (Greek *anthrōpos*, human being), the eating of human flesh by human beings, cannibalism; *geophagy*, the practice in some tribal societies of eating earth. The noun-ending **-phagia** is a less common alternative, as in *polyphagia*, the eating of a varied diet, or *omophagia* (Greek *ōmos*, raw), the eating of raw food, especially raw meat. (*Dysphagia*, on the other hand, difficulty in speaking, derives instead from Greek *phatos*, spoken.)

Related adjectives are formed either with **-phagic** or **-phagous**, though the latter is more common. Examples of the former include *hyperphagic*, an alternative to *bulimic*, relating to insatiable overeating as a medical condition, and *anthropophagic*, cannibalistic. Examples of the latter are *phytophagous*, of a creature that feeds on plants, and *polyphagous*, of an animal that eats many kinds of food.

The ending **-phage** marks organisms that feed or subsist in a given way, as in *saprophage* (Greek *sapros*, putrid), an organism that feeds on or obtains its nourishment from decaying organic matter, and *bacteriophage*, a virus which parasitizes a bacterium by infecting it and reproducing inside it.

The plural ending **-phaga** appears in systematic names for animal groups to indicate a method of feeding, as in *Entomophaga* (Greek *entomon*, insect) a genus of fungi that live on insects; *Phyllophaga* (Greek *phullon*, leaf), a genus of beetles whose larvae feed on plant roots; *Mallophaga* (Greek *mallos*, lock of wool), an order of insects that comprises the biting lice.

phallo- *Penis.* [Greek *phallos*, penis.]

Phalloplasty is plastic surgery performed to construct, repair, or enlarge the penis; a *phallocracy* is a society or system which is dominated by men and in which the male sex is thought superior; *phallocentric* refers to a focus on or concern with the phallus or penis as a symbol of male dominance; *phalloidin* is the toxin present in the death cap toadstool, whose name is taken from the specific part of the species name *Amanita phalloides*, given it because the young toadstool appears like an erect penis.

-phane Also **-phan**. *Having a given appearance.* [Greek *-phanēs*, appearing.]

This appears in several names for minerals, such as *glaucophane* (Greek *glaukos*, bluish-green), a bluish sodium-containing mineral of the amphibole group, and *allophane* (Greek *allos*, otherwise), an aluminium silicate whose colour is lost when heated. Other examples include *lithophane* (Greek *lithos*, stone), a kind of ornamentation of porcelain visible when held to the light; *tryptophan* (sometimes *tryptophane*), an amino acid which is a constituent of most proteins and is associated with *trypsin*, a digestive enzyme, as it is formed during digestion; and *cellophane* (from *cellulose*), a trademarked name for a thin transparent wrapping material made from viscose.

phanero- *Visible.* [Greek *phaneros*, visible, evident.]

The *Phanerozoic* (Greek *zōion*, animal) is the aeon in which animal fossils are known, the whole of time since the beginning of the Cambrian period; a *phanerocrystalline* mineral is one in which the constituent elements can be seen by the naked eye; *phanerogam* is an old-fashioned term for a *spermatophyte*, a plant of a large division comprising those that bear seeds, including the gymnosperms and angiosperms.

pharmac(o)- *Drugs, medicines.* [Greek *pharmakon*, drug, medicine.]

A common term is *pharmacy*; a *pharmacopoeia* (US also *pharmacopeia*) (Greek *-poios*, making) is a publication that contains a list of medicinal drugs with their effects and directions for their use; *pharmacotherapy* is medical treatment by means of drugs. *Pharmacology* is the branch of medicine concerned with the uses, effects, and modes of action of drugs; this has several sub-disciplines, including *pharmacogenetics*, concerned with the effect of genetic factors on reactions to drugs, and *pharmacokinetics*, concerned with the movement of drugs within the body.

pharyng(o)- *Pharynx.* [Modern Latin from Greek *pharunx, pharung-*, pharynx.]

Pharyngitis is inflammation of the pharynx, causing a sore throat; a *pharyngotomy* (Greek *-tomia*, cutting) is a surgical incision into the pharynx; a *pharyngoscope* is a device for examining the pharynx; in phonetics, to *pharyngealize* a sound is to articulate it with constriction of the pharynx; the usual adjective relating to the pharynx is *pharyngeal*.

-phasia Also **-phasic**. *Speech disorder.* [Greek *phanai*, to speak.]

Psychologists use these terms for speech disorders that are mainly caused by brain damage. Examples are *aphasia* (Greek *a-*, not), inability, or impaired ability, to understand or produce speech; *dysphasia* (Greek *dus-*, difficult), deficiency in the generation of speech, and sometimes also in its comprehension; *paraphasia* (Greek *para*, amiss, irregular), jumbling of words and production of meaningless sentences.

Associated adjectives are formed using **-phasic**: *aphasic, dysphasic.* However, some with that ending derive instead from nouns ending in *-phase*, for example *biphasic*, having two phases, or *polyphasic*, consisting of or occurring in a number of separate stages.

phen(o)- Also **phenoxy-**. *Benzene compounds; showing.* [Greek *phaino-*, shining; *phainein*, to show.]

The link between these senses is that the first benzene compounds were obtained from coal-tar, a by-product of the production of illuminating gas.

The key chemical name is *phenol* (adjective *phenyl*), obtained from coal-tar and used in chemical manufacture.

Other examples are *phenobarbitone*, a narcotic and sedative barbiturate drug used chiefly to treat epilepsy, and *phenanthrene*, a crystalline hydrocarbon present in coal-tar.

The compound prefix **phenoxy-** (*see* oxy-) indicates the presence of the radical C_6H_5O—, as in *phenoxyacetic acid*, one of a group that includes the weedkillers 2,4–D and MCPA, and *phenoxybenzamine*, a drug that dilates blood vessels in the treatment of conditions involving poor circulation.

The sense of 'showing' appears in *phenomenon*, and also in *phenotype*, the set of observable characteristics of an organism resulting from the interaction of its genotype with the environment, and *phenocryst* (Greek *krustallos*, crystal), a large or conspicuous crystal in a porphyritic rock.

-phile Also **-phil**, **-philia**, **-phily**, **-philic**, and **-philous**. *Lover of or enthusiast for; having an affinity with a given thing.* [Greek *philos*, loving.]

Several broad groups are linked within this ending. One set denotes an admirer of the customs, people, or institutions of a country: *Anglophile, Francophile, Slavophile, Japanophile*. Another marks an enthusiast for the cultural products of a medium (*audiophile, cinephile, videophile*), or for some subject area (*bibliophile*, a lover of books; *oenophile*, a connoisseur of wines; *technophile*, a person who is enthusiastic about new technology). It also appears in names for abnormal psychological states: a *paedophile* (US *pedophile*) (Greek *pais, paid-*, child, boy) is a person who is sexually attracted to children; a *zoophile* (Greek *zōion*, animal) can be a person with a morbid attraction to animals (though it is also used for a micro-organism that attacks animals).

In biology, the ending often indicates an organism, especially a micro-organism, that prefers a particular habitat, as in *halophile*, one that grows in or can tolerate saline conditions; *thermophile*, one that grows best at higher than normal temperatures; and *extremophile*, one that lives in conditions of extreme temperature, acidity, alkalinity, or chemical concentration.

The ending **-phil** can be a variant spelling, but most commonly names cells that have an affinity for certain dyes, such as *neutrophil*, one readily stained only by neutral dyes; *eosinophil*, a white blood cell containing granules that are readily stained by eosin; *argyrophil* (Greek *arguros*, silver), one readily stained black by silver salts.

Nouns in **-philia** denote the type of affinity: *logophilia* (Greek *logos*, word, reason), a love of words; *haemophilia* (US *hemophilia*) (Greek *haima*, blood), a medical condition in which the ability of the blood to clot is severely reduced; *necrophilia* (Greek *nekros*, corpse), sexual intercourse with or attraction towards corpses. Nouns ending in **-phily** often refer to the collection of items as a hobby or pursuit, for example *cartophily* (French *carte* or Italian *carta*, card), the collecting of picture cards, such as postcards or cigarette cards, or *scriptophily* (English *scrip*, a certificate), the collection of old bond and share certificates.

Adjectives end in **-philic** (*hydrophilic*, having a tendency to mix with, dissolve in, or be wetted by water), or in **-philous** (*entomophilous*, of a plant or flower that is pollinated by insects; *anemophilous* (Greek *anemos*, wind), wind-pollinated).

For their opposites, *see* -PHOBIA.

phil(o)- *Liking for a specified thing.* [Greek *philein*, to love, or *philos*, loving.]

A *philanthropist* (Greek *anthrōpos*, human being) is a person who seeks to promote the welfare of others; a *philogynist* (Greek *gunē*, woman) likes or admires women; someone *philoprogenitive* has many offspring; a *philosopher* is literally a lover of wisdom, from Greek *sophos*, wise; similarly, *philology*, the study of languages, literally means 'love of learning', from Greek *logos*, word or speech; the adjective *philharmonic*, devoted to music, is mainly used in the names of orchestras. The form also marks an admirer of a country or people, as with

philhellene, a lover of Greece and Greek culture, or *philosemitism*, admiration for the Jewish people. However, *philistine*, a person who is hostile or indifferent to culture and the arts, derives from the Hebrew name for the people.

phleb(o)- *A vein.* [Greek *phleps*, phleb-, vein.]

Examples include *phlebitis*, the inflammation of the walls of a vein; *phlebotomy* (Greek *-tomia*, cutting), the surgical opening or puncture of a vein, also called *venesection*; *phlebography*, radiography of the veins; *phlebosclerosis* (Greek *sklērōsis*, from *sklēroun*, harden), hardening of the walls of veins; *phlegothrombosis*, obstruction of a vein by a blood clot.

-phobia Also **-phobic** and **-phobe**. *Extreme or irrational fear or dislike.* [Greek *phobia*, fear or horror.]

A large number of words using this ending have been created in modern psychiatry and related fields. It is possibly also the most fecund in the language for humorous invention, as in *arachibutyrophobia*, fear of peanut butter sticking to the roof of your mouth (from the genus name of the peanut, *Arachis*, plus Latin *butyrum*, butter). See the LIST opposite for some common examples.

Related adjectives are formed in **-phobic** (*claustrophobic*, *technophobic*). Nouns ending in **-phobe** describe a person affected by the condition (*arachnophobe*, *xenophobe*).

For their opposites, *see* -PHILE.

-phone Also **-phonia**, **-phony**, **-phonic**, and **-phonous**. *Sound.* [Greek *phōnē*, sound, voice.]

One group is of musical instruments (*saxophone*, *sousaphone*, *vibraphone*, *xylophone*) or technical terms for types of musical instrument (*aerophone*, a wind instrument; *chordophone*, a stringed instrument). Others are names for devices connected with the production or transmission of sound: *gramophone*, *microphone*, *earphone*, *megaphone*, *telephone*.

Another group is concerned with speech. Some members denote indivi-

-phobia   Extreme or irrational fear or dislike.
Word origins are from Greek unless otherwise stated.

acrophobia	heights	(*akros*, tip or extremity)
agoraphobia	open spaces	(*agora*, marketplace)
arachnophobia	spiders	(*arakhnē*, spider)
chemophobia	chemotherapy	
claustrophobia	enclosed spaces	(Latin *claustrum*, a confined space)
computerphobia	computers or computing	
cyberphobia	computers or technology	(*see* CYBER-)
homophobia	homosexuality and homosexuals	(*homos*, same)
hydrophobia	water, but especially rabies, whose sufferers typically experience great difficulty in swallowing	(*hudōr*, water)
Islamophobia	Islam or Muslims	
neophobia	the new	(*neos*, new)
phonophobia	sound or noises	(*phōnē*, sound, voice)
photophobia	extreme sensitivity to light	(*phōs, phōt-*, light)
Russophobia	Russians or Russia	
technophobia	technology	
triskaidekaphobia	the number 13	(*treiskaideka*, thirteen)
xenophobia	strangers	(*xenos*, stranger)

duals who use a specified language: *francophone, anglophone, lusophone* (Portuguese-speaking, from Lusitania, the ancient Roman province). Others are terms in linguistics, such as *allophone* (Greek *allos*, other), any of the various phonetic realizations of a phoneme in a language, which do not contribute to distinctions of meaning; *homophone* (Greek *homos*, same), each of two or more words having the same pronunciation but different meanings, origins, or spelling.

A few nouns exist in **-phonia**, for example *aphonia*, inability to speak through disease or damage to the larynx or mouth, and *dysphonia*, difficulty in speaking due to a physical disorder. Rather more are formed using **-phony**: *cacophony* (Greek *kakos*, bad), a harsh discordant mixture of sounds; *euphony* (Greek *eu*, well), the quality of being pleasing to the ear, *polyphony* (Greek *polloi*, many), simultaneously combining a number of musical parts in harmony.

Most nouns have related adjectives in **-phonic**: *anglophonic, allophonic; stereophonic* (Greek *stereos*, solid), of sound recording and reproduction using two

or more channels; *symphonic* (Greek *sun*, with), having the character of a symphony or symphony orchestra. Adjectives ending in **-phonous** are less common: *cacophonous, homophonous*.

Other terms ending in **-phone** are considered to be compounds of *phone*, short for *telephone*, rather than examples of this form: *answerphone, cardphone, cellphone, entryphone, speakerphone*.

phon(o)- *Sound.* [Greek *phōnē*, sound, voice.]

A *phonograph* is an early form of gramophone using cylinders; *phonetics* is the study and classification of speech sounds; a *phoneme* is one of the perceptually distinct units of sound in a specified language that distinguish one word from another; *phonotactics* is the study of the rules governing the possible phoneme sequences in a language; *phonics* is a method of teaching people to read by correlating sounds with symbols in an alphabetic writing system; a *phonon* is a quantum of energy or a quasiparticle associated with a compressional wave such as sound or a vibration of a crystal lattice.

-phony: *see* -PHONE

-phore Also **-phor**, **-phora**, **-phoresis**, and **-phorous**. *An agent, bearer, or producer of a specified thing.* [Modern Latin *-phorus*, from Greek *-phoros*, *-phoron*, bearing, bearer, from *pherein*, to bear.]

A common example is *semaphore* (Greek *sēma*, sign), a system of sending messages. Others include *chromophore*, an atom or group whose presence is responsible for the colour of a compound; *siderophore* (Greek *sidēros*, iron), a molecule which binds and transports iron in micro-organisms; and *spermatophore*, a protein capsule containing a mass of spermatozoa, transferred during mating.

A few terms contain the related **-phor**: *iodophor*, any of a group of disinfectants containing iodine in combination with a surfactant; *metaphor* (Greek *metapherein*, to transfer), a figure of speech in which a word or phrase is applied to an object or action to which it is not literally applicable; *phosphor* (Greek *phōs*, light), a synthetic fluorescent or phosphorescent substance.

Terms ending in **-phora** are frequently systematic names for organisms that bear some characteristic, such as *Mastigophora* (Greek *mastix*, *mastig-*, whip), a group of single-celled animals that includes the protozoal flagellates, and *Pteridophora* (Greek *pteris*, *pterid-*, fern), a genus of birds of paradise. Other examples of the ending have figurative senses derived from the Greek root *pherein*, including *anaphora* (Greek, literally 'repetition', from *ana-*, back), the use of a word referring back to one used earlier, to avoid repetition, and *exophora* (Greek *exō*, outside), reference in a text or utterance to something external to it.

A fourth noun-ending, **-phoresis**, appears in a variety of abstract terms, such as *diaphoresis* (Greek, from *diaphorein*, carry off, sweat out, from *dia*, through), sweating to an unusual degree; *electrophoresis*, the movement of charged particles in a fluid or gel under the influence of an electric field; and *iontophoresis*, a technique of introducing ionic medicinal compounds into the body through the skin by applying a local electric current.

Adjectives are formed using **-phoric** (*semaphoric*, *exophoric*, *metaphoric*), or in **-phorous** (*phosphorous*, see the next entry; *odontophorous*, of a cartilaginous projection in the mouth of a mollusc).

phosph(o)- Also **phosphor(o)-**. *Phosphorus; light.* [English *phosphorus*, via Greek *phōsphoros* from *phōs*, light, plus *-phoros*, bringing.]

The element *phosphorus* was given that name because its white form glows in the dark. Both **phospho-** and **phosphoro-** derive from *phosphorus*, the latter being the older and now less common form.

Examples of words containing **phospho-** include *phosphate*, a salt or ester of *phosphoric acid*; *phosphine*, a colourless foul-smelling gaseous compound of phosphorus and hydrogen, analogous to ammonia; *phospholipid*, a lipid containing a phosphate group in its molecule; *phosphocreatine*, a phosphate ester of creatine found in vertebrate muscle.

Phosphoro- appears in a few terms: *phosphorylase*, an enzyme which introduces a phosphate group into an organic molecule, notably glucose; *phosphorolysis* (Greek *lusis*, loosening), a form of hydrolysis in which a bond in an organic molecule is broken and an inorganic phosphate group becomes attached to one of the atoms previously linked; the adjective *phosphorous* refers to phosphorus or something containing it; this has a stricter sense in chemistry, referring to phosphorus in its lower, trivalent state, as in *phosphorous acid*, H_3PO_3.

Some terms relating to the production of light also derive from phosphorus, such as *phosphorescence*, light emitted by a substance without combustion or perceptible heat, and *phosphor*, a synthetic fluorescent or *phosphorescent* substance.

photo- *Light; photography.* [Greek *phōs*, *phōt-*, light.]

A *photochemical* action is caused by the chemical action of light, as for example in *photography*; a *photoelectric* process involves the emission of electrons from a surface by the action of light; a *photophore* (*see* -PHORE) is a light-producing organ in certain fishes and other animals; a *photodetector* responds to or detects incident light. A *photon* is a quantum of light or other electromagnetic radiation, and *photonics* is the branch of technology concerned with the properties and transmission of photons, for example in fibre optics.

In the second sense, relating to *photography*, the form derives from the first element of that word, which also appears in its own right, *photo*. Examples include *photocall*, an occasion on which famous people pose for photographers by arrangement; *photojournalism*, the art or practice of communicating news by photographs, especially in magazines; *photomontage*, a montage constructed from photographic images; *photoreconnaissance*, military reconnaissance carried out by means of aerial photography.

-phrenia Also **-phrenic**. *Mental disorder.* [Greek *phrēn*, mind.]

Examples include *schizophrenia* (Greek *skhizein*, to split), a mental disorder involving a breakdown in the relation between thought, emotion, and behaviour; *hebephrenia* (Greek *hēbē*, youthful beauty, because it was originally associated with behaviour in puberty), a form of chronic schizophrenia involving disordered thought, inappropriate emotions, hallucinations, and bizarre behaviour; *paraphrenia* (Greek *para*, amiss or irregular), a form of mental illness of a paranoid or schizophrenic type. Forms ending in **-phrenic** are either nouns indicating a person with the disorder or adjectives relating to it: *schizophrenic*, *hebephrenic*.

-phyceae Also **-phycean**. *Alga.* [Modern Latin plural, derived from Greek *phukos*, seaweed.]

Terms with this ending are systematic biological names for classes of algae. Examples include *Chlorophyceae* (Greek *khlōros*, green), a large and important group of freshwater green algae; *Dinophyceae* (Greek *dinos*, whirling), the dinoflagellates; and *Phaeophyceae* (Greek *phaios*, dusky), the brown algae. Words

ending in **-phycean** are nouns describing members of such a class: *chlorophycean*.

phyco- *Seaweeds and algae.* [Greek *phukos*, seaweed.]

Phycology is the branch of botany concerned with seaweeds and other algae; a *phycobilin* is one of a group of red or blue photosynthetic pigments present in some algae; *phycomycetes* are lower fungi, so named because of their supposed resemblance to algae; a *phycobiont* is the algal partner in a lichen.

-phyll Also **-phyllous**. *Leaf.* [Greek *phullon*, leaf.]

Two common terms with this ending relate not to leaves themselves, but to chemical compounds they contain: *chlorophyll* (Greek *khlōros*, green), the pigment in plants which absorbs light to provide energy for photosynthesis; *xanthophyll* (Greek *xanthos*, yellow), a yellow or brown pigment which causes the autumn colours of leaves. Others refer to types or parts of leaves, or plants bearing certain types of leaf: *mesophyll* (Greek *mesos*, middle), the inner tissue of a leaf, containing many chloroplasts; *microphyll*, a very short leaf, as in a moss or clubmoss; *sclerophyll* (Greek *sklēros*, hard), a woody plant with evergreen leaves that are tough and thick in order to reduce water loss. Adjectives are usually formed with **-phyllous**: *sclerophyllous*, *microphyllous*; examples with other endings are known (*mesophyllic*, *chlorophylline*), but are much less common.

phyll(o)- *Leaf.* [Greek *phullon*, leaf.]

Examples include *phylloclade*, a flattened branch or stem-joint resembling and functioning as a leaf; *phyllotaxis*, the arrangement of leaves on an axis or stem; *phylloxera* (Greek *xēros*, dry), a plant louse that is a pest of vines; *phylloquinone*, one of the K vitamins, found in cabbage, spinach, and other leafy green vegetables.

phyl(o)- *Race; group.* [Greek *phulon*, *phulē*, race, tribe.]

Phylogeny is the branch of biology that deals with *phylogenesis*, the evolutionary development and diversification of a species or group of organisms; *phylogenetics* is the study of phylogeny and phylogenesis, undertaken by a *phylogeneticist*; a *phylum* in zoology is a principal taxonomic category that ranks above the class and below the kingdom, equivalent to the *division* in botany.

-phyre *Porphyritic rocks.* [A modification of the ending of German *Porphyr*, porphyry.]

Porphyry is a hard igneous rock containing crystals of feldspar in a fine-grained, typically reddish groundmass; its name derives from Greek *porphura*, purple. Examples of the form include *lamprophyre* (Greek *lampros*, bright, shining), a porphyritic igneous rock with phenocrysts chiefly of biotite; *granophyre*, a granitic rock in which feldspar and quartz are intergrown; *vitrophyre*, any of a class of porphyritic rocks characterized by an igneous texture in which phenocrysts are embedded in a glassy groundmass.

physico- *Relating to physics.* [English *physics*.]

The most common form here is *physico-chemical* (also often unhyphenated as *physicochemical*), relating to physics and chemistry or to physical chemistry. Other examples are *physico-mechanical*, pertaining to the dynamics of physical forces, or the branch of science that deals with mechanical phenomena; and *physico-mathematical*, relating to the application of mathematics to physics.

physi(o)- *Nature; physiology.* [Greek *phusis*, nature.]

Physiography is another name for physical geography; *physiognomy* (Greek *gnōmōn*, a judge, interpreter), is a person's facial features or expression, especially when regarded as indicative of character or ethnic origin; the adjective *physiochemical* relates to physiological chemistry. *Physician* and *physics* derive from the same source by different routes.

Physiology is the branch of biology that deals with the normal functions of living organisms and their parts; some words containing **physio-** relate to that sense: *physiotherapy* is the treatment of disease, injury, or deformity by physical methods; *physiopathology* is the study of changes to the body resulting from injury or disease.

physo- *Air or gas.* [Greek *phusallis*, bladder.]

Physostigmine is a compound used medicinally to treat glaucoma; it derives from the Calabar bean, genus *Physostigma*, so named because the style forms a bladder-shaped hood over the stigma in its flowers; *physostegia* is a North American perennial herb, the obedient plant or false dragonhead, named in reference to the inflated sepals of its flowers; *physalis*, a plant of a genus that includes the Cape gooseberry and Chinese lantern, is similarly named; a *physoclistous* teleost fish (Greek *kleistos*, closed) is one in which the air bladder is not connected to the alimentary canal, the opposite of *physostomous* (Greek *stoma*, mouth).

-phyte Also **-phyta** and **-phytic**. *A plant or plant-like organism.* [Greek *phuton*, a plant, from *phuein*, come into being.]

Words ending in **-phyte** divide into two classes. Some describe the way plants live; for example, *epiphytes* (Greek *epi*, upon) grow on other plants. Others refer to specific groups of plants; for example, *bryophytes* (Greek *bruon*, moss) are members of a group that comprises the mosses and liverworts. For more examples, see the LIST opposite.

Members of the latter set are often linked to systematic names for groups that end in **-phyta** (from the Greek plural form *phuta*, plants). Two instances are *Chlorophyta* (Greek *khlōros*, green), a division of lower plants that comprises the green algae, and *Pteridophyta* (Greek *pteris*, *pterid-*, fern), a division of flowerless green plants that comprises the ferns and their relatives.

A less obvious member of the set is *neophyte*, a person who is new to a subject, skill, or belief; this is literally a person 'newly planted' (Greek *neos*, new), whose figurative sense derives from St Paul's use of it for a new convert.

-phyte	A plant or plant-like organism.	
	Word origins are from Greek unless otherwise stated.	
bryophyte	a division of small flowerless green plants which comprises the mosses and liverworts	(*bruon*, moss)
charophyte	a division of lower plants that includes the stoneworts	(Latin *Chara*, a plant of uncertain identity)
dermatophyte	a pathogenic fungus that grows on skin and other body surfaces, causing ringworm and related diseases	(*derma, dermat-,* skin, hide)
endophyte	a plant, especially a fungus, which lives inside another plant	(*endon*, within)
epiphyte	a plant that grows on another plant, especially one that is not parasitic	(*epi*, upon)
gametophyte	the gamete-producing phase of a plant with alternating generations	(English *gamete*)
geophyte	a plant propagated by means of underground buds	(*gē*, earth)
halophyte	a plant adapted to growing in saline conditions, as in a salt marsh	(*hals, halo-,* salt)
hydrophyte	a plant which grows only in or on water	(*hudōr*, water)
macrophyte	a plant, especially an aquatic plant, large enough to be seen by the naked eye	(*makros*, long, large)
osteophyte	a bony outgrowth associated with the degeneration of cartilage at joints	(*osteon*, bone)
saprophyte	a plant, fungus, or micro-organism that lives on dead or decaying organic matter	(*sapros*, putrid)
sporophyte	the asexual phase of plants with alternating generations	(*spora*, spore)
xerophyte	a plant which needs very little water	(*xēros*, dry)

Terms ending in **-phyte** have associated adjectives ending in **-phytic**: *epiphytic, saprophytic, xerophytic.*

phyto- *A plant.* [Greek *phuton*, a plant, from *phuein*, come into being.]

Phytoplankton is plankton consisting of microscopic plants; a *phytotoxin* is a poisonous substance derived from a plant; a *phytochrome* is a blue-green pigment found in many plants, in which it regulates various developmental processes; *phytochemistry* is the branch of chemistry concerned with plants and plant products; *phytogeography*, also called plant geography, is the part of botany that deals with the geographical distribution of plants; *phytopathology* is the study of plant diseases.

pico- *In units of measurement, a factor of* 10^{-12}. [Spanish *pico*, a little bit.]

This is one of the standard SI (Système International) multiples (see the table of WORDS FOR MULTIPLES on page 127). An example is *picosecond*, a millionth of a millionth of a second; others are *picogram*, *picofarad*, and *picocurie*. A rare example in the looser sense of 'extremely small' occurs in *picocell*, a very small area of coverage in a wireless communication system, perhaps only a single room within a building.

picr(o)- *Bitter tasting; picric acid.* [Greek *pikros*, bitter.]

Picrotoxin is a bitter compound sometimes used to stimulate the respiratory and nervous system. A few minerals containing magnesium are named using this form, as magnesium compounds are often bitter tasting; an example is *picrite*, a dark basaltic igneous rock rich in olivine.

Picric acid, also known as trinitrophenol, is a bitter yellow compound used as a dye and in the manufacture of explosives; some words in **picro-** refer specifically to its derivatives: it forms salts called *picrates* and its anion —$C_6H_2(NO_2)_3$ is the *picryl* group; *picramic acid* is a derivative used to make azo dyes.

piezo- *Pressure.* [Greek *piezein*, press or squeeze.]

A substance that is *piezoelectric* is able to convert mechanical signals (such as sound waves) into electrical signals, and vice versa; a *piezometer* measures the pressure of a liquid or gas, or something related to pressure (such as the compressibility of liquid); *piezoresistance* is a change in the electrical resistance of a solid when subjected to mechanical stress.

pil(o)- *Hair.* [Latin *pilus*, hair.]

A plant or animal that is *pilose* is covered with long soft hairs; *pilomotor* nerves act on muscle fibres around the base of hairs in the skin and can cause them to rise, resulting in gooseflesh; the adjective *pilonidal* (Latin *nidus*, a nest) refers to a clump of hair; *pilosebaceous* refers to hair follicles and their related sebaceous glands.

pinn(i)- Also **pinnati-**. *Wings, fins, or feathers.* [Latin *pinna*, *penna*, wing, fin, feather.]

A leaf that is *pinnate* has leaflets arranged on either side of the stem, typically in pairs opposite each other, rather like the barbs of a feather; one that is *pinnatifid* (Latin *fid-*, cleft) is *pinnately* divided, but not all the way down to the central axis, as opposed to a *pinnatisect* one, which is so divided; a *pinniped* (Latin *pes*, *ped-*, foot) is a member of a group of aquatic mammals—the seals, sea lions, and walrus—which have flipper-like limbs. *Pinna* itself is variously used in technical English to refer to the external part of the ear in humans and other mammals (figuratively the 'wing' of the ear), or a primary division of a pinnate leaf, or one of a number of animal structures resembling fins or wings.

pisc(i)- *Fish.* [Latin *piscis*, fish.]

An animal that is *piscivorous* feeds on fish; *pisciculture* is the controlled breeding and rearing of fish; the adjective *piscatorial* is a formal way to refer to fishermen or fishing; the usual adjective relating to fish is *piscine*.

-pithecus *Genera of fossil apes.* [Greek *pithēkos*, ape.]

Some examples are **Australopithecus** (Latin *australis*, southern), a fossil bipedal primate found in Pliocene and Lower Pleistocene deposits in Africa; *Dryopithecus* (Greek *drus*, tree), a fossil anthropoid ape that may be the common ancestor of gorillas, chimpanzees, and humans; *Gigantopithecus* (Greek *gigas*, *gigant-*, giant), a very large fossil Asian ape of the Upper Miocene to Lower Pleistocene epochs; *Ramapithecus* (from *Rama* in the Hindu pantheon), a fossil anthropoid ape of the Miocene epoch, known from remains found in SW Asia and East Africa, and probably ancestral to the orang-utan.

placo- *A plate.* [Greek *plax*, *plak-*, flat plate.]

A *placode* in an embryo is a thickening of the ectoderm that will later develop into specialized sensory organs; a fish scale that is *placoid* is shaped like a plate; a *placoderm* (Greek *derma*, skin) is a fossil fish of the Devonian period, which has the front part of its body encased in broad flat bony plates; a *placodont* (Greek *odous*, *odont-*, tooth) is a fossil reptile of the Triassic period, which has short flat grinding palatal teeth.

plagio- *Oblique.* [Greek *plagios*, slanting, from *plagos*, side.]

Plagioclase (Greek *klasis*, cleavage) is a form of feldspar, whose crystals exhibit two cleavages at an oblique angle; *plagiocephaly* (Greek *kephalē*, head) is a congenital distortion or lack of symmetry in the shape of the head; a plant exhibits *plagiotropism* when a part of it becomes aligned at an angle to the stimulus, usually at an angle to the vertical.

plan(o)- Also **plani-**. *Level or flat.* [Latin *planus*, flat.]

A lens that is *planoconcave* has one surface flat and the opposite one concave, while a *planoconvex* one has the curved face convex; the adjective *planographic* refers to a printing process in which the printing surface is flat, as in lithography; a *planisphere* is a map formed by the projection of a sphere or part of a sphere on a plane; a *planometer* is a flat plate used in metalwork as a standard gauge for plane surfaces, while a *planimeter* is an instrument for mechanically measuring the area of a plane figure; a *planarian* is a type of flatworm; in medicine, *planigraphy* is the process of obtaining a visual representation of a plane section through living tissue.

-plasm Also **-plasia**, **-plasmic**, and **-plast**. *Growth or development; living substance; tissue.* [Greek *plasis* or *plasma*, formation, from *plassein*, to shape or mould.]

Words ending in **-plasm** refer to kinds of cell tissue. Examples are *cytoplasm*, the material within a living cell (excluding the nucleus, whose substance is the *nucleoplasm*); *neoplasm*, a new and abnormal growth of tissue in some part of the body, especially as a characteristic of cancer; *protoplasm*, the colourless material comprising the living part of a cell, including the cytoplasm, nucleus, and other organelles; *ectoplasm*, either the more viscous, clear outer layer of the cytoplasm in amoeboid cells, or a viscous substance that is supposed to exude from the body of a medium during a spiritualistic trance. Associated adjectives are formed with **-plasmic**: *cytoplasmic*, *ectoplasmic*, *protoplasmic*.

The ending **-plasia** forms names for types of cell growth, mostly abnormal. Examples include *dysplasia* (Greek *dus-*, bad or difficult), abnormal growth or development of skin, bone, or other tissues; *hyperplasia* (Greek *huper*, over, beyond), the increased production and growth of normal cells in a tissue or organ; *neoplasia* (Greek *neos*, new), the presence or formation of new, abnormal growth of tissue; *aplasia* (Greek *a-*, not or without), the failure of an organ or tissue to develop or to function normally.

The **-plast** ending refers to components of cells, mostly in plants, such as *plastids* (from the same Greek root), members of a class of small organelles in the cytoplasm of plant cells, containing pigment or food. Examples include *chloroplast* (Greek *khlōros*, green), a plastid in green plant cells which contains chlorophyll and in which photosynthesis takes place; *protoplast* (Greek *prōtos*, first), the protoplasm of a living plant or bacterial cell whose cell wall has been removed; *kinetoplast*, a mass of mitochondrial DNA lying close to the nucleus in some flagellate protozoa; *tonoplast* (Greek *tonos*, tension, tone), a membrane which bounds the chief vacuole of a plant cell.

plasm(o)- *Plasma or plasm.* [Late Latin from Greek *plasma*, mould, formation.]

The relevant sense of *plasma* or *plasm* is that of the colourless fluid part of blood or lymph in which corpuscles or fat globules are suspended. Examples include *plasmolysis* (Greek *lusis*, loosening), contraction of the protoplast of a plant cell as a result of loss of water from the cell, resulting in separation of the plasma membrane from the cell wall; *plasmid*, a genetic structure in a cell that can replicate independently of the chromosomes, typically a small circular DNA strand in the cytoplasm of a bacterium or protozoan; *plasmin*, an enzyme, formed in the blood in some circumstances, which destroys blood clots by attacking fibrin; *plasmodesma* (Greek *desma*, bond, fetter), a narrow thread of cytoplasm that passes through the cell walls of adjacent plant cells and allows communication between them.

-plast: *see* -PLASM

-plasty *Reconstructive surgery.* [Greek *plastos*, formed, moulded.]

Examples include *angioplasty* (Greek *angeion*, vessel), surgical repair or unblocking of a blood vessel, especially a coronary artery; *rhinoplasty* (Greek *rhis*, *rhin-*, nose), plastic surgery performed on the nose; *blepharoplasty* (Greek *blepharon*, eyelid), surgical repair or reconstruction of an eyelid; *otoplasty* (Greek *ous*, *ōt*-, ear), a surgical operation to restore or enhance the appearance of an ear or the ears.

platin(o)- *Platinum.* [English *platinum*, alteration of earlier *platina*, from Spanish, a diminutive of *plata*, silver.]

Platinum is a precious silvery-white metallic element, first encountered by the Spanish in South America. Something *platinized* has been coated with platinum; the adjective *platinous* refers to platinum in its divalent state, as in *platinous oxide*, PtO; *platinic* refers to its tetravalent state, for example *platinic hydroxide*, $Pt(OH)_4$; a *platinocyanide* is one of a series of fluorescent salts containing the anion $=Pt(CN)_4$; *platinoid* is an alloy of copper with zinc, nickel, and sometimes tungsten, used for its high electrical resistance, so named because it resembles platinum.

platy- *Broad or flat.* [Greek *platus*, broad, flat.]

The *platypus* (Greek *pous*, foot) is a semi-aquatic egg-laying mammal of eastern Australia with flat, webbed feet; a *platyhelminth* is a member of a phylum of invertebrates that comprises the flatworms; *platyrrhine* (Greek *rhis*, *rhin*-, nose) refers to primates of a group that comprises the New World monkeys, marmosets, and tamarins, which have nostrils that are far apart and directed forwards or sideways; the *platysma* is a broad sheet of muscle fibres extending from the collar bone to the angle of the jaw.

-plegia Also **-plegic**. *Paralysis.* [Greek *plēgē*, stroke.]

Paraplegia (Greek, from *paraplēssein*, strike at the side, from *para*, beside) is paralysis of the legs and lower body, typically caused by spinal injury or disease; *hemiplegia* (Greek *hēmi*-, half) is paralysis of one side of the body; *quadriplegia* (Latin, from *quattuor*, four) or *tetraplegia* (Greek, from *tettares*, four) is paralysis of all four limbs; *cardioplegia* is the temporary arrest of the heart's action to enable surgery to be carried out; *ophthalmople-gia* (Greek *ophthalmos*, eye) is paralysis of the muscles within or surrounding the eye. Associated adjectives are created using **-plegic**: *paraplegic*, *hemiplegic*.

pleo- Also **pleio-** and **plio-**. *More.* [Greek *pleōn* or *pleiōn*, more.]

Pleonasm (Greek *azein*, breathe hard) is the use of more words than are necessary to convey meaning; *pleocytosis* (Greek *kutos*, vessel) is the presence of an abnormally large number of lymphocytes in the cerebrospinal fluid; *pleiotropy* (Greek *tropē*, turning) is the production by a single gene of two or more apparently unrelated effects; the *Pliocene* (Greek *kainos*, new) epoch, follows the Miocene and precedes the Pleistocene epoch; the *pliosaur* (Greek *sauros*, lizard) is a plesiosaur, so named because of its greater similarity to a lizard than the ichthyosaur.

pleur(o)- *The pleurae; the side of the body.* [Greek *pleura*, side, *pleuron*, rib.]

The *pleurae* (singular *pleura*) are the pair of membranes lining the thorax and enveloping the lungs. *Pleurisy* is inflammation of the pleurae; *pleurodynia* (Greek *odunē*, pain) is severe pain in the muscles between the ribs or in the diaphragm; *pleuropneumonia* is pneumonia complicated with pleurisy.

-plex *Having a given number of parts or units.* [Latin *plicare*, to fold.]

This ending can refer to numerical multiples: *duplex*, something having two parts; *multiplex*, consisting of many elements in a complex relationship; *simplex* (Latin, literally 'single', variant of *simplus*, simple), composed of or characterized by a single part or structure; *googolplex*, equivalent to ten raised to the power of a googol, itself an invented word meaning ten raised to the power of a hundred (10^{100}).

In addition, *duplex* can mean a residential building divided into two apartments, or two houses with a common wall (*semi-detached* in British usage), and a *multiplex* can be a cinema with several separate screens. This meaning, of a group of similar buildings or facilities on the same site, derives from one sense of *complex*, which comes from the same Latin stem.

Other examples—particularly common in North America—are *triplex*, a building divided into three self-contained residences; *fourplex* (also *quadraplex* and *quadriplex*), a building divided into four such residences; *Cineplex*, a trade name for a cinema with several separate screens; and, by extension, *metroplex*, a very large metropolitan area, especially one which is an aggregation of two or more cities. Several of these were originally blends (*Cineplex* from *cinema* and *complex*, for example), but **-plex** seems now to be established as a combining form in this sense.

plio-: *see* PLEO-

-ploid Also **-ploidy**. *The number of sets of chromosomes in a cell.* [From *haploid* and *diploid* (see text).]

The two oldest forms are *haploid* (Greek *haploos*, single), of a cell or nucleus that has a single set of unpaired chromosomes, and *diploid* (Greek *diplous*, double), containing two complete sets of chromosomes, one from each parent. They were formed using the ending -OID, but the last two letters of the Greek stems became attached to it to make a new ending.

Other examples are *triploid*, containing three homologous sets of chromosomes; *tetraploid*, containing four; *hexaploid*, containing six; *polyploid*, containing more than two homologous sets of chromosomes; *aneuploid* (Greek *an-*, not, plus *eu-*, well, good), having an uneven number of chromosomes.

The state of having such chromosome arrangements is expressed by **-ploidy**: *aneuploidy*, *polyploidy*, *triploidy*.

-ploitation *Commercial exploitation in film and other media.* [English *exploitation*.]

Well-established though informal examples are *blaxploitation* (containing a respelled *blacks*), the exploitation of black people, especially with regard to stereotyped roles in films, and *sexploitation*, commercial exploitation of sex, sexual attractiveness, or sexually explicit material. Other inventions include *teensploitation*, poor quality films directed at and exploiting the teenage audience, and *whitesploitation*, contrasted with *blaxploitation*.

plumb(o)- Also **plumbi-**. *Lead.* [Latin *plumbum*, lead.]

Plumbago is an old name for graphite, which produces a lead-coloured mark in pencil leads, but now it more commonly refers to an evergreen flowering shrub or climber, also called *leadwort*, from the colour of its flowers; the adjective *plumbous* refers to lead with a valency or combining power of two, while *plumbic* refers to lead with a valency of four; *plumbism* is another name for lead poisoning; *plumbogummite* and *plumbojarosite* are minerals containing lead.

pluri- *Several.* [Latin *plus*, *plur-*, more, *plures*, several.]

An immature cell that is *pluripotent* (Latin *potent-*, being able) is capable of giving rise to several different cell types; something *pluriform* exists in more than one form; *plurilingual* refers to knowing or using many languages, multilingual; *pluridisciplinary* is equivalent to *multidisciplinary*; *plurinominal* refers to electoral constituencies returning more than one representative through proportional representation. *See also* MULTI-.

pneumo- Also **pneumat(o)-** and **pneumono-**. *The lungs; air or gas; spirit.* [Greek *pneumōn*, lung; *pneuma*, *pneumat-*, wind, breath, spirit.]

Examples referring to the lungs include *pneumonia*, lung inflammation caused by bacterial or viral infection; *pneumoconiosis* (Greek *konis*, dust), a disease of the lungs due to inhalation of dust; *pneumonitis*, inflammation of the walls of the alveoli (air sacs) in the lungs, usually caused by a virus; *pneumonectomy* (Greek *ektomē*, excision), surgical removal of a lung or part of a lung.

Terms indicating the presence of air or gas include *pneumatic*, something containing or operated by air or gas under pressure; *pneumothorax*, the presence of air or gas in the cavity between the lungs and the chest wall, causing collapse of the lung; *pneumocephalus*, the presence of air within the skull, usually resulting from a fracture; *pneumatosis*, the occurrence of gas cysts in abnormal sites in the body.

A rare example of its sense of 'spirit' occurs in *pneumatology*, the branch of Christian theology concerned with the Holy Ghost and other spiritual concepts.

-pnoea (US **-pnea**) *Breath, respiration.* [Greek *pnoē*, breathing.]

Examples are *apnoea*, temporary cessation of breathing, especially during sleep; *dyspnoea* (Greek *dus-*, difficult), difficult or laboured breathing; *tachypnoea* (Greek *takhus*, swift), abnormally rapid breathing; and *orthopnoea* (Greek *orthos*, straight, right), difficulty in breathing except when standing or sitting upright.

pod(o)- *Foot.* [Greek *pous, pod-*, foot.]

Podiatry (Greek *iatros*, physician) is the treatment of the feet and their ailments, chiropody; *podology* is the study of the feet; *podagra* (Greek *agra*, seizure) is gout of the foot, especially the big toe; the *podocarp* (Greek *karpos*, fruit) is a coniferous tree or shrub chiefly native to the southern hemisphere; *podophyllum* (Greek *phullon*, leaf) is the dried rhizome of the May apple or American mandrake, from which *podophyllin* is derived, a caustic resin sometimes used to treat warts.

-pod Also **-poda**, **-pode**, and **-podium**. *Foot or feet.* [Greek *pous, pod-*, foot.]

A few words ending in **-pod** refer to stands or supports with a given number of feet, such as *tripod*, a three-legged one for supporting a camera or other apparatus, and *monopod*, a one-legged support for a camera or fishing rod. However, the majority are names for animals, mostly crustaceans, having particular characteristics; for some common examples, see the LIST opposite.

All the examples in that list are members of groups whose systematic names end in **-poda** (*Arthropoda, Gastropoda, Decapoda*). Other examples are *Chilopoda* (Greek *kheilos*, lip), a class of myriapod arthropods which comprises the centipedes, and *Scaphopoda* (Greek *skaphē*, boat), a class of molluscs that comprises the tusk shells.

A small number of words end in the variant form **-pode**, such as *megapode* (Greek *megas*, great), a large ground-dwelling Australasian and SE Asian bird, and the *antipodes* (Greek *anti*, against), Australia and New Zealand as viewed by inhabitants of the northern hemisphere. Some others end in **-podium**, such as *lycopodium* (Greek *lukos*, wolf, because of the claw-like shape of the root), a plant of a genus that includes the common club-mosses; *parapodium* (Greek *para-*, subsidiary), each of a number of paired muscular bristle-bearing appendages in a polychaete worm.

-poiesis Also **-poietic**. *Production, formation.* [Greek *poiēsis*, making.]

These are medical terms. *Haemopoiesis* (US *hemopoiesis*) or *haematopoiesis* (US *hematopoiesis*) (all from Greek *haima, haimat-*, blood) is the production of blood cells and platelets, which occurs in the bone marrow; *erythropoiesis* (Greek *eruthros*, red) refers specifically to the production of red blood cells; *lymphopoiesis* is the formation of lymphocytes. Associated adjectives are formed with **-poietic**: *erythropoietic, haemopoietic*.

poikilo- *Variegated; variable.* [Greek *poikilos*, variegated, varied.]

In medicine, *poikilocytosis* (Greek *kutos*, vessel) is the presence of abnormally shaped red cells (*poikilocytes*) in the blood; *poikiloderma* (Greek *derma*, *dermat-*, skin, hide) is a condition in which the skin atrophies and becomes pigmented, giving it a mottled appearance. A *poikilotherm* (Greek *thermē*, heat) is a cold-blooded organism, which cannot regulate its body temperature except by behavioural means such as basking or burrowing; in geology, *poikiloblastic* (Greek *blastos*, germ, sprout) denotes the texture of a metamorphic rock in which small crystals of an original mineral occur within crystals of its metamorphic product.

polio- *Tissue in the nervous system; grey matter.* [Greek *polios*, grey.]

-pod A foot or feet.
Word origins are all from Greek.

amphipod	a member of an order of chiefly marine crustaceans, in which some legs are specialized for swimming and some for feeding	(*amphi-*, of both kinds}
arthropod	a member of a large phylum of invertebrate animals that includes insects, spiders, crustaceans, and their relatives	(*arthron*, joint)
brachiopod	a member of a phylum of marine invertebrates that comprises the lamp shells	(*brakhiōn*, arm)
branchiopod	a member of a class of small aquatic crustaceans that includes water fleas and fairy shrimps, which have gills on the feet	(*brankhia*, gills)
cephalopod	a member of a large class of active predatory molluscs comprising octopuses, squids, and cuttlefish, which have a ring of tentacles around a beaked mouth	(*kephalē*, head)
copepod	a member of a large class of small aquatic crustaceans with paddle-like feet	(*kōpē*, handle, oar)
decapod	a member of an order of crustaceans which includes shrimps, crabs, and lobsters, which have five pairs of walking legs	(*deka*, ten)
gastropod	a member of a large class of molluscs which includes snails, slugs, whelks, and all terrestrial kinds	(*gastēr*, *gastr-*, stomach, because of the position of the foot)
hexapod	a member of a class of six-legged arthropods that comprises the insects	(*hex*, six)
macropod	a plant-eating marsupial mammal of an Australasian family that comprises the kangaroos and wallabies	(*makros*, long, large)
myriapod	an arthropod of a group that includes the centipedes, millipedes, and related animals	(*murias*, *muriad-*, from *murioi*, 10,000)
ornithopod	a mainly bipedal herbivorous dinosaur	(*ornis*, *ornith-*, bird)

The *grey matter* is the darker tissue of the brain and spinal cord. Examples of its use include *poliomyelitis* (Greek *muelos*, marrow), an infectious viral disease that affects the central nervous system and can cause paralysis; *polioencephalitis*, infection of the brain by the poliomyelitis virus.

-polis *A city.* [Greek *polis*, city.]

This ending appears in the names of some famous cities of the ancient world, such as *Persepolis* and *Heliopolis*, and in some US placenames created in imitation, such as *Minneapolis*, *Indianapolis*, and *Annapolis*. Other examples include *metropolis* (Greek *mētēr*, *mētr-*, mother), the capital or chief city of a country or region; *necropolis* (Greek *nekros*, dead person), a cemetery, especially a large one belonging to an ancient city; *cosmopolis* (Greek *kosmos*, world), a city inhabited by people from many different countries; *megalopolis* (Greek *megas*, *megal-*, great), a very large, heavily populated city or urban complex.

politico- *Politically; political and …* [Greek *politikos*, civic, political.]

Examples include *politico-economic*, of politics and economics; *politico-religious*, of politics and religion, or relating to politics as affected by religion; similarly *politico-ethical*, *politico-military*, *politico-legal*, and *politico-judicial*.

poly- *Many, much.* [Greek *polus*, much, *polloi*, many.]

A *polyglot* (Greek *glōtta*, tongue) is a person who knows or uses several languages; a *polymath* (Greek *manthanein*, learn) is a person of wide-ranging knowledge or learning; a *polygon* (Greek *-gōnos*, -angled) is a plane figure with at least three straight sides and angles, and typically five or more; *polygamy* (Greek *gamos*, marriage) is the practice or custom of having more than one wife or husband at the same time; *polyphonic* (Greek *phōnē*, voice, sound) refers to producing many sounds simultaneously.

In chemistry, a *polymer* (Greek *meros*, a share) is a substance whose molecular structure has been built up from a large number of similar units bonded together; **poly-** appears in a large number of terms for chemical compounds of this sort, including most substances generically called plastics: *polythene* or *polyethylene*, chiefly used for plastic bags, food containers, and other packaging; *polycarbonate*, a tough material often used as housings for consumer products; *polytetrafluoroethylene* or PTFE, used for the coating on non-stick saucepans and the like; *polyester*, used chiefly to make synthetic textile fibres; *polystyrene* is a polymer of styrene, used chiefly as lightweight rigid foams and films. A substance that is *polyunsaturated*, such as a fat or oil, contains several double or triple bonds between carbon atoms.

porno- Also **porn-**. *Pornography.* [The first element of *pornography*, from Greek *pornē*, prostitute.]

A *pornostar* is a popular featured participant in pornographic materials; a *pornmaster*, less often *pornmeister*, is the person running a pornographic website (from *Webmaster*); *pornotopia*, modelled on *utopia*, is a facetious term for a place in which pornography is widely and easily available; the *pornocracy* is the dominating influence of harlots or prostitutes, especially the government of Rome during the first half of the 10th century. *Porn* and *porno* exist as free-standing words referring to pornography, and some compounds may be derived from these.

por(o)- Also **poros-** *A pore.* [Latin *porus*, pore.]

Porencephaly (Greek *enkephalos*, brain) is an abnormal communication between the lateral ventricle and the surface of the brain; *porokeratosis* (Greek *keras*, *kerat-*, horn) is a skin disease in which lesions develop as annular horny ridges; *porosimetry* is the measurement of the size of pores in materials; a *porometer* is an instrument for estimating the sizes of the stomata of leaves by measuring the rate at which air can be passed through them.

post- *After in time or order.* [Latin *post*, after, behind.]

The form is widely used in hyphenated compounds: *post-natal*, of the period after childbirth; *post-operative*, the period following a surgical operation; *post-war*, occurring or existing after a war, especially World War Two (compare *post-bellum*, from Latin *bellum*, war, most commonly used in connection with the American Civil War); *post-dated*, a document containing a date later than the actual one; *post-industrial*, relating to an economy which no longer relies on heavy industry.

It appears in several terms that refer to a revised view of a subject following some crucial change in circumstances or opinion; it can suggest either dependence on what went before or revolt against it: *postmodernism*, a range of experimental tendencies in art, architecture, the media, and criticism since the 1950s, a departure from modernism; *post-structuralism*, a set of influential cultural theories that rejected much of structuralism on the grounds that meaning is ultimately always indeterminate; *post-feminism*, a cultural theory that moves beyond or rejects some of the ideas of feminism as out of date.

Though most recent terms are hyphenated, older ones generally are not: *posthumous* (Latin *postumus*, last, respelled by association with *humus*, ground), occurring after the death of the originator; *postscript* (Latin *scribere*, write), an additional remark at the end of a letter; *posthypnotic*, of ideas or instructions given to a subject under hypnosis that are intended to affect behaviour after the hypnotic trance ends; *postlude*, a concluding piece of music or a written or spoken epilogue.

Its opposite is ANTE-.

Terms such as *post-haste* and *post-paid* contain *post* in the sense of mail.

postero- *Posterior.* [English *posterior*.]

Terms mainly appear in medicine: *posterolateral*, behind and at the side; *posteroanterior*, of the direction from the back to the front; *posteroinferior*, of a position that is both lower and at the back; *posteroventral*, on the rear or lower part of the abdomen. All can appear hyphenated.

prae-: *see* PRE-

-praxia Also **-praxis** and **-practic**. *Action; practice.* [Greek *praxis*, action.]

Apraxia (Greek *a-*, not or without) or *dyspraxia* (Greek *dus-*, bad or difficult) is inability to perform particular purposive actions, as a result of brain damage; *neurapraxia* is temporary loss of nerve function due to pressure on the nerve, often found in sports injuries; *echopraxia* is pathological imitation of the actions of another person; *eupraxia* (Greek *eu*, well) or *orthopraxis* (Greek *orthos*, straight, right) is correct practice or action, in a spiritual or ethical sense; *parapraxis* (sometimes *parapraxia*) (Greek *para*, beside, amiss, irregular) is the faulty performance of an intended action.

Adjectives based on these are formed with **-practic**: *apractic*, *eupractic*. A rare example of a noun with this ending is *chiropractic* (Greek *kheir*, hand), a system of complementary medicine based on the diagnosis and manipulative treatment of misalignments of the joints.

pre- Also **prae-**. *Prior to; before; earlier; in front of.* [Latin *prae*, before.]

Many words containing this form were created in Latin: *premature* (Latin *praematurus*, very early, from *maturus*, ripe), *pre-*

side (Latin *praesidere*, from *sedere*, sit), *precaution* (Latin *praecavere*, from *cavere*, take heed, beware of), *precinct* (Latin *praecinctum*, from *cingere*, to gird), *preclude* (Latin *praecludere*, from *claudere*, to shut), *preposition* (Latin *ponere*, to place), *prescribe* (Latin *praescribere*, direct in writing, from *scribere*, write).

The form is widely used to form new terms by attaching it to English stems: *prepay*, *preflight*, *prefrontal*. It is frequently hyphenated when the stem begins with a vowel, as in *pre-adolescent*, *prearranged*, *pre-existing*, *pre-ignition*. British English often hyphenates words which in American usage commonly appear without one: *pre-war*, *pre-school*, *pre-book*, *pre-cooked*, *pre-planned*.

The spelling **prae-** is now used only for words which are regarded as Latin or which relate to Roman antiquity: *praetorian*, of each of two ancient Roman magistrates ranking below consul; *praenomen* (Latin *nomen*, name), an ancient Roman's first or personal name.

See also ANTE- and FORE-.

preter- Also **praeter-**. *More than.* [Latin *praeter*, past, beyond.]

The only common words in which this appears are *preternatural*, beyond what is normal or natural, and *preterite* (US also *preterit*) (Latin *ire*, go), a grammatical term expressing a past action or state. Other examples include *preterhuman*, beyond what is human, and *preterition*, the action of passing over or disregarding a matter, especially the rhetorical technique of making summary mention of something by professing to omit it. The spelling **praeter-** is now archaic.

pro-¹ *Favour or support; forwards, out, or away; substitute or deputy.* [Latin *pro*, forward, in front of, on behalf of, instead of, on account of.]

Modern examples in which it has the sense of favouring or supporting include *pro-choice*, advocating the legal right of a woman to choose whether or not she will have an abortion; *pro-European*, favouring or supporting closer links with the European Union.

Words in which it has a sense of motion forwards, out, or away include *proceed* (Latin *procedere*, from *cedere*, go); *propel* (Latin *propellere*, from *pellere*, to drive); and *prostrate* (Latin *prostratus*, thrown down, from *sternere*, lay flat).

In a few words it has the sense of something acting as a deputy or substitute: *proconsul* (Latin *pro consule*, (one acting) for the consul), a governor of a province in ancient Rome, having much of the authority of a consul; *pro-vice-chancellor*, an assistant or deputy vice-chancellor of a university; *procaine*, a synthetic compound used as a local anaesthetic, especially in dentistry, named because it was a substitute for cocaine.

Other examples imported from Latin include *profane* (Latin *profanus*, outside the temple, not sacred, from *fanum*, temple); *prohibit* (Latin *prohibere*, keep in check, from *habere*, to hold); *promise* (Latin *promittere*, put forth, promise, from *mittere*, send); *prospect* (Latin *prospicere*, look forward, from *specere*, to look); and *proverb* (Latin *proverbium*, from *verbum*, word).

See also PUR-.

pro-² *Before in time, place, order, etc.* [Greek *pro*, before.]

Examples from Greek include *problem* (originally a riddle or question put forward for academic discussion; Greek *proballein*, put forth, from *ballein*, to throw), *proboscis* (Greek *proboskis*, means of obtaining food, from *boskein*, (cause to) feed), and *prophet* (Greek *prophētēs* spokesman, from *phētēs*, speaker).

Examples formed in English include *proactive*, causing something to happen rather than responding to it after it has happened; *prokaryote* (Greek *karuon*, nut, kernel), a microscopic single-celled organism which does not have a distinct nucleus, taken to be a more primitive form than one with a nucleus; *prophylaxis* (Greek *phulaxis*, act of guarding), action taken to prevent disease, later extended in sense in *prophylactic* to refer euphemistically to a condom; *prosimian*, a primitive primate of a group that in-

cludes the lemurs; *prophase*, the first stage of cell division.

proct(o)- *Anus or rectum.* [Greek *prōktos*, anus.]

Proctology is the branch of medicine concerned with the anus and rectum; a *proctoscope* is a medical instrument with an integral lamp for examining the anus and lower part of the rectum or carrying out minor medical procedures; *proctitis* is inflammation of the rectum; *proctalgia* is neuralgic pain in it; *proctectomy* (Greek *ektomē*, excision) is its surgical removal.

prop- *A three-carbon chain of atoms.* [Greek *pro*, before, plus *piōn*, fat.]

The first chemical compound to contain this word element was *propionic acid*, C_2H_5COOH, a colourless pungent liquid organic acid produced in some forms of fermentation; it acquired its name because it is the first member of the series of organic acids to form fats. From this, names have been derived for other chemical compounds containing a chain of three carbon atoms, such as the hydrocarbons *propane* and *propylene*, the pesticide *propachlor*, and the alcohol *propanol*. The adjective *propyl* (*see* -YL) refers to the radical C_3H_7— derived from propane, as in *propyl alcohol* (another name for propanol) and *propylbenzene*.

pros(o)- *Towards, forward, anterior.* [Greek *pros*, towards; *prosō*, forwards.]

This appears in a few words imported from Greek, such as *proselyte* (Greek *erkhesthai*, come); *prosody* (Greek *ōidē*, song); and *prosthesis* (Greek *prosthesis*, addition, from *tithenai*, to place), originally the addition of a letter or syllable at the beginning of a word, but now also an artificial body part. A few scientific terms contain it, mostly dating from the 19th century: *prosencephalon* (Greek *enkephalos*, brain), another word for the forebrain; *prosenchyma* (Greek *enkhuma*, infusion), a plant tissue consisting of elongated cells with interpenetrating tapering ends; *prosobranch* (Greek *brankhia*, gills), a member of a group of molluscs which includes the limpets and abalones. It is not an active word forming element.

prosop(o)- *Face; person.* [Greek *prosōpon*, face or person.]

This form occurs in just a few technical English words, of which the most common are *prosopagnosia* (Greek *agnōsia*, ignorance), an inability to recognize the faces of familiar people, typically as a result of damage to the brain; *prosopography* (Greek *-graphia*, writing), sometimes a description of a person's appearance, personality, social and family connections, but more commonly the study of careers and family connections, especially in Roman history; and *prosopopoeia* (Greek *poiein*, to make), a figure of speech in which either an abstract thing is personified, or an imagined or absent person or thing is represented as speaking.

prote(o)- *Protein.* [English *protein* plus -o-.]

A *protease* is an enzyme which breaks down proteins and peptides, a process called *proteolysis* (Greek *lusis*, loosening); a *proteoglycan* is a compound consisting of a protein bonded to mucopolysaccharide groups, present especially in connective tissue; a *proteolipid* is a type of lipoprotein occurring mainly in the brain.

proto- *Original or first; primitive or ancestral.* [Greek *prōtos*, first.]

Examples include *prototype*, a first or preliminary model of something; *protohuman*, a hypothetical prehistoric primate, resembling humans and thought to be their ancestor; *protomartyr*, the first martyr for a cause, especially the first Christian martyr, St Stephen; *protostar*, a contracting mass of gas which represents an early stage in the formation of a star; *protoplast* (Greek *plassein*, to mould), the protoplasm of a living plant or bacterial cell whose cell wall has been removed; *Protozoa* (Latin plural of Greek *zōion*, animal), a phylum or grouping of phyla which comprises the single-celled microscopic animals.

pseud(o)- *False; imitative.* [Greek *pseudēs*, false, *pseudos*, falsehood.]

A *pseudonym* (Greek *onoma*, name) is a fictitious name, especially one used by an author; *pseudoscience* is a collection of beliefs or practices mistakenly regarded as being based on scientific method. The form is widely distributed in technical contexts: a *pseudopodium* (Greek *podion*, little foot) is a temporary protrusion of the surface of an ameboid cell for movement and feeding; *pseudoextinction* is the apparent extinction of a group of organisms but in which modified descendant forms survive; a *pseudorandom* number satisfies some statistical tests for randomness but is produced by a definite mathematical procedure. The form is sometimes used in medicine to describe conditions that mimic others, as in *pseudodementia*, *pseudogout*, *pseudojaundice*, and *pseudopregnancy*.

psilo- *Bare, smooth.* [Greek *psilos*, bald.]

The drugs *psilocybin* (Greek *kubē*, head) and *psilocin* are alkaloid hallucinogenics found in the liberty cap and related toadstools of the genus *Psilocybe*, named from their appearance; *psilomelane* (Greek *melas*, *melan-*, black) is a hydrated oxide of manganese, which occurs in smooth black amorphous masses.

psych(o)- *The mind; psychology.* [Greek *psukhē*, breath, soul, mind.]

Psychology is the scientific study of the human mind and its functions, while *psychiatry* studies and treats mental illness, emotional disturbance, and abnormal behaviour; a *psychopath* is a person suffering from chronic mental disorder with abnormal or violent social behaviour; *psychotherapy* is the treatment of mental disorder by psychological rather than medical means; a *psychedelic* drug (Greek *delos*, clear, manifest) is one, especially LSD, that produces hallucinations and apparent expansion of consciousness.

Several terms relate to cross-disciplinary ubjects involving psychology or perception: *psychoacoustics* is the branch of psychology concerned with the perception of sound and its physiological

---

-ptera Groups of winged animals.
All word origins are from Greek.

Chiroptera	the bats	(*kheir*, hand)
Coleoptera	the beetles	(*koleos*, sheath)
Diptera	the two-winged or true flies	(*di-*, two)
Ephemeroptera	the mayflies	(*ephēmeros*, lasting only a day)
Hemiptera	the true bugs, including aphids, cicadas, and leafhoppers	(*hemi-*, half, because of their forewing structure)
Heteroptera	a group of true bugs comprising those in which the forewings are non-uniform	(*heteros*, other)
Homoptera	a group of true bugs comprising those in which the forewings are uniform in texture, such as aphids	(*homos*, same)
Hymenoptera	a large order of insects that includes the bees, wasps, ants, and sawflies, with four transparent wings	(*humēn*, membrane)
Isoptera	the termites, whose members have four large equal wings	(*isos*, equal)
Lepidoptera	the butterflies and moths, which have wings covered in scales	(*lepis*, *lepid-*, scale)
Neuroptera	the lacewings, alderflies, snake flies, and ant lions, which have four finely veined membranous wings	(*neuron*, veined)
Orthoptera	the grasshoppers, crickets, and their relatives, which have straight and narrow forewings	(*orthos*, straight)

effects; *psychobiology* deals with the biological basis of behaviour and mental phenomena; *psychohistory* interprets historical events with the aid of psychological theory; *psycholinguistics* studies the relationships between linguistic behaviour and psychological processes.

-ptera Also **-pteran** and **-pterous**.
Winged animals. [Greek *pteron*, wing.]

This ending forms systematic names for groups of animals with wings, mainly the insects but also the bats, of which some examples are in the LIST above. Forms ending in **-pteran** are either adjectives relating to the group or names for members of it (*coleopteran*, *dipteran*); other adjectives are formed with **-pterous** (*heteropterous*, *orthopterous*).

pterido- *A fern.* [Greek *pteris*, *pterid-*, fern.]

A *pteridophyte* (Greek *phuton*, plant) is a member of the *Pteridophyta*, a division of flowerless green plants that comprises the ferns and their relatives; *pteridology* is the study of ferns and related plants; and a *pteridosperm* is a fossil plant which is intermediate between the ferns and seed-bearing plants, dying out in the Triassic period.

ptero- *A wing.* [Greek *pteron*, feather, wing.]

A *pterodactyl* (Greek *daktulos*, finger) is a flying reptile of the late Jurassic period, a member of an order of such reptiles of the Jurassic and Cretaceous periods, the *pterosaurs* (Greek *sauros*, lizard); a *pteranodon* (Greek *an-*, without, plus *odous*, *odont-*, tooth) is a large tailless pterosaur of the Cretaceous period, with a long toothless beak. A *pteropod* (Greek *pous*, *pod-*, foot), a sea butterfly, is a small mollusc with wing-like extensions to its body which it uses for swimming; *pteroylglutamic acid* is another term for folic acid, so called because related substances, *pterins*, occur as pigments in insect wings.

pteryg(o)- *Wing-like.* [Greek *pterux*, *pterug-*, wing.]

Something *pterygoid* is wing-shaped, but the word usually appears in the term *pterygoid process* for each of a pair of wing-like projections from the sphenoid bone that forms the base of the cranium; *pterygomandibular* refers to the pterygoid process and the mandible; a *pterygium* is a triangular, wing-like overgrowth of the corner of the cornea by thickened conjunctiva; a *pterygote* is a member of a large group of insects (the **Pterygota**) comprising those that have wings or winged ancestors, including the majority of modern species.

ptyalo- *Saliva; salivary gland.* [Greek *ptualon*, spittle.]

Ptyalin is an enzyme found in saliva that breaks down starch; *ptyalism* is excessive salivation; *ptyalography* is an X-ray examination of the salivary ducts. The equivalent form SIALO- is more common.

pur- *Forwards, out, or away.* [Old French or Anglo-Norman French, from Latin *por-*, *pro-*.]

Such words are closely related in origin and sense to those beginning with **pro-** (*see* PRO-[1]). Examples include *pursue* (Anglo-Norman French *pursuer*, from an alteration of Latin *prosequi*, prosecute), *purloin* (Anglo-Norman French *purloigner*, put away); *purport* (Old French *purporter*, from Latin *portare*, carry or bear); *purchase* (Old French *pourchacier*, seek to obtain or bring about).

py-: *see* PYO-

pycn(o)- Also **pykn(o)-**. *Compact; dense.* [Greek *puknos*, thick.]

A *pycnocline* (Greek *klinein*, to slope) is a layer in a body of water in which water density increases rapidly with depth; a *pycnometer* (sometimes *pyknometer*) measures the relative density of liquids; *Pycnogonida* (Greek *gonu*, knee) is a class of marine arthropods, the sea spiders; someone who is *pyknic* is stocky, with a

rounded body and head, thickset trunk, and a tendency to fat; *pyknosis* is the shrinkage of the nuclear material of a cell into a compact mass, a sign of cell degeneration.

pyel(o)- *The pelvis of the kidney.* [Greek *puelos*, trough, basin.]

The pelvis of the kidney, the renal pelvis, is the broadened top part of the ureter into which the kidney tubules drain. *Pyelography* is an X-ray technique for producing an image of the renal pelvis and urinary tract; *pyelitis* is inflammation of it; *pyeloplasty* is an operation to relieve obstruction at the junction of the kidney and the ureter; *pyelolithotomy* (Greek *-tomia*, cutting) is surgical removal of a stone from the kidney through an incision made in the renal pelvis; *pyelonephritis* is inflammation of the substance of the kidney as a result of bacterial infection.

pyg(o)- *The buttocks.* [Greek *pugē*, rump.]

A *pygidium* is the terminal part or hind segment of the body in certain invertebrates; a *pygostyle* (Greek *stulos*, column) in a bird is a triangular plate, typically supporting the tail feathers; *pygopagus* (Greek *pagos*, fixed) refers to a pair of Siamese twins joined at the buttocks, often back to back.

pylor(o)- *The pylorus.* [Greek *pulē*, gate.]

The *pylorus* is the opening from the stomach into the duodenum; *pyloroduodenal* refers to the pylorus and duodenum together; *pyloroplasty* is a surgical operation to reconstruct it; *pylorospasm* is a muscle spasm that closes it; the usual adjective is *pyloric*.

py(o)- *Pus.* [Greek *puon*, pus.]

Examples include *pyaemia* (US *pyemia*) (Greek *haima*, blood), blood poisoning caused by pus-forming bacteria from an abscess; *pyoderma* (Greek *derma*, skin), a skin infection with formation of pus; *pyogenic*, involving or relating to the production of pus; *pyorrhoea* (US *pyorrhea*) (Greek *rhoia*, flux), another term for periodontitis, inflammation of the tissue around the teeth; *pyuria* (Greek *ouron*, urine), the presence of pus in the urine, typically from bacterial infection.

pyr(o)- *Fire.* [Greek *pur*, fire.]

Pyromania is an obsessive desire to set fire to things; *pyrotechnics* (Greek *tekhnē*, art) is the art of making or displaying fireworks (often figuratively, a brilliant performance or display); *pyracantha* (Greek *akantha*, thorn) is a thorny evergreen shrub, the firethorn, so called from its bright red berries; *pyrography* is the craft of decorating wood by burning a design on the surface; a *pyrometer* is an instrument for measuring high temperatures, especially in furnaces and kilns; *pyrexia* is raised body temperature or fever.

In geology, *pyroclastic* (Greek *klastos*, broken in pieces) denotes fragments of rock ejected from a volcano; *pyrolusite* (Greek *lousis*, washing, because of its use to remove colour from glass) is a black or dark grey mineral with a metallic lustre, consisting of manganese dioxide; *pyrophosphoric acid* is a glassy solid obtained by heating phosphoric acid; *pyrene* is a crystalline aromatic hydrocarbon present in coal-tar.

quadr(i)- Also **quadru-**. *Four; having four parts; square.* [Latin *quadrans*, a quarter, from *quattuor*, four.]

Examples are *quadrilateral*, a shape or figure having four sides; *quadruped*, an animal with four legs; and *quadruple*, fourfold or having four parts; a *quadrangle*, a square or rectangular space, is so called because it has four angles.

The related Latin word for forty, *quadraginta*, appears in the archaic *quadragesimal*, a period of forty days (as in the Lenten fast, hence *Quadragesima*, the first Sunday in Lent) and in *quadragenarian*, a person aged between 40 and 49.

For *quadrillion* see the list of NUMBER WORDS on page 162.

quasi- *Seemingly; apparently but not really; partly or almost.* [From Latin *quasi*, as if, as though, almost.]

In Physics, a *quasicrystal* is one that is locally regular but whose patterns do not repeat themselves indefinitely, and a *quasiparticle* is a packet or quantum of energy that in some respects can behave as a subatomic particle but is not one. A *quasi-judicial* body is one outside the legal system but which has powers of investigation and enforcement that resemble those of a court.

quin-: *see* QUINTI-

quinqu(e)- Also **quin-**. *Five; having five parts.* [From Latin *quinque*, five.]

An event which is *quinquennial* happens once every five years (less usually, it lasts for five years); any period of five years may be called a *quinquennium*; a *quincentenary* is the five-hundredth anniversary of a significant event; a *quincunx* is an arrangement of five objects with four at the corners of a square and the fifth at its centre, like the five on dice. In botany something *quinquefoliate* has five leaves or leaflets.

The related Latin word for fifty, *quinquaginti*, appears in *quinquagenarian*, a person in their fifties, and in *Quinquagesima*, the Sunday before the beginning of Lent, taken to be fifty days before Easter.

quint(i)- *Five; the fifth in a series.* [From Latin *quintus*, fifth.]

If their Latin origins were the only factor, **quinti-** would mean 'fifth' and QUINQUE- would mean 'five', but this distinction has long been lost. A *quintet* contains five members, a *quintile* is any one of five equal groups into which a population can be divided, a *quintuplet* is one of five children born to the same mother at one birth, and to *quintuple* something is to increase it fivefold. For *quintillion*, see the list of NUMBER WORDS on page 162.

R

rach(i)- *The spine.* [Modern Latin *rachis*, from Greek *rhakhis*, spine.]

A *rachis* can be a stem of a plant bearing flower stalks at short intervals, or the spine of an animal, or the cord from which it develops, or the shaft of a feather, especially the part bearing the barbs; *rachilla*, a diminutive of *rachis*, is a spikelet that bears the florets, as in grasses and sedges; *rachitis* is an older medical term for rickets; *rachischisis* is another term for spina bifida.

radio-¹ *Radiation; radio waves.* [The first element of English *radiation* (from Latin *radiat-*, emitted in rays), plus -o-.]

The core sense is that of electromagnetic radiation, such as heat, light, X-rays, and gamma rays. Terms with this sense include *radiometer*, an instrument for detecting or measuring the intensity or force of radiation; *radiology*, the science dealing with X-rays and other high-energy radiation, especially its use for the diagnosis and treatment of disease; and *radiotherapy*, the treatment of disease, especially cancer, using X-rays or similar forms of radiation.

The form is most widely used today in an extended sense in which it refers to the emission of subatomic particles or ionizing radiation from atomic nuclei, as in the adjective *radioactive*, referring to a substance that emits them; a *radio-isotope* is a radioactive isotope of an atom; *radiochemistry* is the branch of chemistry concerned with radioactive substances.

A narrower sense refers to one form of electromagnetic radiation, radio waves (*radio* as a standalone word is an abbreviation of terms like *radio-telephony*, in which *radio-* has the broader sense of radiation); examples are often self-explanatory (*radio-controlled*, *radiotelescope*) and some are now dated (*radiolocation*, an old term for radar).

radio-² *The radius bone.* [Latin *radius*, staff, spoke, ray.]

The *radius* is the thicker and shorter of the two bones in the human forearm; **radio-** is found in a few adjectives that describe the radius in conjunction with some other part of the body: *radio-carpal*, of the radius plus the carpal bones of the wrist; *radio-ulnar*, of the radius and the ulna, the other long bone in the forearm.

-rama: *see* -ORAMA

re- Also **red-**. *Again; back.* [Latin *re-*, *red-*, again, back.]

In principle, **re-** can be added to any verb to make new verbs or verbal derivatives. The most commonly encountered sense, especially in words of modern creation on English stems, is of something happening or being done once more or afresh: *redecorate*, *re-elect*, *repeat*, *re-roof*, *reprint*, *retry*, *rewrite*.

Related ideas are of going back to a previous place or state (*re-establish*, *refund*, *restore*, *return*, *revert*); of withdrawal or reversal (*recant*, *recede*, *resign*, *revoke*); or of pushing back or acting against something, opposing (*react*, *rebel*, *repel*, *resist*)

In a few cases, the older Latin form of *red-* appears, at one time used before vowels: *redolent* (Latin *olere*, to smell), strongly reminiscent or suggestive of something; *redeem* (Latin *emere*, buy), compensate for the faults or bad aspects of something, or gain or regain possession of something in exchange for payment.

Most words beginning with **re-** are written without hyphens, even when the prefix is followed by a stem beginning in a vowel (*reuse*, *reinsure*); however, some do appear hyphenated before *e* (*re-enact*, *re-enter*) though US usage prefers to omit the hyphens.

Hyphenation is used in particular to indicate that repetition is meant, in order to distinguish words with that sense from others with the same spelling with a figurative sense (*re-sign*, to sign again, say a contract to continue a service, versus *resign*, to voluntarily leave a job or other position; *re-form*, to form again, versus *reform*, to make changes in something in order to improve it). Hyphenated terms in such pairs have a stronger stress on the **re-** prefix.

rect(i)- *Straight; right; correct.* [Latin *rectus*, straight.]

Examples are *rectify*, to put right or correct; *rectitude*, morally correct behaviour or thinking; *rectangle* (Latin *angulus*, an angle), a plane figure with four straight lines and four right angles; *rectilinear* (Latin *linea*, line), consisting of or moving in a straight line.

recto- *The rectum.* [English *rectum*.]

A *rectocele* (Greek *kēlē*, tumour or hernia) is a prolapse of the wall between the rectum and the vagina; the *rectosigmoid* is the part of the large intestine around the junction of the sigmoid colon and the rectum; *rectopexy* (Greek *-pexia*, *pexis*, fixing together), is the fixation of a prolapsed rectum. Adjectives often refer to the rectum plus another part of the body: *rectovaginal*, the region between the rectum and the vagina; *rectovesical* (Latin *vesica*, bladder), the rectum and bladder. Such terms are often hyphenated.

-rel Also **-erel**. *Forming nouns.* [Old French *-erel(le)*.]

Words often have a diminutive or derogatory sense: *wastrel*, a wasteful or good-for-nothing person (originally meaning a strip of uncultivated land, so deriving from *waste*); *doggerel*, comic verse composed in irregular rhythm (apparently from a contemptuous sense of *dog*, as in *dog Latin*); *cockerel*, a young domestic cock; *scoundrel* may be similarly derived, but nobody knows for sure. Other words come from a variety of unrelated sources: *mackerel*, *minstrel*, *mongrel*, *squirrel*.

ren(i)- Also **reno-**. *The kidneys; kidney-shaped.* [Latin *ren*, kidney.]

Something *reniform* is kidney-shaped; *renography* is the radiological study of the

kidneys, resulting in a *renogram*. The usual adjective relating to the kidneys is *renal*.

reticulo- *Net-like; reticulated.* [Latin *reticulum*, diminutive of *rete*, net.]

Something *reticulated* contains a fine network or net-like structure, as in a *reticulocyte*, an immature red blood cell without a nucleus, which has a granular or net-like appearance when suitably stained; *reticulocytosis* is an increase in the proportion of such blood cells in the bloodstream. The *reticulum* is a network of tubules or blood vessels in the body, for example in the brain; the adjective *reticuloendothelial* denotes a diverse system of fixed and circulating cells involved in the immune response, spread throughout the body; *reticuloendotheliosis* is overgrowth of some part of this system, causing isolated swelling of the bone marrow and in severe cases the destruction of the bones of the skull; *reticulosis* is abnormal growth of any of the cells of the lymphatic glands or the immune system.

retin(o)- *The retina.* [English *retina*, plus -o-.]

A *retinopathy* (Greek *patheia*, suffering, feeling) is one of various diseases of the retina which results in impairment or loss of vision; a *retinoblastoma* is a rare malignant tumour of the retina, affecting young children; a *retinoscope* is an instrument used to determine errors of refraction in the eye; *retinitis* is inflammation of the retina of the eye.

retro- *Directed backwards; behind.* [Latin *retro*, backwards.]

Some common examples are *retroactive*, taking effect from a date in the past; *retrofit*, to add a component or accessory to something that did not have it when manufactured; *retrograde*, directed or moving backwards; *retrorocket*, a rocket fired in the direction of travel to slow the craft down; *retrospection*, the action of looking back on or reviewing past events or situations, especially those in one's own life. A few words have the sense of 'behind': *retrochoir*, the interior of a cathedral or large church behind the high altar; *retrosternal*, behind the breastbone or sternum. However, in *retrovirus*, any of a group of RNA viruses which insert a DNA copy of their genome into the host cell in order to replicate, the form derives from the initial elements of *reverse transcriptase*.

rhabdo- Also **rhabdomyo-**. *A rod or rodlike structure.* [Greek *rhabdos*, rod.]

Rhabdomancy is dowsing with a rod or stick; a *rhabdom* or *rhabdome* is a translucent cylinder forming part of the light-sensitive receptor in the eye of an arthropod; something *rhabdoid* is rodlike; a *rhabdocoel* (Greek *koilos*, hollow) is a turbellarian worm of the order *Rhabdocoela*; a *rhabdovirus* is any of a group of rod-shaped RNA viruses, including the rabies virus. The compound form **rhabdomyo-** (Greek *mus*, *mu-*, mouse or muscle) is used in medicine to refer to striated or skeletal muscle: *rhabdomyolysis*, the destruction of striated muscle cells; *rhabdomyosarcoma*, a rare malignant tumour involving striated muscle tissue.

-rhagia: *see* -RRHAGIA

-rhea: *see* -RRHOEA

rheo- *Current or flow.* [Greek *rheos*, stream.]

Rheology is the branch of physics that deals with the deformation and flow of matter, especially the non-Newtonian flow of liquids and the plastic flow of solids; a *rheometer* is an instrument for measuring the flow of fluids, especially blood; a *rheostat* is an electrical instrument used to control a current by varying the resistance; *rheotaxis* is the property in a living organism of responding to the stimulus of a flow of water.

rhin(o)- *The nose.* [Greek *rhis*, *rhin-*, nose.]

Rhinitis is inflammation of the mucous membrane of the nose, caused by a virus infection or an allergic reaction; a *rhinovirus* is a member of a group of small RNA viruses, including those that cause some forms of the common cold; *rhinoplasty* is plastic surgery performed on the nose.

The name of the *rhinoceros* derives from the same source, plus Greek *keras*, horn.

rhizo- *A root or roots.* [Greek *rhiza*, root.]

A *rhizome* is a continuously growing horizontal underground stem which puts out lateral shoots and adventitious roots at intervals; a *rhizomorph* is a rootlike aggregation of hyphae in certain fungi; the *rhizosphere* is the region of soil in the vicinity of plant roots in which its chemistry and microbiology is influenced by them; *rhizobium* (Greek *bios*, life) is a nitrogen-fixing bacterium that is common in the soil, especially in the root nodules of leguminous plants.

rhodo- *Rose-coloured.* [Greek *rhodon*, rose.]

Rhododendron literally means 'rose tree', from Greek *dendron*, tree; *rhodopsin* (Greek *opsis*, sight) is a purplish-red light-sensitive pigment present in the retinas of humans and many other animal groups; *rhodochrosite* is a mineral that typically occurs as pink, brown, or grey crystals; *rhodonite* is a brownish or rose-pink mineral; the element *rhodium* was given that name because of the colour of its salts in solution.

rhyncho- *Snout or beak.* [Greek *rhunkos*, snout, beak.]

Terms are found in biology, most commonly in the systematic names of organisms. Examples are *rhynchosaur* (Greek *sauros*, lizard), a tusked herbivorous reptile of the Triassic period; the *Rhynchophora* is a group of beetles with snouts, the weevils; *rhynchosporium* is a fungus which causes barley and rye leaf blotch, so named because of its shape; a *rhynchonellid* is a member of a group of marine invertebrates called brachiopods.

roentgeno- Also **röntgeno-** *X-rays.* [From the name of Wilhelm Conrad Röntgen (1845–1923), the German physicist who discovered X-rays.]

This form is now largely restricted to the US and even there terms are often replaced by equivalents. Examples include *roentgenology*, another term for radiology; *roentgenography*, X-ray photography, which produces a *roentgen-*

ogram. Spellings using the umlaut are rare.

Romano- *Roman; Roman and...* [English *Roman* plus -o-.]

The most common example here is *Romano-British*, relating to the period of the Roman occupation of Britain. Others with similar senses include *Romano-Celtic*, *Romano-Germanic*, and *Romano-Egyptian*.

-rrhagia Also **-rrhagic** and **-rrhage**. *An excessive flow or discharge*. [Greek *-rrhag-*, stem of Greek *rhēgnunai*, to burst.]

Terms often contain the linking vowel -o- before the ending. Examples include *menorrhagia* (Greek *mēn*, month), abnormally heavy bleeding at menstruation; *metrorrhagia* (Greek *mētra*, womb), abnormal bleeding from the womb; and *haemorrhagia* (US *hemorrhagia*) (Greek *haima*, blood), loss of blood from a ruptured blood vessel.

Though adjectives can in theory be formed ending in **-rrhagic**, only *haemorrhagic* is at all common. Similarly, the only common example of a word with the noun suffix **-rrhage** is *haemorrhage*, the usual term for an escape of blood from a ruptured vessel.

-rrhaphy *Surgical sewing or suturing.* [Greek *-rraphia*, from *rhaphē*, a seam.]

These are specialist medical terms; they include *herniorrhaphy*, suturing of a hernia; *colporrhaphy* (Greek *kolpos*, womb), an operation to remove lax and redundant vaginal tissue in cases of prolapse of the vaginal wall; and *tenorrhaphy*, joining a severed tendon with a suture.

-rrhoea Also **-rrhoeic**, and **-rrhoeal** (US **-rrhea**, **-rhea**, **-rrheic**, and **-rrheal**). *Discharge; flow*. [Greek *rhoia*, flow, flux.]

Diarrhoea (Greek *dia*, through) is a condition in which faeces are discharged from the bowels frequently and in a liquid form; *gonorrhoea* (Greek *gonos*, semen) is a venereal disease involving inflammatory discharge from the urethra or vagina; *amenorrhoea* (Greek *a-*, without, plus *mēn*, month) is an abnormal absence of menstruation; *seborrhoea* is excessive discharge of sebum from the sebaceous glands.

The standard US spelling of the ending is **-rrhea** (*diarrhea*, *seborrhea*); it is occasionally spelled with only one *r* (*diarhea*, *amenorhea*).

Adjectives are formed ending in **-rrhoeic** (*seborrhoeic*, *diarrhoeic*), or **-rrhoeal** (*gonorrhoeal*, *amenorrhoeal*).

Russo- *Russian; Russian and...* [English *Russia* plus -o-.]

The form appears in terms such as *Russo-Finnish*, *Russo-Japanese*, and *Russo-Turkish*, often in reference to wars between these countries. A *Russophile* is a person who is friendly towards Russia or fond of Russia and things Russian, especially someone who is sympathetic to the political system and customs of the former Soviet Union; the opposite is *Russophobe*.

-ry: *see* -ERY

s

-s¹ Also **-es**. *Noun plurals.* [Old English plural ending *-as*.]

The **-s** ending forms the plural of most nouns (*crimes*, *doors*, *lamps*). However, nouns that end in *s*, *x*, *z*, *sh*, or *ch* do so in **-es** (*classes*, *boxes*, *chintzes*, *wishes*, *matches*).

-s² Also **-es**. *Third person singular of the present tense of verbs.* [Old English dialect forms, probably from the second person singular present tense ending *-es*, *-as*.]

The usual ending is **-s** (*cuts*, *sews*, *takes*); however, verbs whose stem ends in *s*, *x*, *z*, *sh*, or *ch* use **-es** instead (*blesses*, *fizzes*, *flexes*, *pushes*, *lunches*), as do those ending in *o* (*echoes*, *goes*, *vetoes*).

-s³ *Nicknames or pet names.* [Perhaps suggested by the usual plural ending, *see* -s¹.]

Some examples are: *Babs*, *Fats*, *ducks*, and *Pops*. *See also* -SY *and* Y.

-'s¹ *Possessive forms of nouns.* [Old English endings.]

The suffix is commonly used to mark singular possessive forms of nouns (*the boy's toy*; *the rose's scent*). The usual form with plurals is *-s'*.

-'s² *Various contractions.* [Standard apostrophe usage.]

The ending may indicate a contracted form of *is* (*he's here*, *where's Bill?*), *has* (*she's just left*; *the car's been stolen*), *does* (*what's he do?*), or *us* (*let's go*).

-s' *Plural possessive nouns.* [Old English ending.]

This is the usual possessive ending attached to nouns that take their plurals in *s* or *-es* (*see* -s¹): *the darts' match*, *the hospitals' waiting-lists*.

sacchar(o)- *Sugar.* [Modern Latin *saccharum*, from Greek *sakkharon*, sugar.]

Saccharin is a sweet-tasting synthetic compound used as a substitute for sugar; *saccharose* is an alternative name for sucrose, cane sugar; the adjective *saccharine* refers to something excessively sweet or sentimental. In biochemistry, *saccharides* are the simple carbohydrates, often called *sugars*, whose names end in *-ose* (*see* -OSE²); they are divided into groups according to their complexity (*monosaccharides*, *disaccharides*, *oligosaccharides*, *polysaccharides*).

sacr(o)- *Sacrum.* [Latin *(os) sacrum*, literally 'holy bone'—it was believed to be the nucleus on which the body would be resurrected at the Last Judgement.]

The *sacrum* is a curved triangular element at the back of the pelvis, consisting of five fused vertebrae. The adjective relating to it is *sacral*, as in the *sacral nerves* or the *sacral vertebrae* (it can also refer to sacred rites or symbols); the adjective *sacroiliac* refers to the sacrum and the ilium (especially the sacroiliac *joint*, inflammation in which is *sacroiliitis*, *see* -ITIS), while *sacrococcygeal* relates to the sacrum and the coccyx together.

salping(o)- *Fallopian tube.* [Greek *salpinx*, *salping-*, trumpet (referring to its shape).]

In medicine, *salpingectomy* (Greek *ektomē*, excision) is surgical removal of a Fallopian tube; *salpingitis* is inflammation of one; *salpingostomy* (Greek *stoma*, mouth) is an operation to restore free passage through a blocked one; *salpingo-oophoritis* (Latin *oophoron*, ovary) is inflammation of a Fallopian tube and an ovary.

At one time **salpingo-** could refer to the Eustachian tubes leading from the middle ear to the pharynx, as in *salpingo-nasal*, though this sense is now obsolete. However, a *salpinx* can be either a Eustachian tube or a Fallopian tube.

-san *Japanese honorific.* [Japanese *-sama*, denoting respect.]

This is the usual respectful marker in Japanese, equivalent to English *Mr*, *Mrs*, or *Miss*, which occasionally appears attached to Japanese names in English; it is used after both names and titles. Examples are *mama-san*, *Suzuki-san*, and *samurai-san*.

sangui- *Blood.* [Latin *sanguis*, *sanguin-*, blood.]

Terms here are often poetic or figurative; literal references to blood, as in medicine, are usually marked by HAEMO-. Someone or something *sanguinary* is bloodthirsty or accompanied by bloodshed; an organ that is *sanguineous* contains blood; a person who is *sanguine* is cheerfully optimistic (a term taken from one of the medieval humours, which indicated a constitution associated with the predominance of blood); in heraldry, the word can also refer to a blood-red colour; *sanguinaria* is a plant, known in North America as *bloodroot* from the red dye that can be extracted from its rhizomes.

sapro- *Putrefaction or decay.* [Greek *sapros*, putrid.]

A *saprophyte* (Greek *phuton*, a plant) is a plant that lives on dead or decaying organic matter; the term is a general one which can refer also to fungi and microorganisms; as these last two groups are not plants, some specialists prefer *saprobe* (Greek *bios*, life) for them; a *saprophagous* organism feeds on decaying organic matter; one that is *saproxylic* (Greek *xulon*, wood) lives on dead or decaying wood; *sapropel* (Greek *pēlos*, mud, earth, clay) is sediment laid down in stagnant water; something *saprogenic* is caused or produced by putrefaction or decay.

sarc(o)- *Flesh or fleshy tissue; muscle.* [Greek *sarx*, *sarc-*, flesh.]

A *sarcoma* is a malignant tumour of certain soft tissues; *sarcoidosis* is a chronic disease which causes lymph nodes in many parts of the body to enlarge; the *sarcolemma* (Greek, from *lepein*, to peel) is the fine transparent tubular sheath which envelops the fibres of skeletal muscles; a *sarcomere* (Greek *meros*, part) is a structural part of striated muscle. *Sarcophagus*, a stone coffin, derives from the same root (Greek *sarkophagos*, flesh-consuming, from *-phagos*, eating, because the stone was believed to consume the flesh of the corpse within it), as does *sarcasm*, the use of irony to mock or convey contempt (Greek *sarkazein*, tear flesh).

-saur Also **-saurus**. *Reptiles, especially extinct ones.* [Greek *sauros*, lizard.]

The strict difference between these endings is that **-saurus** indicates a systematic genus name, while **-saur** appears in Anglicized common names. For example, a *tyrannosaur* (Greek *turannos*, tyrant), a carnivorous dinosaur of the late Cretaceous period, is placed in the genus *Tyrannosaurus* (the species best known is actually *Tyrannosaurus rex*). However, it is common for the genus names to be used as common names, but with lower-case initial letter—for example, *brontosaurus* (Greek *brontē*, thunder) is more common than *brontosaur*.

The first such formation was *dinosaur* (Greek *deinos*, terrible) as a general name for the group. Many others exist, such as *ichthyosaur* (Greek *ikhthus*, fish), *mosasaur* (Latin *Mosa*, for the River Meuse near which it was discovered), *plesiosaur* (Greek *plēsios*, near), and *stegosaur* (Greek *stegē*, covering, referring to its bony back plates). All these, except dinosaur itself, have associated genus names ending in **-saurus** (*Ichthyosaurus*, *Stegosaurus*).

saur(o)- *Lizard.* [Greek *sauros*, lizard.]

An animal that is *saurian* is a lizard or like a lizard; as a noun, it refers to any large reptile, but especially a dinosaur or other extinct form; the *saurischians* (Greek *iskhion*, hip joint) are dinosaurs of an order distinguished by having a pelvic structure resembling that of lizards, of which an example is a *sauropod* (Greek *pous*, *pod-*, foot), a very large herbivorous dinosaur; a *sauropterygian* (Greek *pteron*, feather, wing) is one of various extinct aquatic reptiles of the Mesozoic Era.

-saurus: *see* -SAUR

-scape *A specified type of scene, or a representation of it.* [The ending of English *landscape*.]

This combining form is common and active, both to describe real scenes (*cityscape*, *streetscape*) and virtual or imaginary ones (*dreamscape*, *mindscape*). It is frequently employed to make casual formations, often used only once: *Californiascape*, *skyscraperscape*, *plotscape*. See the LIST below.

Escape does not belong here, being formed from Latin *ex-*, out, and *cappa*, cloak, figuratively to take off one's cloak, to throw off restraint.

scaph(o)- *Boat-shaped.* [Greek *skaphos*, boat.]

Scaphocephaly (Greek *kephalē*, head) is a congenital malformation of the head which gives it an unusually long and narrow shape; something *scaphoid* is boat-shaped (as a noun it is the name of a boat-shaped bone in the wrist); a *scaphopod* (Greek *pous*, *pod-*, foot) is a type of burrowing marine mollusc, which has a tusk-shaped shell with both ends open.

scapul(o)- *The shoulder blade.* [Latin *scapula*, shoulder blade.]

The adjective relating to the shoulder blade is *scapular*, which as a noun in ecclesiastial contexts refers to a short cloak covering the shoulders. Several medical terms refer to the shoulder blade plus another part of the body: *scapulohumeral*, the shoulder blade and the humerus, the bone of the upper arm; *scapulocoracoid*, the shoulder blade and the coracoid, the projection from the shoulder blade to which part of the biceps is attached. *Scapulimancy* (sometimes *scapulomancy*) (Greek *manteia*, divination) is divination from the cracks in a burned animal shoulder blade.

scato- *Dung or excrement.* [Greek *skōr*, *skat-*, dung.]

Scatology (adjective *scatological*) can refer to a scientific study of dung to determine, for example, an organism's diet, but more frequently is an interest in or obsession with excrement and excretion; an insect or other animal that is a *scatophage* (Greek *phagein*, eat) feeds on dung; *scatomancy* (Greek *manteia*, divination) is divination based on the examination of faeces.

schisto- *Fissure or split.* [Greek *skhizein*, to split.]

-scape A specified type of scene, or a representation of it.
Terms are based on English stems.

cityscape	the visual appearance of a city or urban area; a city landscape
cloudscape	a scene of clouds
dreamscape	a landscape or scene with the strangeness or mystery characteristic of dreams
interiorscape	the appearance of the inside of a building, especially in relation to interior design; a mental landscape
mediascape	the world as it appears in the broadcasting and print media, considered to be distorted from reality in some respect
mindscape	a mental view of one's surroundings
moonscape	a view of the surface of the Moon, or an area that resembles it in barrenness and desolation
nightscape	a night-time view, say of a city
soundscape	a piece of music considered in terms of its component sounds
streetscape	a view of streets, or an environment of streets, especially in an urban area
timescape	time considered as an unchanging analogue to landscape
townscape	the visual appearance of a town or urban area; an urban landscape
xeriscape	a style of landscape design requiring little or no irrigation or other maintenance, used in arid regions (Greek *xĕros*, dry)

The tropical disease *schistosomiasis*, also called bilharzia, is caused by a parasitic worm of the *Schistosoma* genus (Greek *sōma*, body, so 'divided body'), so called because the adults and young, *schistosomes*, are parasites on different organisms. *Schism*, a split or division between strongly opposed sections or parties, comes from the same Greek root, as does *schist*, a rock which can be split into thin irregular plates.

schiz(o)- *Divided or split.* [Greek *skhizein*, to split.]

The mental disorder *schizophrenia* (Greek *phrēn*, mind, so literally 'split mind') was called that because a part of the sufferer's psyche seems to be split off (the popular usage of *schizophrenic* for inconsistent attitudes is now regarded as misleading or offensive); a *schizotype* in psychiatry is a personality type in which mild symptoms of schizophrenia are present; somebody *schizoid* has a personality type characterized by emotional aloofness and solitary habits.

The form is used also in botany and biology: a *schizocarp* (Greek *karpos*, fruit) is a dry fruit that splits into single-seeded parts when ripe; *schizogony* (Greek *-gonia*, -begetting) is asexual reproduction by multiple fission in some protozoa; a *schizont* is a cell that divides by schizogony to form daughter cells.

scler(o)- *Hard; hardening.* [Greek *sklēros*, hard.]

Sclerosis is abnormal hardening of body tissue, as in *multiple sclerosis*, a disease involving damage to the sheaths of nerve cells; several compound terms exist, an example being *arteriosclerosis*, thickening and hardening of the walls of the arteries. A *scleroderma* (Greek *derma*, skin) is a chronic hardening and contraction of the skin and connective tissue; the *sclera* is the hard outer layer of the eyeball; *sclerotherapy* is treatment of varicose blood vessels using hardening chemicals.

A *scleroprotein* is an insoluble structural protein such as keratin, collagen, or elastin; a *sclerophyll* (Greek *phullon*, leaf) is a woody plant with evergreen leaves that are tough and thick in order to reduce

water loss; *sclerenchyma* (Greek *enkhuma*, infusion) is supporting or protective tissue composed of hardened cells, as in the skeletons of corals.

-scope Also **-scopic** and **-scopy**. *An instrument for observing, viewing, or examining something.* [Greek *skopein*, look at.]

This ending appears in the names of a wide variety of instruments in engineering, medicine, the sciences, and other fields, most containing the linking vowel -o- before the ending. All can have associated adjectives ending in **-scopic**, as in *spectroscopic* or *gyroscopic*. Many have a linked noun-ending in **-scopy** that describes an observation or examination made using the instrument: *laryngoscopy*, *endoscopy* (among those in which the **-scopy** form is rare are *kaleidoscope* and *periscope*, in which names do not represent a scientific instrument). In *horoscope*, the ending has a figurative sense. For more examples, see the LIST on the next page.

Scoto-¹ *Scotland or the Scots; Scotland and…* [Latin *Scōtus*, a Scot.]

Examples include *Scotophile*, someone fond of Scotland and the Scots, and *Scotophobia*, a hatred of Scotland and its people. When referring to an association or link between Scotland and another country the prefix is usually hyphenated, as in *Scoto-Irish* or *Scoto-Norwegian*.

scot(o)-² *Darkness.* [Greek *skotos*, darkness.]

This combining form is particularly associated with human vision, as in *scotopic*, relating to or denoting vision in dim light; and *scotoma*, a partial loss of vision or blind spot in an otherwise normal visual field. In biology or animal husbandry, a *scotophase* is an artificially induced period of darkness. *Scotophobia* is fear of the dark.

scyph(o)- Also **scyphi-**. *Cup-shaped.* [Greek *skuphos*, cup.]

The *Scyphozoa* are the marine jellyfishes, so named from their shape, and a *scyphozoan* is a member of that class; a *scyphistoma* (Greek *stoma*, mouth) is the polyp-like stage in the life cycle of a

-scope An instrument for observing, viewing, or examining something.
Word origins are from Greek unless otherwise stated.

endoscope	an instrument which can be introduced into the body to give a view of its internal parts	(*endon*, within)
gyroscope	a device consisting of a fast-spinning wheel on supports, often used as a compass or to give stability	(*guros*, a ring)
horoscope	a forecast of a person's future based on the positions of the stars and planets at the time of his or her birth	(*hōra*, time)
kaleidoscope	a toy consisting of a tube containing mirrors and pieces of coloured glass or paper	(*kalos*, beautiful, plus *eidos*, form)
laparoscope	a fibre optic instrument which is inserted through the abdominal wall to view the organs in the abdomen or permit small-scale surgery	(*lapara*, flank)
microscope	an optical instrument used for viewing very small objects	(*mikros*, small)
ophthalmoscope	an instrument for inspecting the retina and other parts of the eye	(*ophthalmos*, eye)
oscilloscope	a device for viewing oscillations by a display on the screen of a cathode ray tube	(English *oscillation*)
otoscope	an instrument designed for visual examination of the eardrum and the passage of the outer ear	(*ous*, ōt-, ear)
periscope	a device, as in a submarine, which uses mirrors to observe a scene otherwise out of sight	(*peri*, about, around)
spectroscope	an apparatus for producing and recording spectra for examination	(English *spectrum*)
stethoscope	a medical instrument for listening to the action of someone's heart or breathing	(*stēthos*, breast)
stroboscope	an instrument for apparently stopping movement by shining a bright light at intervals	(*strobos*, whirling)
telescope	an optical instrument designed to make distant objects appear nearer	(*tēle-*, far off)

jellyfish, while a *scyphomedusa* is its medusoid phase. A *scyphus* (plural *scyphi*) is a cup-shaped part, say of a flower; something *scyphate* is cup-shaped.

se- *Apart; without.* [Latin *se, sed*.]
This prefix is not a living one in English, but occurs in a variety of words imported from Latin, most of them verbs, as in **separate** (*parare*, prepare), **secede** (*cedere*, go), **seclude** (*claudere*, to shut), **segregate** (*grex*, flock), **secrete** (*cernere*, to sift), **select** (*legere*, choose), **seduce** (*ducere*, to lead).

seb(o)- *Oil, fat, or grease.* [Latin *sebum*, grease, tallow.]
Sebum is the medical term for an oily secretion from the **sebaceous** glands in the skin; the latter word can also be an adjective referring more generally to oil or fat; **seborrhoea** (US **seborrhea**) (Greek *rhoia*, flow or flux) is excessive discharge of sebum from the sebaceous glands; **sebacic acid** is a white crystalline solid made from castor oil, used to produce candles, lubricants, and plasticizers.

-sect *Divided or cut.* [Latin *sect-*, from *secare*, to cut.]

A *transect* (Latin *trans*, across) is a straight line or thin section through an object or natural feature; to *intersect* (Latin *inter-*, between) is to divide something by passing or lying across it. An *insect* (Latin *in-*, into, hence 'in parts') is named from the threefold form of its body.

To *dissect* something is to cut it up in order to examine it closely (Latin *dis-*, apart); a surgeon may *resect* or remove a small piece of tissue or part of an organ, literally 'cut it back'. The verbs *bisect* (Latin *bi-*, having two) and *trisect* (Latin *tres*, three) refer to dividing an object into parts.

A *sect*, a group having different beliefs from those of a larger group to which it belongs, derives instead from Latin *secta*, a following (from *sequi*, to follow); to *vivisect* (Latin *vivus*, living), to perform operations on live animals for scientific research, is formed from *vivisection*.

seism(o)- *An earthquake.* [Greek *seismos*, earthquake.]

Seismology is the branch of science concerned with earthquakes and related phenomena; the adjective relating to earthquakes is *seismic*; a *seismograph* is an instrument that measures and records earthquakes; the *seismicity* of a region is the extent to which earthquakes occur there; a *seismosaurus* was a huge late Jurassic dinosaur (so named because it was so big it must have shaken the earth when it walked).

selen(o)-¹ *The moon.* [Greek *selēnē*, moon.]

Selenography is lunar geography; *selenology* is the scientific study of the moon; something *selenocentric* has the moon as its centre; *selenodesy* (Greek *daiein*, to divide) is the branch of mathematics dealing with the shape and area of the moon or large parts of it, the lunar equivalent of geodesy; *selenite* is either a colourless and transparent crystalline form of gypsum (so called because it was thought to wax and wane with the moon), or a supposed inhabitant of the moon (but *see* SELENO-²); molar teeth that are *selenodont* have crescent-shaped

ridges on the grinding surfaces, characteristic of ruminants.

selen(o)-² Also **seleni-**. *Selenium.* [English *selenium*.]

The non-metal *selenium*, related to sulphur, was named by its discoverer Berzelius (1779–1848) after the moon (*see* SELENO-¹) to indicate how close its properties are to those of tellurium (Latin *tellus*, *tellur-*, earth). The lower combining power of selenium, divalent or tetravalent, is referred to as the *selenous* or *selenious* form (as in *selenious acid*, H_2SeO_3, whose salts are *selenites*, such as *sodium selenite*, a dietary supplement providing selenium), while the hexavalent form is termed *selenic* (as in *selenic acid*, H_2SeO_4, analogous to sulphuric acid, whose compounds are *selenates*). The compound *selenomethionine* is a marker used in nuclear medicine for detecting tumours.

self- *Oneself, itself.* [Old English *self*.]

Many words incorporating **self-** exist in English, nearly all of them hyphenated. They fall into two broad groups, though the boundary between them is indistinct.

One group has the sense of some action or condition by, for, or in relation to the agent: *self-adhesive*, *self-appointed*, *self-assembly*, *self-defence*, *self-hatred*, *self-pity*, *self-propelled*, *self-respect*, *self-service*.

The other group has a sense of acting automatically or autonomously, by itself or oneself: *self-sealing*, *self-acting*, *self-closing*, *self-fulfilling*, *self-regulating*, *self-starting*.

semi- *Half; a part.* [Latin *semi-*, half.]

The strict sense of a half occurs only in a minority of words, of which examples are *semicircle*; *semidiameter*; *semilunar*, shaped like a half-moon or crescent; and *semiquaver*, in British musical terminology a note having the time value of half a quaver, a sixteenth note. A few terms extend the idea to that of occurring twice in some time period, as in *semi-annual*, occurring twice a year (nominally every half year), and the North American *semi-monthly*, occurring or published twice a month (or every half month). A related idea occurs in *semi-final*, a match or round immediately preceding the final, the 'half-final'.

Most terms in the prefix, however, signal that something is partially or incompletely so: *semi-professional*, *semi-conscious*, *semi-retired*, *semi-literate*, *semi-skilled*, *semi-derelict*, *semiprecious*, *semiconducting* (of a substance that has a conductivity between that of an insulator and that of most metals), and *semipermeable* (of a material or membrane that allows certain substances to pass through it but not others).

semio- Also **semeio-** and **semo-**. *Sign; communication.* [Greek *sēmeion*, sign.]

The key term here is *semiotics* (also *semiology*; less commonly *semeiotics* or *semology*), the study of signs and symbols and their interpretation or use, of which a practitioner is a *semiotician*; *semiosis* is the process of conveying meaning in language or literature; a *semiochemical* is a pheromone or other chemical that conveys a signal from one organism to another. Closely related is *semantic*, relating to meaning in language or logic.

-sepalous *Having sepals of a given type.* [English *sepal* plus -OUS] .

Words formed using this ending are specialist terms in botany: *gamosepalous* (Greek *gamos*, marriage), less commonly *synsepalous* (Greek *sun*, with), having the sepals united; *polysepalous* (Greek *polloi*, many), having a calyx of separate sepals; *oppositisepalous*, of a plant feature situated opposite a sepal.

sept(i)- *Seven.* [Latin *septem*, seven.]

A *septet* is a group of seven people playing music or singing together; *septuplets* are seven children born at one birth. A *septcentenary* is the seven-hundredth anniversary of a significant event; *septennial* can refer to some event recurring every seven years, or to a period of seven years; as a noun *septenary* is a group or set of seven, but as an adjective it refers to something divided into seven. *September* was originally the seventh month of the Roman calendar. For *septillion* see the table of NUMBER WORDS on page 162.

Related words are formed from Latin *septuaginta*, seventy: *septuagenarian*, a person in his or her seventies; *Septuagesima* (literally 'seventieth day'), the third Sunday before Lent and the seventieth day before Easter Sunday; the *Septuagint* is the Greek Old Testament, traditionally attributed to 72 translators working under divine inspiration.

See also HEPTA-.

Words such as *septicaemia* and *septic* come instead from the Greek *sēptikos*, rotten or decayed.

Serbo- *Serbian; Serbian and ...* [English *Serbia*, plus -o-.]

The most common terms here are *Serbo-Croat* and *Serbo-Croatian*, relating to Serbia and Croatia or their common language. Other examples refer to Serbia plus another country: *Serbo-Albanian*, *Serbo-Bulgarian*, *Serbo-Greek*.

seric- Also **seri-**. *Silk.* [Latin *sericum*, silk.]

The production of raw silk by breeding silkworms is *sericulture*, carried out by *sericulturists*; something *sericeous* is silky or covered in fine hairs; *sericin* is a gelatinous protein found in silk; *sericite* is a fine-grained fibrous white mica with a silky lustre. The combining form is irregularly abbreviated to **seri-** in *serigraphy*, a silk-screening process that produces a *serigraph*, and in *serine*, an amino acid found in most proteins, which was first obtained from silk.

sero- *Serum; a serous membrane.* [Latin *serum*, whey.]

Serum is the amber-coloured, protein-rich liquid which separates out when blood coagulates, for which the associated adjective is *serous*; *serology* is its scientific study or diagnostic examination. A *seropositive* individual has a positive result in a test of blood serum, say for the presence of a virus, while someone *seronegative* tests negative; *seroconversion* is the change from the latter state to the former. The *seroprevalence* of a pathogen is its level in a population, as measured in blood serum. *Serotonin* is a neurotransmitter present in blood platelets and serum.

sesqui- *One and one half.* [Latin *semi-*, a half, plus *que*, and.]

A *sesquicentenary* is the one hundred and fiftieth anniversary of a significant event; a *sesquialtera* (Latin *alter*, second) in music denotes a ratio of 3:2, as in an interval of a fifth. A *sesquioxide* is one in which oxygen is present in the ratio of three atoms to two of another element, as for example aluminium oxide, Al_2O_3; a *sesquiterpene* is a member of the terpene family of volatile unsaturated hydrocarbons found in essential oils that has one and a half times as many carbon atoms (15) as a terpene (10). A *sesquipedalian* word (Latin *sesquipedalis*, a foot and a half long) has many syllables; the adjective also describes somebody long-winded or who uses long words.

seti- Also **seta-**. *A bristle.* [Latin *seta*, bristle.]

A *seta* (plural *setae*) is a stiff hair-like or bristle-like structure in an invertebrate, or a stalk supporting the capsule in a moss or liverwort; the adjective is *setaceous*. Something *setose* (less often *setiferous* or *setigerous*) bears bristles. *See also* CHAETO-.

sex(i)- *Six.* [Latin *sex*, six.]

A *sextet* is a group of six people playing music or singing together; *sextuplets* are a set of six children born at one birth; a *sexcentenary* is the six-hundredth anniversary of a significant event; a *sexennial* is an event recurring every six years, or a period of six years; something *sextuple* consists of six parts or things; For *sextillion*, see the table of NUMBER WORDS on page 162. A *sextant*, used for taking altitudes in navigation and surveying, is so named because the measuring arc covers one-sixth of a full circle.

Related words are formed from Latin *sexaginta*, sixty: *sexagesimal* refers to reckoning by sixtieths or a number base of sixty, which survives in angular measurement and in hours and minutes; a *sexagenarian* is a person in his or her sixties; *Sexagesima* (literally 'sixtieth day') is the second Sunday before Lent.

-ship *Forming abstract nouns.* [Old English *-scipe*, *-scype*, related to *shape*.]

This ending is broadly applied and active in the language.

It can denote a quality, condition, or state: *censorship*, *courtship*, *companionship*, *friendship*, *hardship*, *relationship*, *worship*. It can signify status, office, rank, or honour: *ambassadorship*, *citizenship*, *lordship*, *kingship*; this sense overlaps somewhat with the idea of a period or tenure of office, or the office itself: *chairmanship*, *dictatorship*, *directorship*, *headship*, *internship*, *partnership*, *professorship*. A further group indicates a skill in a certain capacity: *authorship*, *curatorship*, *entrepreneurship*, *musicianship*; many terms with this meaning end in -MANSHIP. Some examples denote the collective individuals of a group: *membership*, *readership* (and the more recent *viewership* and *listenership*); however, *township*, originally indicating the inhabitants of a town, now usually refers to an area where people live. Other terms ending in *ship* are compounds of various senses of the word *ship*: *airship*, *midships*, *trans-ship*, *warship*.

sial(o)- Also **siala-**. *Saliva; salivary gland.* [Greek *sialon*, saliva.]

A *sialagogue* (Greek *agōgos*, eliciting) is a drug that promotes the secretion of saliva; *sialorrhoea* (US *sialorrhea*) (Greek *rhoia*, flow, flux) is excessive production of saliva; a *sialolith* (Greek *lithos*, stone) is a calculus, a stony accretion, formed in a salivary gland or duct; *sialography* is radiographic examination of a salivary gland; *sialadenitis* is an inflammation in a salivary gland; *sialic acid* is a substance present in saliva. *See also* PTYALO-.

sider(o)- *Iron.* [Greek *sidēros*, iron.]

A *siderophore* is a molecule in microorganisms which binds and transports iron; a *sideroblast* is an iron-rich red blood cell in the bone marrow; a *siderophile* is something that has an affinity for iron; *sideropenia* is iron deficiency in the body; *siderosis* is a deposition of iron in the lungs, an occupational disease of arc welders; *siderite* is either an ore of iron, or a meteorite consisting mostly of nickel and iron.

A few terms contain instead Latin *sidus*, *sider-*, a star: a *siderostat* is an instrument used for keeping the image of a celestial object in a fixed position; a *siderograph* is a chart of planetary positions used in financial astrology, and *sidereal* is the adjective referring to the stars, as opposed to the sun or planets.

silic(o)- Also **silici-** and **sil-**. *Silicon.* [Latin *silex*, *silic-*, flint.]

Flint is composed of *silica*, silicon dioxide; rocks rich in silica are said to be *silicic*, while those termed *siliciclastic* are broken pieces of older rocks consisting largely of silica. *Silicosis* is a lung disease caused by the inhalation of dust containing silica. A *silicone* is one of a class of synthetic materials which are polymers with a chemical structure based on chains of alternate silicon and oxygen atoms, for which a general name is *siloxane*; a *silicate* is a salt that contains both silicon and oxygen, especially the anion SiO_4^{2-}. A *silane* is a member of the group of silicon halides; *silex* is a heat-resistant glass or brick formed of fused quartz.

sinistr(o)- *Left; the left side; left-handed.* [Latin *sinister*, left.]

Some examples: *sinistral*, of or on the left side or the left hand; the associated abstract noun *sinistrality* often refers specifically to left-handedness; *sinistrorse* (Latin *sinistrorsus*, from *vertere*, to turn), turned or spiralling upwards towards the left like a left-hand thread, or a spiral stair, or a plant curling anticlockwise around a support. The adjective *sinister*, suggestive of impending evil or harm, comes from the idea that something left-handed is inauspicious or unlucky (in heraldry it literally means 'on the left-hand side'). See also DEXTRO-.

sin(o)-[1] Also **sinu-**. *A sinus.* [Latin *sinus*, a curve, bend, or cavity.]

A *sinus* is a cavity within a bone or other tissue; the *sinoatrial node* is a small group of cells in the wall of the right atrium of the heart that acts as a pacemaker; *sinusitis* is inflammation of the sinuses of the face. A *sinusoid* is either a small blood vessel in certain organs, especially the liver, or a curve having the form of a *sine* wave; the name of that trigonometric function comes from the large circle used to calculate its values, the *sinus totus*, the 'complete curve'. Something *sinuous* has many curves and turns.

Sino-[2] *Chinese; China and …* [Greek *Sinai*, the Chinese.]

Sinology is the study of Chinese language, history, customs, and politics (undertaken by a *Sinologist*); *Sinophobia* is a dread or dislike of China and things Chinese. Hyphenated terms usually refer to China in relation to another country: *Sino-Japanese*, *Sino-Soviet*, *Sino-American*. However, *Sino-Tibetan* refers to a large language family which includes Chinese, Burmese, Tibetan, and others from eastern Asia.

-sion: *see* -ION

siphon(o)- *Siphon.* [Greek *siphōn*, pipe.]

The *siphonapterans* are members of an order of insects with sucking mouth parts, comprising the fleas (the name literally means 'wingless pipe', from Greek *apteros*, wingless); *siphonophores* (Greek *pherein*, to bear) are members of an order of colonial marine coelenterates that includes the Portuguese man-of-war; a *siphonostele* is a type of plant whose stems contain a hollow tube of tissue. *Siphuncle*, a tube connecting the chambers of a nautilus, is from the Latin diminutive *siphunculus*, a small tube, rather than from Greek.

-sis: *see* -OSIS

sito- Also **sitio-**. *Food.* [Greek *sitos*, diminutive of *sition*, grain, food.]

Sitology is another name for dietetics, the branch of medicine dealing with nutrition; *sitosterol* is a mixture of sterol derivatives found in plants, especially wheat germ, said to be useful as a dietary supplement to reduce cholesterol levels in the body; *sitiophobia* (less often *sitophobia*) is a morbid aversion to food.

Slavo- *Slavs; Slavonic languages in relation to others.* [Medieval Latin *Sclavus*.]

This form is uncommon. An example is *Slavophile*, someone favourable or friendly to Slavs. Hyphenated examples usually refer to the Slavonic language group in connection with another language or language group, such as *Slavo-Germanic* or *Slavo-Lithuanian*. The Latin root is also the source of *slave*, since Slav peoples had been reduced to that status in the ninth century.

-smith *A skilled worker with a specified material.* [English *smith*.]

Several examples mark a person who works with a metal: *goldsmith*, *silversmith*, *coppersmith*, *tinsmith*. A *blacksmith* works in iron, the black metal, as opposed to a *whitesmith*, who works in tin, the white metal. The ending can also indicate someone skilled with types of articles: *gunsmith*, *locksmith*. Other examples, originally jocular but increasingly accepted as standard terms, indicate a skill in music or writing: *wordsmith*, *songsmith*, *tunesmith*, *jokesmith*.

-soever *Of any kind; to any extent.* [Middle English: originally as the phrase *so ever*.]

The only word containing that is at all common is *whatsoever*, now usually combined with a negative to indicate an emphatic sense of 'nothing at all' (*I have no doubt whatsoever*). Others are either archaic (*whichsoever*, *whithersoever*) or very formal (*howsoever*, *whomsoever*). Several have been replaced by shorter forms (*whoever* is usually preferred to *whosoever*, *whenever* to *whensoever*, *wherever* to *wheresoever*) except in very formal situations.

-sol *Soil.* [Latin *solum*, soil.]

This ending forms specialist names for soil types. Examples are *vertisol* (from *vertical*), a clayey soil that forms deep vertical cracks on drying; *palaeosol* (US *paleosol*), a stratum or soil horizon which was formed as a soil in a past geological age (Greek *palaios*, ancient); and *mollisol*, a soil of temperate grassland with a dark, humus-rich surface layer (Latin *mollis*, soft). One common term of this type, *podzol*, an infertile acidic soil with an ash-like leached subsurface layer, actually derives from Russian (*pod*,

under, plus *zola* ashes), but is often spelled *podsol* to match the others.

Other words ending in **-sol** come from several sources: in *aerosol*, *cytosol*, *hydrosol*, and *plastisol* the ending is the word *sol* (from the first element of *solution*), indicating a fluid suspension of a colloidal solid in a liquid; in *cortisol* and *creosol* it is really -OL, but happens to be preceded by *s*; in *parasol* the last element is Latin *sol*, sun.

somat(o)- *The body.* [Greek *sōma*, *sōmat-*, body.]

The Greek word *soma* is used in English to refer to the parts of an organism other than the reproductive or germ cells, or to the body as opposed to the mind; the adjective in both senses is *somatic* (as in *psychosomatic*, of an illness caused or aggravated by a mental factor such as internal conflict or stress). *Somatoform* disorders are those in which there is a history of physical complaints without any physical basis; in psychiatry, *somatization* refers to the production of recurrent and multiple medical symptoms with no discernible organic cause; a *somatosensory* sensation such as touch can occur anywhere in the body, in contrast to one localized at a sense organ, like sight. A *somatotype* is a category to which people are assigned according to their body type. *See also* -SOME³.

-some¹ *Forming adjectives.* [Old English *-sum*.]

Adjectives variously derive from nouns, adjectives, and verbs. They can suggest something having the character of the stem (*adventuresome*, *quarrelsome*, *wholesome*), or inducing the state suggested by it (*awesome*, *bothersome*, *fearsome*, *flavoursome*, *irksome*, *tiresome*, *troublesome*). The sense of a few is disguised because the stem is no longer current or the adjective has shifted sense: *cumbersome*, unwieldy, comes from *cumber*, a hindrance, obstruction, or burden; *handsome* from *hand*, so originally meant something easy to handle or use. The ending is often used to form words of only momentary usefulness; these frequently imply some stimulus inducing a response: *barfsome*, *cringesome*, *swoonsome*.

-some² *A group of a specified number.* [Old English *sum*, some.]

Examples are *twosome*, *threesome*, *foursome*, and *eightsome*, (in all of which the ending is pronounced /səm/). Particularly in American English, the ending can be added to larger numbers to suggest 'approximately': *twenty-some*, *forty-some*, as in *fifty-some people were there*. In these cases, the suffix is said as though it were a separate word: /sʌm/. *See also* -SOMETHING.

-some³ *Also* **-somal**. *A part of a body, especially a cell.* [Greek *sōma*, body.]

Examples include *chromosome*, *liposome*, and *ribosome*. For details and more examples, see the LIST below. Related adjectives are usually formed

ending in **-somal**: *chromosomal*, *ribosomal*.

-something *A person whose age falls into a given decade.* [English *something*.]

Originally in American English (especially following a television series of the late 1980s called *Thirtysomethings*), and then more widely, this ending has been adopted to create nouns and adjectives that indicate a person whose age falls into a given decade: *twentysomething*, *thirtysomething*, *fortysomething*. These are usually written without a hyphen.

somn(i)- *Sleep.* [Latin *somnus*, sleep.]

A *somnambulist* is a sleepwalker (Latin *ambulare*, to walk), for which the associated noun is *somnambulism*; in medicine, a *somnifacient* is a drug that induces sleep or drowsiness; something *somniferous* tends to induce sleep; *somnolent* can

-some³	A part of a body, especially a cell. *All word origins are from Greek unless otherwise stated.*	
autosome	any chromosome that is not a sex chromosome	(*autos*, self)
centrosome	an organelle near the nucleus of a cell which contains the centrioles	(English *centre*)
chromosome	thread-like structures in the nucleus of cells that carry genetic information, so named because the threads can be stained with dyes for easier viewing under a microscope	(*khrōma*, colour)
liposome	a minute spherical sac of fat molecules enclosing a water droplet, especially one formed artificially to carry drugs or other substances into the tissues	(*lipos*, fat)
lysosome	a structure in some cells containing enzymes enclosed in a membrane that degrades waste material	(*lusis*, loosening)
nucleosome	a structural unit of a chromosome in a cell nucleus	(English *nucleus*)
phagosome	a structure in the cytoplasm of a cell that has enclosed an invading cell or particle prior to destruction by lysosomes	(*phago-*, eating)
ribosome	a minute particle consisting of RNA and associated proteins found in large numbers in the cytoplasm of living cells	(English *ribose*)
schistosome	a parasitic flatworm which needs two hosts to complete its life cycle	(*skhistos*, divided)
trypanosome	a single-celled parasitic protozoan with a trailing flagellum, infesting the blood	(*trupanon*, borer)

refer to a person who is sleepy or drowsy or to something inducing drowsiness.

son(o)- Also **soni-**. Sound. [Latin *sonus*, sound.]

Sonography is the analysis of sound into its component frequencies; it can also be a shortened form of *ultrasonography*, in which ultrasound is used to image an internal body structure or a developing foetus. A *sonobuoy* is a buoy equipped to detect underwater sounds and transmit them by radio; *sonoluminescence* is luminescence excited by the passage of sound waves; a biological sample is *sonicated* when it is subjected to ultrasonic vibration to fragment its parts. Something *sonorous* is capable of producing a deep or ringing sound. The usual adjective relating to sound is *sonic*; *sonics* is the study of sound waves.

-sophy A system of thought. [Greek *sophia*, skill or wisdom.]

The most common word with this ending is *philosophy* (Greek *philos*, loving, hence 'love of wisdom'), the study of the fundamental nature of knowledge, reality, and existence. Others are *theosophy* (Greek *theos*, god), any of a number of philosophies maintaining that a knowledge of God may be achieved through special individual relations; and *anthroposophy* (Greek *anthrōpos*, human being), a system established by Rudolf Steiner that seeks to use mainly natural means to optimize physical and mental health and well-being. Such words form related adjectives ending in *-sophic* (*theosophic*) or *-sophical* (*philosophical*), and adverbs ending in *-sophically* (*anthroposophically*).

-sory: *see* -ORY[1] and -ORY[2].

sous- Subordinate; beneath. [French *sous*, under.]

This prefix occurs hyphenated in words borrowed from French: *sous-chef*, *sous-préfecture*, *sous-lieutenant*, *sous-entendu* (literally 'under-heard', something not said but left to be understood). The French word appears in *sous vide*, used in food science for foodstuffs that are vacuum packed prior to pasteurization.

spasmo- A spasm. [Greek *spasmos*, *spasma*, from *span*, pull.]

In medicine, a *spasmolytic* (Greek *lusis*, loosening) is a drug that relieves spasms of smooth muscle; a *spasmogen* is a substance that can produce smooth muscle contractions; *spasmophilia* is an undue tendency of the muscles to contract. The usual adjective relating to spasms is *spasmodic*, which also has a general sense of something that happens intermittently.

-speak A manner of speaking. [English *speak*.]

This combining form grew out of *Newspeak*, a language described in George Orwell's book *Nineteen Eighty-four*; with lower-case initial that word now refers more generally to ambiguous euphemistic language in political propaganda. *Doublespeak*, to say one thing but mean another, was drawn from the use of *doublethink* in the book, and *oldspeak*, normal English usage as opposed to technical or propagandist language, was coined as a humorous inversion of *Newspeak*. Other examples invented on their model to indicate the language or special vocabulary of a group include *Eurospeak*, jargon in European Union documents or statements; *technospeak*, incomprehensible technical jargon (and *computerspeak*, specifically the technical jargon of computing); *teenspeak*, the language and way of speaking of teenagers; *Airspeak* and *Seaspeak*, formal languages used by pilots and sailors respectively to limit the risk of misunderstanding; and *upspeak*, a tendency to end statements with a raised inflection as though asking a question. The form is active in the language and some short-lived formations employ it: *customerspeak*, *mobspeak*, *therapyspeak*.

spectr(o)- Spectrum. [French *spectre* or Latin *spectrum*, image or apparition.]

A *spectrum* (plural *spectra*) is an arrangement of the components of a complex light or sound source in order of frequency or energy. Most terms beginning with **spectro-** refer to electromagnetic radiation (visible light, X-rays, radio waves, etc); the usual adjective relating to spectra is *spectral* (but see below). *Spectroscopy* is the branch of science concerned with the study of spectra; *spectroscope* is a general term for an instrument used in that work (others are *spectrograph* and *spectrometer*); a *spectrophotometer* measures the intensity of light in a part of the spectrum, especially as transmitted or emitted by particular substances.

Rarely, the combining form can refer to *spectres* (US *specters*), ghosts or apparitions, to which the adjective *spectral* can also be applied; for example, *spectrology* is the study of ghosts.

-sperm *Seed.* [Greek *sperma*, seed.]

Seed-bearing plants are divided into two groups, the *gymnosperms* (Greek *gumnos*, naked), whose seeds are unprotected by an ovary or fruit, and the *angiosperms* (Greek *angeion*, vessel), a much larger group that has flowers and seeds enclosed within a carpel. Other botanical terms with this ending include *endosperm* (Greek *endon*, within), the part of a seed which acts as a food store for the developing plant embryo, and *perisperm* (Greek *peri*, about, around), a mass of nutritive material in some seeds that lies outside the embryo sac. The *pteridosperms* (Greek *pteris*, *pterid-*, fern) are a type of fossil plants intermediate between the ferns and seed-bearing plants, which died out in the Triassic period.

spermat(o)- Also **sperm(a)-**, **spermi(o)-**, and **spermo-**. *Semen or sperm.* [Greek *sperma*, *spermat-*, seed.]

The **spermio-** and **spermo-** forms are irregularly created from the Greek original, and most terms containing them have been replaced by equivalents with **spermato-**.

Semen is the male reproductive fluid; in suspension it contains *spermatozoa* (singular *spermatozoon*) (Greek *zōion*, animal), the mature motile male sex cells (the term is often abbreviated to *sperm*). A *spermicide* is a substance that kills spermatozoa, used as a contraceptive; the adjective *spermatic* relates to sperm or semen.

In biology, including human biology, a *spermatogonium* is a primitive germ cell that gives rise to *spermatocytes*, which divide into *spermatids* and mature into spermatozoa through *spermiogenesis*; the whole process is called *spermatogenesis*. In botany, a *spermatophyte* (Greek *phuton*, a plant) is a plant that bears seeds, including the gymnosperms and angiosperms.

The white waxy substance produced by the sperm whale, *spermaceti* (Greek *kētos*, whale), was given that name from the belief that it was whale sperm.

sphaero-: *see* SPHERO-

sphen(o)- *Wedge-shaped.* [Greek *sphēn*, wedge.]

The *sphenoid bone* (frequently abbreviated to *sphenoid*) forms the base of the cranium behind the eyes; **spheno-** is used in medicine to refer to this bone together with another part of the skull: *sphenopalatine*, the sphenoid plus the palate; *sphenoethmoid*, the sphenoid plus the ethmoid, a square bone at the root of the nose.

Outside medicine, *sphenoid* is a general adjective to describe something wedge-shaped; the *Sphenopsida* is a class of plants including the horsetails (Greek *opsis*, appearance); *sphene* is a mineral that occurs in wedge-shaped crystals; a *sphenogram* is a rather rare term for a wedge-shaped cuneiform character.

-sphere *A broadly spherical object or region.* [English *sphere*, derived from Greek *sphaira*, ball.]

The larger proportion of common words ending in **-sphere** refer to the Earth, such as *atmosphere* or *biosphere*. Several others refer to regions of a star, such as *photosphere*. Others are general terms relating to a spherical object or region: *hemisphere*. For more details and additional examples, see the LIST opposite. Adjectives are formed either with *-speric* (*atmospheric*, *ionospheric*), or less commonly with *-spherical* (*hemispherical*).

spher(o)- Also **sphaero-**. *A sphere; spherical.* [Greek *sphaira*, ball.]

-sphere	A broadly spherical object or region. *Word origins are from Greek unless otherwise stated.*	
atmosphere	the envelope of gases surrounding the earth or another planet	(*atmos*, vapour)
biosphere	the regions of the surface and atmosphere of the earth or another planet occupied by living organisms	(*bios*, life)
hemisphere	a half of a sphere	(*hĕmi-*, half)
ionosphere	the layer of the earth's atmosphere which contains a high concentration of ions and free electrons and is able to reflect radio waves	(English *ion*)
lithosphere	the rigid outer part of the earth, consisting of the crust and upper mantle	(*lithos*, stone)
magnetosphere	the region surrounding the earth or another astronomical body in which its magnetic field is the predominant one	(English *magnet*)
photosphere	the luminous envelope of a star from which its light and heat radiate	(*phōs*, *phōt-*, light)
stratosphere	the layer of the earth's atmosphere above the troposphere, extending to about 50 km above the earth's surface	(Latin *stratus*, strewn)
troposphere	the lowest region of the atmosphere, extending from the earth's surface to a height of about 6–10 km	(*tropos*, turning)

A *spherometer* is an instrument for measuring the curvature of spheres and curved surfaces; something *spheroid* is a sphere-like but not perfectly spherical body; a *spheroplast* is a bacterium or plant cell bound by its plasma membrane. A related term is *spherule*, a small sphere (Latin *sphaerula*, a diminutive of Latin *sphaera*, sphere), from which comes *spherulite*, a small spheroidal mass of crystals, grouped radially around a point, found in obsidian and other glassy rocks. The spelling **sphaero-** is the older one, now almost entirely replaced by **sphero-**.

sphingo- *Compounds isolated from the brain and nervous tissue.* [Greek *Sphinx*, *Sphing-*, Sphinx (a monster in Greek mythology that set people riddles, killing those who could not answer them), originally in the name of the compound *sphingosine*, with reference to its enigmatic nature.]

Sphingosine is a constituent of a number of substances important in the metabolism of nerve cells, especially *sphingomyelins*, which occur widely in brain and nervous tissue; *sphingolipids* are members of a class of compounds which are fatty acid derivatives of sphingosine and occur chiefly in the cell membranes of the brain and nervous tissue.

sphygm(o)- *The pulse.* [Greek *sphugmos*, pulse.]

A *sphygmomanometer* is the standard doctor's instrument for measuring blood pressure by means of an inflatable cuff around the arm linked to some type of pressure gauge or *manometer*; a *sphygmograph* is an instrument which produces a line, on a *sphygmogram*, recording the strength and rate of a person's pulse.

spin(i)- Also **spino-**. *Thorn or spine; the spine or spinal cord.* [Latin *spina*, thorn.]

A plant or animal that is *spinose* or *spinous* has spines or thorns; something *spiniform* has the shape of a spine. The grass called *spinifex* (Latin *-fex*, from *facere*, to make) has that name because it produces spiny flower heads.

In medicine, **spino-** can refer to the spine (itself so named because it has blunt projections on each vertebra) in connection with another part of the body, as in *spinocerebellar*, the spine and cerebellum, or *spinothalamic*, the spine and the thalamus. The Latin original occasionally appears as a formal word for the spine, especially in *spina bifida*, a congenital malformation in which one or more vertebrae fail to close fully over the meninges of the spinal cord.

spir(o)-¹ *Spiral; coiled.* [Latin *spira*, Greek *speira*, a coil.]

This occurs in a number of names for organisms: a *spirochaete* (US *spirochete*) (Greek *khaitē*, long hair) is a spirally twisted bacterium, especially one that causes syphilis; a *spirogyra* (Greek *gura*, round) is a green alga that contains chlorophyll in spiral bands; the shrub called the *spiraea* is so named from its coiled fruits; *spirillum* is a bacterium with a rigid spiral structure; *spirulina* (Latin *spirula*, small spiral) is filamentous cyanobacteria which form tangled masses, so called from their corkscrew shape.

spir(o)-² *The breath; breathing.* [Latin *spirare*, to breathe.]

A *spirograph* is an instrument for recording breathing movements, as is a *spirometer*, both of which record their results on *spirograms*; the process of investigation is called *spirometry*. (*Spirograph* is also the name given to a toy for drawing intricate curved patterns, from SPIRO-¹.) In zoology, a *spiracle* is an external respiratory opening, for example on an insect.

splanchn(o)- *The viscera; intestines.* [Greek *splankhna*, entrails.]

The adjective *splanchnic* refers to the viscera or internal organs, especially those of the abdomen; *splanchnology* is the scientific study of the viscera and its organs; the *splanchnocranium* comprises those bones and cartilages of the head and face that are derived from visceral arch elements. A *splanchnopleure* (Greek *pleura*, side) is a layer of tissue in a vertebrate embryo, which gives rise to the gut, lungs, and yolk sac.

splen(o)- *The spleen.* [Greek *splēn*, spleen.]

A *splenectomy* (Greek *ektomē*, excision) is a surgical operation to remove the spleen; *splenitis* is inflammation of it; *splenomegaly* (Greek *megas*, *megal-*, great) is abnormal enlargement of it. The adjective is *splenic*. A person may be *splenetic*, bad-tempered or spiteful, a term which derives from the belief once held that such behaviour was caused by a diseased spleen.

The *splenius*, any of two pairs of muscles attached to the vertebrae in the neck and upper back which draw back the head, derives its name instead from Greek *splēnion*, a bandage, because of the way it appears to wrap around the back of the head. Words such as *splendid* and *splendour* come instead from Latin *splendere*, to shine, be bright.

spondyl(o)- *A vertebra.* [Latin *spondylus*, vertebra, from Greek *spondulos*.]

Spondylitis is inflammation of the joints of the backbone (*ankylosing spondylitis* is a form of spinal arthritis); *spondylosis* is a painful condition of the spine resulting from the degeneration of the discs in the joints between the vertebrae; *spondylolisthesis* (Greek *olisthēsis*, slipping) is the forward displacement of a vertebra relative to the one below it; *spondylosyndesis* (Greek *syn-*, together, plus *desis*, binding) is the fusion of the joints between the vertebrae by surgery; a *spondylopathy* (Greek *patheia*, suffering, feeling), refers in general to a disorder of the spine.

spongi(o)- Also **spongo-**. *A sponge; sponge-like.* [Latin *spongia*, from Greek.]

Something *spongiform* has a porous structure or consistency resembling that of a sponge, as in *bovine spongiform encephalitis* (BSE or *mad cow disease*), a neural disease which renders the brain spongy. A *spongioblastoma* (also called a *glioblastoma*) is a kind of spongy malignant tumour, usually of the brain or optic nerve. *Spongin* is the horny or fibrous substance found in the skeleton of many sponges. A *spongolite* is a rock formed almost entirely of siliceous sponge spicules.

-spore *A spore.* [Greek *spora*, spore.]

Examples include *zoospore* (Greek *zōion*, animal) a spore of certain algae, fungi, and protozoans, capable of swimming by means of a flagellum; *megaspore* (Greek *megas*, great), the larger of the two kinds of spores produced by some ferns (the smaller being a *microspore*); *oospore* (Greek *ōion*, egg), the thick-walled zygote of certain algae and fungi, formed by fertilization of an oosphere; *zygospore* (Greek *zugon*, yoke), the resting cell of certain fungi and algae, arising from the fusion of two similar gametes.

spor(o)- Also **spori-**. *A spore.* [Greek *spora*, spore.]

An organism that produces spores is said to be *sporogenous* (Greek *genos*, a kind) or *sporiferous* (Latin *-fer*, producing); a *sporophore* (Greek *phorēsis*, being carried) is the spore-bearing structure of a fungus; a *sporangium* (Greek *angeion*, vessel) is a receptacle in which asexual spores are formed, for example in fungi, algae, mosses, and ferns; A *sporicide* is a substance used to kill spores. *Sporadic* does not belong in this set, as it derives instead from Greek *speirein*, to sow.

squam(o)- *A scale.* [Latin *squama*, scale.]

The adjective *squamous* can refer to something having scales (*Squamata* is a taxonomic order that includes the snakes and lizards), to a layer of tissue that consists of very thin flattened cells (as in *squamous cell carcinoma*, a form of skin cancer), or the flat portion of the temporal bone which forms part of the side of the skull. The adjective *squamocolumnar* refers to a junction between layers of stratified squamous cells and columnar cells in epithelial tissue; a *squamule* is a small scale.

-st: *see* -EST[2]

stann(o)- *Tin.* [Latin *stannum*, tin.]

In chemistry, *stannous* and *stannic* refer respectively to tin having a valency of two and four, as in *stannous fluoride* (SnF$_2$), used to fluoridate toothpaste, and *stannic chloride* (SnCl$_4$), used as a conductive coating and in ceramics. An ore or mineral containing tin is said to be *stanniferous*. A *stannary* was formerly a tin-mining district in Cornwall or Devon, whose miners were regulated by a *stannary court*.

staphyl(o)- *The uvula; a bunch or cluster.* [Greek *staphulē*, bunch of grapes.]

When swollen, the *uvula*—an extension of the soft palate at the back of the mouth—can fancifully resemble a bunch of grapes. In medicine, *staphylectomy* (Greek *ektomē*, excision) is surgical removal of the uvula. Bacteria of the *staphylococcus* group (Greek *kokkos*, berry), many types of which cause disease, are spherical and tend to form irregular clusters; the adjective relating to such bacteria is *staphylococcal* (sometimes abbreviated to *staph*); *staphylokinase* is an enzyme produced by certain strains of such bacteria that tends to stop blood clotting. A *staphyloma* is an abnormal bulging of the cornea or sclera of the eye, usually as a result of inflammation.

-stasis *Slowing down; stopping.* [Greek *stasis*, standing, stoppage.]

The ending is most common in medical terms, such as *bacteriostasis*, the prevention of the growth of bacteria; *haemostasis* (US *hemostasis*) (Greek *haima*, blood), the stopping of a flow of blood; *cholestasis* (Greek *kholē*, bile), failure of normal amounts of bile to reach the intestines, leading to jaundice; *fungistasis*, inhibition of the growth of fungi; *epistasis* (literally 'stoppage', from Greek *ephistanai*, to stop), the interaction of genes that are not alleles, in particular the suppression of the effect of one such gene by another. However, *metastasis* (Greek *methistanai*, to change) is the development of secondary malignant growths at a distance from a primary site of cancer. An example from outside medicine is *iconostasis*, a screen bearing icons, separating the sanctuary of many Eastern churches from the nave.

-stat *Something that maintains a controlled state.* [Greek *statikos*, causing to stand.]

Most terms refer to an instrument, such as *thermostat*, one that automatically regulates temperature; *rheostat*

(Greek *rheos*, stream), one that controls a current by varying the resistance; *humidistat*, a device that regulates the humidity of the air in a room or building; *cryostat* (Greek *kruos*, frost), one that maintains a very low temperature; *haemostat* (US *hemostat*) (Greek *haima*, blood), an instrument for preventing blood flow by compression of a blood vessel.

Others refer to a substance that controls a chemical system, or a system so controlled, such as *chemostat*, a system in which the chemical composition is kept at a controlled level, especially for the culture of micro-organisms, or *bacteriostat*, a substance that stops bacteria multiplying without destroying them. The *appestat* is the region of the hypothalamus of the brain which is believed to control a person's appetite for food.

stato- *Resting; equilibrium; balance.* [Greek *statos*, standing.]

A *statoblast* is a reproductive body in certain bryozoans that can survive unfavourable conditions in a state of rest or stasis; a *statocyst* is an organ of balance and orientation in some invertebrates; a *statocyte* is an equivalent organ in some plants; both contain *statoliths*, particles that sense gravity; a *statoscope* is a form of aneroid barometer adapted for recording small changes in aircraft altitude.

steat(o)- Also **stear-**. *Fat.* [Greek *stear*, *steat-*, tallow or fat.]

The condition called *steatopygia* (Greek *pugē*, rump) is the accumulation of large amounts of fat on the buttocks; *steatosis* is the infiltration of liver cells by fat as a result of a medical condition; *steatorrhoea* (Greek *rhoia*, flow, flux) is the excretion of abnormal quantities of fat with the faeces owing to reduced absorption of fat by the intestine. *Stearic acid* is a solid saturated fatty acid obtained from animal or vegetable fats, which forms salts called *stearates*; a glyceryl ester of stearic acid, *stearin*, is a white crystalline substance which is the main constituent of tallow and suet; the mineral called *steatite* is a consolidated form of talc, also called *soapstone* from its slippery feel. *See also* LIPO-.

stego- Also **stegano-**. *Covered; hidden.* [Greek *stegē*, covering; *steganos*, covered or enclosed.]

Steganography is a form of secret writing in which the existence of the message is hidden (for example, invisible inks or microdots). Other terms with these combining forms occur in the names of animals: the order of the pelicans is the *Steganopodes* (Greek *pous*, *pod-*, foot), so named because they have webbed feet; a *stegosaur*, of the genus *Stegosaurus*, is a dinosaur of the Jurassic and early Cretaceous periods, covered with a double row of large bony plates or spines along the back; *Stegomyia* is the old genus name of tropical mosquitoes responsible for dengue, encephalitis, and yellow fever.

steno- *Small; constricted.* [Greek *stenos*, narrow.]

This combining form appears in *stenography* and its relatives, for the process of writing in shorthand. *Stenosis* is the abnormal narrowing of a passage in the body. In ecology, *stenohaline* (Greek *halinos*, of salt) refers to an organism able to tolerate only a narrow range of salinity, *stenothermal* to one that can tolerate only a small range of temperature, and *stenotopic* (Greek *topos*, place) to one able to exist in only a restricted range of habitats or ecological conditions; all can be contrasted with terms beginning in EURY-.

step- *A relationship resulting from a remarriage.* [Old English *stēop-*, from a Germanic base meaning bereaved, or orphaned.]

Terms beginning in **step-** refer to a person in a family relationship but unrelated biologically. Originally it referred only to relationships resulting from remarriage after the death of a spouse; in the 19th century terms were extended to refer to any relationship resulting from remarriage, say following divorce. Examples include *stepmother* and *stepfather* (together, *stepparent*) *stepbrother* and *stepsister* (together, *stepsibling*), *stepson* and *stepdaughter* (together, *stepchild*) and *stepfamily*.

-ster *A person or thing associated with an activity or quality.* [Old English *-estre*, *-istre*, etc.]

Early examples referred to a woman engaged in an occupation, such as *brewster*, *maltster*, and *spinster*, this last originally 'a woman who spins' (the ending was the feminine equivalent of words ending in *-ere*, which later became *-er*; see -ER[1]). It has long been extended to activities undertaken by men, such as *chorister* or *teamster*. Words in which it refers to a characteristic of the person include *youngster* and the US-derived *oldster*, as well as *hipster* (a person who is *hip*, who follows the latest trends and fashions). Less often, the ending refers to objects, *roadster* being a rare example.

It often has a derogatory sense: *tipster*, *rhymester*, *prankster*. Many of these are more common in the US than Britain: *gamester*, *gangster*, *huckster*, *jokester*, *mobster*, *punster*, *trickster*. Such terms continue to be formed, again most frequently in the US: *popster*, *hypester*, *soulster*, *scamster*.

Master comes from Old English *mæg(i)ster*, but derives from Latin *magister* (see also -MEISTER); others that derive from Latin words with the same ending include *minister* and *barrister* (formed from *bar* in imitation of *minister*), as do nouns ending in -ASTER (such as *poetaster*). In words such as *boaster*, *jester*, *broadcaster*, and *protester*, the suffix is *-er* (see -ER[1]) on a stem ending in *st*.

See also -STRESS.

sterco(r)- *Faeces; dung.* [Latin *stercus*, *stercor-*, dung.]

Most words in this form are archaic. Exceptions are *stercoraceous*, consisting of or resembling dung or faeces; *stercobilin*, the colouring matter of faeces, a breakdown product of the bile pigment bilirubin; the adjective *stercoral* usually appears in *stercoral ulcer*, an ulcer of the colon caused by faecal material. The genus of tropical trees, *Sterculia*, gains its name from the foetid odour of the blossoms or timber of some species.

ster(eo)- *Solid; three-dimensional.* [Greek *stereos*, solid.]

Sound that is *stereophonic* (*stereo* for short) seems to be distributed in space; *stereochemistry* is concerned with the three-dimensional arrangement of atoms and molecules; a *steradian* is the SI unit of solid angle; *stereography* (adjective *stereographic*) is the representation of three-dimensional things by projection on to a flat surface, for example in map-making or crystallography. A *stereoscope* is a device by which two photographs can be viewed together to create an impression of depth; the derived adjective *stereoscopic* refers to something having an appearance of solidity or relief. *Stereotype*, now usually meaning a fixed and oversimplified image or idea, comes from an older sense of a relief printing plate cast from type.

stern(o)- *The breastbone or sternum.* [Greek *sternon*, chest.]

Several terms refer to the breastbone plus another part of the body: *sternothyroid*, the sternum and the thyroid cartilage; *sternoclavicular*, the sternum and the clavicle or collar bone; *sternocleidomastoid*, of muscles that connect the sternum, clavicle, and mastoid process of the temporal bone. The *sternebra* (plural *sternebrae*) is one of the four parts that fuse during development to form the body of the sternum; *sternotomy* (Greek *-tomia*, cutting) is surgical cutting of the breastbone to allow access to the heart. The adjective relating to the breastbone is *sternal*.

-sterol *A sterol.* [The second element of *cholesterol*, the first member of the group to be identified, derived from Greek *stereos*, stiff or solid.]

The *sterols* are naturally occurring unsaturated steroid alcohols, typically waxy solids. An example is *lanosterol*, a precursor in the biosynthesis of cholesterol and a component of lanolin. Sterols that come from plants are collectively called *phytosterols* (Greek *phuton*, a plant), examples being *ergosterol*, from ergot and many other fungi, and *sitosterol* (Greek *sitos*, grain, food), a group of sterols obtained from various plant sources, including corn oil.

-sterone *A steroid hormone.* [A blend of *steroid* with *ketone*.]

Such compounds are steroids that are also ketones, containing a carboxyl group (—CO—). Examples include the naturally occurring sex hormones ***progesterone*** (Latin *pro* plus the first part of *gestation*), ***testosterone*** (Latin *testis*, a witness (to fertility)), and ***androsterone*** (Greek *anēr*, *andr-*, man). Other examples are ***aldosterone*** (English *aldehyde*), a corticosteroid hormone which stimulates absorption of sodium by the kidneys and so regulates water and salt balance, and ***corticosterone***, a hormone secreted by the adrenal cortex.

stib(o)- Also **stibio-**. *Antimony.* [Latin *stibium*, black antimony, antimony trisulphide.]

The Latin name for this antimony compound, once used as a cosmetic, has supplied the element's chemical symbol, Sb. ***Stibnite*** is antimony sulphide, the chief ore of antimony; ***stibine*** is the poisonous, colourless gas, antimony hydride, SbH_3; ***stibogluconate*** (in full *sodium stibogluconate*) is useful in the treatment of leishmaniasis. ***Stibiopalladinite*** and ***stibiotantalite*** are minerals containing antimony in association with, respectively, palladium and tantalum.

stomat(o)- *The mouth; a opening.* [Greek *stoma*, *stomat-*, mouth.]

In medicine, ***stomatitis*** is inflammation of the mucous membrane of the mouth; ***stomatology*** is the study of the mouth and its diseases; and ***stomatogastric*** relates to the mouth and stomach. ***Stoma*** (plural ***stomas*** or ***stomata***) is used in botany and zoology for various openings, such as the minute pores in the epidermis of the leaf or stem of a plant. *Stomach* derives from the related Greek word *stomakhos*, gullet.

-stome Also **-stomous**. *A mouth.* [Greek *stoma*, mouth.]

This ending appears in some specialist words in zoology for animals with certain kinds of mouths, as in ***cyclostome***, an eel-like jawless vertebrate with a circular sucking mouth, such as a lamprey or hagfish; ***protostome*** (Greek *proto-*, primitive), a multicellular organism whose mouth develops from a primary embryonic opening, such as a mollusc or arthropod; the ***peristome*** (Greek *peri-*, around) is the part surrounding the mouth of various invertebrates. Such nouns have associated adjectives ending in **-stomous**, such as ***physostomous*** (Greek *physa*, bladder), having the mouth and air bladder connected by an air duct. *See also* -TOME.

-stomy *A surgical operation to create an opening in an organ.* [Greek *stoma*, mouth.]

Terms always contain the linking vowel -o-. Several examples refer to operations in which a part of the digestive system is opened, either for drainage or to introduce food: ***colostomy***, an opening in the colon; ***ileostomy***, in the ileum, a part of the small intestine; ***gastrostomy*** (Greek *gastēr*, *gastr-*, stomach), in the stomach; and ***jejunostomy***, in the jejunum, another part of the small intestine. Examples relating to other parts of the body include ***nephrostomy*** (Greek *nephros*, kidney), surgical creation of an opening to drain urine directly from the kidney, and ***salpingostomy*** (Greek *salpinx*, *salping-*, trumpet), surgical unblocking of a blocked Fallopian tube. A general term for any operation of this type is ***ostomy***. *See also* -TOMY and -ECTOMY.

strat(i)- Also **strato-**. *A layer; layered.* [Latin *stratum*, something spread or laid down; *stratus*, strewn.]

The ***stratosphere*** is the layer of the earth's atmosphere from about 6–50km. above the earth's surface. ***Stratigraphy*** is the branch of geology concerned with the order and relative position of strata; something ***stratiform*** is arranged in layers. In meteorology, ***stratocumulus*** is cloud in a low layer of clumped or broken grey masses, while ***stratus*** is a continuous horizontal grey sheet of cloud, often with rain or snow. The adjective ***stratal*** refers to strata or a stratum; something ***stratified*** is formed or arranged into strata.

However, *stratocracy* is government by the army (Greek *stratos*, army); *strategy* and its relatives derive from the related *stratēgos*, a general (Greek *agein*, to lead).

strepto- *Twisted.* [Greek *streptos*, twisted, from *strephein*, to turn.]

A *streptococcus* (Greek *kokkos*, berry; plural *streptococci*) is a bacterium of a genus that includes pathogens causing various infections such as scarlet fever and pneumonia. The bacteria form chains, and the genus was named in 1877 by the German pathologist Billroth, who took the Greek word to mean 'chain'. The genus *Streptomyces* (Greek *mukēs*, *mukēt-*, fungus), another bacterial genus, was similarly named; they occur chiefly in soil as aerobic saprophytes resembling moulds and several of them are important sources of antibiotics, such as *streptomycin* and *streptozotocin*. The enzyme *streptokinase*, produced by some streptococci, is used to treat inflammation and blood clots; another active substance from streptococci, *streptolysin* (Greek *lusis*, loosening), removes haemoglobin from red blood cells.

-stress *A female person associated with a specific activity.* [English -STER, plus -ESS.]

The most common examples here are *seamstress*, a woman who sews, especially one who earns her living by sewing; and *mistress* (actually formed from Old French *maistresse*, from *maistre*, master). The same considerations of gender that are working against words ending in -ESS apply here and no new examples are being created using it; however, some remain in active use, such as *headmistress* and *songstress*.

-style¹ *In a characteristic manner.* [English *style*.]

This suffix forms adjectives and adverbs indicating something resembling or characteristic of a particular style, as in *church-style*, *family-style*, *home-style*, *Japanese-style*, *new-style*, *peasant-style*, and *regency-style*.

-style² *Having columns of a specified type.* [Greek *stulos*, column or pillar.]

A *hypostyle* (Greek *hupo*, under) is a building whose roof rests on pillars; an *epistyle* (Greek *epi*, upon) is a main beam resting across the tops of columns; a *peristyle* is a row of columns surrounding a space within a building. Other terms refer to the number of columns in a building or portico, such as *hexastyle*, six, or *tetrastyle*, four.

Some examples refer to forms of animal bones: *pygostyle* (Greek *pugē*, rump), a triangular plate in a bird that typically supports the tail feathers; *urostyle* (Greek *oura*, tail), a long bone formed from fused vertebrae at the base of the vertebral column in some lower vertebrates, especially frogs and toads.

stylo-¹ Also **styli-**. *Style; stylus.* [Latin *stilus*.]

The Latin word referred to a writing instrument, and also figuratively to a manner or technique of literary composition. The latter sense is preserved in English *style*, and the former in *stylus*. Both words were respelled under the influence of Greek *stulos*, a column or pillar, whose meaning has also affected the usage of *style*.

Examples of **stylo-** in various senses include *stylometry*, the statistical analysis of variations in literary style between one writer or genre and another; *stylophone*, a miniature electronic musical instrument that employs a stylus; and *stylograph*, a kind of fountain pen having a fine perforated tube instead of a split nib. The adjective *styliform* refers to something slender and pointed.

stylo-² Also **styli-**. *A column, pillar, or tube.* [Greek *stulos*, pillar.]

Something *styloid* (Latin *styloides*, derived from Greek) is like a thin rod or stylus; a *styloid process* in anatomy is a slender projection of bone, such as that from the lower surface of the temporal bone of the skull. In geology, a *stylolite* is an irregular surface or seam within limestone or other sedimentary rock, creating columnar formations. In classical Greek architecture, a *stylobate* (Greek *bainein*, to walk) was a continuous base supporting a row of columns. A *stylite* was an early Christian ascetic who lived on top of a pillar.

sub- Also **suc-**, **suf-**, **sug-**, **sup-**, **sur-**, and **sus-**. *A lower level or position;*

somewhat or nearly; secondary action. [Latin *sub*, under, close to, to some degree.]

This is a common prefix, both in words which have come from Latin with it already attached, and also in many examples coined in English.

One set contains the literal idea of something moving to or being at a lower level or position, as in *submarine*, *subconscious*, *subcutaneous* (Latin *cutis*, skin), *substratum*, and *subtitle*; this leads into a sense of being lower in rank, of secondary status, or a part of something larger: *subaltern*, *subcommittee*, *sub-human*, *sublieutenant*, *subordinate*, *subculture*, *subframe*, *subset*, *suburb*.

A second set contains the idea of something imperfect or incomplete, which suggests that a thing is less than, somewhat, or nearly like another: *subarctic*, *subclinical*, *subequatorial*, *submarginal*, *sub-orbital*, *subsonic*.

In some verbs (and associated nouns) the prefix marks a later or secondary action of the same kind: *subcontract*, *sublet*, *subdivide*. It can be used informally to suggest something is in an inferior version of another style: *sub-Wordsworthian*, *sub-Marxist*. In chemistry, **sub-** is included in the names of compounds containing a relatively small proportion of a component, as in *suboxide*.

Some examples where **sub-** became attached in Latin, and in which it has a figurative association in English, include *subdue* (*ducere*, to lead or draw); *sublime* (in which the second element may be related to *limen*, threshold); *subscribe* (*scribere*, to write); *subjugate* (*jugum*, yoke); *submit* (*mittere*, to send, put); and *subsequent* (*sequi*, to follow).

Several variant forms of the prefix occur before certain consonants in words adopted from Latin. It becomes **suc-** before *c*: *succinct* (*cingere*, to gird); **suf-** before *f*: *suffocate* (*fauces*, throat); **sug-** before *g*: *suggest* (*gerere*, to bring); **sup-** before *p*: *support* (*portare*, to carry); **sur-** before *r*: *surreptitious* (*rapere*, to seize), but *see also* SUR-; **sus-** before *c, p,* or *t*: *susceptible* (*capere*, to take), *suspend* (*pendere*, to hang), *sustain* (*tenere*, to hold).

sulpha- (US **sulfa-**). *A drug derived from sulphanilamide.* [The first element of *sulphanilamide*.]

Sulphanilamide (from *sulphur*, plus *aniline*, of which it is a derivative, plus *amide*) is a synthetic compound with antibacterial properties which is the basis of the sulphonamide (or *sulpha*) drugs. Though they have for many purposes been replaced by antibiotics, a substantial group of them is still in use, of which some examples are *sulphacetamide*, *sulphadiazine*, *sulphadimidine*, *sulphamethoxazole*, *sulphapyridine*, and *sulphasalazine*.

sulph(o)- (US **sulf(o)-**). *Sulphur.* [Latin *sulfur*, sulphur.]

Sulphurous acid forms *sulphites*, while *sulphuric* acid forms *sulphates*. *Sulphonic* acid is an organic acid containing the group —SO_2OH, which forms *sulphonates*; the process of conversion of compounds into sulphonates is *sulphonation*. *Sulphides* are compounds of sulphur with another component, usually a metallic element. *See also* THIO-.

sup-: *see* SUB-

super- *Above, over, or beyond; great or large; of a higher kind.* [Latin *super*, above, beyond.]

Though a number of words have been imported from Latin with this prefix already attached, most have been formed in English, particularly because it has become a popular way of forming superlatives in recent decades.

The most common sense refers to something having greater influence, capability or power than another of its kind, or exhibiting some quality to a greater degree: *superabundant*, *superbug*, *supercharger*, *supercomputer*, *superconductor*, *supercool*, *superfluid*, *superglue*, *superhero*, *superman*, *supermodel*, *superpower*, *superstar*, *superwoman*.

Other examples suggest something extra large of its kind: *supercontinent*, *supermarket*, *superstore*, *supertanker*. Some imply a position or status above or beyond another: *superstructure*, *supersonic*, *supernatural*, *superscript*, *superstra-*

tum, *supertitles*. In systematic classifications of the living world, it indicates a higher level, as in *superfamily*, *superclass*, and *superorder*. In chemistry, it is occasionally used to suggest an element is in greater proportion than usual: *superoxide*.

Examples in which the prefix was attached in Latin have often lost a direct reference to such senses in English, though sometimes it peeps through: *supercilious* (*cilium*, eyelid, so linked to the idea of someone raising his eyebrows), *superficial* (*facies*, face, originally something associated with the surface, hence its outward appearance), *superior* (*superus*, that is above), *superlative* (*latus*, carried, so a person or thing borne above others), and *supervise* (*videre*, to see, therefore to 'look over' another's work).

See also HYPER- and SUR-.

supra- *Over or above; transcending.* [Latin *supra*, above, beyond.]

In medicine in particular, this often has a sense of a thing that is located physically over, above, or on top of another: *suprarenal*, above the kidneys; *suprahyoid*, above the hyoid bone; *supraorbital*, above the orbit of the eye, the eye socket.

In other examples, the sense is of going beyond or transcending something, often figuratively: *supramolecular*, relating to or denoting structures composed of several or many molecules; *supranational*, having power or influence that transcends national boundaries or governments; *supramundane*, transcending or superior to the physical world.

sur- *Over, above, beyond; additional.* [French *sur*, from Latin *super*.]

Few words have been formed in English using this prefix, most examples having entered the language from French with it already attached. Examples are *surcharge*, an additional charge or payment; *surface* (from *face*), *surmount*, to overcome some difficulty or obstacle, *surfeit*, *surpass*, *survive* (Old French *sourvivre*, from Latin *vivere*, to live), *surtax*, and *surrender* (Old French *rendre*, from an alteration of Latin *reddere*,

to give back). Though spelled differently, *sirloin*, indicating the choicer part of a loin of beef, came into English by the same route (its spelling may have been influenced by a story of an English king who facetiously knighted a roast joint of beef). Many words beginning *surr-* are examples instead of an assimilated form of SUB-. *See also* SUPER-.

sus-: *see* SUB-

-sy *Forming nouns and adjectives.* [Origin uncertain, perhaps a combination of -s¹ and -Y².]

This ending is added to proper names to provide an affectionate version: *Betsy*, *Patsy*, *Topsy*. It can also be added to a variety of nouns, such as *antsy*, *ballsy*, *gutsy*, *popsy*, *footsie*, and *tootsy*. Some adjectives suggest smallness: *eensy* (and *eensy-weensy*), *itsy-bitsy*, *teensy* (and *teensy-weensy*). Other adjectives have a dismissive or contemptuous sense: *artsy-fartsy*, *bitsy*, *booksy*, *cutesy*, *folksy*, *mumsy*, *newsy*, *rootsy*. Occasionally, the spelling is -*zy*, as in *ditzy*.

syn- Also **syl-**, **sym-**, and **sys-**. *United; acting or considered together; alike.* [Greek *sun*, with, together.]

A *synapse* (Greek *hapsis*, joining) is a junction between two nerve cells; a *syndrome* (Greek *dramein*, to run) is a group of symptoms which consistently occur together; *synthesis* (Greek *thesis*, placing) has various senses meaning combination or composition; a *synonym* (Greek *onoma*, name) is a word or phrase that has nearly the same meaning as another; *syntax* (Greek *tassein*, arrange), is the arrangement of words and phrases to create well-formed sentences in a language; a *synagogue* is literally a place where people come together, from Greek *agein*, to bring; *synod*, an assembly of the clergy and sometimes also the laity, derives from Greek *hodos*, way.

In many words brought into English through Latin, the prefix changes its final letter before certain consonants. Before *l*, it becomes **syl-**: *syllable* (Greek *lambanein*, take); before *b*, *m*, or *p*, it becomes **sym-**: *symbiosis* (Greek *bios*, livelihood), *symmetry* (Greek *metron*, measure), *sympathy* (Greek *pathos*, feeling). Before *s*, it becomes **sys-**, though examples are rare: *syssarcosis*, the joining or attachment of bones by means of muscle (Greek *sarx*, flesh).

synchro- *Synchronous.* [The first part of English *synchronous*, from Greek *sun-*, together, plus *khronos*, time.]

Something *synchronous* exists or occurs at the same time as some other event. Examples of **synchro-** include *synchromesh*, a system for changing gear easily, short for *synchronized mesh*; *synchroflash*, in which the opening of the camera shutter is synchronized with the firing of a flash gun; *synchrotron*, a cyclotron in which the magnetic field strength increases in time with the energy of the particles to keep their orbital radius constant. *Synchro* as a free-standing word can be an abbreviation of *synchromesh* or *synchronized swimming*, or refer in general to synchronized operations.

syndesmo- *Connective tissue, especially* ligaments. [Greek *sundesmos*, binding, fastening, from *syn*, together, and *desmos*, bond or connection.]

A *syndesmosis* is an immovable joint in which bones are joined by connective tissue, for example between the fibula and tibia at the ankle; a *syndesmophyte* is a bony growth attached to a ligament; *syndesmology* is the branch of anatomy that deals with ligaments.

syring(o)- *A tube or long cavity; a fistula.* [Greek *surinx*, *suring-*, tube, channel.]

Syringomyelia (Greek *muelos*, marrow) is a chronic progressive disease in which longitudinal cavities form in the cervical region of the spinal cord, an extension of which into the lower brainstem is a *syringobulbia*; *syringoma* is a condition in which multiple benign tumours of the sweat glands appear. The Greek word appears in *syrinx*, the lower larynx or voice organ in birds, for which the adjective is *syringeal*.

sys-: *see* SYN-

T

-t: *see* -ED²

tach(o)- Also **tacheo-** and **tachisto-**. *Speed.* [Greek *takhos*, speed.]

A *tachometer* is an instrument which measures the working speed of an engine (especially in a road vehicle); a similar device which produces a printed record is a *tachograph*, used particularly of the device that measures the speed of a goods vehicle and the distance it has travelled. A *tachistoscope* (Greek *takhistos*, swiftest, plus *skopein*, look at) is an instrument used for exposing objects to the eye for a very brief measured period of time; *tacheometry* (also called *tachymetry*, see the next entry) is a method of surveying an area quickly using instruments designed for the purpose.

tachy- *Rapid.* [Greek *takhus*, swift.]

In medicine, *tachycardia* (Greek *kardia*, heart) is an abnormally rapid heart rate; *tachyphylaxis* (Greek *phulaxis*, act of guarding) occurs when repeated doses of a drug cause responses that are progressively and rapidly less effective; *tachypnoea* (US *tachypnea*) (Greek *pnoē*, breathing) is abnormally rapid breathing. A *tachyon* is a hypothetical particle that travels faster than light.

-tactic: *see* -TAXIS

taeni- In the US, sometimes **teni-**. *Ribbon; tapeworm.* [Greek *tainia*, band, ribbon.]

This form appears in a few medical terms related to tapeworms of the genus *Taenia*, especially *taeniasis*, infestation by them; a *taeniafuge* (Latin *fugare*, cause to flee) or *taeniacide* (Latin *caedere*, kill) is an agent that eliminates them from the body. A term reflecting the original Greek sense is *taenia*, of which one sense is a flat ribbon-like structure in the body.

talo- Also **tali-** *The ankle bone.* [Latin *talus*, the ankle bone.]

Some examples are adjectives that refer to the ankle bone or *talus* plus an associated bone, such as *talofibular*, of the talus plus the fibula (one of the two bones between the knee and the ankle). *Talipes* (Latin *pes*, foot) is the technical term for club-foot. *Talon*, a claw, derives from the same source. *See also* TARSO-.

tarso- *The tarsus.* [Greek *tarsos*, a flat surface.]

The medical term *tarsus* either refers to the seven bones that form the ankle and upper part of the foot, or to a thin sheet of fibrous connective tissue which supports the edge of each eyelid. Examples of medical terms are *tarsorrhaphy* (Greek *rhaphē*, a seam), an operation in which the upper and lower eyelids are joined together to protect the cornea; *tarsitis*, inflammation of the eyelid; and *tarsectomy* (Greek *ektomē*, excision), either surgical removal of the tarsal bones of the foot, or of a section of the tarsus of the eye.

A *tarsometatarsus* (adjective *tarsometatarsal*) is a long bone in the lower leg of birds and some reptiles, formed by fusion of tarsal and metatarsal structures.

-tastic *Something outstanding, superb, or excellent.* [The ending of *fantastic*.]

This is a relatively recent colloquial formation, whose survival is as yet in doubt. The earliest example, still the most common, is *poptastic*, something superlative in pop music; others that have been formed on the same model (but which are much less common) include *cybertastic*, *sextastic*, and *babetastic*.

tauro- *Ox or bull.* [Greek *tauros*, bull.]

Taurine is a sulphur-containing amino acid important in the metabolism of fats, so named because it was originally obtained from ox bile; *taurocholic acid* is a bile acid formed by the combination of taurine with cholic acid. *Tauromachy* is an alternative term for bullfighting.

tauto- *The same.* [Greek *tauto*, contraction of *to auto*, the same.]

A *tautology* occurs when the same thing is said twice in different words; a *tautomer* (Greek *meros*, a share) is each of two or more isomers of a compound which exist together in equilibrium; a *tautonym* is a taxonomic name in which the same word is used for both the genus and species elements, for example *Coccothraustes coccothraustes*, the hawfinch.

taxi-: *see* TAXO-

-taxis Also **-taxy**, **-taxia**, **-tactic**, and **-taxic**. *Arrangement or order; movement in response to an external stimulus.* [Greek *taxis*, orientation, arrangement.]

The senses of **-taxis** are derived from those of the free-standing word *taxis*.

Examples in the first sense include *phyllotaxis* (Greek *phullon*, leaf), the arrangement of leaves on an axis or stem, and *stereotaxis* (Greek *stereos*, solid), the use of medical devices that accurately place probes within the body. In linguistics, *taxis* can also refer to the arrangement of linguistic items in sequence, as in *parataxis* (Greek *para-*, beside), the placing of clauses or phrases one after another without words to indicate coordination or subordination.

Examples in the second sense include *geotaxis*, the motion of a motile organism or cell in response to the force of gravity; *phototaxis*, movement in response to light; and *thigmotaxis* (Greek *thigma*, touch), motion or orientation in response to touch.

Words ending in **-taxy** derive from the same source, but are equivalent to those ending in **-taxis** only in the sense of arrangement: *phyllotaxy*; *stereotaxy*; *epitaxy*, the growth of crystals on a crystalline substrate that determines their orientation. With the exception of *epitaxy*, forms ending in **-taxy** are usually less common than their counterparts ending in **-taxis**. *Ataxy* is a variant form of *ataxia*, the medical term for a loss of full control of bodily movements (literally 'without order', at first referring to an irregularity of function); terms ending in **-taxia** are otherwise rare.

Adjectives are commonly formed from these nouns using **-tactic**: *geotactic*, *hypotactic*, *paratactic*, *stereotactic*. A few also occur in the less common spelling **-taxic**: *stereotaxic*, *thermotaxic*, of an organism that moves in response to changes in temperature. However, *ataxia* has *ataxic* as its usual adjective.

One noun that does not belong with this set is *epistaxis*, bleeding from the nose, which is from Greek *epi*, upon, in addition, plus *stazein*, to drip.

taxo- Also **taxi-**. *Order, arrangement, classification.* [Greek *taxis*, orientation, arrangement.]

The only common words in these forms are *taxonomy* (Greek *-nomia*, distribution), the branch of science concerned with classification, especially of organisms, and *taxidermy* (Greek *derma*, skin), the art of preparing, stuffing, and mounting the skins of animals with lifelike effect. *Taximeter* derives instead from French *taxe*, a tariff.

-taxy: *see* -TAXIS

tebi-: see the table of WORDS FOR MULTIPLES on page 127

-technics Also **-techny**, **-technical**, and **-technic**. *A technology or skill.* [Greek *tekhnē*, art, craft.]

Terms ending in **-technics** may be regarded as based on *technics*, technical terms, details, and methods. It and its compounds, though in form plural, are treated as singular.

Examples are *geotechnics* (Greek *gē*, earth), the branch of civil engineering concerned with the study and modification of soil and rocks; *pyrotechnics* (Greek *pur*, fire), the art and technology of making fireworks; *electrotechnics*, the application of electricity in technology; *zootechnics* (Greek *zōion*, animal), the art of rearing animals.

The ending **-techny** has the same meaning as **-technics**, but its compounds are less common: *pyrotechny*, *zootechny*.

Related adjectives are formed either with **-technical** (*geotechnical*, *electro-technical*), or less commonly with **-technic** (*geotechnic*, *biotechnic*). A *poly-technic*, however, is a British institution of higher education, now only an historical term.

techno- *Technology, especially its impact or implications.* [Greek *tekhnē*, art, craft.]

Some examples are *technocracy* (Greek *-kratia*, power or rule), the government or control of society or industry by an elite of technical experts; *technophile*, a person who is enthusiastic about new technology (the opposite being a *technophobe*); *technothriller*, a suspense novel in which the manipulation of sophisticated technology plays an important role. Informal or short-lived terms beginning in **techno-** are common; they often focus on the implications of technology for individuals or society, especially in relation to computer technology, and are frequently disparaging: *technostress*, stress or psychosomatic illness caused by working with computer technology on a daily basis; *technobabble*, incomprehensible technical jargon; *technonerd*, a person overly absorbed in technical matters, especially in computing. *Techno*, an abbreviation of *technology*, is a style of fast, heavy electronic dance music.

tectono- *Tectonics.* [English *tectonics* (Greek *tektoníkos*, from *tektōn*, carpenter, builder), plus -o-.]

In geology, *tectonics* is the name given to large-scale processes that affect the structure of the earth's crust. *Tectonophysics* deals with the forces that cause movement and deformation in the crust; the adjective *tectonostratigraphic* refers to the correlation of rock formations with each other in terms of their connection with a tectonic event; something *tectonothermal* involves both tectonism and geothermal activity.

-teen Also **-teenth**. *Forming the names of numerals from 13 to 19.* [Old English inflected form of *ten*.]

Examples are *fourteen* and *nineteen*. A *pre-teen* is a young person below the age

of *thirteen*. The form **-teenth** (*see* -TH[1]) appears in the associated ordinal numbers; the noun *Juneteenth* refers to a celebration of 19 June, the anniversary of the emancipation of slaves in Texas on 19 June 1865. Words such as *velveteen* and *sateen* derive instead from French words ending in *-ine* (*see* -EEN).

tele- *To or at a distance.* [Greek *tēle-*, far off.]

Terms formed directly from the Greek root include *telescope*, *telegraph*, *telegram*, *telephone*, *television*, *telemetry*, the transmission of instrument readings by radio, and *telekinesis* (Greek *kinēsis*, motion), the supposed ability to move objects at a distance by mental power.

The general term for communication over a distance by electronic means is *telecommunications*. On the model of this and related terms, **tele-** has in recent decades taken on the sense of something that acts or occurs at a distance by means of an electronic link, especially computer-mediated: *telecommuter*, a person who works from home, using the telephone, fax, or the Internet to connect to the workplace; *telecottage*, a room or building, especially in a rural area, containing computer equipment for the shared use of people living in the area; *teleconference*, a conference with participants in different locations linked by communication devices; *telemedicine*, the remote diagnosis and treatment of patients by such technology; *telematics*, the branch of information technology which deals with the long-distance transmission of computerized information; *telepresence*, the use of virtual reality technology, especially for remote control of machinery or for apparent participation in distant events.

The form also more specifically refers to a single telecommunications medium. Examples relating to television include *telethon*, a very long television programme, typically one broadcast to raise money for a charity; *televangelist*, an evangelical preacher who appears regularly on television; *telegenic*, having an appearance or manner that is appealing on television; *telecine*, apparatus used to broadcast cinema films on television. Some refer to the telephone: *telebanking*, banking over the telephone; *telesales* and *telemarketing*, the selling of goods or services by means of telephone calls.

teleo- *Perfect; complete.* [Greek *teleos*, complete.]

This form is rare, with the only common term being *teleost* (Greek *osteon*, bone), a fish of a large group that comprises all ray-finned fishes, so named because their skeletons are completely turned into bone. A *teleosaur* (Greek *sauros*, lizard) is an extinct marine crocodile of the Triassic and Jurassic periods. Words such as *teleology* contain a related Greek word: *see* TELO-.

tellur(o)- *Tellurium; the earth.* [Latin *tellus*, *tellur-*, earth.]

The semi-metal *tellurium* was named by its discoverer, the German chemist Martin Klaproth (1743–1817), as a deliberate contrast to *uranium* (Greek *ouranos*, heavens), which he had discovered previously. Most terms in this form relate to tellurium: a *telluride* is a compound of divalent tellurium, analogous to a sulphide; *tellurite* is a salt of the anion TeO_3^{2-}; the adjectives *tellurous* and *telluric* can refer respectively to tellurium with combining powers of four and six. However, a few words retain the original Latin sense of the earth: a *tellurian* is an inhabitant of the earth; telluric can also refer to the earth as a planet or to the soil; a *tellurometer* is a microwave long-distance surveying instrument.

telo- Also **teleo-**. *End; purpose.* [Greek *telos*, end.]

A *telomere* (Greek *meros*, part) is a compound structure at the end of a chromosome; a *telogen* is the resting phase of a hair follicle; the *telophase* is the final phase of cell division; the adjective *telolecithal* (Greek *lekithos*, egg yolk), refers to an egg or egg cell that has a large yolk situated at or near one end.

Examples spelled **teleo-** are rarer: *teleology* is the explanation of phenomena by the purpose they serve rather than by

postulated causes; *teleonomy* is an impression of purpose in living organisms as a result of adaptation through natural selection. For another sense of this spelling, *see* TELEO-.

temporo- *The temporal bones.* [Latin *tempora*, plural of *tempus*, temple of the head.]

The *temporal* bones are the flat parts on either side of the head between the forehead and the ear. Compounds are adjectives that refer to these bones in connection with another part of the head, as in *temporomandibular*, of the temporal bone and the lower jaw or mandible; *temporoparietal*, of the temporal and parietal bones; *temporo-occipital*, of the temporal and occipital bones. The first two terms are often hyphenated.

tendino-: *see* TENO-

-tene *Stages in cell division.* [Greek *tainia*, band, ribbon.]

This ending appears in four terms for the successive steps in the first stage of division of a cell, the *prophase*, in which the chromosomes separate. The four steps are *leptotene* (Greek *leptos*, fine, thin, delicate), in which each chromosome becomes visible as two fine threads (chromatids); *zygotene* (Greek *zugon*, yoke), in which homologous chromosomes begin to pair; *pachytene* (Greek *pakhus*, thick), in which the paired chromosomes shorten and thicken, the two chromatids of each separate, and exchange of segments between chromatids may occur; and *diplotene* (Greek *diplous*, double), in which the paired chromosomes begin to separate into two pairs of chromatids.

teno- Also **tendin(o)-**. *A tendon.* [Greek *tenōn*, tendon; Latin *tendin-*, *tendo*, a tendon.]

Examples are *tenosynovitis*, inflammation and swelling of a tendon, typically in the wrist, often caused by repetitive movements such as typing; *tenotomy* (Greek *-tomia*, cutting), the surgical cutting of a tendon, especially as a remedy for club foot; *tenodesis*, the operation of suturing the end of a tendon to a bone. A few words contain **tendino-**: *tendinous*, of the nature of a tendon; *tendinitis*, inflammation in a tendon (also often as *tendonitis*, formed from English *tendon*).

tephr(o)- *Ash; ash-coloured.* [Greek *tephra*, ash, ashes.]

In geology, the form can refer to *tephra*, rock fragments and particles ejected by a volcanic eruption, as in *tephrochronology*, the dating of volcanic events by studying layers of tephra; *tephroite* is a manganese silicate, occurring in crystalline masses of an ashy grey or reddish colour; *tephrite* is a fine-grained basaltic rock.

ter- *Three; having three.* [Latin *ter*, thrice.]

A *tercentenary* is the three-hundredth anniversary of a significant event. Otherwise, the form occurs mainly in chemical names, but not commonly even then: the *terphenyls* contain three linked benzene rings; a chemical reaction that is *termolecular* involves three molecules; a *tervalent* chemical radical has a combining power of three; *terbutaline* (from elements of its formal chemical name, *see also* BUT-) is a drug used especially in the treatment of asthma. The form has largely been replaced by TRI-.

tera- *In units of measurement, a factor of 10^{12}, a million million.* [Greek *teras*, monster.]

This is one of the standard SI (Système International) multiples (see the table of WORDS FOR MULTIPLES on page 127). It occurs in terms such as *terahertz*, a frequency of a million million cycles per second, and *terawatt*, a million million watts. In computing, it strictly has a sense of 2^{40}, but in terms such as *terabyte* it often means a million million bytes. The unit of computing speed, the *teraflop*, is always equal to one million million floating-point operations per second.

terato- *Monsters or abnormal forms.* [Greek *teras*, *terat-*, monster.]

Though *teratology* can be a collection of tales about fantastic creatures and monsters, it is also the scientific study of congenital abnormalities and abnormal formations. Most terms beginning in **terato-** have this medical sense, as in *teratogenesis*, the process by which congenital malformations are produced in an embryo or foetus, such as by a *teratogen*; a *teratoma* is a tumour composed of tissues not normally present at the site; a *teratocarcinoma* is a form of malignant teratoma occurring especially in the testis.

-teria Also **-ateria** and **-eteria**. *A self-service establishment.* [The final element of *cafeteria*, from Latin American Spanish *cafetería*, a coffee shop.]

This ending is rather variable in form, and some terms using it have been formed irregularly. The first example, in North America at the beginning of the 20th century, was *groceteria* (sometimes *grocerteria*), a small self-service grocery store, a term that is now only historical; the only example in common use today is *washeteria* (also commonly *washateria* in parts of the US), another name for a laundrette.

tetan(o)- *Tetanus.* [Greek *tetanos*, muscular spasm.]

Tetanospasmin and *tetanolysin* (Greek *lusis*) are toxins produced by tetanus bacteria in an infected wound; the former causes the spasms typical of the disease while the latter causes local destruction of tissues. Adjectives relating to tetanus are *tetanoid* and *tetanic*.

tetr(a)- Also **tetarto-**. *Four; having four.* [Greek, from *tettares*, four.]

This form is widely used. Some examples are *tetrathlon* (Greek *athlon*, contest), in which each contestant competes in four events; *tetraplegic*, a person paralysed in all four limbs; *tetrameter* (Greek *metron*, measure), a verse of four measures; and *tetrad*, a group or set of four.

It is common in scientific contexts, for example in *tetrahedron*, a solid having four plane triangular faces; *tetrapod* (Greek *pous*, *pod-*, foot), a four-footed animal; *tetrapterous* (Greek *pteron*, wing), of an insect that has two pairs of wings.

In chemistry it indicates the presence of four atoms or groups of a particular kind: **tetroxide**, an oxide containing four atoms of oxygen in its molecule or empirical formula; **tetracycline**, any of a group of antibiotics with a molecular structure containing four rings; **tetrafluoroethylene**, a dense gas which is polymerized to make plastics; **tetrahydrocannabinol**, a crystalline compound that is the main active ingredient of cannabis.

The form **tetarto-** (from Greek *tetartos*, fourth) now only occurs with any frequency in *tetartohedral*, a term in crystallography for a crystal that has only a quarter of the number of faces required for full symmetry.

-th¹ Also **-eth**. *Forming ordinal and fractional numbers.* [Old English *-(o)tha.*]

The ending is added to numbers from four onwards to make ordinal numbers that define a thing's position in a series: **fourth**, **fifth**, **eighth**, **twenty-ninth**, **hundredth**. When the number ends in *y*, that letter changes to *i* and the ending becomes **-eth**: **twentieth**, **fiftieth**, **nineti-eth**. The same form is used in fractions: *two fifths*, *three eighths*. See also -TEEN (for -*teenth*).

-th² *Forming nouns.* [Old English *-thu, -tho, -th.*]

Some have been formed from verbs: **berth** (from *bear*), **growth** (from *grow*), and **stealth** (from *steal*). Others derive from adjectives: **breadth** (from obsolete *brede*, related to *broad*), **depth** (from *deep*), **health** (from a Germanic stem related to *whole*), **truth** (from *true*), and **width** (from *wide*). Though the ending is not currently active, one example that has returned from obscurity in the latter part of the 20th century is **coolth**, coolness; another sometimes found is the archaic **heighth**, a modern mis-spelling of *height* on the pattern of these others.

thalam(o)- *The thalamus.* [Greek *thalamos*, an inner room.]

The *thalamus* is one of two masses of grey matter that lie deep in the forebrain and which are the junction points for all sensory messages entering the brain. Two examples of the form are **thala-mocortical**, designating sensory nerve fibres running from the thalamus to the cerebral cortex, and **thalamotomy** (Greek *-tomia*, cutting), an operation in the brain involving a cut in part of the thalamus.

thalasso- *The sea.* [Greek *thalassa*, sea.]

Thalassaemia (US **thalassemia**) (Greek *haima*, blood) is a member of a group of hereditary diseases caused by faulty haemoglobin synthesis, so named because they were first found around the Mediterranean; **thalassotherapy** is medical and cosmetic treatment by bathing in sea water; **thalassocracy** (Greek *-kratia*, power, rule) is sovereignty over the seas.

thall(o)- *A thallus; thallium.* [Greek *thallos*, green shoot.]

A *thallus* is a plant body that is not differentiated into stem and leaves, typical of algae, fungi, lichens, and some liverworts. A **thallophyte** (Greek *phuton*, a plant) is a plant that consists of a thallus; linked adjectives are **thalloid** and **thalline**. The element **thallium** was given its name by its discoverer Sir William Crookes (1832–1919) because of a bright green line in its spectrum; the adjective **thallous** refers to that metal in its monovalent state (as in *thallous oxide*, Tl_2O), while **thallic** refers to trivalent thallium (as in *thallic chloride*, $TlCl_3$).

thanato- *Death.* [Greek *thanatos*, death.]

Thanatos in Freudian theory is the death instinct, often expressed in violent aggression; **thanatology** is the scientific study of death and the practices associated with it; **thanatopsis** (Greek *opsis*, sight) is a view or contemplation of death; **thanatophobia** (Greek *phobos*, fear) is a morbid fear of death.

thaumato- *Wonder or miracle.* [Greek *thauma, thaumat-,* marvel.]

Thaumaturgy is the performance of wonders or miracles, carried out by a **thaumaturge** (both words are from Greek *-ergos*, -working); a **thaumatrope** is a 19th-century scientific toy consisting of a rotating disc that causes two pictures to superimpose; **thaumatology** is the description or study of miracles.

-thelium *A layer of body tissue.* [Greek *thēlē*, teat.]

The first term with this ending, on which others are modelled, was *epithelium* (Greek *epi*, upon), the thin tissue that forms the outer layer of a body's surface or which lines a cavity, that on a teat being taken as the model. Other examples: *endothelium* (Greek *endon*, within) is the tissue which forms a single layer of cells lining various organs and cavities of the body, especially the blood vessels, heart, and lymphatic vessels; *mesothelium* (Greek *mesos*, middle) is the epithelium that lines the pleurae, peritoneum, and pericardium; the *urothelium* (Greek *ouron*, urine) is similarly the epithelium that lines the urinary tract, especially that of the bladder.

theo- *God or deities.* [Greek *theos*, god.]

Some examples are *theology*, the study of the nature of God and religious belief; *theocracy*, a system of government in which priests rule in the name of God or a god; and *theophany* (Greek *phainein*, to show), a visible manifestation to humankind of God or a god.

The alkaloid called *theobromine* derives its name indirectly from the same source, as it occurs in seeds of the cocoa plant, whose genus is *Theobroma* (Greek *brōma*, food, hence 'food of the gods'). However, *theodolite*, the surveying instrument, comes from another source, possibly the same root that is in words like *theorem*—Greek *theōrein*, to look at.

-theria: *see* -THERIUM

theri(o)- Also **thero-**. *An animal.* [Greek *thērion*, wild animal; *thēr*, beast.]

Something *theriomorphic* (Greek *morphē*, form) has an animal form; a deity that is *therianthropic* (Greek *anthrōpos*, human being) combines the form of an animal with that of a man; a *therian* is a member of a major group of mammals that comprises the marsupials and placental animals, belonging to the subclass *Theria* (the plural of *thērion*). A *theropod* (Greek *pous*, *pod-*, foot) is a member of a group of carnivorous dinosaurs.

-therium Also **-theria**. *An animal genus.* [Greek *thērion*, wild animal.]

Most such names are of fossil genera, one exception being *Ceratotherium* (Greek *keras*, *kerat-*, horn), the genus containing the white rhino. Examples of fossil species are *Deinotherium* (Greek *deinos*, terrible), an elephant-like mammal found mainly in the Pliocene epoch; *Hyracotherium* (Greek *hurax*, shrew-mouse), the earliest fossil ancestor of the horse from the Eocene epoch; and *Megatherium* (Greek *megas*, great), an extinct giant ground sloth of the Pliocene and Pleistocene epochs in America. Names for fossil genera are often written with lower-case initial letter as a general term for a member of the genus and can then be made plural, either ending in **-theria** (*megatheria*) or by adding *-s*.

-therm Also **-thermal**, **-thermy**, **-thermic**, and **-thermia**. *Temperature; heat.* [Greek *thermē*, heat.]

Most terms in **-therm** categorize animals on the basis of the way they adapt to changes in ambient temperature: an *ectotherm* (Greek *ektos*, outside) is dependent on external sources of body heat; an *endotherm* (Greek *endon*, within) is capable of internal generation of heat; a *poikilotherm* (Greek *poikilos*, variegated, varied), cannot regulate its body temperature except by its behaviour, such as basking or burrowing. A term with a separate sense is *isotherm* (Greek *isos*, equal), a line on a map connecting points having the same temperature at a given time.

Such nouns often have related adjectives ending in **-thermal**: *endothermal*, *isothermal*. Other examples are found in geology, based on the adjective *thermal*: *geothermal*, produced by the internal heat of the earth; *hydrothermal*, denoting the action of heated water in the earth's crust. Some adjectives are formed using **-thermic**: *homeothermic*, *poikilothermic*. *Exothermic* and *endothermic* have specific senses in chemistry for reactions that are accompanied respectively by the release or absorption of heat.

Nouns ending in **-thermy** are usually abstract terms for the state: *ectothermy*, *poikilothermy*, except that *diathermy* (Greek *dia*, through) is a medical technique involving the production of heat in the body by high-frequency electric currents. Some nouns have the ending **-thermia**, for medical states linked to temperature: *hyperthermia* (Greek *huper*, over, beyond), the condition of having a body temperature greatly above normal; *hypothermia* (Greek *hupo*, under), the reverse condition, of having an abnormally (typically dangerously) low body temperature.

therm(o)- *Heat; temperature.* [Greek *thermos*, hot, *thermē*, heat.]

A *thermometer* (Latin *-metrum*, measure) measures temperature; a *thermostat* automatically regulates temperature; a *thermocouple* consists of two wires of different metals and also measures temperature, using the *thermoelectric* effect in which electricity is generated by a difference of temperatures; a *thermoplastic* substance becomes plastic on heating and hardens again on cooling; *thermonuclear* processes are nuclear reactions that occur only at very high temperatures; *thermodynamics* is the branch of physical science that deals with the relations between heat and other forms of energy; the adjective *thermionic* relates to electrons emitted from a substance at high temperatures. The usual adjective relating to heat is *thermal*.

-thermy: *see* -THERM

thio- *Sulphur* [Greek *theion*, sulphur.]

The form is used in chemistry to indicate the replacement of oxygen in a molecule by sulphur: a *thiosulphate* (US *thiosulfate*) is a salt containing the anion $S_2O_3^{2-}$, equivalent to a sulphate with one oxygen atom replaced by sulphur; *thiourea* is the sulphur analogue of urea, $SC(NH_2)_2$, used in photography and in making synthetic resins; a *thiocyanate* is a salt containing the anion SCN^-; the adjective *thionyl* denotes the divalent radical $=SO$.

-thon: *see* -ATHON

thorac(o)- *The chest or thorax.* [Greek *thōrax, thorāc-*, chest.]

A *thoracotomy* (Greek *-tomia*, cutting) is a surgical incision into the chest wall; the adjective *thoracolumbar* refers to the *thoracic* and lumbar regions of the spine; a *thoracostomy* (Greek *stoma*, mouth) is an incision made into the chest wall for drainage.

thrombo- *Blood clotting.* [Greek *thrombos*, blood clot.]

Thrombosis is local coagulation or clotting of the blood in the circulatory system; *thrombolysis* (Greek *lusis*, loosening) is the dissolution of a blood clot; a *thromboembolism* is obstruction of a blood vessel by a blood clot that has become dislodged from another site in the circulation; *thrombocyte* is another name for a platelet, a small disc-shaped cell fragment involved in clotting; *thrombocytopenia* (Greek *penia*, poverty), is a deficiency of platelets in the blood.

-thymia *A condition of the mind.* [Greek *thumos*, state of mind.]

Examples include *dysthymia* (Greek *dus-*, bad or difficult), persistent mild depression; *cyclothymia* (Greek *kuklos*, circle), a mental state in which there are marked swings of mood between depression and elation; and *alexithymia* (*a-*, without, plus Greek *lexis* speech), a disorder marked by inability to recognize or express emotions.

thym(o)- *The thymus.* [Greek *thumos*, excrescence like a thyme bud, thymus gland.]

The *thymus* is a gland in the neck which produces T-lymphocytes for the immune system. A *thymocyte* (Greek *kutos*, vessel) is a lymphocyte within the gland; a *thymoma* is a rare, usually benign tumour arising from thymus tissue; *thymectomy* (Greek *ektomē*, excision) is surgical removal of the thymus gland. The usual adjective referring to the thymus or its functions is *thymic*. *Thymine* is one of the four constituent bases of nucleic acids, so named because a related compound was first extracted from the thymus.

thyro- *The thyroid.* [Greek *(khondros) thur-*

eoeidēs, shield-shaped (cartilage), from *thureos*, oblong shield.]

The *thyroid* is a ductless gland in the neck which secretes hormones regulating growth and development, the main one being **thyroxine**, generated from a protein called **thyroglobulin**. **Thyrotropin** (also **thyrotrophin**) is a hormone secreted by the pituitary gland which regulates the production of thyroid hormones. **Thyrotoxicosis** is a condition caused by an excess of thyroid hormones in the bloodstream.

tibio- *The tibia.* [Latin *tíbia*, shin bone.]

Terms here are adjectives that refer to the *tibia*, the larger bone of the lower leg, together with another part of the skeleton. Examples include **tibiofibular**, of the tibia plus the fibula, the other long bone in the lower leg; **tibiofemoral**, of the tibia plus the femur, the thigh bone. Terms are often hyphenated. The **tibiotarsus** is the bone in a bird's leg that corresponds to the tibia, fused at the lower end with some bones of the tarsus at the ankle.

-tic: *see* -ATIC, -ETIC, -IC, -ITIC, and -OTIC

-tide *A festival of the Christian Church; a specified time or season.* [Old English *tíd*, time, period, era.]

Festivals include *Eastertide*, the period around Easter; *Whitsuntide*, the weekend or week including Whit Sunday; *Shrovetide*, Shrove Tuesday and the two days preceding it; and *Ascensiontide*, the period of ten days from Ascension Day to Whitsun Eve. These are still in use within the Christian Church, but other examples are now only poetic or literary: *eventide*, *noontide*, *springtide*, *winter-tide*, *Yuletide* (the Christmas period).

-tion: *see* -ION

-tious: *see* -ITIOUS

titano-¹ *Gigantic, huge.* [Greek *Titan*, one of the older generation of gods in Greek mythology, who preceded the Olympians and whose size and power was outstandingly great.]

Some words refer to fossil species: a **titanosaur** (Greek *sauros*, lizard) is one of several gigantic Cretaceous dinosaurs; a **titanothere** (Greek *thērion*, wild animal) is a very large extinct horned mammal species related to the rhinoceros. Other examples refer directly to the Greek gods: *Titanism* is a spirit of revolt against the established order or convention, in reference to the war of the Titans against the Olympian gods, called *Titanomachy* (Greek *-makhia*, fighting). The usual adjective referring to great size is **titanic** (but see the next entry for another sense).

titano-² *Titanium.* [The element *titanium* was named by the German chemist Martin Klaproth (1743–1817) from Greek Titan (see the previous entry).]

A **titaniferous** rock or mineral is one that contains titanium, such as its ores **titanomagnetite** and **titanite** (also called *sphene*). A **titanate** is a salt containing the anion $TiO_3{}^{2-}$; the adjectives **titanous** and **titanic** refer respectively to titanium with a combining power of three and four.

toco- Rarely also **toko-**. *Childbirth; reproduction.* [Greek *tokos*, offspring.]

A **tocolytic** drug (Greek *lusis*, loosening) is used to suppress premature labour; a **tocodynamometer** is an electronic device for monitoring and recording uterine contractions in labour; the **tocopherols** (Greek *pherein*, to bear) are a group of closely related compounds, collectively called Vitamin E, needed for normal reproduction and growth; **tocology** (sometimes spelled **tokology**) is an uncommon alternative term for obstetrics.

-tome *An instrument for cutting; a section or segment.* [The first sense is from Greek *-tomon*, that cuts; the second is from Greek *tomē*, a cutting, both from *temnein*, to cut.]

The most common terms in the first sense are **microtome** (Greek *mikros*, small), an instrument for cutting extremely thin sections of material for examination under a microscope, and **osteotome** (Greek *osteon*, bone), a surgical instrument for cutting bone, typically resembling a chisel. Others exist in surgery, usually closely related to terms for a procedure that ends in -TOMY or -ECTOMY, but they are relatively rare.

Terms with the second sense include three for sections of embryos that give rise to particular parts of the body: *dermatome* (Greek *derma*, skin), the part that develops into the connective tissue of the skin; *myotome* (Greek *mus*, *mu-*, muscle), into the skeletal musculature; *sclerotome* (Greek *sklēros*, hard), into bone or other skeletal tissue.

Epitome, a person or thing that is a perfect example of a particular quality or type, or a summary of a written work, derives from Greek *epitemnein*, to make an incision into, hence abridge.

Terms such as *cyclostome* and *protostome* contain the ending -STOME instead.

-tomy Also **-otomy**. *Cutting.* [Greek *-tomia*, cutting, from *temnein*, to cut.]

Dichotomy, a contrast between two things represented as being opposed or entirely different, derives from Greek *dikho-*, in two or apart, hence 'cutting in two'. The subject of *anatomy*, concerned with the bodily structure of humans, animals, and other living organisms, was so named because it relied heavily on dissection (Greek *ana-*, up, so 'cutting up'). Most other examples refer to medical procedures that involve an incision. Some common ones are given in the LIST below. All contain the linking vowel -o- before the ending, making it in effect *-otomy. See also* -ECTOMY and -STOMY.

-tonia Also **-tonic**. *Muscle tone or tension; a personality state.* [Greek *tonos*, tone or tension.]

Examples of the first sense include *dystonia* (Greek *dus-*, bad or difficult), a state of abnormal muscle tone resulting in muscular spasm and abnormal posture; *hypotonia* (Greek *hupo*, under), a state of abnormally low muscle tone (it can also refer to a condition of lower osmotic pressure); *myotonia* (Greek *mus*, *mu-*, muscle), inability to relax voluntary muscle after vigorous effort. A common example of the second sense is *catatonia* (Greek *kata*, badly), abnormal movement and behaviour arising from a disturbed mental state, especially schizophrenia.

Adjectives are formed ending in **-tonic**: *catatonic, dystonic, myotonic*. Some adjectives with this ending do not have analogous nouns ending in **-tonia**: *isotonic* (Greek *isos*, equal) refers to muscle action that takes place with normal contraction; a person who is *syntonic* (Greek *sun*, with) is responsive to and in harmony with their environment.

tono- Tension; tone. [Greek *tonos*, tension, tone.]

A *tonometer* is either a tuning-fork or other instrument for measuring the pitch of musical tones, or an instrument for measuring the pressure in a part of

-tomy A cut or incision.		
craniotomy	removal of a portion of the skull	(Greek *kranion*, skull)
episiotomy	a cut made at the opening of the vagina during childbirth to aid a difficult delivery	(Greek *epision*, pubic region)
keratotomy	a surgical operation involving cutting into the cornea of the eye	(Greek *keras*, *kerat-*, horn)
laparotomy	an opening made into the abdominal cavity	(Greek *lapara*, flank)
lobotomy	an incision into the prefrontal lobe of the brain	(English *lobe*)
osteotomy	the surgical cutting of a bone	(Greek *osteon*, bone)
phlebotomy	the surgical opening or puncture of a vein in order to withdraw blood	(Greek *phleps*, *phleb-*, vein)
thoracotomy	making an opening into the chest wall	(Greek *thōrax*, *thorāc-*, chest)
tracheotomy	an incision in the windpipe made to relieve an obstruction to breathing	(English *trachea*, windpipe)

the body; a **tonoplast** (Greek *plastos*, formed) is a membrane around the vacuole of a plant cell; **tonology** is the branch of linguistics that deals with tones and intonation in speech.

-topia Also **-topic** and **-topian**. *A place with specified characteristics.* [Greek *topos*, place.]

The key term here is **utopia** (Greek *ou*, not), an imagined place or state of things in which everything is perfect; **dystopia** (Greek *dus-*, bad) was later invented as its opposite.

In recent decades, more words with this ending have appeared, such as **ecotopia**, a community whose environment is organized on ecological and environmentally sensitive principles; **subtopia** (from *suburb*), a British term for an unsightly, sprawling suburban development; and **technotopia** (from *technology*), a vision of a utopia brought about by science and technology.

Early examples were blends of delimiting words with *utopia*, but several short-lived inventions in recent years (**digitopia**, **pornotopia**) suggest a combining form is appearing. The ending appears in a few other words, such as **ectopia** (Greek *ektos*, outside), the presence of organs in an abnormal place or position, in which the sense is of something being in a place, rather than a place itself.

The last term is more commonly encountered as the adjective **ectopic**; however, most such words form their related adjectives using **-topian** (*utopian*, *dystopian*).

topo- *Place; position.* [Greek *topos*, place.]

Topology is the study of geometrical properties and spatial relations; **topography** is the arrangement of the natural and artificial physical features of an area; a **toponym** (Greek *onuma*, a name) is a place name, with **toponymy** being their study; **topoisomerase** is an enzyme which alters the supercoiled form of a DNA molecule.

-tor: *see* -OR[1]

-tory: *see* -ORY[1] and -ORY[2].

tox(i)- Also **toxico-** and **toxo-**. *Toxin; toxic.* [Latin *toxicum*, poison, from Greek *toxikon (pharmakon)*, (poison for) arrows, from *toxon*, bow.]

Toxicology is the branch of science concerned with the nature, effects, and detection of poisons; **toxaemia** (US **toxemia**) (Greek *haima*, blood) is blood poisoning by toxins from a local bacterial infection; **toxaphene** (from the second element of the related compound *camphene*) is a synthetic substance used as an insecticide; something **toxigenic**, such as a bacterium, produces a toxin or toxic effect. **Toxocara** (Greek *kara*, head) is a parasitic nematode worm which can cause **toxocariasis** (Greek *kara*, head), an illness that can lead to a risk of blindness; similarly **toxoplasmosis** is a disease caused by protozoa called **toxoplasmas**, transmitted chiefly through undercooked meat, soil, or in cat faeces. The original Greek sense survives in the rather rare **toxophily** (Greek *-philos*, loving), a love or enthusiasm for archery.

trache(o)- *The trachea.* [Greek *trakheia (artēria)*, rough (artery), from *trakhus*, rough.]

The *trachea* is the windpipe. **Tracheotomy** (Greek *-tomia*, cutting), also **tracheostomy** (Greek *stoma*, mouth), is an incision in it to relieve an obstruction to breathing; **tracheitis** is inflammation of it. The eye disease **trachoma** derives from the same Greek root: the eyelashes turn inwards and roughen the surface of the eye, eventually leading to blindness if untreated.

trans- *Across; beyond; through.* [Latin *trans*, across.]

The key sense in this widely distributed form is that of being on the other side of something or moving across or straddling something. Modern examples relating to physical locations include **transatlantic**, **transborder**, and **trans-Pacific**; the area in Romania called **Transylvania** literally means 'beyond the forest' in Latin. Some examples, such as **transalpine**, situated in the area beyond the Alps (in particular as viewed from Italy), are often contrasted with forms beginning in CIS-.

Some examples imply a movement to another place, position, or situation: *transmit* (Latin *mittere*, send); *transfer* (Latin *ferre*, to bear); *transpose* (Latin *poser*, to place); *transition* (Latin *transire*, go across).

There can be an implication of change into another state or condition: *transform* (Latin *formare*, to form), *translate* (Latin *translatus*, carried across); *transmute* (Latin *mutare*, to change), change in form, nature, or substance; *transsexual*, a person having the physical characteristics of one sex but a strong and persistent desire to belong to the other.

Trans- can imply something surpassing: *transcend* (Latin *scandere*, climb), be or go beyond the range or limits of something; *transhistorical*, going beyond historical boundaries, eternal; *transfinite*, in mathematics relating to or denoting a number corresponding to an infinite set.

Many words imported from Latin, or based on Latin elements, now have senses that are figurative: *transact* (Latin *agere*, do, lead), conduct or carry out business; *transfix* (Latin *figere*, fix, fasten), cause someone to become motionless with horror, wonder, or astonishment; *transgress* (Latin *gradi*, go), infringe some established standard of behaviour.

In some cases, the form became truncated to *tra-* or *tre-* in Latin, or in its passage from Latin into English: *tradition* (Latin *dare*, give), *traverse* (Latin *vestire*, clothe), *trespass* (Latin *transpassare*), *traduce* (Latin *ducere*, to lead).

In chemistry, **trans-** refers to a molecule in which two atoms or groups lie on opposite sides of a given plane in the molecule, as in *trans-fatty acid*, an unsaturated fatty acid with this arrangement of the carbon atoms next to its double bonds; other examples are *transaminase*, an enzyme; *trans-2-butene*; *trans-1,2-dichlorocyclopentane*; *trans* is often used as a word in its own right to refer to such arrangements. Its opposite is CIS-.

tri- *Three; having three.* [Latin *tres*, Greek *treis*, three.]

Some examples are *triangle*, literally 'three-cornered' (Latin *angulus*, corner);

triathlon, an athletic contest consisting of three different events; *tripod* (Latin *pous, pod-*, foot), a three-legged stand for supporting a camera or other apparatus; *trilingual*, able to speak three languages (Latin *lingua*, tongue); *tripartite* (Latin *partitus*, divided), consisting of three parts; the fossil animal called a *trilobite* (Greek *lobos*, lobe) had a segmented hindpart divided longitudinally into three lobes; *triplicate* (Latin *triplex, triplic-*, threefold), refers to something existing in three copies or examples. The form is widely used in chemistry to indicate the presence of three atoms or groups of a given type: *trichloroacetic acid*, *triiodothyronine*, *trisaccharide*. See also TRITO-.

-triene: *see* -ENE

trib(o)- *Friction.* [Greek *tribos*, rubbing.]

Triboelectricity is electric charge generated by friction; *triboluminescence* is emission of light from a substance caused by rubbing, scratching, or similar frictional contact; *tribology* is the study of friction, wear, lubrication, and the design of bearings; a *tribometer* is an instrument for measuring friction in sliding.

-trice: *see* -TRIX

tricho- *Hair.* [Greek *thrix, trikho-*, hair.]

Trichology is medical and cosmetic study and practice concerned with the hair and scalp (*trichologist* is sometimes used facetiously to mean a hairdresser); *trichotillomania* (Greek *tillesthai*, pull out) is a compulsive desire to pull out one's hair; *trichiasis* is ingrowth of the eyelashes; *trichoepithelioma* (Greek *epi*, above, plus *thēlē*, teat) is a cancerous tumour derived from hair follicle cells; a *trichocyst* is any of numerous minute rod-like structures found near the surface of ciliates and dinoflagellates.

-trichous *Hairy; having hair.* [Greek *thrix, trikho-*, hair, plus -OUS.]

A variety of specialist adjectives contain this, usually in reference to cilia or flagella on the surface of microorganisms: *peritrichous* (Greek *peri*, about, around), a bacterium that has flagella distributed over the whole cell surface;

hypotrichous (Greek *hupo*, under), having cilia mainly on the lower part of the body; *monotrichous* (Greek *monos*, alone), having a single flagellum; *lophotrichous* (Greek *lophos*, crest), having several flagella in a bundle at one end of the cell.

trito- *Third.* [Greek *tritos*, third.]

In ancient Greek drama, the *tritagonist* (Greek *agōnistēs*, actor) was the person third in importance, after the protagonist and deuteragonist; *tritium* is a radioactive isotope of hydrogen with a mass approximately three times that of the usual isotope; the *tritocerebrum* is the third and hindmost segment of an insect's brain. *See also* TRI-.

-trix Also **-trice**. *Forming feminine agent nouns.* [Latin suffix corresponding to masculine *-tor*.]

Though many words with this suffix have been created since the 15th century, few have been common; those few that do appear mostly now do so only in formal legal contexts: *executrix* (the female equivalent of *executor*), *administratrix* (of *administrator*), and *testatrix* (of *testator*). One that has come back into use in the latter part of the 20th century after a long fallow period is *dominatrix*, a dominating woman who takes the sadistic role in sadomasochistic sexual activities. Other examples, now only historical, are *aviatrix*, a female aviator; *editrix*, a female editor; and *proprietrix*, a female proprietor. The spelling **-trice** is an alternative form, via French, now almost totally archaic. The plural of words ending in **-trix** is either *-trices* or *-trixes*.

trocho- *Wheel-like.* [Greek *trokhos*, wheel.]

A *trochophore* (Greek *-phoros*, *-phoron*, bearing; bearer) is one of the planktonic larvae of certain invertebrates, having a roughly spherical body, a band of cilia, and a spinning motion; a *trochosphere* is the planktonic larva of any of various invertebrates, including certain molluscs and polychaete worms, having a spheroidal body with a ring of cilia in front of the mouth; something *trochoidal* is wheel-like, in various applications.

-tron *A subatomic particle; an instrument or device.* [The ending of *electron*.]

This appears in the names of a few subatomic particles: *neutron*, *positron* (for others, *see* -ON[1]). It has also been used to create the names of various thermionic tubes or valves, such as *ignitron*, *klystron* (Greek *kluzein*, *klus-*, wash over), and *magnetron*. It occurs in the names of particle accelerators, such as *cyclotron*, *synchrotron*, and *bevatron* (from *BEV*, billions of electron volts). The ending was generalized to mean some high-tech device in *orgasmatron*, in Woody Allen's 1973 film *Sleeper*. This has had a few short-lived imitators, and also appears in *perceptron*, a computer model or computerized machine devised to represent or simulate the ability of the brain to recognize and discriminate.

-trope *Form; type; affinity.* [Greek *tropos*, turning.]

Words ending in **-trope** are nouns for organisms or objects that exhibit some characteristic whose abstract name ends in -TROPISM or -TROPY, or for which an adjective exists in -TROPIC. An *allotrope* is one of two or more different physical forms in which an element can exist, an instance of *allotropy*; an *isotrope* (Greek *isos*, equal) is a substance that is *isotropic*, having the same composition in every direction; a *phototrope* is a plant that exhibits *phototropism*, growth or movement in response to light.

Heliotrope (Greek *hēlios*, sun) is now the name of a purple-flowered plant, but the term was once applied to various plants whose flowers turn towards the sun, a phenomenon called *heliotropism*; a *lipotrope* (Greek *lipos*, fat) is a substance that has an affinity for lipids and thus prevents excess fat from accumulating in the liver.

The ending also appears in a few names for 19th-century scientific toys, in which the ending has the literal sense of 'turning': *thaumatrope* (Greek *thauma*, marvel), a disc with pictures on its sides, which appear to combine into one when the disc is spun; *zoetrope* (Greek *zōē*, life), a cylinder with a series of pictures on the inner surface that give an impression of continuous motion when viewed through slits with the cylinder rotating.

-trophic Also **-trophy**, **-trophism**, **-troph**, and **-trophe**. *Nutrition; feeding.* [Greek *trophíkos*, from *trophē*, nourishment.]

Terms ending in **-trophic** are adjectives: a *heterotrophic* (Greek *heteros*, other) organism derives its nutritional requirements from complex organic substances; a lake that is *eutrophic* (Greek *eu*, well) is rich in nutrients and supports many plants, whose decomposition kills animal life by depriving it of oxygen; an organ that is *hypertrophic* (Greek *huper*, over, beyond) has grown because its cells have increased in size, not because their number has risen.

Nouns ending in **-trophy** and **-trophism** name the state or condition associated with such adjectives, the former being more common than the latter: *atrophy* (Greek *a-*, not), wasting away of body tissue or an organ (adjective *atrophic*); *dystrophy* (Greek *dus-*, bad), a disorder in which an organ or tissue of the body wastes away (adjective *dystrophic*).

Nouns ending in **-troph** refer to instances of the state or condition: *auxotroph* (Latin *auxílium*, help), a mutant organism that requires a particular additional nutrient which the normal strain does not. Some can appear spelled **-trophe**: *oligotrophe*, an instance of a lake which is relatively poor in plant nutrients and containing abundant oxygen in the deeper parts, from Greek *oligoi*, few.

Apostrophe, *catastrophe* and their relatives derive instead from Greek *strophē*, turning.

troph(o)- *Nourishment.* [Greek *trophē*, nourishment.]

Examples include *trophoblast* (Greek *blastos*, germ, sprout), a layer of tissue on the outside of a mammalian blastula, supplying the embryo with nourishment; *trophozoite* (Greek *zoion*, animal), a growing stage in the life cycle of some sporozoan parasites, when they are absorbing nutrients from the host; *tro-phallaxis* (Greek *allaxis*, exchange), the mutual exchange of regurgitated liquids between adult social insects or between them and their larvae.

-tropic Also **-tropous**. *Turning; changing; affecting.* [Greek *tropē*, turn, turning.]

Adjectives with both these endings are closely related to nouns ending in -TROPISM and -TROPY in their various senses. Examples include *isotropic* (Greek *isos*, equal), having a physical property which has the same value when measured in different directions; *thixotropic* (Greek *thixis*, touching), of a substance that becomes less viscous when subjected to an applied stress; *psychotropic* (Greek *psukhē*, breath, soul, mind), denoting drugs that affect a person's mental state.

Adjectives ending in **-tropous** have a similar sense, but are much less common; two examples are *orthotropous* (Greek *orthos*, straight, right), of an ovule, part of the ovary of the plant, that is growing straight; *campylotropous* (Greek *kampulos*, bent), having an ovule that is partially inverted and curved.

-tropism *Preferential growth or movement of an organism.* [Greek *tropē*, turning.]

Words ending in **-tropism** usually contain the sense of *tropism*, the growth or movement of an organism in a particular direction in response to an external stimulus. Examples include *geotropism* (Greek *gē*, earth), growth in response to gravity; *heliotropism* (Greek *hēlios*, sun), directional growth in response to sunlight; *phototropism* (Greek *phōs*, *phōt-*, light), orientation in response to light; *thigmotropism* (Greek *thigma*, touch), the turning or bending of a plant or other organism in response to a touch stimulus; *chemotropism*, growth or movement in response to a chemical stimulus. One instance that stands aside from this group is *neurotropism*, the tendency of a virus, toxin, or chemical substance to attack or affect the nervous system preferentially. Associated adjectives are formed using -TROPIC.

tropo- *Turning; change.* [Greek *tropos*, turning.]

The *troposphere* is the lowest region of the atmosphere, which exhibits convection; it extends from the earth's surface to the *tropopause*, the interface between the troposphere and the stratosphere; *tropomyosin* is a protein involved in muscle contraction, myosin, and occurs together with a related protein, *troponin*, in the thin filaments of muscle tissue. *Tropology* is the figurative use of language; a *trope* is a figurative or metaphorical use of a word or expression.

-tropous: *see* -TROPIC

-tropy *Forming nouns that correspond to adjectives ending in* -TROPIC. [Greek *tropos*, turning.]

Examples include *isotropy* (Greek *isos*, equal), having a physical property which has the same value when measured in different directions; *pleiotropy* (Greek *pleiōn*, more), the production by a single gene of two or more apparently unrelated effects; *thixotropy* (Greek *thixis*, touching), the property of becoming less viscous when subjected to an applied stress, shown for example by some gels which become temporarily fluid when shaken or stirred; *allotropy* (Greek *allo-*, other), the existence of two or more different physical forms of a chemical element.

tubo- Also **tubi-**. *A tube.* [Latin *tubus*, tube.]

In medicine, the term *tubo-ovrian* (also *tuboovarian*) refers to a Fallopian tube together with an ovary, and *tuboplasty* is the surgical repair of one or both Fallopian tubes. *Tubocurarine* is an alkaloid used to relax voluntary muscles, so named because its precursor, curare, was at one time transported in bamboo tubes in South America. A *tubifex* worm (Latin *-fex* from *facere*, make) is a small worm that lives in fresh water, partly buried in the mud, an example of a *tubicolous* worm, one living in a tube.

-tude Also **-tudinous**. *Forming abstract nouns.* [French *-tude*, from Latin *-tudo*.]

Examples include *altitude*, *fortitude*, *gratitude*, *latitude*, *magnitude*, *multitude*, *platitude*, and *solitude*. A few have adjectives ending in **-tudinous**: *multitudinous*, *platitudinous*.

turbo- *A turbine.* [Latin *turbo*, *turbin-*, spinning top, whirl.]

A *turbine* is a power-generating machine in which a wheel is driven round by a stream of air, water, steam, or other fluid. Compounds indicate either the presence of a turbine or a device driven by one: *turbocharger*, a turbine powered by the engine's exhaust gases, so increasing its power; *turbofan*, a jet engine in which a turbine-driven fan provides additional thrust; *turbojet*, a jet engine in which the jet gases also operate a turbine-driven compressor for compressing the air drawn into the engine; *turboprop*, a jet engine in which a turbine is used to drive a propeller.

Turco- Also **Turko-**. *Turkish; Turkish and...* [English *Turkey*.]

Examples include *Turco-German*, *Turco-Russian*, and *Turco-Italian*. Such compounds are much less commonly spelled **Turko-**. A *Turcophile* is someone who favours Turkish culture or people.

-ty¹ *Forming nouns.* [Via Old French from Latin *-tas*, *-tat-*.]

Examples include *anxiety* (Latin *anxietas*), *difficulty* (Latin *difficultas*), *honesty* (Latin *honestas*), *modesty* (Latin *modestus*, keeping due measure), *poverty* (Latin *paupertas*, from *pauper*, poor); others are *casualty*, *penalty*, and *sobriety*. Some, such as *beauty*, *royalty*, and *warranty*, were formed in French. However, *travesty* comes through French from Italian *travestire*, from Latin *trans-*, across, plus *vestire*, clothe. *See also* -ITY.

-ty² *Groups of ten.* [Old English *-tig*, denoting ten, the second element of the decade numerals from 20 to 90.]

This suffix appears in all the English words for multiples of ten from *twenty* up to *ninety*: *thirty*, *fifty*, *eighty*, etc.

tympan(o)- *The eardrum.* [Greek *tumpanon*, drum.]

The formal name for the eardrum is *tympanum*; medical terms that refer to it include *tympanoplasty*, surgical repair of defects of the eardrum or the ossicles of the middle ear; *tympanometry*, the measurement, for diagnostic purposes, of changes in the compliance of the *tympanic* membrane as the air pressure is altered in the passage of the external ear, leading to the production of a *tympanogram*, a graphical record of the pressure changes; *tympanosclerosis* is thickening of the tympanic membrane, and of the connective tissue in the tympanic cavity. However, the condition called *tympanides* is swelling of the abdomen with air or gas so that it becomes resonant or drumlike. The *timpani* or *tympani* are the kettledrums, especially when played by one musician in an orchestra.

-ual: *see* -AL[1]

über- or **uber-**. *Superior*. [German *über*, over.]

The model for this combining form is German *Übermensch*, superman, which dates from the beginning of the 20th century. From the 1980s on, a few short-lived words began to be created, suggesting a superior version of a given personal type, but usually in a mildly derogatory or tongue-in-cheek way: *überconcept*, *uberbabe*, *übercouple*, *ubergeek*. The umlaut is often left off.

-ubility, **-uble**, or **-ubly**: *see* -ABLE

-ula Also **-ular**. *Forming diminutive nouns*. [Latin feminine ending *-ula*.]

Examples include *auricula* (diminutive of Latin *auris*, ear), an Alpine primula whose leaves supposedly resemble bears' ears; *cannula* (diminutive of Latin *canna*, reed), a thin tube inserted into a vein or body cavity during surgery; *spatula* (diminutive of Latin *spatha*, a broadsword), an implement with a broad, flat, blunt blade. However, *peninsula* derives from Latin *insula*, island; others come from a variety of sources.

Words ending in **-ular** are adjectives, derived from the Latin adjectival ending *-ularis*. They are sometimes related to diminutive nouns ending in -ULE or **-ula** (*fistular*, *globular*, *macular*, *molecular*, *pustular*). Others are linked to a variety of English nouns that have various endings with no diminutive sense (*angular*, *irregular*, *muscular*, *oracular*, *perpendicular*).

-ule Also **-ulum** and **-ulus**. *Forming nouns*. [Latin endings *-ulus*, *-ula*, *-ulum*.]

Many words ending in **-ule** were created in Latin as diminutives, though this sense is often not present in modern English terms derived from them, as with *schedule* (Latin *schedula*, a slip of paper, a diminutive of *scheda*, paper); or *ferrule* (Latin *viriola*, a diminutive of *viriae*,

bracelets). Some where a sense of smallness persists are *globule* (Latin *globulus*, diminutive of *globus*, a spherical object or globe), a small round particle of a substance; *capsule* (Latin *capsula*, diminutive of *capsa*, a case), a small case or container; and *molecule* (Latin *molecula*, diminutive of *moles*, mass), a group of atoms bonded together.

Words ending in **-ulum** derive from Latin neuter nouns: *pendulum* (literally, 'a little hanging thing' from Latin *pendulus*, hanging down); *curriculum* (Latin *curriculum*, course, racing chariot, from *currere*, to run); *pabulum* (Latin, derived from *pascere*, to feed), bland or insipid intellectual fare or entertainment. Words ending in **-ulus** are similarly from Latin masculine nouns: *stimulus* is from the Latin word meaning a goad, spur, or incentive; *cumulus*, a type of cloud, derives from the Latin word for a heap; *homunculus* (diminutive of Latin *homo*, *homin-*, man) is a very small human or humanoid creature. Other examples with both endings are mostly specialist words in the sciences.

See also -OLE[2].

-ulent *Abounding in; full of*. [Latin *-ulentus*.]

Some words ending in **-ulent** were created in Latin and a few others have been generated in English on their model, though the ending is not particularly active. Examples are *corpulent*; *flatulent*; *flocculent* (Latin *floccus*, tuft of wool), having or resembling tufts of wool; *fraudulent*; *opulent*; *succulent*; *truculent*; and *turbulent*. Associated nouns end in **-ulence**: *corpulence*, *opulence*, *turbulence*. *See also* -LENT.

ulno- *The ulna*. [Latin *ulna*, plus -O-.]

The *ulna* is the thinner and longer of the two bones in the human forearm; terms beginning with **ulno-** refer to the ulna plus another part of the arm, as in *ulnocarpal*, of the ulna plus the carpus bones of the wrist; *ulnoradial*, of the ulna plus the radius, the other long bone of the forearm; *ulnohumeral*, of the ulna plus the humerus, the bone of the upper arm. These terms sometimes appear hyphenated.

-ulose: *see* -OSE[1] *or* -OSE[2]

-ulous: *see* -OUS

ultra- *Beyond; extreme.* [Latin *ultra*, beyond.]

The form is common in scientific terms, such as *ultraviolet*, of electromagnetic radiation beyond the violet end of the visible spectrum; *ultrasonic*, involving sound waves too high-pitched for humans to hear; *ultrashort*, of radio waves that have a wavelength shorter than about 10 metres; *ultracentrifuge*, a very fast centrifuge used to precipitate large biological molecules from solution.

In non-technical terms, it often refers to something taken to an extreme, as in *ultraleft*, of an individual or group holding opinions at the extreme left of the political spectrum; *ultraist*, a holder of extreme opinions; *ultrafeminine*, being feminine to an extreme extent; *ultraportable*, a type of personal computer that is extremely small.

In a few words the sense is of something figuratively lying beyond another in physical position, as in the deep blue pigment *ultramarine*, which derives from Latin *ultramarinus*, beyond the sea, something obtained from overseas; *ultramontane* (Latin *mons*, *mont-*, mountain) refers to advocacy of supreme papal authority in matters of faith and discipline (originally it denoted a representative of the Roman Catholic Church north of the Alps, beyond the Alps from the viewpoint of Rome).

un- *Negation; reversal of a state.* [Old English prefixes *un-* and *on-*, of Germanic origin.]

This prefix occurs extremely widely; the majority of adjectives, adverbs, and verbs (and many nouns) can in principle be given it to create a new word indicating an opposite or a reversal.

A very few of the many examples in the sense of 'not' are *unconnected*, *unenclosed*, *unfashionable*, *unhappy*, *unloved*, *unmade*, *unsuitable*, and *unwilling*. In this sense, **un-** often has a stronger and less neutral force than just negation (so it is not equivalent to NON-): *unkind* can mean active cruelty rather than a simple lack of kindness; to say someone is *un-American* can imply an active antagonism to American ways.

With verbs, it usually has the sense of reversing some state: *unblock*, *unburden*, *unhook*, *unlace*, *unsettle*, *unstick*, *untie*, *unwind*, *unzip*.

Un- is closely related in sense to **in-** (*see* IN-[1]), but although the latter prefix is common it is no longer active. There is no good rule to decide which is the right form in any given situation and terms have to be learnt. To confuse matters somewhat, some noun-adjective pairs use different prefixes: *instability* corresponds to *unstable*; *inequality* to *unequal*; *injustice* to *unjust*. In a few cases, pairs of adjectives exist in both prefixes with similar senses: *inadvisable* and *unadvisable*; *incommunicative* and *uncommunicative*. In a few other pairs, members have significantly different senses, as with *unhuman*, not resembling or having the qualities of a human being, versus *inhuman*, lacking human qualities of compassion and mercy.

-uncle *Forming nouns, chiefly diminutives.* [Old French *-oncle*, *-uncle*, or from Latin *-unculus*, a special form of *-ulus*.]

This form occurs in a few words, but is not active. Examples are *carbuncle* (Latin *carbunculus*, small coal), a severe abscess or multiple boil in the skin; *peduncle*, the stalk bearing a flower or fruit (Latin *pedunculus*, from Latin *pes*, *ped-*, foot); *furuncle*, a technical term for a boil (Latin *furunculus*, literally 'petty thief', also 'a knob on a vine', regarded as stealing the sap, from *fur*, thief).

undec(a)- *Eleven.* [Latin *undecim*, eleven.]

An *undecagon* (Greek *-gōnos*, angled) is a plane figure with eleven straight sides and angles; *undecane* (*see* -ANE) is a hydrocarbon of chemical formula

$C_{11}H_{24}$; the related fatty acid is **undecanoic acid**, one form of which, produced from castor oil and used in perfumery, is commonly called **undecylenic acid**.

under- *Below.* [Old English *under-*.]

Some terms refer to something being placed—literally or figuratively—underneath something else: **underclothes**, **undercover**, **undergrowth**, **underpass**. The sense of lower position can figuratively refer to someone in a subordinate role: **undersecretary**, **understudy**, **undersheriff**. Some have lost a direct link to position: **understand**, **undertake**.

A related and common sense is of something that is insufficient or incomplete: to **underachieve** is to do less well than expected; a firm that is **undercapitalized** has insufficient funds to achieve its desired results; a person who is **undernourished** lacks enough food for good health; an area that is **underpopulated** has an insufficient or very small population.

uni- *One; having or consisting of one.* [Latin *unus*, one.]

Some examples taken from Latin include **unicorn** (Latin *cornu*, horn); **unify** (Latin *unificare*, make into a whole); **uniform** (Latin *uniformis*); **universe** (Latin *universus*, combined into one, whole); and **university** (Latin *universitas*, the whole, in late Latin referring to a society or guild).

The form is widely used: **unisex** refers to something, especially clothing or hairstyles, designed to be suitable for both sexes; a **unipod** is a one-legged support for a camera; a **unitard** is a one-piece garment, a version of a leotard; something **unidirectional** moves or operates in a single direction; an action that is **unilateral** is performed by only one party in a situation, so is not mutually agreed; in chemistry, something **unimolecular** consists of or involves a single molecule.

See also MONO-.

unnil- *Also* **unun-**. *Certain transuranic elements.* [Latin *unus*, one, plus *nil*, nothing.]

During a long-standing dispute over what names to give to artificially synthesized transuranic elements of atomic number over 100, temporary names were assigned by the International Union of Pure and Applied Chemistry. Names used **unnil-** to indicate *10*, plus a Latin or Greek numeral for the final digit, plus -IUM indicating an element. So **unnilquadium** (Latin *quattuor*, four), was element 104, now *rutherfordium*; **unnilhexium** (Greek *hex*, six) was element 106, now *seaborgium*. The dispute has been resolved and this naming convention is now reserved for a few elements of atomic number above 110 that have not yet been given formal names; these are formed using **unun-** (representing *11*), as in **unununium** for element 111, **ununquadium** for 114.

-uous: *see* -OUS

up- *Up; upwards; higher; increased.* [Old English *up-*.]

The prefix is attached to verbs and nouns, forming new verbs, nouns, adjectives, and adverbs. In some cases, a literal sense of movement upwards or to a higher position is meant, as in **updraught**, **uphill**, **upland**, **upriver**, **upslope**, **upswing**, **uptown**, and **upwind** (the wind being considered as flowing downhill like a river). In a few, a sense of inversion appears, as in **upend** and **upturn**. Many examples are figurative, as in **upbringing**, **upgrade**, **upmarket**, **upbeat**, and **upstart** (a person, often behaving arrogantly, who has risen suddenly to wealth or high position).

-up *An activity.* [English *up*.]

Some nouns have been formed from phrasal verbs that include *up*, as **sign-up**, the action of enrolling for something, comes from the verb phrase *to sign up*, or **warm-up**, a period or act of preparation for a match or performance, from *to warm up*; others are **chat-up** and **take-up**. Many others have been created on this model, mostly informal terms: **booze-up**, **cock-up**, **frame-up**, a conspiracy to falsely incriminate someone; **knees-up**, a party or lively gathering; **lace-up**, a shoe or boot that is fastened with laces; **mix-up**, a confusion of one thing with another;

pick-me-up, a restorative; *toss-up*, a situation in which any of two or more outcomes is equally possible or attractive.

ur- *Primitive; original; earliest.* [From German.]

An *urtext* is an original or the earliest version of a text, to which later versions can be compared; an *ur-novel* is the earliest example of a novel in modern form, or one written in a deliberately primitive style; an *ur-language* (often also *Ursprache* from German) is a hypothetically reconstructed parent language.

urano-¹ *The heavens; the palate.* [Greek *ouranos*, heavens, sky; roof of the mouth.]

Terms relating to the heavens are archaic (*uranography*, the branch of astronomy concerned with describing and mapping the stars). The same stem occurs in the family of fishes called the *Uranoscopidae*, the stargazers, so called because their eyes are on top of their heads.

Words relating to the palate are specialist and relatively uncommon. Examples are *uranoplasty*, plastic surgery on the hard palate, and *uranoschisis* (Greek *skhistos*, divided), the technical term for a cleft palate.

uran(o)-² *Uranium.* [The stem of English *uranium* plus -o-.]

The radioactive element *uranium* was named after the then newly discovered planet *Uranus*, whose name in turn was taken from that of the Greek god who was ruler of the universe, so it ultimately derives from the same stem as that in the previous entry. The *uranyl* cation is UO_2^{2+}, present in some compounds of uranium; *uranic* compounds contain uranium with a combining power of six, while in *uranous* ones it has a combining power of four; *uranophane* (Greek -*phanēs*, appearing) is an ore of uranium.

ur(e)- *Urea.* [Greek *ourein*, urinate.]

Urea is a nitrogen-containing substance excreted in urine. *Uraemia* (US *uremia*) (Greek *haima*, blood) is a raised level in the blood of urea and other nitrogenous waste compounds that are normally eliminated by the kidneys; *urease* is an enzyme that catalyses the conversion of urea to carbon dioxide and ammonia; a *ureide* is any of a group of compounds which are acyl derivatives of urea; *urethane* (also called *ethyl carbamate*) is a synthetic crystalline-derived compound from urea used in making pesticides and fungicides, which polymerizes to make the resin *polyurethane*, used in paints, varnishes, and adhesives.

-ure¹ *Forming nouns.* [Latin -*ura*; French -*eure* and other endings.]

Nouns with this ending that derive from Latin broadly denote an action, instrument, process, or result, of which some examples are *censure*, *closure*, *creature* (something that has been created), *gesture*, *lecture*, *rupture*, and *scripture* (literally, something written).

Some words with this ending derive from French suffixes (such as -*eure*, -*ir*, -*or*, and -*our*) and have taken on the -**ure** ending in English by imitation: *enclosure*, *moisture*, *pleasure*, *nurture*, *treasure*. Others derive from Latin words with other endings: *ordure*.

-ure² *Forming nouns.* [Greek *oura*, tail.]

The best-known example is *cynosure* (Greek *kuōn*, *kun-*, dog, originally the constellation Ursa Minor or the pole star, used for navigation), a person or thing that is the centre of attention or admiration. Several examples are alternative names for animals: *gymnure* (Greek *gumnos*, naked), the moonrat; *zonure* (Greek *zōnē*, girdle), the girdled lizard; *dasyure* (Greek *dasus*, rough, hairy), another name for the quoll.

-uret *A binary compound.* [Latin ending -*uretum*.]

This is an archaic chemical suffix for compounds of two elements, for which the standard ending is now -IDE. Examples that may be encountered in older writings, especially in geology and mining, include *sulphuret*, a compound of sulphur with another element, a sulphide; *carburet*, one containing carbon, a carbide.

ureter(o)- *The ureter.* [English *ureter* (from Greek *ourein*, urinate), plus -o-.]

The *ureter* is one of a pair of tubes by which urine passes from the kidneys to the bladder. *Ureteritis* is inflammation of it; *ureterostomy* (Greek *stoma*, mouth) is the surgical creation of an external opening to it; *ureterectomy* (Greek *ektomē*, excision) is its surgical removal; a *ureterocele* hernia (Greek *kēlē*, tumour) occurs when its lower end slips down into the bladder.

urethr(o)- *The urethra.* [English *urethra* (from Greek *ourein*, urinate), plus -o-.]

The *urethra* is the tube by which urine passes out of the body from the bladder. *Urethritis* is inflammation of it; *urethroplasty* (Greek *plastos*, formed, moulded) is its surgical repair; *urethrography* (Greek *-graphia*, writing) is X-ray examination of it, after introducing a radiopaque fluid.

-urgy Also **-urge**. *The art or process for working with something.* [Greek *-ourgia*, working.]

This ending appears in a small set of words derived from Greek, but is not active in the language. Examples include *metallurgy* (Greek *metallon*, metal), the branch of science and technology concerned with the production and purification of metals; *dramaturgy*, the theory and practice of dramatic composition; *liturgy* (Greek *lēitos*, public), a form by which public religious worship is conducted; *thaumaturgy* (Greek *thauma*, marvel), the working of wonders and performing of miracles; *zymurgy* (Greek *zumē*, leaven), the study or practice of fermentation in brewing and associated fields. A person engaged in the activity is sometimes indicated by **-urge**: *dramaturge*, *thaumaturge*.

-uria Also **-uric**. *A substance present in the urine, especially in excess.* [Greek *-ouria*, from *ouron*, urine.]

This ending is common in medicine; a few examples are *proteinuria*, the presence of abnormal quantities of protein in the urine, which may indicate damage to the kidneys; *bacteriuria*, the presence of bacteria in the urine; *polyuria* (Greek *polus*, much), production of abnormally large volumes of dilute urine, as opposed to *oliguria* (Greek *oligos*, small), the production of abnormally small

amounts; *haematuria* (US *hematuria*) (Greek *haima*, blood), the presence of blood in urine. Associated adjectives are formed ending in **-uric**: *polyuric*, *haemauric*, *glycosuric* (Greek *glukus*, sweet), of a condition in which there is too much sugar in the urine.

urino- *Urine; the urinary system.* [English *urine* (from Latin *urina*), plus -o-.]

Urinalysis is the analysis of urine to detect abnormal constituents; a *urinoma* is a cyst containing urine; *urinogenital* refers to the organs concerned with excretion and reproduction; A *urinometer* measures the specific gravity of urine. *See also* URO-².

uro-¹ *The tail or the tail part of the body.* [Greek *oura*, tail.]

The *uropod* (Greek *pous*, *pod*-, foot) is the sixth and last pair of abdominal appendages of lobsters and related crustaceans, forming part of the tail fan; the *uropygium* (Greek *pugē*, rump) is the rump of a bird, supporting the tail feathers; a *urostyle* is a long bone at the base of the vertebral column in frogs and toads.

uro-² *Urine or the urinary organs.* [Greek *ouron*, urine.]

Urodynamics is the diagnostic study of pressure in the bladder, in treating incontinence; the adjective *urogenital* denotes both the urinary and genital organs; *urolithiasis* is the formation of stony concretions in the bladder or urinary tract; *urology* is the branch of medicine and physiology concerned with the function and disorders of the urinary system. *See also* URINO-.

uter(o)- *The uterus.* [English or Latin *uterus* plus -o-.]

Many instances are adjectives that refer to the uterus plus another part of the body, such as *uteroplacental* of the placenta and uterus; *uterovaginal*, of the uterus and vagina; *uterocervical*, of the cervix, the neck of the uterus. Such terms are often hyphenated. A *uterotomy* (Greek *-tomia*, cutting) is a surgical incision into the uterus, as in a caesarean section; *uterosalpingography* (*see* SALPINGO-) is an X-ray examination of the interior of the womb and the Fallopian tubes.

-ution *Forming nouns.* [French from Latin words ending in *-utio(n-)*.]

Nouns have a similar sense to those formed with -ATION, denoting an action, or an instance of an action, or its result. Examples include *absolution*, *contribution*, *diminution*, *institution*, *persecution*, *pollution*, *retribution*, *resolution*, and *solution*. However, *electrocution* is an accidental spelling, derived from *electrocute* by adding -ION.

V

vagin(o)- *The vagina.* [Latin *vagina*, literally 'sheath, scabbard'.]

Vaginosis is a bacterial infection of the vagina; *vaginitis* is inflammation of it; *vaginography* is the examination of the vagina using X-rays. The prefix also appears in terms referring to the vagina and an associated part of the body, as in *vaginolabial*, of the vagina and labia. *See also* COLPO-.

vago- *The vagus nerve.* [Latin *vagus*, wandering, uncertain.]

The *vagus nerve* is heavily branched and connects the brain with the heart, lungs, and stomach and to other upper digestive organs. The most common term is *vagotomy*, a surgical operation in which one or more branches of the vagus nerve are cut, typically to reduce gastric secretion in treating peptic ulcers; a person or animal subjected to this has been *vagotomized*. Something *vagolytic* acts to disrupt or impede the action of the vagus nerve.

-valent *Combining power.* [Latin *valent-*, being strong, present participle of *valere*, to be worth.]

This ending is common in chemistry to indicate the combining power or *valency* of an element or radical. Though it is possible to use either Latin or Greek number prefixes, the Greek ones are much more common: *monovalent* (a combining power of one), *divalent* (of two), and so on (see the list of NUMBER PREFIXES on page 161); one with a valency of three or more is *polyvalent* (Greek *polloi*, many). The ending also appears in terms indicating the nature of the combination, as in *covalent*, bonding by sharing electrons, as opposed to ionic or *electrovalent*, bonding where the attraction is electrostatic.

Outside chemistry, the same ending occurs in *ambivalent* (Latin *ambi-*, on both sides), *equivalent* (Latin *aequi-*, equally), and *prevalent* (Latin *praevalere*, have greater power, from *prae*, before).

varico- Also **varici-**. *A varicose vein.* [Latin *varix*, *varic-*, dilated vein.]

A *varicocele* (Greek *kēlē*, swelling) is a collection of dilated veins in the spermatic cord; *varicosis* is the condition of having varicose veins, usually in the legs; something *variciform* resembles a varicose vein.

vas(o)- *A vessel.* [Latin *vas*, vessel.]

Most terms are medical ones relating to blood vessels and hence to blood pressure: *vasoconstriction* is the constriction of blood vessels, which increases blood pressure (the opposite is *vasodilation*); *vasopressin* (from *pressor*, something causing pressure) is a pituitary hormone which acts to increase blood pressure. However, *vasectomy* (Greek *ektomē*, excision), refers to the surgical cutting of the *vas deferens*, ducts which convey sperm from the testicles, typically as a means of sterilization.

ven(o)- Also **vene-** and **veni**. *A vein.* [Latin *vena*, vein.]

In medicine, *venipuncture* (sometimes *venepuncture*) is the puncture of a vein for any therapeutic purpose; *venography* is X-ray examination of a vein after injection of a radiopaque fluid, so producing a *venogram*; *venesection* (sometimes *venisection*) is another name for phlebotomy, the letting of blood by cutting a vein. *See also* PHLEBO-.

ventricul(o)- *A ventricle.* [Latin *ventriculus*, diminutive of *venter*, belly.]

A *ventricle* is a hollow or cavity in an organ, in particular the main chambers of the heart and four natural cavities in the brain; the adjective for either of these is *ventricular*. Medical terms containing this form usually refer to those in the brain: *ventriculography* is radiography of them; *ventriculostomy* (Greek *stoma*, mouth) is an operation to introduce a hollow needle into a ventricle for a variety of purposes, such as draining cerebrospinal fluid.

vermi- *A worm.* [Latin *vermis*, worm.]

Something **vermiform** resembles or has the form of a worm (as in *vermiform appendix*, the full name for the human appendix). A **vermicide** (Latin *caedere*, kill) is a substance that kills worms; a **vermifuge** (Latin *fugare*, cause to flee) is a medicine that kills intestinal parasitic worms; **vermiculture** is the cultivation of earthworms.

Several terms have figurative links: **vermicelli** is the Italian name for pasta made in long slender threads; the mineral called **vermiculite** comes from Latin *vermiculari*, full of worms, because on heating it expands and throws out what look like small worms; the dye called **vermilion** (Latin *vermiculus*, a small worm) was originally produced from the dried bodies of an insect, mistakenly thought to be a worm.

vesic(o)- Also **vesiculo-**. *A blister; the urinary bladder.* [Latin *vesica*, bladder.]

A **vesicle** can be any of a variety of fluid-filled or air-filled cavities or sacs, including a small blister full of clear fluid. A **vesicant** is an agent that causes blistering.

Most medical terms use **vesico-** to refer to the urinary bladder, for which the adjective is **vesical**; **vesicoureteric reflux** (Greek *ourein*, to urinate) is a flow of urine from the bladder back into the ureters, caused by defective valves; **vesicostomy** (Greek *stoma*, mouth) is a surgical procedure that creates a passage between the bladder and the skin to allow urine to pass; **vesicovaginal** refers to the bladder and the vagina.

Terms ending in **vesiculo-** (Latin *vesicula*, diminutive of *vesica*) refer to the seminal vesicles, as in **vesiculitis**, inflammation of them.

vibro- Also **vibra-**. *Oscillation; shaking.* [Latin *vibrare*, to tremble or shake.]

The Latin word is the source of *vibration*, *vibrant*, and the musical term *vibrato* for a rapid, slight variation in pitch. A **vibraphone** (sometimes called a **vibraharp**, formerly a US proprietary name) is a percussion instrument containing a motor-driven rotating vane or electronic circuits that give a vibrato effect. A **vibrometer** is a device for measuring the movements of a vibrating body; the adjective **vibrotactile** refers to the perception of vibration through touch.

vice- *Deputy; assistant.* [Latin *vice*, in place of.]

Numerous formations exist, of which a few are **vice-president**, an official or executive ranking below and deputizing for a president; **vice-chancellor**, a deputy chancellor, especially one of a British university who discharges most of its administrative duties; **vice-chairman**, a deputy chairman; **viceroy** (Latin *roi*, king), a ruler exercising authority in a colony on behalf of a sovereign, for which the adjective is **viceregal**.

viginti- *Twenty.* [Latin *viginti*, twenty.]

This prefix is rare. Something **vigintennial** occurs every twenty years; for **vigintillion** see the table of NUMBER WORDS on page 162.

-ville *A fictitious place indicating some quality.* [French *ville*, town.]

This suffix is of US origin, where many real place names end in **-ville**. Examples are usually used humorously and negatively: **dullsville**, the quintessentially dull provincial town, hence something or somewhere boring; **nowheresville**, an isolated place where there is no prospect of success or opportunity for advancement, so a job or position with these qualities; **pleasantville**, the archetypal nice place to be (also the name of a film in 1998 and the name of several real towns in the US). The suffix is active, generating transient forms such as **bribesville** for a place where corruption is endemic. Sometimes words are given initial capitals, as though they were actual place names.

vin(i)- Also **vino-**. *Wine.* [Latin *vinum*, wine.]

Viniculture is the cultivation of grapevines for winemaking; **vinification** is the conversion of grape juice into wine by fermentation (for which the verb is *vinify*); *vinology* is the scientific study of grapevines; the adjective associated with wine is *vinous*.

vir(o)- Also **viri-** and **viru-**. *A virus*. [Latin *virus*, poison.]

Viraemia (also *viremia*) is the presence of viruses in the blood; a *virucide* or *viricide* is a substance that kills viruses; a *virion* is the complete, infective form of a virus outside a host cell; *virology* is the branch of science that studies viruses.

English *virulent* shares the same Latin root. However, *virile* and *virility* come instead from Latin *vir*, man, while *viridian* and *viridescent* derive from Latin *viridis*, green.

viscero- *The viscera*. [Latin *viscera*, the plural of *viscus*.]

The *viscera* are the internal organs in the main cavities of the body, especially those in the abdomen (the singular is *viscus*). A *viscerotropic* micro-organism is one that tends to attack the viscera; a *viscerosomatic* reaction is a muscular response to a stimulus in a visceral organ; *visceromotor* impulses control the smooth muscle in the viscera. The adjective relating to the viscera is *visceral*, though it also has a figurative sense relating to deep inward feelings rather than to the intellect.

visco- *Sticky; thick*. [English *viscous*, from Latin *viscum*, birdlime.]

Viscosity is the state of being thick and sticky in consistency (for which the adjective is *viscous*), or a quantity expressing the ease with which a substance flows. A substance that is *viscoelastic* exhibits both elastic and viscous behaviour; a *viscometer* is an instrument for measuring the viscosity of liquids; *viscose* is a viscous orange-brown solution used to make rayon fibre and transparent cellulose film.

visuo- *Sight; vision*. [Latin *visus*, sight.]

This prefix appears in a number of adjectives relating to vision, of which the most common are *visuospatial*, relating to visual perception of the relative positions of objects, and *visuomotor*, relating to the coordination of movement and visual perception by the brain.

vitell(i)- Also **vitello-**. *The yolk of an egg*. [Latin *vitellus*, yolk.]

In medicine and zoology, the *vitellus* (plural *vitelli*) is the yolk of an egg or ovum; the adjective relating to the yolk is *vitelline* (as in the *vitelline membrane*, a transparent membrane surrounding and secreted by the fertilized ovum, preventing the entry of further spermatozoa); *vitellogenin* is a protein present in the blood, from which the substance of egg yolk is derived; *vitellin* is a protein found in the yolks of eggs; *vitellogenesis* is the formation of yolk.

vitr(o)- Also **vitri-**. *Glass; glassy*. [Latin *vitrum*, glass.]

The adjective *vitreous* refers to some substance like glass in appearance or physical properties; the *vitreous humour* is the transparent tissue filling the eyeball behind the lens, hence *vitrectomy* (Greek *ektomē*, excision) for the surgical operation of removing or replacing it. *Vitrophyre* (German *Porphyr*, porphyry) is a type of igneous rock containing embedded glassy particles; *vitrification* is the conversion of a material into a glass-like substance, typically through heat. The Latin phrase *in vitro* (literally 'in glass') refers to processes taking place in a test tube, culture dish, or elsewhere outside a living organism, the opposite of *in vivo*.

vivi- *Alive; living*. [Latin *vivus*, alive.]

An animal that is *viviparous* (Latin *parus*, bearing) bears live young which have developed inside the body of the parent; to *vivify* is to enliven or animate; *vivisection* (Latin *secare*, to cut, literally to dissect living things), is a pejorative term for the practice of performing operations on live animals for experimentation or scientific research.

-vore Also **-vora** and **-vorous**. *An organism living on a given type of food*. [Latin *-vorus*, from *vorare*, to devour.]

Examples include *carnivore* (Latin *caro*, *carn-*, flesh), a flesh-eating animal; **herbivore** (Latin *herba*, herb, green vegetation), an animal that eats plants; and *omnivore*

(Latin *omnis*, all), an animal or person that eats a variety of food of both plant and animal origin.

The associated ending **-vorous** (*see* -ous) supplies adjectives: *carnivorous*; *insectivorous*, feeding on insects; *nectarivorous*, feeding on nectar.

The suffix **-vora** appears in the names of animal classifications: *Carnivora* is an order of flesh-eating mammals that includes the cats, dogs, and hyenas; *Insectivora* is an order of small mammals that live on insects, such as the shrews, moles, and hedgehogs.

vulv(o)- *The female external genitals, the vulva.* [Latin *vulva*, literally 'womb'.]

Vulvitis is inflammation of the vulva; *vulvodynia* (Greek *odunē*, pain) is chronic pain in the vulva; *vulvectomy* (Greek *ektomē*, excision) is its surgical removal. Some terms refer to the vulva plus another part of the body, as in *vulvovaginal*, the vulva plus the vagina.

-ward Also **-wards**. *In a specified direction.* [Old English *-weard*, from a Germanic base meaning 'turn'.]

These two forms are virtually identical in meaning, the choice between them often being one of euphony or personal inclination. However, there is a strong tendency in British English for words ending in **-wards** to be adverbs (*his car shot forwards*), while those ending in **-ward** are more likely to be adjectives (*she was a backward child*), or occasionally nouns (*let us look to the eastward*). In American English, **-ward** is more usual in all cases.

The suffixes can be added to nouns that relate to some place or direction, and to adverbs that refer to a direction. They make adverbs and adjectives that indicate movement in some direction (*backwards*, *eastward*, *towards*, *upward*). A few refer to movement in time (*afterwards*). Examples are created as needed in the modern language: *futurewards*, *holeward*, *lakewards*, *planetward*, *riverwards*.

-ware *Items of a specified type or for a given purpose; classes of computer applications.* [Old English *waru*, commodities.]

This ending generates group nouns describing items of a particular type, such as *chinaware*, *earthenware*, *glassware*, *hardware* (traditionally, items made of iron), *silverware*, and *stoneware*. The suffix is also applied collectively to items intended for a specific purpose, such as *tableware*, *kitchenware*, *giftware*, *ovenware*, and *sanitaryware*.

Computer specialists in the 1950s made a distinction between *hardware*, the equipment, and *software*, the sets of numerical instructions that tell the systems what to do. On their model, many terms for types of software have since been created, such as *firmware*, which is permanently programmed into a read-only memory; *middleware*, which

sits between applications from different sources to ensure they work together; *groupware*, which assists a group of people to work collectively; *shareware*, which may be freely copied and shared for evaluation purposes, but for which a fee is required if it continues to be used; and *freeware*, free software.

The suffix is extremely active in computer contexts, often giving rise to humorous formations: *vapourware* (US *vaporware*; also *brochureware*), software that is advertised, often as a spoiler to competitors, but which does not (yet) exist; *bloatware*, software with excessive or unnecessary functions that takes up valuable storage space and memory; *wetware*, human brains; *liveware*, human beings; *shelfware*, computer applications purchased but never used.

-ways Also **-way**. *Way, direction, or manner.* [Middle English *wayes*, the genitive of *way*.]

Examples of the first form include *edgeways*, *lengthways*, *sideways*, and *widthways*. *Anyway* is the only common British English example of a word without the final *s*, though *everyway*, *someway*, and *noway* are found in North America (even here, however, the final *s* is not unknown, at least on the last two). *Leastways* is now dialect or informal. Though once common, no new forms ending in **-ways** are being created, -WISE being preferred.

-wide *Extending throughout the specified area or scope.* [Old English *wīd*, spacious or extensive.]

Some well-established words with this ending, such as *worldwide*, *nationwide*, *countrywide*, and *statewide*, have now been joined by a variety of others coined in the last decade or so, of which a few examples are *enterprisewide*, *campuswide*, *networkwide*, and *householdwide*. Examples continue to be actively formed.

-wise *In a given way or manner; with respect to or concerning.* [Old English *wīse*, manner or custom.]

The first sense has long been represented in English: *clockwise*, *crabwise*, *lengthwise*, *likewise*, *otherwise*. The suffix has in the past century largely taken over the function, and some of the territory, of -WAYS. A few pairs are in use: *edgewise* and *edgeways*; *breadthwise* and *breadthways*; *crosswise* and *crossways*. However, new forms always employ **-wise**.

In the past half century, the suffix has taken on an informal sense of 'in connection with something': *careerwise*, *clotheswise*, *plotwise*, *realitywise*, *successwise*, *timewise*. This originated in American English and is still more common there than in other varieties of the language. Such words are frequently created in informal contexts, but are often deprecated in formal writing.

Forms such as *streetwise*, having the skills and knowledge necessary for dealing with modern urban life, are compounds using the adjective *wise*, not examples of the suffix.

with- *Away, back, against, in opposition to.* [Old English *wiþ-*, against or away, also the source of the preposition *with*.]

There were once many words that contained this prefix, but only a few now survive in the language—*withdraw*, *withstand*, *withhold*—and no new ones are being created.

-woman *Woman.* [English *woman*.]

This ending appears in a variety of terms denoting a woman who has a given place of residence, nationality, association, occupation, role, or skill: *Englishwoman*, *Yorkshirewoman*, *laywoman*, *saleswoman*, *oarswoman*. Such terms are now frequently considered to be sexist and gender-neutral alternatives are preferred. *See also* -MAN, -MANSHIP, and -PERSON.

-womanship: *see* -MANSHIP

-word *In reference to a word that may be offensive.* [English *word*]

People use this suffix to generate euphemisms for taboo terms: the *C-word*, the *F-word*. It is used facetiously, especially in political and journalistic contexts, with the implication that to say a word in full would be 'talking dirty': *L-word* (*liberal*), *E-word* (*Europe*).

Many other examples of terms ending in **-word** exist, such as *foreword*, *buzzword*, *password*, and *watchword*, but these are considered to be compounds of *word*.

-work *Things made of a specified material or in a particular way.* [English *work*.]

Some examples denote things or parts made of a specified material, with specified tools, or specified techniques: *basketwork*, *beadwork*, *brickwork*, *needlework*, *fretwork*, *knotwork*, *paintwork*, *plasterwork*, *silverwork*, *wickerwork*. Others mark a mechanism or structure of a specified kind: *bridgework*, *clockwork*, *coachwork*, *earthwork*, *firework*, *latticework*. Those words in which the focus of attention is on the activity of working are considered to be compounds of *work* instead: *housework*, *homework*, *teamwork*.

-worthy *Deserving; suitable or fit for.* [English *worthy*.]

The first sense appears in *blameworthy*, *praiseworthy*, *trustworthy*, *noteworthy*, and *creditworthy*; the second in *airworthy*, *newsworthy*, and *roadworthy*. The ending is rarely used to create new forms, and many words containing it are now archaic, such as *laughworthy* and *thankworthy*.

-x *Forming the plural of many nouns ending in -u taken from French.* [French plural form.]

Some French words ending in *-eau* or *-eu* brought into English have retained their French plural forms: *bureaux, châteaux, milieux, plateaux, tableaux*. It is increasingly common to see these with the standard English plural *-s* instead (*see* -s¹), especially in American English, though *châteaux* has been least affected. Some have completed the shift: *adieus, portmanteaus, purlieus, trousseaus*. *See also* -TRIX.

xanth(o)- *Yellow.* [Greek *xanthos.* yellow.]

A *xanthoma* is an irregular yellow patch or nodule on the skin, caused by deposition of lipids; *xanthene* is a yellowish crystalline compound, whose derivatives include brilliant, often fluorescent dyes such as fluorescein; *xanthophyll* (Greek *phullon*, leaf) is a yellow or brown carotenoid plant pigment which causes the autumn colours of leaves; organic salts containing the ion $=OCS_2$ are *xanthates*, because the first example known produced a yellow precipitate with copper sulphate.

xeno- *Foreign; different.* [Greek *xenos*, stranger, foreigner.]

Xenophobia is an intense or irrational dislike or fear of people from other countries or cultures; *xenotransplantation* is the process of grafting or transplanting organs or tissues between members of different species; a substance that is *xenobiotic* is foreign to the body or to an ecological system. The chemical element *xenon* was so named because it is a heavy inert gas that occurs only in tiny quantities in the atmosphere.

xero- *Before a vowel* **xer-**. *Dry.* [Greek *xĕros*, dry.]

Xerography is a dry copying process, to which the trade name *Xerox* refers; a *xerophyte* is a plant which needs very little water; a *xeriscape* is a style of landscape design requiring little or no irrigation or other maintenance, used in arid regions; a *xeroderma* is one of various diseases involving extreme dryness of the skin; the adjective *xeric* means very dry.

-xion: *see* -ION

xiph(o)- *Also* **xiphi-**. *Sword; sword-shaped.* [Greek *xiphos*, sword.]

The *xiphoid process* or *xiphoid cartilage* is the cartilaginous section at the lower end of the breastbone, also known as the *xiphisternum*, which is not attached to any ribs, and gradually ossifies during adult life. *Xiphias* is the genus containing the swordfish; *Xiphosura* (Greek *oura*, tail, so literally 'sword-tail'), is the sub-class of the horseshoe crabs, for which the related adjective is *xiphosuran*.

xylo- *Wood.* [Greek *xulon*, wood.]

A *xylophone* is a musical instrument played by striking wooden bars with hammers; *xylem* is the tissue in plants which conducts water upwards from the root and also helps to form the woody element in the stem; something *xylophagous*, such as an insect larva or mollusc, feeds on or bores into wood; *xylene* is a volatile liquid hydrocarbon obtained by distilling wood, coal-tar, or petroleum; *xylose* is a five-carbon sugar found in plants, sometimes called *wood sugar*. *See also* LIGNO-.

y- *An archaic form marking the past participle.* [Old English *ge-*.]

In Old English *ge-* marked the past participle of verbs, as it does in modern German. By the 14th century, this had dwindled to **y-** (*ybaptised*, *yblamed*), or had vanished altogether. Writers from the 15th century have used it as a conscious anachronism in forms such as *yclept*, 'called or named'.

-y¹ Also **-ey**. *Full of; having the quality of; inclined to; apt to.* [Old English *-ig*, of Germanic origin.]

Adjectives in this ending divide broadly into three groups. In one they straightforwardly denote the quality of the nouns from which they derive: *icy, inky, juicy, mossy, sandy, speedy, waxy*. A second group are to some extent dismissive or disparaging, often with a figurative or indirect association, such as *beery, boozy, dreamy, mousy, tinny*. A third set indicates a close attachment or mild addiction to something, as in *booky, doggy, horsy*. A few are formed from verbs rather than nouns: *dangly, sticky*.

The origins of some are now puzzling because their sources are archaic (*happy* is from *hap*, luck or fortune; *jolly* from a Old Norse word related to *yule*); some have developed figurative senses that obscure their origin (as *flighty* has from *flight*, or *shirty* from *shirt*).

The ending is active and is often used to create informal terms which may be mildly negative in tone, frequently in an attempt to communicate some quality that might be hard otherwise to describe briefly: *bacony, dancey, designery, Internetty, jargony, plasticky, tabloidy*.

The rules for spelling require that this ending appears as **-ey** when it is attached to a noun that already ends in *y*—*clayey* from *clay*, *skyey* from *sky*, *sprayey* from *spray*.

-y² Also **-ie** and **-ee**. *Forming affectionate or pet names, or nouns that imply smallness.* [Scots *-ie*, used in names but of uncertain origin, taken over in Middle English.]

The ending appears in affectionate versions of people's names (*Johnny, Sandy, Tommy*), in names for objects or people associated with childhood (*dolly, kitty, tummy*), in familiar terms of address (*ducky, sonny, lovey*), or affectionate names for objects (*hanky, telly* for television in British usage).

The **-ie** and **-y** endings exist in parallel in modern English and it is often a matter of taste which is used. As both endings have plurals of *-ies* (*frillies, kiddies, sweeties*) there is a tendency for the **-ie** ending to be taken as the usual singular form, especially in newer creations (*Brummie*, a person from Birmingham, *druggie*, a drug-taker, *veggie*, a vegetarian). However, some older words usually take **-y**: *baby, daddy, granny, mummy*. Reflecting its Scots origin, certain words associated with Scotland usually take the **-ie** ending: *beastie, laddie, lassie, caddie* (in the golfing term; *caddy* when it is a container of tea).

A few terms are spelled **-ee**, perhaps a variant spelling of **-ie**: *bootee, chickadee, coatee, townee*. *Goatee*, a beard like that on a goat's jaw, might belong in this set, as might *bargee*, though the latter may well have been influenced by the other sense of **-EE**, indicating a person given charge of a barge.

See also -SY.

-y³ *A quality, state, action, or entity.* [Old French *-ie*, deriving from Latin *-ia*.]

Many common English nouns that were brought into the language from French in medieval times and later contain this ending. It is not an active word-forming element itself, but is often found in compound ones that are, such as -CRACY or -GRAPHY. Examples are *blasphemy, courtesy, family, glory*, *honesty*, *jealousy*, *library*, *misery*, *navy*, *orthodoxy*, *society*, *story*, *subsidy*, and *victory*. See also entries for other compound suffixes containing this form: -ANCE (for -*ancy* and -*ency*) -CY, -ERY, -GEN (for -*geny*), -ITY, -LOGY, -TOMY, -TY. See -IA for words that retain the Latin ending.

-yer: *see* -IER

yester- *Yesterday.* [Old English *geostran*, of Germanic origin.]

Compounds containing **yester-** are now archaic or poetical; the only common example surviving in the language is *yesterday*. Instances of rarer or dialect forms are *yestereve*, *yestermorn*, *yester-year*, and *yesternight*. The word can exist alone as the adjectives *yester* or *yestern*, but these too are now only dialectal or poetic.

-yl Also **-oyl**. *Forming names of chemical radicals.* [Greek *hulē*, material, matter.]

Examples include *acetyl*, the radical CH_3CO- derived from acetic acid; *benzyl*, the $C_6H_5CH_2-$ group from toluene; *carbonyl*, the $CO-$ group; *ethyl*, the C_2H_5- group from ethane; *hydroxyl*, the $-OH$ group; *methyl*, the CH_3- group from methane; and *phenyl*, the C_6H_5- group from benzene.

The ending **-oyl** forms the names of acid radicals from associated carboxylic acids, whose names end in -OIC: *benzoyl* from *benzoic acid*, *caproyl* from *caproic acid*, *pantoyl* from *pantanoic acid*.

-ylene: *see* -ENE[1]

-yne *Hydrocarbons containing a triple bond.* [Latin feminine form -*ina*.]

These are systematic names of open-chain (aliphatic) hydrocarbons that contain carbon-carbon triple bonds; they are named by replacing the -ANE ending of the equivalent saturated hydrocarbon with **-yne**. Examples include *ethyne* (common name *acetylene*), *butyne*, and *propyne* (common name *allylene*). The general term for a member of the series, with formula C_nH_{n-2}, is *alkyne*. A *polyyne* is an organic compound containing two or more carbon-carbon triple bonds. *See also* -ENE.

yocto-: see the table of WORDS FOR MULTIPLES on page 127

yotta-: see the table of WORDS FOR MULTIPLES on page 127

Z

zepto-: see the table of WORDS FOR MULTIPLES on page 127

zetta-: see the table of WORDS FOR MULTIPLES on page 127

-zoa or **-zoan**: *see* -ZOON

-zoic¹ *Relating to a given geological aeon or era.* [Greek *zōē*, life, plus -IC.]

Among other divisions of geological time are the *Proterozoic* aeon (Greek *proteros*, former) from about 2,500 million years ago to 570 million years ago, after which follows the *Phanerozoic* aeon (Greek *phaneros*, visible, evident), covering the whole of time since then, and comprising the *Palaeozoic* (Greek *palaios*, ancient), *Mesozoic* (Greek *mesos*, middle), and *Cenozoic* (Greek *kainos*, new) eras, the last of which began 65 million years ago.

-zoic²: *see* -ZOON

zoo- *Animal; animal life.* [Greek *zōion*, animal.]

Zoology is the scientific study of animals, for which the adjective is *zoological*; *zooplankton* is plankton consisting of small animals and the immature stages of larger animals; a *zoospore* is a spore of certain algae, fungi, and protozoans, capable of swimming and so somewhat animal-like; a *zoonosis* (Greek *nosos*, disease) is a disease which can be transmitted to humans from animals; *zoomorphic* (Greek *morphē*, form) refers to the representation of animal forms or gods of animal form.

-zoon Also **-zoa**, **-zoan**, and **-zoic**. *Types of animal.* [Greek *zōion*, animal.]

Examples of this ending include *bryozoon* (Greek *bruon*, moss), a group of sedentary aquatic invertebrates that comprises the moss animals; *protozoon* (Greek *prōtos*, first), a single-celled microscopic animal, such as an amoeba, ciliate, or sporozoan; *spermatozoon* (Greek *sperma*, *spermat-*, seed), the mature motile male sex cell of an animal, by which the ovum is fertilized.

A common plural for these is **-zoa** (*bryozoa*, *spermatozoa*); this ending also occurs in the taxonomic names for some groups of animals, of which examples include *Anthozoa* (Greek *anthos*, flower), a large class of sedentary marine coelenterates that includes the sea anemones and corals, and *Hydrozoa* (Greek *hudōr*, water), a class of coelenterates which includes hydras and Portuguese men-of-war.

Forms ending in **-zoan** are primarily adjectives, but can also act as nouns; as nouns, they are sometimes more common than the alternatives ending in **-zoon**: *bryozoan*, *hydrozoan*, *protozoan*.

Adjectives relating to these and other types of animal are formed using **-zoic**: *cryptozoic* (Greek *kruptos*, hidden), relating to small invertebrates living on the ground but hidden in the leaf litter, under stones or pieces of wood; also *epizoic*, *hydrozoic*, *protozoic* and others. For the names of geological periods in the same ending, *see* -ZOIC¹.

zygo- *Joining or pairing.* [Greek *zugon*, yoke.]

A *zygote* (Greek *zugōtos*, yoked) is a diploid cell, a fertilized ovum, resulting from the fusion of two haploid gametes; a bird that is *zygodactyl* (Greek *daktulos*, finger) has a pair of toes pointing forward and another pair backward, like a parrot; the *zygomatic* bone forms the prominent part of the cheek and the outer side of the eye socket, at the junction between the cranial and facial bones; a *zygospore* is the thick-walled resting cell of certain fungi and algae, arising from the fusion of two similar gametes.

zym(o)- *Enzymes or fermentation.* [Greek *zumē*, leaven.]

Enzymes are substances produced by living organisms which act as catalysts to bring about a specific biochemical reaction. Terms include *zymase*, a mixture of enzymes which catalyse the breakdown of sugars in alcoholic fermentation; *zymogen* (also called a *proenzyme*), an inactive substance which is converted into an enzyme when activated by another enzyme; *zymurgy*, the study or practice of fermentation in brewing, winemaking, or distilling.

Selective Thematic Index

Biochemistry and drugs
See also BODY, MEDICINE AND SURGERY

-ase	Enzyme.
-ergic	Neurotransmitter.
-globin	Globin.
-kinin	Hormone.
nucleo-	Nucleic acid.
plasmo-	Plasma; plasm.
proteo-	Protein.
sero-	Serum.
-sterol	Sterol.
-sterone	Steroid hormone.
sulpha-	Sulphanilamide drug.
zymo-	Enzyme.

Biological classifications
See also LIVING WORLD

-acea	Animals.
-aceae	Seed-bearing plants.
-ales	Plants.
-bacter	Bacteria.
clado-	Branch; branching.
-coccus	Spherical bacterium.
-ella	Bacteria; algae.
-fera	Animal orders or phyla.
-formes	Animal orders.
-ida	Animal and plant groups.
-idae	Animal and plant groups.
-ides	Plant and animal genera.
-ina	Plant and animal genera.
-inae	Animal subfamilies.
-monas	Simple microorganisms.
-morpha	Animal groups.
-myces	Bacteria or fungi.
-phyte	Plant.
-pithecus	Fossil ape.
-ptera	Winged animal.
-saur	Reptile.
taxo-	Classification.
-therium	Animals.
-zoon	Animals.

Body
See also MEDICINE AND SURGERY

abdomino-	Abdomen.
adeno-	Gland.
adipo-	Fat; fatty tissue.
adreno-	Adrenal gland.
amnio-	Amnion.
angio-	Blood vessel.
arterio-	Artery.
arthro-	Joint.
bili-	Bile.
blepharo-	Eyelid.
brachio-	Arm.
broncho-	Bronchi.
bucco-	Cheek.
cardio-	Heart.
-cardium	Heart tissue.
cephalo-	Head.
-cephalic	Head.
cerebro-	Brain.
cervico-	Cervix; neck.
chaeto-	Hair.
cheilo-	Lip.
chiro-	Hand.
chole-	Bile; gall.
chondro-	Cartilage; grain.
chorio-	Chorion; choroid.
-coel	Body cavity.
colo-	Colon.
colpo-	Vagina.
copro-	Dung; faeces.
costo-	Rib.
cranio-	Cranium.
cysto-	Urinary bladder.
dacryo-	Tears.
dactylo-	Fingers; toes.
-dactyly	Fingers; toes.
denti-	Tooth; tooth-like.
-derm	Skin.
dermato-	Skin.
digiti-	Finger.
dorsi-	Back.
duodeno-	Duodenum.
embryo-	Embryo.
encephalo-	Brain.
-enchyma	Cellular tissue.
entero-	Intestine.
feto-	Fetus.
fronto-	Forehead.
ganglio-	Ganglion.
gastro-	Stomach.
gingivo-	Gums.
glio-	Glia.
glosso-	Tongue.
gnatho-	Jaw.
gono-	Sexual; reproductive.
-gonium	Reproductive organs.
-head	Head.
haemo-	Blood.
hepato-	Liver.

noo-	Mind.
hymeno-	Hymen.
hystero-	Uterus.
ileo-	Ileum.
ilio-	Ilium.
irido-	Iris of eye.
ischio-	Ischium.
jejuno-	Jejunum.
kerato-	Cornea.
labio-	Lip.
laparo-	Abdominal wall.
laryngo-	Larynx.
lipo-	Fat.
lumbo-	Lower back; loin.
luteo-	Corpus luteum.
lympho-	Lymph.
mammo-	Breast.
masto-	Breast.
maxillo-	Jaw.
meningo-	Meninges.
meno-	Menstruation.
metro-[1]	Uterus.
musculo-	Muscle.
myo-	Muscle.
myelo-	Bone marrow; spinal cord.
myringo-	Eardrum.
naso-	Nose.
nephro-	Kidney.
neuro-	Nerve; nervous system.
noo-	Mind.
occipito-	Occipital bone.
oculo-	Eye; vision.
odonto-	Tooth.
-odont	Tooth; toothed.
oesophago-	Oesophagus.
omphalo-	Navel; umbilical cord.
onycho-	Nail.
oophoro-	Ovary.
ophthalmo-	Eye.
orchido-	Testis; testicle.
oro-[2]	Mouth.
osteo-	Bone.
oto-	Ear.
ovario-	Ovary.
palato-	Palate.
pancreato-	Pancreas.
papillo-	Papilla.
papulo-	Papule.
pedi-	Foot.
pelvi-	Pelvis.
phallo-	Penis.
pharyngo-	Pharynx.
phlebo-	Vein.
pilo-	Hair.
pneumo-	Lung.
-pnoea	Breath, respiration.
podo-	Foot.
poro-	Pore.

procto-	Anus or rectum.
prosopo-	Face.
pygo-	Buttocks.
rachi-	Spine.
radio-[2]	Radius bone.
recto-	Rectum.
reni-	Kidney.
retino-	Retina.
rhino-	Nose.
sacro-	Sacrum.
salpingo-	Fallopian tube.
sarco-	Flesh; muscle.
scapulo-	Shoulder blade.
sebo-	Oil, fat.
sialo-	Saliva; salivary gland.
sino-[1]	Sinus.
somato-	Body.
somni-	Sleep.
spermato-	Sperm; semen.
spini-	Spine; spinal cord.
splanchno-	Viscera; intestine.
spleno-	Spleen.
spondylo-	Vertebra.
staphylo-	Uvula.
steato-	Fat.
sterno-	Breastbone.
stetho-	Chest.
talo-	Ankle bone.
tarso-	Ankle; eyelid.
temporo-	Temporal bone.
teno-	Tendon.
thalamo-	Thalamus.
thymo-	Thymus.
tibio-	Tibia.
tracheo-	Trachea.
tricho-	Hair.
-trichous	Hairy; having hair.
tympano-	Eardrum.
ulno-	Ulna.
urano-[1]	Palate.
uretero-	Ureter.
urethro-	Urethra.
urino-	Urine; urinary system.
uro-[2]	Urine; urinary organs.
utero-	Uterus.
vagino-	Vagina.
veno-	Vein.
viscero-	Viscera.
vulvo-	Vulva.

Chemical elements
See also SUBSTANCES

anthraco-	Carbon.
argento-	Silver.
arseno-	Arsenic.
auri-	Gold.
azo-	Nitrogen.

benzo-	Benzene.
boro-	Boron.
bromo-	Bromine.
carbo-	Carbon.
chalco-	Copper
chloro-	Chlorine.
chromo-	Chromium.
chryso-	Gold.
cupro-	Copper.
eka-	Unknown element.
ferro-	Iron.
halo-	Halogen.
fluoro-	Fluorine.
hydro-[2]	Hydrogen.
iodo-	Iodine.
-ium	Chemical element.
mangano-	Manganese.
natro-	Sodium.
-on[2]	Inert gas.
oxy-[2]	Oxygen.
platino-	Platinum.
plumbo-	Lead.
seleno-[2]	Selenium.
sidero-	Iron.
silico-	Silicon.
stanno-	Tin.
stibo-	Antimony.
sulpho-	Sulphur.
telluro-	Tellurium.
thallo-	Thallium.
thio-	Sulphur.
titano-[2]	Titanium.
unnil-	Transuranic element.
urano-[2]	Uranium.

Chemical radicals
See also SUBSTANCES

aceto-	Acetyl group.
acido-	Acid.
-al[2]	Aldehyde.
aldo-	Aldehyde.
amido-	Amido group.
amino-	Amine group.
-ane	Saturated hydrocarbon.
but-	Four-carbon chain.
carboxy-	Carboxyl group.
chemo-	Chemical reaction.
cyano-	Cyanide.
dehydro-	Loss of hydrogen.
deoxy-	Loss of oxygen.
-ene[1]	Hydrocarbons.
eth-	A two-carbon chain of atoms.
ethoxy-	The ethoxyl radical.
hydroxy-	Hydroxyl or hydroxide.
-idine	Ring containing nitrogen.
imido-	Amine derivative.
indo-[2]	Indole.

-itol	Polyhydric alcohol.
keto-	Ketone.
mercapto-	Mercaptan.
meta-	Substitution.
metallo-	Metal.
metho-	Methyl radical.
methoxy-	Methoxyl radical.
naphtho-	Napthalene.
nitro-	Nitrogen compounds.
nor-	Parent compound.
-oic	Carboxyl group.
-ol	Alcohol or phenol.
-ole[1]	Organic compound.
-one	Ketones etc.
-onic	Organic acid.
organo-	Organic compound.
ortho-	Substitution.
-ose[2]	Sugar; carbohydrate.
oxy-[1]	Acid.
para-	Substitution.
pheno-	Benzene compound.
phospho-	Phosphorus.
prop-	Three-carbon chain.
-uret	Binary compound.
-valent	Combining power.
-yl	Chemical radical.
-yne	Triple-bond hydrocarbon.

Colours

alb-	White.
chloro-	Green.
-chrome	Colour.
chromo-	Colour.
-chroic	Colour.
chryso-	Gold.
cyano-	Blue.
erythro-	Red.
flavo-	Yellow.
leuco-	White.
luteo-	Yellow.
melano-	Black.
nigro-	Black.
rhodo-	Rose-coloured.
tephro-	Ash-coloured.
xantho-	Yellow.

Culture and society
See also RELIGION AND SPIRIT

-aholic	Person excessively fond of something.
-aire	Person of given type.
arch-	Chief; pre-eminent.
-archy	Government; rule.
-ast	Person connected with a pursuit.
-athon	Event.

-ati	Groups of people.
-cade	Procession or show.
-cide	Killing.
cine-	Cinema; film.
-core	Musical genre.
-cracy	Government; rule; influence.
-delic	Type of experience.
demo-	People.
docu-	Documentary.
-ene[2]	Inhabitant.
ethno-	Nation; people; culture.
-fest	Festival; gathering.
-gamy	Marriage.
-gate	Political scandal.
geronto-	Old age; old people.
grand-	Parentage; descent.
homo-[2]	Man; human being.
-hood	Group of people.
-ier	Person in an occupation.
-in[2]	Protest gathering.
-ista	Supporter.
klepto-	Thieving.
-logue	Communication; debate.
-machy	Fighting.
-manship	Skill.
matri-	Mother.
-meister	Master; skilled person.
metro-[3]	Large urban area.
-monger	Dealer or trader.
-nap	Abduct for ransom.
necro-	Death; a corpse.
nomo-	Law.
-orama	Display or spectacle.
paedo-	Child; children.
patri-	Father.
phylo-	Race; group.
-phile	Lover of; enthusiast for.
-phobia	Irrational fear.
-ploitation	Commercial exploitation.
-polis	City.
politico-	Politically
porno-	Pornography.
-praxia	Action; practice.
-san	Japanese honorific.
step-	Relationship from remarriage.
-teria	Self-service establishment.
-topia	Place.
über-	Superior.
-ville	Fictitious place.
vice-	Deputy; assistant.
xeno-	Foreign.

Diminutives

-een	
-en[5]	
-ino	
-kin	
-ling	

Direction and movement

-ad[2]	Towards a body part.
ante-	Before; preceding.
antero-	Towards front of body.
dextro-	On or to the right.
dia-	Through, across.
ento-	Within; inside.
extro-	Outwards.
fore-	Before; in front of.
fronto-	Front part of body.
gyro-	Rotation.
in-[2]	In, into.
infra-	Below; beneath.
intra-	Inside; within.
intro-	Into, inwards.
kinesio-	Movement.
-kinesis	Movement.
laevo-	On or to the left.
ob-	Towards.
-petal	Seeking; moving towards.
proso-	Towards, forward.
retro-	Directed backwards.
trans-	Across; beyond; through.
-ward	In a specified direction.
-ways	Way; direction.

Food and drink

galacto-	Milk.
glyco-	Sugar.
hydro-[1]	Water.
lacto-	Milk.
oeno-	Wine.
sito-	Food.
saccharo-	Sugar.
vini-	Wine.

Gender

andro-	Male or maleness.
-androus	Maleness.
-elle	Feminine nouns.
-enne	Nouns denoting females.
-ess	Female person.
-ette	Female gender.
gynaeco-	Female; relating to women.
-gynous	Female characteristics.
-ine[2]	Feminine nouns.

-man	Male person.
-person	Gender-neutral term.
-stress	Female person.
-trix	Nouns denoting females.
-woman	Woman.

Knowledge

-gnosis	Knowledge or recognition.
-ics	Subject of study, branch of knowledge.
-logical	Branch of knowledge.
-logist	Person skilled in a branch of study.
-logy	Subject of study or interest.
-nomy	Specified area of knowledge.
-pedia	Compendium of information.
-sophy	A system of thought.

Language and communication

-eme	Linguistic unit.
glosso-	Speech, language.
-gram	Written or recorded.
grapho-	Writing; images.
-graphy	Writing; images.
-lect	Language variety.
-lepsis	Figure of speech.
logo-	Words; speech.
-logue	Communication; debate.
-onym	Kinds of words.
-phasia	Speech disorder.
semio-	Sign; communication.
Slavo-	Slavonic languages.
-speak	Manner of speaking.
-word	Offensive word.

Living world
See also BIOLOGICAL CLASSIFICATIONS

acaro-	Mite; tick.
angio-	Seed vessel.
-angium	Container.
antho-	Flower.
anthropo-	Human.
-anthropy	Human; humankind.
arachno-	Spider.
arbori-	Tree.
auxo-	Growth, increase.
avi-	Bird, flight.
bacill-	Bacillus.
bacterio-	Bacterium.
basidio-	Basidium.
bio-	Life; living things.

-biosis	Mode of life.
-blast	Immature or embryonic cell.
blasto-	Germination.
botryo-	Bunch of grapes.
branchio-	Gill.
bryo-	Moss.
-carp	Fruit.
-chaete	Bristle, seta.
cheli-	Claw.
cirro-	Tuft, curl, tendril.
cocci-	Bacterium.
-colous	Preferring a given environment.
copro-	Dung; faeces.
cyno-	Dog.
-cyte	Cell.
cyto-	Cell.
dendro-	Tree.
-dendron	Shrub; tree.
eco-	Ecology; natural environment.
entomo-	Insect.
flori-	Flower.
franken-	Genetically modified.
fructi-	Fruit.
fungi-	Fungus.
gamo-	Fertilization; reproduction.
-gamy	Fertilization; reproduction.
hippo-	Horse.
hylo-	Wood; matter.
ichthyo-	Fish; fishlike.
-idium	Plant or animal structure.
ligno-	Wood.
limno-	Fresh water.
myco-	Fungi; fungal.
myrmeco-	Ant.
myxo-	Mucus.
-nasty	Nastic movement.
nuci-	Nut.
oo-	Egg or ovum.
ophio-	Snake.
ornitho-	Bird.
ovi-	Eggs, ova.
-parous	Bearing; producing.
partheno-	Reproduction without fertilization.
-ped	Foot.
pedi-	Foot.
-petal	Seeking; moving towards.
phago-	Feeding; eating.
-phagy	Feeding.
-phyceae	Alga.
phyco-	Seaweed; alga.

phyllo-	Leaf.
-phyll	Leaf.
-phyte	Plant; plant-like.
phyto-	Plant.
pinni-	Wings; fins; feathers.
pisci-	Fish.
-plasm	Living substance; tissue.
-pod	Foot.
pterido-	Fern.
ptero-	Wing.
pterygo-	Wing-like.
rhizo-	Root.
rhyncho-	Snout; beak.
sapro-	Putrefaction; decay.
-saur	Reptiles.
sauro-	Lizard.
scato-	Dung; excrement.
-sepalous	Sepals of a given type.
seti-	Bristle.
siphono-	Siphon.
-sperm	Seed.
spongio-	Sponge; sponge-like.
sporo-	Spore.
-spore	Spore.
squamo-	Scale.
stomato-	Mouth; opening.
-stome	Mouth.
tauro-	Ox or bull.
-taxis	Movement in response to stimulus.
-tene	Stages in cell division.
thanato-	Death.
therio-	Animal.
-trichous	Hairy; having hair.
tropho-	Nourishment.
-trophic	Nutrition; feeding.
-tropism	Preferential growth or movement.
uro-[1]	Tail; tail part.
uredo-	Rust fungus.
vermi-	Worm.
vitelli-	Yolk.
-vore	Living on a given food.
vivi-	Alive; living.
zoo-	Animal; animal life.
zygo-	Joining; pairing.

Medicine and surgery
See also BIOCHEMISTRY AND DRUGS, BODY

-acusis	Condition of hearing.
-aemia	Substance in excess in the blood.
-agogue	Leading, promoting.
-agra	Pain.
-algia	Pain.
algo-	Pain.
anthraco-	Carbuncle.

-asis	Disease.
athero-	Atheroma.
-blast	Immature or embryonic cell.
carcino-	Cancer.
-cele	Tumour, hernia.
-centesis	Puncture or perforation.
-derma	Skin disorder.
-ectomy	Surgical removal.
febri-	Fever.
fibrino-	Fibrin.
geronto-	Old age.
hernio-	Hernia.
histo-	Organic tissue.
-iatric	Medical practice; treatment.
iatro-	Physician; medical treatment.
immuno-	Immunity; immunology.
ino-	Fibrous tissue, muscle.
-itis	Inflammatory disease.
karyo-	Cell nucleus.
-lagnia	Morbid sexual arousal.
-lalia	Speech condition or disorder.
-lepsy	Seizure.
-lysis	Disintegration; decomposition.
-malacia	Abnormal softening of a tissue.
-mania	Mental abnormality or obsession.
medico-	Medicine plus another field.
-megaly	Abnormal enlargement of an organ.
-melia	Abnormal condition of a limb.
-metropia	Condition of the eye.
muco-	Mucus.
narco-	Stupor; drowsiness.
neuro-	Nerves or the nervous system.
noci-	Pain.
noso-	Disease.
-odontics	Specialism in dentistry.
-odynia	Pain.
-oma	Tumour; abnormal growth.
onco-	Tumour.
-onychia	Condition of the nails.
-opia	Visual disorder.
-opsia	Defect of vision.
-opsy	Medical examination.
-osis	Disease.

-osmia	Abnormal condition of sense of smell.
paedo-	Child; children.
-pagus	Conjoined twins.
parieto-	Body cavity.
patho-	Disease.
-pathy	Disease or disorder; treatment of disease.
-penia	Deficiency in a component of the blood.
pero-	Deformity.
-pexy	Operation to fix an organ in position.
phaco-	Lens of the eye.
pharmaco-	Drugs, medicines.
-phasia	Speech disorder.
-phobia	Extreme or irrational fear or dislike.
-phrenia	Mental disorder.
-plasty	Reconstructive surgery.
-plegia	Paralysis.
pleuro-	Pleurae; side of body.
-ploid	Chromosomes in a cell.
-poiesis	Production, formation.
poikilo-	Variegated; variable.
polio-	Nervous system tissue; grey matter.
-praxia	Action; practice.
psycho-	Mind; psychology.
ptyalo-	Saliva; salivary gland.
pyo-	Pus.
pyelo-	Pelvis of kidney.
pyloro-	Pylorus.
-rrhagia	Excessive flow or discharge.
-rrhaphy	Surgical sewing or suturing.
-rrhoea	Discharge; flow.
sangui-	Blood.
schizo-	Divided; split.
-some[3]	Cell.
spasmo-	Spasm.
sphygmo-	Pulse.
spiro-[2]	Breath; breathing.
-stomy	Operation to create an opening.
syndesmo-	Connective tissue, especially ligaments.
syringo-	Fistula.
taeni-	Tapeworm.
terato-	Monsters; abnormal forms.
tetano-	Tetanus.
-thelium	A layer of body tissue.
thrombo-	Blood clotting.
-thymia	A condition of the mind.

thyro-	Thyroid.
toco-	Childbirth; labour.
-tome	Cutting instrument.
-tomy	Incision in an organ.
-tonia	Muscle tone; personality state.
toxi-	Toxin; toxic.
-uria	Substance in excess in the urine.
varico-	Varicose vein.
vaso-	Vessel.
ventriculo-	Ventricle.
vesico-	Blister; urinary bladder.
viro-	Virus.
vitelli-	Yolk.

Negatives

a-[1]
anti-
dis-
dys-
in-[1]
mal-
mis-
nega-
non-
un-

Numbers and multiples

atto-	10^{-18}
bi-	Two; having two; doubly.
centi-	Hundredth.
chili-	Thousand.
deca-	Ten.
decem-	Ten.
deci-	One tenth.
demi-	Half; partially.
deutero-	Second; secondary.
di-	Twice; two; double.
dodeca-	Twelve.
duo-	Two.
duodeci-	Twelve; twelfth.
ennea-	Nine.
exa-	10^{18}.
femto-	10^{-15}.
giga-	10^{9}.
haplo-	Single.
hecto-	One hundred.
hemi-	Half; part.
hendeca-	Eleven.
hepta-	Seven.
hexa-	Six.
icos-	Twenty.
kilo-	Thousand.
mega-	Million.
micro-	One millionth.

milli-	Thousandth; thousand.
mono-	One; alone; single.
nano-	10^{-9}.
nona-	Nine.
octo-	Eight.
penta-	Five.
peta-	10^{15}.
pico-	10^{-12}.
quadri-	Four.
quinque-	Five.
quinti-	Five; fifth.
semi-	Half.
septi-	Seven.
sesqui-	One and one half.
sexi-	Six.
-teen	Thirteen to nineteen.
ter-	Three.
tera-	10^{12}.
tetra-	Four.
tri-	Three.
trito-	Third.
-ty[2]	Multiples of ten.
undeca-	Eleven.
viginti-	Twenty.
uni-	One.

Physical world

actino-	Ray; beam.
aero-	Atmosphere.
anemo-	Wind.
areo-	Mars.
astro-	Star.
-clase	Minerals.
clino-	Inclined; monoclinic.
cosmo-	World; universe.
crystallo-	Crystal.
dynamo-	Power.
electro-	Electricity.
ergo-	Work; energy.
fluvio-	River.
galvano-	Electric current.
geo-	Earth.
glacio-	Glacier.
helio-	Sun.
hygro-	Moisture; humidity.
irido-	Rainbow.
-lite	Mineral; fossil.
litho-	Stone.
-lith	Stone; stony structure.
-lithic	Stone.
magneto-	Magnetism; magnet.
metallo-	Metal.
nepho-	Cloud.
nocti-	Night.
nycto-	Night.
-ode[2]	Electrical conductor.

ombro-	Rain; moisture.
-on[1]	Subatomic particles; quanta.
opto-	Light.
oro-[1]	Mountain.
osmo-	Osmosis.
pedo-[1]	Soil; soil type.
petro-	Rocks; petroleum.
-phyre	Porphyritic rocks.
physio-	Nature; physiology.
physico-	Physical.
piezo-	Pressure.
pyro-	Fire.
radio-[1]	Radiation; radio waves.
rheo-	Current; flow.
roentgeno-	X-rays.
seismo-	Earthquake.
seleno-[1]	Moon.
-sol	Soil.
sono-	Sound.
spectro-	Spectrum.
-sphere	Spherical object or region.
tectono-	Tectonics.
thermo-	Heat; temperature.
-therm	Heat; temperature.
telluro-	Earth.
thalasso-	Sea.
tribo-	Friction.
-tron	Subatomic particle.
urano-[1]	Heavens.

Places and peoples

Afro-	Africa, African.
Anglo-	English, British.
Austro-[1]	Austria
Austro-[2]	Australia.
Euro-	Europe.
Franco-	France, French.
Gallo-	France, French.
Germano-	Germany, German.
Graeco-	Greece, Greek.
Hiberno-	Irish.
Hispano-	Spanish.
Ibero-	Iberian.
Indo-[1]	India.
Italo-	Italian.
Judaeo-	Jewish.
Malayo-	Malay.
Romano-	Roman.
Russo-	Russian.
Serbo-	Serbian.
Sino-[2]	China, Chinese.
Slavo-	Slav, Slavonic.
Turco-	Turkish.

Position

acro-	Tip; extremity.

ambi-	On both sides; around.
amphi-	On both sides; around.
bathy-	Depth.
centri-	Centre.
-centric	Central.
circum-	Around; about.
cis-	On this side of.
-clinic	Oblique; at an angle.
clino-	Inclined; monoclinic.
ecto-	External; outside.
enantio-	Opposite; opposing.
endo-	Internal; within.
epi-	Upon; above.
exo-	External; from outside.
extra-	Outside; beyond.
-form	Form.
gonio-	Angle.
hapto-	Binding; fastening.
hind-	Back; posterior.
hypso-	Height; elevation.
inter-	Between; among.
juxta-	Near.
lepto-	Small; narrow.
medio-	Middle.
-mer	Part; segment.
meso-	Middle.
mid-	Middle.
omni-	In all places.
opistho-	Behind; to the rear.
ortho-	Straight; correct; upright.
para-[1]	Beside; adjacent to.
peri-	Round; about.
plagio-	Oblique.
postero-	Posterior.
pre-	In front of.
pro-[2]	Before.
proso-	Anterior.
recti-	Straight; right-angled.
sinistro-	Left; the left side.
sub-	Lower level or position.
super-	Above; over; beyond.
supra-	Over; above.
sur-	Above; over; beyond.
ultra-	Beyond.
under-	Below.
up-	Up; upwards; higher.
tele-	To or at a distance.
telo-	End.
topo-	Place; position.
-wide	Extending throughout.

Proportions

aniso-	Unequal; dissimilar.
dicho-	Paired.
diplo-	Double.
equi-	Equal; equally.
-fid	Divided.

giganto-	Great size.
-grade	Division.
holo-	Whole; complete.
iso-	Equal; isomeric.
macro-	Long; large.
magni-	Large; great.
maxi-	Very large or long.
mega-	Large; great.
meio-	Less or fewer.
mero-	Partly; partial.
meso-	Intermediate.
midi-	Medium-sized.
mini-	Very small.
multi-	More than one; many.
oligo-	Small number; having few.
pluri-	Several.
poly-	Many, much.
semi-	Part.
titano-[1]	Gigantic, huge.

Qualities
See also SENSATIONS

bene-	Good; well.
brachy-	Shortness.
brady-	Slowness.
caco-	Unpleasant; bad.
calli-	Beautiful.
crypto-	Concealed; secret.
dino-	Terrible; frightful.
eigen-	Proper; characteristic.
elasto-	Elastic.
equi-	Equal; equally.
eu-	Well; easily.
eury-	Variety.
gymno-	Bare; naked.
haplo-	Single; simple.
hetero-	Different.
holo-	Whole; complete.
homeo-	Similar.
homo-[1]	Same.
hyalo-	Glassy; transparent.
hyper-	Excessive; above normal.
hypo-	Below normal.
ideo-	Idea.
idio-	Personal; own.
-mania	Extreme enthusiasm.
miso-	Hatred.
nudi-	Naked.
neo-	New.
normo-	Normal; close to average.
nulli-	Nothing.
-oid	Like; resembling.
-opsis	Resemblance; likeness.
pachy-	Thick.

pan-	All-inclusive.		audio-	Hearing.
pene-	Almost; nearly.		baro-	Pressure.
per-	Through; all over; completely.		cryo-	Cold.
			echino-	Spiny.
phaeo-	Dusky.		eroto-	Sexual desire.
-phane	Having a given appearance.		-geusia	Taste.
philo-	Liking for something.		noci-	Pain.
placo-	Plate-like.		malaco-	Soft.
pleo-	More.		oculo-	Vision.
preter-	More than.		oneiro-	Dreams; dreaming.
pseudo-	False; imitative.		opto-	Vision.
pycno-	Compact; dense.		phanero-	Visible.
quasi-	Seemingly; apparently; partly.		phono-	Sound.
			-phone	Sound.
recti-	Right; correct.		photo-	Light.
schizo-	Divided; split.		picro-	Bitter tasting.
stego-	Covered; hidden.		psilo-	Bare, smooth.
steno-	Small; constricted.		scoto-	Darkness.
tacho-	Speed.		thermo-	Heat; temperature.
tachy-	Rapid.		-therm	Heat; temperature.
-tastic	Outstanding; superb; excellent.		vibro-	Oscillation; shaking.
			visco-	Sticky; thick.
tauto-	Same.		visuo-	Sight; vision.
teleo-	Perfect; complete.		xero-	Dry.
tono-	Tension; tone.			
vitro-	Glassy.			
xeno-	Foreign; different.			
-wise	Given way or manner.			
-worthy	Deserving.			

Shapes

ankylo-	Bent; crooked.
astro-	Star-shaped.
cyclo-	Circle.
denti-	Tooth; tooth-like.
disco-	Disc; disc-shaped.
dolicho-	Long.
falc-	Sickle-shaped.
-gon	Plane figure.
-hedron	Geometrical solid.
helico-	Spiral; screw.
kypho-	Humped.
lamino-	Thin layer.
lopho-	Crested.
morpho-	Form.
-morph	Form.
nemato-	Thread-like.
phaco-	Lens-shaped.
plano-	Level; flat.
platy-	Broad; flat.
reni-	Kidney-shaped.
reticulo-	Net-like.
rhabdo-	Rod-like.
scapho-	Boat-shaped.
sclero-	Hard.
scypho-	Cup-shaped.
spheno-	Wedge-shaped.
sphero-	Sphere; spherical.
spiro-[1]	Spiral; coiled.
stereo-	Solid, three-dimensional.
strepto-	Twisted.
trocho-	Wheel-like.

Religion and spirit

Christo-	Christ.
demono-	Demon.
hagio-	Saints; holiness.
hiero-	Sacred; holy.
icono-	Image; likeness.
-latry	Worship of something.
-mancy	Divination.
mytho-	Myth.
necro-	Death.
onto-	Existence; being.
telo-	Ultimate purpose.
thanato-	Death.
thaumato-	Wonder; miracle.
theo-	God; deities.
-tide	Christian festival.

Sensations
See also QUALITIES

acantho-	Spiny; thorny.
acido-	Sharp; sour.
acousto-	Hearing.
-agra	Pain.
-algia	Pain.
alb-	Bright.
algo-	Pain.

tubo-	Tube.
xipho-	Sword; sword-shaped.

Substances
See also CHEMICAL ELEMENTS, CHEMICAL RADICALS

acrylo-	Acrylic.
amylo-	Starch.
aqua-	Water.
calci-	Lime, calcium.
-cide	Substance that kills.
fibro-	Fibre.
galacto-	Milk.
glyco-	Sugar.
granulo-	Granule.
hydro-[1]	Water.
indo-[2]	Indigo.
lacto-	Milk.
oeno-	Wine.
oleo-	Oil.
physo-	Air or gas.
pneumo-	Air or gas.
saccharo-	Sugar.
sebo-	Oil, fat.
seric-	Silk.
ure-	Urea.
vitro-	Glass.
xylo-	Wood.

Technology

aero-	Aircraft.
agro-	Farming, cultivation.
auto-[2]	Motor vehicle.
cyber-	Computer-mediated communications.
e-[1]	Electronic communications.
-flop	Measures of computing speed.

heli-	Helicopter.
mechano-	Mechanical.
-meter	Measurement.
metro-[2]	Measurement.
-ode[2]	Electrical conductor.
-scope	Instrument.
-smith	Skilled worker with a material.
-stat	Something maintaining a controlled state.
-ster	Person linked to an activity.
-technics	Technology.
techno-	Technology.
turbo-	A turbine.
-urgy	Art or process.
-ware	Computer application.

Time

afore-	Before; previously.
ante-	Before; preceding.
après-	After an activity.
archaeo-	Ancient; prehistoric.
-chronic	Time.
chrono-	Time.
-cene	Division of geological time.
-ennium	Period of years.
eo-	Early, primeval.
palaeo-	Ancient.
palin-	Again.
post-	After in time or order.
pre-	Prior to; before; earlier.
proto-	Primitive; ancestral.
synchro-	Synchronous.
ur-	Primitive; original; earliest.
yester-	Yesterday.
-zoic[1]	Geological era.